EXPLORER'S GUIDES

Virginia Beach, Richmond & Tidewater Virginia

Including Williamsburg, Norfolk and Jamestown

A Great Destination

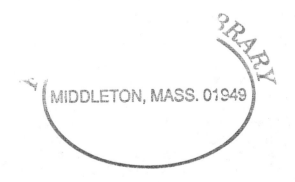

Virginia Beach, Richmond & Tidewater Virginia

Including Williamsburg, Norfolk and Jamestown

A Great Destination

Renee Wright

with photographs by the author

The Countryman Press ✳ Woodstock, Vermont

91755

We welcome your comments and suggestions. Please contact Explorer's Guide Editor, The Countryman Press, P.O. Box 748, Woodstock, VT 05091, or e-mail countrymanpress@wwnorton.com.

Interior photographs by the author unless otherwise specified
Maps by Erin Greb Cartography, © The Countryman Press
Book design by Joanna Bodenweber
Composition by PerfecType, Nashville, TN

Published by The Countryman Press, P.O. Box 748, Woodstock, VT 05091

Distributed by W. W. Norton & Company, Inc., 500 Fifth Avenue, New York, NY 10110

Virginia Beach, Richmond, and Tidewater Virginia: A Great Destination

978-1-58157-106-6

Printed in the United States of America

10 9 8 7 6 5 4 3 2 1

To my mom and dad,
who both contributed in their unique ways
to my love of history, books, and travel,
as well as to my deep roots in the South;

and to Kaylee, my sister,
companion on many adventures
and tap dancer extraordinaire.

EXPLORE WITH US!

The one hundred miles covered by this guide—from the fall line at Richmond to the seawall where the Atlantic laps at the skirt of Virginia Beach—has a natural unity, based on history and industry, and reinforced by the road system. Many people who go to Richmond to see the Civil War battlefields and museums will also want to visit the *Monitor* museum in Newport News and tour the Navy Yard in Norfolk. Families who come to Williamsburg for history also want to spend time at Virginia Beach.

In this book, we set a southeasterly course through the region, basically following the route of I-64 from Richmond to the beach. Along the way, we suggest some side trips that will take you through towns forgotten by modern progress but alive with history.

Special chapters on the natural and cultural history of the region and the best ways to get there and get around are at the beginning. Toward the end, you'll find lots of useful information, including local newspapers, television and radio stations, and recommended reading.

Watch for our Wright Choice selections throughout the book, marked with a special star, ✪ for the area's best bets for dining, lodging, attractions, and fun.

Wherever possible, we've included a Web site address for more information. We also list places with free Wi-Fi access where you can get connected.

You'll find lots of specific information for the major attractions in the region, and this information was checked as close to publication as possible. However, change is the one constant, so please use the phone numbers provided to check for current hours before you set out on a long trip to a particular place.

A NOTE ON PRICES

The accommodations and restaurants in this book represent a wide selection of price points. Rather than give specifics, we use categories based on a range of prices. This range is based on the nightly room rate for hotels and per unit for cottages or other rental units. For meals, the range reflects the typical price of a dinner entrée, not including appetizer, dessert, drinks, tax, and tip.

LODGING

Inexpensive	up to $80
Moderate	$80 to $150
Expensive	$150 to $200
Very expensive	$200 and up

DINING

Inexpensive	under $10
Moderate	$10 to $20
Expensive	$20 to $25
Very expensive	$25 and up

In addition to the dining price ranges, the *Where to Eat* listings in each chapter include information on what meals are served, using the following abbreviations:

B   Breakfast
L   Lunch
D   Dinner
SB   Sunday brunch

KEY TO SYMBOLS

☙ **Special value.** The special-value symbol appears next to lodgings and restaurants that offer a quality not often found at the price charged.

🐾 **Pets.** The pet symbol indicates places, activities, and lodgings that accept pets. Almost all lodging accommodations require that you inform them of a pet when you make a reservation and often request an additional fee.

✎ **Child-friendly.** The crayon symbol appears next to places or activities that accept and/or appeal to young children, or have a children's menu.

♿ **Handicapped access.** The wheelchair symbol appears next to lodgings, restaurants, and attractions that are partially or completely handicapped accessible. U.S. law requires that all restaurants, hotels over three stories tall, and public attractions be accessible to wheelchairs.

☂ **Rainy-day activity.** The rainy-day symbol shows places of interest and things to do that are appropriate for inclement-weather days.

💍 **Weddings.** The wedding-ring symbol indicates establishments that specialize in weddings.

🍸 **Bars.** The martini-glass symbol appears next to establishments that have choice selections of beers, wines, and other alcoholic beverages.

(¹) **Wi-Fi.** The WiFi symbol indicates lodgings that offer wireless Internet connections or data ports. In many cases, the more expensive hotels charge a fee for this while B&Bs and inns do not.

▼ **Gay-friendly.** The inverted triangle symbol indicates lodgings, nightclubs, and attractions that go out of their way to welcome LGBT travelers.

❧ **Eco-friendly.** Many hotels, restaurants, and attractions attained certification as "Virginia Green" by adopting special sustainable and ecologically friendly practices. Find a complete listing at www.virginia.org/green.

✪ **Wright Choice.** The Wright Choice symbol indicates the area's best bets in every category.

We would appreciate any comments or corrections. Please write to Explorer's Guide Editor, The Countryman Press, P.O. Box 748, Woodstock, VT 05091, or e-mail countrymanpress@wwnorton.com.

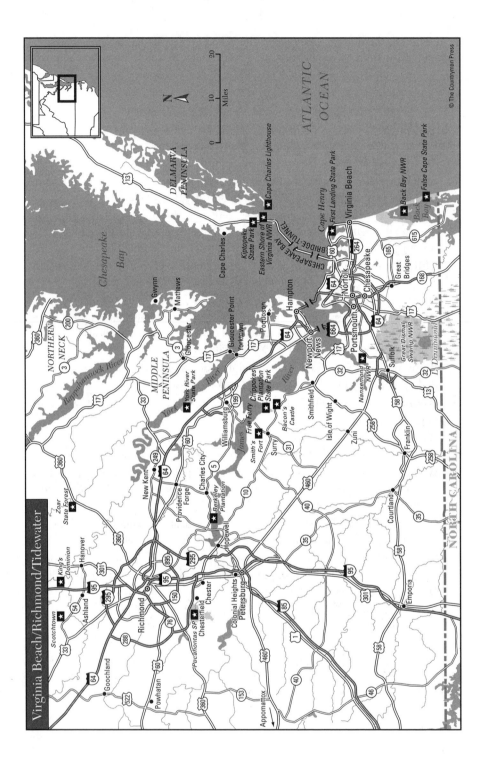

Virginia Beach/Richmond/Tidewater

CONTENTS

ACKNOWLEDGMENTS

A book such as this, bringing together so much information on so many different topics, required the help and insights of numerous people.

My thanks to all those who shared their favorite things about the Virginia Tidewater, including Erin Filarecki of the Norfolk Convention & Visitors Bureau; Lois Chapman of the Smithfield & Isle of Wight Convention & Visitors Bureau; Suzanne Pearson of the Newport News Tourism Development Office; Erin Bagnell of the Richmond Metropolitan Convention and Visitors Bureau; Ron Kuhlman of the Virginia Beach Convention & Visitors Bureau; Kari Journigan from Boom Your Brand, who ably handles Virginia Beach's press relations; Donna Bozza, director of tourism for Virginia's Eastern Shore; Becky Cutchins of the Portsmouth Convention and Visitors Bureau; Kate Hoving and Meagan Nicholas from the Greater Williamsburg Chamber & Tourism Alliance; Sharon Rogers of the Colonial Williamsburg Foundation; Alexis Wyrofsky of Mfa Marketing and Public Relations; Stacy Royal of Lou Hammond & Associates; Tamra Talmadge-Anderson and Richard Lewis of the Virginia Tourism Corporation; Ryan LaFata and Mary Fugere of the Hampton Convention & Visitor Bureau; and all the photogenic pirates who invade Hampton every summer.

Like many travelers, I frequently find that the best advice comes from folks who operate bed & breakfast inns. Thanks to Robert Epstein and Ke Jing Jang of Norfolk's Freemason Inn Bed and Breakfast, and Richmond innkeepers Anna Currence of the Museum District Bed & Breakfast and Pat Daniels and Mike Rodhe of the William Miller Bed and Breakfast, for sharing their expert insight into local best bets.

A special thanks to Sharon Owen, manager and founder of the exceptional Gallery at York Hall in Yorktown. Working full time as a volunteer, she exhibits a great love for history and her town, and offers a welcome to every visitor.

Thanks also to Eric Coulson of the Surf & Adventure Co. in Virginia Beach, who took us into the surf at Sandbridge and on a paddle into Back Bay, and to Andrea Battin of Wild River Outfitters for introducing us to the idyllic calm of Lynnhaven Bay.

To Joan and Dub Ham; Holley and Tom Odahl; Irene Karras Long; Michael, Grace, and Gavin Voelzow; Linda George; and Wayne Sweatt, thanks for your understanding, patience, and encouragement, and for making it fun to come home.

Thanks go as well to Allan Maurer, my editor at *North Carolina Magazine, Charlotte's Best,* and *Charlotte Magazine,* and my friend for many years, who launched me on my writing career and continues to offer fine editorial advice.

A brave few joined in my voyages of discovery. Thanks to Kaylee and Paul, Sue and Jack, and, of course, my mom, the best traveling companion of all. Special thanks also to Caitlin and Jan Snead, my mates for all pirate adventures and sundry voyages on land and sea.

In addition, I'd like to thank all the people at Countryman Press and W. W. Norton who helped make this book a reality, especially Kim Grant and Kermit Hummel, for their great patience and faith in our project.

INTRODUCTION

Heaven and Earth never agreed better to frame a place for Man's habitation. —Capt. John Smith, 1608

From the time John Smith first set foot on the shores of the Great Tidewater of Virginia, the region played a vital role in our nation's history.

In Jamestown, and nearby Hampton, the first successful English colonies took root, spreading branches up and down the Eastern Seaboard.

At Williamsburg, the royal governor came into conflict with the cream of the Tidewater's gentry, sparking revolution and a new nation.

A TRIP ON THE FREE JAMESTOWN-
SCOTLAND FERRY IS A FAVORITE DAYTRIP
FOR FAMILIES VISITING WILLIAMSBURG.

Nearby at Yorktown, that revolution came to a victorious close, as Cornwallis surrendered to Washington and turned the world upside down.

At Richmond, the Confederacy raised its battle flag, challenging the federal government to beat it down. More than a hundred blood-soaked Civil War battlefield sites hallow the surrounding countryside. In the waters of Hampton Roads, the most famous naval battle of all time took place as the ironclads *Merrimack* and *Monitor* clashed, ushering in a new era of naval warfare.

Once the U.S. military arrived, it found Hampton Roads the perfect base of operations and never left. The area bulges with military installations, from the great Norfolk Naval Base, home of the mighty Atlantic Fleet, to Langley

Field, site of numerous flight tests of experimental aircraft and birthplace of NASA.

Those military men and women needed a place to play, and Virginia Beach grew up to fill the bill. Today this year-round resort, one of the top beach destinations on the Eastern Seaboard of the United States, burgeons with restaurants, nightlife, outdoor activities, and annual events.

This part of Virginia doesn't just remember its past. It celebrates it. Numerous museums and annual events recognize the area's rich legacy as well as its vibrant future.

In this guide, you'll find detailed instructions to help you find sites where you can immerse yourself in the beginnings of our nation's history, experience the unique Tidewater culture, and enjoy nature and outdoor recreation available to visitors year-round.

THE REVOLUTIONARY CITY PROGRAMS IN WILLIAMSBURG RECREATE EVENTS LEADING UP TO THE FOUNDING OF THE UNITED STATES.

WHAT'S WHERE IN VIRGINIA BEACH, RICHMOND & TIDEWATER VIRGINIA

ALCOHOL, SMOKING, AND DRIVING REGULATIONS Only people 21 and older may purchase alcohol, including wine and beer. Photo IDs are required and will be checked for all customers who appear to be under the age of 30. While beer and wine are widely available at convenience stores and specialty shops, liquors and distilled beverages are sold only at state-operated **Virginia ABC Stores,** where you'll also find large selections of Virginia wines. Locate the nearest store at www.abc.virginia.gov. Hours are generally Monday–Saturday 10–9, Sunday 1–6.

In December, 2009, Virginia banned all smoking in restaurants anywhere in the state. Many restaurants have installed open-air patios where smoking is permitted. Bars and lounges are also smoke-free, since all bars in Virginia must serve food in order to qualify for an on-premises ABC license.

Pedestrians should be aware that in Virginia, motorists must yield—but not stop—for pedestrians in crosswalks if the speed limit is 35 mph or less. If the speed limit is over 35, motorists have the right of way at crosswalks.

AREA CODES Area codes 800, 866, 877, and 888 indicate a toll-free number. Dial 1 first to access the long-distance system.

CLIMATE AND SEASONS The Tidewater and Piedmont regions of Virginia enjoy a humid, subtropical climate, with high temperatures and humidity during the summer, and occasional freezes, even snow, during the winter months. Average daytime and nighttime temperatures in the Richmond and Williamsburg areas range from 45 to 25 degrees in January and 88 to 67 in July. In Virginia Beach and Norfolk, the water along the coasts moderates average temperatures, with winter a few degrees warmer and summer a few degrees cooler. January averages run from highs of 48 to lows of 32; while July sees highs averaging 85 with night temps in the 70s.

Winds along the coast frequently make temperatures feel several degrees cooler in both summer and winter, so an extra sweater or windbreaker is always a good idea. Thunderstorms are possible all year, especially in spring and summer, with August the wettest month.

FISHING REGULATIONS AND CHARTERS A **Virginia Saltwater Fishing License** is required for any sort of fishing—rod and reel, cast net, handline, spear, or gig—in Virginia's offshore ocean waters, Chesapeake Bay, the tidal James River below a line running from Hog Island to College Creek, the tidal Elizabeth River, the York River system below the VA 33 bridges, and the lower Piankatank. A saltwater license good for a year costs $12.50 for Virginia residents or $25 for nonresidents. A 10-day temporary license costs $5 for residents, $10 for nonresidents. You can buy your license online at www.mrc.virginia.gov, by phone (866-721-6911 Monday–Friday), or at a licensed agent. Anglers under 16 and seniors 65 and older do not require a saltwater license.

The numerous freshwater lakes and rivers above the saltwater line provide fishing opportunities from bank, pier, or boat. A **Virginia Freshwater Fishing License** is required for all anglers except for residents of Virginia under 16 years old, nonresidents under 12

years old, and legally blind persons. Visit www.dgif.virginia.gov or call 866-721-6911 for current prices, regulations, and more information.

Combination fresh- and saltwater licenses are also available. If you are going out on a charter boat or head boat, or fishing from a commercial pier, you probably won't need to buy a license as boats and piers usually have a blanket license to cover everyone casting a line. Most marinas and sporting goods stores sell licenses, as do Food Lion groceries, Kmart, Walmart, and Bass Pro Shops.

Additional permits for specific species such as trout may be required at some locations. Each fish species is governed by different regulations, and these change frequently. Check with the local experts at area tackle shops, or visit www.mrc.virginia.gov (for saltwater species) and www.dgif.virginia.gov (for freshwater species).

In addition, the federal government now requires all those fishing in salt water to be listed with the **National Saltwater Angler Registry.** Anglers or spearfishers under the age of 16, anglers aboard licensed charter or head boats, or anglers who hold a Highly Migratory Species Angling Permit are exempt. Sign up by telephone at 888-674-7411 or online at www.countmyfish.noaa.gov. A fee may apply.

Charter boats generally carry up to six anglers. If you aren't with a group and don't want to pay for the entire charter yourself, ask about a makeup charter where you are paired with other anglers with similar interests. Bait and tackle, ice, and a blanket fishing license are usually included in the price. Visit www.hrfishingguide.com for an online listing of charter boat captains.

For a worry-free, budget-conscious introduction to fishing, sign up for a half day on a head boat. These boats charge per person or per "head" and sometimes carry as many as a hundred anglers. Bait, tackle, and license are all taken care of, and there's friendly help nearby to help you bait your hook and reel in your catch. Children are welcome on most head boat trips, and it's a great way for them to find out about fishing. You get to keep what you catch.

GUIDANCE For the contact information of chambers of commerce and town and county governments relevant to the specific regions covered by this guide, please see the *Guidance* section in each chapter. The following chambers and visitors information centers can guide you to more general information about Virginia as well as other sites of interest within the state: **Appomattox County Chamber of Commerce** (434-352-2621; www .appomattoxchamber.org; P.O. Box 704, Appomattox 24522), **Appomattox Visitor Information Center** (434-352-8999 or 877-258-4739; www.tour appomattox.com; 214 Main Street, Appomattox 24522), **The Eastern Shore of Virginia Chamber of Commerce** (757-787-2460; www.esva chamber.org; 19056 Parkway, Melfa 23410), **Eastern Shore of Virginia Tourism Commission** (757-787-8268; www.esvatourism.org; P.O. Box 72, Tasley 23441), **Fredericksburg Regional Chamber of Commerce** (540-373-9400; www.fredericksburg chamber.org; P.O. Box 7476, Fredericksburg 22404), **Greater Fredericksburg Tourism Partnership** (540-373-1776 or 800-678-4748; www .visitfred.com; 706 Caroline Street, Fredericksburg 22401), **Northern Neck Tourism Council** (804-333-1919 or 800-393-6180; www.northern neck.org; P.O. Box 1707, Warsaw 22572), and **Virginia Tourism**

Corporation (804-545-5586 or 800-VISITVA; www.virginia.org; 901 E. Byrd Street, Richmond 23219), the state division of tourism.

HUNTING REGULATIONS Limited hunting is permitted on public lands in Virginia. Visit www.findgame.org to get more information on hunts, then apply online, by telephone at 877-VAHUNTS (877-824-8687), or by mailing your application to **Virginia Quota Hunts,** c/o CyberData, Inc., P.O. Box 9009, Hicksville, NY 11802. Participants for quota hunts are selected by lottery, with a day-of-hunt drawing held on-site to fill no-show spots. Hunt participants must meet all state hunting license requirements and must purchase a refuge permit. Visit www .dgif.virginia.gov for more information.

MEDICAL EMERGENCY In addition to the emergency rooms and urgent care clinics listed in the *Medical Emergency* section of each chapter, you can get treatment for common illnesses and minor injuries at **Minute Clinics** (www.minuteclinic.com) located inside CVS pharmacies, and at **Patient First** (www.patientfirst.com), with facilities throughout the Hampton Roads and Richmond regions.

For emergency assistance, dial 911.

NEWSPAPERS AND OTHER PUBLICATIONS

The major publications for the area follow. For a more comprehensive list, see Appendix A.

Hampton Roads: **Hampton Roads Magazine** (757-422-8979; www.hrmag.com), 1264 Perimeter Parkway, Virginia Beach 23454. Associated publications include *Hampton Roads Bride* (www.hamptonroadsbride.com) and *Virginia Wine Lover Magazine* (www.virginiawinelover.com).

Newport News Daily Press (757-247-4600; www.dailypress.com), 7505 Warwick Boulevard, Newport News 23607. Daily covers the cities on and around the Virginia Peninsula.

Virginian-Pilot (757-446-2000; www.thevirginianpilot.com or www.pilotonline.com), Norfolk. The largest daily newspaper in the state of Virginia, covering southeastern Virginia, the Eastern Shore, northeastern North Carolina, and Hampton Roads.

Williamsburg Yorktown Daily (757-565-1079; www.wydaily.com), 5000 New Point Road, Williamsburg 23188. Daily covers Williamsburg and James City and York counties.

Richmond Region: **Richmond Magazine** (804-355-0111; www.richmondmagazine.com), 2201 W. Broad Street, Suite 105, Richmond 23220. Monthly four-color glossy covering Richmond past, present, and future.

Richmond Times-Dispatch (804-644-4181 or 800-468-3382; www2.timesdispatch.com or www2.richmond.com), 300 E. Franklin Street, Richmond 23219. Daily is the primary paper of the state's capital, commonly considered the "newspaper of record" for the state of Virginia. Extensive online archives at www.richmond.com.

Style Weekly (804-358-0825; www.styleweekly.com), 1313 E. Main Street, Richmond 23219. Richmond's alternative weekly for news, arts, culture, and opinion. Published on Wed.

RADIO AND TELEVISION

Cox Cable (ww2.cox.com) serves Virginia Beach, Chesapeake, Norfolk, Portsmouth, Newport News, Hampton, York, Williamsburg, and Mathews. **Verizon FiOS** (www22.verizon.com) serves Norfolk, Virginia Beach, Portsmouth, Chesapeake, Hampton, and Newport News. **Charter Cable** (www.buycharter.com) serves Suffolk; Franklin; Smithfield; the Eastern Shore, including Cape Charles; and parts of North Carolina's Outer Banks. **Comcast** (www.comcast.com) serves Richmond and Chesterfield County. Some hotels offer the **Dish Network** (www.dishnetwork.com) or **DirecTV**

(www.directv.com). For a list of specific television stations, see Appendix A.

The area's major radio stations include the following (for a more comprehensive list, see Appendix A):

WHOV 88.1 FM (757-727-5670), Hampton. Hampton University jazz station.

WCVE 88.9 FM (804-320-1301; www.ideastations.org/radio), Richmond. Public radio, jazz, swing.

WHRV 89.5 FM (757-889-9400; www.whro.org), Norfolk public radio. Jazz, blues, Americana.

The Tide 92.3 FM (757-565-1079; www.tideradio.com), Williamsburg. Handpicked music and local events.

WVBW The Wave 92.9 FM (757-671-1000; www.929thewave.com), Virginia Beach. Adult contemporary.

WPTE The Point 94.9 FM (757-497-2000; www.pointradio.com), Virginia Beach. Adult contemporary hits.

WGH The Eagle 97.3 FM (757-671-1000; www.eagle97.com), Newport News. Country music.

WTVR 98.1 FM (Lite 98) (804-474-0000; www.lite98.com), Richmond. Soft rock, local events.

WYFI 99.7 FM (757-420-9505; www.bbnradio.org), Norfolk. Bible Broadcasting Network home station.

WRXL 102.1 FM (The X) (804-474-0000; www.1021thex.com), Richmond. New rock.

WXTG 102.1 FM (www.1021thegame.com), Virginia Beach. Sports radio. Also 1490 AM.

WMXB 103.7 FM (804-330-5700; www.mix1037.com), Richmond. Adult contemporary; local entertainment and event news.

WDZY 1290 AM (804-353-7200; www.radiodisney.com), Colonial Heights. Radio Disney.

ROAD DESIGNATIONS In Virginia, as elsewhere, there are state roads, preceded by "VA" in this guide. However, in addition there are roads called State Secondary Routes—which elsewhere might be called County Routes. These are designated "SR" on little signs across the state, and we have followed suit in this guide to indicate that these roads are smaller, harder to find, and harder to follow than the major Virginia highways.

SCENIC BYWAYS AND TRAILS
Captain John Smith Adventures on the James and Pamaunk Flu Driving and Water Trails (www.johnsmithtrail.org). Follow Smith's explorations of the James and York river valleys by land and sea, with quotes from Smith's journals and letters. Three land and water loops are mapped out along the James (Powhatan Flu), from the Falls of the James to Newport News. Land routes travel along both sides of the James, visiting many historic points and nature preserves. The **Pamaunk Trails** explore the Pamunky, Mattaponi, and York rivers.
Chesapeake Bay Gateways Network (410-260-2488; www.baygateways.net), 410 Severn Avenue, Suite 314, Annapolis, MD 21403. This listing of more than 160 parks, wildlife refuges, museums, sailing ships, his-

toric communities, and water, hiking, and driving trails on the Chesapeake Bay and its rivers is administered by the National Park Service. Driving tours include **Early Settlement in Virginia,** from Jamestown Island to the Pamunkey Indian Reservation, plus themed tours on boatbuilding, watermen, and waterfowling.

Civil War Trails (www.civilwar-va .com). Several Civil War trails run through the Tidewater, following the routes of the Peninsula Campaign of 1862, Lee vs. Grant 1864–1865, and Lee's Retreat.

Colonial Parkway (757-898-2410; www.nps.gov/colo). Scenic 24-mile parkway connects Historic Jamestowne and Yorktown Battlefield with no commercial development along the way.

Dismal Swamp Canal Trail (757-382-6411; www.cityofchesapeake.net).

Multiuse 8.5-mile paved trail running along the Dismal Swamp Canal is open for biking, hiking, running, horseback riding, and boating (in the canal). The trailhead in Chesapeake is at the intersection of Old Route 17 and Dominion Boulevard.

Road to Revolution Heritage Trail (888-742-4666; www.roadto revolution.com). Sites associated with Virginia patriot Patrick Henry stretch across the state, from his birthplace in Hanover County to his last home and burial place at **Red Hill** (www.patrick henry.com).

Virginia Birding and Wildlife Trails (804-367-1000; www.dgif .virginia.gov/vbwt), 4010 W. Broad Street, Richmond 23230. Numerous loops lead to the region's rich natural heritage sites.

Virginia Capital Trail (www .virginiacapitaltrail.org), P.O. Box 17966, Richmond 23226. New 55-mile, paved multiuse path connecting the former and current Virginia capitals of Williamsburg, Jamestown, and Richmond runs alongside scenic VA 5, the John Tyler Highway. The annual **Cap2Cap bike ride** (http://cap2cap .virginiacapitaltrail.org) follows the route each May.

Virginia Scenic Byways (www .virginiadot.org). A map of Virginia's designated scenic byways can be downloaded or ordered online. Significant routes in southeast Virginia include **VA 5,** running past the plantations of Charles City County; the **Green Sea Byway,** through the Pungo region south of Virginia Beach; and **SR 600,** an alternate route up the Delmarva Peninsula.

Virginia Wine Trails (www .virginiawine.org). With more than 150 wineries and more than a dozen wine trails spread across the state, Virginia presents lots of options for wine lovers.

HISTORY AND CULTURE

As William Byrd II famously said, "In the beginning, all America was Virginia." Perhaps no other statement better sums up the importance of this region in our nation's history.

Here English settlers first encountered the Native Americans who had lived on these lands for thousands of years. Elizabeth I, the English queen, gave those first comers freedom to settle all of Virginia, described as stretching from the Atlantic to the Pacific oceans (believed to be a matter of a few hundred miles) and along the coast from Cape Fear to Canada.

Barely one hundred years later, the Virginia colony, grown rich on tobacco, gave birth to a generation of young revolutionaries—Washington, Jefferson, Patrick Henry, Madison, believers in the universal Rights of Man—who would lead America in its fight for independence from the English crown and through its early years as a republic.

The world would never be the same. The English fife and drum corps recognized the fact when they played "The World Turned Upside Down" at the surrender of General Cornwallis in Yorktown.

One hundred years more, and descendants of many of the same families would fight another war on Virginia soil in the cause of states' rights, but also over the "peculiar institution" of slavery, a fatal paradox in a society that bases its identity on the idea that all men are created equal.

Nearly 150 years after Lee's surrender at Appomattox, Richmond, the Virginia Peninsula, and Hampton Roads form the most populous area of the state. Virginia Beach is Virginia's largest metropolitan area, and Richmond is once again the prosperous and cultivated capital of one of the largest and most important states in the country.

But despite the modern boom, history runs too deep here to be forgotten. For about one hundred miles, from the mouth of Chesapeake Bay to the Falls of the James River, where the view reminded William Byrd II of England's Richmond-upon-Thames, costumed interpreters wait at dozens of locations, eager to share the stories of the people who lived here and the world-changing events they participated in.

Williamsburg, the largest living-history museum in the country, re-creates the days of the Revolution. Jamestown and the Citie of Henricus preserve memories of the earliest settlements. American Indians explain the traditions of their ancestors next to mat huts and longhouses. Hoop-skirted ladies lead tours of elegant antebellum homes. Uniformed men, in both blue and gray, stand guard over the many battlefields that dot the land.

Nowhere better can a visitor experience firsthand the events and personalities that shaped, and continue to shape, our nation.

IT CAME FROM OUTER SPACE: THE BIG BANG

The natural history of the Virginia Tidewater began, literally, with a bang.

About 35 million years ago, tropical forests of palms, oaks, and walnut trees covered the land that would become eastern Virginia. Shallow ocean waters reached inland as far as today's Richmond city limits.

Traveling faster than a speeding bullet, an extraterrestrial rock a mile wide crashed into this quiet landscape, landing in the waters just offshore. Penetrating through thousands of feet of sediment and mud, the meteorite fractured the bedrock to a depth of 7 miles before vaporizing in a flash of steam and setting off a series of massive tsunamis.

The explosion left behind a crater 96 miles across and more than a mile deep. Scientists found the center of the crater directly beneath the little town of Cape Charles on the Eastern Shore. Although the crater soon filled with new sediments and cannot be seen on the surface today, the event caused a subsidence of the area, a low spot that endured to form Chesapeake Bay.

The impact is credited with causing a distinctive right angle bend to the north in the lower reaches of the James River as it passes over the rim of the ancient crater. This sharp bend harbors Hampton Roads, one of the greatest deepwater ports in the world.

THE TIDEWATER:
WHERE LAND AND WATER MEET

All of the land east of I-95, which runs along Virginia's fall line, is considered the **Tidewater.** Here the land is fertile, and the rivers follow the rise and fall of the tides. Many streams, including the James and York, are salty far upstream.

A series of falls and rapids marks the western edge of the Tidewater and the beginning of the hilly **Virginia Piedmont.** Several important cities, including Richmond, Petersburg, and Fredericksburg, developed at the fall line to take advantage of water power to run mills and factories.

Stretching southeast from the fall line at Richmond, a long peninsula bordered on either side by the York and James rivers extends toward the Chesapeake Bay. On the shores of these rivers the first lasting English settlements in the New World took root. Thanks to this preeminence, the land between the rivers became known as the **Virginia Peninsula,** heart of the English crown's richest American colony.

Today, communities on the Virginia Peninsula include rural Charles City County and New Kent County, on the outskirts of Richmond; Williamsburg; Yorktown; Poquoson; and, at the southern tip, Hampton and Newport News.

Across the James River lies the area known to locals as the **Southside,** once the quiet home of plantations and truck farms, today the most populous section of Virginia and home of the great Atlantic Fleet. Communities here include the independent cities of Virginia Beach, largest in the state; the Navy ports of Norfolk and Portsmouth; rural Chesapeake; and Suffolk, the peanut capital; as well as the counties of Surry and Isle of Wight, where the unincorporated town of Smithfield rules the land of ham.

Between the tip of the Virginia Peninsula and the Southside lies the great **Hampton Roads,** a deep anchorage or roadstead, named by the colonists for Henry Wriothesley (pronounced *Risley*), third Earl of Southampton, a prominent member of the Virginia Company of London and an important patron of William Shakespeare. Today, the name Hampton Roads is applied to the entire region lying along the shores of this deep, crater-created harbor.

The Virginia Peninsula is the longest and most southern of the necks of land

THE GREAT DISMAL

For many miles along the Virginia–North Carolina border, swamps create a tangled jungle, named "dismals" by the early settlers for their dim light and murky water. Meandering blackwater streams, their waters dyed dark by tannic acid from dropping leaves, thread these marshy woodlands of cypress, juniper, cedar, and tupelo gum.

William Byrd II first surveyed the area, establishing a dividing line between the colonies in 1728. He found the swamp a "horrible desert" and unsuitable for human habitation. George Washington, who made his own survey in 1763, saw something entirely different—"a glorious paradise"— and headed a company that bought 40,000 acres of the swamp, intending to drain it and establish a huge plantation. Although several ditches were dug, the drainage effort failed, so the company concentrated on lumbering off the cypress trees and turning the cedars into shingles, industries that con-tinued for 150 years.

Washington also proposed digging a canal through the swamp to con-nect the Chesapeake Bay with Albemarle Sound in North Carolina. Dug mostly with slave labor, today the Dismal Swamp Canal is an alternate route on the Atlantic Intracoastal Waterway and the country's oldest man-made canal still in operation.

Many travelers visited the Dismal Swamp during the 19th century, including some prominent literary figures. Edgar Allan Poe wrote his poem "The Lake" after visiting Lake Drummond, reputedly haunted, in the heart of the swamp. Robert Frost came here with a broken heart, seeking an equally gloomy landscape. Edna Ferber wrote her novel *Showboat,* the inspiration for the famous musical, after seeing performances aboard the James Adams' Floating Theatre on the canal.

Before the Civil War, the Great Dismal became a refuge for enslaved people seeking freedom. Henry Wadsworth Longfellow published a poem titled "The Slave in the Dismal Swamp" in 1842, and Harriet Beecher Stowe followed up her successful *Uncle Tom's Cabin* with a second novel, *Dred: A* that jut into the Chesapeake Bay. To the north, the **Middle Peninsula** lies between the York and Rappahannock rivers. A mostly rural area, with few industries and no cities, this region, sometimes called the **River Country** (www.visit rivercountry.org), is also the location of several small American Indian reservations, among the few to survive from colonial days.

The **Northern Neck** (www.northernneck.org), a narrow peninsula lying between the Rappahannock and Potomac rivers, developed a sophisticated plantation society early in colonial times. Many of Virginia's gentry were born in what was called the Athens of the New World, including George Washington at **Pope's**

Tale of the Great Dismal Swamp, in 1856. Today, the Great Dismal is part of the **Underground Railway Network to Freedom** (www.nps.gov/ugrr).

Originally estimated to have covered some 2,200 square miles, the Great Dismal has been reduced to about 600 square miles today, still the largest wilderness area on the Eastern Seaboard. Although considerably drier than in previous centuries due to logging and ditching, the swamp is still home to a great variety of wildlife, including black bears, bobcats, otters, and white-tailed deer, plus 70 species of reptiles and amphibians. Nearly 100 species of birds nest here, with another 100 migrating through, and 43 species of butterflies have been sighted, including the rare Hessel's Hairstreak.

Today, much of the Great Dismal is protected in a series of national, state, and private preserves, including the **Great Dismal Swamp National Wildlife Refuge** (www.fws.gov), the largest at 111,000 acres. Parts of the swamp, however, are still privately owned, including 6,000 acres purchased by the military contractor formerly known as Blackwater Worldwide for use as their private training ground.

DEEP CYPRESS SWAMPS, CALLED DISMALS, ONCE OCCUPIED MUCH OF THE VIRGINIA TIDEWATER.

VIRGINIA'S INDIAN TRIBES TODAY

Although many of the tribes living in Virginia before the arrival of the English have been lost or displaced, the rivers running into Chesapeake Bay reveal the distribution of the Native American peoples. The Chickahominy; the Appomattox; the Pamunkey and Mattaponi; the Piankatank; the Nottaway, Nansemond, and Meherrin; and the great Rappahannock and Potomac rivers all were named for the tribes that once lived along their shores.

After the various conflicts with the English, most Tidewater tribes were resettled on treaty lands in **King William County** (www.kingwilliamcounty .us) between the Mattaponi and Pamunkey rivers.

Despite the heavy toll of war, displacement, disease, and racial prejudice, eleven tribes of **Virginia Indians** (http://virginiaindians.pwnet.org) have survived to the current day and are recognized by the state of Virginia (www.indians.vipnet.org). Two tribes, the Mattaponi and the Pamunkey, occupy remnants of tribal lands granted by the Virginia General Assembly in 1658. Other tribes gradually lost or sold their reservation lands and migrated back to their traditional homes. Ten of the recognized tribes can be found in the Tidewater region.

The **Pamunkey** (804-843-4792; www.pamunkey.net; 175 Lay Landing Road, King William 23086), one of the most powerful tribes in the Powhatan Confederacy, today hold 1,200 acres of land on the banks of their namesake river, about 25 miles from Richmond. On the reservation visitors can take a driving tour of historic sites, including the reputed burial mound of Powhatan; visit the Shadfish Hatchery and the Pamunkey Indian Museum; and see pottery made using traditional techniques and local clay.

The **Mattaponi** (804-769-4508; http://sites.communitylink.org/Mattaponi; 1467 Mattaponi Reservation Circle, West Point 23181) continue to live on reservation lands along the Mattaponi River, one of the most pristine streams in the eastern United States. A museum here is open to the public, along with a pottery shop, trading post, and a fish hatchery and marine science facility dedicated to the American shad, a fish important in the traditional Mattaponi lifestyle. A related band, the **Upper Mattaponi Indian Tribe** (804-769-3378; www.uppermattaponi.org; 13383 King William Road, King William 23086), lives nearby and hosts a Tribal Pow-Wow and Festival every May.

The **Rappahannock Tribe** (804-769-0260; www.rappahannocktribe.org; 5036 Indian Neck Road/SR 623, Indian Neck 23148) owns lands in King and Queen County (www.kingandqueenco.net). The tribal museum holds items found in archaeological digs, including early trade beads. A Tribal Pow-Wow is held every October.

Members of the **Chickahominy** (www.chickahominytribe.org) and **Eastern Chickahominy** (www.cied.org) tribes returned to their ancestral lands on the Virginia Peninsula, once a rich center of corn production. Today, the tribes own land in neighboring Charles City and New Kent counties. An annual Fall Festival and Powwow is held in September at the **Chickahominy Tribal Center** (804-829-2027; 8200 Lott Cary Road, Providence Forge 23140). Other annual events include a Crab Feast in October and the Six Nations Pow-Wow the first weekend in May.

The **Nansemond Indian Tribe** (www.nansemond.org) lives today, as it did in the past, in the Chuckatuck area along the Nansemond River, near today's Suffolk. The tribe hosts an American Indian Festival every June in association with the Chesapeake Parks Department (757-382-8466), and a Tribal Pow Wow in August at Lone Star Lakes Lodge in Suffolk. The **Suffolk Center for Cultural Arts** (www.suffolkcenter.org) displays an exhibit of Nansemond artifacts.

The **Monacan Indian Nation** (434-946-5391; www.monacannation.com; 2009 Kenmore Road, Amherst 24521), a Siouan-speaking tribe descended from the peoples that once roamed the Virginia Piedmont, have a tribal center and museum at Bear Mountain, near Lynchburg.

Several tribes received state recognition in 2010. The **Cheroenhaka** (757-562-7760; www.cheroenhaka-nottoway.org; P.O. Box 397, Courtland 23837) have reestablished their reservation lands in Southampton County, where they will build a tribal cultural center, museum, historic village, and powwow grounds. The Green Corn Dance celebration is held every July. The nearby **Nottoway of Virginia** (434-658-4454; www.nottowayindians.org; P.O. Box 246, Capron 23829) hold their powwow in September.

Another tribe recognized in 2010, the **Patawomeck** (540-371-9452; www.patawomeckindians.org; 534 Fagan Drive, Fredericksburg 22405), live mostly in Stafford County and the Northern Neck, and continue to build traditional dugout canoes.

Other tribes, including the **Halawa-Saponi** (www.haliwa-saponi.com) and **Meherrin** (www.meherrintribe.com), live on the border between Virginia and North Carolina and have been recognized by the state of North Carolina.

Every year on the day before Thanksgiving, representatives of the Mattaponi and Pamunkey tribes arrive at the Governor's Mansion in Richmond to present tributes of pottery, deer, and other game, as specified in the treaties of 1646 and 1677, in return for their reservation lands.

Creek Plantation (www.nps.gov/gewa) and Robert E. Lee at **Stratford Hall** (www.stratfordhall.org).

NATIVE TRIBES: BEFORE AND AFTER POCAHONTAS

By the time the English began to arrive in the early 1600s, Native American tribes had inhabited the Tidewater of Virginia for many thousands of years. In fact, archaeologists working at Cactus Hill, 45 miles south of Richmond on the Nottaway River, recently discovered artifacts dated to 15,000–17,000 years ago, lying below newer deposits left by the Clovis people, long considered the first humans to inhabit the New World.

By 1607, on the eve of the English arrival, the Tidewater was densely populated by Algonquian tribes, including 30 in a confederacy controlled by a paramount chief called Powhatan, plus several independent tribes including the Chickahominy, the Rappahannock, the Nansemond, and the Meherrin. The Native American population in the Tidewater is estimated to have numbered 15,000–21,000 people precontact. Above the fall line, a similar number of Siouan-speaking peoples of the Monacan confederacy occupied the Virginia Piedmont.

Relations between the English and the native tribes were rocky from the start. In the winter of 1609, after Capt. John Smith returned to England, the Powhatan tribes would no longer provide corn for the settlers, triggering the Starving Time, when all but 60 of the 500 colonists died. Only the arrival of a supply fleet commanded by Baron Delaware saved the colony from failure.

By 1610, the Kecoughtan tribe, despite hosting the first Chesapeake oyster roast enjoyed by the newcomers and many other acts of hospitality, were driven from their rich fields in today's Hampton area, and the pattern repeated across the Peninsula as English numbers increased.

CAPT. JOHN SMITH EXPLORED MUCH OF THE CHESAPEAKE BAY AND FOUNDED THE EARLIEST VIRGINIA COLONIES.

A period of peace followed the marriage of Powhatan's daughter to colonist John Rolfe in 1614, but after the death of Pocahontas and her father, the new chief sought to drive the English away, attacking unexpectedly in 1622, killing 350–400 settlers, about one third of their total number, and destroying the Citie of Henricus and several other settlements. The colonists retaliated, burning Indian villages and fields. A peace was negotiated, but more than two hundred Indian warriors were poisoned at the signing ceremony in Jamestown.

A second surprise attack in 1644 killed another four hundred settlers, by this time just a tenth of the English population. Fierce retaliations followed, and the subsequent Treaty of 1646 gave the English control of all the land between the York and the Blackwater rivers, including the entire Virginia Peninsula as far inland as the Falls of the James. Land on the Middle Peninsula was reserved for the tribes but was soon overrun by a new wave of English settlers.

By 1669, records indicate that disease and warfare had reduced the native population of the Tidewater from some 20,000 to approximately 1,800.

The James River, formerly known as Powhatan Flu, was renamed for the king of England, and the Pamunkey below the fall line became the York, name changes that symbolized the supplanting of the once-powerful Native American tribes.

EARLY EXPLORERS AND FIRST SETTLEMENTS

With the death of Queen Elizabeth I, the Virgin Queen, in 1603, the patent of Sir Walter Raleigh to plant settlements in Virginia expired and colonization rights passed to the favorites of the new king, James I. The Virginia Company of London, chartered in 1606, wasted no time sending three ships, the *Susan Constant,* the *Godspeed,* and the *Discovery,* carrying about one hundred men and boys, to found a colony. On April 26, 1607, the company landed on the south side of the mouth of Chesapeake Bay near today's Virginia Beach, naming the cape there for Henry, Prince of Wales. The cape on the north side of the bay's mouth was named for his brother, Charles, Duke of York.

Under orders to found their colony away from the Atlantic, where it might be better protected from the Spanish, Captains Goswold, Smith, and Newport proceeded up the James River, with a stop in today's Hampton region, where they enjoyed the hospitality of the local Kecoughtan tribe. The low and swampy island they selected for their settlement, named James Towne in honor of the king, proved to be insect-ridden and poor for farming but had the advantages of a deep anchorage and no previous native inhabitants.

A REPLICA OF THE *SUSAN CONSTANT* AT JAMESTOWN SETTLEMENT SHOWS HOW THE ENGLISH CROSSED THE ATLANTIC.

BACON'S REBELLION

In 1675, one of Virginia's wealthy colonists, Nathaniel Bacon, organized an army to defy Royal Governor William Berkeley's policy of containment and cooperation with the remaining American Indians in the colony. Bacon demanded that the Indians living on treaty-protected lands be driven out or killed and accused Berkeley of corruption and favoritism.

Bacon's militia invaded Jamestown twice, first holding the House of Burgesses and the governor at musketpoint, then, in September 1676, returning to burn the colonial capital to the ground. The rebel leader died of dysentery a month later, and his men dispersed, evacuating the properties they had occupied, including impressive **Bacon's Castle** (www.apva.org/baconscastle) on the south side of the James.

THE JACOBEAN ARCHITECTURE OF BACON'S CASTLE MADE IT AN IDEAL FORTRESS DURING THE 1675 REBELLION.

The Spanish had explored these waters much earlier, establishing a Jesuit mission named Ajacan on the York River in 1570. The Powhatan tribes wiped out the mission, ending Spanish settlement attempts.

Despite its unfavorable situation, James Towne remained the capital of the Virginia colony until 1699, surviving many near disasters, including the 1609 Starving Time, Indian massacres in 1622 and 1646, and Bacon's Rebellion in 1676. Under orders to make a profit for their investors in England, the colonists fruitlessly prospected for silver and gold, and tried many other industries, including glassmaking in America's first factory.

Capt. John Smith, who claimed that Pocahontas saved him from being beheaded by her father, Powhatan, is credited with the early survival of the colony, but John Rolfe, the man who married Pocahontas, gave the colony the cash crop it needed to survive. Rolfe planted a sweet strain of tobacco that found favor in the European markets and began exporting it in 1612. Soon, other colonists followed suit, making their fortunes from a plant that would bring prosperity to Virginia for four hundred years.

Smith and Newport made many voyages around the Chesapeake Bay seeking sites for other settlements. A fort was established at Old Point Comfort, near today's city of Hampton, in 1610. In 1611, Sir Thomas Dale and three hundred settlers founded the Citie of Henricus (www.henricus.org), a palisaded town near today's Richmond.

Soon both shores of the James were populated by settlements called hundreds, sponsored by venture capitalists back in England who received 100 acres of land for each colonist they sent to Virginia. The Bermuda Hundred, located near Henricus on the land between the James and the Appomattox rivers, was the earliest, founded in 1613.

By 1632, the entire lower Peninsula was in English hands. To protect their settlements and cattle from Indian attack, the English built a wooden palisade completely across the Peninsula from the James to the York rivers. A fort and community established here, named Middle Plantation, developed around the only gate through the palisade. Native Americans seeking to enter the protected area had to obtain a pass at the gate.

In 1694, the College of William and Mary began classes at Middle Plantation under a royal charter. After an accidental fire in 1699 burned the Jamestown statehouse, the capital of the colony moved to Middle Plantation, renamed Williamsburg in honor of King William III. It remained the capital of Virginia until 1780, when Governor Thomas Jefferson moved the state government to Richmond during the Revolutionary War.

THE STORY OF POCAHONTAS SYMBOLIZES THE CLASH BETWEEN NATIVE AMERICAN INDIAN AND ENGLISH CULTURES.

TIDEWATER ARISTOCRACY

By the 1700s, large estates lined the shores of the James, York, and Potomac rivers, mostly tobacco plantations embellished with palatial homes occupied by the cream of the Tidewater aristocracy. Many of the families descended from younger sons of the English gentry, who came to America to find land of their own. During the English Civil War (1642–1660), these included many Royalists and Cavaliers opposed to Oliver Cromwell. King

Charles II referred to the Virginia colony as his "Old Dominion," a nickname still used today.

William Byrd, son of a London goldsmith, became a prominent fur trader in Virginia, with trading posts near the falls of the James and Appomattox rivers. His son William Byrd II built the impressive Westover plantation house on the James and founded the cities of Richmond and Petersburg, besides becoming one of the colony's most prolific authors.

The descendants of this early Tidewater aristocracy became known as Virginia's First Families, and many have played important roles in the nation's history. One of William Byrd's descendants, Adm. Richard E. Byrd, gained fame for his daring flights over both the North and South poles.

REVOLUTIONARY FIREBRANDS

Boston, Massachusetts, is frequently called the Cradle of Liberty, but the name belongs perhaps equally to Williamsburg, Virginia, where many of the future nation's Founding Fathers gathered in the years leading up to the Revolution. Serving in the Virginia House of Burgesses, these young men included George Washington, Thomas Jefferson, Patrick Henry, George Mason, and others who would soon take their places on the world stage.

EDGAR ALLAN POE: THE RAVEN OF RICHMOND

Although born in Boston, Massachusetts, and buried in Baltimore, Maryland, Edgar Allan Poe, originator of detective fiction and master of the horror story, had deep roots in the fertile ground of Richmond, Virginia. His mother, an actress, died in the city and was buried at St. John's Episcopal, leaving young Edgar, just three, an orphan in 1811. The well-to-do Allan family took the boy in and added their name to his, although never formally adopting him.

EDGAR ALLAN POE STILL ATTRACTS THE LADIES AT THE POE MUSEUM IN RICHMOND.

As a teenager, Poe formed an attachment with Elmira Royster, who lived nearby. The pair would meet under the linden trees in a garden on Franklin

Many of the future patriots attended the College of William and Mary in Williamsburg, where they came under the influence of George Wythe, the first professor of law in America. Wythe was a proponent of John Locke's philosophy of natural rights, holding that men are by nature free and equal, with inalienable rights to life, liberty, and property. These ideas later influenced documents drafted by Wythe's students, including the Declaration of Independence and the Virginia Statute of Religious Freedom, both written by Thomas Jefferson, and George Mason's Virginia Declaration of Rights, a direct precursor to the United States Bill of Rights.

As early as 1765, Patrick Henry's resolutions condemning the Stamp Act set the colony on fire. In June 1774, the royal governor dissolved the Burgesses when they voted to show solidarity with Boston, where royal decree had closed the port. The members met instead at nearby Raleigh Tavern, voting to support Massachusetts and suggesting the formation of a Continental Congress of all the colonies. In August 1774 the first Virginia Convention voted to suspend all trade with Great Britain, and in November, Yorktown had its own Tea Party, with two chests of imported tea dumped into the York River.

The second Virginia Convention met in March 1775 at St. John's Church in Richmond. Delegates voted to arm the Virginia militia after Patrick Henry declared, "Give me liberty or give me death."

Street owned by Poe's father, today the site of the Linden Row Inn. The young couple entered into an engagement when Elmira was just 15, but the romance was soon broken up by the girl's father, who intercepted and destroyed the letters Poe sent his sweetheart from college.

Elmira married another, a Mr. Shelton, but the story of the lost letters and parental interference later became widespread in the city. Poe, broken-hearted, left for the North, pursuing a writing career at publications in Boston, New York, Baltimore, and Philadelphia, and gaining fame as a poet, short story writer, and reviewer. The couple, now both widowed, met again in 1848, when Poe returned to town on a lecture tour. They became engaged, but Poe died under mysterious circumstances in Baltimore just weeks before the wedding.

Elmira's influence on Poe's writings continues to be debated by biographers; however, it seems sure that his favorite themes of lost love, dark tragedy, and enchanted gardens were suggested by this early romance. Certainly, Poe's first published work, *Tamerlane,* and his last, *Annabel Lee,* can be directly attributed to Elmira's inspiration, justifying her reputation in Richmond as Poe's first and last love.

The **Poe Museum** (www.poemuseum.org), occupying the city's oldest stone house, preserves many unique relics donated by the people of Richmond, including much information on Elmira Royster Shelton and Poe's other lady loves.

On April 20, 1775, the day following the Battles of Lexington and Concord outside of Boston, Lord Dunmore, the royal governor of Virginia, secretly ordered his troops to remove gunpowder stored in the Williamsburg Magazine to a ship in the York River. An enraged company of militia, led by Patrick Henry, marched on Williamsburg.

By June 1775, Dunmore was sufficiently impressed by the insurrection to flee to the safety of a British man-of-war and retreat to Norfolk, then a center of Loyalist sentiment thanks to its large merchant population. In November, the governor issued a proclamation offering freedom to any enslaved person who would leave their patriot masters and join the British forces, the first mass emancipation of slaves in North America.

A month later, on December 11, 1775, patriot troops from Virginia and North Carolina routed Dunmore's forces at the **Battle of Great Bridge** (www.gbbattle field.org), 12 miles south of Norfolk. On New Year's Day, 1776, the fleet commanded by Dunmore opened fire on the town of Norfolk, bombarding it for eight hours before sailing up the coast to New York City, abandoning Virginia to the patriots.

Most of the action in the Revolution took place to the north and south of Virginia until December 1780, when Benedict Arnold, now a British brigadier general, sailed up the James, capturing and burning Richmond, and defeating an outnumbered Continental force in the Battle of Petersburg on April 25, 1781.

Cornwallis reached Petersburg on May 20 and moved toward Williamsburg, followed closely by Lafayette's forces. The July 6 Battle of Green Spring, near Jamestown, was the last major land engagement of the war before Cornwallis dug in at Yorktown.

On September 5, a fleet of French warships defeated 19 British ships of the line in a naval battle just outside the mouth of Chesapeake Bay. This victory, called the Battle Off the Capes, or Battle of the Chesapeake, cut Cornwallis off from rescue or resupply.

To trap Cornwallis at Yorktown, George Washington and the Comte de Rochambeau marched their armies 450 miles from New York in just over a month. Their route across six states, now called the **Washington-Rochambeau Revolutionary Route** (www.w3r-us.org), is a designated National Historic Trail.

After a month of siege, heavy bombardment from American and French artillery, and several sharp battles, Cornwallis surrendered his army on October 19, 1781, effectively ending hostilities in the American Revolution and ensuring the liberty of the United States of America.

THE CIVIL WAR: GROUND ZERO

No state saw more battles during the Civil War than Virginia, where hundreds of engagements took place throughout the four-year conflict. The presence of the Confederate Capital in Richmond ensured that the Union viewed it as the ultimate prize, the one place that had to fall before the war could end.

Many of the most famous, and bloodiest, battles of the war took place on the roads leading to Richmond—Cold Harbor, the Crater, Malvern Hill, Chancellorsville, the Wilderness—as well as some of the most renowned feats of heroism, including J. E. B. Stuart's ride around McClellan's army. It was a war that saw many innovations—including trench warfare, aerial surveillance from balloons, repeating rifles, and ironclad warships—and a war that signaled the end of an agrarian way of life based on the plantation system and the labor of enslaved people.

As you travel the Virginia Civil War Trails, you'll meet many famous names, such as Lee and Grant, Stonewall Jackson, Jeff Davis, and Abraham Lincoln, and see the graves of many others whose names history has forgotten—those who crossed paths here, debating with force of arms whether the United States, founded less than a hundred years before, would survive.

AFRICAN AMERICANS IN THE TIDEWATER

The first Africans arrived in the Virginia colony on August 1, 1619, aboard pirate ships that removed them from a Portuguese slave ship en route from Angola. The pirates traded the Africans for provisions, beginning a slave trade that would last for centuries.

At first, Africans had the status of indentured servants, who earned their independence after a term of service, typically three to seven years. But during the late 1600s, racial slavery became widespread, and enslaved people of African descent no longer could gain their freedom. Several slave insurrections followed. In 1705, a new Virginia code declared that "all Negro, mulatto and Indian slaves within this dominion" should be enslaved for life, as the property of their owners, and inflicted severe punishments for rebellion. Other laws made slavery hereditary.

As the Virginia plantation system grew, it became ever more dependent on enslaved labor. By 1730, slaves formed a quarter of Virginia's population, and by 1830, 40 percent of the state was of African descent.

The Constitution of the United States outlawed the importation of slaves from abroad after 1808, but the sale of slaves continued between the states, and Richmond emerged as a major slave trading center. The **Manchester Slave Trail** (804-646-7955; www.jamesriverpark.org) follows the route taken from the docks to Lumpkin's Slave Jail, where the final slave auction took place the day before Richmond fell to Union forces in 1865.

The industrial mills in Petersburg attracted people looking for work, and by 1860 the city had the largest population of free blacks in the South. Many of them lived on **Pocahontas Island,** and some participated in the Underground Railroad. Another route to freedom ran through the Dismal Swamp to Norfolk, where sympathetic ship captains could be found to take escaped slaves to northern ports.

During the Civil War, **Fort Monroe** became a refuge for enslaved people escaping from the Confederate states. After the war, Hampton Normal and Agricultural Institute, today **Hampton University** (www.hamptonu.edu), educated many of the newly freed people, counting among its alumni Booker T. Washington and many other prominent African Americans. Some of the graduates, including lawyers, journalists, and politicians, lived nearby in the affluent **East End** neighborhood of Newport News. Several house museums as well as the campus of Hampton University are open for tours.

In Richmond, **Jackson Ward** developed into a thriving African American business and cultural center, sometimes referred to as the Black Wall Street and the Harlem of the South. Walking tours of the neighborhood begin at the **Black History Museum** (www.blackhistorymuseum.org).

In the wake of the 1954 Brown v. Board of Education Supreme Court decision

THE CIVIL WAR IN THE VIRGINIA TIDEWATER AND RICHMOND REGION: A TIME LINE

This time line lists the major engagements of the Civil War that took place in the region covered by our guide, along with locations that give additional insight into the war years. Union forces made two main thrusts up the Virginia Peninsula, first in 1862 under General McClellan, and again in 1864 under General Butler. Neither was successful in capturing Richmond.

Meanwhile, Lincoln sent armies every year to attack Richmond overland from the north. None made it farther than Fredericksburg, until General Grant's bloody campaign in 1864 kept moving south, no matter what the cost.

Several established Civil War driving tours crisscross the region, often following the same roads used by the opposing troops. Visitors approaching from the north down I-95 may want to follow the **Lee vs. Grant 1864 Overland Campaign** driving tour, detailing the battles that led from the Wilderness to the Siege of Petersburg and Lee's eventual defeat. History buffs beginning their tour from the Virginia Beach or Williamsburg areas can follow the **1862 Peninsula Campaign** driving tour toward Richmond. Other driving tours in the region follow **Lee's Retreat** from Richmond to Appomattox, the cavalry action that concluded at **Trevilian Station,** and the **Wilson-Kautz Raid** through Southside Virginia.

Details of all these driving tours, as well as podcast tours of specific battlefields, are available for download free at www.civilwartraveler.com. The region's **National Battlefield Parks** (www.nps.gov) each has its own driving tours, with maps available at the visitors centers or online.

Another invaluable resource for the history traveler is the **Historical Marker Database** (www.hmdb.org), with its searchable listings of roadside markers found throughout the region (and beyond). Each marker, many with GPS coordinates, is linked to a map of its location, a critical aide in navigating the many winding country roads of Virginia.

A good place to begin any tour of Civil War sites in the region is the **Civil War Visitor Center at Tredegar Iron Works** (804-226-1981; www.nps .gov/rich; 470 Tredegar Street) in downtown Richmond. More information on attractions mentioned in the time line can be found in the individual chapters of this book.

1861

April 1861: Fort Monroe in Hampton reinforced. With Fort Wool across the harbor, it controls the entrance to Hampton Roads throughout the war.

The **Casemate Museum** (757-788-3391; www.monroe.army.mil) at Fort Monroe is open daily. Cruises aboard the *Miss Hampton II* from the Hampton waterfront include a stop at **Fort Wool.**

April 20, 1861: Norfolk Navy Yard (Gosport) burns. The Union Navy sets fire to the Gosport Shipyard in Portsmouth, destroying nine ships, including the USS *Merrimack.* Confederates raise the *Merrimack,* converting her into the CSS ironclad *Virginia.*

The **Portsmouth Naval Shipyard Museum** (757-393-8591; www.portsnaval museums.com), on the waterfront in Portsmouth, tells of the role played by the shipyard in local and national history.

May 18–19, 1861: Battle of Sewell's Point. Two Union gunboats make an inconclusive attack on the Confederate batteries near Norfolk.

Sewell's Point is today the location of the **Norfolk Naval Base,** home of the Atlantic Fleet. Tours by bus and boat are available. **Fort Norfolk** (www.norfolk historical.org; 810 Front Street), on the waterfront near downtown, originally built in 1794 and occupied by both Confederate and Union forces during the war, is open for self-guided tours.

May 27, 1861. Maj. Gen. Benjamin Butler, in command of Fort Monroe, declares escaping slaves seeking refuge at the fort to be contraband of war.

The **James A. Fields House** (757-245-1991; 617 27th Street), in Newport News, was built by one of these former slaves, later a representative to the Virginia House of Delegates. Other information on the contrabands can be found at Fort Monroe, Hampton City Museum and Hampton University in Hampton, and at Endview Plantation in Newport News. Norfolk's **Elmwood Cemetery** (757-441-2576; Princess Anne Road) contains one of the few monuments to African American soldiers who fought in the Civil War.

June 10, 1861: Battle of Big Bethel. The first land battle of the war in Virginia takes place in York County, near Tabb.

August 7, 1861. Confederates burn the town of Hampton to prevent it being used as a Union base.

The **Hampton History Museum** (757-727-1610) includes exhibits on the Battle of Big Bethel and dramatic photos of the ruins of the town after the fire. **St. John's Church** (www.stjohnshampton.org), the lone survivor of the destruction, is open for tours.

Winter 1861–1862. Confederate commander John "Prince" Magruder, with 13,000 troops, establishes three defensive lines of earthworks across the Virginia Peninsula from the York to the James rivers.

1862

March 8–9, 1862: Battle of Hampton Roads. The ironclads USS *Monitor* and CSS *Virginia* face off in a battle that changes naval warfare. On March 8, the *Virginia* attacks and destroys two wooden Union ships, the *Cumberland* and the *Congress.* On March 9, the *Monitor* arrives and engages the Confederate ironclad in a battle that ends in a draw.

The ***Congress* and *Cumberland* Overlook,** in **Christopher Newport Park,** between 26th and 28th streets on the Newport News waterfront, is directly opposite the site of the March 8 battle. Many observers watched the March 9 battle from the beach near today's ***Monitor-Merrimack* Overlook Park,** 16th Street and Oak Avenue off VA 167.

The **USS *Monitor* Center/Mariners' Museum** (800-581-7245; www .monitorcenter.org), in Newport News, contains many artifacts rescued from the wreck of the *Monitor,* including its distinctive "cheesebox" turret, plus a walk-in model of its interior.

March 17, 1862. McClellan's Army of the Potomac, more than 120,000 strong, arrives at Fort Monroe to begin the **Peninsula Campaign.**

MANY SPECTATORS WATCHED THE BATTLE BETWEEN THE IRONCLADS FROM THIS LOOKOUT IN NEWPORT NEWS. TODAY, IT IS A POPULAR SPOT FOR FISHING.

April 4, 1862: Skirmish at Causey's Mill. The Warwick Road, now US 60, is the Union's main avenue of advance.

Located next to the Riverside Regional Medical Center on Warwick Boulevard (US 60) in Newport News, **Causey's Mill** sits beside Lake Maury in the **Abernathy Garden. Young's Mill,** farther down US 60, was the site of a major Confederate camp, part of Magruder's first Peninsula line. The 1810 **Warwick Court House** (1401 Old Courthouse Way) was used as a Union headquarters during the campaign. From here, Thaddeus Lowe, chief aeronaut of the Army of the Potomac, made daily reconnaissance assents in the hot-air balloon *Constitution.*

April 5–May 4, 1862: Battle of Yorktown. McClellan's forces encounter Magruder's second defensive line stretching from Yorktown across the Peninsula to Mulberry Island on the James. Shore batteries at Yorktown and Gloucester Point block the York River to Union warships.

Tyndall's Point, a Gloucester County park on the north side of the US 17 bridge over the York, contains remains of earthworks and interpretive signs.

April 5, 1862: Battle of Lee's Mill. Thanks to clever Confederate troop movements during this battle, McClellan overestimates the forces opposing him and settles in for a siege. The Union's new Ager rapid-fire gun is first used in this battle.

At **Lee's Mill Battlefield Park,** off US 60 at 180 River Ridge Circle, Newport News, a short trail leads to well-preserved earthworks on a 40-foot bluff overlooking the Warwick River.

Confederate generals Magruder and Johnston rented **Lee Hall** (757-888-3371; www.leehall.org), in Newport News, as their headquarters. A Peninsula Campaign museum is located on the ground floor. Nearby **Endview Plantation** (757-887-1862; www.endview.org) served as a hospital for both Confederate and Union wounded.

April 16, 1862: Battle of Dam No. 1. Strong Confederate fortifications turn back McClellan's only serious attack of the siege.

Explore the battle's well-preserved earthworks, including a covered way built by George Armstrong Custer, via the Two Forts interpretive trail in **Newport News Park,** near the Newport News Visitor Center.

April 19, 1862: Battle of South Mills. Confederate troops repulse Union efforts to capture the southern end of the Dismal Swamp Canal.

Interpretive information is available at the **Dismal Swamp Canal Visitor Center** (252-771-8333) on US 17, 3 miles south of the Virginia border, and at the battle site on Canal Drive in South Mills, North Carolina. Other Civil War markers are located along the **Dismal Swamp Canal Trail** (Old Route 17) and at **Deep Creek Lock Park** (300 Luray Street, Chesapeake 23323) off US 17, commemorating the Dismal Swamp Rangers.

May 4, 1862. General McClellan prepares to attack Yorktown with more than 70 siege guns, the greatest concentration of heavy artillery ever massed in a single spot up to that time in history. However, the Confederates slip away on the night of May 3, retreating to Magruder's third defensive line near Williamsburg. Yorktown becomes a major Union port for the rest of the war.

The 1820s **Archer Cottage** on the Yorktown waterfront is the only structure surviving "Under the Hill" from the period. Information on the Civil War battles in the area can be found at the **Yorktown Visitor Center** (757-898-3400) of the Colonial National Park (www.nps.gov/colo).

May 5, 1862: The Battle of Williamsburg. The first heavy fighting of the campaign takes place around Fort Magruder, a bloody rear-guard action along the Williamsburg Road, as the Confederates retreat toward Richmond.

Many of the earthworks that made up the Confederate's third defensive line can still be seen. In Williamsburg, the site of **Fort Magruder,** on Penniman Road (SR 641), and **Redoubt Park,** on Quarterpath Road off US 60, preserve remnants of Confederate fortifications. The northern end of the Williamsburg line, including Redoubts 11, 12, and 13, is off Lakeshead Drive near the entrance of **New Quarter Park** (757-890-3500; www.yorkcounty.gov). Earthworks at the southern end of the line can still be seen in the national park on Jamestown Island.

May 5, 1862. President Lincoln, dissatisfied with the progress of the campaign, arrives in Hampton Roads to take command in the field. The next day he directs gunboat operations in the James River, and on May 8 he orders the *Monitor* and other Union ships to shell Confederate batteries at Sewell's Point.

May 9, 1862. Lincoln personally reconnoiters Sewell's Point and chooses a landing site near Willoughby Spit. Troops embark from Fort Monroe and land the next day, finding Sewell's Point abandoned.

May 10, 1862. Confederates burn the Gosport Shipyard. Union forces under General Wool occupy Norfolk. The crew of the CSS *Virginia,* unable to go up the James River because of her deep draft, scuttles the ironclad off Craney Island on May 11.

May 15, 1862: Battle of Drewry's Bluff. Union gunboats, including the ironclads *Monitor* and *Galena,* are repulsed by heavy fire at Fort Drewry (called Fort Darling by Union forces), 7 miles downstream from Richmond.

At **Drewry's Bluff** (7600 Fort Darling Road), part of **Richmond National Battlefield Park** (www.nps.gov/rich), visitors can enjoy a great view of the James and walk through the still-intact fort, site of the Confederate Naval Academy.

May 17, 1862: Capture of Forts Boykin and Huger. Confederate forts on the south side of the James fall to Union warships.

Fort Boykin (757-301-4007; 7410 Fort Boykin Trail, Smithfield 23430), built in the shape of a seven-pointed star, remains largely intact high on its bluff above the James about 6 miles upstream from Smithfield. An interpretive trail leads to an impressive view of the **Atlantic Ghost Fleet** from atop the bluff.

Fort Huger (757-301-4007; 15080 Talcott Terrace), about 2 miles farther up the James, was recently restored with an interpretive trail, cannon emplacements, and decks for viewing the Atlantic Ghost Fleet across the river.

May 27, 1862: Battle of Hanover Court House. A Confederate force of about 4,000 troops meet a Union force of 12,000 in a brief but bloody battle 4 miles southwest of Hanover near Slash Church, the first but far from the last battle in Hanover County.

Slash Church (804-798-4520; www.slashcc.org; 11353 Mount Hermon Road, Ashland 23005), where Confederate troops camped before the battle, is the oldest frame church in Virginia, erected in 1729 and still standing, about 15 miles north of Richmond.

May 31–June 1, 1862: Battle of Seven Pines. Confederate troops attack the Union forces south of the Chickahominy River. Despite inconclusive results, McClellan's march on Richmond is stalled and Confederate commander Johnston wounded, soon replaced by Gen. Robert E. Lee.

Markers in Sandston, near Richmond International Airport, interpret the disorganized battle. Several are in front of the Sandston Branch of the **Henrico County Library** (804-737-3728; 23 E. Williamsburg Road/US 60). The **Seven Pines National Cemetery** (804-795-2031; 400 E. Williamsburg Road), just east of town, is located on a portion of the battlefield.

June 12–15, 1862: J. E. B. Stuart's Ride. Lee's favorite cavalry commander completes a daring reconnaissance ride of nearly 100 miles, completely encircling McClellan's army.

Much of Stuart's route passed through **New Kent County** south of Richmond. A driving tour following Stuart's route accompanied by the officer's own commentary from his report to Lee is available at www.usa-civil-war .com and www.newkent.net.

June 26–July 1, 1862: Seven Days Campaign. The battles of Beaver Dam Creek, Gaines' Mill, Glendale (Frayser's Farm), and Malvern Hill, planned by Robert E. Lee, save Richmond and send McClellan's troops into retreat.

The Dabbs House Museum (804-652-3406; 3808 Nine Mile Road, Henrico 23223), served as Lee's first headquarters after taking command of the Army of Northern Virginia.

June 26, 1862: Battle of Beaver Dam Creek. Confederate forces under A. P. Hill attack Union forces in Hanover County.

The **Richmond National Battlefield Park** (804-771-2145; www.nps.gov/ rich) preserves two sites relating to the events of June 26. At **Chickahominy Bluff** (4300 Mechanicsville Turnpike, Richmond 23223), an audio exhibit on an overlook near where Robert E. Lee watched the opening of his offensive gives an introduction to the battle. A driving tour begins here, following many of the same roads used by the opposing forces in 1862. The park unit at **Beaver Dam Creek Battlefield** (7423 Cold Harbor Road, Mechanicsville 23111) preserves a section of the 2-mile front.

June 27, 1862: Battle of Gaines' Mill or First Cold Harbor. Confederate forces mount a coordinated attack, convincing McClellan to retreat to the James River and giving Lee his first major victory in the war.

At the **Gaines' Mill Battlefield Unit** (6283 Watt House Road, Mechanicsville 23111) of the **Richmond National Battlefield Park** (www.nps.gov/ rich), a trail passes rifle pits, artillery positions, and the historic Watt House, used as Union headquarters. An electric map of the Gaines' Mill battle can be found inside the **Cold Harbor Battlefield and Visitor Center** (5515 Anderson-Wright Drive, Mechanicsville 23111).

June 30, 1862: Battle of Glendale or Frayser's Farm. Disorganized Confederate attacks against the retreating Union forces allow McClellan's units to regroup.

The **Glendale Battlefield Visitor Center,** open seasonally inside the Glendale National Cemetery (804-795-2031; 8301 Willis Church Road, Richmond 23231) interprets the final two battles of the Seven Days Campaign with an electric map and exhibits. A driving tour covering both battlefields begins here.

July 1, 1862: Battle of Malvern Hill. Confederates are repulsed with heavy losses in attacks against strong Union positions.

Malvern Hill Battlefield (9175 Willis Church Road, Richmond 23231), another unit of **Richmond National Battlefield Park** (www.nps.gov/rich), features a trail following the route taken by Confederate forces into the face of the Union guns above them on the hill.

July–August 1862: Occupation of Harrison's Landing. Union forces, reunited with their commander McClellan, occupy the grounds of Berkeley Plantation and next door Westover Plantation under the protection of gunboats patrolling the James River. Abraham Lincoln arrives twice during the summer to review the troops and consult with McClellan.

Berkeley Plantation (804-829-6018 or 888-466-6018; www.berkeleyplantation .com), the location of Harrison's Landing, is open for tours. The grounds include a monument to the immortal "Taps" bugle call, composed here in July 1862.

December 11–16, 1862: Battle of Fredericksburg. Gen. Ambrose Burnside, the newly appointed commander of the Army of the Potomac, crosses the Rappahannock River with 120,000 men and attacks Lee's entrenched positions on the hills surrounding Fredericksburg. After sustaining more than 12,000 casualties, Burnside retreats.

The **Fredericksburg Battlefield Visitor Center** (540-373-6122; www.nps.gov/ frsp; 1013 Lafayette Boulevard, Fredericksburg 22401) preserves and interprets large sections of the December 1862 battlefield, including the Sunken Road and Stone Wall where two-thirds of the Union casualties occurred.

The **Fredericksburg Visitor Center** (540-373-1776 or 800-678-4748; www.visit fred.com; 706 Caroline Street), in downtown, offers self-guided walking tours interpreting the street fighting during the battle and the assault on Marye's Heights. Other sites interpreting the battle include the **White Oak Civil War Museum** (540-371-4234; www.whiteoakmuseum.com; 985 White Oak Road, Falmouth 22405) and **Chatham Manor** (540-654-5121; 120 Chatham Lane, Falmouth 22405), used by Union forces as a headquarters and hospital.

December 31, 1862. The USS *Monitor* sinks in a storm off Cape Hatteras while under tow to join the blockade at Beaufort, North Carolina.

1863

April 11–May 4, 1863: Siege of Suffolk. Confederate forces under Longstreet, Hood, and Pickett attempt to retake this agricultural center.

    Riddick's Folly (757-934-1390; www.riddicksfolly.org), in Suffolk, served as Union headquarters during the unsuccessful siege and retains Civil War–era graffiti.

April 30–May 6, 1863: Battles of Chancellorsville and Second Fredericksburg. In a two-pronged attack, Joseph Hooker, the new commander of the Army of the Potomac, sends his troops against the Confederates at Fredericksburg while the major part of his force meets Lee's troops at the nearby crossroads of Chancellorsville. Despite outnumbering the Confederates five to one, the Union suffers one of its greatest defeats of the war.

    The **Chancellorsville Battlefield Visitor Center** (540-786-2880; www.nps .gov/frsp; 9001 Plank Road, Fredericksburg 22407) is located near the spot where Gen. "Stonewall" Jackson received his wound on May 2. Driving tours include unpaved roads used by Jackson in his brilliant flanking maneuver.

May 10, 1863: Death of "Stonewall" Jackson. Following a wound from friendly fire, Jackson's arm is amputated. He contracts pneumonia and dies eight days later.

    The building at Guinea Station where Jackson died has been preserved virtually intact as the **Stonewall Jackson Shrine** (804-633-6076; 12019 Stonewall Jackson Road/SR 606, Woodford 22580). Although Jackson is buried in Lexington, Virginia, his amputated left arm was interred by his chaplain in the graveyard at **Ellwood,** near Chancellorsville battlefield. Both Ellwood and the shrine are operated by the National Park Service.

1864

January 31–February 1, 1864: Battle of Smithfield. Confederate forces destroy a Union gunboat attacking the town. Smithfield is the only town on the James below Richmond to remain in Confederate hands throughout the war.

    The **Isle of Wight County Museum** (757-356-1223; www.smithfield -virginia.com), in Smithfield, displays the gilded eagle that adorned the gunship before its destruction.

May 4, 1864: The Overland Campaign Begins. Ulysses S. Grant, now general-in-chief of the Union forces, crosses the Rapidan River near Fredericksburg with 120,000 men, beginning the bloodiest march in American history.

A driving-tour map of Grant's decisive campaign is available at www.civil wartraveler.com.

May 5–20, 1864: The Bermuda Hundred Campaign. Gen. Benjamin Butler lands with 30,000 troops at Bermuda Hundred, near the junction of the James and Appomattox rivers, to begin the Union advance on Richmond from the east. After a series of inconclusive battles, Butler retires behind his line of fortifications called the Bermuda Hundred Line. The Confederates build the opposing Howlett Line, bottling up Butler's forces.

Much of the Bermuda Hundred Campaign took place in **Chesterfield County** (804-777-9663; www.chesterfieldtourism.com), on the southeast side of Richmond. Parks preserve several battle sites and earthworks, including Confederate emplacements at **Howlett Line Park** (804-751-4664; 14100 Howlett Line Drive, Colonial Heights 23834) and **Battery Dantzler History Park** (804-751-4664; 1820 Battery Dantzler Road, Chester 23836); and Federal emplacements at **Bermuda Hundred** (VA 10/E. Hundred Road, Hopewell 23860) and **Dodd Park at Point of Rocks** (804-748-1623; 201 Enon Church Road, Hopewell 23860), where Butler established his headquarters.

Butler proved a prolific builder, digging the **Dutch Gap Canal** (804-748-1623; 301 Henricus Park Road, Chester 23836), now the main channel of the James, and building **Fort Wead** (804-751-4664; 1107 Greyledge Boulevard, Chester 23831), behind his lines. The final engagements of this campaign took place May 12–20 near **Fort Stevens Historical Park** (804-751-4664; 8900 Pams Avenue, Richmond 23237) and at **Ware Bottom Church** (804-751-4664; 1600 Old Bermuda Hundred Road, Chester 23836).

Parker's Battery (804-226-1981; 1801 Ware Bottom Spring Road, Chester 23831) and **Drewry's Bluff** (7600 Fort Darling Road, Richmond 23237), both now units of the **Richmond National Battlefield Park,** also saw important action during Butler's campaign. For more information on these battles and on Lee's Retreat through the area, visit the **Chesterfield County Museum** (804-796-1479; www.chesterfieldtourism.com; 10201 Iron Bridge Road, Chesterfield 23832).

May 5–6, 1864: Battle of the Wilderness. Grant is outflanked by Lee on a battlefield just a few miles west of the one where Lee met Hooker the year before. However, instead of retreating back to the north, Grant leads his men south toward Richmond, a pattern he will repeat after each battle of the 1864 Overland Campaign.

The Battle of the Wilderness was largely fought between two roads, the Orange Turnpike (VA 20) and Orange Plank Road (SR 621). A 5-mile driving trail linking the two sectors of the battlefield begins near the **Battlefield Exhibit Shelter** (www.nps.gov/frsp) on VA 20.

May 6–7, 1864: Battle of Todd's Tavern. Delaying action by cavalry units under J. E. B. Stuart and Fitzhugh Lee allows Confederate forces to reach Spotsylvania Court House before Grant.

A short driving tour on the **Brock Road**, now SR 613, connects the sites of the Todd's Tavern conflict. Maps are available at the Fredericksburg and Chancellorsville visitors centers and online at www.nps.gov/frsp/todds.htm.

May 8–21, 1864: Battle of Spotsylvania Court House. Bloody fighting along 4 miles of trenches leads to heavy casualties for both Lee and Grant.

The **Spotsylvania History Trail,** beginning at the Battlefield Exhibit Shelter on SR 613, has several walking and driving options, including the **Bloody Angle** loop. Many trenches survive, including **Lee's Final Line,** where the log construction has been restored. The **Spotsylvania Visitors Center** (540-891-8687 or 877-515-6197; www.spotsylvania.va.us; 4704 Southpoint Parkway, Fredericksburg 22407), off I-95 in Massaponax, offers information and maps.

May 11, 1864: Battle of Yellow Tavern. J. E. B. Stuart, the Confederacy's dashing cavalry commander, is mortally wounded.

A **J. E. B. Stuart Monument** stands near the point where he was wounded, off Telegraph Road, in the residential area of Lakeside in the north Richmond suburbs. An impressive equestrian statue of Stuart can be found on Richmond's **Monument Avenue.** Stuart is buried in Richmond's **Hollywood Cemetery.**

May 23–26, 1864: Battle of North Anna. Union and Confederate forces, nearly equal in strength, reach a stalemate at the North Anna River. An ill Robert E. Lee misses perhaps his best chance to stop Grant's advance.

At the **North Anna Battlefield Park** (804-365-4695 or 804-788-8062; www.co.hanover.va.us/parksrec; 12075 Verdon Road/SR 684, Doswell 23047), an interpreted trail visits well-preserved Confederate earthworks. A driving tour, available at www.nps.gov/frsp/nanna.htm, leads past other battle sites in the area.

May 24, 1864: Battle of Wilson's Wharf. Fitzhugh Lee's cavalry attacks the Union supply depot at Wilson's Wharf on the James River and is repulsed by two black Union regiments.

Now called **Fort Pocahontas** (804-829-9722; www.fortpocahontas.org), the well-preserved earthen fort is open for group tours of 10 or more, and for an annual reenactment of the battle and living-history event every May.

May 31–June 12, 1864: Battle of Cold Harbor. Grant sends his troops in frontal assault against Lee's heavily entrenched Confederate lines just 10 miles from Richmond in one of the bloodiest battles of the war, with more than 12,000 Union troops killed.

The **Cold Harbor Battlefield and Visitor Center** (804-226-9181; www.nps.gov/ rich; 5515 Anderson-Wright Drive, Mechanicsville 23111) contains an excellent electronic map of the battle and is the starting spot for driving and walking tours of the battlefield. A nearby Hanover County park, **Cold Harbor Battlefield Park** (804-365-4695; www.co.hanover.va.us/parksrec; 6005 Cold Harbor Road, Mechanicsville 23111) has a paved, fully accessible trail past Union rifle pits and trenches, as well the **Garthright House,** a landmark in the battle. Just across the street lies the **Cold Harbor National Cemetery** (804-795-2031; www.cem.va.gov), the final resting place of many of the battle's casualties.

June 11–12, 1864: Battle of Trevilian Station. Cavalry battle diverts attention from Grant's forces as they move south to the James River.

A driving tour of the battle runs from **Louisa Court House** (www.louisa county.com; W. Main Street/SR 666, Louisa 23093) to **Oakland Cemetery** (West Street/SR 666, Louisa 23093), where casualties of the battle are buried. Tour directions are available at www.civilwartraveler.com and from the National Park Service (www.nps.gov/frsp/trev.htm).

June 15, 1864. Grant crosses the James River and establishes his headquarters at City Point.

Grant ferried two corps across the James by steamship from the landing at what is now **Lawrence Lewis, Jr. Park** (www.charlescity.org; 12400 and 12580 Willcox Wharf Road), in Charles City County. Other troops crossed a pontoon bridge 3 miles downstream at Weyanoke Point. The **City Point Unit of the Petersburg National Battlefield** (804-458-9504; www.nps.gov/pete; 1001 Pecan Avenue, Hopewell 23860) preserves the log cabin that served as Grant's headquarters during the 10-month Siege of Petersburg as well as other period structures. The **City Point National Cemetery** (804-795-2031; 10th Avenue and Davis Street) containing seven thousand Civil War dead, lies nearby. The U.S. Department of Veteran Affairs (www.cem.va.gov) maintains a database of all known interments in national cemeteries.

June 15, 1864–April 2, 1865: Siege of Petersburg. For 292 days, Grant seeks to break the Confederacy's lines south of Richmond and turn Lee's flank. The opposing armies fight more than a hundred engagements in nine major offensives across 176 square miles before the decisive battle at Five Forks.

The **Eastern Front Visitor Center** (804-732-3531; www.nps.gov/pete; 5001 Siege Road off VA 36, Petersburg 23803) offers an overview of the siege with exhibits and videos, plus many ranger-led programs, including Segway tours of the battlefield. A driving tour, beginning here, follows VA 36 to US 301, passing the interpreted sites of **Fort Stedman** and the bloody **Battle of the Crater,** July 30, 1864.

More than six thousand Union soldiers who fell during the siege rest in **Poplar Grove National Cemetery** (8005 Vaughan Road, Petersburg 23805), also the location of the **Western Front Visitor Center,** open seasonally. The **Siege Line Driving Tour,** beginning here, passes forts, a monument marking the site of A. P. Hill's death, and the Peebles Farm and White Oak Road battlefields. Additional defensive earthworks, part of the Dimmock Line extending south and east of Petersburg, can be seen at **Lee Park** (804-733-2404; 1616 Defense Road).

Robert E. Lee made his headquarters during the siege at **Violet Bank** (804-520-9395; www.colonial-heights.com; 303 Virginia Avenue, Colonial Heights 23834), today a house museum exhibiting guns, swords, furniture, and other artifacts of the era. Nearby, **Fort Clifton** (804-520-9224; www .colonial-heights.com; 5501 Conduit Road, Berberich Park), attacked many times by Union gunboats but never defeated, still stands on its bluff above the Appomattox River.

More than 30,000 Confederate dead are interred at **Blandford Church and Cemetery** (804-733-2396; www.petersburg-va.org/tourism; 111 Rochelle Lane, Petersburg 23803), where 15 Tiffany windows are dedicated to the Confederate dead. Tours of the church and cemetery are offered daily. The **Siege Museum** (804-733-2404; www.petersburg-va.org/tourism; 15 W. Bank Street, Petersburg 23803) explores the civilian side of the longest siege in U.S. history.

September 29, 1864: Capture of Fort Harrison. Union forces capture this key fort in the Richmond defensive line, but the Confederates hold the adjacent forts in heavy fighting, leading to six more months of siege warfare.

The **Richmond National Battlefield Park** (www.nps.gov/rich) preserves these forts and miles of earthworks along **Battlefield Park Road,** off VA 5 southeast of Richmond. A driving tour connects the forts, with short walking trails at Forts Harrison and Brady. A visitors center, open seasonally, is located next to Fort Harrison.

1865

March 31, 1865: Battle of White Oak Road. An interpreted walking trail of the **White Oak Road Battlefield,** located near the intersection of White Oak Road (SR 613) and SR 631 in Petersburg, visits well-preserved Confederate trenches.

April 1, 1865: Battle of Five Forks. The Confederate loss during a cavalry action at this key crossroads finally exposes the South Side Railroad, Lee's last avenue of supply, to attack and forces the evacuation of Richmond.

A new visitors center at the **Five Forks Battlefield** unit of the Petersburg National Battlefield (804-469-4093; www.nps.gov/pete; 16302 White Oak Road, Dinwiddie 23885) is the beginning of a short driving tour of the battle sites.

April 2, 1865: Breakthrough Battle and Evacuation of Petersburg. Lee evacuates his troops from Richmond and Petersburg as other units fight holding actions to permit his withdrawal.

Pamplin Historical Park and the National Museum of the Civil War Soldier (804-861-2408 or 877-726-7546; www.pamplinpark.org; 6125 Boydton Plank Road, Petersburg 23803) presents a multimedia account of the events of April 2 in its Breakthrough Theater, as well as an excellent museum of artifacts unearthed on the site. Outside, three loops of the **Breakthrough Trail** let visitors explore the battlefield, assisted by podcasts at many interpretive exhibits. The park also displays the **Banks House,** used by Grant as his headquarters on April 2, 1865; the interactive **Museum of the Civil War Soldier;** an accurate reconstruction of field fortifications; a Civil War military encampment; and much more.

On US 460 at Namozine Road, west of Petersburg, **Sutherland Station** was the scene of a battle as Lee's forces sought to hold the South Side Railroad. Near the wayside exhibit, the **Historic Fork Inn** (804-265-8141; 19621 Namozine Road/SR 708, Sutherland 23885), used as a Union army hospital, is open for guided tours.

April 2–9, 1865: Lee's Retreat. Following the fall of Richmond, Lee is forced to withdraw westward. One major battle takes place during the retreat. On April 6, Lee loses 7,700 men, including eight generals, at the **Battle of Sailor's Creek.**

South Side Station (River Street and Cockade Alley), in Old Towne Petersburg, marks the beginning of the **Lee's Retreat Driving Tour.** Following the route taken by Lee's forces, it includes more than 25 wayside exhibits, each with short-range radio messages available on 1620 AM, also online at www .civilwartraveler.com, along with maps of the route.

Sailor's Creek Battlefield Historical State Park (434-315-0349; www.dcr.virginia.gov/state_parks/ sai.shtml; SR 617/Saylers Creek Road, Rice 23966) is situated about halfway between Petersburg and Appomattox. The **Overton-Hillsman House,** used as a field hospital, is open for tours. A commemoration of the battle is held each April.

ABRAHAM LINCOLN AND HIS SON TAD VISITED RICHMOND ON THE DAY AFTER ITS SURRENDER, AN EVENT COMMEMORATED BY THIS STATUE AT THE TREDEGAR IRONWORKS.

mandating public school integration, U.S. senator Harry F. Byrd Sr., a descendant of one of Virginia's founding families, organized a movement dubbed Massive Resistance opposing racial desegregation. A series of laws were passed in Virginia cutting public funds and even closing schools that followed the Supreme Court order. The issue came to a head in 1958 when 17 African American students enrolled in previously segregated public schools in Norfolk, and the governor of Virginia ordered the schools closed, leaving ten thousand children without education. The federal courts ruled the action unconstitutional, and the schools reopened in February 1959, marking the end of Massive Resistance.

The city of Norfolk (www.norfolk.gov/emr) celebrated the 50th anniversary of the defeat of this divisive policy in 2009 and plans a permanent memorial to the Norfolk 17, the students who led the desegregation effort despite physical and emotional abuse.

Desegregation in the region proceeded at a very slow pace, however, and in 1968, a new Supreme Court ruling in the case of Green v. School Board of New Kent County addressed the inequalities still found within the system. Today, a driving tour (www.newkent.net/historygreen.html) visits the two schools that figured in the case, New Kent High School and G. W. Watkins School, both now National Historic Landmarks.

April 4–5, 1865: Lincoln's Visit to Richmond. Just a day after the Confederate government evacuates its capital, Lincoln and his son Tad tour the smoldering ruins.

A map and podcast of the walking tour, **Lincoln Visits Richmond,** are available at www.civilwartraveler.com. A life-sized statue depicting Lincoln and Tad can be seen outside the **Tredegar Iron Works Civil War Visitor Center.** The wall behind the statue bears words from Lincoln's second inaugural address: To Bind Up the Nation's Wounds.

April 9, 1865: Lee surrenders at Appomattox Court House. Finding his army without supplies and cut off by a superior force, Lee meets with Grant at the McLean House to arrange for the surrender of the Army of Northern Virginia.

Located about 95 miles west of Richmond, **Appomattox Court House National Historical Park** (434-352-8987; www.nps.gov/apco; VA 24) includes many original historic buildings, including the McLean House. The visitors center in the reconstructed courthouse houses exhibits and a theater. For more information on the historic town of Appomattox, visit www.tourappomattox.com or www.appomattoxchamber.org.

MILITARY MIGHT

The U.S. military maintains an impressive number of facilities—more than two dozen—in the Hampton Roads and Virginia Peninsula areas, with every service represented and many special commands.

Norfolk's name is synonymous with the U.S. Navy. The largest naval base in the world, **Naval Station Norfolk,** home of the powerful Atlantic Fleet, lies along the city's shores. Across the Elizabeth River in Portsmouth, the **Norfolk Naval Shipyard** has been building, repairing, and refitting ships since the 1600s. In Newport News, **Northrop Grumman** builds ships under contract for the Navy, including nuclear aircraft carriers and submarines. Visitors to Virginia Beach can't miss the fighter wings flying overhead as they land and take off at **Naval Air Station Oceana,** the East Coast's largest master jet base.

The U.S. Army maintains a presence at several historic locations. **Fort Monroe,** a Training and Command Base scheduled for decommission in the next several years, is the largest moated stone fort ever built in the United States. **Fort Story Military Reservation** in Virginia Beach occupies Cape Henry, the site of two lighthouses. **Fort Eustis** in Newport News is home of the U.S. Army Transportation Corps, providing our troops with all important logistical support by road, rail, sea, and air. **Fort Lee,** in Petersburg, is home to the U.S. Army Quartermaster Corps.

In Hampton, the U.S. Air Force's **Langley Air Force Base,** the first military base in the country built specifically for air power, served as the birthplace of NASA.

For a visitor, this bonanza of bases creates a unique opportunity to see our armed forces at work and to explore their heritage. Several of the bases permit tours with proper ID; others maintain museums either on or off base.

THE WEALTH OF THE SEA

Although they came looking for silver and gold, it didn't take the first English settlers long to realize what the Native Americans knew all along—the real wealth of the region comes from it abundant waters. The rivers flowing into the Chesapeake Bay, the shallow waters of the bay itself, and the rich ocean flats just offshore contribute more than 400 tons of seafood annually to commercial markets. More than 90 percent of this seafood is caught by dayboats, ensuring its arrival on area tables direct from the dock.

No visit to the region can be complete without sampling Virginia seafood (www.virginiaseafood.org). Some 80 species of shellfish and finfish are sold commercially. More than one-third of all blue crabs are caught in Chesapeake Bay. Entrepreneurs farm local varieties of oysters and clams in coastal waters. This bounty inspires chefs around the region and makes seafood the featured item on most local menus.

TRADITIONAL CHESAPEAKE SEAFOOD BAKE

Since John Smith first discovered Native Americans roasting oysters over a fire, the oyster bake has been a popular meal for visitors and residents alike. Shop at local seafood and farmer's markets for authentic flavors, then fire up the grill.

Ingredients: oysters, clams, crabs, fish (spot, croaker, mackerel, bluefish), corn on the cob, white or sweet potatoes; strawberries or watermelon for dessert.

Place oysters and clams in a foil pan on a hot grill until they pop open. Steam crabs in Old Bay seasoning and about 2 inches of water in a pot on the grill, covered, for 15 minutes. Brush fish with marinade and grill over hot coals till flakey. Pull back husks and remove silk from corn, then soak in water, wrap in husks, and grill, 10–15 minutes. Roast potatoes on the grill or wrap in foil and bury in coals until done.

GETTING THERE
AND GETTING AROUND

I n colonial times, and for many years thereafter, most transportation in Tide-water Virginia was by water, with packet boats steaming down the James and up Chesapeake Bay. Canals were dug, several at the suggestion of George Washington, for circumnavigating the rapids on the James River and the swamps of the Great Dismal, and to speed the products of plantations upstream to European markets.

Norfolk, Portsmouth, Yorktown, Petersburg, and City Point (now Hopewell) all developed as important ports before the Civil War. The region continues to play a dominant role in commercial shipping today with the deepest harbor on the East Coast. **Port of Virginia** facilities (www.portofvirginia.com) at Norfolk, Portsmouth, and Newport News include more than a dozen Suez-class cranes, the largest and most efficient in the world. Take a harbor tour for a close-up look at these monster movers in action.

Fifteen percent of all East Coast shipping can be seen coming and going through the mouth of Chesapeake Bay. An afternoon spent at the fishing pier on the **Chesapeake Bay Bridge-Tunnel** (www.cbbt.com) will yield views of a wide variety of shipping, both commercial and military, under way. Cruisers, battleships, submarines, and aircraft carriers from the great Atlantic Fleet make a strong show amid the container ships. You may even see one of the cruise ships now docking at Norfolk's **Half Moone Cruise Center** (www.cruisenorfolk .org) on the downtown waterfront or a tall ship under sail headed for Norfolk's yearly HarborFest.

By any means, see Hampton Roads

GIANT CARGO CRANES LINE THE SHORES OF THE PORT OF VIRGINIA.

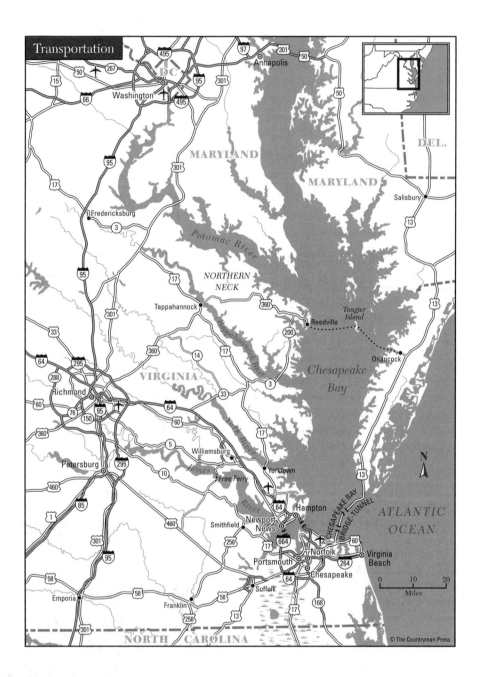

from a boat or bridge. These waters, wide and deep, form the lifeblood of this region that for hundreds of years has offered refuge and recreation to sailors, settlers, and visitors from around the world.

NUCLEAR SUBMARINES COME AND GO THROUGH HAMPTON ROADS.

GETTING THERE Most visitors come to the Virginia Tidewater by private automobile, and a car maximizes your touring options. However, getaways without an auto can be enjoyed at any of the region's popular pleasure craft ports—Hampton, Norfolk, Portsmouth—as well as in downtown Richmond, in the Williamsburg Historic District, and along the Virginia Beach Boardwalk, all of which offer plenty of public transportation. Train and bus service, as well as numerous air flights from around the world, are available to the region.

For online information on touring in Virginia, visit the official Virginia tourism Web site, **Virginia is for Lovers** (www.virginia.org), or call toll free 800-847-4882 (800-VISIT-VA).

By air: In addition to the airports within the Tidewater region listed below, many visitors arrive via **Washington Dulles International Airport (IAD)** and **Ronald Reagan Washington National Airport (DCA)** in the metropolitan Washington area (www.metwashairports.com). Another option is **Baltimore Washington International Airport (BWI)** (www.bwiairport.com), with connections to AMTRAK train service via free shuttles from the airport terminal to the BWI Marshall Rail Station.

More information on airports within Virginia can be found at www.flyvirginia.com and www.doav.virginia.gov.

COMMERCIAL AIRPORTS Newport News/Williamsburg International **Airport (PHF)** (757-877-0221; www.nnwairport.com), 900 Bland Boulevard, Newport News 23602. Conveniently located off I-64 at exit 255-B (Jefferson Avenue/VA 143), this field was formerly part of the U.S. Army's Camp Patrick Henry, a staging area for troops shipping out to Europe during World War II. Travelers enjoy complimentary luggage carts and parking shuttle; free "no-tips" skycap service, Wi-Fi, and a cell phone waiting lot; and a regional welcome center and excellent meals at the **Blue Sky Café** (757-369-0925), in the main lobby.

Norfolk International Airport (ORF) (757-857-3351; www.norfolkairport.com), 2200 Norview Avenue, Norfolk 23518. Located between Norfolk and Virginia Beach, this international airport includes a variety of shops and restaurants, including the full-service **Phillips Seafood Restaurant** (757-858-9601; www.phillipssea food.com) in the main lobby; currency exchange and business services; visitor information center; and barber shop, shoe shine, and hair salon. Wi-Fi available

for a fee. The Airport Connection shuttle (757-963-0433 or 866-823-4626; www
.onetransportationsolution.com) provides service to all area cities as far north as
Williamsburg.

Richmond International Airport (RIC) (804-226-3000; www.flyrichmond.com),
Airport Drive, Richmond 23250. Convenient to I-64 (exit 197A) or I-295 (exit 31),
this airport on the east side of Richmond offers flights from many discount carriers, as well as Air Canada service from Toronto. Visitors center, free Wi-Fi and cell
phone lot. The **Virginia Aviation Museum** (804-236-3622; www.vam.smv.org) is
next door. Limousine service is available from CMC Limousine (804-360-2122;
www.cmclimo.com) and Groome Transportation (804-222-7222 or 800-552-7911;
www.groometransportation.com).

GENERAL AVIATION AIRPORTS Campbell Field Airport (9VG) (757-442-
7519; www.campbellfieldairport.com), 9114 Bayford Road, Weirwood 23413. Historic airport on the Eastern Shore has grass runways, free courtesy car and
campsites, and sponsors Soup-on-Sunday fly-ins. The **Eastern Shore Hang Gliding Center** (757-752-8811 or 757-442-7510; www.easternshorehanggliding.com),
based here, takes gliders up to a mile high.

Chesapeake Regional Airport (CPK) (757-432-8110; www.chesapeakeairport
.com), 2800 Airport Drive, Chesapeake 23323. Lighted runway, jet charter service
(www.jetaircharter.net), aircraft rentals and repair, car rentals, two flight schools,
and **Chesapeake Skydive Adventures** (804-421-9245 or 800-615-9084; www
.skydivechesapeake.com) at the closest general aviation airport to Virginia Beach.

Chesterfield County Airport (FCI) (804-743-0771; www.chesterfield.gov), 7511
Airfield Drive, Richmond 23237. The closest executive airport to downtown Rich-
mond offers aircraft rentals and flight training available through Heart of Virginia
Aviation (804-271-2231; www.flyhova.com), and rental cars and air charters through
Dominion Aviation Services (804-271-7793; www.dominionaviation.com). **King's
Korner** (804-743-9333; www.kingskornercatering.com) serves a daily lunch buffet.

Dinwiddie County Airport (PTB) (804-861-0128; www.ptbairport.com), 6775
Beck-Chappell Drive, Petersburg 23803. Airport 20 miles south of Richmond next
to I-85 and US 460, used as a Navy Air Ferry station during World War II, offers
charter flights and aircraft maintenance.

Emporia-Greensville Regional Airport (EMV) (434-634-9400; www.emporia
greensvilleairport.com), 139 Airport Drive, off US 58, Emporia 23847. Friendly
rural airport has no landing fees.

Franklin Municipal Airport (FKN) (757-562-8764; www.franklinva.com), 32470
John Beverly Rose Drive, Franklin 23851. Free aircraft parking, courtesy car, and
pilot amenities.

Hampton Roads Executive Airport (PVG) (757-465-0260; www.hamptonroads
executiveairport.com), 5172 W. Military Highway, Chesapeake 23221. Full-service
airport near Portsmouth offers charter flights, flight instruction, business center,
Wi-Fi, and meals in the **BlueSkies Grille** (757-405-3313; www.blueskiesgrille.com).

Hanover County Municipal Airport (OFP) (804-798-6500; www.co.hanover
.va.us), 11152 Air Park Road, Ashland 23005. Aircraft rental, air charters, flight
training, aircraft repair, and fueling through Heart of Virginia Aviation (www.fly
hova.com). Rental cars available by prior arrangement.

Louisa County Airport/Freeman Field (LKU) (540-967-5380). Field northwest of Richmond near Lake Anna is home of **Skydive Virginia** (540-967-3997 or 540-941-8085; www.skydive-virginia.com) and an annual air show.

Middle Peninsula Regional Airport (FYJ) (804-785-9725; www.fly-fyj.com), 1000 Airport Road, Mattaponi 23110. Home of **West Point Skydiving Adventures** (804-785-9707; www.skydivewestpoint.com).

New Kent County Airport (W96) (804-932-3984; www.w96.org or www.newkent aviation.com), 6901 Terminal Road, Quinton 23141. Airport situated between Williamsburg and Richmond offers first flight lessons, sight-seeing flights, and airplane rentals.

Suffolk Executive Airport (SFQ) (757-514-4411; www.suffolk.va.us/airport), 1200 Gene Bolton Drive, Suffolk 23434. Home of **Skydive Suffolk** (757-539-3531 or 800-SKYDIVE; www.skydivesuffolk.com), the **Throttle Back Cafe** (757-514-4410), and the **Fighter Factory** (757-539-8440; www.fighterfactory.com), a leading aviation-maintenance school specializing in the restoration of World War II–era propeller aircraft. Free Wi-Fi.

Williamsburg-Jamestown Airport (JGG) (757-229-9256; www.williamsburg airport.com), 100 Marclay Road, Williamsburg 23185. Family-run airport near the Williamsburg Winery offers aircraft charters and repairs, pilot shop, plus lunch served daily in the award-winning **Charly's Airport Restaurant** (757-229-6855). Rental cars at special rates available by advance arrangement.

By bus: **Greyhound Bus Service** (800-231-2222; www.greyhound.com) is available throughout the region, with service from Richmond (804-254-5910) to Petersburg (804-732-2905), Williamsburg (757-229-1460), Hampton (757-722-9861), Newport News (757-872-4405), Norfolk (757-625-7500), Suffolk (757-539-6937), and Virginia Beach (757-422-2998), connecting with points throughout the United States, Canada, and Mexico. Another bus route travels up the Delmarva Peninsula to Wilmington, Delaware, and points north.

By car: The broad waters of the James River define travel in the region. Downstream from the bridges in Richmond, and the I-95 and I-295 highrises, only two bridges cross the James: the **Benjamin Harrison Memorial Bridge** (VA 156), connecting Hopewell and Charles City County, and the **James River Bridge,** carrying US 17, US 258, and VA 38, 50 miles downriver in Newport News. Between the two, the only way across the James is the **Jamestown-Scotland Ferry,** connecting Jamestown and Surry County. This free car ferry runs daily year-round. For schedule information, call 800-VA-FERRY.

THE PATIO AT CHARLY'S RESTAURANT, NEXT TO THE RUNWAY AT THE WILLIAMSBURG–JAMESTOWN AIRPORT, IS A POPULAR LUNCH STOP FOR LOCALS AND VISITORS ALIKE.

I-95, running along the fall line from Washington, D.C., to the North Carolina border, passes through downtown Richmond and historic Petersburg, where I-85 forks off to the west. Virginia Welcome Centers can be found on both interstates at the North Carolina line. Approaching from the north, travelers will find a Virginia Welcome Center at mile 131 on I-95 southbound in Fredericksburg.

I-64 from western Virginia passes through Richmond and straight down the high ground of the Virginia Peninsula past Williamsburg and Hampton before leaping Hampton Roads on the Hampton Roads Bridge-Tunnel to Norfolk and Virginia Beach beyond. The **East Coast Virginia Welcome Center** (804-966-7450) is located at mile 213 eastbound in New Kent County.

Although I-64 is the major route into the Tidewater, traffic is often very heavy, especially when holiday or summer traffic intersects with the region's busy rush hours. Planning to take an alternate route can take you past many interesting sights that the interstate misses and may even save you time.

Below are a few of our favorite routes for shunpiking.

From the Northeast

Bypass the Washington-Baltimore region by crossing the Potomac on the Governor Harry W. Nice Memorial toll bridge (US 301) to reach the Richmond area. Or turn east on US 17 down the Middle Peninsula to Yorktown, crossing the **George P. Coleman Toll Bridge** (US 17), the only bridge across the York. Tolls are $2 for passenger vehicles; E-ZPass (877-762-7824; www.ezpassva.com) accepted.

For a very pleasant way to reach Hampton Roads, follow US 13 down the **Delmarva Peninsula** (www.delmarvausa.com) past Chincoteague and the **Assateague Island National Seashore** (www.nps.gov/asis), home of the famous wild horses, the Victorian railroad town Cape Charles, and numerous small Eastern Shore fishing villages. The **New Church Welcome Center** (757-824-5000) is located on US 13 at the Virginia-Maryland border. At the tip of the peninsula, the 17.6-mile-long **Chesapeake Bay Bridge-Tunnel** (757-331-2960; www.cbbt.com) crosses spectacularly from the Eastern Shore to the Virginia Beach–Norfolk area. Tolls for passenger vehicles are $12 each way, and E-ZPass is accepted.

THE FREE FERRY BETWEEN JAMESTOWN AND SURRY COUNTY RUNS EVERY DAY ALL YEAR.

From the South

I-85 and I-95 join in Petersburg and provide the major route from points south and west. Turn off on US 58, now mostly four-lane divided highway, to travel due east to the Norfolk and Virginia Beach area through Peanut Country.

If you are coming from eastern North Carolina or the Outer Banks, several routes provide scenic opportunities. Take US 17 through the **Great Dismal Swamp National Wildlife Refuge** (http://greatdismalswamp.fws .gov) or get to Virginia Beach the back

THE CBBT: A DRIVE BETWEEN SEA AND SKY

Nearly 20 miles long, the Chesapeake Bay Bridge-Tunnel (CBBT) is considered one of the Seven Engineering Wonders of the Modern World, the largest bridge-tunnel complex on the planet. Two 1-mile-long tunnels and two four-lane high-rise bridges connect a string of man-made islands and a portion of the **Fisherman Island National Wildlife Refuge** (http://eastern shore.fws.gov). Along the way, the CBBT crosses the major shipping channels used by commercial cargo ships as well as Navy ships, aircraft carriers, and submarines on their way to Norfolk Naval Station and Shipyard.

Built in 1964 to replace a car ferry service, the causeway provides a unique opportunity to see the Atlantic Ocean and Chesapeake Bay, far from the nearest shore. Numerous fishing boats gather around the pilings of the bridge to cast for schools of fish that haunt the depths. On the **Sea Gull Fishing Pier**, located on the southernmost island, 3.5 miles from the Virginia Beach shore, you can angle for deep-sea fish without boarding a boat. The handicapped-accessible, 625-foot pier has cleaning tables and a weigh station. No fishing license is required.

A restaurant with indoor and outdoor dining and gift shop next to the pier make this a pleasant stop on your way across the bay. Exhibits highlight U.S. Navy history in Hampton Roads. Another rest area and scenic overlook is located at the north end of the bridge-tunnel.

MANY TRAVELERS STOP AT THE RESTAURANT NEXT TO THE SEAGULL PIER ON THE CBBT TO SAMPLE THE LOCAL SEAFOOD.

Besides remarkable views of ships and sunsets, a drive across the CBBT yields excellent birding, some of the best on the East Coast. Many migrating species, including peregrine falcons, pelicans, oystercatchers, ducks, and gulls, stop here to rest during their long migrations.

Free northbound and southbound podcast driving tours are available for download at the CBBT Web site (www.cbbt.com).

way by taking the free ferry to Knotts Island and following Princess Anne Road (SR 615) through the **Mackay Island National Wildlife Refuge** (www.fws .gov/mackayisland). The fastest route to or from the Outer Banks is VA 168, a toll road.

From the West

I-64 and the Hampton Roads Bridge-Tunnel carry more than a hundred thousand cars a day during the height of tourist season, and backups are frequent and time-consuming. To avoid the traffic, take VA 5, a scenic byway on the north bank of the James, to Williamsburg. Here you can cross to the south bank of the James via the

UNIQUE VIRGINIA PEANUTS ARE AVAILABLE AT ROADSIDE STANDS ALONG US 58 AND US 460.

US 58 AND US 460: JOURNEYS THROUGH PEANUT COUNTRY

Think a peanut is just a peanut? You'll change your tune after trying the unique Virginia variety. Larger than any other strain, with a distinctive texture and flavor, these peanuts are like no other.

More than four hundred Virginia farmers, nearly all of them living between the James River and the North Carolina border, grow some 100 million of the gourmet goobers each year.

Peanuts and pork go hand in hand. Local experts say the distinctive flavor of Virginia pork is due to the hogs being fattened on peanuts foraged from the fields, rather than on the usual corn.

While Virginia peanuts and hams are readily available by mail order and at local stores, a trip south of the James, along highways US 58 or US 460, lets you buy them from the source, meet the farmers themselves, and sample local delicacies such as peanut soup, peanut pie, and locally cured country ham and sausage on sweet potato biscuits. At farmer's markets and roadside stands, look for boiled green peanuts, a local delicacy.

US 58 runs through the heart of the richest peanut-growing region in the country, from Emporia on I-95 to Suffolk on the outskirts of Norfolk. Landmarks free Jamestown-Scotland Ferry and follow VA 10 through Surry County, Smithfield, and Isle of Wight before meeting up with I-64/I-664 around Norfolk, no tunnels required.

This route, or the alternate of following I-64 or US 60 down the Peninsula to cross the James River Bridge in Newport News, is the best route to and from the Southside for RVs and campers, which must stop at each tunnel to have their propane tanks checked.

Locals from the Richmond area frequently head for Virginia Beach down US 460, a real, but well-maintained, back road through peanut fields and blackwater swamps.

to look for include the **Peanut Patch Gift Shop** (757-653-2028 or 800-544-0896; www.feridies.com; 27478 Southampton Parkway/US 58, Courtland 23837); **Belmont Peanuts of Southampton** (434-658-4613 or 800-648-4613; www.belmontpeanuts.com; 23195 Popes Station Road, Capron 23829), on the Marks family farm; and the **Gurganus Peanut Outlet** (434-658-4263 or 888-922-1166; www.gurganus-peanuts.net; US 58 at SR 654, Capron 23829). Stop for lunch at **Porky's BBQ** (434-658-3131; 23218 Main Street) in Capron.

Visit the Web site of **Southampton County** (www.southamptoncounty .org) for a complete list of peanut outlets and local attractions.

US 460 splits off from US 58 in Suffolk, running northeast along the railroad tracks to Petersburg and I-95. Along the way, find peanuts at the **Zuni Gourmet Peanut & Plant Shop** (757-242-3112 or 800-965-4550; www.zuni peanuts.org; 5213 Homegrown Lane, Zuni 23898), a nonprofit carrying products from the Zuni Presbyterian Homes residential community; or **Adams Peanuts & Country Store** (757-899-8651; www.adamspeanuts.com; 9243 US 460, Waverly 23890). Stop for lunch at the nearby **Cowling's BBQ** (804-834-3100; 7019 US 460, Waverly 23890), where they've been smoking pork over white oak coals since 1972, or visit the **Virginia Diner** (757-899-3106; www .vadinerrestaurant.com; 408 County Drive, Wakefield 23888), serving home-style meals, Virginia ham biscuits, and a famous peanut pie since 1929.

In Waverly, the **Miles B Carpenter Museum Complex** (804-834-3327 or 804-834-2151; 201 Hunter Street, Waverly 23890) includes the First Peanut Museum in the United States as well as a folk art museum displaying the work of acclaimed wood carver and outsider artist Miles Carpenter.

Begin or end your journeys down US 58 and US 460 at the famous Mr. Peanut statue in the center of **Suffolk** (www.suffolk-fun.com). The town hosts the world's largest **Peanut Festival** (www.suffolkfest.org) every October. Emporia has its own peanut festival (www.thevirginiapeanutfestival .com) in September, as well as the **Virginia Pork Festival** (www.vaporkfesti val.com) in June. For more peanut information, visit www.aboutpeanuts.com.

I-64: The Road that Eats Its Tail

Motorists caught in any of the frequent backups on I-64 can attest to its serpent status, but navigating around the region often requires a trip on this notorious highway that leaves many first-time visitors dazed and confused. After running straight down the Virginia Peninsula from Richmond and crossing the Hampton Roads Bridge-Tunnel, I-64 turns into a beltway, looping around the city of Norfolk, until it merges into I-664 and heads back across the Monitor Merrimac Memorial Bridge-Tunnel, meeting itself in the city of Hampton.

I-264, another tangle in this interstate snarl, starts just blocks from the ocean in Virginia Beach, crossing I-64 before running straight into and through downtown Norfolk, and over the Elizabeth River to Portsmouth via the Downtown Tunnel and Berkley Bridge. Backups are frequent on this route, as well as at the nearby Midtown Tunnel on US 58, and locals in the know usually follow the I-64/I-664 beltway around the city unless business takes them to downtown Norfolk.

Keep an eye on the frequent construction projects on the region's highways at the **Virginia Department of Transportation Travel Center** (866-MY-511-VA; www.virginiadot.org) or tune in to 610 AM on your radio. Up-to-the-minute accident, road condition, and weather info is available by dialing 511 (out of state 800-578-4111) or by visiting www.511virginia.org.

By train: **AMTRAK** (800-872-7245; www.amtrak.com), the nation's railroad service, provides access to many destinations in the Tidewater. The **Northeast Regional Route** runs from Boston (BOS), New York City (NYP), BWI Airport (BWI), and Washington, D.C. (WAS), to Newport News (NPN), with stops at Fredericksburg (FBG), Ashland (ASD), Richmond's Staples Mill (RVR), and Main Street (RVM) stations, and Williamsburg (WBG). Bus connections are available from Newport News to Norfolk and Virginia Beach. Morning trains run hourly from Richmond's Staples Mill station to Union Station in Washington, D.C.

The **Carolinian** travels daily between Charlotte, North Carolina (CLT), and New York City (NYP), with stops in Raleigh, North Carolina (RGH), Petersburg (PTB), Richmond (RVR), Fredericksburg (FBG), Washington, D.C. (WAS), Baltimore (BAL), and Philadelphia (PHL).

Palmetto and Silver Service trains running from New York City to Florida make stops at Richmond's Staples Mill Road station (RVR) and Petersburg (PTB).

AMTRAK Vacations (800-AMTRAK-2; www.amtrakvacations.com) offer package tours to Williamsburg that include accommodations, passes to Colonial Williamsburg, and round-trip rail travel.

MILEAGE TO VIRGINIA BEACH FROM AMERICAN AND CANADIAN CITIES	
Atlanta	578 miles
Boston	583 miles
Chicago	886 miles
New York City	348 miles
Raleigh, North Carolina	202 miles
Richmond	104 miles
Washington, D.C.	200 miles
Williamsburg	50 miles
Montreal	765 miles
Toronto	800 miles

GETTING AROUND *By bicycle:* Tidewater Virginia is crossed by several national long-distance bike routes.

U.S. Bicycle Route 76, otherwise known as the **TransAmerica Trail,** runs from the Atlantic to the Pacific. The Virginia portion leads along quiet country roads from Charlottesville, through Goochland and Louisa counties, to Ashland, north of Richmond, before heading down the Peninsula along the north bank of the James through Williamsburg, ending in Yorktown. A group **Cross State Ride** (www .vabike.org) takes place every May.

U.S. Bicycle Route 1, also known as the **Atlantic Coast Bike Route,** follows back roads for 2,535 miles from Maine to Florida. The Virginia section begins in Arlington, outside Washington, D.C., and travels south through Fredericksburg, Ashland, and Richmond, before heading down the south side of the James River to Hopewell, Suffolk, and points south.

Another popular bike route leads up the Delmarva Peninsula along US 13 and other quiet roads. Bicycles aren't permitted on the Chesapeake Bay Bridge-Tunnel, but a shuttle van is available for cyclists with advance reservations. The cost is $12, the same as a passenger-car toll.

Bikes are welcome on the several ferries in Virginia, including the free Jamestown-Scotland Ferry across the James, the Paddlewheel Ferry between Norfolk and Portsmouth, and the Tangier Island Ferry connecting the Northern Neck with the Eastern Shore.

THE PADDLEWHEEL FERRY BETWEEN NORFOLK AND PORTSMOUTH PROVIDES AN INEXPENSIVE WAY TO SEE THE SHIPS IN HAMPTON ROADS.

More information on the national long-distance bike routes can be found on the Web site of the **Adventure Cycling Association** (www.adventurecycling.org). Download or order an official *Bicycling in Virginia* map, featuring these and other trails, free at www.virginiadot.org/bikemap.

On the south side of the James, **Smithfield** and **Isle of Wight County** have developed miles of biking routes visiting Forts Boykin and Huger, Bacon's Castle, and a Nike missile site via the area's quiet country roads. Download maps at www.visitsmithfieldisleofwight.com.

On the Middle Peninsula, the **Mathews County Visitor & Information Center** (804-725-4BAY or 877-725-4BAY; www.visitmathews.com; 239 Main Street, Mathews 23109) sells a *Bicycle Routes Guide* detailing five routes passing scenic small towns, historic sites, and several unique galleries ($6).

Additional multiuse trails in Virginia can be found on the Web sites of the **Rails to Trails Conservancy** (www.traillink.com) and the **East Coast Greenway** (www .greenway.org).

By boat: With thousands of miles of shoreline on ocean and bay plus numerous navigable rivers, the Virginia Tidewater is one of the great boating destinations in the world. The Chesapeake Bay, more than 200 miles long, is fed by a dozen major rivers mingling their freshwaters with salt water flowing in through the bay's mouth. Recreational boaters enjoy exceptional opportunities for fishing, exploring historic sites, viewing lighthouses far from shore (www.cheslights.org), and searching for "Chessie," the legendary monster of the bay. The *Chesapeake Bay Magazine* (www.chesapeakeboating.net) provides specialized information on marinas, destinations, fishing, and events of interest to boaters. The **Chesapeake Bay Foundation** (www.cbf.org) gives up-to-date information on the health of the bay ecosystem.

Norfolk is Mile 0 of the Atlantic Intracoastal Waterway (ICW), stretching south through protected channels to Key West, Florida. Connecting water routes lead north as far as Boston.

From Norfolk, two ICW channels head south, connecting Albemarle Sound in North Carolina with the Southern Branch of the Elizabeth River and the Chesapeake Bay beyond. The older of the two, the **Dismal Swamp Canal,** begun in 1793 at the request of George Washington, is about 6 feet deep and popular with recreational boaters, including kayaks and canoes. It runs straight south from **Deep Creek Locks** (757-487-0831) in Chesapeake to **South Mills Locks** (252-771-5906), site of a Civil War battle, before emptying into North Carolina's Pasquotank River at Elizabeth City.

The **Albemarle & Chesapeake Canal,** begun in 1855, is a more easterly route, and with a maintained depth of 12 feet is the usual route for commercial vessels. The canal stretches from **Great Bridge Locks** (757-547-3311; www.chesapeake .va.us), site of a Revolutionary War battle, to a conjunction with the North Landing River, before entering Currituck and Albemarle sounds.

Boaters can take a pleasant loop trip, going down one canal and returning through the other. A brochure describing the route is available on the Elizabeth City Web site, www.discoverec.org.

For more information on the ICW, visit the Web site of the Atlantic Intracoastal Waterway Association (www.atlintracoastal.org), the ICW Facilities Web site

ELIZABETH CITY: HARBOR OF HOSPITALITY

Visiting boaters receive a warm welcome at this friendly North Carolina port on the Pasquotank River, just south of the Dismal Swamp Canal on the ICW. **Mariner's Wharf** on the downtown waterfront offers free dockage for 48 hours, with free Wi-Fi access throughout the harbor area. The famous Rose Buddies (www.elizcity.com/rose) greet boaters with wine, cheese, and expert advice.

The nearby streets, perfect for a walking tour, are lined with historic houses and inns, including one of the largest collections of antebellum buildings in the state, plus revitalized shops, restaurants, and even a restored movie palace. Across from the waterfront, the free **Museum of the Albemarle** (252-335-1453; www.museumofthealbemarle.com; 501 S. Water Street, Elizabeth City, NC 27909) explores ten thousand years of ecology and culture in the region.

Several bed & breakfasts can be found within walking distance of the harbor, including the award-winning **Culpepper Inn** (252-335-9235; www.culpepperinn.com; 609 W. Main Street, Elizabeth City, NC 27909).

This is the home of the **United States Coast Guard Support Center Elizabeth City** (252-335-6540), the country's largest Coast Guard base, and **TCOM** (252-330-5555; www.tcomlp.com), a company that builds lighter-than-air craft, otherwise known as blimps. Tours of both facilities are available on a limited basis with advance reservations.

Elizabeth City is located at the junction of US 17 and US 158. For more information, contact the **Elizabeth City Info Center** (252-335-5330 or 866-324-8948; www.discoverec.org; 400 S. Water Street, Elizabeth City, NC 27909).

THE ROSE BUDDIES GREET BOATERS ARRIVING AT ELIZABETH CITY'S FRIENDLY WHARF.

(www.icwfacilitiesguide.com), and the site of the U.S. Army Corps of Engineers (www.nao.usace.army.mil/pao/brochure.pdf), which maintains the ICW.

By Paddle Trail and Blueway: To see the Tidewater from the perspective of John Smith and the early settlers, nothing beats a journey on one of the region's rivers. Many historic sites, hard to reach by road, front on the James, the York, and other area streams.

Captain John Smith Chesapeake National Historic Trail (410-260-2470; www.nps.gov/cajo or www.smithtrail.net), 410 Severn Avenue, Suite 314, Annapolis, MD 21403. The first national water trail follows Smith's historic 1607–1609 voyages throughout the Chesapeake watershed, based on the captain's own letters, maps, and journals. Stretching over 3,000 miles, the trail's many branches can be followed by boat or on land, visiting Native American, colonial, and natural sites along the way. Smart buoys throughout the bay broadcast cultural, geographic, and historical information as well as real-time scientific data, also accessible on the Web at www.buoybay.org or by calling 866-BOUYBAY. Contact the Friends of the John Smith Chesapeake Trail (443-482-2826; www.friendsofthejohnsmithtrail.org) for current updates.

James River Water Trails (804-788-8811; www.jamesriverassociation.org), 9 S. 12th Street, fourth floor, Richmond 23219. Waterproof maps of the Middle and Lower James available from the James River Association help navigate the river from Lynchburg to Chesapeake Bay, detailing access points, amenities, and historic landmarks. Get a preview at www.virginia.org/johnsmithtrail.

Mathews Blueways Water Trails (877-725-4BAY; www.mathewsblueways.org). More than 90 miles of interconnected water trails in Mathews County, a peninsula jutting into Chesapeake and Mobjack bays, pass **New Point Comfort Light,** abandoned steamship wharves, fishing villages, and bird sanctuaries. The **Piankatank River Trail** travels upstream to Dragon's Run, draining a pristine cypress swamp.

Seaside Water Trail (www.deq .state.va.us/coastal/seasidewatertrail). This 70-mile paddle trail runs down the Eastern Shore behind Virginia's barrier islands. Water trails on the bay side of the Eastern Shore include a 14-mile loop beginning at the **Onancock** (www.onancock.org) town dock and paddle trails in the **Saxis Wildlife Management Area** (www.dgif .virginia.gov/wmas).

York River Water Trail (804-769-0841; www.mpra.org). Follows the Lower Mattaponi and Pamunkey Rivers Water Trail through Native American lands, then enters the tidal York, past the site of White House, once the home of Martha Custis Washington, and York River State Park to the Yorktown waterfront.

⚓ BECOME A VIRGINIA TIME TRAVELER

Indulge your hunger for history by participating in the Virginia Time Travelers program, collecting stamps on a special passport at six (or more) historic sights and attractions throughout the state to earn special patches and other prizes. The **TimeTravelers** Web site (www.timetravelers.org) lists hundreds of participating sites. Many are free or offer discounts to passport visitors.

By bus: **Greater Richmond Transit Company** (804-358-4782; www.ridegrtc .com). Bus service to and from Richmond International Airport, and throughout the Richmond region. The free Lunch Time Express circles the downtown Mon.–Fri. 11:30–2:30, with stops near popular restaurants. An Extended Express Service provides direct access to Petersburg, Ashland, and Fredericksburg.

Hampton Roads Transit (HRT) (757-222-6100; www.gohrt.com). Provides service throughout the Hampton Roads region, including bus connections within and between the Southside communities of Norfolk, Chesapeake, Portsmouth, Suffolk, and Virginia Beach, and the Peninsula communities of Newport News and Hampton. Free or low-cost electric bus service is available in downtown Norfolk (Norfolk Electric Transit), downtown Portsmouth (the Loop), and the Virginia Beach oceanfront (VB Wave). Most buses have free bike racks. HRT also operates the low-cost Paddlewheel Ferry between Norfolk and Portsmouth; the Max Metro Area Express; and **The Tide** (www.ridethetide.com), a new light rail line in Norfolk scheduled to begin service in 2011. Future expansion will extend the Tide line to Virginia Beach. Tickets for all HRT services can be purchased from conveniently located ticket vending machines. Single tickets, one-day and seven-day passes, and senior and student fares are available.

Williamsburg Area Transport (757-220-5493; www.williamsburgtransport.com). Service throughout James City County, the city of Williamsburg, the Bruton District of York County, and Surry County across the James, including a daily shopping trolley.

By rental car: **Alamo** (800-462-5266; www.alamo.com).

Avis (800-831-2847; www.avis.com).

Budget (800-527-0700; www.budget .com).

Colonial Rent a Car (757-220-3399 or 800-899-2271; www.colonialrenta car.com), Colonial Williamsburg Train Station, 468 N. Boundary Street, Williamsburg 23185.

Dollar (800-800-4000; www.dollar .com).

Enterprise (800-736-8227; www .enterprise.com).

Hertz (800-654-3131; www.hertz.com).

National (800-227-7368; www .nationalcar.com).

Thrifty (800-367-2277; www.thrifty .com).

By taxi and limo: Newport News/Hampton: **Affinity Limousine Service** (757-850-0089; www .affinitylimousine.net).

All City Taxi (757-380-8300).

HAMPTON ROADS TRANSIT PROVIDES SHUTTLE BUSES TO MANY POPULAR ATTRACTIONS.

Associated Cabs (757-887-3412).

Hops Cabs (757-245-3005).

North End Cab (757-244-4000).

Orange Cab (757-369-8977).

Yellow Cab (757-855-1111; www.yellowcabofnewportnews.com).

Norfolk: **Andy's Cab** (757-461-8880 or 866-840-6573; www.andystaxigroup.com).

City Wide Cabs (757-622-2227).

Executive Pathway Transportation (757-461-1331; www.limova.com).

Waterside Taxi Company Inc. (757-328-1250).

Norfolk Checker (757-855-3333; www.norfolkcheckertaxi.com).

Oceanside Executive (757-455-5996).

Southside Cab Co. (757-423-0154).

Richmond Region: **Deb's Taxi Service** (804-439-2232; www.debstaxiservice.com).

Diamond Taxi Cab (804-901-9557; www.richmonddiamondcab.com).

Gentleman Taxi (804-839-8400 or 866-668-8549; www.gentlemantaxi.com).

Richmond Taxi (804-439-0009; www.richmondvataxi.com).

Veterans Cab (804-275-5542; www.veteranscabrichmond.com).

Virginia Beach: **Al's Taxi** (757-467-1180 or 757-328-3652).

Atlantic Limousine (757-518-0080 or 877-518-0080; www.atlantic-limos.com).

Beach Taxi (757-486-6585).

NEW KENT COUNTY: CROSSROADS OF HISTORY

For most of its 50 miles between Richmond and Williamsburg, I-64 passes through **New Kent County** (www.newkent.net or www.co.new-kent.va.us), one of Virginia's oldest. Still largely rural, this area makes for a relaxing side trip through a region rich in history. Drive down quiet country lanes where Lafayette played cat and mouse with Cornwallis, and, a century later, J. E. B. Stuart made his famous ride around McClellan's army. Two first ladies were born in New Kent: Martha Custis Washington and Letitia Tyler. You can visit **St. Peter's Parish Church,** where George and Martha took their vows in 1759, and the **Old Jail,** on the Court House grounds were British and American troops camped on their way to Yorktown.

Maps and other information are available at the **New Kent Visitors and Commerce Center** (804-966-9631; www.visitnewkent.com; 324 Vineyards Parkway/VA 106, Talleysville 23124), off I-64 at exit 211. Just past the welcome center, the **New Kent Winery & Vineyards** (804-932-8240; www.new kentwinery.com) offers tastings of Virginia wines.

Black Top Taxi (757-724-9999; www.blacktoptaxiva.com).

Orange Peel Airport Shuttle and Transportation (757-463-7500; www.orange peeltransportation.com).

Williamsburg: **Dreams in Motion Luxury Limousines** (757-817-1122; www .motionlimo.com).

Historic Taxi (757-258-7755).

Triangle Taxi (757-564-6969).

By motorcycle: **Eaglerider of Central Virginia** (866-892-6990; www .eagleridercva.com), with locations in Richmond (Velocity Motorcycles, 804-353-3456; 1202 N. Boulevard, Richmond 23230) and Virginia Beach (Southside Harley Davidson, 757-802-1741; 385 N. Witchduck Road, Virginia Beach 23462) rents motorcycles by the day, weekend, or week for self-guided tours of the region.

Virginia Piedmont

1

A TALE OF TWO RIVER CITIES—
RICHMOND AND PETERSBURG

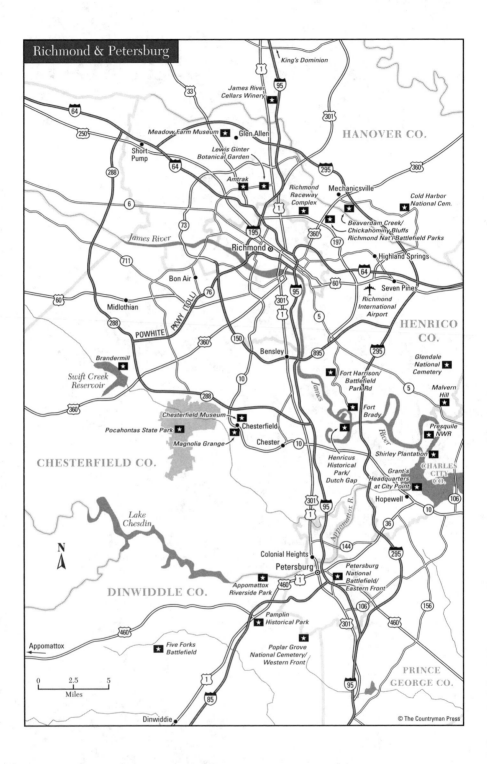

Richmond & Petersburg

A TALE OF TWO RIVER CITIES— RICHMOND AND PETERSBURG

Home to some of the earliest English settlements in the region and site of many of the decisive battles of the Civil War, the lower reaches of the James and Appomattox rivers offer visitors an experience steeped in history.

Richmond and Petersburg, just 23 miles apart, are located where the Piedmont meets the coastal plain—Richmond at the Falls of the James, Petersburg at the Falls of the Appomattox. At the time of the Civil War, they were the two largest cities in Virginia, the heart of a budding industrial area with iron foundries and warehouses brimming with tobacco and cotton.

After the defeat of the Confederacy, Richmond recovered swiftly, becoming the skyscraper-laden city of today. In Petersburg, however, history took a different course. In the Old Towne district, never razed for urban development, two-hundred-year-old buildings now house art galleries and antiques shops, offering visitors a chance to wander streets largely unchanged from that day to this.

RICHMOND: DAUGHTER OF THE JAMES

Today and always, the story of Richmond is very much about the great river that runs through its heart. Long the source of commercial wealth, the river and its shores today are preserved as the **James River Park** (www.jamesriverpark.org), an urban playground where residents and visitors enjoy swimming, hiking, mountain biking, white-water river running, fishing, and even rock climbing.

The **city of Richmond** (www.richmondgov.com) occupies both banks of the James at the fall line. Many of its historic sites are located in a compact downtown area on the north bank of the river within a loop of expressways formed by I-95, I-64, I-195, and the Downtown Expressway. Because of a history of catastrophic floods, the banks of the James are now lined with tall levy walls, with walkways along the top offering scenic views of the river and rapids below.

Richmond's recorded history began in 1607 when Capt. Christopher Newport, exploring up the James River, landed in the area today called **Shockoe Slip** (www.shockoeslip.org). The name derives from the Powhatan word *Shacquohocan*, referring to large, flat stones found in a nearby stream. A replica of the cross erected by Newport stands on the Canal Walk.

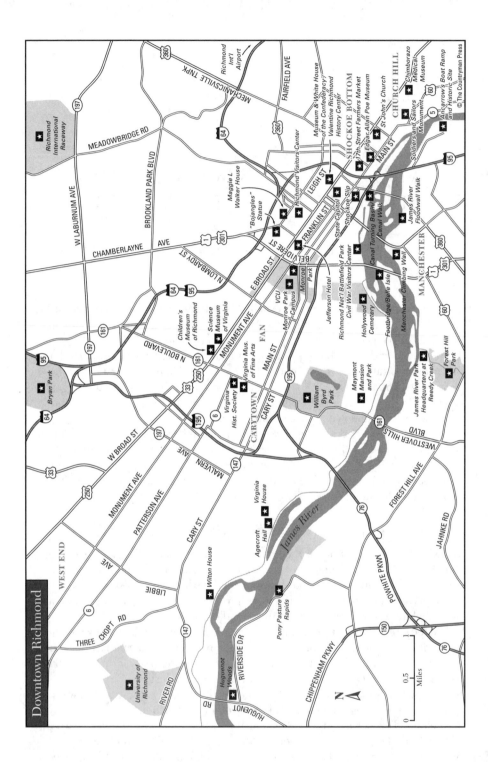

Downtown Richmond

In 1676, William Byrd established a trading post across the river in today's Manchester district and, after the Indian Wars, acquired extensive property in the region. His son, William Byrd II, is credited with founding both Richmond in 1737 and Petersburg in 1748.

Early development in Richmond concentrated in Shockoe Slip and the adjacent Shockoe Bottom. Today called the **River District** (www.richmondriverdistrict.com or www.riverdistrictnews.com), this is an area of cobblestone streets and restored tobacco warehouses housing a vibrant nightlife and dining scene, as well as shops, galleries, condominiums, and museums.

St. John's Church, the city's oldest house of worship, occupies **Church Hill** (www.churchhillrichmond.com or www.chpn.net), just east of Shockoe Bottom. Virginia's first revolutionary congress met here in 1775, when Patrick Henry delivered his famous "liberty or death" rallying cry for independence. Today, Church Hill contains one of the largest intact 18th-century communities in the country, with many antebellum structures.

The government of the newly independent state of Virginia moved permanently to Richmond from Williamsburg in 1780 to escape the British. Soon after the war ended, Thomas Jefferson designed an elegant state capitol based on a Roman temple. Construction began on the crest of Shockoe Hill in 1788. At the time of its construction, and for many years thereafter, Virginia statesmen enjoyed a magnificent view of the James River from the capitol portico.

To get a bird's-eye view of the city and river today, visit the free **Observation Deck** (804-646-7000; www.richmondgov.com; 900 E. Broad Street) on the 18th

THE OBSERVATION DECK ATOP RICHMOND'S CITY HALL GIVES A PANORAMIC VIEW OF CAPITOL HILL, THE JAMES RIVER, AND THE SURROUNDING COUNTRYSIDE.

floor of Richmond's City Hall. From here you can see the many hills that caused Richmond to be compared to imperial Rome, as well lots of local landmarks.

Thomas Jefferson wasn't the only Founding Father to leave his mark on Richmond. George Washington personally surveyed and lobbied for the **Kanawha Canal** (www.venturerichmond.com) bypassing the Falls of the James. Many of the early structures along the canal succumbed to fire as the Confederates retreated from the city in 1865, leaving behind "the burnt district" stretching from the river to the very edge of the capitol grounds. The ruins were soon replaced by huge brick warehouses, including the impressive **Tobacco Row.** Today, you can take a boat ride along the partially restored canal and stroll the Canal Walk past exhibits on area history.

After the Revolution, many lawyers settled in **Court End** just north of Capitol Square. The neighborhood, now dominated by the Medical College of Virginia, contains several attractions, including the home of John Marshall, first chief justice of the U.S. Supreme Court; the Valentine Museum of History; and the White House of the Confederacy.

By the time of the Civil War, fine town houses and mansions stretched west from Capitol Square, with Broad Street the major financial and business thoroughfare. North of Broad, **Jackson Ward** (www.hjwa.org or www.cjwn.net) developed as an important center of African American culture, with its own banks, businesses, and fraternal orders, becoming known as the Harlem of the South. Here you'll find soul food restaurants, museums detailing the neighborhood's black heritage, and a statue of Bill "Bojangles" Robinson, a Jackson Ward native.

Broad Street remains an important commercial corridor today, lined with restored theaters, condo-converted department stores, and museums, as well as such necessities as gasoline stations and drugstores. It is also the best way to navigate from the center of Richmond to the Far West End without encountering one-way streets.

Used as a military camp during the Civil War, **Monroe Park** (www.monroepark .com) today sits in the center of the **Virginia Commonwealth University** (www .vcu.edu) campus and marks the eastern edge of the Victorian neighborhood called the **Fan** (www.fandistrict.org or www.fdhub.net), containing many restaurants and inns. A few blocks from the park, Franklin Street changes into storied **Monument Avenue,** considered one of the most beautiful streets in America and a great place for a stroll or jog.

West of the Fan, **Boulevard** borders the **Museum District** (www.museum district.org), home of the Virginia Museum of Fine Arts and the Virginia Historical Society and **Carytown** (carytownrva.org), the city's hippest shopping and dining neighborhood.

Upscale communities west of I-295 include the **Near West End** (www.near westendnews.net), site of medieval Agecroft Hall; **The Avenues** (www.libbie grove.com) shopping district; and the campus of the **University of Richmond** (www.richmond.edu). Beyond lies Richmond's hottest new neighborhood, **Short Pump** (www.downtownshortpump.com), in the Far West End.

When giving directions, Richmond residents refer to the **East End** (Shockoe Bottom and beyond); the **West End,** stretching west from Capitol Square; the **North Side** (www.northrichmondnews.com), a group of former streetcar suburbs, including **Ginter Park** (www.historicginterpark.org) and the **South Side** (www .southsiderichmond.org), across the James, where you'll find **Manchester,** a river-

side industrial district undergoing revival, and **Forest Hill** (www.foresthill
neighborhood.com), site of a popular public park.

Over the years, metropolitan Richmond has absorbed a number of surrounding
communities with historic pasts. On the south side of the river, these include
Chesterfield County (www.chesterfield.gov); trendy **Midlothian** (www.mid
lothianva.org), once a coal mining region; and **Brandermill** (www.brandermill
.com) on Swift Creek Reservoir.

On the north side of the James, historic **Henrico County** (www.henrico
historicalsociety.org or www.co.henrico.va.us) wraps around the city. **Glen Allen,**
10 miles northwest of downtown Richmond, is a major destination along I-295,
with upscale shopping, hotels, and restaurants. Beyond Henrico lie **Goochland
County** (www.co.goochland.va.us), the area's horse country to the west; **Hanover
County** (www.co.hanover.va.us), stomping grounds of Patrick Henry, to the north;
and **Charles City County** (www.co.charles-city.va.us), where plantation houses
line the James, east of town, along Scenic Byway 5.

Today, Richmond presents a vibrant urban face to the world. Often called River
City or the RVA by its residents, the metropolitan area offers the latest in shopping, dining, and nightlife options, layered upon beloved traditions and enormous
historical depth.

THE TRI-CITIES: PETERSBURG, COLONIAL HEIGHTS, AND HOPEWELL

Although founded at nearly the same time, the **city of Petersburg** (www.peters
burg-va.org) presents a strong contrast to Richmond's sprawling urban presence.
The historic **Old Towne district** (www.oldtownepetersburg.com) on the banks of
the Appomattox is surrounded by a compact collection of historic neighborhoods,
while earthworks raised by Confederate and Union forces during the Civil War
occupy much of the rest of the city's acreage. Many miles of fortifications are preserved in the Petersburg National Battlefield and in various state and local parks.
The military maintains a presence in Petersburg at **Fort Lee** (www.lee.army.mil),
home of the U.S. Army Quartermaster Corps Center and School, as well as several
military museums.

In the years before the Civil War, the factories located at the Falls of the Appomattox brought great prosperity to the area, and by 1860, Petersburg was home to
the largest community of free African Americans in Virginia. The heart of the free
black community lay on **Pocahontas Island,** a peninsula in the Appomattox River,
now on the National Register of Historic Places. The city played major roles in the
Underground Railroad before the Civil War and in the Civil Rights Movement of
the 1960s. Petersburg was the first city in the nation to declare the birthday of
Martin Luther King Jr. a holiday, after the Civil Rights leader's assassination in
1968.

Across the Appomattox, the **city of Colonial Heights** (www.colonial-heights
.com) takes its name from the artillery emplacements the Marquis de Lafayette
placed here during the Revolutionary War. Late in the Civil War, Robert E. Lee
established his headquarters on those same heights overlooking the besieged city
of Petersburg.

The **city of Hopewell** (www.hopewellva.gov) occupies the point of land where
the Appomattox joins the James River. Formerly called City Point, the area served

as the headquarters of Gen. Ulysses S. Grant and the staging point for the siege of Petersburg during the closing days of the Civil War.

GUIDANCE Ashland (804-798-9219; www.town.ashland.va.us), 101 Thompson Street, Ashland 23005.

Ashland and Hanover County Visitors Center (804-752-6766 or 800-897-1479; www.co.hanover.va.us); 112 N. Railroad Avenue, Ashland 23005.

Charles City County (804-652-4701; www.co.charles-city.va.us), 10900 Courthouse Road, Charles City 23030.

Charles City County Visitor Center and Courthouse Complex (804-652-4701; www.charlescity.org), 10760 Courthouse Road, Charles City 23030.

Chesterfield County (804-748-1161; www.chesterfield.gov), 9901 Lori Road, Chesterfield 23832.

Chesterfield County Chamber of Commerce (804-748-6364; www.chester fieldchamber.com), 9330 Iron Bridge Road, Chesterfield 23832.

Civil War Visitor Center at Tredegar Iron Works (804-771-2145; www.nps .gov/rich), 470 Tredegar Street, Richmond 23219. Supplies information on Civil War sites operated by the National Park Service.

Colonial Heights (804-526-5872; www.colonial-heights.com), 201 James Avenue, Colonial Heights 23834.

Eastern Front Visitor Center (804-732-3531; www.nps.gov/pete), 5001 Siege Road, Petersburg 23803. Main unit of the Petersburg National Battlefield.

Goochland County (804-556-5800; www.co.goochland.va.us), 1800 Sandy Hook Road, P.O. Box 10, Goochland 23063.

Goochland County Chamber of Commerce (804-556-3811; www.goochland chamber.org), 2941 River Road W., Goochland 23063.

Hanover County (804-365-6000; www.co.hanover.va.us), P.O. Box 470, 7497 County Complex Road, Hanover 23069.

Henrico County (804-501-7500; www.co.henrico.va.us), 4301 E. Parham Road, Henrico 23228.

Henrico County Visitor Center (804-652-3406; www.co.henrico.va.us/rec/), Dabbs House Museum, 3812 Nine Mile Road/VA 33, Richmond 23223.

Hopewell (804-541-2461; www.hopewellva.gov), 300 N. Main Street, Hopewell 23860.

Hopewell–Prince George Chamber of Commerce (804-458-5536; www.hpg chamber.org), 210 N. Second Avenue, Hopewell 23860.

Hopewell Visitor Center (804-541-2461 or 800-863-8687; www.hopewellva.gov), 4100 Oaklawn Boulevard/VA 36, Hopewell 23680. Just off I-295 exit 9A. Has driving-tour brochures that can also be downloaded from the Web site.

King George County (540-775-9181; www.king-george.va.us), 10459 Courthouse Drive, King George 22485.

King William County (804-769-9619; www.kingwilliamcounty.us), 227 Horse Landing Road, King William 23086.

Louisa County (540-967-0401 or 866-325-4131; www.louisacounty.com), P.O. Box 160, Louisa 23093.

New Kent County (804-966-9861; www.co.new-kent.va.us), 12007 Courthouse Circle, New Kent 23124.

New Kent County Chamber of Commerce (804-932-4063; www.newkent chamber.org), P.O. Box 119, Providence Forge 23140.

New Kent Visitors and Commerce Center (804-966-9631; www.visitnewkent .com), 324 Vineyards Parkway/VA 106, Talleysville 23124.

Petersburg (804-733-2402; www.petersburg-va.org), 15 W. Bank Street, Petersburg 23803.

Petersburg Area Information Center, at the Carson rest stop on I-95 (mile 36) northbound. Closed Tues.

Petersburg Area Regional Tourism (804-861-1666 or 877-730-7278; www.petersburgarea.org), P.O. Box 1776, Petersburg 23805.

Petersburg Chamber of Commerce (804-733-8131; www.petersburgvachamber .com), 325 E. Washington Street, Petersburg 23804.

Petersburg Visitors' Center (804-733-2400 or 800-368-3595; www.petersburg-va .org), 19 Bollingbrook Street, Petersburg 23803. In the 1817 Farmers Bank in Old Towne.

Powhatan County (804-598-5611; www.powhatanva.gov), 3834 Old Buckingham Road, Powhatan 23139.

Powhatan County Chamber of Commerce (804-598-2636; www.powhatan chamberofcommerce.org), 3829 Old Buckingham Road, Powhatan 23139.

Prince George County (804-722-8600; www.princegeorgeva.org), 6602 Courts Drive, Prince George 23875.

Richmond (804-646-7000; www.richmondgov.com), 900 E. Broad Street, Richmond 23219.

↬ **Richmond Metropolitan Convention and Visitors Bureau** (804-783-7450 or 888-RICHMOND; www.visitrichmondva.com), 405 N. Third Street, Richmond 23219. Additional branches are located in the baggage claim area of the Richmond International Airport (804-236-3620), open daily, and in Bass Pro Shops (804-615-5412; 11550 Lakeridge Parkway, Ashland 23005), open Thurs.–Mon.

Sussex County (434-246-1000; http://sussexcounty.govoffice.com), 15080 Courthouse Road, Sussex 23884.

Sussex County Chamber of Commerce (804-246-4503; www.sussexvachamber .org), P.O. Box 1371, Sussex 23884.

Virginia Tourism Corporation (800-VISITVA; www.virginia.org), 901 E. Byrd Street, Richmond 23219.

↬ **Virginia Welcome Center—Bell Tower** (804-545-5586), 101 N. Ninth Street, Richmond 23219. Located in the historic Bell Tower in the southwest corner of Capitol Square. Mon.–Fri. 9–5.

Other helpful Web sites include www.chesterfieldtourism.com, www.allthingsrich mond.blogspot.com, and www.discoverrichmond.com.

MEDICAL EMERGENCY Bon Secours Richmond Health System (www .bonsecours.com). Richmond facilities operated by the Sisters of Bon Secours include: **Memorial Regional Medical Center** (804-764-6000; 8260 Atlee Road, East End of Richmond, near I-295, Mechanicsville 23116), **Richmond Community Hospital** (804-225-1700; 1500 N. 28th Street, Church Hill, Richmond 23223), **St. Francis Medical Center** (804-594-7300; 13710 St. Francis Boulevard, Chesterfield County, Midlothian 23114), and **St. Mary's Hospital** (804-285-2011; 5801 Bremo Road, West End, Richmond 23226).

Children's Hospital (804-228-5818; www.childrenshosp-richmond.org), 2924 Brook Road, Richmond 23220.

Henrico Doctors' Hospitals (www.henricodoctors.com), three locations: **Henrico Doctors' Hospital** (804-289-4500; 1602 Skipwith Road, Richmond 23229), **Parham Doctors' Hospital** (804-747-5600; 7700 E. Parham Road, Richmond 23294), and **Retreat Doctors' Hospital** (804-254-5100; 2621 Grove Avenue, Richmond 23220).

Southside Regional Medical Center (804-765-5000; www.srmconline.com), 200 Medical Park Boulevard, Petersburg 23805.

VCU Medical Center (804-828-9000; www.vcuhealth.org), 1250 E. Marshall Street, Richmond 23298.

✳ To See

Richmond and Petersburg are superb destinations for history and architecture buffs, besides having top-quality arts organizations presenting performances year-round.

ARCHITECTURE Historic preservation comes naturally to the residents of Richmond, where history takes up so much of the popular imagination. Century-old factories in Tobacco Row and Shockoe Slip along the Kanawha Canal now house shops, restaurants, condominiums, and entertainment venues. Ornate old movie palaces have been turned into performance spaces, while one, the **Byrd** (2908 W. Cary Street), is still showing movies after nearly 90 years of operation. The **Old Stone House** (1914 E. Main Street) circa 1740, now home to the Poe Museum, is thought to be the oldest surviving residence in the city. Nearby, the 1787 **Mason's Hall** (1807 E. Franklin Street), a wooden Palladian building, is the oldest Masonic hall in continuous use in the country.

Surviving neoclassical mansions include the magnificently restored **Wickham-Valentine House** (1015 E. Clay Street), designed by Alexander Parris in 1811. Parris also designed the 1814 **Virginia Governor's Mansion,** the oldest executive residence in continuous use in the country. The 1845 **Linden Row** (100 block, E. Franklin Street), now a hotel, is the city's most spectacular set of Greek Revival townhomes.

The 1814 **Monumental Church** (1224 E. Broad Street), designed by architect Robert Mills, is his only surviving circular church in the country. Nearby, the 1845 **Egyptian Building** (E. Marshall and College streets), designed by Thomas Stewart and now part of the VCU Medical School campus, is considered the country's finest example of Egyptian Revival.

In 1919, John Russell Pope, architect of the Jefferson Memorial in Washington, D.C., completed two quite different Richmond landmarks just a few blocks from each other: the domed neoclassical **Broad Street Station** (2500 W. Broad Street), now home of the Science Museum of Virginia, and the **Branch House** (2501 Monument Avenue), a Tudor-style mansion now housing the Virginia Center for Architecture.

Other architects closely associated with Richmond include Charles M. Robinson (www.charlesmrobinson.com) and Colonial Revival designer William Lawrence Bottomley, who crafted seven houses along Monument Avenue.

In the years after the Civil War, Richmond's wealthy citizens, flush with tobacco dollars, became fascinated with the Tudor and Gothic styles, importing antiques, interiors, and even entire buildings from the English countryside and building castlelike homes of their own. **Agecroft Hall** (4305 Sulgrave Road) and **Virginia House** (4301 Sulgrave Road), both in the Windsor Farms neighborhood, are excellent examples of this trend.

Many residences in downtown neighborhoods, especially Jackson Ward and Church Hill, exhibit cast-iron balconies and other architectural details thanks to the iron foundries that once thrived in Richmond. The interior of the 1887 **Old City Hall** (1001 E. Broad Street), itself an outrageous example of High Victorian Gothic, houses a magnificent three-story wrought-iron courtyard. The 1866 **Donnan-Asher Building** (1211 E. Main Street) is a rare surviving example of iron front construction.

At the height of the turn-of-the-20th-century enthusiasm for eclectic designs drawn from many different eras, Lewis Ginter hired Carrere and Hastings, the renowned New York architectural firm that designed the Fifth Avenue Public Library and the Frick Museum, to construct his **Jefferson Hotel** (www.jefferson hotel.com; 101 W. Franklin Street), considered one of the finest Beaux-Arts buildings in the country. The châteaulike 1901 **Main Street Station** (1520 E. Main Street), recently restored, is another ornate example of this style.

For detailed explorations of the architecture found in Richmond's historic districts, visit the Web sites of the **Historic Richmond Foundation** (www.historicrich mond.com) and the **Alliance to Conserve Old Richmond Neighborhoods** (www.richmondneighborhoods.org). Descriptions of all the area buildings on the National Register of Historic Places can be found at www.nps.gov/history/nr/travel.

The **Historic Petersburg Foundation** (804-732-2096; www.historicpetersburg .org) has saved and restored more than two hundred buildings dating to all eras of that city's past, including the 1783 **John Baird, Jr. House** (420 Grove Avenue), now the organization's headquarters. Seven historic districts have achieved designated status in the city, and guides to several of them are available for a small fee at the Petersburg Visitor Center or from the organization.

The Crescent Hills community in **Hopewell** (804-541-2461; www.hopewellva.gov) contains a large number of **Sears Catalog Homes** (www.searsarchives.com), mostly located along Crescent, Oakwood, and Prince George avenues, as well as several of the less well-known **Aladdin Kit Homes** (www.aladdintown.com).

ART MUSEUMS & VISUAL ARTS CENTERS Harnett Museum of Art and Print Study Center (804-289-8276; www.richmond.edu), Modlin Center for the Arts, 28 Westhampton Way, University of Richmond, Richmond 23173. The university's public gallery presents exhibitions, lectures, workshops, concerts, and symposia. The **Harnett Print Study Center** houses a permanent collection of prints, drawings, and photographs. Closed Mon. and school breaks. Free.

Museum Galleries at Virginia Union University (804-257-5660; www.vuu .edu), 1500 N. Lombardy Street, Richmond 23220. Galleries in the Wilder Library contain collections of African and South Pacific art objects and African American folk art. Tues.–Thurs., or by appointment. Free. The university's **Belgian Building,** originally constructed for the 1939 New York World's Fair, is decorated with sculptures representing the Congo. Student-led tours of the campus available (804-342-3579).

Petersburg Area Art League (806-861-4611; www.paalart.com), 7 E. Old Street, Petersburg 23803. Monthly exhibitions feature the work of local artists. Closed Mon. Free.

Petersburg Regional Arts Center (804-733-8200; www.pracarts.com), 132 N. Sycamore Street, Petersburg 23803. Studios of more than 50 artists in Old Towne Petersburg, plus a gallery with juried shows that change monthly. Open Wed.–Sat. Free.

Robins Gallery of Design from Nature (804-289-8276; www.richmond.edu), Boatwright Memorial Library, University of Richmond, Richmond 23173. Cultural artifacts from around the world include rare gems and minerals, prehistoric shells, and dinosaur fossils; glass by Dale Chihuly; and an impressive collection of Chinese ceramics. Closed Mon. and school breaks. Free.

✪ **Virginia Museum of Fine Arts (VMFA)** (804-340-1400; www.vmfa.state .va.us), 200 N. Boulevard, Richmond 23220. The VMFA reopened in May 2010 after a major renovation with new galleries devoted to art nouveau, art deco, modern, and contemporary art, plus a new sculpture garden. The museum is noted for its collections of French impressionist, post-impressionist, and British sporting art; works by African American artists; and galleries devoted to English silver and the Pratt Collection of Russian Imperial Jewels by Fabergé. Events include Art After Hours and Third Thursdays. Free Highlights tour daily; excellent café on-site. Closed Mon. and Tues. Free.

CINEMA ✪ Byrd Theatre (804-353-9911 or 804 358-3056; www.byrdtheatre .com), 2908 W. Cary Street, Richmond 23221. Carytown 1928 landmark survives complete with its Mighty Wurlitzer organ, still showing films 365 days a year, including second-run movies ($2), indies, midnight movies, film festivals, and silent films with organ accompaniment. Live organ concerts precede Sat. evening shows.

Movieland at Boulevard Square (804-354-6099; www.bowtiecinemas.com), 1301 N. Boulevard, Richmond 23230. Stadium-style theater inside a historic locomotive factory shows first-run films on 17 screens, plus a free children's summer film series, Movies and Mimosas Classic Films, and Insomnia Theater Cult Classics.

CIVIL WAR SITES AND MUSEUMS Literally hundreds of Civil War–related sites, including earthworks, cemeteries, museums, battlefield markers, and walking and driving tours, can be found in this region, where the most intense fighting of the conflict took place. For additional suggestions on touring these sites, see *The Civil War in the Virginia Tidewater and Richmond Region: A Time Line* sidebar in the "History and Culture" chapter.

Petersburg Area

Blandford Church and Cemetery (804-733-2396; www.petersburg-va.org), 111 Rochelle Lane, Petersburg 23803. Open: Daily. Admission: Adults $5, seniors and active military $4, children under seven free. Built in 1735, this chapel was renovated after the Civil War as a monument to the 30,000 Confederate dead who rest in the adjacent cemetery. Louis Comfort Tiffany's studio designed the 15 windows dedicated to each of the Confederate states. Tours of the church and cemetery are offered daily. A reception center houses exhibits and a gift shop.

Chesterfield County Civil War Sites (804-796-7121; www.chesterfieldtourism .org/civilwar.shtml). Open: Daily sunrise–sunset. Admission: Free. Many Civil War sites, including batteries overlooking the James River and fortifications associated with the 1864 Bermuda Hundred Campaign, are administered by the Chesterfield County Department of Parks and Recreation. Visit the Chesterfield Tourism Web site for locator maps.

✪ **Pamplin Historical Park and the National Museum of the Civil War Soldier** (804-861-2408; www.pamplinpark.org), 6125 Boydton Plank Road, Petersburg 23803. Open: Daily in summer; call for winter hours. Admission: Adults $10, children 6–12 $5, under six free. Located on the battlefield of Apr. 2, 1865, where Union troops finally broke through the Confederate lines, this sprawling park provides a unique perspective on the realities of the Civil War from the viewpoints of average soldiers on both sides of the struggle, facing the monotony of camp, the misery of the march, and the test of courage in the face of fire. Visitors select a soldier—Yankee or Confederate—to follow through the museum as podcasts and interactive exhibits tell of the soldier's life and his eventual fate. Outside, trails lead to the 1812 **Tudor Hall** plantation house; barns filled with heritage animals; exhibits on the life of field slaves; the **Banks House,** used by Grant as his headquarters; a military encampment with log cabins; accurate, full-scale models of the fortifications that ringed Petersburg; and the **Battlefield Center,** where exhibits and several excellent films discuss the events of Apr. 2. In the grounds beyond, the **Breakthrough Trail** explores the bat-

CABINS AT PAMPLIN HISTORICAL PARK RE-CREATE LODGINGS CONSTRUCTED BY UNION AND CONFEDERATE TROOPS DURING THE BITTER WINTER OF THE PETERSBURG SIEGE.

tlefield itself, while the peaceful 1.5-mile **Headwaters Trail** provides information on local ecology. Allow a full day to completely explore this unique and moving park. For those looking for total immersion, the **Civil War Adventure Camp** allows individuals and families to experience the life of a soldier, spending the night in typical shelters, eating around campfires, and learning to fire reproduction rifles and mortars.

Petersburg National Battlefield (804-732-3531; www.nps.gov/pete), headquarters: 1539 Hickory Hill Road, Petersburg 23803. Open: Daily, except Thanksgiving, Christmas, and New Year's Day. Admission: $3 per individual or $5 per car, good for seven days, at the Eastern Front Main Unit; other park units are free. This park commemorates the 10-month siege of Petersburg and the final days of the Confederacy. A 33-mile driving tour of the many battlefields includes 13 separate interpreted sites with three visitors centers and takes a full day to complete.

The park unit farthest east is **Grant's Headquarters at City Point** (804-458-9504; 1001 Pecan Avenue, Hopewell 23860), where the Union army established an enormous supply depot to provision the siege. A visitors center in Appomattox Manor overlooking the river houses interpretive displays. The restored log cabin Grant used as his headquarters is open daily.

The **Eastern Front Visitor Center** (804-732-3531; 5001 Siege Road, Petersburg 23803), the main unit of the park, offers an overview of the siege with exhibits and videos. Highlights of the Eastern Front driving tour include trails to the Dictator mortar, Colquitt's Salient at Fort Stedman, and the Crater battlefield.

The driving tour continues to the **Poplar Grove National Cemetery Contact Station** (8005 Vaughan Road, Petersburg 23805), open summer weekends, which interprets the Western Front of the siege. More than six thousand Union soldiers are interred here. An alternate **Confederate Defense Line Tour** passes Battery Pegram and Fort Lee.

The new **Five Forks Battlefield Visitor Center** (804-265-8244; 16302 White Oak Road, Dinwiddie County 23885) interprets the final days of the siege when General Sheridan's cavalry victory ensured the fall of the Confederate capital. A short driving tour visits sites of the conflict.

The National Park Service offers many ranger-led programs, including walking and driving tours. Segway tours of the battlefield are offered on Sunday. Contact **Segway of Richmond** (804-343-1850; www.segwayofrichmond.biz) to make reservations. Biking is a popular activity in the park, with bike lanes along the Battlefield Road in the Eastern Front Unit. Fishing is permitted from pier and shore in the City Point unit of the park, with a valid freshwater fishing license.

The Siege Museum (804-733-2404; www.petersburg-va.org), 15 W. Bank Street, Petersburg 23803. Open: Daily. Admission: Adults $5, seniors and active military $4, children under seven free. The 1839 Exchange Building contains exhibits detailing the 10-month siege of Petersburg (June 1864–Apr. 1865), the longest ever endured by a U.S. city. Special children's activities.

Violet Bank Museum (804-520-9395; www.petersburgarea.org or www.colonial-heights.com), 303 Virginia Avenue, Colonial Heights 23834. Open: Tues.–Sun. Admission: Free; donations requested. Robert E. Lee established his headquarters at this charming Federal farmhouse overlooking Petersburg during the long siege. The interior displays many Civil War–era artifacts as well as fine Adams-style moldings.

✪ The American Civil War Center at Historic Tredegar (804-780-1865; www.tredegar.org), 500 Tredegar Street, Richmond 23219. Open: Daily, except Thanksgiving, Christmas, and New Year's Day. Admission: Adults $8, seniors (65-plus) and students $6, children 7–12 $4, under seven free; parking fee in the adjacent lot waived with museum admission. Housed in the ruins of the historic Tredegar Ironworks, this new museum uses films, podcasts, and interactive exhibits to explore the beliefs and events leading up to the Civil War, its costs, and its results from the perspective of every American—Yankee and Confederate, man and woman, rich and poor, black and white, enslaved and free. Telling the whole story of the war is an audacious undertaking, but this museum makes it work.

Museum of the Confederacy and the White House of the Confederacy (804-649-1861; www.moc.org), 1201 E. Clay Street, Richmond 23219. Open: Daily, except Thanksgiving, Christmas, and New Year's Day; Confederate White House closed Jan.–Feb. Admission to either the museum or the Confederate White House: Adults $8, seniors (62-plus) $7, students 7–13 $4, under seven and active military in uniform free; combination tickets for both: adults $11, seniors $10, students $6. Parking free with validated ticket at the MCVH Visitor Patient Parking Deck across the street. Exhibits in the three-story museum draw on the world's largest and most comprehensive collection of Confederate artifacts, including E. B. D. Julio's famous oil, *The Last Meeting of Lee and Jackson,* and the personal effects of many famous Confederates, including Jefferson Davis, Robert E. Lee, "Stonewall" Jackson, and J. E. B. Stuart. The White House of the Confederacy, next door to the museum, has been restored to its appearance when Davis and his wife, Varina, were in residence, with more than half of the original furnishings. The **Eleanor S. Brockenbrough Library,** open to researchers on a fee basis, contains an unexcelled collection of Confederate documents, letters, maps, currency, periodicals, and books.

✪ Richmond National Battlefield Park (804-226-1981; www.nps.gov/rich), 3215 E. Broad Street, Richmond 23223. Open: Daily, except Thanksgiving, Christmas, and New Year's Day. Admission: Free. With 11 park units and five visitors centers within the city of Richmond and surrounding Henrico, Hanover, and Chesterfield counties, this battlefield park interprets several different campaigns of the war, including the Seven Days battles of 1862—Lee's first in command of the Army of Northern Virginia—and the Overland Campaign of 1864, which brought Grant to the outskirts of the city. An 80-mile driving tour connects most units of the park and takes at least a full day. An Earth-Cache program is also available.

Begin your visit at the free **NPS Civil War Visitor Center at Tredegar Iron Works** (804-771-2145; 470 Tredegar Street, Richmond 23219), in the

J. E. B. STUART'S CAVALRY HAT, COMPLETE WITH OSTRICH PLUME, IS ONE OF THE TREASURES OF THE MUSEUM OF THE CONFEDERACY.

same complex as the American Civil War Center. Here films, maps, and interactive exhibits introduce you to Richmond at the time of the war and the many battlefields in the region. National Park Service rangers are on hand daily, offering programs, walks, and maps to help you plan your visit.

Nearby, in Church Hill on the east side of Richmond, **Chimborazo Medical Museum and Visitor Center** (804-226-1981; 3215 E. Broad Street, Richmond 23223) commemorates the site of one of the largest military hospitals of the war. Films and exhibits explore medical treatment of the period. Open all year.

One battlefield saw action in both the 1862 and 1864 campaigns: the infamous Cold Harbor. The **Cold Harbor Battlefield and Visitor Center** (804-226-1981; 5515 Anderson-Wright Drive, Mechanicsville 23111), open all year, interprets both battles with electronic maps, walking and driving trails, and ranger programs.

An audio exhibit atop **Chickahominy Bluff** (4300 Mechanicsville Turnpike, Richmond 23223) interprets the site where Lee watched his forces assemble on the first day of the 1862 Seven Days Battle. A short trail at the **Beaver Dam Creek Battlefield** (7423 Cold Harbor Road, Mechanicsville 23111) explains troop movements that day.

The final conflicts of the Seven Days campaign are interpreted at the **Glendale Battlefield Visitor Center** (804-226-1981; 8301 Willis Church Road, Richmond 23231), located inside Glendale National Cemetery and open in summer. A driving tour connects the cemetery with nearby **Malvern Hill Battlefield** (9175 Willis Church Road, Richmond 23231), the best preserved in the Richmond area, with extensive interpretive walking trails.

Another unit of the park, 7-mile **Battlefield Park Road** off VA 5 southeast of Richmond, winds between opposing Confederate and Union trenches and past the remains of several forts that saw action in 1864. Short interpretive trails are located at Fort Harrison and at Fort Brady overlooking the James River. The **Fort Harrison Visitor Center** (804-226-1981; 8621 Battlefield Park Road, Richmond 23231), open seasonally, offers a map, film, and exhibits.

Drewry's Bluff (7600 Fort Darling Road, Richmond 23237), on the south side of the James, is the site of the decisive May 1862 battle that repulsed the Union Navy, including the ironclad USS *Monitor,* as well as the location of the Confederate Naval Academy. The largely intact fort offers walking trails and numerous exhibits, plus a sweeping view of the river.

DANCE The Concert Ballet of Virginia (804-798-0945; www.concertballet .com), many venues. Classically oriented ballet company stages traditional and contemporary ballets, plus original Storybook Series for children.

The Dance Space (804-673-3326; www.thedancespace.com), 6004 W. Broad Street, Richmond 23230. Public ballroom dances held on a 1,600-square-foot wooden floor.

Dog Town Dance Theatre (804-314-9644; www.dogtowndancetheatre.com), 109 W. 15th Street, Richmond 23224. The former Bainbridge School Gymnasium in Old Manchester is the city's newest venue for modern dance, including the **Ground Zero Dance Company** (www.groundzerodance.org).

Jammin' on the James (www.jamminonthejames.com), various venues, Richmond. Annual Lindy dance weekend held in Oct.

K Dance (804-270-4944; www.kdance.org), 10601 Three Chopt Road, Richmond
23233. Contemporary modern company presents dance concerts, films, and master
classes, including the "Yes, Virginia—Dance" Invitational in Sept.

Latin Ballet of Virginia (804-379-2555; www.latinballet.com), Cultural Arts Center at Glen Allen, 2880 Mountain Road, Glen Allen 23060. Company presents programs of Flamenco, classical Spanish, Latin American, and Caribbean dances, including its annual holiday production, *The Legend of the Poinsettia.*

Richmond Ballet (804-344-0906; www.richmondballet.com), 407 E. Canal Street, Richmond 23219. The repertory of the official State Ballet of Virginia includes ballets by George Balanchine and an annual *Nutcracker,* plus new commissioned works by top choreographers.

Richmond Shag Club (804-359-0497; www.richmondshag.homestead.com). Dances and lessons Tues. and Thurs. nights at **Visions Dance Club** in the Holiday Inn Select—Koger South (804-379-3800; http://hiselectrva.com; 10800 Midlothian Turnpike, Richmond 23235). The **Richmond Beach Music Festival** (www.richmondbeachmusicfestival.com) is held annually in Sept.

Richmond Tango (www.richmondtango.org). Milongas at **Fuego** (804-282-0207; 6008 W. Broad Street, Richmond 23230), a Mexican restaurant downstairs from Dance Space.

Traditional American Dance and Music Society (804-748-6602; www.tadams va.org). Contra dances on the second and fourth Sat. of each month at the Lewis Ginter Recreation Center. Beginners welcome.

USA Dance Richmond (www.usadancerichmond.org). Ballroom dances monthly in Richmond and Colonial Heights.

GALLERIES More than a dozen of Richmond's downtown galleries, plus shops, restaurants, and other public venues, located in or near the Broad Street Art District participate in the monthly **First Friday Art Crawl** (www.firstfridays richmond.com). Some of the same venues are also open for a more low-key Second Saturday crawl. Richmond's largest art show and sale, **Arts in the Park** (www.richmondartsinthepark.com), is held every May at the Carillon in Byrd Park.

In **Old Towne Petersburg** (www.oldtownepetersburg.com), many galleries, shops, restaurants, and museums participate in **Friday for the Arts,** held the second Friday of each month. The venues, all within walking distance of each other, host music, special menus, and art openings.

art6 Gallery (804-343-1406; www.art6.org), 6 E. Broad Street, Richmond 23219. Nonprofit gallery showcases visual and performing arts, including open mic poetry.

Artspace at Plant Zero Art Center (804-232-6464; www.artspacegallery.org), 31 E. Third Street, Richmond 23224. Co-op gallery south of the James with monthly exhibitions.

Chasen Galleries of Fine Art and Glass (804-204-1048 or 800-524-2736; www.chasengalleries.com), 3554 W. Cary Street, Richmond 23221. Internationally recognized gallery hosts receptions for artists from around the world.

Crossroads Art Center (804-278-8950; www.crossroadsartcenter.com), 2016 Staples Mill Road, Richmond 23230. Monthly gallery openings present the work of more than 225 local and regional artists.

Gallery 5 @ Virginia Fire and Police Museum (804-644-0005; www.gallery 5arts.org), 200 W. Marshall Street, Richmond 23220. Jackson Ward gallery, voted Best in Richmond, presses the boundaries of creativity in Virginia's oldest fire station.

Main Street Gallery (804-355-6151; www.mainartsupply.com), 1537 W. Main Street, Richmond 23220. Monthly openings showcase local artists.

Quirk (804-644-5450; www.quirkgallery.com), 311 W. Broad Street, Richmond 23220. Uninhibited art and unique gifts from around the world.

Reynolds Gallery (804-355-6553; www.reynoldsgallery.com), 1514 W. Main Street, Richmond 23220. Important contemporary artists and emerging local stars.

✪ 1708 Gallery (804-643-1708; www.1708gallery.org), 319 W. Broad Street, Richmond 23220. Edgy nonprofit founded by artists from Virginia Commonwealth University. Satellite gallery inside the **Linden Row Inn** (100 E. Franklin Street).

GARDENS Brandon Plantation Gardens (757-866-8486), 23500 Brandon Road, Spring Grove 23881. A 1765 Palladian plantation house surrounded by 30 acres of formal gardens leading down to the James River. Gardens open daily. $8.

Bryan Park Azalea Garden (804-646-5733; www.friendsofbryanpark.org), 4300 block of Hermitage Road, Richmond 23227. Garden with a half million azaleas is open for driving tours Apr. 1–May 15. Free.

✪ Lewis Ginter Botanical Garden (804-262-9887; www.lewisginter.org), 1800 Lakeside Avenue, Richmond 23228. Flowers bloom all year at this garden just off I-95. Highlights include the 1,800-bush rose garden; Medieval, sunken, Asian, wetlands, and Victorian specialty gardens; and a conservatory featuring an orchid wing. In the children's garden, kids can visit an international village, harvest vegetables, or visit a handicapped-accessible tree house. The Robins Visitors Center houses galleries, a garden shop, and the Garden Cafe. Special events include Flowers After 5 wine and jazz series and the holiday GardenFest of Lights. Open daily, with extended hours Tues. and Thurs. summer evenings. Adults $10, seniors (55-plus) $9, children 3–12 $6. The visitors center and café are free.

Marie Bowen Gardens (804-732-2096; www.pgcvirginia.org), located between Arch and Fairfax streets, Petersburg. Walnut Hill neighborhood park features azaleas, camellias, rhododendrons, and flowering trees in a natural setting.

Meadowview Biological Research Station (804-633-4336; www.pitcherplant .org), 8390 Fredericksburg Turnpike, Woodford 22580. Facility researching carnivorous pitcher plants and longleaf pines is open by appointment.

National Donor Memorial Garden (804-782-4800; www.donormemorial.org), 700 N. Fourth Street, Richmond 23219. Butterfly garden and walls of remembrance honor organ and tissue donors.

St. John's Mews (804-643-7407; www.gcvirginia.org), Broad and Grace streets, between N. 23rd and N. 24th, Richmond. Located west of historic St. John's Church, this picnic spot incorporates cast-iron work produced by Richmond foundries rescued from other locations.

Tuckahoe Plantation (804-379-9554; www.tuckahoeplantation.com), 12601 River Road, Richmond 23238. The grounds and gardens of Thomas Jefferson's boyhood home are open for self-guided tours daily. Admission $5. Guided tours available by prior arrangement.

Downtown Richmond

Beth Ahabah Museum and Archives (804-353-2668; www.bethahabah.org), 1109 W. Franklin Street, Richmond 23220. Located next to the Byzantine-style sanctuary, the museum contains exhibits on Richmond's Jewish community from the 18th century. Guided tours available. Closed Fri.–Sat. Suggested $5 donation.

Bolling Haxall House (804-643-2847; www.twcrichmond.org), 211 E. Franklin Street, Richmond 23219. This 1858 Italianate mansion, the home of the Women's Club of Richmond, can be visited by prior arrangement.

Cole Digges House (804-648-1889; www.apva.org/coledigges), 204 W. Franklin Street, Richmond 23220. Built by a Revolutionary War hero in 1805, this house is now the home of Preservation Virginia. Open by appointment.

Confederate War Memorial Chapel (804-740-4479), 2900 Grove Avenue, Richmond 23221. Gothic Revival chapel located behind the Museum of Fine Arts contains many Confederate artifacts. Open Wed.–Sun. 11–3. Free.

Kent-Valentine House (804-643-4137; www.gcvirginia.org), 12 E. Franklin Street, Richmond 23219. The headquarters of the Garden Club of Virginia and Virginia's **Historic Garden Week** (www.vagardenweek.org), this 1845 mansion exhibits prints by 18th-century naturalist Mark Catesby. Open weekdays by appointment.

Museum of Virginia Catholic History at the Cathedral of the Sacred Heart (804-359-5661 or 804-359-5651; www.richmondcathedral.org), 18 N. Laurel Street, Richmond 23220. Guided tours of the cathedral and exhibits in the Baptistery Gallery and Crypt available free by appointment. Walk-ins welcome.

Old City Hall, 1001 E. Broad Street, Richmond 23219. Dramatic granite building built in High Victorian Gothic, 1887–1894, boasts turrets and towers outside and a three-story cast-iron courtyard inside. Open to visitors during business hours.

✪ **St. John's Episcopal Church** (804-648-5015; www.historicstjohnschurch.org), 2401 E. Broad Street, Richmond 23223. The oldest surviving wooden church in Virginia, it hosted the Second Virginia Convention in 1775. Daily year-round (except on major holidays), costumed interpreters conduct tours of the church and cemetery where Declaration of Independence signer George Wythe, Edgar Allan Poe's mother, and many other historic figures are buried. Tours: Adults $8, seniors (62-plus) $5, students 7–18 $4. Free reenactments of Patrick Henry's famous "Give me liberty or give me death" speech take place at 2 PM every Sun. from Memorial Day through Labor Day.

St. Paul's Episcopal Church (804-643-3589; www.stpauls-episcopal.org), 815 E. Grace Street, Richmond 23219. Robert E. Lee and Jefferson Davis both worshiped at this 1844 church on Capitol Square, where Westminster chimes still toll the quarter hours. The interior contains 10 windows and one mosaic by Tiffany. Free guided tours after the 11:15 AM service on Sun. Lunch is served daily during Lent, with a jazz series during the Easter season.

Sixth Mt Zion Baptist Church (804-648-7511; www.smzbc.org), 14 W. Duval Street, Richmond 23220. Founded in 1867 by Rev. John Jasper, born a slave in 1812. Tours by appointment. Free.

Stewart-Lee House (804-643-2797; www.hbav.com), 707 E. Franklin Street, Richmond 23219. Gen. Robert E. Lee and his family occupied this 1844 town house during the war and for two months after Appomattox. Today it's the headquarters of the Home Builders Association of Virginia. Visits by appointment.

Virginia Center for Architecture (804-644-3041; www.virginiaarchitecture.org), 2501 Monument Avenue, Richmond 23220. Architect John Russell Pope designed this magnificent 1918 Tudor Revival mansion, today the home of the Virginia Society of the American Institute of Architects, containing exhibits on architecture, a permanent display on Pope and his work, and an excellent book and gift shop in the vaulted chapel. Tours available. Closed Mon. Free.

✪ **The Virginia State Capitol and Governor's Mansion** (804-698-1788; www .virginiacapitol.gov), Bank and 10th streets, Richmond 23219. Open Mon.–Sat. 8–5, Sun. 1–5. Free. Occupying a majestic hill overlooking the city, the Virginia State Capitol, designed by Thomas Jefferson, recently underwent a $74 million face-lift that gave it a new entrance on Bank Street, with a tunnel, elevators, and ramps that make the building fully accessible. Displays on the history of the building and the city, including Native American exhibits, as well as a gift shop and a café (804-698-7438), both open Mon.–Fri., line the tunnel.

Highlights include the **Rotunda,** containing a bust of Lafayette and a full-length statue of George Washington by Jean-Antoine Houdon, both done from life and considered the best likenesses of these men in existence; and the **Old House Chamber,** with statues and busts of prominent Virginians. Free guided and self-guided tours are available daily. Public galleries in the House and Senate chambers are open when the legislature is in session, usually for 46–60 days beginning in mid-Jan.

The extensive capitol grounds contain numerous other statues of prominent Virginians, including a spectacular equestrian statue of George Washington, a thoughtful Edgar Allan Poe, and a moving Civil Rights memorial. Pleasant walks

THE VIRGINIA STATE CAPITOL, DESIGNED BY THOMAS JEFFERSON AND FILLED WITH IMPORTANT STATUES AND HISTORIC ARTIFACTS, IS OPEN DAILY FOR FREE TOURS.

lead downhill to a fountain and the 1824 **Bell Tower** (804-545-5586), now a Virginia State Welcome Center and gift shop, open Mon.–Fri.

Other buildings open to visitors in Capitol Square include the **General Assembly Building** (Ninth and Capitol streets), where a sixth-floor cafeteria serves breakfast and lunch, and the recently restored 1814 **Executive Mansion** (804-371-8687; www.executivemansion.virginia.gov), open for tours Tues.–Thurs. Free.

Petersburg Area

Battersea (804-733-2400; www.petersburg-va.org/revwar), 1289 Upper Appomattox Street, Petersburg 23803. This 1768 neo-Palladian Colonial villa is the site of an annual reenactment of the Apr. 25, 1781, Revolutionary War Battle of Petersburg. Open for tours by appointment. Admission.

THE STATUE OF GEORGE WASHINGTON ON THE CAPITOL GROUNDS WAS ORIGINALLY INTENDED TO TOP THE FIRST PRESIDENT'S TOMB.

Dinwiddie County Courthouse (804-469-5346; www.dinwiddieva.us), 14101 Boydton Plank Road (US 1 at SR 619), Dinwiddie County 23841. Union general Sheridan used this 1851 courthouse as his headquarters during the Battle of Five Forks. Open for tours Tues. and Thurs.

Farmer's Bank (804-733-2400 or 800-368-3595; www.apva.org/farmersbank or www.petersburg-va.org/tourism), 19 Bollingbrook Street, Petersburg 23803. Now housing one of the few bank museums in the country, as well as the Old Towne Petersburg Visitor Center, this bank survived the Civil War by printing its own money. Open daily.

Merchant's Hope Church (804-458-1356; www.princegeorgevahistoricalsociety.org), 11500 Merchant's Hope Road, Prince George County 23860. One of the country's oldest Episcopal churches, established in 1657, is still in use. Open by appointment.

Old Brick House (804-520-9476 or 804-526-2695; www.petersburgarea.org), 131 Waterfront Drive, Colonial Heights 23834. This 1685 house is thought to be the oldest surviving brick house in Virginia. Tours by appointment.

✪ **Olgers Store** (804-304-4200), US 460 at Namozine Road/SR 708, Sutherland 23885. Country store/museum stuffed with unusual items, including a sheet metal statue of Robert E. Lee, is hosted by Confederate descendant Jimmy Olgers, usually to be found on the store's front porch "talking story." Nearby, the **Historic Fork Inn** (804-265-8141; 19621 Namozine Road), also occupied by Olgers family members, served as a Union hospital and is open for tours.

VIRGINIA PIEDMONT

Metropolitan Richmond Area

Belle Isle (804-646-5733; www.richmondgov.com/parks), off the Canal Walk at the west end of Tredegar, Richmond. Now the city's favorite playground for hiking and biking, the island has many interpretive signs telling of its past as a Civil War prison camp, plus the remains of an iron foundry and quarry.

Bojangles Triangle, Leigh Street and Chamberlayne Avenue, Richmond. Park in Jackson Ward features a great statue of tapdancer Bill "Bojangles" Robinson, who grew up nearby.

The Carillon at Byrd Park (804-646-5733; www.richmondgov.com/parks), 1300 Blanton Avenue, Richmond 23221. The bells in the 240-foot tower, built in 1924 as a memorial to World War I veterans, play concerts on patriotic holidays. The first floor is used for art exhibits. Nearby stands a statue of Christopher Columbus, the first in the South.

Great Shiplock Park (804-646-5733; www.richmondgov.com/parks), Canal and Pear streets, Richmond. Unit of James River Park preserving the ruins of the

PATRICK HENRY: VIRGINIA'S FIREBRAND PATRIOT

When Patrick Henry declared "Give me liberty, or give me death!" his fiery oratory inspired revolutionary sentiments and consolidated opposition to British rule. Born just north of present-day Richmond in Hanover County, Henry later served as the first governor of the independent state of Virginia. The **Road to Revolution Heritage Trail** (www.roadtorevolution.org) leads to sites important in Henry's career, and in our nation's history as well.

Hanover Courthouse (804-537-5815 or 804-837-4900; www.co.hanover.va.us), County Complex Road off US 301, Hanover 23069. Patrick Henry practiced law in this 1735 courthouse, now open by appointment. Reenactments of Henry's first famous case, the **Parson's Cause** (www.parsonscause.org), are performed on summer weekends.

✪ **Hanover Tavern** (804-537-5050; www.hanovertavern.org), 13181 Hanover Courthouse Road, Hanover 23069. The original 1732 tavern, operated by Patrick Henry's father-in-law, provided lodging for lawyers presenting cases at the nearby courthouse. The current building dates to 1781 and hosts performances of the **Barksdale Theatre** (804-282-2620; www.barksdale richmond.org) as well as historical exhibits and an on-site pub. Free self-guided tours daily.

Historic Polegreen Church (804-266-6186; www.historicpolegreen.org), 6411 Heatherwood Drive, Mechanicsville 23116. Site of one of the first Dissenter congregations in the colony, where Patrick Henry worshiped during his final lock at the eastern end of the Kanawha Canal offers hiking trails and great fishing.

Jefferson Park (804-646-5733; www.richmondgov.com/parks), 21st and E. Marshall streets, Richmond. A steam train, trapped by a landslide in 1925, remains buried with workers still on board in this reputedly haunted park. Nice place for a picnic, with a playground, exercise trail, and great views of the city's East End.

Libby Hill Park (804-646-5733; www.richmondgov.com/parks), 28th and E. Franklin streets, Richmond. The Confederate Soldier and Sailor Monument keeps watch from atop this hill in the East End. Trails circling the hill provide good hiking, with striking views from the top.

Monroe Park (www.monroepark.com), Franklin, Main, Laurel, and Belvidere streets, Richmond. The city's oldest park is today the heart of the VCU campus, hosting many concerts and community events, including the **Really Really Free Market** (www.myspace.com/rvafreemarket), a swap meet held the last Sat. of the month.

✪ **Monument Avenue.** Running east to west through the heart of the city, Monument Avenue (a continuation of Franklin Street) contains some of Richmond's

---

teens, has a Time Line of Religious Freedom and exhibits in a pleasant park setting.

Historic Shelton House (804-226-1981; www.nps.gov/rich), Studley Road, Mechanicsville 23116. Patrick Henry married his first wife, Sarah Shelton, in this house, also known as Rural Plains, in 1754. In May 1864, the battle of Totopotomoy Creek raged around the property. The house is now the newest unit of Richmond National Battlefield Park.

✪ **St. John's Church** (804-648-5015; www.historicstjohnschurch.org), 2401 E. Broad Street, Richmond 23223. The oldest church in Richmond, built on Church Hill in 1741, hosted the Second Virginia Convention attended by George Washington, Thomas Jefferson, and Patrick Henry. It was here, on Mar. 23, 1775, that Henry delivered his famous "liberty or death" speech. Every Sun. from Memorial Day through Labor Day, reenactors re-create this decisive event. Performances begin at 2 PM; doors open an hour earlier. Free. Tours of the church and cemetery (adults $8, seniors 62-plus $5, students 7–18 $4) offered daily all year.

Scotchtown (804-227-3500; www.apva.org/scotchtown), 16120 Chiswell Lane, Beaverdam 23015. Patrick Henry lived in this unusual house, now furnished with period antiques, including some owned by the Henry family. Open Fri.–Sun., Mar.–Dec., or by appointment. Adults $8, seniors $6, students $4.

Virginia Patriots, Inc. (804-272-7775; www.virginiapatriots.com). Professional actors interpreting the lives of famous Virginians present numerous performances around the region. Check Web site for schedule.

most famous landmarks and has been named one of the Ten Top Streets in the country. Originally a parade of Confederate greats, in recent years the avenue has taken a more inclusive tone, although not without heated debate, with the addition of African American tennis star Arthur Ashe. From east to west, the statues and their cross streets are: J. E. B. Stuart (1907) at Lombardy, Robert E. Lee (1890) at Allen Street, Jefferson Davis (1907) at Davis Avenue, "Stonewall" Jackson (1919) at Boulevard, famous oceanographer Matthew Fontaine Maury (1929) at Belmont Avenue, and Arthur Ashe (1996) at Roseneath Road.

Pumphouse Park (804-646-5733; www.richmondgov.com/parks), 1708 Pump House Drive, Richmond 23221. Another part of James River Park, this one at its western end, on the north shore off Blanton Road, preserves an impressive 1883 Victorian Gothic pumphouse.

✪ **Virginia War Memorial** (804-786-2050; www.vawarmemorial.org), 621 S. Belvidere Street, Richmond 23220. A 23-foot-tall white marble statue titled *Memory* stands guard over glass and stone walls engraved with the names of nearly 12,000 Virginia war dead from World War II to the present. Also on-site, a visitors center, exhibits, rose garden, auditorium showing films, and a stunning view of the James River far below. Open daily. Free.

Regional Sites

Chesterfield Museum Complex (804-777-9663; www.chesterfieldhistory.com), 10201 Iron Bridge Road/VA 10, Chesterfield 23832. Several historic sites are located close together on VA 10: **Castlewood,** an early Federal building housing the historical society's extensive library; the 1822 plantation, **Magnolia Grange;** the 1892 **Old Jail;** and the **Chesterfield County Museum.** The museum and Castlewood are free; tours of Magnolia Grange are $5.

Eppington Plantation (804-748-1624; www.chesterfieldtourism.org), 14201 Eppes Falls Road, Chesterfield 23838. Early Federal-style house has many connections with Thomas Jefferson. Open by appointment, and on the second Sat. in Oct. for Colonial Heritage Day.

Falling Creek Ironworks Park (804-748-1623; www.fallingcreekironworks.org), 6407 Jefferson Davis Highway, Richmond 23234. Site of the first ironworks in English North America.

Henrico County Historic Sites (804-501-7275; www.co.henrico.va.us). The county of Henrico is caretaker for several historic sites open to the public, including the 1915 **Armour House and Gardens at Meadowview Park;** the **Clarke-Palmore House Museum;** and the 1825 **Walkerton Tavern,** location of a popular summer concert series.

Historic springs. Richmond's position on the fall line means that the area has many spots where freshwater flows to the surface—another reason both Native Americans and English settlers chose to live here. Several of these springs, now protected in parks, still pour out drinkable water: **Fonticello Park** (804-646-5733; 28th Street and Bainbridge, Richmond), also known as Carter Jones Park; **Spring Park** (804-501-7275; Lakeside and Park avenues, Richmond), near Bryan Park; and **Wayside Spring Park** (804-646-5733; New Kent and Prince George roads, Richmond). Bring your own jugs.

Mid-Lothian Mines Park (804-748-1623; www.midlomines.org), 13301 N. Wool-

HOUSE MUSEUMS

Petersburg Area

Centre Hill Museum (804-733-2401; www.petersburg-va.org), 1 Centre Hill Court, Petersburg 23803. Open: Daily. Admission: Adults $5, seniors and active military $4, children under seven free. This opulent 1836 Greek Revival mansion houses exhibits on the history of Petersburg and the Bolling family.

Weston Manor (804-458-4682; www.historichopewell.org), N. 21st Avenue and Weston Lane, Hopewell 23860. Open: Daily, Apr.–Oct. Admission: $5. Plantation-style home built in 1789 overlooking the Appomattox River still has 85 percent of its original interior details, plus a ghost.

Richmond Area

✪ **Agecroft Hall** (804-353-4241; www.agecrofthall.com), 4305 Sulgrave Road, Richmond 23221. Open: Tues.–Sun.; closed national holidays. Admission: Adults $8, seniors (65-plus) $7, students $5, under six free. Step back in time five hundred years at this Tudor mansion, originally built in the late 15th century in Lancastershire, England, now standing on the banks of the James River. Taken apart, crated, and shipped across the Atlantic by a wealthy Richmond resident, the once dilapidated manor house has been restored to its original condition and filled with authentic pieces dating from 1485 to 1660. Around it stretch extensive gardens re-created on plans of the period. Admission includes an introductory film and a tour of the house by costumed guides. The Richmond Shakespeare Festival presents plays under the stars in the Agecroft Courtyard every summer.

The John Marshall House (804-648-7998; www.apva.org/marshall), 818 E. Marshall Street, Richmond 23219. Open: Fri.–Sun., Mar.–Dec.; by appointment Jan.–Feb. Admission: Adults $10, seniors (55-plus) and children 4–18 $7, children under four free. Chief Justice John Marshall lived in this Federal town house in the Court End from 1788 until his death in 1835. Occupied by his family until bought by the City of Richmond in 1911, it retains many original furnishings and personal belongings used by Marshall. The grounds include a fine herb and flower garden. Special events include a series of brown bag lunch tours.

Maggie L. Walker National Historic Site (804-771-2017; www.nps.gov/mawa), 3215 E. Broad Street, Richmond 23223. Open: Mon.–Sat. Admission: Free. In 1903, Mrs. Walker founded the first bank established by a woman in the United States. Today, it is the Consolidated Bank and Trust Company, the country's oldest financial institution continuously operated by African Americans. Guided tours of her house in Jackson Ward, furnished throughout with original family pieces, tell Walker's inspiring story. Special children's activities.

✪ **Maymont Mansion and Gardens** (804-358-7166; www.maymont.org), 1700 Hampton Street, Richmond 23220. Open: Tues.–Sun.; last tour 4:30 PM. Admission: Free; suggested donation $5. Romanesque Revival combines with picturesque Queen Anne styles in this unique and lovely mansion built at the height of the Gilded Age. The furnishings and decor are completely intact, including a magnificent 15-foot Tiffany window illuminating the central hall. Belowstairs, self-guided exhibits introduce the domestic staff that cared for the 33-room mansion. The estate's 100 acres are landscaped in a blend of natural areas and formal gardens, including a Japanese garden, Butterfly Trail, and an arboretum containing trees from around the world. A Normandy-style granite carriage house displays 20 different horse-drawn vehicles; carriage rides ($3–5) are offered on a regular basis. On weekends, trams ($2–3) make a loop through Maymont's gardens and nature preserve.

Virginia House and Gardens (804-353-4251; www.vahistorical.org/vh/Virginia _House.htm), 4301 Sulgrave Road, Richmond 23221. Open: By appointment. Admission: Adults $5, seniors $4, students $3. Located next door to Agecroft Hall, this 1928 mansion combines elements of Sulgrave Manor, ancestral home of George Washington; the 12th-century Priory of Warwick; and Wormleighton Manor, seat of the Churchill family. The interior is equally eclectic, with decor elements collected by the owners on their world travels. Magnificent gardens containing more than a thousand types of ornamental plants descend in a series of terraces to the James River.

Wilton House Museum (804-282-5936; www.wiltonhousemuseum.org), 215 S. Wilton Road, Richmond 23226. Open: Tues.–Sun.; last tour at 3:45 PM. Admission: Adults $10, seniors and students $8, children under seven free. Built about 1752 for William Randolph III, one of the colony's richest men, this Georgian plantation house was moved 15 miles up the James in 1933 by the Colonial Dames to save it from demolition. The uniquely designed building is fully paneled, with many walls painted a luscious (and authentic) Prussian Blue. The parlor, with its fluted pilasters and arches, is considered among the one hundred most beautiful rooms in America. Special events include a Colonial Kids' Camp in Aug. and Jammin' on the James outdoor jazz concerts on summer Saturdays.

KIDS' CULTURE ⚓ ⟰ **Children's Museum of Richmond** (804-474-7000; www.c-mor.org), 2626 W. Broad Street, Richmond 23220. Open: Daily Memorial Day–Labor Day; closed Mon. and some holidays Labor Day–Memorial Day. Admission: Adults and children $8, seniors $7, under one year free. Designed for children from birth to age eight, this museum provides fun and educational environments that take kids back to the basics of play. Kids can visit the art studio, climb trees, explore caves, float a miniature boat, and play in an outdoor backyard with fountains for cool summer fun. Role-playing environments include a village square and Little Farm, designed for toddlers.

⚓ **Meadow Farm Museum** at Crump Park (804-501-5520; www.co.henrico.va.us/rec), 3400 Mountain Road, Glen Allen 23060. Open: Tues.–Sun. afternoons, Mar.–Nov.; weekends Dec.–Feb.; closed early Jan. Admission: Free. Costumed interpreters re-create life in the rural South at this 1860s farmhouse and working farm with sheep, horses, and more.

⟰ ⤳ **Science Museum of Virginia** (804-864-1400 or 800-659-1727; www.smv .org), 2500 W. Broad Street, Richmond 23220. Open: Daily in summer; closed Mon. except holidays the rest of the year. Admission: Adults $10; youth (4–12), seniors (over 60), and active military $9; IMAX only $8.50. Combo ticket: adults $15, youth $14. Carpenter Science Theater: $3, feature films: $10. Free parking. Hundreds of hands-on experiences let you float on air, help build a space station, and walk inside a strand of DNA. Housed under the dome in the former Broad Street Station, this uplifting museum offers nature movies, planetarium shows, and full-length features on an IMAX screen; live theater performances; summer camps; plus a gift shop and Cafe Portico with free Wi-Fi on-site (museum admission not required).

LIVING HISTORY AND HISTORY MUSEUMS

Petersburg Area

City Point Early History Museum at St. Dennis Chapel (804-458-2564; www.historichopewell.org), 600 Brown Avenue, Hopewell 23860. Open: Daily, Apr.–Oct. Admission: $3. Housed in an 1887 chapel, this museum tells the story of Hopewell from the founding of City Point in 1613 through the present day, including exhibits on the World War I DuPont factory and the Hopewell China Factory (1920–1945).

✪ ✿ **Henricus Historical Park** (804-748-1613; www.henricus.org), 251 Henricus Park Road, Chester 23836. Open: Daily, except early Jan., Thanksgiving Day, Christmas Eve, and Christmas Day. Admission: Adults $7; seniors, military, and teachers $6; children 3–12 $5; under three free. Conveniently located off VA 10 between I-95 and I-295, this living-history museum re-creates the 1611 Citie of Henricus, the second English colony after Jamestown, closely associated with the story of Pocahontas. Costumed interpreters portray Native Americans, soldiers, and other settlers. With its historically accurate Indian and English villages, tobacco farm, protective palisade, and the forest pressing in on every side, Henricus offers a more authentic and hands-on experience of life in the New World than can be found at attractions farther down the James. The **Dutch Gap Conservation Area,** with excellent hiking, boating, and birding opportunities, shares the same parking lot and gift shop.

Prince George County Regional Heritage Center (804-863-0212 or 804-458-4319; www.princegeorgevahistoricalsociety.org), 6404 Courthouse Drive, Prince George 23875. Exhibits in the 1883 Courthouse detail the history of one of the country's oldest counties. Open daily. Free.

U.S. Army Quartermaster Museum (804-734-4203; www.qmmuseum.lee.army.mil), 1201 22nd Street, Fort Lee 23801. Open: Tues.–Sun.; closed winter holidays. Admission: Free. Museum at Fort Lee preserves the history of the U.S. Army Quartermaster Corps, the Army's oldest logistic branch, founded in 1775, with a massive collection detailing Quartermaster operations in every U.S. battle action. To visit Fort Lee, you must present photo identification, proof of vehicle insurance, and vehicle registration.

U.S. Army Women's Museum (804-734-4327; www.awm.lee.army.mil), 2100 A Avenue, Fort Lee 23801. Open: Tues.–Sun.; closed winter holidays. Admission: Free. Museum honors women's contributions to the U.S. Army from the Revolutionary War to the present, with interactive exhibits and videos. To visit Fort Lee, you must present photo identification, proof of vehicle insurance, and vehicle registration.

Richmond Area

Black History Museum and Cultural Center of Virginia (804-780-9093 or 804-780-9107; www.blackhistorymuseum.org), 00 Clay Street, Richmond 23219. Open: Tues.–Sat.; closed major holidays. Admission: Adults $5; seniors (60-plus), students, and teachers $4; children 12 and under $3. Located in the heart of

Jackson Ward, this historic house contains exhibits on the history of the neighborhood; artworks by Sam Gilliam, John Biggers, and P. H. Polk; African artifacts and textiles; and extensive information on the Black experience in Virginia.

Dabbs House Museum (804-652-3406; www.co.henrico.va.us/rec/dabbs.html), 3812 Nine Mile Road/VA 33, Richmond 23223. Open: Wed.–Sun. Admission: Free. Henrico County's Visitor Center occupies the house Robert E. Lee used as his headquarters when he first took command of the Army of Northern Virginia. Research library open by appointment.

✪ ♂ **Edgar Allan Poe Museum** (804-648-5523 or 888-213- 2763; www.poe museum.org), 1914-16 E. Main Street, Richmond 23223. Open: Tues.–Sun. Admission: Adults $6, seniors and students $5. Even though he never lived there, Edgar Allan Poe's ghost seems to haunt this little stone house in Shockoe Bottom, one of the oldest structures to survive in the city. It and several other buildings, some created from bricks rescued from places where Poe lived and worked, are stacked to the eaves with a remarkable collection of Poe memorabilia, including many rare editions of little-known works, early photos, personal possessions, and information on his many lady loves. The moody Enchanted Garden, guarded by a bust of the poet, is a popular spot for weddings. An excellent self-guided audio tour can be downloaded from the Web site.

The Fed Experience (804-697-8110; www.thefedexperience.org), 701 E. Byrd Street, Richmond 23219. Interactive exhibits bring the role of the Federal Reserve in our economy to life. Open Mon.–Fri. Free.

A BUST OF EDGAR ALLAN POE OVERLOOKS THIS MOODY GARDEN BEHIND THE POE MUSEUM, A FAVORITE SPOT FOR WEDDINGS.

First Freedom Center (804-643-1786; www.firstfreedom.org), 1321 E. Main Street, Richmond 23219. An exhibit, "Faces of Religious Freedom," examining the history and progress of this important human right around the world, occupies historic buildings in Shockoe Slip. Open by appointment. Free.

↑ "1" **Library of Virginia** (804-692-3500; www.lva.virginia.gov), 800 E. Broad Street, Richmond 23219. Closed Sun. Admission: Free. Collections include many important documents, including Virginia's original copy of the U.S. Bill of Rights. Orientation film and tour available by advance arrangement (804-692-3527).

Richmond Railway Museum (804-231-4324; www.odcnrhs.org), 102 Hull Street, Richmond 23219. Open: Sat. and Sun. Admission: Donation. Currently housed in a restored Railway Express car, the museum will soon move into the Southern Railway Station, being renovated next door. Exhibits and photos explore Richmond's railroad history, including the famous Triple Crossing, the Church Hill tunnel collapse, and Richmond's streetcar system, the first successful one of its kind. Sign up for spring and fall train excursions.

✪ **Valentine Richmond History Center and Wickham House Museum** (804-649-0711; www.richmondhistorycenter.com), 1015 E. Clay Street, Richmond 23219. Open: Tues.–Sun.; closed holidays. Admission: Adults $8; seniors (55-plus), children (7–18), and students with ID $7; under seven free. Free parking with admission in the lot on 10th Street behind the museum. Providing an excellent introduction to the many people who played a part in Richmond history, this museum in Court End offers exhibits on the city's growth, important social movements, and the Valentine family, early collectors who turned their home into a museum. Admission includes a tour of the connected 1812 **Wickham House,** one of the most lavish of its time, with original wall paintings based on classical Greek and Roman motifs. Behind the mansion, a courtyard makes a pleasant spot for lunch from the on-site **Cafe Richmond** (804-649-9550). Also located off the courtyard is the **Sculpture Studio of Edward V. Valentine,** the artist who created the statue of Thomas Jefferson in the Jefferson Hotel.

Verizon TelecomPioneers Museum of Virginia (804-772-1118, 540-966-1444, or 800-423-3422; www.jackmansystems.com/telephonemuseum), 713 E. Grace Street, Richmond 23219. Extensive collection of telephone equipment, phones, and other memorabilia dating back to the late 1800s. Open by appointment.

✈ **Virginia Aviation Museum** (804-236-3622; www.vam.smv.org), 5701 Huntsman Road, Richmond Airport, Richmond 23250. Open: Tues.–Sun.; closed holidays. Admission: Adults $6, youth (4–12) and senior (60-plus) $5, under four free. Airplane buffs will enjoy this hangar stuffed with historic planes, including the 1927 Fairchild FC-2W2 used by Virginian Adm. Richard E. Byrd on his Antarctic expeditions, a home-built 1928 Pietenpol Air Camper, a 1917 Curtiss "Jenny," and many more. Dioramas trace air combat's role in World War II, including exhibits on the Tuskegee Airmen and Women's Airforce.

✪ **Virginia Historical Society** (804-358-4901; www.vahistorical.org), 428 N. Boulevard, Richmond 23220. Open: Tues.–Sun.; closed major holidays. Admission: Free; free parking. The museum's signature exhibit, "The Story of Virginia: An American Experience," leads visitors on a path from the mastodons that once roamed the region to the tennis triumphs of Arthur Ashe, with plenty of interesting historical facts along the way. Other permanent exhibits include collections of Virginia silver, firearms manufactured in Richmond, and the murals *Four Seasons of the Confederacy* by French artist Charles Hoffbauer. *The War Horse,* a bronze memorial to Civil War horses, stands on the front lawn.

Virginia Holocaust Museum (804-257-5400; www.va-holocaust.com), 2000 E. Cary Street, Richmond 23223. Open: Daily. Admission: Free. Recommended for children nine and above. Dedicated to promoting tolerance through education, this museum presents 28 permanent exhibits on the Holocaust, including a ghetto, concentration camp, cattle car, and the *St. Louis* refugee ship, plus replicas of the famed Chor Schul synagogue in Lithuania and the Nuremberg Trials Courtroom. Film and lecture series, plus many special events, are open to the public. Free parking.

MUSIC AND CONCERT SERIES Brown's Island (804-788-6466; www.browns island.com or www.venturerichmond.com), Seventh and Tredegar streets, Shockoe Slip, Richmond. Free Fri. evening concerts on the Canal Walk.

Dogwood Dell Festival of Arts (804-646-DELL or 804-646-1437; www .richmondgov.com/parks), 700 Blanton Avenue, Richmond 23221. Summer-long celebration of the arts features free art exhibits, concerts, dance, and theater in Byrd Park.

Innsbrook After Hours (804-423-6589 or 804-794-6700; www.innsbrookafter hours.com), 4901 Lakebrook Drive, Glen Allen 23060. National acts perform under a giant tent every summer.

✍ **Pocahontas Premieres** (804-796-4255 or 800-933-PARK; www.dcr.virginia .gov), 10301 State Park Road, Chesterfield 23832. Sat.-night concerts at Pocahontas State Park's outdoor amphitheatre. $8–10; children under 13 free.

Richmond Jazz Society (804-643-1972; www.vajazz.org). Complete listings of area jazz clubs and radio stations. Find local jazz concerts at www.rvajazz.com.

Richmond Philharmonic (804-673-7400; www.richmondphilharmonic.org). Community orchestra founded in 1972 presents Great Works concerts on the VCU campus.

Richmond Symphony (804-788-1212; www.richmondsymphony.com). Professional orchestra performs more than two hundred concerts a year at many venues.

Summer Interlude Concerts (804-340-1405; www.vmfa.state.va.us), 9201 W. Huguenot Road, Richmond 23235. Classical concerts by the Richmond Chamber Players at **Bon Air Presbyterian Church** (804-272-7514; www.bonairpc.org).

Virginia Opera (866-673-7282; www.vaopera.org). State opera company presents four classics a year in the Carpenter Theatre at CenterStage.

NIGHTLIFE See our listings under *Dance, Galleries,* and *Where to Eat—Breweries and Brewpubs* for more nightlife suggestions.

Metro Richmond

Alley Katz (804-643-2816; www.alleykatzrva.com), 10 Walnut Alley, Richmond 23223. Live-music club in Shockoe Bottom has plenty of room to dance, lounge, and listen. Full kitchen.

The Camel (804-353-4901; www.thecamel.org), 1621 W. Broad Street, Richmond 23220. Entertainment includes music by local bands, art, poetry, video, and political forums; casual menu.

The Canal Club (804-643-2582; www.thecanalclub.com), 1545 E. Cary Street, Richmond 23219. Upstairs concert venue, downstairs lounge with food and free Wi-Fi.

Cary Street Cafe (804-353-7445; www.carystreetcafe.com), 2631 W. Cary Street, Richmond 23220. Carytown hippie bar and homegrown music venue features live jam bands, reggae, bluegrass, rock, and alt-country, plus vegetarian dishes and box lunches.

Emilio's Restaurante Espanol (804-359-1224; www.emiliosrichmond.com), 1847 W. Broad Street, Richmond 23220. Tapas, paella pit, and Spanish dishes complement live Latin music, jazz, and salsa lessons at this club in the Fan. Additional locations in Short Pump and Woodlake.

Funny Bone Comedy Club and Restaurant (804-521-8900; www.richmond funnybone.com), Short Pump Town Center, 11800 W. Broad Street, Richmond 23233.

Hat Factory (804-788-4281; www.hatfactoryva.com), 140 Virginia Street, Richmond 23219. Live music venue in Shockoe Slip hosts shows for all ages.

Lulu's (804-343-9771; www.lu-lusrichmond.com), 21 N. 17th Street, Richmond 23219. Cool spot created by the Millie's team across from the 17th Street Farmers Market hosts evenings of jazz accompanied by comfort-food buffets; Sun. brunch.

Martini Kitchen & Bubble Bar (804-254-4904; www.martinikitchenrichmond va.com), 1911 W. Main Street, Richmond 23220. Sophisticated club in the Fan hosts live jazz and R&B.

The National (804-612-1900; www.thenationalva.com), 708 E. Broad Street, Richmond 23219. Restored and updated historic theater hosts national music acts. Full-service **Gibson's Grill** (804-644-2637; www.gibsonsgrill.com; 700 E. Broad Street) next door.

✪ **Poe's Pub** (804-648-2120; www.poespub.com), 2706 E. Main Street, Richmond 23223. Cool roadhouse in the East End offers music from bluegrass to Beatles covers, plus great food.

Rare Olde Times Irish Public House (804-750-1346; www.rareoldetimespub .com), 10602 Patterson Avenue, Canterbury Shopping Center, Richmond 23238. Short Pump club owned by musicians.

Siné Irish Pub (804-649-7767; www.sineirishpub.com), 1327 E. Cary Street, Richmond 23219. Traditional Irish pub fare meets live music in Shockoe Slip.

✪ **The Tobacco Company** (804-767-1837 or 804-782-9555; www.thetobacco company.com), 1201 E. Cary Street, Richmond 23219. Landmark club in a Shockoe Slip warehouse hosts live music, happy hours, and dancing amid stained glass and Victorian decor.

Regional

Ashland Coffee & Tea (804-798-1702; www.ashlandcoffeeandtea.com), 100 N. Railroad Avenue, Ashland 23005. Live acoustic music Wed.–Sat. Free Wi-Fi.

County Seat Food & Gathering Place (804-598-5000; www.thecountyseat .com), 3883 Old Buckingham Road, Powhatan 23139. Live bluegrass and rockabilly music on Sat. nights and Southern country cooking daily at this family-friendly spot across from the Powhatan courthouse.

The Ironhorse (804-752-6410; www.ironhorserestaurant.com), 100 S. Railroad Avenue, Ashland 23005. Local and regional bands play jazz, bluegrass, folk, and blues on weekend nights. Open mic; bar menu. No cover.

Longstreet's Deli (804-722-4372; www.myspace.com/longstreets), 302 N. Sycamore Street, Petersburg 23803. Live bands on weekend nights.

✪ **Sycamore Rouge** (804-957-5707; www.sycamorerouge.org), 21 W. Old Street, Petersburg 23803. Unique venue in Olde Towne hosts live theater, jazz, Parisianstyle cabaret, and classic films; dining and full bar.

White Hawk Music Café (804-556-3388; www.whitehawkmusiccafe.com), 1940 Sandy Hook Road, Goochland 23063. Coffee bar hosts live bluegrass, blues, and jazz bands. Free Wi-Fi.

Metropolitan Richmond

Elegba Folklore Society (804-644-3900; www.elegbafolkloresociety.org), 101 E. Broad Street, Richmond 23219. Exhibits and performances celebrate African and African American culture.

Grace Street Theater (804-828-2020; www.vcu.edu), 934 W. Grace Street, Richmond 23220. Restored 1935 movie house serves as a venue for VCU's Department of Dance, as well as films and community events.

Landmark Theater (804-646-0546; www.landmarktheater.net), 6 N. Laurel Street, Richmond 23220. Better known as the Mosque, this historic building opened in 1927 as the Temple of the Mystic Shrine, complete with minarets, gold leaf dome, and Saracen decor inside and out. Now a city property, it seats nearly four thousand people for stage shows and boasts the largest proscenium stage on the East Coast.

Modlin Center for the Arts at the University of Richmond (804-289-8980; http://modlin.richmond.edu), 28 Westhampton Way, Richmond 23173. Hosts student-written and -produced plays, music and dance performances, plus national touring acts, performance series, and changing art exhibits.

✪ **Richmond CenterStage** (804-343-0144; www.richmondcenterstage.com), box office at the corner of Sixth and Grace, Richmond. New downtown venue hosts many local art organizations, as well as touring Broadway shows. The 1928 **Carpenter Theatre** enjoyed a complete refit, with state-of-the-art sound and lights, world-class acoustics, and 1,800 comfortable, new seats.

Richmond Coliseum (804-780-4956; www.richmondcoliseum.net), 601 E. Leigh Street, Richmond 23219. Multipurpose venue hosts a wide variety of events.

Robinson Theater Community Arts Center (804-562-9133; www.robinson theater.org), 2903 Q Street, Richmond 23223. Art deco theater provides a venue for variety shows, films, jazz bands, and more in the Church Hill neighborhood.

Regional Venues

Beacon Theatre (804-458-6551; www.beacontheatre.org), 401 N. Main Street, Hopewell 23860. Gorgeous art deco movie palace presents performing arts and special events.

The Cultural Arts Center at Glen Allen (804-261-2787; www.artsglenallen .com), 2880 Mountain Road, Glen Allen 23060. Music and dance performances, plus two art galleries.

Hanover Arts and Activities Center (804-798-2728; www.hanoverarts.org), 500 S. Center Street, Ashland 23005. Former Baptist church, built in 1859, hosts a summer theater camp, outdoor summer concerts, and musical variety shows. The summer series of **Ashland Street Parties** (www.ashlandstreetparties.com) takes place nearby.

Henrico Theatre (804-328-4491; www.co.henrico.va.us/rec), 305 E. Nine Mile Road, Highland Springs 23075. This 1938 art deco movie palace screens a Cinema Classics series ($1) the first weekend of each month and hosts a variety of performing arts.

Petersburg Area

Lee Playhouse (804-734-6629; www.leemwr.com), Building 4300, Mahone Avenue, Fort Lee 23801. The resident theater on Fort Lee is open to the public, presenting mainstage productions as well as KidKapers children's theater.

○ **Swift Creek Mill Theatre** (804-748-5203; www.swiftcreekmill.com), 17401 Jefferson Davis Highway, Colonial Heights 23834. Theater company housed in a converted three-hundred-year-old gristmill presents popular comedies, musicals, revues, and a children's series.

Richmond Area

African American Repertory Theatre (804-355-2187; www.africanamerican theatre.org), Pine Camp Cultural Arts Center, 4901 Old Brook Road, Richmond 23227. Professional company led by award-winner Derome Smith presents plays illuminating the African American experience.

○ **Barksdale Theatre** (804-282-2620; www.barksdalerichmond.org). Central Virginia's leading professional theater company presents seasons of Broadway musicals, comedies, and dramas at several locations, including historic **Hanover Tavern** (www.hanovertavern.org; 13181 Hanover Courthouse Road, Hanover 23069), site of the nation's first dinner theater.

Chamberlayne Actors Theatre (804-262-9760; www.cattheatre.com), 319 Wilkinson Road, Richmond 23227. Established in 1964, this nonprofit company presents quality productions using professional talent from the community.

Firehouse Theatre Project (804-355-2001; www.firehousetheatre.org), 1609 W. Broad Street, Richmond 23220. Theater company in a renovated firehouse presents recent off-Broadway shows not previously seen in the region, plus original works and the annual Festival of New American Plays.

HATTheatre (804-343-6364; www.hattheatre.org), 1124 Westbriar Drive, Richmond 23238. Eclectic selection of plays, including many Richmond premieres, performed in a Greenwich Village–style black box theater.

Henley Street Theatre (804-340-0115; www.henleystreettheatre.org). Ensemble-based professional theater company performs classical and contemporary plays.

Mystery Dinner Playhouse (804-649-2583 or 888-471-4802; www.mysterydinner .com), Crown Plaza Hotel–Richmond West, 6531 W. Broad Street, Richmond 23230. Comedies that are fun for the whole family.

○ **Richmond Shakespeare Theatre** (804-232-4000 or 866-227-3849; www.rich mondshakespeare.com). Company dedicated to the Bard presents summer outdoor productions, as well as a summer Shakespeare camp, in the courtyard at **Agecroft Hall** (www.agecrofthall.com) and a fall season indoors at the new CenterStage.

▼ **Richmond Triangle Players** (804-346-8113; www.richmondtriangleplayers .com), 1300 Altamont Avenue, Richmond 23260. Critically acclaimed company presents works relevant to the gay, lesbian, bisexual, and transgender communities at its new theater in **Scott's Addition** (www.scottsaddition.com).

♪ **Theatre IV: The Children's Theatre of Virginia** (804-344-8040; www .theatreivrichmond.org), 114 W. Broad Street, Richmond 23220. Professional company stages plays and summer camps for young audiences in the beautifully restored 1911 Empire Theatre.

Theatre VCU (804-828-6025; www.vcu.edu/arts), Raymond Hodges Theatre, Singleton Center for Performing Arts, 922 Park Avenue, Richmond 23284. Student productions by the Virginia Commonwealth University theater department feature guest artists; cutting-edge plays.

✴ To Do

Downtown Richmond is an anomaly among metropolitan areas. Within just a few blocks of the State Capitol Building, you can enjoy hiking, mountain biking, rock climbing, fishing, and world-class white-water rafting in James River Park. Nearby, the Petersburg region offers excellent boating and hiking along the banks of the Appomattox.

BEACHES AND SWIMMING ✍ **Cobblestones Water Park** (804-798-6819; www.cobblestonespark.com), 13131 Overhill Lake Lane, Richmond 23059. Water park offers acres of sandy beach, floating hippos, water slides for all ages, aquacycles, and the largest concrete swimming pool in Virginia. Open Memorial Day–Labor Day. $10–12; children under two free.

✍ **Hadad's Lake** (804-795-2659; www.hadadslake.com), 7900 Osborne Turnpike, Richmond 23231. Nostalgic natural water park offers swimming in freshwater pools with sandy bottoms, water trampoline, rope swing, paddleboats, picnic areas, and lake fishing. Lifeguards on duty. $12.

○ **James River Park** (804-646-8911; www.jamesriverpark.org), Richmond. The Pony Pasture beach off Riverside Drive remains the favorite spot for locals to get wet in the summer, but parking can be impossible on weekends. Other spots to swim or boulder-hop on the south bank include small sandy beaches at the Wetlands and Huguenot Woods, and the beach and rock pools near the 42nd Street entrance. On the north bank, Belle Isle, with a sandy beach at the east end, is the most popular spot, while Texas Beach at the end of Texas Avenue is the choice for locals looking for privacy. Wherever you enter the water, be sure to wear water shoes or old sneakers. Snorkeling is often interesting, especially when the water is low in summer.

Pocahontas State Park Pool and Aquatic Recreation Center (804-796-4255; www.dcr.virginia.gov/parks), 10301 State Park Road, Chesterfield 23832. Swimming daily, Memorial Day–Labor Day, in three pools, including a kiddie pool with slides. Ages 3–12 $5–7, over 13 $6–8.

Richmond City Pools (804-646-1174; www.richmondgov.com/parks). The city maintains numerous pools around town, most outdoors and open seasonally. For indoor swimming, visit the **Calhoun Pool** (804-780-4751; 436 Calhoun Street, Richmond 23227) or the **Swansboro Pool** (804-646-8088; 3160 Midlothian Turnpike, Richmond 23224).

BICYCLING The Richmond area, with its hilly terrain and dense vegetation, is a particularly good one for biking both on and off road. The parks that line the banks of the James River offer both challenging single-track and semirural paved routes where you'll encounter light traffic along with great scenery. In addition, the many acres of national battlefields in the region are laced with roads appropriate for bike touring.

To join a group ride during your visit, contact the **Richmond Area Bicycling Association** (www.raba.org), sponsoring organized rides for all ability levels throughout the region. Visitors are welcome. Route maps are available on the association Web site.

BEST BIKE ROUTES **Battlefield Park Road, Richmond National Battle-field Park** (www.nps.gov/rich). Winding, 7-mile road off VA 5 links several forts and miles of earthworks, ending at Fort Brady on the James River.

Petersburg National Battlefield (804-732-3531; www.nps.gov/pete), 5001 Siege Road, Petersburg 23803. A bike lane runs alongside the Park Tour Road, leading to dirt trails and roads suitable for biking to historic points of interest.

Virginia Capital Trail (www.virginiacapitaltrail.org), P.O. Box 17966, Richmond 23226. The first phase of the Richmond Riverfront section connects Canal Walk with Great Shiplock Park (Dock and Pear streets), where free parking is available. Other phases of the Richmond section follow the James River through the village of Rockett's Landing into Henrico County, with a spur to the new Randolph Landing Park. Eventually, this 55-mile multiuse paved trail, paralleling VA 5, will allow bikers and hikers to travel from Richmond to Williamsburg. Completion is expected by 2014.

BIKE SHOPS AND RENTALS **Bunnyhop Bicycle Shop** (804-248-5878; www.bunnyhop.org), 1387 W. Broad Street, Richmond 23220. Great prices on new and used bikes, tires repaired and wheels built, in the Fan near VCU.

Carytown Bicycle Company (804-440-2453; www.carytownbicyclecompany .com), 3224 W. Cary Street, Richmond 23221. Friendly sales and service in the heart of Carytown. Group ride Fri. afternoons.

Pedal Power Bicycles (804-730-9197; www.pedalpowerbicycles.com), 7034 Lee Park Road, Mechanicsville 23111. Rents road, mountain, and hybrid cruiser bikes.

Riverside Outfitters (804-560-0068; www.riversideoutfitters.net), 6836 Old Westham Road, Richmond 23225. Mountain bikes available for rent by the hour or day.

BMX TRAILS AND MOUNTAIN BIKING Richmond has some of the best, most challenging mountain bike action in the nation right in the heart of the city, as well as at many outlying locations. Visit www.cycleva.com for maps and advice.

Deep Run Park (804-501-7275; www.co.henrico.va.us/rec), 9900 Ridgefield Parkway, off I-64 at Gaskins Road, Richmond 23233. More than 5 miles of challenging single-track, plus nature and exercise trails, nature pavilion, and boardwalk.

Dorey Park (804-795-2334; www.co.henrico.va.us/rec), 7200 Dorey Park Drive, Richmond 23231. About 5 miles of fun single-track, plus disc golf, exercise and hiking trails, tennis, fishing pier.

Forest Hill Park (804-646-5733 or 804-646-5942; http://foresthillpark.rrp foundation.org), 4100 Forest Hill Avenue, Richmond 23225. Nearly 4 miles of challenging trails connect with the Buttermilk trails in James River Park.

Gillies Creek Park (804-646-4309; www.richmondbmx.com), Stoney Run Drive and Williamsburg Road, Richmond 23227. BMX trails, plus disc golf.

James River Park (804-646-8911; www.jamesriverpark.org), Richmond. Located on both sides of the James, this park contains more than 15 miles of mountain bike trails for every ability level, including many used in XTERRA competition. Main routes include the Belle Isle trails, where an intermediate to advanced route with many drops leads over a mountain, while an easier trip skirts the shore; the technical Buttermilk and Buttermilk Heights trails on the south bank of the James; and the 3-mile North Trail, running along the north bank of the river. Ambitious riders can make an 8-mile loop by crossing the Belle Isle and Nickel (Boulevard) bridges. Easier trails suitable for family biking are found in the Pony Pasture area on the south bank.

Pocahontas State Park (804-796-4255; www.dcr.virginia.gov/parks), 10301 State Park Road, Chesterfield 23832. More than 10 miles of mountain bike trails, including the 6-mile Old Mill Bicycle Trail circling Beaver Lake, and the challenging Lakeview Trail along Swift Creek.

Poor Farm Park (804-365-4695; www.co.hanover.va.us/parksrec), 13400 Liberty School Road, Ashland 23005. More than a dozen miles of challenging single-track make this one of the top mountain-bike destinations in the region for experienced riders.

Powhite Park (804-646-5733; www.richmondgov.com/parks), 7200 Jahnke Road, Richmond 23235. Southside park is a favorite with expert riders, offering challenging jumps and a tricky half-pipe.

BOATS & BOATING In addition to its many lakes, the region is crisscrossed with seven protected Virginia Scenic Rivers (www.dcr.virginia.gov), providing exceptional opportunities for water recreation.

Because of its location on the fall line of the James, Richmond can claim the only class IV white-water rapids in the country within the city limits of a major metropolitan area. White-water enthusiasts can take on class III–IV rapids with the skyline of the city as a backdrop.

BOAT RENTALS ✍ **Byrd Park** (804-646-5733; www.richmondgov.com/parks), 0 South Boulevard, Richmond 23221. In summer, rent a paddleboat for a spin around Fountain Lake at this downtown park.

Pocahontas State Park (804-796-4255; www.dcr.virginia.gov/parks), 10301 State Park Road, Chesterfield 23832. Canoes, kayaks, pedal boats, and rowboats for rent from Memorial Day to Labor Day on Swift Creek Lake. Private boats can also launch on the lake. Electric motors allowed.

Riverside Outfitters (804-560-0068; www.riversideoutfitters.net), 6836 Old Westham Road, Richmond 23225. Rent oversized tubes, sit-on-top kayaks, and canoes for a couple of hours or a full day from this outfitter close to the Pony Pasture. Free equipment shuttle from various take-outs along the James.

Canoeing, Kayaking, Tubing, and White-Water Rafting
Appomattox Canal and River Loop (804-861-1666; www.folar-va.org). Put in at **Appomattox Riverside Park** (877-730-7278; www.petersburgarea.org; Appomat-

tox River Park Road off Ferndale Road/Pickett Avenue, Petersburg) for a peaceful paddle up the historic Upper Appomattox Canal to the Abutment Dam. From there, enter the white-water rapids of the river itself for a 2-mile run back to the parking area. Or continue farther downstream through a final set of class II–IV rapids just before the Campbell's Bridge take-out, a distance of about 7 miles. Water levels are best in winter and early spring.

Dutch Gap Conservation Lagoon Water Trail (804-748-1621 or 804-706-9690; www.chesterfield.gov), 251 Henricus Park Road, off SR 615, Chester 23836. This 4-mile paddle trail leads through a labyrinth of sunken wooden barges, as well as bald cypress wetlands, home to herons, ospreys, and kingfishers.

✪ **James River Park** (804-646-8911; www.jamesriverpark.org), Richmond. Paddlers who prefer flat water can put in at the Huguenot Woods launch and paddle upstream about 1.5 miles to Bosher's Dam, or downstream to the Pony Pasture take-out, a slightly more exciting ride, with a portage around the Z Dam. Both Huguenot Woods and the Pony Pasture are popular put-ins for tubing as well.

A novice white-water run stretches from the Pony Pasture to Park Headquarters at Reedy Creek. It's a good idea to do this stretch with someone experienced as the half-dozen class II rapids can be tricky to navigate. The same goes for the stretch of class II–IV whitewater that stretches from Reedy Creek to the Mayo take-outs near the 14th Street bridge, recommended only for experienced river runners. Several alternate routes are possible, and rescues are frequent, especially during times of high water. Detailed descriptions of the rapids can be found at www .americanwhitewater.org.

The difficulty of the rapids varies with the water level, so always check before entering the water. When the water level is 5 feet or above, everyone entering the river must wear a life jacket. When the water level reaches 9 feet, the river is closed to recreational use, unless you obtain an expert permit (experience with class V rapids required) at Fire Station No. 1 (804-646-4229; 308 N. 24th Street, Richmond 23223). Water levels are posted at every river access point, or check before you go by calling the River Level Hotline at 804-646-8228.

Lower Appomattox River Blueway (804-861-1666; www.folar-va.org), P.O. Box 1808, Petersburg 23805. Put in below the Temple Avenue Bridge in Petersburg or at White Bank Park on Swift Creek for a flatwater paddle down to Hopewell's **Appomattox River Trailhead** at the junction of the Appomattox and James rivers. (See listing under *Hiking.*)

Upper James Flatwater Paddle (www.jamesriverassociation.org). Put in at Watkins Landing (SR 625 in Powhatan County) and paddle 4 miles downstream to a take-out at **Robious Landing Park** (804-751-4696; 3800 James River Road, Midlothian 23113), or continue south and take out at Bosher's Dam.

The following are canoeing, kayaking, and rafting outfitters in the region:

Adventure Challenge (804-276-7600; www.adventurechallenge.com). Classes in white-water kayaking and special women's classes include trips on the James River.

Mattaponi Canoe & Kayak (769-144-9562 or 800-769-3545; www.mattaponi.com), P.O. Box 146, Aylett 23009. Mattaponi rents kayaks and canoes, and conducts guided tours Apr.–Oct. on the Mattaponi, Pamunkey, and Chickahominy rivers, and into the legendary Dragon Swamp.

River City Rafting (804-232-7238; www.rivercityraft.com), 100 Stockton Street, Richmond 23224. Guided white-water rafting and tubing trips on the Upper and Lower Falls of the James. Tube rentals available.

Riverside Outfitters (804-560-0068; www.riversideoutfitters.net), 6836 Old Westham Road, Richmond 23225. Guided flatwater canoe trips, flatwater and class II rapids trips aboard sit-on-top kayaks, and white-water rafting on the rapids of the Upper James (class I–II) and Lower James (class II–IV), plus twilight paddles and tree-climbing lessons. Wet suits provided for winter trips. Rents tubes, sit-on-top kayaks, canoes, mountain bikes, and river boards.

Marinas

Anchor Point Marine Services (804-541-6200; www.anchorpointcondos -marina.com), 303 Beacon Ridge Drive, Hopewell 23860. Transient slips include water and cable; fuel, marina store, and shower house available.

Appomattox Small Boat Harbor (804-733-5770; www.appomattoxboatharbor .com), 1604 Fine Street, Prince George 23875. Family-owned marina offers transient slips and a boat ramp open 24 hours.

Hopewell City Marina (804-541-2353; www.hopewellva.gov), 1051 W. Riverside Avenue, Hopewell 23860. Boat ramps, pump-out service.

Jordan Point Yacht Haven (804-458-3398; www.jordanpoint.com), 101 Jordan Point Road, Hopewell 23860. Full-service marina on the Lower James offers slip rentals, snack bar, pool, ships store, concrete boat ramps.

Public Boat Ramps

In the city of Richmond, **James River Park** (www.jamesriverpark.org) offers several boat launches on the south side of the river, including a boat slide for canoes, kayaks, and inner tubes at **Huguenot Woods,** west of the Huguenot Bridge, off Southampton Street; and a concrete boat ramp below the rapids at historic **Ancarrow's Landing** on Maury Street.

In Chesterfield County, south of Richmond, the **Appomattox Canoe Launch** (21400 Chesdin Road, Petersburg 23803) provides water access to both the river and Lake Chesdin. A concrete ramp for motorized boats and a fishing pier lie on the other side of the lake in Dinwiddie County, off SR 776. Additional facilities are found at **Lake Chesdin Park** (12900 Lake Chesdin Parkway, Chesterfield 23838).

The **Dutch Gap Boat Ramp** (804-748-1623; 441 Coxendale Road, Chester 23831), off VA 10 between I-95 and I-295, is also the trailhead for a walk along the banks of the James River. **Robious Landing Park** (804-323-1700; 3800 James River Road, Midlothian 23113), with a boat slide for small craft, provides access to the Upper James behind Bosher's Dam. For additional information, call 804-748-1623 or visit www.chesterfield.gov.

In Henrico County east of Richmond, several boat ramps access the Lower James River and its tributaries. **Deep Bottom Landing** (9525 Deep Bottom Road, off VA 5, Richmond 23231) has two concrete boat ramps into the James and a canoe launch into Four Mile Creek. **Osborne Landing and Park** (9680 Osborne Turnpike, Richmond 23231), site of many BASS Masters events, has three double boat slips and a canoe launch, as well as a fully accessible fishing pier, trails, boardwalk, playground, and picnic area. For additional information and directions, call 804-501-5108 or visit www.co.henrico.va.us/rec.

Hanover County (www.co.hanover.va.us/parksrec) provides boat slides suitable for canoes, kayaks, and other light craft into the Pamunkey River at Little Page Bridge (US 301), and into the South Anna River at both the Ground Squirrel Bridge (US 33) and at 13151 W. Patrick Henry Road (VA 54) in Ashland. A canoe ramp at 17600 Washington Highway/US 1, Ashland 23005, provides access to the North Anna River.

FAMILY FUN Confederate Hills Croquet Club (804-737-2859), 302 Lee Avenue, Highland Springs 23075. Learn to play croquet or shuffleboard at the Confederate Hills Recreation Center.

Ironbridge Sports Park (804-748-7770; www.ironbridgesportspark.com), 11400 Ironbridge Road, Chester 23831. Lots of fun in one spot with a covered driving range, batting cages, miniature golf course, go-carts, arcade, on-site restaurant, Friday Classic Car Cruise-In.

✪ **Kings Dominion** (804-876-5000; www.kingsdominion.com), 1600 Theme Park Way (I-95 exit 98), Doswell 23047. Begin your visit with a bird's-eye view atop the 275-foot replica of the Eiffel Tower to see all the fun in store. Attractions include one of the best collections of coasters on the East Coast, including the new Intimidator 305 giga-coaster, new Planet Peanuts themed children's area, several live shows, and the 20-acre Waterworks water park. Open Apr.–Oct. Discounts available online.

Lucky Lake Gem & Mineral Mine of Virginia (804-478-5468; www.luckylakeva.com), 4125 Harpers Road, McKenney 23872. Natural pegmatite mine off I-95 south of Richmond offers flume panning and free stone identification.

Maymont Children's Farm (804-358-7166; www.maymont.org), 2201 Shields Lake Drive, Richmond 23220. Kids can meet and feed domestic animals raised on Virginia farms, including goats, pigs, donkeys, and horses, plus rare breeds, such as Scotch Highland cows and Barbados Blackbelly sheep. Free.

Ravenchase Adventures (804-218-0551 or 888-702-9039; www.raven chase.com), 3126 W. Cary Street, #139, Richmond 23221. Richmond-based company designs treasure hunts that will take you to undiscovered spots in the city.

A REPLICA OF THE EIFFEL TOWER FORMS THE CENTERPIECE OF KINGS DOMINION THEME PARK.

⊤ **SkateNation Plus** (804-364-1477; www.skatenationplus.com), 4350 Pouncey Tract Road, Glen Allen 23060. Ice rink in Short Pump offers public skating, laser tag, arcade games, and a rock climbing wall.

𝄢 ⊤ **Swader's Sports Park** (804-733-3700; www.swaders.com), 4725 Whitehill Boulevard, Prince George 23875. Family fun center with go-cart tracks, batting cages, miniature golf, and a golf driving range, plus an enormous indoor facility with laser tag, Playsmart indoor playground, arcade, and 4D thrill rides.

O Three Lakes Park Nature Center and Aquarium (804-262-5055 or 804-261-8230; www.co.henrico.va.us/rec), 400 Sausiluta Drive, Richmond 23227. A 50,000-gallon outdoor freshwater aquarium has an underwater viewing window; smaller tanks hold turtles, snakes, and amphibians. Short, shady nature trails lead around the lakes. Fishing permitted from the shore or fishing pier. Free.

West Point Skydiving Adventures (804-785-9707; www.skydivewestpoint.com), Middle Peninsula Regional Airport, Airport Road, Shacklefords 23156. Tandem jumps for first timers, plus free fall and instructor-assisted jumps.

Winter fun (www.richmondgov.com/parks). If your visit to Richmond coincides with one of the area's rare snowfalls, join the locals for sledding in Bryan Park or Forest Hill Park.

Disc Golf Courses

Dorey Park (804-795-2334; www.co.henrico.va.us/rec), 2999 Darbytown Road, Richmond 23231.

Dunncroft/Castlepoint Park (804-501-7275; www.co.henrico.va.us/rec), 4901 Francistown Road, Richmond 23294. Nine-hole course.

Gillies Creek Park (804-646-4309; www.richmondgov.com/parks), Stoney Run Drive and Williamsburg Road, Richmond 23227.

Goyne Park (804-748-1623; www.chesterfield.gov), 5300 Ecoff Avenue, Chester 23831.

Pharaoh's Tomb at White Bank Park (804-520-9224; www.colonial-heights .com), White Bank Road, Colonial Heights 23834.

Skate Parks

Colonial Heights Skate Park (804-520-9204; www.colonial-heights.com/ RecParks.htm), 3451 Conduit Road, Colonial Heights 23834. Located behind the Colonial Heights Technical Center. $1–2.

Hopewell Skateboard Park (804-541-2353; www.ci.hopewell.va.us), 100 W. City Point Road, Hopewell 23860. New facility with ramps and jumps.

Laurel Skate Park (804-672-6273; www.co.henrico.va.us/rec), 10301 Hungary Spring Road, Richmond 23228. Lighted park is free for skateboarders, inline skaters, and freestyle bikers; safety equipment required.

Pella Virginia Skate Park (804-276-9622; www.ymcarichmond.org), 7540 Hull Street, Richmond 23235. Nice park at the Manchester YMCA. Annual community membership $25, plus $7 per session.

FISHING The James River and its tributaries, along with the many freshwater lakes in the area, provide plenty of opportunities to drop a line. During the spring, the river through downtown Richmond is the scene of a fine run of American and

Hickory shad, while hard-fighting striped bass arrive spring and fall. And Richmond is one of the best places in the country to catch trophy-sized smallmouth bass.

In the tidal regions of the James below Richmond, gigantic blue catfish, many weighing more than 80 pounds, create a world-class fishing opportunity. Visit the **James River Cats** Web site (www.jamesrivercats.com) for more information.

The Appomattox River, slower moving than the James, produces sizeable largemouth bass and chain pickerel, and is one of the few streams in the East where spotted or Kentucky bass are caught.

Fishing Lakes & Piers

All these fishing locations require a Virginia freshwater fishing license, unless otherwise stated. In addition, stocked trout lakes require a special trout license between November 1 and April 30 each year. For more information, contact the **Virginia Department of Game and Inland Fisheries** (866-721-6911; www.dgif.virginia.gov; 4010 W. Broad Street, Richmond 23230).

& **Amelia Lake** (804-367-6796; www.dgif.virginia.gov), between US 60 and US 360, 25 miles southwest of Richmond. Noted for a high density of largemouth bass, bluegill, and sunfish. Boat ramp and handicapped-accessible fishing pier. River fishing in late winter and spring for striped bass and walleye, plus spotted bass above US 360.

 & **Bryan Park** (804-646-5733; www.richmondgov.com/parks or www.friendsof bryanpark.org), 4300 Hermitage Road, Richmond 23227. Handicapped-accessible shoreline fishing at two lakes stocked annually with channel catfish.

& **Byrd Park** (804-646-5733; www.richmondgov.com/parks), 0 South Boulevard, Richmond 23221. Downtown park has two lakes for shoreline fishing: **Shields Lake,** stocked with channel catfish and trout, and **Swan Lake,** stocked with channel catfish.

& **Dory Park Lake** (804-501-7275; www.co.henrico.va.us/rec), 2999 Darbytown Road, Richmond 23231. Popular lake, stocked annually with channel catfish and trout, has a handicapped-accessible fishing pier and a walking trail circling the lake.

Lake Chesdin (804-748-1623; www.chesterfield.gov), 12900 Lake Chesdin Parkway, Petersburg 23803. This 3,100-acre reservoir on the Appomattox River offers excellent fishing for largemouth bass, crappie, and channel catfish. Walleye and striped bass are stocked annually. Three marinas, with concessions, boat rentals, and other amenities, are located on the lake: **Cozy Cove Campground and Marina** (804-265-9000; 713 Sutherland Road, Church Road 23833), **Seven Springs Marina and Store** (804-590-3671; 8631 River Road, Petersburg 23803), and **Whippernock Marina and Campground** (804-265-5252; 2700 Sutherland Road, Sutherland 23885).

 Powhatan Wildlife Management Area (804-367-6796; www.dgif.virginia.gov), off US 60 or VA 13, Powhatan Court House. About 25 miles west of Richmond, this preserve contains two lakes, plus the Bass, Sunfish, and Catfish ponds, good spots for young anglers looking for a lot of action. Boats with electric motors allowed. Hiking trails offer glimpses of beavers and wildfowl.

Fishing Outfitters

Hanover Fly Fishers (804-537-5036; www.hanoverfly.com), Box 525, Hanover 23069. Join the experts for largemouth bass and panfish on a private stocked lake at **Elsing Green Plantation** (www.elsinggreen.com). Instruction in fly casting available.

✐ **James River Fishing School** (804-938-2350; www.jamesriverfishing.com), 7239 Lookout Drive, Richmond 23235. Guided trips for flathead and blue catfish, shad, and striped bass. Lessons and special parent/child short courses available.

Old Dominion Outdoors (804-539-8023 or 804-795-4335; www.olddominionout doors.com), Eberly's Store, 5164 New Market Road, off VA 5, Richmond 23231. Join Capt. Neil Renouf to look for huge blue cats, or visit **Eberly's Store** for expert advice, refreshments, and Virginia-made products.

Virginia Fishing Adventures (804-687-1869; www.virginiafishingadventures .com), 4525 E. Seminary Avenue, Richmond 23227. Guided float trips for smallmouth bass in the James or Rappahannock; evening fishing on the James with fly rods or light spinning tackle. Lessons and kids' camp available.

Tackle Shops

Castaway Sporting Goods (804-706-9100; www.castawaysportinggoods.com), 11600 Jefferson Davis Highway, Chester 23831. Sponsors of the Castaway Tournament Trail, the largest fishing tournament in the region.

Greentop Hunting and Fishing (804-550-2188; www.greentophuntfish.com), 10193 Washington Highway/US 1, Glen Allen 23059. Locally owned store in business for 60 years.

Orvis (804-253-9000; www.orvis.com), 800 W. Broad Street, Richmond 23233. Fly-fishing equipment, lessons, and seminars.

Pope's Bait and Tackle (804-737-7707; www.popesbaitandtackle.com), 320 E. Williamsburg Road, Sandston 23150. Shop east of Richmond International Airport known for its huge bloodworms, live crickets, minnows, and eels. Licenses available.

GOLF With more than two dozen public courses, and an equal number of distinguished private courses, the Richmond region has enough golf for the most dedicated player. Our listings include some of the favorite local courses. Consult the Web site of the **Richmond Golf Association** (www.rgaweb.org), as well as the golf listings in the "Williamsburg, Jamestown, and Yorktown" chapter, for additional options.

Belmont Golf Course (804-501-4653; www.co.henrico.va.us), 1600 Hilliard Road, Richmond 23228. Henrico County public course designed by Albert Warren Tillenghast in 1916, then redesigned by Donald Ross.

Dogwood Trace Golf Course (804-732-5573; www.dogwoodtracegolf.com), 3108 Homestead Drive, Petersburg 23805. Petersburg's municipal course enjoyed a complete redesign by golf architect Tom Clark.

The First Tee Chesterfield (804-275-8050; www.thefirstteerichmondchesterfield .org), 6736 Hunting Creek Drive, Richmond 23237. One of the few First Tee facilities to offer 18 holes, as well as a short par 3 course, driving range, and practice green.

The First Tee Richmond (804-646-4074; www.thefirstteerichmondchesterfield

.org), 400 School Street, Richmond 23222. All-weather heated and covered practice area, two six-hole par 3 courses designed by Lester George, pro shop, grill, close to downtown Richmond.

Independence Golf Club (804-594-0261; www.independencegolfclub.com), 600 Founders Bridge Boulevard, Midlothian 23113. Daily fee course designed by Tom Fazio with 18 championship holes, plus a nine-hole short course, receives the nod as a Best Place to Play from *Golf Digest*. The **Charles House Bar & Grill** (804-594-0378) and the **Harry W. Easterly Museum of Virginia Golf History** occupy the clubhouse.

Sycamore Creek Golf Course (804-784-3544; www.sycamorecreekgolfcourse .com), 991 Manakin Road, off W. Broad Street, Manakin-Sabot 23103. Signature Michael Hurdzan design, considered the best area course by locals, is noted for its excellent greens conditions and the frosty pints at its bar.

✔ **Windy Hill Sports Complex** (804-794-0010; www.windyhillsports.com), 16500 Midlothian Turnpike, Midlothian 23113. Challenging nine-hole course has some of the lowest greens fees in the region, plus a lighted par 3 for night play, driving range, minigolf, go-carts, and batting cages.

HEALTH & FITNESS CLUBS AND TRAILS Many of Richmond's downtown hotels offer free passes to the **Downtown YMCA** (804-644-9622; www.downtown richmondymca.org; 2 W. Franklin Street, Richmond 23220) or the **James Center YMCA** (804-200-6070; www.jamescenterymca.org; 1051 E. Cary Street, Richmond 23219) in Shockoe Slip.

In Carytown, **Pilates, Dance and More** (804-354-0600; www.pilatesdanceand more.com; 3122 W. Cary Street, Richmond 23221), in the Cary Court Park & Shop, welcomes walk-ins.

Numerous fitness trails can be found in area parks. The mile-long Vita Trail at **Byrd Park** (804-646-5733; www.richmondgov.com/parks; 0 S. Boulevard, Richmond 23221) is most convenient to downtown.

HIKING **James River Park trails** (804-646-8911; www.jamesriverpark.org). James River Park contains many hiking trails, including the **Manchester Slave Trail,** beginning at Ancarrow's Landing; the **Floodwall Walk,** along the top of the cement levy; the **Buttermilk Trail,** following the ancient shoreline of the James; and the **Wetlands Trail,** all on the south side of the river, and the trails on **Belle Isle,** accessed from the north bank via a pedestrian bridge under Lee Bridge.

Pocahontas State Park Trails (804-796-4255; www.dcr.virginia.gov/parks), 10301 State Park Road, Chesterfield 23832. Extensive system of trails winds over heavily wooded hills. Parking $2–3.

✪ **Richmond Canal Walk** (804-648-6549; www.richmondriverdistrict.com). A 1.25-mile paved walking path stretches along either side of the Kanawha and Haxall canals from Seventh Street at Belle Isle and the Tredegar Ironworks to 17th Street in Shockoe Bottom. Walk down to the river's edge on Brown's Island to the **Pipeline Trail,** a metal catwalk with views of the river's fiercest rapids and heron rookeries.

Upper Appomattox Canal Trail (804-861-1666; www.folar-va.org), P.O. Box 1808, Petersburg 23805. From **Appomattox Riverside Park** (877-730-7278;

www.petersburgarea.org; Appomattox River Park Road off Ferndale Road/Pickett Avenue, Petersburg), also known as Old Ferndale, follow the towpath along the canal up to the abutment dam, or head east along a series of trails 4 miles to a new park at the ruins of Campbell Bridge.

The planned **Lower Appomattox Greenway** will stretch 22 miles from the Lake Chesdin dam to City Point in Hopewell. Completed sections of the greenway on the south side of the river can be found at **Appomattox River Regional Park** (804-733-2646; www.princegeorgeva.org; River Road, between I-295 and the Riverside Regional Jail); at the **Appomattox River Trailhead** (804-541-2353; www.ci.hopewell.va.us; off Appomattox Street, Hopewell), with a trail to Civil War sites at City Point; and on **Pocohontas Island** (804-733-2400; 810 Logan Street, Petersburg 23803), north of the US 1/US 301 bridge between Petersburg and Colonial Heights.

On the north side of the river, trails are found at **Ettrick Riverside Park** (804-748-1623; www.chesterfield.gov; 21514 Chesterfield Avenue, Ettrick 23803), near the Virginia State University campus; at **White Bank Park** (804-520-9224; www.colonial-heights.com; White Bank Road, Colonial Heights 23834); and at nearby **Fort Clifton/Berberich Park** (804-520-9224; www.colonial-heights.com; Brockwell Lane, Colonial Heights 23834), where trails offer scenic views from the bluffs above the river.

The **Colonial Heights Appomattox River Trail System** (804-520-9275; www.colonialheightstrails.org), now under construction on the north bank of the river, will stretch about 2 miles from **Appamatuck Park,** just west of the US 1/301 bridge, to **Roslyn Landing Park,** off E. Roslyn Road. Both parks will have launch areas for small boats and canoes, picnic areas, and fishing areas.

HORSEBACK RIDING Blue Ridge Stables (804-798-6686; www.blueridge stables.com), 11483 Cedar Lane, Ashland 23005. Riding lessons, horse day care, layover suite next to the barn available for owners by the night.

Beaver Hollow Farm (804-240-2545; www.beaverhollowfarm.com), 9501 Woodpecker Road, Chesterfield 23838. Overnight boarding, lessons, and trail rides at nearby Pocahontas State Park, Petersburg National Battlefield, or Hatteras Island, North Carolina.

✍ **Brandywine Farms & Pony Rides** (804-590-2305; www.brandywinefarmva.com), 13705 Bundle Road, Chesterfield 23838. Hunt seat lessons, summer camps, trail and pony rides.

Pocahontas State Park (804-796-4255; www.dcr.virginia.gov/parks), 10301 State Park Road, Chesterfield 23832. Nine miles of equestrian trails, plus the Bright Hope day-use horse complex with access to the Bright Hope multiuse trail. No overnight facilities.

Reedy Creek Hounds (804-478-5119), Reedy Creek Farm, McKenney. Experienced riders can join twice-weekly hunts, Aug.–Apr.

Shangrila Retreat (434-517-0888; www.shangrilaretreat.us), 3219 Cluster Springs Road, South Boston 24592. All-inclusive packages include lodging, meals, and daily horseback riding. Trail and wagon rides for day visitors available by appointment.

The White Horse Stables (804-932-4684; www.thewhitehorsestables.com), 4900 Huntsman Trail, Quinton 23141. Lessons in equitation and fox hunting, trail rides.

HUNTING AND SHOOTING **Amelia Wildlife Management Area** (804-367-6796; www.dgif.virginia.gov), between US 60 and US 360, about 25 miles southwest of Richmond. Annual hunts for deer, turkey, rabbit, quail, and squirrel; 28 acres of dove fields; three free shooting ranges with a clay-bird shotgun range and archery range. Open Sept. 1–Mar. 31.

Hunt's Game/Training Preserve (434-246-2067; www.huntsgamepreserve.com), 19039 Walkers Mill Road, Jarratt 23867. Quail-hunting preserve offers lodging and dog rental, or will train your dogs for the hunt.

Southbound Sporting Preserve (434-447-8363; www.southboundpreserve.com), 1077 Dry Creek Road, South Hill 23970. Private resort near the North Carolina border provides professional guides for hunting, horseback riding, and fishing; upland clays target shooting; quail and pheasant hunting; and hunting-dog training.

Virginia Elite Outdoors (804-543-7168; www.vaeliteoutdoors.com). Spring gobbler hunts, deer hunts, guided fishing trips for largemouth bass and catfish.

RACQUET SPORTS & TENNIS **The City of Richmond Parks and Recreation** (804-646-5733; www.richmondgov.com/parks) maintains some 140 tennis courts throughout the metro area, most available on a first come, first served basis. **Byrd Park** (804-647-4651; 0 S. Boulevard, Richmond 23221) has 12 lighted courts downtown.

Courtside West (804-740-4263; www.courtsidewest.com; 1145 Gaskins Road, Richmond 23238) has indoor tennis and racquetball courts.

ROCK CLIMBING **Belle Isle** (804-646-8911; www.jamesriverpark.org). This island was used as a quarry during the construction of Richmond, leaving behind several rock faces used by climbers for practice and training, as well as areas suitable for bouldering.

Manchester Wall (804-646-8911; www.jamesriverpark.org), off US 60 at the Manchester Bridge. The remnants of the old Richmond and Petersburg Railroad Bridge, located on the south side of the James in downtown Richmond, provide some challenging climbs. More than 40 different routes, ranked easy to advanced, have been mapped up the 60-foot granite wall and its three adjacent piers.

⚓ ☂ **Peak Experiences Indoor Climbing Center** (804-897-6800; www.peakexperiences.com), 11421 Polo Circle, Midlothian 23113. One of the largest indoor climbing walls on the East Coast.

SNORKELING & SCUBA **Atlantis Divers** (804-320-7000; www.atlantisdiversva.com), 9990 Robious Road, Richmond 23235. Top equipment brands come with instruction and pool time.

The Dive Shop (804-270-0700; www.thediveshoprichmond.com), 9320 W. Broad Street, the Shops at Tripps, Richmond 23294. PADI and Technical Dive classes; free seminars on scuba.

♻ **Lake Rawlings Scuba Park** (804-478-9000 or 800-583-3781; www.lakerawlings.com), 1 Quarry Lane (I-85 exit 39), Rawlings 23876. Named one of the top 50 dive sites in the United States, this former granite quarry is a favorite with regional divers thanks to its clear, warm water, 65-foot depth, and many underwater attractions, including sunken boats, automobiles, and even an airplane. The on-site dive shop offers equipment rentals and PADI courses. Camping and cabin rentals available. The lake is open for swimming and snorkeling on weekdays. Scuba diving $12–25; swimming/snorkeling $5–7.

SPAS Legends Salon & Day Spa (804-359-5512; www.legendssalon.com), 3148 W. Cary Street, Richmond 23221. Spa in Cary Court with a full menu of treatments.

Main Street Day Spa & Salon (804-644-1084; www.mainstreetspa.com), 519 E. Main Street, Richmond 23219. Spa in the Fan offers couples massage, wedding packages, castor oil packs, and herbology.

Retreat Salon & Spa (804-861-8104; www.retreatsalon.com), 12 W. Old Street, Petersburg 23803. Spa in Old Towne Petersburg was selected one of the top two hundred spas in the United States by *Salon Today*.

Utopia Spa (804-732-1234; www.theutopiaspa.com), 115 N. Sycamore Street, Petersburg 23803. Petersburg spa offers many reasonably priced add-ons.

SPECTATOR SPORTS Professional sports have had a rocky road of late in Richmond. During the last few years, the city lost minor league teams in hockey (the Richmond Riverdogs and the Richmond Renegades), indoor football (Richmond Bandits), and, most recently, their beloved Triple-A baseball team, the Richmond Braves, which relocated to Gwinnett County, Georgia, in 2009, rather than face another season in the venerable, but outdated, **Diamond Stadium** (3001 N. Boulevard, Richmond 23230).

All, however, is not lost. An AA ball club affiliated with the San Francisco Giants relocated to Richmond in 2010, where it will play at least the first few seasons at the Diamond. A fan contest named the team the **Flying Squirrels** (www.squirrels baseball.com), and sales of tickets and team memorabilia are brisk.

Indoor football returned to the city in 2010 as well, as the **American Indoor Football League** brought the **Richmond Raiders** (www.richmondraiders profootball.com) to the **Richmond Coliseum** (804-780-4956; www.richmond coliseum.net; 601 E. Leigh Street, Richmond 23219).

The **Richmond Kickers Professional Soccer Club** (804-644-5425; www .richmondkickers.com) remains the city's longest standing pro team, playing from April to August at the University of Richmond stadium.

Local colleges conduct active sports programs. The **Virginia Commonwealth University Rams** (804-828-RAMS; www.vcuathletics.com) are powerhouses in men's and women's basketball, playing at the **Seigel Center** in the heart of the city. The **University of Richmond Spiders** (804-289-8388 or 877-SPIDER-1; www.richmondspiders.com) won the 2008 National Football Championship. Their annual match against the William and Mary Tribe is a hot ticket. The **Virginia Union University Panthers** (804-342-1493; http://vuusports.vuu.edu) play in the Central Intercollegiate Athletic Association Conference and have sent a number of players on to the pros.

Colonial Downs (804-966-7223; www.colonialdowns.com), Virginia's only parimutuel horse racetrack, is located halfway between Richmond and Williamsburg in New Kent County at I-64 exit 214. The track hosts thoroughbred racing during the summer and harness racing every fall. The **Strawberry Hill Races**

(804-569-3232; www.strawberryhillraces.com) steeplechase meet is held there every spring.

If auto racing is more your speed, **Richmond International Raceway** (866-455-7223; www.rir.com; 600 E. Laburnum Avenue, Richmond 23222) hosts NASCAR Sprint Cup meets in May and September and IndyCar racing in June under the lights on the unique 0.75-mile oval. If you feel the need for speed yourself, catch a ride or take a driving class with the **Richard Petty Driving Experience** (800-237-3889; www.drivepetty.com) or **Drivetech Racing School** (877-226-7223; www.theracingschool.com). Both offer frequent sessions in Richmond.

Short track racing takes place most Friday nights from April to Labor Day at the **Southside Speedway** (804-744-2700; www.southsidespeedway.com; 12800 Genito Road, Midlothian 23112). Or catch the hot-rod action most Friday and Saturday nights all year at the **Richmond Dragway** (804-737-1193; www.richmonddragway .com; 1955 Portugee Road, Sandston 23150).

At the **Virginia Motorsports Park** (804-862-3174; www.virginiamotorsportspk .com; 8018 Boydton Plank Road, Petersburg 23803), you can enjoy your choice of drag racing, mud bog, BMX, or motocross action, plus truck and tractor pulls.

TOURING Several discount tickets help cut costs. The **Richmond Civil War Pass** ($12) gives access to the Museum of the Confederacy, Confederate White House, and American Civil War Center at Historic Tredegar. The $10 **Court End Passport** provides entrance for a year to four attractions near the state capitol: the Valentine Richmond History Center, the 1812 Wickham House, the John Marshall House, and the Black History Museum and Cultural Center of Virginia, plus complimentary parking behind the Valentine Center.

In Petersburg, combination tickets ($9–11) are available for three of the city's top attractions: the Siege Museum, Blandford Church, and Centre Hill Mansion.

By air: ✪ **Balloons Over Virginia** (804-798-0080; www.balloonsovervirginia .com), 9988 Lickinghole Road, Richmond 23005.

Dominion Aviation Services (804-271-7793; www.dominionaviation .com), 7511 Airfield Drive, Richmond 23237. Day or night air tours from Chesterfield Airport in a four-seat craft.

By automobile: **African American Driving Tour of Petersburg** (804-733-2396; www.petersburg-va.org). Visits 26 sites, ranging from Gillfield Baptist Church, one of the oldest black congregations in the country, to a house used by the Underground Railroad.

✪ **Hollywood Cemetery Driving Tour** (804-648-8501; www.hollywood cemetery.org), 412 S. Cherry Street, Richmond 23220. A painted blue line

COLONIAL DOWNS, IN NEW KENT COUNTY HALFWAY BETWEEN RICHMOND AND WILLIAMSBURG, HOSTS BOTH HARNESS AND FLAT RACING, AS WELL AS STEEPLECHASE MEETS.

leads visitors through this enormous cemetery on the bluffs above the James River, passing a 90-foot granite pyramid commemorating the 18,000 Confederate dead buried here; Presidents' Circle, with the tombs of James Monroe and John Tyler; the grave of Jefferson Davis; a black cast-iron dog guarding the grave of a little girl; and much more. Open daily. Free. A map ($1) is available at the office, open weekdays.

By bicycle or on foot: **Capital Creepers Eerie Nights Walking Tour** (804-833-1845; www.eerienights.com). Ghost tour of Shockoe Bottom led by a band of the living dead. May–Nov. $13.

City Point Open Air Walking Tour (804-541-2461 or 800-863-8687; www.hope wellva.gov). Self-guided tour passes 24 Civil War sites, as well as lovely homes and gardens. Brochure available at the visitors center.

Jackson Ward African-American Heritage Walking Tour (804-780-9093; www.blackhistorymuseum.org). Self-guided tours of this historically black neighborhood begin at Richmond's Black History Museum.

✪ **Haunts of Richmond** (804-343-3700 or 866-782-2661; www.hauntsofrichmond .com), 1914 E. Main Street, Richmond 23223. Tours explore the darker side of Richmond's past, including Shadows of Shockoe, Haunted Capitol Hill, and a Spirits & Spirits Pub Crawl (over 21 only). May–Nov.; $15.

Historic Richmond Tours (804-649-0711; www.richmondhistorycenter.com). Guided walking tours visit many neighborhoods, including daily **City Center Walks,** and tours of **Hollywood Cemetery.** Dog-friendly History Hounds tours also available. $10.

Historic Tours of Richmond and the Civil War Battlefields (804-272-8888 or 866-808-1861; www.owensandramsey.com). Marc Ramsey, Civil War buff and owner of one of the top historical bookstores in the South, offers personalized tours in the Richmond area.

GENERATIONS OF RICHMOND CITIZENS, INCLUDING PRESIDENTS MONROE AND TYLER, CONFEDERATE PRESIDENT JEFF DAVIS, AND CAVALRY HERO J. E. B. STUART, NOW REST ON THE BLUFFS OVERLOOKING THE FALLS OF THE JAMES IN HOLLYWOOD CEMETERY.

Manchester Slave Trail (804-646-8911 or 804-646-3012; www.james riverpark.org). This 1.3-mile self-guided tour begins at **Ancarrow's Landing** (south side of the James, I-95, Maury Street exit), at the old Manchester Docks where many enslaved individuals arrived from Africa. The mostly wooded path connects with the **Floodwall Walk,** winding along the top of the cement levy with great views of the river, then crosses the Mayo Bridge to the Reconciliation Statue (15th and Main streets) before ending at the 1841 First African Baptist Church (www.aaheritageva.org; College Street at E. Broad). Guided tours available.

By boat: **Eagle Cruises** (804-222-0223; www.eaglecruises.net), 3101 Wharf Street, Richmond 23223. Lunch, dinner, and moonlight cruises on the James River by prior arrangement.

James River Bateau Festival (www.batteau.org). Every June, crews pole replicas of 18th-century bateau boats about 120 river miles from

MORE THAN 18,000 CONFEDERATE SOLDIERS LIE BURIED NEAR THIS PYRAMID IN RICHMOND'S HOLLYWOOD CEMETERY.

Lynchburg to Maiden's Landing just west of Richmond, camping along the way. Many canoes and kayaks join the weeklong event.

✪ **Richmond Canal Cruises** (804-649-2800 or 804-788-6466; www.venturerich mond.com), Turning Basin, on Virginia Street, between 14th and Dock streets. Narrated 40-minute tours aboard a covered, handicapped-accessible canal boat along the Kanawha Canal. Weekends spring and fall; Wed.–Sun. in the summer. Adults $5, children (5–12) and seniors (65 and up) $4, under five free.

By bus, minivan, or limo: **African American Tours** (804-683-6630; www.african americantours.com).

Historic Richmond Tours (804-649-0711; www.richmondhistorycenter.com). Bus tours explore aspects of the city's history, from nightlife to Jewish and African American culture. Reservations required.

Museum of the Confederacy Bus Tours (804-649-1861; www.moc.org), 1201 E. Clay Street, Richmond 23219. Join experts for a specialized tour of regional Civil War sites.

Richmond City Guided Van Tours (804-744-1718; www.richmondcitytours .com). Full- and half-day tours cover Richmond's history, museums, gardens, and war memorials. Special **Richmond Film Tour** (www.virginiafilmtours.com) visits locations used in movies and television.

A TRIP BY CANAL BOAT PROVIDES A UNIQUE PERSPECTIVE ON RICHMOND HISTORY.

Tacky Lights Tour (804-358-9466 or 800-296-9466; www.winnbus.com). Enjoy the Christmas lights in Richmond neighborhoods and the Grand Illumination at the James Center aboard a limo or a van.

By Segway: ✪ ✧ **Segway of Richmond** (804-343-1850; www.segwayofrichmond.biz), 1301 E. Cary Street, Richmond 23219. Guided tours of Richmond's downtown attractions, including Shockoe Slip, Capitol Hill, Court End, and the Canal Walk, are offered daily, departing from the Richmond Regional Visitors Center (405 N. Third Street, Richmond 23219). Other tours explore Hollywood Cemetery, Monument Avenue, Church Hill, and Petersburg National Battlefield. Segways are also available for rent by the hour, day, or week for self-guided touring.

WILDERNESS CAMPING Primitive camping can be found at several state parks in central Virginia, including **James River** and **Bear Creek Lake state parks,** both about 60 miles west of Richmond. Visit www.dcr.virginia.gov for further information. Farther west, the **George Washington and Jefferson national forests** (540-265-5100 or 888-265-0019; www.fs.fed.us; 5162 Valleypointe Parkway, Roanoke 24019) contain numerous campgrounds, some located beside lakes and streams.

Backcountry camping along some 500 miles of trails, including the Appalachian Trail, can be found in **Shenandoah National Park** (540-999-3500; www.nps.gov/shen), with many trailheads along Skyline Drive. A free camping permit is required. Suggested backcountry itineraries are available on the National Park Service Web site.

WILDLIFE- AND BIRD-WATCHING Richmond Audubon Society Bird Walks (804-257-0813; www.richmondaudubon.org). Nonmembers are welcome to join the society's monthly meetings and bird walks, including regularly scheduled outings to Bryan Park on the first Sun. of the month.

✦ **Richmond Metro Zoo** (804-739-5666; www.metrorichmondzoo.com), 8300 Beaver Bridge Road, Moseley 23120. More than six hundred animals, including lions and tigers, kangaroos, camels, and more than two hundred monkeys, live in naturalistic settings in Chesterfield County. Visitors can feed a giraffe by hand, pet zebras and antelopes, and observe the feeding behavior of African penguins. The Safari Train and Sky Ride make the animals accessible to all. Closed Sun. $9–11.

✪ ✐ **Robins Nature & Visitor Center and Robert M. Freeman Bald Eagle Habitat & Raptor Valley at Maymont** (804-358-7166; www.maymont.org), 2201 Shields Lake Drive, Richmond 23220. Among Maymont's many attractions are open-air wild-animal habitats containing birds of prey, bison, elk, bobcats, and a very popular pair of black bears, plus an aviary with more than two hundred species of birds. In the nature center, 13 linked aquariums are home to river otters, turtles, and native fish. All the animals and birds have suffered an injury and are unable to survive in the wild, and are species found in Virginia, either now or in the past. Admission free; $4 donation suggested. A café in the visitors center serves lunch Tues.–Sat.

✳ Wilder Places

Dragon Flats Preserve and Dragon Run (804-644-5800; www.nature.org or www.dragonrun.org). A cooperative effort between the Nature Conservancy and private conservationists protects Virginia's most pristine blackwater stream and surrounding bald cypress swamp. Access to the Middle Peninsula preserve is restricted, except for the short **Mascot Loop Trail,** where Dragon Run crosses SR 603. Canoes can put in at the Ware Bridge on SR 602. Contact the **Friends of Dragon Run** (www.dragonrun.org; P.O. Box 882, Gloucester 23061) for information on trails, guided hikes, and paddle trips.

✪ **Dutch Gap Conservation Area** (804-748-1623; www.chesterfield.gov), 251 Henricus Park Road (off SR 615), Chester 23831. Land and water trails and viewing blinds adjacent to Henricus Historical Park offer exceptional birding opportunities, including views of a blue heron rookery and tidal freshwater marsh.

James River National Wildlife Refuge (804-829-9020; www.fws.gov/refuges), Flowerdew Hundred Road/SR 639, Prince George 23831. Each summer this refuge, about 30 miles southeast of Richmond, is home to more than two hundred roosting bald eagles. Visits to the refuge require reservations made at least 72 hours in advance. Canoe and pontoon boat tours of this refuge and nearby **Presquile National Wildlife Refuge** are scheduled on a regular basis.

R. Garland Dodd Park at Point of Rocks (804-530-2459; www.chesterfield .gov), 201 Enon Church Road/SR 746, Chester 23831. Trails and boardwalks thread the lower level of this historic park along the Appomattox River, providing excellent birding. Picnic area, playground, and tennis courts.

Richard Bland College Nature Trail (804-862-6247; www.rbc.edu), 11301 Johnson Road, Petersburg 23805. Nature trail beginning next to Ernst Hall leads to a beaver pond where green herons nest. Migrating songbirds frequent the pecan grove at the college entrance in spring.

Rockwood Park (804-276-6661; www.chesterfield.gov), 3401 Courthouse Road/SR 653, Richmond 23236. Nature trails and boardwalks, several fully accessible, wind through woodlands and wetlands. Nature center, tennis courts, archery range, the Ruff House Dog Park.

✳ Lodging

Visitors to the Richmond area have a wide variety of lodgings to choose from in numerous locations. Chain hotels and motels line the interstates, especially the I-95 corridor between Richmond and Petersburg. In downtown Richmond, the upscale chain hotels in Shockoe Slip and Capitol Square make convenient places to stay when you are touring the city.

To truly participate in Richmond's traditions, plan to stay at one of the city's many historic inns or bed & breakfasts. These range from the grand Jefferson Hotel to modest homes once occupied by average citizens, but each has its own history and charm. Richmond's innkeepers pride themselves on their hospitality and knowledge of the city, which they are glad to share with guests. In addition to the inns listed here, find additional options at the Web site of the Bed and Breakfast Association of Virginia (www.inn virginia.com).

Price Categories

Inexpensive	up to $80
Moderate	$80 to $150
Expensive	$150 to $200
Very expensive	$200 and up

HOTELS & RESORTS 🐾 🐕 🐈 ⚲ ⁕

Best Western Kings Quarters (804-876-3321; www.bestwesternkings quarters.com), 16102 Theme Park Way (I-95 exit 98), Doswell 23047. Price: Inexpensive to moderate. Credit cards: Yes. Special features: Free Wi-Fi, seasonal outdoor pool, indoor and outdoor game areas, business services, coin laundry, free parking and shuttle service, pets under 25 pounds allowed with fee. If **Kings Dominion** (www.kings dominion.com) is on your travel itinerary, this motel, located on the theme park property, can maximize your fun

time. Standard hotel rooms, most with two queen beds, surround a pool courtyard with seasonal tiki bar. The pool and outdoor recreation area, with lighted tennis courts, putting green, and playground, are open until midnight. An indoor recreation room with video games and Ping-Pong is open 24 hours, as is the Denny's Restaurant on-site. The free Kings Dominion shuttle, running every day the park is open, saves guests the park's $10 parking fee. Discount park tickets and packages available.

🐈 ⚲ ⁕ **Commonwealth Park Suites Hotel** (804-343-7300; www .commonwealthparksuites.com), 901 Bank Street, Richmond 23219. Price: Moderate. Credit cards: Yes. Special features: Free Wi-Fi, valet parking, fitness center with sauna, business center, guest laundry, pets allowed with fee. Conveniently located across the street from the new entrance to the Virginia State Capitol and about four blocks (uphill) from Shockoe Slip, this 11-story hotel built in 1912 was recently completely refurbished with modern amenities and updated bedding. Historic photos of Richmond at the end of the Civil War, including the "burnt district," of which the hotel property was part, are displayed in the public spaces. Spacious suites and guest rooms are equipped with refrigerators, microwaves, coffeemakers, and big-screen TVs. European-style bathrooms have bidets and granite vanities. The on-site Maxine's Café serves full breakfasts daily. Book online to receive a complimentary meal.

❂ ⚲ 🍴 🐕 🍷 ⁕ ↝ **The Jefferson** (804-788-8000 or 800-424-8014; www.jeffersonhotel.com), 101 W. Franklin Street, Richmond 23220. Price: Very expensive. Credit cards: Yes. Special features: Indoor pool, health club, gift shop, salon, flower shop, valet and concierge services, babysitting, 24-hour business center and room service, free parking, complimentary city shuttle, museum, free Wi-Fi, smoke-free. Designed in 1895 for tobacco magnate Lewis Ginter by renowned New York architectural firm Carrere and Hastings, the ornate Jefferson Hotel is considered one of the world's finest examples of the Beaux-Arts style. In the upper lobby, a magnificent marble statue of Thomas Jefferson by Richmond sculptor Edward V. Valentine presides over the famous Palm Court under a Tiffany stained-glass dome. Nearby, the Grand Staircase, often compared to the stairs featured in the movie *Gone with the Wind,* leads to the lower lobby. The hotel is furnished throughout with original antiques, paintings, and art objects. Self-guided tours of the hotel's public areas are available, and a small museum displays interesting items from the Jefferson's history.

A consistent winner of both the Mobil Five Star and AAA Five Diamond awards, the Jefferson is a required stop for every history buff and an excellent choice for deluxe accommodations while visiting Richmond. The 262 high-ceilinged rooms and suites are equipped with mahogany furnishings, plush bathrobes, and marble baths. Dining is available in the recently renovated **Lemaire** (804-649-4672; www .lemairerestaurant.com), featuring contemporary Southern cuisine with an emphasis on local products, a bar menu of small plates, and daily happy hours, as well as the casual **TJ's** off the lower lobby, famous for its peanut soup and fried house-made Paw Paw's pickles. Afternoon tea (804-649-4661) is served in the Palm Court Fri.–Sun.; the legendary **Sunday Champagne Brunch** (804-649-4677) is a Richmond tradition.

✪ ☻ ♿ ♂ "🍴" ✣ **Linden Row Inn** (804-783-7000; www.lindenrowinn .com), 100 E. Franklin Street, Richmond 23219. Price: Moderate. Credit cards: Yes. Special features: Free Wi-Fi, valet parking, free local shuttle, continental breakfast included, complimentary health club passes and business services, handicapped-accessible rooms. Located in a row of town houses built in the 1840s, the Linden Row Inn offers a unique historical experience in the heart of the city. Once occupied by the cream of Richmond society, the eight town houses are connected by a rear veranda overlooking a shady garden courtyard. Seven two-room parlor suites occupy the original main floors, with high-ceilinged sitting rooms outfitted with period antiques, marble fireplaces, pocket doors, and gasolier lighting; bedrooms with king-sized beds, microwaves, and refrigerators; and granite baths. The suites are being renovated to reflect their historic past; the David Jones historical novel *Two Brothers: One North, One South* describes a party that took place in Ms. Pegram's Parlour Suite. Garden guest rooms in the original carriage house are more modest both in size and price. Several packages are available, including one featuring Edgar Allan Poe, highlighting the author's connections with the site.

✪ ☻ "🍴" ✣ **Museum District Bed & Breakfast** (804-359-2332; www .museumdistrictbb.com), 2811 Grove Avenue, Richmond 23221. Innkeeper: Anna Currence. Price: Expensive. Credit cards: Yes. Special features: Free Wi-Fi, free long-distance calls to the United States and Canada, off-street parking. Occupying a 1922 brick house directly across the street from the Virginia Museum of Fine Arts, this welcoming B&B makes the perfect base for your Richmond visit. Innkeeper Anna Currence serves ample breakfasts featuring fresh baked goods and bacon cured by a nearby butcher, plus coffee on the front porch and convivial afternoon wine and cheese gatherings, and will help personalize your tour with maps and suggestions tailored to your interests. Upstairs, the luxurious Judge Rhea's Suite features a sitting room with big-screen TV; office with refrigerator; sleeping porch with room-darkening shades; and a fabulous bath with two-person claw-foot soaking tub, large steam shower, and bidet. Three other bedrooms on the second floor can be rented separately or as a suite with private access to the large upstairs porch. The moderately priced Carriage House offers complete privacy in its own building off the back patio.

✇ ♿ ⅄ ⅌ ↪ **The Omni Richmond** (804-344-7000 or 800-843-6664; www.omnihotels.com), 100 S. 12th Street, Richmond 23219. Price: Very expensive. Credit cards: Yes. Special features: Free Wi-Fi for Select Guest members (free membership), valet or self parking, business center, indoor pool and sundeck, free airport shuttle, turndown service, room service, pet-friendly (fee), complimentary Sensational Kids program and health club passes. Situated directly across the street from the landmark Tobacco Company in the heart of Shockoe Slip, this 19-story hotel overlooks the James River, with luxury bedding, coffeemaker, and big-screen TV in each room. The on-site **Trevi's Restaurant and Lounge** serves breakfast, lunch, and dinner, plus a lounge menu, inside or on the patio. Rooms on the Omni Club level include complimentary breakfast buffet and evening hors d'oeurves. Bargain-priced packages available online.

✪ ⅌ ↪ **William Miller Bed and Breakfast** (804-254-2928 or 804-405-1248; www.williammillerhouse

.com), 1129 Floyd Avenue, Richmond 23220. Innkeepers: Pat Daniels and Mike Rohde. Price: Expensive. Credit cards: Yes. Special features: Free Wi-Fi, off-street parking, corporate and military rates available, Virginia Green lodging. Beautifully restored 1869 home at the eastern end of the Fan features original marble mantles carved by its builder, the proprietor of a prominent 19th-century marble-works, as well as art objects collected by the innkeepers on their journeys around the world. Numerous small touches make guests feel welcome, including a tray with Perrier and hand-dipped chocolates in each room, and afternoon refreshments featuring Virginia wines and local cheeses. Two large, second-floor rooms each feature pillow-top mattresses, flat-screen TVs, and private baths. The couple-friendly Regency King room has a king bed and double whirlpool tub. Innkeeper Mike Rohde studied cooking in France and creates gourmet breakfasts, featuring organic eggs, bacon, and sausage from a local farm, which are the highlight of any stay.

INNS AND RETREATS Brightly Bed and Breakfast (804-556-5070; www.brightlybandb.com), 2844 River Road W., Goochland 23063. Historic plantation B&B 30 miles west of Richmond in horse country also accommodates visiting horses.

🐴 **Dellwood Plantation** (804-590-0995; www.dellwoodplantation.com), 6100 Woodpecker Road, Chesterfield 23838. An 1820 plantation house surrounded by formal gardens.

The Destiny Inn (804-722-1016 or 877-834-8422; www.thedestinyinn .com), 517 High Street, Petersburg 23803. This 1897 B&B in Old Towne Petersburg serves afternoon tea by appointment.

♂ **Henry Clay Inn** (804-798-3100; www.henryclayinn.com), 114 N. Railroad Avenue, Ashland 23005. Located next to the AMTRAK station in the heart of historic Ashland, this is an exact replica of the 1858 original—except for the modern baths and an in-house art gallery.

The High Street Inn (804-733-0271; www.thehighstreetinn.com), 405 High Street, Petersburg 23803. Elaborately decorated Victorian near Old Towne offers six moderately priced rooms, including one in a turret.

La Villa Romaine (804-861-2285; www.lavilla.tierranet.com), 29 S. Market Street, Petersburg 23803. Italianate 1858 mansion decorated with French antiques offers European-style lodgings and murder-mystery weekends.

Richmond Hill (804-783-7903; www.richmondhillva.org), 2209 E. Grace Street, Richmond 23223. Individual overnight retreats available within the peaceful walled gardens of this former monastery, now a nondenominational center for urban spirituality.

Scents of Cedar Bed & Breakfast (804-732-9632; www.scentsofcedar.com), 15126 Providence Road, Petersburg 23805. Cedar log cabins in a forested setting in Prince George County, next to a pond with boating and fishing.

Winterham Plantation (804-561-4519 or 866-561-4519; www.winterham.com), 11441 Grub Hill Church Road, Amelia 23002. Antebellum 1855 mansion turned B&B is located along the Lee's Retreat Civil War Trail.

RV RESORTS See our listings in "Williamsburg, Jamestown, and Yorktown" for campgrounds between Richmond and Williamsburg.

Amelia Family Campground (804-561-3011; www.ameliafamilycampground.com), 9720 Military Road (VA 153), Amelia 23002. Campground 25 miles west of Richmond offers swimming, fishing, nature trails, and bluegrass festivals twice a year.

Americamps—Richmond North (804-798-5298 or 800-628-2802; www.americamps.com), 11322 Air Park Road, Ashland 23005. Full-service park off I-95 exit 89 offers free Wi-Fi, cable TV, swimming pool, and recreation room.

Camptown Campground (804-469-4569), 22802 Camptown Drive, Petersburg 23803. Resort for tents and RVs with free Wi-Fi, full hookups.

Christopher Run Campground (540-894-4744; www.christopherruncampground.com), 7149 Zachary Taylor Highway, Mineral 23117. Campground on the shores of Lake Anna with tent and RV sites, rental cabins, marina, boat ramps, fishing pier, boat rentals, lake swimming.

Cozy Acres Campground (804-598-2470; www.cozyacres.com), 2177 Ridge Road (SR 627), Powhatan 23139. Family-owned campground with rental cab-

RICHMOND INNS ARE RENOWNED FOR THEIR GOURMET BREAKFASTS.

ins, RV and tent sites, swimming pool, catfish pond.

♂ ◈ ☺ ⁰¦⁰ **Kings Dominion Campground** (804-876-5355 or 800-922-6710; www.kingsdominion.com), 10061 Kings Dominion Boulevard, Doswell 23047. Full-service Good Sam park with swimming pool, lodge with free Wi-Fi, free shuttle to Kings Dominion theme park.

◈ **Lake Rawlings Scuba Park** (804-478-9000 or 800-583-3781; www.lakerawlings.com), 1 Quarry Lane, Rawlings 23876. Tent and RV camping, plus rental cabins, next to a lake with scuba, snorkeling, and swimming, off I-85 exit 39.

● **Pocahontas State Park** (804-796-4255 or 800-933-PARK [reservations]; www.dcr.virginia.gov), 10301 State Park Road, Chesterfield 23832. Water and electric hookups for RVs and tents; swimming, fishing, hiking, rental kayaks, canoes, and rowboats; 20 miles south of Richmond.

Ponderosa Mobile Home and RV Park (804-271-1727 or 804-271-8333; www.ponderosamobilehome.com), 7725 Jefferson Davis Highway, Richmond 23237. Small, quiet park with full hookups, no public facilities; off I-95 exit 64, close to downtown Richmond.

South Forty Camp Resort (877-732-8345; www.southfortycampresort.com), 2809 Courtland Road, Petersburg 23805. Fishing, rental boats, swimming pool, restaurant, rental cabins and trailers; off I-95 exit 41.

✳ Where to Eat

Literally hundreds of restaurants in every price range make Richmond a great dining destination for foodies. Talented local chefs combine the bounty of local farms in exciting new ways, creating a New South cuisine worth exploring.

Shockoe Slip and Shockoe Bottom house concentrations of some of the city's finest establishments, including many of the upscale chains, while Carytown features many unique, even funky, spots, such as outer-space-themed **Galaxy Diner** (804-213-0510; 3109 W. Cary Street), frequented by the neighborhood's somewhat quirky locals.

The Fan is another neighborhood with many interesting dining destinations, coffee shops, and vegetarian venues scattered among the restored residences. Look for concentrations around the VCU campus and on Strawberry Street, where restaurants, take-out spots, gourmet groceries, and a wine store crowd a few short blocks.

Maverick restaurateur Ed Vasaio operates a popular family of Italian restaurants in the Fan and nearby Oregon Hill known for great food and low prices, including the take-out only 8½ (804-358-8505; 401 Strawberry Street); the acclaimed **Mamma Zu** (804-788-4205; www.myspace.com/mammazu; 501 S. Pine Street); and **Edo's Squid** (804-864-5488; 411 N. Harrison Street), combining seafood and Italian specialties.

For a fast and inexpensive lunch while touring Court End, check out the seasonal pushcarts offering a wide variety of cuisine, including many healthy choices, on Marshall and Broad streets near the Medical College of Virginia. The nearby grounds of the State Capitol make a great place for a picnic.

Richmond is a city that takes its traditions, food and otherwise, seriously, with many family restaurants offering the same menu for decades. One of the oldest is **Byram's Lobster House** (804-355-9193; www.byrams.com; 3215 W. Broad Street), serving fresh seafood and steaks, plus Greek and Italian specialties, since 1943.

Box lunches are another distinctive Richmond tradition. Available for pickup or delivery, the boxes typically contain a sandwich made from one of the region's famous salads—chicken, ham, or pimento cheese—plus a deviled egg and a cupcake.

For more contemporary fare, Richmonders frequent the restaurants designed by Michelle Williams and Jared Golden, the creative team behind the Richmond Restaurant Group (www.richmondrestaurantgroup.com). Considered some of the city's finest dining options, these include upscale seafood spot **The Hard Shell** (804-643-2333; www.thehardshell.com; 1411 E. Cary Street) and the nearby **Europa Italian Café and Tapas Bar** (804-643-0911; www.europarichmond.com; 1409 E. Cary Street) in Shockoe Slip; **The Hill Café** (804-648-0360; www.thehillcafe.com; 2800 E. Broad Street), a neighborhood spot with daily blue plates in Church Hill; the stylish **deLux Diner and Lounge** (804-353-2424; www.deluxrichmond.com; 2229 W. Main Street) in the Fan; and the new **Water Grill** (804-353-3411; www.thewatergrill.com; 3411 Cary Street), a casual seafood spot in Carytown. The team also designed the concepts at **Cha Cha's Cantina** (804-726-6296; www.chachascantina.com; 1419 E. Cary Street) and **The Lucky Buddha** (804-648-5100; www.theluckybuddha.com; 1421 E. Cary Street), two popular nightspots that sit side by side in Shockoe Slip.

Richmond's dining scene is constantly changing, with new spots opening every season. Check the dining pages at Richmond Good Life (www.richmondgoodlife.com) for the hottest new spots, plus local recommendations. Dedicated foodies should plan their visit during the annual **Richmond Restaurant Week** (www.richmondrestaurantweek.com) in late October, when some two dozen of the city's hottest restaurants offer meals at special prices.

Price Categories

Inexpensive	under $10
Moderate	$10 to $20
Expensive	$20 to $25
Very expensive	$25 and up

The listings in this section also include information on what meals are served, using the following abbreviations:

B	Breakfast
L	Lunch
D	Dinner
SB	Sunday brunch

DINING OUT ✪ ♿ ⚲ ¶ **The Boathouse at Sunday Park** (804-744-2545; www.boathouserichmond.com), 4602 Millridge Parkway, Midlothian 23112. Open: Daily. Credit cards: Yes. Serving: D, SB. Price: Moderate. Cuisine: Seafood, pizza. Handicapped access: Yes. Special features: Full bar, Fri. happy hour, live entertainment, patio dining, smoking area, wine tastings, call-ahead seating. Occupying an idyllic site on the shores of Swift Creek Reservoir, the Boathouse's wide decks provide a perfect view of the sunset, as well as excellent cuisine at reasonable prices. The menu, featuring fresh seafood, steaks, and crabmeat in numerous combinations—crab "puppies," steaks and lobsters "double stuffed" with crab, crab-topped pizzas and salads—rarely tops $20. A wood-fired oven turns out gourmet Neapolitan-style pizzas and endless Pizzookies, the Boathouse's signature dessert: a tender, baked to order chocolate-chip cookie topped with ice cream and dark chocolate syrup.

While the effort to locate this romantic restaurant in the wilds of Midlothian is well worth the time (call for directions), you can now enjoy a very similar menu and stunning waterfront views at the new **Boathouse at Rocketts Landing** (804-622-2628; 4708 E. Old Main Street), much closer to downtown in the historic Power Plant building, part of the upscale **Rocketts Landing** (www.rockettsvillage.com) mixed-use community just east of Shockoe Bottom on the shores of the James River. The new location's futuristic patios and wall of windows provide Richmond's only riverfront dining experience, as well as a look at the city's impressive skyline.

♪ ☀ ⴲ ♈ **Can Can Brasserie** (804-358-7274; www.cancanbrasserie.com), 3120 W. Cary Street, Richmond 23221. Open: Daily. Credit cards: Yes. Serving: B, L, D, SB. Price: Expensive. Cuisine: French, seafood. Handicapped access: Yes. Special features: Patio dining; full bar; separate lounge; morning coffee bar; afternoon café menu; children's menus; daily specials; bakery on-site; weekly wine, beer, and cocktail tastings. One of Carytown's favorite spots, this bistro does its best work when it adheres to its French inspiration. Enjoy fresh-baked beignets and steamy cups of café au lait in the morning, or croque monsieur or a nice salad niçoise with a glass of white Bordeaux in the afternoon on one of the streetside patios. For dinner, choose from a menu replete with classics: moules frites, coq au vin, garlicky escargots, beefy onion soup. Or join the local crowd at the classic 50-foot zinc bar for martinis and a "Grand Plateau" of fresh chilled seafood. Whatever you order, be sure to sample the boutique breads baked in-house. Expect high-decibel noise levels around the bar as the hour grows late and conversations get serious.

✪ ⴲ ♈ **Capital Ale House** (804-780-2537; www.capitalalehouse.com), 623 E. Main Street, Richmond 23219.

Open: Daily. Credit cards: Yes. Serving: L, D, SB. Price: Moderate. Cuisine: American and German. Handicapped access: Yes. Special features: Outdoor beer garden, live entertainment, free parking in deck at Sixth and Main after 4 PM weekdays and all day weekends, game room with pool and darts, late-night menu. With nearly 50 beers from around the world on tap, plus two hand-pumped casks and more than two hundred bottled brews, this is a must-stop for beer lovers. Housed in a hundred-year-old downtown building, this superpub features a "zamboni" ice strip down the middle of the bar to keep your beer cold and a beer garden out back. Excellent food complements the brews, from mustard-crusted rack of lamb to stuffed pretzels. The Music Hall next door hosts a free After Work Brews & Blues series on Fri., and many special events.

The Capital Ale House has additional locations, featuring even more beers on tap. Near the Innsbruck Pavilion, the **Innsbruck Capital Ale House** (804-780-ALES; 4024-A Cox Road at W. Broad, Glen Allen 23060) has 77 taps, an Innsbruck After Hours concert series, and a beer garden with duck pond. The new **Midlothian Capital Ale House** (804-780-2537; 13831 Midlothian Turnpike, Midlothian 23114) taps a staggering 80 brews. Hint: This is not the place to ask for a sampler.

ⴲ **Comfort** (804-780-0004; www.comfortrestaurant.com), 200 Broad Street, Richmond 23220. Open: Mon.–Sat.; closed Sat. lunch. Credit cards: Yes. Serving: L (Mon.–Fri.), D. Price: Moderate. Cuisine: Southern. Handicapped access: Yes. Special features: Full bar, counter service; no reservations. Uncomplicated Southern home cooking served in generous portions make this storefront just two blocks from the toney Jefferson Hotel one of

Richmond's most popular restaurants. The inexpensive lunch menu features thick slabs of meat loaf, tender roasted chicken, pork chops, and fried catfish with your choice of vegetables grown on local farms. At dinner, fancier dishes, such as Kobe skirt steak, shrimp and grits, venison, and duck, join in. Evening entrées, with two or three sides, skid up near the $20 mark. And, no matter how good the mac and cheese or squash casserole may be, a three-veggie plate priced at $16 is not a comforting thought. So come for lunch, and save room for the excellent banana pudding.

  よ ♈ **Croaker's Spot** (804-269-0464; www.croakersspot.com), 1020 Hull Street at 11th, Richmond 23224. Open: Daily. Credit cards: Yes. Serving: L, D. Price: Inexpensive. Cuisine: Seafood. Handicapped access: Yes. Special features: Full bar, counter service, take-out. Long a landmark in Jackson Ward, this soul food restaurant operated by the Eggleston family recently closed its doors downtown, but it continues to operate a new location across the river in the Manchester neighborhood. Huge squares of sweet corn bread still accompany meals, and the signature fish boats, composed of fried lake trout topped with sautéed green peppers and onions, remain enormous and the restaurant's claim to fame. Other menu offerings include shrimp or scallops and grits, a unique seafood chili, baked trout topped with mushrooms, po'boys, and an excellent Southern sautéed chicken. Wash your meal down with homemade lemonade or limeade, with or without a splash of vodka, and save room for a piece of the famous layer cake. If you're in a rush, call ahead for take-out.

  ❦ ♈ **Curbside Café** (804-355-7008; www.curbsiderichmond.com), 2525 Hanover Avenue, Richmond 23220.

Open: Daily. Credit cards: Yes. Serving: L, D, weekend brunch. Price: Inexpensive. Cuisine: American. Handicapped access: Yes. Special features: Patio dining, full bar, late-night hours, daily specials. Laid-back neighborhood spot in the Fan, just steps from the Museum District, is famous for its "cheap eats" and friendly vibe. A creative menu of sandwiches and burgers is supplemented after 5 PM with a short list of entrées, topped by racks of baby back ribs slow roasted in beer. On Sat. and Sun., regulars head down for brunch, featuring a Tidewater Omelet stuffed with crabmeat and Virginia ham accompanied by discount mimosas, screwdrivers, and Bloody Marys.

  よ ♂ ♈ **Julep's New Southern Cuisine** (804-377-3968; www.juleps.net), 1719 E. Franklin Street, Richmond 23223. Open: Mon.–Sat. Credit cards: Yes. Serving: D. Price: Expensive. Cuisine: Southern. Handicapped access: Yes. Special features: Seasonal menus, full bar, wine dinners, valet parking on weekends; reservations suggested. Scarlett and Rhett would feel right at home, sipping mint juleps from silver cups while dining on fried green tomato beignets, shrimp and grits, and broiled quail or rack of lamb, at this spot in Shockoe Bottom that is both romantic and historic. Extensive renovation turned the 1817 brick commercial building, oldest surviving in the city, into an attractive, two-story restaurant serving Southern classics with imaginative twists. Scarlett and Rhett would undoubtedly opt to finish their meal with flaming bananas Foster, prepared tableside. The excellent wine list received the *Wine Spectator* Award of Excellence. **The Mint,** a new speakeasy on-site, offers designer cocktails and a light menu on Fri. and Sat. nights after the restaurant closes (call 804-651-8621 for admission).

& **Millie's** (804-643-5512; www
.milliesdiner.com), 2603 E. Main
Street, Richmond 23223. Open: Tues.–
Sun. Credit cards: Yes. Serving: L, D,
weekend brunch. Price: Very expensive. Cuisine: American. Handicapped
access: Yes. Special features: Daily specials, full bar, counter service, open
kitchen, outdoor patio. Locals consistently rate this Shockoe Bottom spot
the best restaurant in Richmond and
are ready to stand in line, sometimes
for hours, to have weekend brunch in
its two tiny dining rooms or on its
postage-stamp-sized patio. If you can
score a seat, Millie's is indeed cool,
nestled down at the base of Church
Hill on Main Street, just before it
turns rural. The music is awesome and
self-serve from tabletop Select-O-
Matic units connected to a Seeburg
stuffed with eclectic singles. The menu
is unusual and constantly changing,
created by hot young chefs you can
watch at work in the tiny open kitchen.
The Devil's Mess, an open-face omelet
topped with cheddar and avocado, is
the most popular dish at lunch and
brunch, when prices drop from big
splurge to quite a bargain. If lines here
are just too long, cross the street to
Poe's Pub (804-648-2120; www
.poespub.com; 2706 E. Main Street),
where you'll find a friendly welcome
and great Reubens.

& Y **Sensi Italian Chop House** (804-
648-3463; www.sensirestaurant.com),
2222 E. Cary Street, Richmond 23223.
Open: Daily. Credit cards: Yes. Serving: D. Price: Very expensive. Cuisine:
Steak and seafood, Italian. Handicapped access: Yes. Special features:
Nightly specials, happy hour, online
reservations, prix fixe and tasting
menus, separate lounge, outdoor patio,
gated parking. Understated and stylish
spot in a renovated warehouse along
the James serves upscale steaks,
seafood, and Italian specialties with a

big-city vibe. Steaks, veal chops, and
the shelled whole Maine lobster come
highly recommended, and the pastas
and risottos feature delightful flavor
combinations. Finish your meal with
authentic tiramisu or budino with coffee or port on the outside terrace. The
three-course prix fixe menu, available
nightly, is a real bargain.

**BAKERIES Jean-Jacques Bakery
Cafe** (804-355-0666; www.carytown
bakery.com), 3138 W. Cary Street,
Richmond 23221. Carytown bakery
offers classic French breads, pastries,
and fruit tarts.

Montana Gold Bread Co. (804-359-
7700; www.montanagoldbread.com),
3543 W. Cary Street, Richmond 23221.
Everything is done on-site at this Carytown bakery, from milling the wheat to
kneading the dough by hand. Box
lunches available Mon.–Sat.

Two Sweet (804-360-4284; www.two
sweetrichmond.com), 3422 Lauderdale
Drive, Richmond 23233. Boutique
bakery near Short Pump offers delicious takes on traditional and filled
cupcakes. Open Tues.–Sat.

BARBECUE Bill's Barbecue (804-
788-1261; www.billsbarbecue.net),
700 E. Main Street, Richmond 23219.
Chopped pork, homemade chocolate
pie, and hand-squeezed limeades in
downtown Richmond since 1930.
Open weekdays 7–3 only.

Buz & Ned's Real Barbecue (804-
355-6055; www.buzandneds.com),
1119 N. Boulevard, Richmond 23230.
Considered by many to have the best
ribs in the city. Full bar.

Y "I" **Grandpa Eddie's Alabama
Ribs & BBQ** (804-270-7427; www
.grandpaeddiesbbq.com), 11129 Three
Chopt Road, Richmond 23233. Texas-
style beef, North Carolina–style pork,
Alabama-style ribs, Kansas City burnt

ends, plus live music and happy hour. Free Wi-Fi.

King's Famous Barbecue (804-732-0975; www.kingsfamousbarbecue.com), 2910 S. Crater Road, Petersburg 23805. Hickory-smoked meats topped with a secret sauce, served by the same family since 1946.

Little Pig Barbecue (804-861-4046), 3329 W. Washington Street, Petersburg 23803. The Rawlings family has been smoking pork, and topping it with a mustardy South Carolina–style sauce, since 1932.

BOX LUNCHES AND TAKE-OUT

Chez Foushee (804-648-3225; www.chezfoushee.com), 2 W. Grace Street, Richmond 23220. One of Richmond's favorite lunch spots offers gourmet lunches, including a famous pimento cheese, and box lunches for pickup or delivery, Mon.–Fri.

Homemades by Suzanne (www.homemadesbysuzanne.com). Gourmet box lunches by a top caterer available at two convenient locations: near the depot in Ashland (804-798-8331; 102 N. Railroad Avenue, Ashland 23005) and at the **Colony Club** (804-775-2323; www.colonyclubandcatering.com; 10 E. Franklin Street, Richmond 23219), where you can also enjoy luncheon on weekdays, 11:30–2:30.

May Fair House at St. Stephen's Episcopal (804-282-3004; www.saintstephensrichmond.net), 6000 Grove Avenue, Richmond 23226. Southern delicacies prepared by the Women of St. Stephen's include biscuits, pies, and pimento cheese.

Mrs. Marshall's Carytown Cafe (804-355-1305; www.mrsmarshalls.com), 3125 W. Cary Street, Richmond 23220. Famous for potato salad since 1923, this box-lunch spot makes delicious deviled eggs and chicken and ham salads.

Sally Bell's Kitchen (804-644-2838; www.sallybellskitchen.com), 708 W. Grace Street, Richmond 23220. Nationally famous for box lunches, which always include a deviled egg and one of Sally Bell's legendary cupcakes. Delivery available.

↪ **Savor** (804-527-2867; www.savorcompany.com), 201 W. Seventh Street, Richmond 23224. Cosmopolitan spot in Old Manchester offers box lunches, wine dinners. Delivery available.

Strawberry Street Market (804-353-4100; www.strawberrystreetmarket.com), 415 N. Strawberry Street, Richmond 23220. Grocery in the Fan is locally famous for its fried chicken and blue plate specials.

BREAKFAST AND MORE ✪ The

Black Sheep (804-648-1300; www.theblacksheeprva.com), 901 W. Marshall Street, Richmond 23220. Enormously creative breakfast menu, from salmon hash to chocolate hazelnut French toast, served until 2 PM; plus battleship-sized subs, soups, enticing dinner entrées, vegetarian options.

✪ ♈ **Dixie Diner** (804-732-7425; www.dixiedinerrocks.com), 250 N. Sycamore Street, Petersburg 23803. Diner in Old Towne Petersburg serves three meals a day, plus live music most nights.

Joe's Inn (804-355-2282; www.joesinn.com), 205 N. Shields Avenue, Richmond 23220. Traditional diner in the Fan serves breakfast anytime.

McLean's Restaurant (804-358-0369; www.billofare.com), 4001 W. Broad Street, Richmond 23230. Southern-style breakfasts come with complimentary grits and tiny checks at this Richmond legend.

Perly's Restaurant (804-649-2779), 111 E. Grace Street, Richmond 23219. Diner serving breakfast and lunch for more than 40 years offers great value, vegetarian options.

3rd Street Diner (804-788-4750; www.billofare.com), 218 E. Main Street, Richmond 23219. Breakfast and blue plate specials served 24/7. Full bar.

Ψ **The Village Cafe** (804-353-8204; www.villagecafeonline.com), 1001 W. Grace Street, Richmond 23220. Inexpensive spot featured on the Food Network serves breakfast until 2 AM, plus daily specials; happy hour.

BREWERIES AND BREWPUBS
Commercial Taphouse & Grill (804-359-6544), 111 N. Robinson Street, Richmond 23220. English-style pub in the Fan keeps 15 or so craft and import beers on tap, plus one cask selection.

Extra Billy's Barbecue (804-379-8727; www.extrabillys.com), 1110 Alverser Drive, Midlothian 23113. Named for a famous politician, Extra Billy's has been serving meat smoked over wood fires since 1985. The Southside location, just west of Chesterfield Towne Center, has the on-site brewery. The **Downtown Extra Billy's** (804-282-3949; 5205 W. Broad Street, Richmond 23230) just pulls the taps.

Hops Restaurant, Bar & Brewery (804-794-2727; www.hopsrestaurants .com), 1570 W. Koger Center Boulevard, Richmond 23235. Chain pub behind Chesterfield Towne Center brews on-site and has some terrific happy hour deals.

✪ Ψ **Legend Brewing Company** (804-232-3446; www.legendbrewing .com), 321 W. Seventh Street, Richmond 23224. Virginia's oldest and largest microbrewery occupies a spectacular site on the south side of the James, with great views of the river and city skyline from its deck. Live music some nights.

Penny Lane Pub (804-780-1682; www.pennylanepub.com), 421 E. Franklin Street, Richmond 23219. Downtown pub offers a dozen or so Brit brews on tap, British pub grub, darts, pool, and soccer on the telly; free Wi-Fi.

CANDY, CHOCOLATES, AND SWEETS de Rochonnet Delights (804-794-1551; www.derochonnet delights.com), 13228 Midlothian Turnpike, Village Marketplace, Midlothian 23113. Parisian-style chocolate shop with handmade truffles and chocolates; fabulous chocolate ice cream.

Ψ "❶" **The Desserterie** (804-639-9940; www.thedesserterie.com), 6161 Harbourside Center Loop, Midlothian 23112. Southside café with European pastries, gelato and sorbetto, patio dining, free Wi-Fi, live music on summer evenings.

For the Love of Chocolate (804-359-5645), 2820 W. Cary Street, Richmond 23221. Carytown shop stocks chocolates and candies from around the world.

Gearharts Fine Chocolates (804-282-1822; www.gearhartschocolates .com), 306 Libbie Avenue, Richmond 23226. Made in Virginia artisanal chocolates at the corner of Libbie and Grove avenues.

COFFEEHOUSES Ψ "❶" **Aurora** (804-644-5380; www.aurorarichmond .com), 401 E. Grace Street, Richmond 23219. Sophisticated café in City Center offers European pastries and desserts baked on-site, tapas, live jazz, full bar, free Wi-Fi.

♿ "❶" **Cafe Portico** (804-864-1414; www.smv.org), 2500 W. Broad Street, Richmond 23220. Convenient location just outside the Science Museum of Virginia has free Wi-Fi and parking.

"T" Ellwood's Coffee (804-612-1827; www.ellwoodscoffee.com), 10 S. Thompson Street, Richmond 23221. In Carytown, organic coffees and teas, local wines and beers, a fully organic menu, live music, free Wi-Fi.

Y "T" GlobeHopper Coffeehouse & Lounge (804-523-8083; www.globe hoppercoffee.com), 2100 E. Main Street, Richmond 23223. French press coffees, European pastries, free Wi-Fi, live jazz, coffee tastings, and happy hour.

"T" Lift Coffee Shop (804-344-5438; www.liftcoffeeshop.com), 218 W. Broad Street, Richmond 23220. Hip coffeehouse in the Arts District hangs contemporary art. Free Wi-Fi.

Rostov's Coffee & Tea (804-355-1955; www.rostovs.com), 1618 W. Main Street, Richmond 23220. Fifty varieties of fresh roasted coffee and 60 loose teas.

"T" Shockoe Espresso & Roastery (804-648-3734), 104 Shockoe Slip, Richmond 23219. Try the Shockoe Shake for an energy boost on a hot day. Free Wi-Fi with purchase.

COOKING CLASSES The Compleat Gourmet (804-353-9606; www .thecompleatgourmet.com), 3030 W. Cary Street, Richmond 23221. Kitchenware store offers cooking classes on a wide variety of cuisines.

Mise En Place (804-249-1332; www .miseenplaceshockoe.com), 104 Shockoe Slip, Richmond 23219. Hands-on classes and wine tastings in a historic setting.

✍ Sur La Table (804-272-7094; www .surlatable.com), 9200 Stoney Point Parkway, Richmond 23235. Cooking classes for adults, plus kids' and teens' summer baking camps.

DELIS & SPECIALTY FOODS ✪ Belmont Butchery (804-422-8519;

www.belmontbutchery.com), 15 N. Belmont Avenue, Richmond 23221. Tanya Cauthen's nationally praised butcher shop offers hand-cut, locally raised meats; bacon and sausage cured in-house; plus pâtés, confits, and other charcuterie items.

✪ Coppola's Deli (804-359-6969; www.coppolasdeli.com), 2900 W. Cary Street, Richmond 23221. Italian sandwich shop in Carytown carries cheeses, Italian wines, and groceries, with vegetarian options.

Olio Bistro and Market (804-355-5182; www.oliorichmond.com), 2001½ W. Main Street, Richmond 23220. Extensive list of cheeses, pâtés, caviars, and antipasto, in addition to prepared dishes to eat in or take out.

Padow's Hams & Deli (804-648-4267; www.padows.com), 1009 E. Main Street, Richmond 23219. Location in the historic 1858 Ironfronts Building downtown is one of a dozen in the Richmond area. Dine in or carry out more than 75 menu items including country ham biscuits and box lunches, or fill your basket with made in Virginia foods.

FARMS, FARMER'S MARKETS & VEGETABLE STANDS The region around Richmond is renowned for its fine produce. Regional Saturday-morning farmer's markets include the **Ashland Farmers Market** (804-921-0243; www.town.ashland.va.us; VA 54/Duncan Street, Ashland 23005), behind the Ashland Town Hall; the **Chester Farmers Market** (804-748-9650; www.chesterfarmersmarket.com; Chester Village Green at Centre Street, Chester 23831); **Goochland Farmers Market** (804-332-3144; www.centerforruralculture.org; 2955 River Road W., Grace Episcopal Church, Goochland Courthouse 23063), in Richmond's horse country;

TAKING TEA

Becky's Tea Cafe at the Virginia Pantry (804-598-6656; www.beckystea cafe.com), 2652 Anderson Highway, Powhatan 23139. Gift shop serves cream, fruit, and high tea by reservation.

Carytown Teas (804-358-8327; www.carytownteas.com), 24–26 S. Nansemond Avenue, Richmond 23220. Sells more than a hundred kinds of tea.

⁰ᵀ⁰ **Feathernesters Tea Room & Gifts** (804-262-7305; www.feathernesters .com), 6118 Lakeside Avenue, Richmond 23228. Charming spot near Lewis Ginter Gardens serves lunch and weekend brunch. Afternoon tea by reservation only. Free Wi-Fi.

✪ **Jefferson Hotel** (804-649-4661; www.jeffersonhotel.com), 101 W. Franklin Street, Richmond 23220. Enjoy afternoon tea in the historic Palm Court, Fri.–Sun., by reservation. Monthly Teddy Bear and Chocolate Lovers' teas.

AFTERNOON TEA AT THE JEFFERSON HOTEL IS AN ELEGANT AFFAIR.

🌿 **Lavender Fields Herb Farm** (804-262-3386; www.lavender fieldsfarm.com), 11300 Winfrey Road, Glen Allen 23059. Lovely farm on the banks of the Chickahominy River offers herbal cooking classes and afternoon tea.

⁰ᵀ⁰ **TeaCo Unique Café and Lounge** (804-775-9595; www.tea -co.com), 902 W. Broad Street, Richmond 23220. Tearoom near VCU. Free Wi-Fi.

and the **West End Farmers Market** (804-364-8213; www.westendfarmers market.com; Gayton Road and Ridge-field Parkway, Richmond 23238) in Henrico County, also open Wed. mornings with free kids' programs.

The Market Umbrella (www.the marketumbrella.com) sponsors several European-style markets around the Richmond area, including the **Quirk Gallery Evening Market** (311 W. Broad Street; first Friday of the month). See the Web site for other locations.

The season for farmer's markets usually runs May–October, with special holiday markets in November and December, but some operate all year. Find a full listing at www.vdacs.virginia.gov.

Brookview Farm (804-784-3131; www.brookviewfarm.com), 854 Dover Road, Manakin-Sabot 23103. Sat. morning market at this organic farm sells grass-fed beef, free-range chicken, eggs, raw honey, and produce.

*Chesterfield Berry Farm and Market** (804-739-3831; www.chesterfieldberryfarm.com), 26000 Pear Orchard Road, Moseley 23120. Pick-your-own strawberries, blackberries, tomatoes, herbs, flowers, and pumpkins, plus a farm market, fall corn maze, and seasonal events.

*Gallmeyer Farms** (804-795-9979; www.gallmeyerfarms.com), 3622 Darbytown Court, Richmond 23231. Pick your own fruits, vegetables, greens, and pumpkins in a low-key family setting.

Petersburg Farmer's Market (804-733-2400; www.petersburg-va.org), 9 E. Old Street, Petersburg 23803. Historic octagonal building in Old Towne hosts Sat. morning markets.

✪ **17th Street Farmers Market** (804-646-0310; www.17thstreet farmersmarket.com), 100 N. 17th Street, at Main, Richmond 23219. Shockoe Bottom market has been a gathering spot since 1737 and is one of the oldest farmer's markets in the nation. Open weekends Apr.–Dec., Thurs. through Oct., with many special events, including Fri. evening beer tastings.

FAST FOOD Christopher's Run-Away Gourmay (804-400-3663; www.christophersrunawaygourmay.com), Eighth, 10th, 12th, and Main streets, and in Court End. Seasonal carts in the downtown business district offer healthy, low-priced pastas, salads, and fruit and cheese plates for weekday lunch.

*Joey's Hot Dogs** (804-651-4108; www.joeyshotdogs.com), 10400 Ridgefield Parkway, Richmond 23233. Hot dogs and homemade chili at this little counter inside a gas station have been earning raves since 1939.

Nate's Taco Truck (www.twitter.com/natestacotruck). Richmond's favorite taco stand can usually be found on the VCU campus or at a local farmer's market. Check Twitter for daily locations.

*Ray's Dog House** (804-644-3848), 401 N. First Street, Richmond 23219. Best spot for a quick dog downtown.

Stuffy's Subs (804-359-6800; www.stuffysubs.com), 411 N. Harrison Street, Richmond 23220. Local sandwich chain with lots of veggie offerings; seven other locations in addition to this one near VCU.

ICE CREAM Bev's Homemade Ice Cream (804-204-2387; www.billofare.com), 2911 W. Cary Street, Richmond 23221. Carytown favorite near the Byrd Theatre serves yummy flavors such as pear sorbet and espresso Oreo.

*"1" The Dairy Bar Restaurant** (804-355-1937; www.dairybar restaurant.com), 1602 Roseneath Road, Richmond 23230. Old-fashioned soda fountain just north of Broad serves ice cream specialties, breakfast, lunch, and limeades. Free Wi-Fi.

Gelati Celesti Ice Cream Makers (804-346-0038), 8906 W. Broad Street, Richmond 23294. Homemade ice cream in more than a hundred flavors is worth the drive to the West End. Or find their ice cream in town at **Boyer's Ice Cream and Coffee** (804-288-4088; 5720 Patterson Avenue, Richmond 23226).

Scotty's Ice Cream & Snack Bar
(804-520-8642), 106 N. Sycamore
Street, Petersburg 23803. Old Towne
landmark serves shakes, sundaes,
cones, and light lunches.

Southern Railway Deli (804-343-
1770; www.southernrailwaydeli.com),
111 Virginia Street, Richmond 23219.
Stop by on a hot day in Shockoe Slip
for house-made gelato in a variety of
flavors. Design-your-own pastas and
salads, plus pizzas and subs, make this
a family-friendly lunch spot, near the
corner of 14th and Canal streets.

**NATURAL FOODS AND VEGE-
TARIAN MENUS ✪ Cafe Guten-
berg** (804-497-5000; www.cafeguten
berg.com), 1700 E. Main Street, Richmond 23223. Award-winning bookstore
and café continues its "eat local" policy, offering plenty of choices for veg-
ans, including brunch served all day.
Free Wi-Fi.

**🍴 ⌇ ❝T❞ Cous Cous Mediterranean
Moroccan Cuisine** (804-358-0868;
www.couscous900.com), 900 W.
Franklin Street, Richmond 23220.
Cool spot above the Virginia Book
Store offers a weekly Vegetarian Night;
many vegan dishes, free Wi-Fi, compli-
mentary tapas nightly.

*❝T❞ Crossroads Coffee & Ice
Cream** (www.crossroadsrva.com), two
locations: the Fan across from the
VCU campus (804-355-3559; 26 N.
Morris Street, Richmond 23220) and
Forest Hill across from the park (804-
231-2030; 3600 Forest Hill Avenue,
Richmond 23225). Lots of vegetarian
breakfast and lunch dishes. Free Wi-
Fi.

Ellwood Thompson's Local Market
(804-359-7525; www.ellwood
thompsons.com), 4 N. Thompson
Street, at Ellwood, Richmond 23221.
The largest independent organic grocery in Virginia carries the city's largest

selection of local produce, plus organic
wines, craft beers, organic groceries,
salad and hot buffets, juice bar. Weekend wine tastings.

Harrison Street Coffee Shop (804-
261-5656; www.harrisonstcoffeeshop
.com), 402 N. Harrison Street, Richmond 23220. Completely vegetarian
restaurant serves vegan brunch on
weekends.

Ipanema Café (804-213-0190; www
.ipanemaveg.com), 917 W. Grace
Street, Richmond 23219. Creative vegetarian and vegan menus for lunch,
dinner, and Sun. brunch; wine happy
hours; bakery. In the heart of the VCU
campus.

Panda Garden (804-359-6688), 948
W. Grace Street, Richmond 23220. All
the popular Chinese and Japanese
dishes made without meat.

Positive Vibe Café (804-560-9622;
www.positivevibecafe.com), 2825
Hathaway Road, Richmond 23225.
Nonprofit restaurant in the Stratford
Hills Shopping Center off Forest Hill
Avenue trains and employs people with
disabilities and serves a menu created
from local foods.

PIZZA & MORE *Bottoms Up
Pizza** (804-644-4400; www.bottoms
uppizza.com), 1700 Dock Street, Richmond 23223. Create your own pizza,
pasta, or portobello at this Shockoe
Bottom spot, then enjoy it outside with
a view of the famous "Triple Cross"
railroad crossing. Delivery available.

8½ (804-358-8505), 401 Strawberry
Street, Richmond 23220. Italian take-
out spot in the Fan gets high marks for
great food and low prices.

Mad Italian Pasta & Steak House
(804-732-9268; www.craterroad.com),
2545 S. Crater Road, Petersburg
23805. Longtime Petersburg favorite
serves Italian and Greek specialties.

Mary Angela's Pizzeria (804-353-2333; www.maryangelaspizzeria.com), 3345 W. Cary Street, Richmond 23221. Carytown favorite serves Sicilian- and New York–style pizzas, pastas, and subs.

℣ **Tarrant's Café and Tarrantino's Pizzeria** (804-225-0035; www.tarrants cafe.org), 1 W. Broad Street, Richmond 23220. Unique restaurant in a renovated 1873 drugstore serves New York–style pizza, Sun. brunch; full bar. Delivery available.

SPORTS BARS ⁙ **Mulligan's Sports Grille** (804-744-8686; www .mulligansportsgrille.com), 1146 Hull Street, Midlothian 23112. TVs at every booth, plus high-def big screens and 52 feeds. Free Wi-Fi, pool tables, darts, trivia boxes.

℣ **The Pump Pour House** (804-364-9083; www.thepourhouse.us), 3438 Pump Road, Richmond 23233. Fifty TVs tuned to sports, live music on Sat., partying crowd.

✎ ℣ **The Triple** (804-359-7777; www .richmondbilliards.com), 3306 W. Broad Street, Richmond 23230. Family-friendly venue combines food, art, and music by local musicians, with pool tables suitable for all ages. Sister club **The Playing Field** (804-755-7700; 7801 W. Broad Street, Richmond 23294) is home to local, state, and national tournaments in billiards, Foosball, darts, and poker, as well as an award-winning chili.

WINE BARS & WINE AND BEER SHOPS ℣ **Barrel Thief Wine Shop and Cafe** (www.barrelthiefwine.com), two locations: Short Pump (804-364-0144; 11747 W. Broad Street, Richmond 23233) and Patterson & Libbie (804-612-9232; 5805 Patterson Avenue, Richmond 23226). Wines by the bottle or glass, nice menu of go-withs, plus tastings, classes, and live music.

℣ **Bin 22 @ Betsy's** (804-358-4501; www.bin22carytown.com), 3200 W. Cary Street, Richmond 23221. Carytown spot is a coffeehouse by day, popular wine bar by night.

J. Emerson Fine Wines and Cheese (804-285-8011; www.jemersonfine wine.com), 5716 Grove Avenue, Richmond 23226. Monthly tastings. Many unusual and rare vintages.

Once Upon a Vine (804-726-9463; www.onceuponavine.us), 4009 MacArthur Avenue, Richmond 23227. One of the top beer retailers in the world, with brews from six continents.

River City Cellars (804-355-1375; www.rivercitycellars.com), 2931 W. Cary Street, Richmond 23221. Carytown store offers free beer and wine tastings, many wines under $10, imported cheeses.

Strawberry Street Vineyard (804-355-1839; www.strawberrystreet.com), 407 Strawberry Street, Richmond 23220. Pick up a bottle of wine here to go with Italian take-out from **8½**, just down the block.

WINERIES & VINEYARDS Dozens of Virginia wineries participate in Richmond's annual **James River Wine Festival** (www.jamesriverwine festival.com) every April, and in Powhatan's **Festival of the Grape** (www.powhatanchamberofcommerce .org) and the **Carytown Food and Wine Festival** (www.carytownrva.org), both held in October. To find more wineries and wine trails, visit www .virginiawine.org.

❧ **Heart of Virginia Wine Trail** (www.hovawinetrail.com). Winding north from Richmond, this trail visits four wineries before returning to I-95. In addition to James River Cellars listed below, wineries on the tour include **Greyhaven Winery** (804-556-3917;

www.grayhavenwinery.com; 4675 E. Grey Fox Circle, Gum Spring 23065), **Cooper Vineyards** (540-894-5253; www.coopervineyards.com; 13372 Shannon Hill Road, Louisa 23093), and **Lake Anna Winery** (540-895-5085; www.lawinery.com; 5621 Courthouse Road, Spotsylvania 22551). A $10 passport buys a souvenir glass, tastings at each winery, and a gift.

James River Cellars Winery (804-550-7516; www.jamesrivercellars.com), 11008 Washington Highway, Glen Allen 23059. Just 10 miles north of Richmond, this winery, which uses all Virginia-grown grapes, is open for tastings and tours seven days a week.

New Kent Winery (804-932-8240 or 877-932-8240; www.newkentwinery.com), 8400 Old Church Road (I-64 exit 211), New Kent 23124. Lovely new winery between Richmond and Williamsburg hosts tastings and tours. Buy a bottle and enjoy it with cheese and crackers on the spacious covered deck.

Rosemont Vineyards and Winery (434-636-9463; www.rosemontof virginia.com), 1050 Blackridge Road, LaCrosse 23950. Just off I-85 near the North Carolina border, this winery with a unique four-level gravity flow system offers tastings, winery tours, and overnight accommodations.

Woodland Vineyard (804-739-2774; www.woodlandvineyard.com), 15501 Genito Road, Midlothian 23112. Family-operated farm winery on the outskirts of Richmond is Virginia's smallest. Tastings by appointment.

✳ Selective Shopping

While upscale mixed-use shopping and entertainment destinations have arrived in the Richmond suburbs in force, downtown the city can boast one of the finest streets of unique shops in the country—known as Carytown to its many fans. Other historic downtowns around the region are returning to their previous prosperity as well, most notably Old Towne Petersburg, where a dozen or so antiques stores occupy centuries-old buildings.

Richmond has been a wealthy town for most of its existence, making for great antiques shopping, as well as good consignment, thrift, and flea market opportunities.

NEIGHBORHOOD SHOPPING DISTRICTS ✪ Carytown (804-422-2279; www.carytownrva.org), 3126 W. Cary Street, Richmond 23221. Nicknamed the Mile of Style, the nine blocks of W. Cary from Thompson Street to Boulevard make up the region's best place to window-shop with a varied and colorful selection of locally owned shops, boutiques, and restaurants. The Carytown Merchants Association hosts **First Thursday Fashion First** events with shops open until 8 PM, the annual Watermelon Festival in Aug., and the Carytown Food and Wine Festival in Oct.

Richmond's first shopping center, the recently refurbished 1938 **Cary Court Park & Shop,** occupying the 3100 block between S. Belmont and S. Auburn streets, makes a convenient landmark with plenty of parking (there's more behind the center), fun shops, and dining options, including the Can Can Brasserie. In addition to on-street parking, free parking decks can be found at Crenshaw and Dooley, and at Sheppard and Colonial.

✪ Old Towne Petersburg (804-733-4955; www.oldtownepetersburg.com), Sycamore and Old streets, Petersburg. Stretching along the southern bank of the Appomattox River, the old section of Petersburg is experiencing a revival as antiques shops, cafés, galleries, and restaurants—even trendy tapas/sushi spot **Wabi Sabi** (804-862-1365;

www.eatwabisabi.com; 29 Bolling-brook Street, Petersburg 23803)—move into the historic buildings. Most are open late on the second Fri. of every month during **Friday for the Arts!** (held 6–10 PM. Free parking is available in the visitors center lot at the corner of Sycamore and Old streets.

"On The Avenues": Libbie and Grove/Libbie and Patterson

(www.libbiegrove.com), Libbie, Grove, and Patterson avenues, Richmond. Upscale neighborhood in Richmond's West End is home to numerous wine shops, jewelry and clothing stores, salons, and the **Westhampton Regal Theater** (804-288-9068; 5706 Grove Avenue, Richmond 23226).

SHOPPING CENTERS & MALLS

Chesterfield Towne Center (804-794-4661; www.chesterfieldcenter .com), 11500 Midlothian Turnpike, Richmond 23235. Major shopping destination on the Southside with 140 stores, including Macy's and Sears; many dining options; and free Wi-Fi in the food court.

✪ ✨ **Short Pump Town Center** (804-360-1700; www.shortpumpmall .com), 11800 W. Broad Street, Richmond 23233. Expansive, open-air shopping and entertainment destination hosts all the national upscale chains, from Nordstrom to the Cheesecake Factory, plus 140 specialty shops and eateries, the Funny Bone Comedy Club, a summer concert series, and **Hotel Sierra** (804-360-7021; www .hotel-sierra.com). Kids enjoy rides aboard the Short Pump Express train.

✛ **Southpark Mall** (804-526-3900; www.southparkmall.com), 230 Southpark Circle (I-95 exit 54), Colonial Heights 23834. Anchored by Macy's, Dillard's, Sears, and JCPenney, this mall, 20 miles south of Richmond, has

more than 70 shops, plus a new food court, laser tag, and the **Regal Cinemas Stadium 16** (804-744-2600).

Stony Point Fashion Park (804-560-7467; www.shopstonypoint.com), 9200 Stony Point Parkway, Richmond 23235. Stylish open-air center with 90 upscale shops and restaurants, including the area's only Saks Fifth Avenue, Anthropologie, and Smith & Hawken. Summer Sounds concerts and free coupon books from the customer service center.

ANTIQUES **Antique Village** (804-746-8914; www.antiquevillageva.com), 10203 Chamberlayne Road/US 301, Mechanicsville 23116. More than 50 vendors located about 20 miles north of downtown Richmond, off I-295 at exit 41A. Closed Wed.

Caravati's Inc (804-232-4175; www.caravatis.com), 104 E. Second Street, Richmond 23224. The oldest architectural salvage company in a city of really old architecture has a warehouse in Old Manchester crammed with stained glass, mantles, and much more.

Disputanta Antiques Depot (804-991-9323; www.disputantaantiquesdepot .com), 10032 County Drive/US 460, Disputanta 23842. Store in Prince George County, just off I-295, with a huge selection nostalgia items, antiques, and collectibles of every sort.

Heritage Antiques & Collectibles (804-262-0284; www.heritageantiques andcollectiblesmall.com), 7521 Staples Mill Road, Richmond 23228. Shop under the glow of crystal chandeliers as you enjoy complimentary refreshments and roam the carpeted aisles of this mall of tempting treasures.

✪ **Old Towne Petersburg antiques shops** (www.oldtownepetersburg.com or www.petersburgarea.org). Cluster of antiques stores in Petersburg's Olde

Towne makes for excellent browsing. Among them: **Patricia Dillard's Antiques** (www.patriciadillardantiques .com), **Penniston's Alley Antiques** (www.pennistonsalley.com), the **Oak Antique Mall** (www.theoakantiques .com), **Kimberly Ann's** (www.shop kimberlyanns.com), **Rivers Edge** (www.riversedgeinteriors.com), and **Second Hand Rose** (www.n2vintage clothing.com), a vintage clothing store.

↑ **West End Antiques Mall** (804-359-1600; www.westendantiquemall .com), 2004 Staples Mill Road, Crossroads Shopping Center, Richmond 23230. Packed with more than 250 vendor booths, the city's largest selection.

BOOKS & MUSIC Aquarian Bookshop (804-353-5575; www.theaquarian bookshop.com), 3519 Ellwood Avenue, Richmond 23220. New Age bookstore in Carytown stocks metaphysical books, candles, crystals, and incense, and offers psychic readings and Mayan Healing training.

Barnes & Noble @ VCU Bookstore (804-828-1678; www.vcu.bncollege .com), 1111 W. Broad Street, Richmond 23284; plus numerous other locations (www.barnesandnoble.com).

Borders Books and Music (804-965-0733; www.borders.com), 9750 W. Broad Street, Glen Allen 23060.

Black Swan Books (804-353-9476; www.blackswanbooks.com), 2601 W. Main Street, Richmond 23220. Used and rare books, including leatherbound volumes, books on Virginiana and the Civil War, art, gardening, and cookbooks, at wallet-friendly prices.

Book People (804-288-4346; www .bookpeoplerichmond.com), 536 Granite Avenue, Richmond 23226. Friendly bookstore in the West End offers new and used titles, including many foreign-language books. Frequent author signings and book swaps.

Chop Suey Books (804-422-8066; www.chopsueybooks.com), 2913 W. Cary Street, Richmond 23221. Used books in Carytown across from the Byrd Theatre.

Fountain Bookstore (804-788-1594; www.fountainbookstore.com), 1312 E. Cary Street, Richmond 23219. Independent bookstore in Shockoe Slip with a fine selection of local authors and books on Richmond history and the Civil War hosts frequent readings and signings.

Owens & Ramsey Historical Booksellers (804-272-8888 or 866-808-1861; www.owensandramsey.com), 2728 Tinsley Drive, Richmond 23235. Huge catalog of new, used, and rare volumes on military, political, and social history, specializing in the Civil War.

Plan 9 Music (804-353-9996; www .plan9music.com), 3012 W. Cary Street, Richmond 23221. Independent music seller carries three hundred titles on consignment from local bands and sponsors in-store performances.

Virginia Book Company (804-359-1222; www.vabookco.com), 900 W. Franklin Street, Richmond 23220. New and used titles, plus Greek and VCU logo wear. The popular **Cous Cous Mediterranean Restaurant** (804-358-0868; www.couscous900.com) is upstairs.

CLOTHING Bygones Vintage Clothing (804-353-1919; www.by gonesvintage.com), 2916 W. Cary Street, Richmond 23221. Men's and women's fashions from 1900 to 1970 next to the historic Byrd movie palace.

Need Supply Co. (804-355-5880; www.needsupply.com), 3010 W. Cary Street, Richmond 23221. Vintage denim and contemporary fashions for men and women in Carytown.

Pink (804-358-0884; www.pinkstore.com), 3158 W. Cary Street, Richmond 23221. Dresses and bags in bold colors popular with the Carytown fashionista crowd.

CONSIGNMENT **Baggio** (804-754-1163; www.baggioconsignment.com), Gayton Crossing Shopping Center, 9744 Gayton Road, Richmond 23238. Consignment boutique carries designer-label clothes and accessories.

Clementine (804-358-2357; www.sweetclementine.com), 3118 W. Cary Street, Richmond 23221. Brand-name women's clothing, shoes, and handbags, plus one-of-a-kind jewelry by local designer the Bead Poet, in Carytown.

The Hall Tree (804-358-9985; www.thehalltreerichmond.com), 12 S. Thompson Street, Richmond 23221. Carytown landmark is one of the largest consignment shops in the nation.

Rumors (804-726-9944; www.rumorsrva.com), 404 N. Harrison Street, Richmond 23220. Recycled clothing, plus locally designed clothing and accessories, selected for the city's hippest crowd.

FLEA MARKETS & THRIFT SHOPS **Bellwood Drive-In Flea Market** (804-275-1187), 9201 Jefferson Davis Highway/US 1, Richmond 23237. Lots of vendors make this a fun place to browse on a nice weekend.

The Clothes Rack (www.jlrichmond.org), two locations: **Carytown** (804-358-4693; 2618 W. Cary Street, Richmond 23220) and **Stratford Hills** (804-323-6270; 6780 Forest Hills Avenue, Richmond 23225). Junior League thrift shops sell fashionable household goods and clothes for a good cause.

▼ **Diversity Thrift** (804-353-8890; www.diversitythrift.org), 1407 Sherwood Avenue, Richmond 23220. Store in the rainbow-striped Gay Community Center of Richmond carries stylish furniture, clothing, books, music, jewelry, and art, at bargain prices.

Goodwill Second Debut (804-254-7623; www.goodwillrichmond.org), 3114 W. Cary Street, Richmond 23221. Previously owned and new designer-label fashions and accessories.

GIFTS **Purple Passion** (804-863-1943; www.purplepassionva.com), 29 W. Bank Street, Petersburg 23803. Eclectic Old Towne shop stocks personalized sterling-silver gifts, hand-knit sweaters, and a whole room of lavender and purple items.

✪ **The Shops at 5807** (804-288-5807; www.shop5807.com), 5807 Patterson Avenue, Richmond 23226. More than two dozen individual boutiques under one roof.

Very Richmond Gallery and Gifts (804-644-3613; www.veryrichmondgifts.com), James Center Atrium, 1051 E. Cary Street, Richmond 23219. Quality souvenirs, from gourmet foods to pewter to art prints, relating to Richmond and Virginia.

World of Mirth (804-353-8991; www.worldofmirth.com), 3005 W. Cary Street, Richmond 23220. Unusual and eclectic shop carries wonderful toys for all ages.

HOME DECOR **La Difference** (804-648-6210; www.ladiff.com), 125 S. 14th Street, Richmond 23219. Three stories of stylish contemporary furniture and accessories in Shockoe Bottom.

Signature Style Polish Pottery Shop (804-733-4495; www.polish

potteryshop.com), 13 W. Old Street, Petersburg 23803. Boleslawiec folk art stoneware in regular and signature designs, plus other unique decor items.

Tweed (804-249-3900; www.tweed athome.com), 11743 W. Broad Street, Richmond 23233. Gifts and home accessories in the Shoppes at Westgate, across from Short Pump Town Center.

JEWELRY Bachrach's Jewelers (804-648-7830; www.bachrachsjewelers .com), 111 E. Broad Street, Richmond 23219. Selling estate and antique jewelry, sterling flatware and hollowware, and clocks since 1887.

Dransfield Jewelers (804-643-0171; www.dransfieldjewelers.com), 1308 E. Cary Street, Richmond 23219. Jeweler in Shockoe Slip specializes in hand-crafted, contemporary designs.

Stevens Jewelers (804-527-2890; www.stevens-jewelers.com), Parkside Marketplace, 10877 W. Broad Street, Glen Allen 23060. Exclusive designs include Virginia and Richmond landmark charms in sterling silver or gold, and the popular Richmond sterling bead bracelet.

✳ Special Events

For up-to-date calendars of events in the Richmond area, visit www.weekly rant.com, www.rvanews.com, www .venturerichmond.com, or www .flavorcalendar.com. The Richmond Raceway Complex hosts numerous events; see its schedule at www .richmondracewaycomplex.com.

January: **Richmond Fishing Expo** (804-228-7500; www.richmondraceway complex.com), Richmond Raceway Complex.

Virginia Boat Show (www.agievents .com), Greater Richmond Convention Center.

February: **Virginia Wine Expo** (www .virginiawineexpo.com), Greater Richmond Convention Center.

WomanKind (www.womankind richmond.com), St. James's Episcopal Church. Held every two years.

March: **Church Hill Irish Festival** (804-356-1093; www.churchhill irishfestival.com), St. Patrick's Church, N. 25th Street, Richmond.

French Film Festival (804-827-3456; www.frenchfilm.vcu.edu), Byrd Theatre, Richmond.

James River Film Festival (804-355-6537; www.rmicweb.org), Byrd Theatre and other venues.

Monument Avenue 10K (www .sportsbackers.org). Voted the best road race in the Southeast.

Richmond Home and Garden Show (804-228-7500; www.agievents .com), Richmond Raceway Complex.

April: ✪ **Battersea Revolutionary War Reenactment** (804-733-2402; www.petersburg-va.org), Petersburg.

✪ **Easter on Parade** (804-788-6466; www.venturerichmond.com), Monument Avenue, Richmond.

Historic Garden Week (www.va gardenweek.org), statewide.

James River Wine Festival (804-353-1525; www.jamesriverwinefestival .com), Innsbrook Pavilion, Glen Allen.

National Duathlon Festival (804-285-9495; www.duathlonnationals .com), Richmond.

Southern Women's Show (804-228-7500; www.southernshows.com), Richmond Raceway Complex.

May: **Arts in the Park** (www.rich mondartsinthepark.com), Byrd Park, Richmond.

A Taste of New Kent Wine Festival (804-932-8240; www.newkentwinery .com), New Kent Winery, 8400 Old Church Road, New Kent.

Asian American Celebration (804-245-4974; www.aasocv.org), Greater Richmond Convention Center.

Dominion Riverrock (804-285-9495; www.sportsbackers.org), Brown's Island. Unique mix of sports, music, and fun on the downtown riverfront.

○ Fort Clifton Festival (804-520-9224; www.colonial-heights.com), Brockwell Lane, Colonial Heights.

NASCAR Sprint Cup Series Race (804-228-7500 or 866-455-7223; www.rir.com), Richmond International Raceway.

Richmond Greek Festival (804-358-5996; www.greekfestival.com), Saints Constantine and Helen's Greek Orthodox Cathedral, 30 Malvern Avenue, Richmond.

Strawberry Hill Races (804-569-3232; www.strawberryhillraces.com), Colonial Downs, New Kent County.

June: **Beer, Bourbon & BBQ Festival** (800-830-3976; www.beerandbourbon.com), Richmond Raceway Complex.

Richmond Vegetarian Festival (804-672-1457; www.veggiefest.org), Azalea Gardens at Bryan Park, Richmond.

July: **Hanover Tomato Festival** (www.hanovertomatofestival.com), Pole Green Park, Mechanicsville.

○ Shockoe Tomato Festival (804-646-0477; www.17thstreetfarmersmarket.com), 17th Street Farmers Market, Richmond.

August: **○ Carytown Watermelon Festival** (804-422-2279; www.carytownrva.com). One of Richmond's favorite festivals, with 2,500 watermelons consumed.

Chesterfield County Fair (804-768-0148; www.chesterfieldcountyfair.org), Courthouse and Krause roads, Chesterfield.

Down Home Family Reunion (804-644-3900; www.efsinc.org), Abner Clay Park, Richmond. Celebration of African American culture sponsored by the Elegba Folklore Society.

Richmond Nationals (www.nsra-usa.com), Richmond Raceway Complex. Sponsored by the National Street Rod Association.

September: **ChesterFest** (www.chesterfest.org), Chester Village Green. Free family festival.

Festival of Grapes and Hops (804-733-8131; www.petersburgvachamber.com), Old Towne Petersburg.

One Last Race to Make the Chase Sprint Cup Series Race (804-228-7500 or 866-455-7223; www.rir.com), Richmond International Raceway.

Que Pasa Festival of Virginia (804-378-4099; www.quepasafestival.com), Science Museum of Virginia, Richmond. Free Hispanic cultural festival.

JAMES RIVER DAYS

This festival, featuring events along the James, stretches from April to December, with activities for all ages. Take a guided walk or boat tour; paddle or tube the river; celebrate the return of spawning fish; view nesting eagles; learn to fish, kayak, or rock-climb; or make your own rain barrel. Highlights include **Riverfest** in June, **Jammin' on the James** concerts all summer, living history at Drewry's Bluff, the **Odyssey Bike Tour** in August, **Publick Days** at the Citie of Henricus in September, and the **James River Parade of Lights** every December. Call 804-717-6681 or visit www.jamesriveradvisorycouncil.com for more information.

Richmond Beach Music Festival (www.richmondbeachmusicfestival .com).

✍ **State Fair of Virginia** (804-994-2800; www.statefair.com), Meadow Event Park, I-95 exit 98, Doswell.

October: **Chesterfield Regional Air Show** (804-796-7045; www.chester fieldtourism.com), Chesterfield County Airport.

Civil War Symposium (804-861-2408 or 877-PAMPLIN; www.pamplinpark .org), Pamplin Historical Park, Petersburg.

Eppington Heritage Day (804-748-1624; www.chesterfieldtourism.com), Chesterfield.

❂ **Food and Wine Festival: A Taste of Carytown** (804-422-2279; www .carytownrva.com), Richmond.

Jammin' on the James (www .jamminonthejames.com), Richmond. Annual Lindy dance weekend.

Meadow Highland Games & Celtic Festival (804-994-2800; www.rich mondceltic.com), Meadow Event Park, I-95 exit 98, Doswell.

Powhatan's Festival of the Grape (804-598-2636; www.powhatan winefestival.com), Courthouse Square, Powhatan.

❂ **Richmond Folk Festival** (804-788-6466; www.richmondfolkfestival .org), downtown Richmond riverfront. One of Virginia's largest festivals. Free.

Richmond Italian Street Festival (www.richmonditalianfestival.com), Horticultural Gardens, Richmond International Raceway Complex.

Richmond Restaurant Week (www.richmondrestaurantweek.com).

Second Street Festival (804-788-6466; www.cjwn.net), Jackson Ward. A celebration of jazz and Richmond's historic African American community.

November: **Annual Powhatan Presentation of Tribute to the Governor** (804-769-2194), Governor's Mansion, Capitol Square, Richmond.

East Coast Bowl Game (804-722-0141; www.ecb.petersburgsports.com), Cameron Field, Petersburg. All-star college bowl features seniors from throughout the East Coast.

December: ✍ **Capital City Kwanzaa Festival** (804-644-3900; www.efsinc .org), the Showplace, 3000 Mechanicsville Turnpike, Richmond.

Christmas Homes Tour (804-732-2096; www.historicpetersburg.org), Historic Petersburg.

Church Hill Holiday House Tour (www.churchhillrichmond.com), Richmond.

❂ ✍ **Court End Christmas** (804-649-0711; www.richmondhistorycenter .com), Richmond. Free.

GardenFest of Lights (804-262-9887; www.lewisginter.org), Lewis Ginter Botanical Garden, Richmond. Thanksgiving weekend through early Jan.

Grand Illumination (www.venture richmond.com), James Center. Annual tree-lighting and festival in the River District kicks off the holiday season.

James River Parade of Lights (804-717-6681; www.jamesriveradvisory council.com), Richmond.

THE PLANTATION ROAD: ROUTE 5 SCENIC BYWAY

Stretching from Richmond to Williamsburg, Virginia's Route 5 Scenic Byway, also known as the John Tyler Memorial Highway, provides a pleasant alternate route between these two destinations, with plenty of historic sites along the way, minus the congestion of the I-64 corridor.

Route 5 is still a quiet, shady country road, passing occasional country stores, some of them in business for a century or more, and country lanes leading down to the shores of the James River, where the colonial aristocracy established their estates.

These estates were owned by some of the most prominent, and wealthy, families of colonial society. The Randolphs, the Byrds, the Hamiltons, and the descendants of Robert "King" Carter, wealthiest man of his day, all had houses here, and their cousins, Thomas Jefferson and George Washington, among others, visited frequently. William Henry "Tippecanoe" Harrison, born at Berkeley Plantation, and his neighbor, John Tyler of Sherwood Forest, went off to Washington in 1841, ending up the ninth and 10th presidents of the United States.

Several of the historic houses are still occupied by the original families, including Shirley, home of the Hill-Carters; Sherwood Forest, home of the Tylers; and North Bend, still occupied by Hamiltons.

The **James River Plantation Gardens and Grounds Pass** (www.piney grove.com) provides admission to the grounds of four plantations: Piney Grove at Southall's, Westover, North Bend, and Edgewood, for $9. Call 804-829-2196 to purchase in advance.

The **Charles City County Visitor Center and Courthouse Complex** (804-652-4701; www.charlescity.org; 10760 and 10702 Courthouse Road, Charles City 23030), just off VA 5, is a good place to gather information about the region. The visitors center, in the 1901 Clerk's Office, offers exhibits, county maps, and informative brochures. Next door is the **Charles City County Center for Local History** (804-652-1516).

A 7-mile section of the new paved **Virginia Capital Trail** (www.virginia capitaltrail.org), for bikers and hikers, begins at the visitors center, running past many of the plantations and other historic sites.

The National Park Service Web site (www.nps.gov/nr/travel/jamesriver/index.htm) details 33 historic properties along both sides of the Tidewater James. Other good sources of information include www.jamesriver plantations.org, www.co.charles-city.va.us, and www.baygateways.net.

Belle Air Plantation (804-829-2431), 11800 John Tyler Memorial Highway/VA 5, Charles City 23030. Built circa 1670, this is one of the oldest frame houses in the country, with a fine Jacobean staircase and 5 acres of gardens. Open during **Historic Garden Week** (www.vagardenweek.org) and by appointment.

○ **Berkeley Plantation** (804-829-6018 or 888-466-6018; www.berkeley plantation.com), 12602 Harrison Landing Road, Charles City 23030. First occupied in 1619, raided by Indians and British turncoat Benedict Arnold, and occupied by Union troops during the Civil War, this land also witnessed the first recorded Thanksgiving celebration in the New World (1619), the first bottle of bourbon whiskey distilled this side of the Atlantic (1621), and the first playing of the bugle call "Taps" (1862). Abraham Lincoln reviewed his troops here; William Henry Harrison, ninth President of the United States, was born here. The first floor of the mansion house is open for guided tours by costumed interpreters; a museum with many artifacts and a film about the house's history occupies the basement. Adults $11, senior and military $10, students (ages 13–16) $7.50, children (ages 6–12) $6.

Charles City Tavern (804-829-5004), 9220 John Tyler Memorial Highway, Charles City 23030. One of the few restaurants in the county—and it's a good one. Enjoy lunch or dinner on the pleasant screened porch or in the historic dining room. Open Tues.–Sun.

Cul's Courthouse Grille (804-829-2205; www.culscourthousegrille.com), 10801 Courthouse Road, Charles City 23030. Casual restaurant in a historic building across from the visitors center serves country classics seven days a week for lunch and dinner.

Edgewood Plantation (804-829-2962; www.edgewoodplantation.com), 4800 John Tyler Memorial Highway, Charles City 23030. This 1849 Carpenter Gothic mansion houses a bed & breakfast inn. History, ghost, picnic, and candlelight tours; Victorian tea parties; and Thanksgiving and Christmas dinners available.

Fort Pocahontas (804-829-9722; www.fortpocahontas.org), Sturgeon Point Road/SR 614, Charles City 23030. The site of the Battle of Wilson's Wharf, where two companies of black Union soldiers repulsed the Confederate cavalry, is a well-preserved earthen fort, now owned by the family of President John Tyler. Open for group tours of 10 or more, and for an annual reenactment of the battle every May.

Harrison Lake National Fish Hatchery (804-829-2421; www.fws.gov/fisheries), 11110 Kimages Road, Charles City 23030. Nature preserve contains 20 fish rearing ponds and trails winding along Herring Creek through mixed hardwoods that attract woodland songbirds, plus a free gravel boat ramp and handicapped-accessible fishing pier on Harrison Lake.

Haupt's Country Store (804-829-2418), 11911 John Tyler Memorial Highway, Charles City 23030. Family operated since 1893, this old-fashioned store near the Charles City Courthouse has a full deli, fresh cut meat, and produce.

Kittiewan Plantation (804-829-2272; www.kittiewanplantation.org), 12104 Weyanoke Road/SR 619, Charles City 23030. One of the oldest properties on the James River is now the headquarters of the Archeology Society of Virginia. The restored plantation house and visitors center with a museum of Americana is open for tours by appointment.

✪ **Lawrence Lewis Jr. Park** (804-652-1601; www.baygateways.net), 12400 and 12580 Willcox Wharf Road, Charles City 23030. Historic landing where the army of Gen. U. S. Grant crossed the James provides public access to the river on two levels, with comfort station, picnic area with grills, bird-viewing platforms, wetlands boardwalk, and fishing pier. Bald eagles and ospreys, as well as a blue heron rookery, can be sighted from the park. Free.

Lazare Gallery (804-829-5001; www.lazaregallery.com), 4641 Kimages Wharf Road, Charles City 23030. Gallery on the shores of the James showcases a superb collection of Russian realist paintings. A cottage on the grounds accommodates overnight guests.

North Bend Plantation (804-829-5176; www.northbendplantation.com), 12200 Weyanoke Road/SR 619, Charles City 23030. Still owned by Harrison descendants, this is considered the best example of Greek Revival architecture in the county. Open daily for self-guided tours of the grounds; house tours by appointment; bed & breakfast lodging in very elegant digs available.

✪ **Piney Grove at Southall's Plantation** (804-829-2480 or 804-829-2196; www.pineygrove.com), 16920 Southall Plantation Lane (off Glebe Lane/SR 615), Charles City 23030. Current owners rescued many historic buildings from around the region, including manor houses, a church, slave quarters, and a smokehouse, and reconstructed them on the grounds of the original Piney Grove plantation house (1790). The plantation offers bed & breakfast accommodations, as well as progressive dinners including tours of the restored buildings. The grounds and gardens are open daily for self-guided tours. Adults $3.

✐ **Renwood Fields and Farm Museum** (804-829-5399; www.renwoodfieldsmaze.com), 17575 Sandy Point Road, Charles City 23030. Cornfield maze, tractor rides, and antique farm museum on a working farm. Seasonal hours.

SHIRLEY PLANTATION HAS BEEN OCCUPIED BY THE SAME FAMILY FOR 11 GENERATIONS.

River's Rest Marina & Resort (804-829-2753; www.riversrest.com), 9100 Willcox Neck Road, Charles City 23030. Located on the Chickahominy River, this secluded resort has a marina, rental pontoon boats, a motel, and the **Blue Heron Restaurant** (804-829-9070), a family-style spot with a great waterfront view that specializes in steaks and fresh local seafood.

Sherwood Plantation (804-829-5377; www.sherwoodforest.org), 14501 John Tyler Memorial Highway, Charles City 23030. John Tyler bought this plantation in 1842, during his term as 10th president of the United States. Additions made by Tyler to the plantation house made it the longest frame residence in America, and it is still occupied by his descendants, as well as a very well-documented ghost. The grounds include more than 80 varieties of trees. Self-guided tours of the grounds ($10) available daily; house tours ($35) by appointment.

✪ **Shirley Plantation** (804-829-5121 or 800-232-1613; www.shirleyplantation .com), 501 Shirley Plantation Road, Charles City 23030. Considered the most intact 18th-century estate in Virginia, Shirley presents a unique opportunity to visit a home occupied by the same family for 11 generations. Guided tours of the 1738 Great House feature original family furnishings, portraits, silver, and hand-carved woodwork. The self-guided tour of the grounds includes eight original outbuildings, including a schoolhouse attended by Robert E. Lee. Special programs during the Christmas and Halloween seasons, including tours guided by the family ghost. Adults $11, seniors $10, youth (ages 6–18) $7.50, under six free.

VCU Rice Center for Environmental Life Sciences (804-827-5600; www.vcu .edu/rice), 3800 John Tyler Memorial Highway, Charles City 23030. Research facility operated by Virginia Commonwealth University offers lectures and field trips on environmental issues for the general public.

Westover Church (804-829-2488; www.westoverparish.org), 16401 John Tyler Memorial Highway, Charles City 23030. The "new" parish church, built in 1731, and its graveyard are open daily for visits.

Westover Plantation (804-829-2882; www.jamesriverplantations.org), 7000 Westover Road, Charles City 23030. Built circa 1730 by William Byrd II, this outstanding example of Georgian architecture, next door to Berkeley Plantation, opens its grounds for self-guided tours daily. Highlights include the 1744 tomb of William Byrd I; the signature Westover doorway; and 18th-century wrought-iron gates, considered the finest in the country. A brief lane from the parking lot leads west to the original sites of the Charles City Courthouse and Westover Parish Church and graveyard, with a number of early graves. A path from the East Gate leads to a marsh with excellent birding. $2.

Virginia
Peninsula

2

HISTORY COMES TO LIFE—
WILLIAMSBURG, JAMESTOWN, AND
YORKTOWN

CROSSROADS OF THE WORLD—
HAMPTON AND NEWPORT NEWS

HISTORY COMES TO LIFE— WILLIAMSBURG, JAMESTOWN, AND YORKTOWN

A visit to Virginia's **Historic Triangle** provides an unparalleled opportunity to learn a lot about our nation's early history quickly and easily, at a number of fun, family-oriented attractions. Within just a few miles of each other, you'll find the site of the earliest successful English colony in North America, the colonial capital where the rebellion against English rule began, and the little town where British general Cornwallis surrendered his army, signaling the end of the American Revolution.

Both the national and state governments are actively involved in interpreting the history here. The National Park Service protects and maintains the actual sites of the events in the **Colonial National Historical Park** (www.nps.gov/colo), with visitors centers at **Historic Jamestowne** and **Yorktown Battlefield** tied together by the 24-mile **Colonial Parkway,** designed to minimize modern scenery. Park service rangers offer interpretive tours at these ongoing archaeological sites.

The Commonwealth of Virginia sponsors the Jamestown-Yorktown Foundation (www.historyisfun.org), with living-history centers at **Jamestown Settlement** and the **Yorktown Victory Center.** At these interactive museums, located close to the national park units, visitors can step inside history and explore accurate re-creations of the historic sites inhabited by costumed interpreters.

FIRST SETTLEMENT: JAMESTOWN

Recently the focus of America's 400th anniversary celebration, the Jamestown site has several new museums and exhibits. Visitors can watch as archaeologists uncover the ancient town, largely abandoned after the Virginia capital moved to Williamsburg in 1699. The Preservation Virginia Web site, www.apva.org, has the latest updates on the Jamestown Rediscovery Project.

Close by, the docks at **Jamestown Settlement** are home to replicas of the *Susan Constant, Godspeed,* and *Discovery,* ships that brought the first settlers to the New World. One of the best views of the ships and Jamestown Island is from the water, aboard the free **Jamestown-Scotland Ferry** (www.virginiadot.org/travel), crossing the James River to Surry County and the peanut fields beyond—a highly recommended side trip.

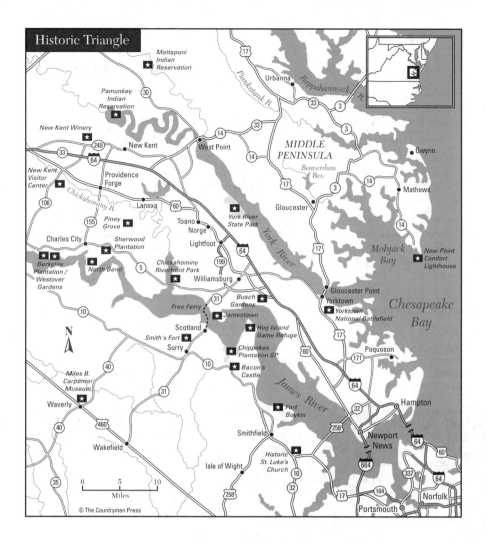

Historic Triangle

VICTORY'S BATTLEFIELD: YORKTOWN

Established in 1691 on a bluff above the deep York River, Yorktown was once one of the colony's most important ports. Impressive inns, houses, and public buildings overlooked the wharves, warehouses, and taverns of "York Under the Hill" along the waterfront.

The layout of the town is largely unchanged today, although the town was nearly pounded out of existence by bombardment during the Revolution and suffered further damage during the Civil War. **Water Street** runs at the foot of the bluff along the riverfront, passing docks occupied by a sailing sloop offering public sails, a fishing pier, several pubs, and a public beach.

Above, the village of Yorktown is a mere two blocks wide by six blocks long, a walkable town with antiques shops, galleries, cafés, and museums, some in restored or rebuilt historic structures. The **Riverwalk,** a new complex of shops and restaurants, with a free parking deck, occupies the western end of the waterfront. Above it all, the Coleman Bridge arches over the York, providing scenic views by day or night.

COLONIAL CAPITAL: WILLIAMSBURG

Between Jamestown and Yorktown, the colonial capital of **Williamsburg** (www .history.org), the largest living-history museum in the nation, provides a unique opportunity to walk streets that look the same today as they did in 1776, to eat and drink at authentic taverns, and to talk with costumed interpreters immersed in the history of the era.

As in 1776, Duke of Gloucester Street, recently named one of the Ten Great Streets in America by the American Planning Association, remains the main thoroughfare of Williamsburg, running from the Colonial Capitol building to the Wren Building on the College of William and Mary (W&M) campus. Along Duke of Gloucester lie numerous shops operated by costumed interpreters creating trade goods using traditional methods, as well as taverns and coffeehouses offering period fare and entertainments. Merchants Square, at the street's western end, provides more modern shops and food options.

WILLIAMSBURG'S DUKE OF GLOUCESTER STREET APPEARS MUCH AS IT DID IN 1775, ON THE EVE OF THE AMERICAN REVOLUTION.

Being a university town from its earliest days, before the colonial capital moved from Jamestown to the settlement then known as Middle Plantation, Williamsburg has picked up some college slang along the way. Locals typically refer to the historic restored area of town as "CW," a nod to the omnipresent Colonial Williamsburg Foundation, and may call Duke of Gloucester Street "DoG." You may even hear the town referred to as "Billyburg."

But there's more than just "CW" to modern Williamsburg. Now a major tourism destination, the area is replete with shopping and dining options, hotels, time-share resorts, and some of the nation's best golf courses. Fortunately, the majority of new development lies along the Bypass, VA 199, an expressway off I-64 that whisks traffic around the city while leaving the historic area untouched. Among the many shopping centers located adjacent to the Bypass, **New Town** (www.new townwilliamsburg.com), a mixed-use development off Monticello Avenue, stands out.

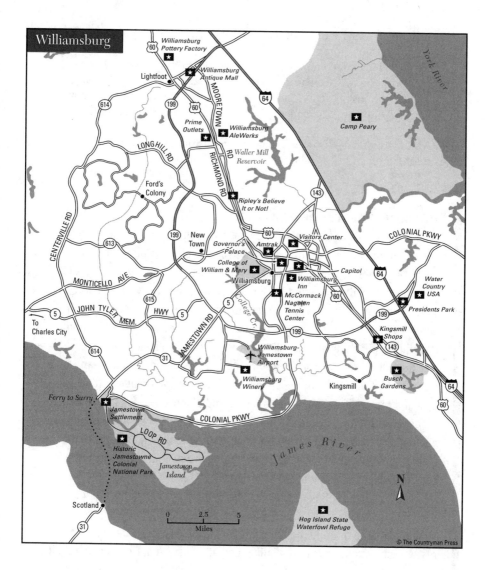

With its numerous historical resources, excellent parks for biking and hiking, paddle trails for kayaking or canoeing, and two of the nation's top theme parks, **Busch Gardens Williamsburg** and **Water Country USA,** the Historic Triangle stacks up as one of the finest destinations in the United States for a family vacation.

NORTH OF THE YORK, SOUTH OF THE JAMES

The Historic Triangle extends beyond the Virginia Peninsula to the regions north of the York River and south of the James River.

Just over the US 17 toll bridge in Yorktown, **Gloucester County** and other areas of the Middle Peninsula provide a pleasant drive where the crowds of

Williamsburg fall away. See the *In the Land of Pocahontas: Virginia's Middle Peninsula* sidebar for more details.

A free ferry, highly recommended for all visitors to the region, connects Jamestown with **Surry County** and the many attractions south of the James River, where history was just as active, but modern development is largely unknown. See the *Smithfield and Surry: Adventures in the Land of Ham* sidebar for details.

GUIDANCE America's Historic Triangle (www.historictriangle.com). Web site offers information on historical attractions, accommodations, and tours.

WILLIAMSBURG: THE RESTORATION

When Rev. Dr. W. A. R. Goodwin accepted a position as rector of Bruton Parish Church in 1903, he found Williamsburg a sleepy Southern college town. Many of its historic buildings were in a state of decay, and the 1715 church itself, with its soaring vault and rosette windows, was in a sorry state. Goodwin determined to restore the church to its former glory and began researching records and raising funds. The restoration of Bruton Parish Church, completed in 1907, was the first in Williamsburg.

Rev. Goodwin returned to the area in 1923 as a department head at the College of William and Mary. The further deterioration of the town's buildings and the proliferation of gas stations and electric wires on Duke of Gloucester Street shocked the dedicated historian. He began a drive to rescue what remained and to restore Williamsburg to its appearance at the time of the Revolutionary War, when George Washington, Thomas Jefferson, and other patriots walked its streets.

In 1926, John D. Rockefeller Jr., one of the country's richest men, brought his family to visit Williamsburg at the urging of Rev. Goodwin. After a midnight stroll through the ancient town, Rockefeller decided to fund the restoration with the aim of reminding and educating Americans about their heritage of freedom. In subsequent years, his family would pour many millions of dollars into the project, and Rockefeller and his wife, Abby, would spend much time at Basset Hall, their Williamsburg home.

The authenticity of the restoration depended in large part on the famous Bodleian Plate, an engraved copperplate dated to 1740 discovered in Oxford's Bodleian Library in 1929. The plate shows the Wren Building and its companions, as well as the Governor's Palace and the capitol, two buildings of which only the foundations remained.

John D. Rockefeller Jr. called the Bodleian Plate the "foundation upon which we have based the restoration" and said, "Without it, we would have been acting in the dark; with it, we have gone forward with absolute certainty and conviction."

East Coast Gateway Welcome Center (804-966-7450), I-64 East at mile marker 213. Provides a wealth of information, maps, and hotel reservations.

Gloucester County Chamber of Commerce (804-693-2425; www.gloucesterva chamber.org), 3562 George Washington Memorial Highway, Hayes 23072.

Gloucester County Parks, Recreation and Tourism (804-693-0014 or 804-693-2355; www.gloucesterva.info), 6467 Main Street, Gloucester 23061.

Gloucester Visitor Center (804-693-3215 or 804-693-0014; www.visitgloucester va.info), 6509 Main Street, Gloucester 23061.

Greater Williamsburg Chamber and Tourism Alliance (757-229-6511 or 800-368-6511; www.williamsburgcc.com), P.O. Box 3495, Williamsburg 23187. Provides information about the arts, and sporting and other events.

James City County Parks and Recreation (757-259-3200; www.jccegov.com), 101 Mounts Bay Road, Williamsburg 23185.

King and Queen County (804-769-5000; www.kingandqueenco.net), P.O. Box 177, King & Queen Court House 23085. Web site lists 101 points of historical interest.

Mathews County (804-725-7172; www.co.mathews.va.us), 50 Brickbat Road, Mathews 23109.

Mathews County Chamber of Commerce (804-725-9009; www.mathews chamber.org), P.O. Box 1126, Mathews 23109.

Mathews County Information Center (804-725-4BAY; www.visitmathews.com), 239 Main Street, Mathews 23109.

River Country (Middle Peninsula Tourism Council) (800-527-6360; www .visitrivercountry.org). Tourism information on the entire Middle Peninsula, including the counties of Essex, Gloucester, Mathews, Middlesex, King and Queen, and King William.

Surry County (757-294-5271; www.surryva.gov), P.O. Box 65, Surry 23883.

Surry County Chamber of Commerce (757-294-0066 or 877-290-0066; www.surrychamber.org), P.O. Box 353, Surry 23883.

Surry County Tourism (www.toursurryva.com).

Visitor Center at Colonial Williamsburg (757-229-1000 or 800-447-8679; www.history.org), 101 Visitor Center Drive/VA 132Y, Williamsburg 23185. Serves as the official information center for the entire region.

West Point (804-843-3330; www.west-point.va.us), 329 Sixth Street, West Point 23181.

West Point/Tri-Rivers Chamber of Commerce (804-843-4620; www.westpoint vachamber.com), 925 Main Street, West Point 23181.

Williamsburg (757-220-6100; www.williamsburgva.gov), 401 Lafayette Street, Williamsburg 23185.

Williamsburg Area Destination Marketing Committee (800-211-7165; www.visitwilliamsburg.com). Provides information on Williamsburg; James City County, where Williamsburg and Jamestown are located; and York County, with suggested itineraries and a page dedicated to the latest deals and packages.

Williamsburg Map (www.williamsburgmap.com). An interactive site that has coupons and is helpful for getting around.

Williamsburg Weekends (www.williamsburgweekends.com) has up-to-date event listings, coupons and discounts, and other information.

York County (757-890-3300; www.yorkcounty.gov), 224 Ballard Street, Yorktown 23690.

York County Chamber of Commerce (757-877-5920; www.yorkcountychamber va.org), 5731 George Washington Memorial Highway, Yorktown 23692.

GETTING AROUND The Historic Triangle has an excellent system of public transit available to visitors free or at very low cost.

The National Park Service (757-898-2410; www.nps.gov/colo) provides free bus service daily from mid-Mar. to Nov. 1 along several routes. The **Historic Triangle Shuttle** runs from the Colonial Williamsburg Visitor Center to Jamestown and Yorktown, along the Colonial Parkway. The Jamestown bus stops at both Historic Jamestowne and the Jamestown Settlement. The Yorktown bus stops at both the Yorktown Battlefield Visitor Center and the Yorktown Victory Center.

Once at Jamestown, visitors can ride the free **Jamestown Area Shuttle,** with continuous service between Historic Jamestowne, the Glasshouse, Jamestown Settlement, and the Jamestown Information Station parking area. Yorktown visitors can board the free **Yorktown Trolley** (www.yorkcounty.gov/tourism) for service between the Yorktown Battlefield Visitor Center and the Yorktown Victory Center, with several stops in the historic village, including Riverwalk Landing. Service on all these lines is generally 9–5, but check for current schedules.

The air-conditioned, handicapped-accessible **Williamsburg Trolleys** (www .williamsburgtransport.com), operated by Williamsburg Area Transit, run from Merchants Square to Williamsburg Shopping Center, High Street, and New Town, with stops at the College of William and Mary, seven days a week all year, 3–10 PM, with extended hours on weekends. Adults $0.50; seniors 60 and over $0.25. Exact change required.

Williamsburg Area Transit (WAT) also runs buses on regular routes with stops at various area hotels and shopping centers, connecting with Colonial Williamsburg, the Williamsburg Outlet Mall, Lee Hall in Newport News, and other area attractions. One route crosses to Surry County aboard the free ferry. Summer service is available between the **Transportation Center** (7239 Pocahontas Trail, Williamsburg 23185), Busch Gardens, and Water Country USA. Fares are $1.25 one way, plus $0.25 for transfers. Exact change required. Find route maps and schedules at the WAT Web site, www.williamsburgtransport.com, or call 757-220-5493.

MEDICAL EMERGENCY Med Express (757-564-3627; www.medx-online.com), 120 Monticello Road, Williamsburg 23185.

Med Express (757-890-6339; www.medx-online.com), Grafton Square, 4740 George Washington Memorial Highway, Yorktown 23692.

Sentara Gloucester Medical Arts (804-210-1005; www.sentara.com), 5659 Parkway Drive (off US 17), Gloucester 23061.

Sentara Williamsburg Regional Medical Center (757-984-6000; www.sentara .com), 100 Sentara Circle, Williamsburg 23188.

A center for higher education and the arts since the founding of the College of William and Mary in the late 1600s, the Historic Triangle is an especially good destination for those interested in architecture, music, and handcrafted art and decor. Visit during the Christmas season to see the famous Williamsburg-style holiday decorations adorning every door and window.

ARCHITECTURE Walking the streets of Colonial Williamsburg, you enter the 18th-century capital of Virginia, as accurately reconstructed as devoted scholarship and immense funds can achieve.

Architecturally, the star of the show is the **Wren Building** on the William and Mary campus, the oldest academic building in the United States still in use. Its design is attributed to Sir Christopher Wren, architect of St. Paul's Cathedral in London. Dated to 1695–1699, the Wren was the first structure restored by Rockefeller in Colonial Williamsburg. Two other original early Georgians, the Brafferton (1723) and the President's House (1733), flank the Wren at the head of Duke of Gloucester Street.

The octagonal **Magazine** is another 18th-century building that survived. Built in 1715 by Governor Spotswood, the structure was the sparking point of the Revolution in Virginia after then-governor Dunmore seized the citizens' gunpowder stored there on April 20, 1775.

Other original buildings in the Historic District include the 1771 Courthouse; the often overlooked 1704 Public Gaol; the 1715 Peyton Randolph House, containing some excellent original walnut paneling; and the **George Wythe House,** a classic Georgian, dating to the mid-1750s. Experts believe the Wythe to be the work of Richard Taliaferro (pronounced *tolliver*), the Virginia architect responsible for many important plantation houses, including Rosewell, Berkeley, Westover, Powhatan, and Carter's Grove. Taliaferro was George Wythe's father-in-law.

The **Prentis Store,** built in 1740, was being used as a gas station when the restoration began. **Wetherburn's Tavern,** just down the street, is one of Williamsburg's most thoroughly restored buildings, thanks to a detailed inventory taken in 1760.

Altogether, 88 original buildings have been restored to their 18th-century appearance in Colonial Williamsburg. Along with hundreds of houses, shops, taverns, and outbuildings reconstructed on their original foundations, they occupy some 301 acres, about 85 percent of Williamsburg's area in 1775.

And the reconstruction continues. **Charlton's Coffeehouse,** a gathering spot for the elite thanks to its proximity to the capitol, opened in 2009, once again serving chocolate and coffee to Williamsburg visitors. The coffeehouse, an exact reproduction built on the foundations of the 1760 original, is based on painstaking archaeological and documentary research.

Visit http://research.history.org/ewilliamsburg to see an interactive map with information on nearly every structure in the Historic District, plus links to documents exploring the history and architecture of Williamsburg.

ART MUSEUMS & VISUAL ARTS CENTERS ☂ **The Muscarelle Museum of Art** (757-221-2700; www.wm.edu/muscarelle), 603 Jamestown Road, Lamberson Hall, Williamsburg 23185. Open: Tues.–Sun. Admission: $5, free for college students and children under 12; additional charge for some special exhibitions; free parking permits available by request. The art gallery of the College of William and Mary displays important traveling exhibitions, as well as selections from the museum's large permanent collections of 17th- and 18th-century English and American art, Japanese prints, works by German expressionist Hans Grohs, and Mrs. Jean Outland Chrysler's collection of American abstract expressionists. The star of the collection is Georgia O'Keeffe's *White Flower.* Docent-led tours are offered weekends at 1 PM. Film and music series are open to the public.

Nearby in Andrews Hall, the **Andrews Gallery** (757-221-1452; www.wm.edu/as/andrewsgallery) hangs eight to 12 exhibitions a year of works by invited artists, students, and faculty.

✪ ↑ **The Museums of Colonial Williamsburg** (757-229-1000 or 800-HISTO-RY; www.history.org), 325 W. Francis Street, Williamsburg 23185. Open: Daily. Single-day museum pass that includes Bassett Hall: Adults $10, youths 6–17 $5, under six free; museum admission is included with most Colonial Williamsburg general admission passes. In the past decade, Colonial Williamsburg moved its two major museums into the same facility. Entry is through the Public Hospital of 1773, where exhibition cells show the conditions endured by early mental patients. Down an elevator, an underground concourse leads to a different world: the **Dewitt Wallace Decorative Arts Museum** and the **Abby Aldrich Rockefeller Folk Art Museum.**

The 15 galleries of the Dewitt Wallace exhibit the world's largest collection of Virginia furniture, as well as the largest collection of English pottery outside of England. Most of the pieces have exceptional provenance, tracing ownership to prominent families such as the Reveres of Boston, and the Byrd and Custis clans of Virginia. Among the many treasures are the famed Tompion's Clock made for King William III and Charles Willson Peale's portrait of George Washington as commander in chief.

The collection of Abby Aldrich Rockefeller, rich in weathervanes, American stoneware jugs, primitive paintings, toys, musical instruments, quilts, and needlework, forms the heart of the holdings of the Folk Art Museum. Special exhibits are designed especially for children.

The Museum Café and Museum Store offer refreshments and gifts. Guided introductions to the collections are offered daily, free with admission. "Teen Takes: A New Angle on Art," an hour-long audio tour, recorded for teens by teens, but of interest to all, is available free at the front desk.

This Century Art Gallery/Williamsburg Visual Art Center (757-229-4949; www.thiscenturyartgallery.org), 219 N. Boundary Street, Williamsburg 23185. Open: Tues.–Sun. Admission: Free. Currently located in a 1920 Sears Roebuck house near Merchants Square, this affiliate of the Virginia Museum of Fine Arts hangs new exhibitions monthly. An award-winning art lecture series is presented at the **Williamsburg Regional Library Theatre** (757-259-4070; www.wrl.org; 515 Scotland Street, Williamsburg 23185). The Library also hosts many concerts, including the Dewey Decibel series, Celtic and Italian film festivals, and theater performances, and has its own art gallery presenting exhibitions of painting, crafts, and photography, as well as exhibits on local and regional history. Open daily.

DANCE **Colonial Shag Club** (www.colonialshagclub.com), P.O. Box 12104, Newport News 23612. Weekly socials and lessons in dancing to beach music at local clubs, plus **Shagging on the Riverwalk** (www.yorkcounty.gov), a weekly summer series in Yorktown.

Country Bootleggers Dances (757-898-1922; www.countrybootleggers.com), 7201A George Washington Memorial Highway (US 17), Yorktown 23692. Fri.-night dances open to the public.

Orchesis (757-221-2674; www.wm.edu/theatre), Phi Beta Kappa Hall, College of William and Mary. Performance company of W&M's dance program presents original modern works.

Williamsburg Chapter USA Dance (757-273-0796; www.williamsburgusadance.com). Ballroom dances at the **Quarterpath Recreation Center** (202 Quarterpath Road, Williamsburg 23185) on the first Sat. of each month. Nonmembers welcome.

Williamsburg Heritage Dancers (757-229-1775), 710 S. Henry Street, Williamsburg 23185. English country dancing weekly at the **Newport House Bed and Breakfast** (www.newporthousebb.com). Beginners and spectators welcome.

FAMILY ATTRACTIONS ✪ ✪ ✎ ✧ **Busch Gardens Williamsburg** (800-343-7946; www.buschgardens.com), 1 Busch Gardens Boulevard, Williamsburg 23187. Open: Late Mar.–Oct. Admission: Adults $60, children (three to nine $50, under three free; seven-day Discovery ticket to both Busch Gardens and Water Country USA, $80 for ages three and up; seven-day Bounce ticket including Colonial Williamsburg, adults $123, children $102; Christmas Town $20; parking $12. When you're ready to step outside American history for a while, head over to Busch Gardens, just 3 miles from Colonial Williamsburg, and spend the day in a fanciful version of Europe, where you can journey inside a leprechaun-infested mountain, ride a dragon, or Escape from Pompeii. The park is divided into sections representing England, Scotland, France, Germany, Italy, and Ireland, and each section has its signature roller coaster thrill ride (some of the scariest in the nation), rides for younger children, and a live show; plus gift shops and restaurants themed to the country's culture. Avoid the sometimes lengthy waits by purchasing a $25 Quick Queue card, giving you priority status on all the most popular rides, including the atmospheric Curse of DarKastle special effects ride and Griffon, one of the world's tallest dive coasters.

This theme park is consistently rated the most beautiful in the country, with deep wooded ravines, lovely landscaping, and scenic architecture. Highlights include the enormous **Das Festhaus,** where you can enjoy German sausages and red cabbage washed down with Anheuser-Busch beer; the new **Sesame Street Forest of Fun,** aimed at the youngest guests; and **Wolf Valley,** where a pack of endangered gray wolves performs the only show of its kind in the world.

Busch Gardens hosts **Howl-O-Scream** weekends in Oct. and **Christmas Town** (www.christmastown.com) from Thanksgiving through Christmas.

✎ ☂ ✧ **Ripley's Believe It Or Not! Museum and 4-D Theater** (757-220-9220; www.ripleys.com or www.williamsburgripleys.com), 1735 Richmond Road, Williamsburg 23185. Open: Daily; late-night hours in summer. Admission: Combo ticket, adults $23, children $20, children under five free; add $3 for double film feature;

museum only, adults $16, children (5–12) $12, seniors $15; films only, ages five and up $12, double feature $15. Eleven galleries of oddities collected from around the world, some shocking, some beautiful, some just downright weird, range from two-headed birds and calves to art made of matchsticks or nails, shrunken heads, and painted bats, plus statues and videos of some of the world's most unusual people, none stranger than Robert Ripley himself. Through the Vortex Tunnel, the 4-D Theater takes you inside the action in films on dinosaurs and other kid favorites.

❦ ✎ **Water Country USA Water Park** (800-343-7946; www.watercountryusa .com), 176 Water Country Parkway, Williamsburg 23187. Open: Mid-May–Labor Day; hours vary. Admission: Adults $42, children (three to nine) $35, under three free; seven-day Discovery Pass to both Busch Gardens and Water Country USA, $80 for ages three and up; seven-day Bounce ticket including Colonial Williamsburg, adults $123, children $102; parking $12. More than just a place to get wet, this huge water park, the largest in the mid-Atlantic region, takes you back in time to the era when rock 'n' roll was king and surfer dudes ruled the waves. Kick back in a tube on one of the Lazy Rivers, catch a wave in Virginia's largest wave pool, zip through a flume to the piped in sounds of '50s and '60s music, or chill out on one of 1,500 lounge chairs. Lockers, bathhouse, and casual dining available, along with free life vests and inner tubes.

GALLERIES Art-cade Gallery (757-565-7424 or 800-627-8223; www.artcade online.com), 1321 Jamestown Road, Williamsburg Office Park, Williamsburg 23185. Original illustrations and reproductions, plus Mickey Sego's People of Williamsburg collection.

art café 26 (757-565-7788; www.artcafe26.com), 5107-2 Center Street, New Town, Williamsburg 23188. Owner Sibilla Dengs integrates feng shui, cutting-edge Continental cuisine, and international art in New Town's first art gallery.

A Touch of Earth (757-565-0425 or 800-865-3639; www.touchofearthgallery .com), 6580 Richmond Road, Gallery Shops, Williamsburg 23188. Award-winning gallery specializes in fine crafts by American artists.

✪ **Gallery at York Hall** (757-890-4490; www.yorkcounty.gov/tourism), 301 Main Street, Yorktown 23691. Nonprofit gallery exhibits a wide variety of works by local artists, including exquisitely carved birds, handmade quilts, music CDs, fine oils, and watercolors.

Gallery on Merchants Square (757-564-1787; www.galleryonmsq.com), 440A Duke of Gloucester Street, Williamsburg 23185. Original paintings and prints of regional historical and maritime subjects, plus heirloom antiques.

Kinks, Quirks & Caffeine (757-229-5889; www.kinksandquirks.com), 1303 Jamestown Road, Colony Square, Williamsburg 23185; and **Kinks & Quirks Contemporary Handcrafts** (757-877-8787), 327 Water Street, Riverwalk Landing, Yorktown 23690. Enjoy a specialty coffee while browsing one-of-a-kind handcrafted works by more than four hundred artisans.

✪ **Nancy Thomas Gallery** (757-259-1938 or 877-645-0601; www.nancythomas .com), two locations: 402 W. Duke of Gloucester Street, Merchants Square, Williamsburg 23185, and 145 Ballard Street, Yorktown 23690. Nationally known for her own whimsical art, Yorktown resident Nancy Thomas features outsider and visionary/self-taught artists from around the country. Frequent artist signings.

Prince George Art and Frame (757-229-7644; www.williamsburgart.com), 107
Colony Square, 1303 Jamestown Road, Williamsburg 23185. Specializing in local
original art including signed giclée prints of Colonial Williamsburg by Fred Miller,
plus fine local crafts.

Trimble Collection (757-220-3456; www.thetrimblecollection.com), 1915 Poco-
hantas Trail, Village Shops at Kingsmill, Williamsburg 23185. Art elegantly presented by master framer Tom Trimble, a specialist in the lost art of hand-painted
French matting. Trimble's work is also displayed at **Center Street Grill** (757-220-
4600; www.centerstreetgrill.com), 5101 Center Street in New Town.

Vernon Wooten Studio and Gallery (757-229-6144; www.huntprints.com), 1315
Jamestown Road, Williamsburg Office Park, Williamsburg 23185. Local artist specializes in fox hunting, Williamsburg, and carousel horse themes.

GARDENS College of William and Mary Plant Tour (757-221-5433; www.wm
.edu/as/biology/planttour), various sites on campus. Highlights of the Henley Tour
of College Plants include the Wildflower Refuge, behind Swem Library, with four
trillium species and several rare wildflowers rescued from construction sites; and a
statue of Thomas Jefferson set amid a majestic grove of oaks.

Colonial Williamsburg Gardens (757-229-1000 or 800-447-8679; http://blogs
.history.org/garden), various sites. Like every other aspect of this remarkable living-
history center, the gardens of Colonial Williamsburg are meticulously researched.
The dozens of gardens in the Historic District include herb and perennial gardens,
cottage gardens, secret gardens, the formal evergreen maze and topiary at the
Governor's Palace, the restored Colonial Revival gardens at Bassett Hall, the
Reid and **Shield learning gardens,** and the **Sunken Garden** at the Williamsburg Spa. The **Colonial Nursery** on Duke of Gloucester Street sells 18th-century
garden plants and reproduction gardening tools. Master gardeners lead garden
tours during the warmer months, with an annual Garden Symposium every spring.

Melissa's Meadow (757-564-2170; www.jccwmg.org/melissas.htm), 705 S. Henry
Street, Williamsburg 23185. Meadow of native plants on the campus of the W&M
next to the McCormack-Naglesen Tennis Center.

Native Habitat Garden (757-566-4300; www.claytonvnps.org), Stonehouse Elementary School, 5316 Rochambeau Road/VA 30, Williamsburg 23188. Garden contains more than 70 species of native plants. Visitors welcome during non–school
hours.

Williamsburg Botanical Garden at Freedom Park (757-259-5360; www
.williamsburgbotanicalgarden.org), 5535 Centerville Road, Williamsburg 23188.
The Ellipse Garden includes wildflower and patriotic meadows, wetlands, woodlands, a fernery, and a butterfly garden.

HISTORIC ATTRACTIONS AND SITES

Williamsburg

Bassett Hall (757-229-1000 or 800-HISTORY; www.history.org), 522 E. Francis
Street, Williamsburg 23187. Open: Daily except Wed. Admission: Adults $10,
youths 6–17 $5, under six free, for single-day museum pass that also includes
entrance to the Dewitt Wallace Decorative Arts Museum and the Abby Aldrich
Rockefeller Folk Art Museum; admission is included with most Colonial Williams-

burg general admission passes. This two-story farmhouse, built in the mid-18th century, served as the home of John D. Rockefeller Jr. and his wife, Abby, during the 1930s and '40s while the restoration of Colonial Williamsburg was under way. The house is decorated much as they left it, accented by 125 charming pieces of folk art, Mrs. Rockefeller's favorites from her collection. The property also includes a teahouse and original smokehouse, kitchen, and dairy, plus extensive Colonial Revival gardens.

✪ **Bruton Parish Church** (757-229-2891; www.brutonparish.org), 200 Duke of Gloucester Street, Williamsburg 23185. Open: Mon.–Sat. 10–4, Sun. 12:30–4:30. Admission: Free. One of the oldest buildings in Williamsburg, the Bruton Parish Church dates to 1715 and has an unusual cruciform design, attributed to Governor Alexander Spotswood. A gallery, added in 1718 for the students of William and Mary, still displays their carved graffiti. The church welcomes visitors daily, except during weekday worship services, which visitors are invited to join. Volunteer guides are on hand to share the church's history. A gift shop is located in the Parish House (757-220-1489; 331 Duke of Gloucester Street). Visitors are also welcome at the free Candlelight Concerts, held every Sat. at 8 PM, and most Tues. and Thurs. evenings.

College of William and Mary (757-221-4000; www.wm.edu), 116 Jamestown Road, Williamsburg 23185. Open: Daily. Admission: Free. Founded in 1693, the College of William and Mary is the United States' second-oldest educational institution and played its part in the nation's history. George Washington received his surveyor's license from the college. Presidents Thomas Jefferson, James Monroe, and John Tyler all received their baccalaureate degrees here. The Phi Beta Kappa society was founded here in 1776.

Construction began on W&M's oldest building, now called the Sir Christopher Wren Building, between 1695 and 1699. It served as a hospital for the French during the Battle of Yorktown and for the Confederates during the Civil War. An exhibition on the first floor of the Wren explores the building's history.

A bronze statue of Norborne Berkeley, Baron de Botetourt, friend and patron of the college during his tenure as royal governor (1768–1770), stands in the College Yard. He is buried in the Wren Chapel vault, and a 1773 marble statue of him, which formerly stood in the yard, can be found in the Botetourt Gallery of the college's Swem Library.

Behind the Wren, buildings of the Old Campus surround the **Sunken Garden.** Just beyond lies the **Crim Dell Bridge,** voted one of the most romantic spots on any college campus. Bronze statues and other art dot the grounds, making for a pleasant stroll. Refreshments from sushi to subs are available at the Campus Center and the Sadler Center.

✪ ✿ ♿ **Colonial Williamsburg** (757-229-1000 or 800-HISTORY; www.history .org), 101A Visitor Center Drive (VA 132Y), Williamsburg 23185. Open: Daily, including holidays. Admission: Varies with season; generally adults $25–35, youths 6–17 $12–17, for single-day tickets; two-day tickets, including entrance to the Governor's Palace, $5–10 more; children under six free. Liberty passes, good for one year; special packages and discounts for Williamsburg resort guests; and multiattraction passes available. Begin your visit to Colonial Williamsburg at the visitors center, where you'll find plenty of free parking, dining and shopping, ticket sales, and an introductory movie, *Williamsburg—The Story of a Patriot.* From here, catch a shuttle bus to the historic area or follow a pedestrian pathway that leads past **Great Hope Plantation,** where interpreters raise heirloom crops and construct buildings using period tools. Between 20 and 40 historic buildings are open for touring by pass holders on a typical day, plus shops and taverns, which are open to the general public. Union Jack flags hang outside open buildings.

Your admission pass allows you to ride the shuttles for free well into the evening. On their route they run close to all of Colonial Williamsburg's main attractions, and they are wheelchair accessible.

Pass holders can also take the highly recommended Orientation Tour, a 30-minute walk providing an overview of the Historic District and the day's programs, dining, and shopping options. Pick up a *Colonial Williamsburg This Week* map and program guide for a listing of tours and performances available during your visit. Get tickets for other tours, many of them free for pass holders, or sign up for a carriage ride, at the Lumber House ticket office. These are offered only on a same-day reservation system, so make your plans early in the day.

Highlights of a visit include a tour of the **Capitol,** a trial at the **Courthouse,** and visits to the Magazine and the museums. Historic trades demonstrations include a blacksmith, brickmaker, wigmaker, print shop, and post office, where your mail will receive an 18th-century postmark.

At the **Raleigh Tavern,** where the Founding Fathers plotted rebellion over punch and ale, you can participate in dancing and games. Pass holders can also visit the **Randolph House** and the **Wythe House,** home of Thomas Jefferson's mentor and reputedly haunted.

Sitting at the head of the Palace Green, the **Governor's Palace,** an ornate three-story Georgian, is a faithful replica of the building occupied by seven royal governors, as well as Patrick Henry and Thomas Jefferson, the first two governors of the independent state of Virginia. A two-day or plus ticket is currently required to tour the palace and the elegant formal gardens behind.

Each day, Duke of Gloucester Street becomes the setting for **Revolutionary City,** an exciting series of living-history scenes re-creating events in Williamsburg before and during the American Revolution. General and Mrs. Washington, Lafayette, Cornwallis, and many other historical personages—some famous, some ordinary townsfolk—take part.

Automobiles are not permitted on Duke of Gloucester and Nicholson streets until after the historic buildings close for the day. Several paid parking lots and a parking deck are located along Henry Street near Merchants Square.

Freedom Park (757-259-5360; www.jccegov.com), 5535 Centerville Road, Williamsburg 23188. Open: Daily. Admission: Free. This county park is the site of the 1781 Revolutionary War Battle of Spencer's Ordinary as well as one of the earliest free black settlements in America. Three historically accurate cabins are furnished with items from the 1803–1850 period.

☀ ᕱ **Historic Jamestowne** (757-229-1733 or 757-898-2400; www.nps.gov/colo or www.historicjamestowne.org), 1368 Colonial Parkway, Jamestown 23081. Open: Daily, except Thanksgiving, Christmas, and New Year's days. Admission: $10 for a seven-day pass that includes Yorktown Battlefield; children under 16 free. Ranger-led and self-guided tours visit the archaeological traces of the Olde and New

A HORSE–DRAWN COACH TOUR IS ONE OF THE MOST POPULAR WAYS TO SEE COLONIAL WILLIAMSBURG.

Townes, including the recently discovered 1607 triangular fort. Highlights include statues of John Smith and Pocahontas; the **Voorhees Archaearium,** a museum using forensic techniques to interpret skeletons and other archaeological finds; the **Jamestown Memorial Church,** incorporating a 1690 tower, the only surviving 17th-century structure; and the remains of Confederate earthworks. A new **visitors center** offers an introductory film and exhibits on Jamestown's history. Meals are available in the **Dale House Cafe** overlooking the James River. The 5-mile **Island Drive** gives a glimpse of the scenery the first settlers faced on their arrival. Near the park entrance, don't miss the **Jamestown Glasshouse,** where craftsmen blow glass, one of the colony's first industries, using traditional techniques. Samples of the lovely green glass are for sale.

✪ ✎ ♿ ➷ **Jamestown Settlement** (757-253-4838 or 888-593-4682; www.historyisfun.org), 2218 Jamestown Road 31 S., Williamsburg 23185. Open: Daily, except Christmas and New Year's days. Admission: Adults $14, children 6–12 $6.50; combination tickets with Yorktown Victory Center, adults $19.25, children $9.25; under six free. An extensive museum contains excellent exhibits and a documentary film tracing the English, African, and Native American roots of the cultures that converged in Jamestown. Outside, costumed reenactors go about their daily tasks in a typical Powhatan village, in a re-creation of the first English fort with thatch-roofed buildings and wooden palisade, and in riverfront fields where tobacco is the major crop. The three brightly painted ships, *Susan Constant,* *Godspeed,* and *Discovery,* replicas of the fleet that brought the first settlers across the Atlantic, can be boarded at docks along the James River. Free guided tours are offered daily; café and gift shop on-site.

↑ **The Manor at Powhatan Plantation** (757-220-1200; www.powhatan plantation.com), 3601 Ironbound Road, Williamsburg 23188. Open: Daily. Admission: Free. Built in 1735 by Virginia's most renowned colonial architect, Richard Taliaferro (pronounced *tolliver*), as his personal residence, this three-story brick Georgian is a classic of its kind. Beautifully restored inside and out, and the centerpiece of the Historic Powhatan Plantation time-share resort, the manor is open to the public for tours. Sign in at the security gate. The **Kitchen at Powhatan** (www.kitchenatpowhatan .com), located in one of the outbuildings, serves gourmet meals on weekends.

✔ ♂ ↝ **Presidents Park** (757-259-1121 or 800-588-4327; www.presidents park.org), 211 Water Country Parkway, Williamsburg 23185. Open: Daily. Admission: Adults $12.75, children $8. Unique outdoor museum dedicated to the U.S. presidency displays huge, 16- to 18-foot-tall busts of each of the presidents created by internationally known sculptor David Adickes. Each bust is accompanied by informative signage telling of events during the president's term and many interesting facts. Other exhibits include re-creations of gowns worn by the First Ladies, a replica of the Oval Office, and a special section on White House pets. A free summer evening concert series and birthday celebrations for each president are among the special events.

Redoubt Park (757-259-3760; www.williamsburgva.gov), Quarterpath Road, Williamsburg 23185. This 22-acre park preserves two of the redoubts constructed by soldiers and slaves along the right flank of the Confederates' Williamsburg Line during the Peninsula Campaign of 1862.

Yorktown

Custom House (804-642-7447; www.comtedegrasse-dar.org), 410 Main Street, Yorktown 23690. Open: Sun. afternoons in summer and fall, or by appointment. Admission: Free. This large brick building, built circa 1720 and recently determined by the National Park Service to be the oldest building in Yorktown, was the first custom house in America. It is on the National Register of Historic Places and owned by the Comte de Grasse Chapter of the Daughters of the American Revolution, which operates a museum and gift shop on the property.

Grace Episcopal Church (757-898-3261; www.gracechurchyorktown.org), 111 Church Street, Yorktown 23690. Open: Daily. Admission: Free. Built in 1697 of native marl, this ancient—and reputedly haunted—church was the site of the first confirmation service in Virginia. Among the graves in the atmospheric old churchyard is that of Thomas Nelson Jr., a signer of the Declaration of Independence. The church and a book and gift shop in the Parish House are open daily.

○ **Watermen's Museum** (757-887-2641; www.watermens.org), 309 Water Street, Yorktown 23690. Open: Tues.–Sun., Apr.–Nov.; Sat.–Sun., Dec.–Mar. Admission: Adults $4, students K–12 $1. Museum on the Riverwalk preserves the traditions of fishing, crabbing, oystering, and clamming in Chesapeake Bay. Exhibits include a lovely wood-paneled room full of ship models, and examples of boats used in the bay from the log canoes of the Native Americans to the classic deadrise still

REENACTORS BRING HISTORY TO LIFE ON THE STREETS OF WILLIAMSBURG DURING THE DAILY REVOLUTIONARY CITY PROGRAMS.

popular among commercial fishermen. Classes in nautical lore are offered in the boathouse, and special events are held on the deck and pier facing the river.

York County Historical Museum (757-898-4910 or 757-890-3508; www .yorkcounty.gov/ychm), 301 Main Street, Yorktown 23690. Open: Tues.– Sun. Admission: Free. Museum on the lower level of York Hall displays artifacts from every era of local history, from Native American tools to exhibits on the USS *Yorktown* and the Naval Weapons Station. York Hall, a modern interpretation of a 1733 courthouse, also contains a gallery of local art and a visitor information area. More exhibits are housed in the **Museum on Main** (408 Main Street), open seasonally.

✪ ♿ **Yorktown Battlefield** (757-898-2410; www.nps.gov/colo), Colonial Parkway, P.O. Box 210, Yorktown 23690. Open: Daily, except Thanksgiving, Christmas, and New Year's days. Admission: $10 for a seven-day pass that includes Historic Jamestowne; children under 16 free. Occupying the actual battlefield where the combined French and American forces defeated the English under Cornwallis in 1781, the park's visitors center offers an introductory film and many exhibits, including campaign tents used by General Washington. Several restored houses, including the **Moore House,** on a bluff overlooking the York River, and the **Nelson House,** on Main Street, are open for viewing. Two driving tours cross the battlefield, the 7-mile **Battlefield Tour Road,** past original redoubts and Surrender Field, and the 9-mile **Encampment Tour Road,** past the site of Washington's headquarters. The Village of Yorktown contains a number of restored and reconstructed buildings, plus the Yorktown Victory Monument and the interesting **Poor Potter's Archaeological Site,** an ongoing exploration of an illegal salt-glazed pottery factory, one of the largest in the colonies.

CAPT. JOHN SMITH STILL KEEPS WATCH AT HISTORIC JAMESTOWNE.

THE JAMESTOWN SETTLEMENT INCLUDES THE RE-CREATION OF A NATIVE AMERICAN VILLAGE.

KID'S CULTURE ✏ ⛵ **Dolls of Diane Gift Shop and Display** (757-345-0029 or 888-202-3518; www.dollsofdiane.com), 2850 Sandy Bay Road, Williamsburg 23185. Mary Diane Dawson, a lifelong doll collector, shares her huge collection of dolls from around the world. Fee for exhibit area.

✏ ⛵ **Williamsburg Doll Factory** (757-564-9703 or 800-609-5727; www.dollfactory.com), 7441 Richmond Road, Williamsburg 23188. Home of the Lady Anne dolls and other nationally known collectible dolls. Tour the factory to see dolls being made or bring your doll to be autographed by designer Margaret Anne Rothwell.

✏ ♿ ⛵ **Yorktown Victory Center** (757-253-4838 or 888-593-4682; www.historyisfun.org), 260 Water Street, Yorktown 23690. Open: Daily, except Christmas and New Year's days. Admission: Adults $9.25, children 6–12 $5; combination tickets with Jamestown Settlement, adults $19.25, children $9.25; under six free. Museum and living-history center vividly tell the story of the colonies' journey to independence. Indoor galleries and a film introduce the ideas that led to the Declaration of Independence, a radical document in its time, and people from many walks of life tell in their own words how the Revolution affected them. Artifacts recovered from the British fleet scuttled in Yorktown harbor and exhibits on the American, French, British, and German forces bring the three-week siege to life. Outside, costumed reenactors lead visitors through a Continental Army camp and demonstrate musket fire.

THE MANOR AT POWHATAN PLANTATION, DESIGNED BY ARCHITECT RICHARD TALIAFERRO, IS CONSIDERED ONE OF THE BEST EXAMPLES OF THE CLASSIC GEORGIAN STYLE.

LIBRARIES ⬆ "ℹ" **Earl Gregg Swem Library** (757-221-3072; www.swem.wm.edu), 1 Landrum Drive, Williamsburg 23187. W&M's Swem Library treasures include manuscripts by alumni Thomas Jefferson, James Monroe, John Marshall, and John Tyler; rare books on Virginiana, printing, and papermaking; the Wark collection of fore-edge paintings; and memorabilia of the late Chief Justice Warren E. Burger. iPod tours available. Free Wi-Fi for guests for one 24-hour period per week.

John D. Rockefeller Jr. Library (757-565-8510; www.research.history.org), 313 First Street, Williamsburg 23185. One of the world's definitive collections on the history and culture of colonial British America, the American Revolution, and the early United States. Open weekdays. The **Department of Archaeological Research** (757-220-7334) is open by appointment Mon.–Fri. Tours of the Archeological Laboratory, offered to the public on Tues., include a look at artifacts from recent excavations. Reservations required.

Williamsburg Regional Library (757-259-4040; www.wrl.org), 515 Scotland Street, Williamsburg 23185. Library close to the Historic District offers a wide range of programs, including free concerts, film series, theatrical performances, art exhibits, a poetry series, and programming for children and teens. Apply for a free temporary library card to use computers with Internet access. The **James City County Library** (757-259-7753; www.wrl.org; 7770 Croaker Road, Williamsburg 23188) also has free public computer terminals but does not require a library card or reservations.

THE ENORMOUS BUSTS AT PRESIDENTS PARK EACH OFFER FASCINATING TIDBITS OF UNITED STATES HISTORY.

MUSIC AND CONCERT SERIES ✪
Bruton Parish Church Music Performances (757-229-2891; www.brutonparish.org), 200 Duke of Gloucester Street, Williamsburg 23185. Candlelight Concerts featuring instrumental and choral groups from around the world are held at 8 PM every Sat., and most Tues. and Thurs. evenings. Monthly Peter Pelham Concerts, often featuring early instruments, are preceded by a dinner. Free admission to concerts; dinners are reservation only and require a fee.

Chamber Music Society of Williamsburg (757-229-2901; www.chambermusicwilliamsburg.org), Williamsburg Regional Library Arts Center Theater, 515 Scotland Street, Williamsburg, 23185.

THE DOUBLE-ENDED SHARPIE IS ONE OF THE LOCAL BOATS ON DISPLAY AT THE WATERMEN'S MUSEUM ON THE YORKTOWN WATERFRONT.

College of William and Mary's Ewell Concert Series and Lively Arts Series (757-221-2674; www.wm.edu/music), Ewell Concert Hall and other venues. Most performances are free and open to the public.

✐ ♈ **Dean Shostak's Crystal Concert** (757-565-8670 or 800-588-3326; www.crystalconcert.com), Kimball Theatre, 428 Duke of Gloucester Street, Williamsburg 23185. Concerts feature the glass armonica, invented by Benjamin Franklin, as well as rare and antique glass instruments from around the world.

Fifes and Drums of York Town (757-898-9418; www.fifes-and-drums.org), various venues. Young musicians wearing 18th-century regimental uniforms perform regularly at Yorktown attractions.

Friday Nights Under the Veranda Lights (757-645-2000; www.colonialheritageclub.com), Colonial Heritage Golf Club, 6500 Arthur Hills Drive, Williamsburg 23188. Free concerts on Fri. evenings, Apr.–Aug.

Lake Matoaka Summer Concert Series (www.matoakasummerconcerts.com), Lake Matoaka Amphitheatre, Williamsburg. Held every other Fri. night next to the lake on the W&M campus.

Live Off Five! Concert Series (757-220-6830; www.wuu.org), 3051 Ironbound Road, Williamsburg 23185. All are welcome at this concert series presented by the Williamsburg Unitarian Universalists.

Merchants Square Concerts (757-259-0209; www.merchantssquare.org). Summer Breeze Concert series in July and Aug., plus holiday music in Dec.

✪ **Riverwalk Concert Series** (757-890-3500; www.riverwalklanding.com). Free Yorktown concerts include the winter **Cabin Fever Concert Series;** summer's Fri.-night **Shagging on the Riverwalk;** and the jazzy **Rhythms on the Riverwalk,** held in the fall.

Toano Acoustic Jam (757-566-1910), Toano Fire House, 3135 Forge Road, Toano 23168. Session on the last Fri. of the month is open to all who enjoy singing or playing acoustic music. Donation benefits the firehouse.

Virginia Symphony Orchestra Classics at St. Bede Concert Series (757-892-6366; www.virginiasymphony.org), 3686 Ironbound Road/SR 615, Williamsburg 23188. Classical music at St. Bede Catholic Church (www.bedeva.org).

Williamsburg Baptist Church Concert Series (757-229-1217; www.williamsburgbaptist.com), 227 Richmond Road, Williamsburg 23185.

Williamsburg Choral Guild (757-220-1808; www.williamsburgchoralguild.org), P.O. Box 1864, Williamsburg 23187. Chorus with more than 80 voices hosts "Summer Sings" open to all.

Williamsburg Consort (757-229-5337; www.wmbgconsort.org). Annual Sept. symphonic band festival hosts ensemble concerts and swing band dances.

Williamsburg Field Musick (757-253-1796; www.fifeanddrum.info), Williamsburg General Store and other venues. Fife and drum group in regimental uniforms plays at many regional venues.

Williamsburg Music Club (www.williamsburgmusicclub.org), Lewis Hall, Bruton Parish Church, Williamsburg. Meetings and concerts on the third Wed. of the month, Sept.–May, are free and open to the public.

Williamsburg Symphonia (757-229-9859; www.williamsburgsymphonia.org), Kimball Theatre (428 Duke of Gloucester Street, Williamsburg) and other venues. Professional chamber orchestra performs three masterworks concerts each year.

✪ **Wren Chapel Historical Concerts** (757-229-2891; www.brutonparish.org), Christopher Wren Chapel, College of William and Mary. Weekly organ concerts of historical music on Sat. at 10 AM. Free.

NIGHTLIFE 🍸 **Bourbon Street Bar & Grille** (757-229-4100; www.clarionhotel.com), 351 York Street, Clarion Hotel Historic District, Williamsburg 23185. Dance club with karaoke, DJs on the weekends, big-screen TV, pool tables, and darts.

🍸 **Buon Amici Ristorante and Pizzeria** (757-220-8188; www.buonamiciwilliamsburg.com), 5201 Center Street, Williamsburg 23188. Live jazz and dancing several nights a week on a heated patio in New Town.

🍸 **Chez Trinh Vietnamese Cuisine** (757-253-1888; www.chez-trinh.com), 157 Monticello Avenue, Williamsburg 23185. Live folk, gospel, and Korean music accompany a pan-Asian menu.

🍸 **The Corner Pocket** (757-220-0808; www.thecornerpocket.us), 4805 Courthouse Street, Williamsburg 23188. Upscale billiards spot in New Town books local and national blues and zydeco bands.

🍸 **J. M. Randalls Classic American Grill and Tavern** (757-259-0406; www.jmrandalls.com), 4854 Longhill Road, Williamsburg 23188. Blues, jazz, and rock bands most nights. Free Wi-Fi; happy hour.

The Library Tavern (757-229-1012), 1330 Richmond Road, Williamsburg 23185. Student favorite serves pizza and subs named for literary icons; occasional music; open late.

🍸 **Second Street—An American Bistro** (757-220-2286; www.secondst.com),

140 Second Street, Williamsburg 23185. Upscale bar with outdoor patio and fire pits. Free Wi-Fi; great burgers.

Williamsburg Inn Regency Room (757-229-2141 or 800-HISTORY; www .colonialwilliamsburgresort.com), 136 E. Francis Street, Williamsburg 23185. Music accompanies elegant dinners of culinary classics; dancing on Fri. and Sat.

✪ ♉ **Williamsburg Lodge Lounge** (757-229-2141 or 800-HISTORY; www .colonialwilliamsburgresort.com), 310 S. England Street, Williamsburg 23185. Cozy lounge has interesting bar menus and live music.

THEATER College of William and Mary Theatre Department (757-221-2674; www.wm.edu/theatre), Phi Beta Kappa Hall, 601 Jamestown Road, Williamsburg 23185. Student productions range from musical theater to Shakespeare.

CrossWalk Community Church (757-258-2825; www.crosswalk.cc), 7575 Richmond Road, Williamsburg 23188. Christian-themed theatricals presented in the former Music Theatre of Williamsburg.

♬ **Haunted Dinner Theater** (757-258-2500; www.wmbgdinnertheater.com), Capt. George's Restaurant, 5363 Richmond Road, Williamsburg 23188. Families enjoy haunting a 71-item all-you-can-eat buffet while participating in a spooky interactive performance. Seasonal.

Mystery Dinner Playhouse (888-471-4802; www.mysterydinner.com), Clarion Inn & Suites, 5351 Richmond Road, Williamsburg 23188. Four-course dinner accompanies a hilarious evening of murder most foul. Year-round performances by a professional cast.

Virginia Premiere Theatre (866-430-1630; www.vptheatre.com), Kimball Theatre, 428 Duke of Gloucester Street, Merchants Square, Williamsburg 23185. Professional theater company specializes in new play development and world premieres.

Virginia Shakespeare Festival (757-221-2674; www.wm.edu/vsf), Phi Beta Kappa Hall, 601 Jamestown Road, College of William and Mary, Williamsburg 23185. For more than 30 years, W&M has hosted professional productions of Shakespeare classics for six weeks every summer, plus weeklong summer camps for young actors ages nine to 17.

Williamsburg Players (757-229-0431; www.williamsburgplayers.org), 200 Hubbard Lane, Williamsburg 23187. Community theater group founded in 1957.

✴ To Do

While the majority of visitors come to the Williamsburg area for its historic sights, the region also offers a wide range of outdoor recreation options—including exceptional biking and kayaking, a nationally known fishery for giant blue catfish, and some extraordinary golf—that provides a welcome diversion from educational activities.

BEACHES Although far removed from the oceanfront, the shores of the York and James rivers, here still salty and subject to tides, provide pleasant beaches for sunning, sand castle building, and swimming.

On the Yorktown Waterfront, located at the bottom of the bluff that edges the north side of town, you'll find **Yorktown Beach** (757-830-3500; www.york county.gov; Water Street, Yorktown), a nice 2-acre sandy strand backed by a 10-acre grass picnic area. Restrooms and showers open seasonally; no lifeguards on duty. Free parking. The area also has several waterfront restaurants, a fishing pier, and boat docks. The beach area has a magnificent view of the George P. Coleman Bridge, leading to Gloucester Point and the Middle Peninsula, where **Gloucester Point Beach Park** (804-642-9474; www.gloucesterva.info; 1255 Greate Road, Gloucester Point 23061) faces Yorktown Beach across the river.

On the James River, **Jamestown Beach Park** (757-259-5360; www.jccegov.com; 2205 Jamestown Road, Williamsburg 23185) is open year-round during daylight hours with a small sandy beach, picnic tables, and grills. Free.

BICYCLING The Historic Triangle's rolling terrain, based on ancient dunes, makes for some challenging rides. A brochure of recommended bike routes can be downloaded from the Web site of the **Greater Williamsburg Chamber and Tourism Alliance** (757-229-6511; www.williamsburgcc.com; 421 N. Boundary Street, Williamsburg 23187).

The **Williamsburg Area Bicyclists** (www.wabonline.org) lead on-the-road group bike rides nearly every weekend, including special rides for families and an annual **Pedal the Parkway** event in May. Road racers can contact **James River Velo Sport** (www.jrvs.org) for fast-paced rides, races, and training opportunities. The **Peninsula Bicycling Association** (www.pbabicycling.org) conducts rides for all abilities on the Peninsula and beyond.

For mountain bikers, visit the Web site of the **Eastern Virginia Mountain Biking Association** (www.evma.org) for information on group rides, trail conditions, and volunteer opportunities.

BEST BIKE ROUTES One of the favorite roads to bike is the **Colonial Parkway** (757-898-2410; www.nps.gov/colo), a 24-mile route that runs from Historic Jamestowne to Yorktown Battlefield, passing under Colonial Williamsburg in a tunnel that bikes must bypass. Although bicycles share the road with cars, the speed limit is 45 mph maximum along this scenic route. Designed to look like a colonial-era roadway, the three-lane parkway is paved with a cobble aggregate, which may make for a bumpy ride.

At the Jamestown end of the parkway, the scenic **Island Loop Drive,** one-way paved loops of 3 or 5 miles open to bicycles, hikers, and motor vehicles, makes an easy family ride.

The Yorktown Battlefield has two tour roads popular for biking, the 7-mile **Battlefield Tour Road** and the 9-mile **Encampment Tour Road.** Maps are available at the Battlefield Visitor Center. An extension leads to the campground and bike trails of Newport News Park, where bike rentals are available.

The new **Virginia Capital Trail** (www.virginiacapitaltrail.org; P.O. Box 17966, Richmond 23226), a 55-mile paved multiuse path connecting the former and current Virginia capitals of Williamsburg, Jamestown, and Richmond, follows scenic VA 5, the John Tyler Highway. The trail is complete from Jamestown to the Chickahominy River, a distance of 8 miles. Parking is available behind Jamestown High School (3751 John Tyler Highway, Williamsburg 23185), where a spur connects

HISTORICAL ENTERTAINMENTS

✪ ⚓ **Chowning's Tavern Gambols** (757-229-2141 or 800-HISTORY; www.colonialwilliamsburgresort.com), 109 E. Duke of Gloucester Street, Williamsburg 23185. Enjoy old-style ales and porters, hard ciders, mint juleps, colonial punch, and homemade draft root beer during an evening of 18th-century entertainment featuring balladeers playing period instruments, sing-alongs, and games of the day. From 5 to 8 PM, the entertainment is geared toward families, taking a more bawdy turn from 8 to closing.

⚓ **Colonial Evening Programs** (757-229-1000 or 800-HISTORY; www.history.org), various venues. Participate in a grand ball at the Governor's Palace, listen to concerts ranging from harpsichord music to African drumming, witness trials for witchcraft or piracy conducted by candlelight, or take a lantern tour of historic buildings to look for ghosts. Many different evening programs are offered nightly. Advance tickets are required and can be bought at any ticket sales location or by phone.

Kimball Theatre (757-565-8588 or 800-447-8679; www.kimballtheatre.com), 428 Duke of Gloucester Street, Merchants Square, Williamsburg 23185. Restored 1933 movie palace, built by John D. Rockefeller Jr. in the style of his Radio City Music Hall, hosts live music, dance, and theater performances; an 18th-century play series; and indie films.

with the east end of the trail, and at **Chickahominy Riverfront Park** (757-258-5020; www.jccegov.com/recreation; 1350 John Tyler Highway, Williamsburg 23185) at the western end, where parking, as well as camping, boat rentals, and swimming, are available. Another 7-mile section of the trail has been completed beginning at **Charles City County Visitor Center and Courthouse** (804-652-4701; www.charlescity.org; 10760 Courthouse Road, Charles City 23030), running past many of the plantations and other historic sites.

BIKE SHOPS AND RENTALS BikeBeat (757-229-0096; www.bikebeatonline.com), 4640-9B Monticello Avenue, Monticello Marketplace, Williamsburg 23188. Weekly rides include mountain bike rides for women. Download route maps online.

Bikes Unlimited (757-229-4620; www.bikewilliamsburg.com), 141 Monticello Avenue, Williamsburg Shopping Center, Williamsburg 23185. Group rides begin near the Historic District. Rentals available.

Williamsburg Lodge and **Woodlands Hotel** (757-253-2277 or 800-HISTORY; www.colonialwilliamsburgresort.com). Williamsburg Lodge: 310 S. England Street, Williamsburg 23185; Woodlands Hotel: 105 Visitor Center Drive, Williamsburg 23185. Rental bikes available.

BIKING AND MOUNTAIN BIKING TRAILS Freedom Park (757-259-5360; www.jccegov.com/recreation), 5535 Centerville Road, Williamsburg 23188. More than 5 miles of scenic mountain bike trails wind through historical sites and forests, with some challenging climbs, twists, and turns.

𝒮 **New Quarter Park** (757-890-3500; www.yorkcounty.gov), 1000 Lakeshead Drive, Williamsburg 23185. Challenging **Redoubt Run** mountain bike trail is more than 7 miles long, with several technical trail features. A shorter multiuse trail is good for family biking.

Upper County Park (757-566-1451; www.jccegov.com/recreation), 180 Leisure Road, Toano 23168. Four-mile mountain bike trail with some challenging features.

Wahrani Trails (804-966-8502; www.co.new-kent.va.us), off I-64 at exit 220, near West Point. Extensive trail system in New Kent County for mountain biking, hiking, and jogging.

Warhill Sports Complex (757-259-5360; www.jccegov.com/recreation), 5700 Warhill Trail, Williamsburg 23188. Gravel multiuse trail winds through mature forests and streams.

York River State Park (757-566-3036; www.dcr.virginia.gov), 5526 Riverview Road, Williamsburg 23188. Six bicycle trails in the park include two exclusively for mountain bikes: the 6-mile **Marl Ravine Trail** for advanced riders, and the less difficult 2-mile **Laurel Glen Trail.**

BOATS & BOATING Bracketed by the York and James rivers, with plenty of marshy streams, lakes, and ponds in between, the Historic Triangle offers families and anglers many opportunities to get out on the water.

The lovely **Chickahominy River,** rich in history, defines the northern section of this region. John Smith explored the Chick, as the locals call it, in 1607, thinking to find a passage to the Pacific. Instead, it led him into the heart of Powhatan's

YORKTOWN BEACH IS A POPULAR AND SCENIC SPOT TO RELAX.

empire and to his fateful meeting with Pocahontas. Running some 237 miles before it meets the James, the Chick becomes a broad river in its lower reaches, lined with bald cypress and heron rookeries. Upstream, it passes through hardwood forests, farms, and wetlands. Several marinas located along its banks make for good point-to-point excursions.

Boat Rentals

✪ **Chickahominy Riverfront Park** (757-258-5020; www.jccegov.com), 1350 John Tyler Highway, Williamsburg 23185. Kayaks, canoes, and motorboats rent by the hour or the day.

Kingsmill Resort Marina (757-253-3919; www.kingsmill.com), 1010 Kingsmill Road, Williamsburg 23185. Paddleboats, kayaks, jon boats with electric motors, and fishing equipment available for daily rental.

Little Creek Reservoir (757-566-1702; www.jccegov.com), 180 Lakeview Drive, Toano 23168. Rental canoes, kayaks, and jon boats.

Waller Mill Reservoir (757-259-3778; www.williamsburgva.gov), SR 645/Airport Road, Williamsburg 23188. Canoes, kayaks, pedal boats, rowboats, and electric motors for rent.

York River State Park (757-566-3036; www.dcr.virginia.gov), 5526 Riverview Road, Williamsburg 23188. Paddleboats, jon boats, canoes, and kayaks can be rented for use on Woodstock Pond. Canoes and kayaks are available for rent at Taskinas Creek. Seasonal.

Canoeing & Kayaking

Paddle enthusiasts can choose to explore the York, the James, their many tributary streams, or one of the area's numerous lakes.

In York County, a map of suggested water trails can be downloaded from the Parks and Recreation Web site: www.yorkcounty.gov/parksandrec. Launch at **Back Creek Park** to circumnavigate Goodwin Island, an extensive marsh that is part of the Virginia Birding and Wildlife Trail. Yorktown's **Riverwalk Landing** (www.riverwalklanding.com), with its many dining and entertainment options, is a favorite destination when paddling on the York River.

One of the most popular paddles on this section of the James is the circumnavigation of historic Jamestown Island. The put-in at **Powhatan Creek Park and Blueway** (757-259-5360; www.jccegov.com; 1831 Jamestown Road, Williamsburg 23185) leads you directly downstream to the river. Paddle a short distance upstream to see the replica ships at Jamestown Settlement, then head south past the statue of John Smith and loop around the island. You can also paddle upstream from the put-in; Powhatan Creek is listed on the Natural Resources Inventory as the most biodiverse creek on the Peninsula.

Another nice paddle launches from **Chickahominy Riverfront Park** (757-258-5020; www.jccegov.com; 1350 John Tyler Highway, Williamsburg 23185). The shores of the lower Chick, one of the least spoiled rivers in the region, are dense with bald cypress and home to many birds, including ospreys, bald eagles, and great blue herons.

The launch areas at **New Quarter Park** (757-890-3500; www.yorkcounty.gov; 1000 Lakeshead Drive, Williamsburg 23185) give access to historic Queens Creek, a marshy waterway that is home to a great blue heron rookery.

Close to Williamsburg's Historic District, you can put in at **College Landing Park** (757-259-3760; www.williamsburgva.gov; S. Henry Street), just down the street from W&M, for a paddle on College Creek, a marshy waterway with many birds. Best at high tide.

The following includes canoe and kayak outfitters in the region:

🛶 **Bay Trails Outfitters** (804-725-0626 or 888-725-7225; www.baytrails.com), 2221 Bethel Beach Road/SR 609, Onemo 23130. Mathews County outfitter leads numerous themed kayak trips across the region, including picnic, twilight, full moon, stargazing, and fireworks tours, even a paddle to pick blueberries at a local farm. Two-day Kids Kayak Camp.

Chesapeake Experience (757-890-0502; www.chesapeakeexperience.org), 103 Industry Drive, Yorktown 23693. Naturalists lead ecopaddles to Goodwin Island, and Queens, Powhatan, and Chickahominy creeks. Five-day camps for children and teens.

York River State Park (757-566-3036; www.dcr.virginia.gov), 5526 Riverview Road, Williamsburg 23188. Guided paddle experiences on Taskinas Creek and the York River.

Marinas and Docks

James and Chickahominy Rivers: **Colonial Harbor Marina** (804-966-5523; www.colonialharbor.com), 14910 Marina Road, Lanexa 23089. Family-run marina on the Chickahominy with boat ramp, docking, seasonal restaurant with weekend entertainment.

Jamestown Beach Yacht Basin (757-229-8309; www.jccegov.com), 2080 Jamestown Road, Williamsburg 23185. Marina near historic Jamestown with 90 wet slips, a boat ramp, ships store, and fuel dock.

Kingsmill Resort Marina (757-253-3919; www.kingsmill.com), 1010 Kingsmill Road, Williamsburg 23185. Fifteen slips for transients. Boats and fishing tackle for rent. The **Marina Bar & Grille** (757-253-3900), open seasonally, offers dockside dining and live entertainment.

River's Rest Marina & Resort (804-829-2753; www.riversrest.com), 9100 Willcox Neck Road, Charles City 23030. Located on the Chickahominy River with easy access to the James, this secluded resort has hookups for transients, boat ramp, pool, and rental pontoon boats. The resort includes a motel, along with the **Blue Heron Restaurant** (804-829-9070), serving fresh local seafood and steaks with a great waterfront view.

York River: **Riverwalk Landing** (757-890-3370; www.riverwalklanding.com), 425 Water Street, P.O. Box 219, Yorktown 23690. Located at the foot of the bluff below one of the country's most historic towns, two piers and nine mooring balls are available for visiting boaters.

Wormley Creek Marina (757-898-5060; www.wormleycreekmarina.com), 1221 Waterview Road, Yorktown 23692. Slips accommodate transients up to 60 feet.

🍴 **York River Yacht Haven** (804-642-2156; www.yryh.net), 8109 Yacht Haven Road, Gloucester Point 23062. Boatyard welcomes transients up to 160 feet. Free Wi-Fi, repair shop, custom rod shop, discount ships store, pool with lifeguards, airport limo service and rental cars, and the **Rivers Inn Restaurant and Crab Deck** (804-642-6161; www.riversinnrestaurant.com), offering dining with a view and courtesy docking.

James City County's public boat ramps are located at **Brickyard Landing** (757-259-5360; 990 Brickyard Road, Toano 23168) and **Chickahominy Riverfront Park** (757-258-5020; 1350 John Tyler Highway, Williamsburg 23185), both with access to the Chickahominy River. A boat ramp at the **Jamestown Beach Yacht Basin** (757-229-8309; Greensprings Road, Williamsburg 23185) provides access to Powhatan Creek and the James River for motorized craft. Contact **James City County Parks and Recreation** (757-259-3232; www.jccegov.com) for additional information.

Croaker Landing in **York River State Park** (757-566-3036; www.dcr.virginia.gov; 5526 Riverview Road, Williamsburg 23188) has a boat ramp and fishing pier on the York River. Launch and parking fees apply.

York County maintains motorized boat ramps at **Back Creek Park** (3000 Goodwin Neck Road/VA 173, Seaford 23696), where there is also a pier for crabbing; **Rodgers A. Smith Landing and Fishing Pier** (Tide Mill Road, Tabb 23693), a free, handicapped-accessible facility on the Poquoson River; and **Old Wormley Creek Landing** (110 Old Wormley Creek Road, Yorktown 23692). For more information, visit www.yorkcounty.gov/parksandrec or call 757-890-3500.

Across the US 17 toll bridge, **Gloucester Point Beach Park** (804-642-9474; www.gloucesterva.info; 1255 Greate Road, Gloucester Point 23061) has several boat ramps for public use. For additional boat ramp locations, see *Marinas and Docks*.

FAMILY FUN ✝ **AMF Williamsburg Lanes** (757-565-3311; www.amf.com), 5544 Olde Towne Road, Williamsburg 23188. Bumper bowling, snack bar, late-night Xtreme bowling with lights and music.

⊘ **Go-Karts Plus Action Park** (757-564-7600; www.gokartsplus.com), 6910 Richmond Road (US 60), Williamsburg 23188. Eight acres of family fun, next to the Williamsburg Pottery Factory, with go-carts, bumper boats, thrill rides, minigolf, blaster boats, Kiddieland for ages two to nine, snack bar, and more.

✝ **Hampton Roads Iceplex** (757-877-7539; www.hriceplex.com), 401 Village Avenue, Yorktown 23693. Open ice-skating sessions, late-night skating.

James City County Skate Park and Multi Use Trail (757-259-4200; www.jccegov.com), 5301 Longhill Road, Williamsburg 23188. Free and open year-round for skateboards, in-line skates, scooters, and bikes.

⊘ **Jumping Joey's Fun Center for Kids** (757-565-5867; www.jjfuncenter.com), 124 Waller Mill Road, Kmart Shopping Center, Williamsburg 23185. Inflatable rides for children 10 and under, special toddler section, Kid's Night Out, Friday Night Frolic parties.

⊘ **Mid County Park** (757-229-1232; www.jccegov.com/recreation), 3793 Ironbound Road, Williamsburg 23188. Kidsburg playground is a local favorite.

⊘ ♿ **My Place Playground** (757-259-5360 or 757-259-5410; www.jccegov.com/recreation), 5301 Longhill Road, Williamsburg 23188. Fully accessible playground at the Williamsburg–James City County Community Center is designed for children with disabilities. Open to all.

New Quarter Park Disc Golf Course (757-564-9586; www.yorkcounty.gov), 1000 Lakeshead Drive, Williamsburg 23185. Challenging course set in a scenic old-growth forest laced with Civil War earthworks is one of Virginia's best. Pro shop carries rental discs, refreshments, and complimentary bug spray. $3 to play all day.

🏌 **Pirates Cove Miniature Golf** (757-259-4600; www.piratescove.net), 2001 Mooretown Road, Williamsburg 23185. Adventure golf course winds under waterfalls and through caves, all while dodging cannon fire.

🛉 **Quarterpath Recreation Center** (757-259-3760; www.williamsburgva.gov), 202 Quarterpath Road, Williamsburg 23185. Drop-ins welcome for open play basketball, volleyball, billiards, and table tennis. Fees $2 or less.

🏌 **Ranger Rick's Lighted Practice Facility** (757-565-4653), 301 Lightfoot Road, Williamsburg 23188. Golf driving range and sand trap; batting cages; minigolf; snack bar serving hot dogs, ice cream, and beer. Open all year.

🛉 **Shake Rattle and Roll Roller Skating** (757-890-3500; www.yorkcounty.gov/parksandrec), Dare Elementary School Gymnasium, 300 Dare Road, Yorktown 23692. Low-cost skate nights on Fri. evenings Sept.–May. In-line skates available.

Williamsburg Inn Lawn Bowling Club (757-345-5729; www.williamsburg lawnbowling.org), 136 E. Francis Street, Williamsburg 23185. Discover the game of bowls on the green behind the Williamsburg Inn, open daily 3–6 PM, Apr. 1–Nov. 1. Free.

FISHING The James River is nationally known for its huge blue catfish. The fishing spots require a Virginia Freshwater Fishing License, unless otherwise noted. The freshwater-saltwater license line runs across the James from Hog Island to College Creek. Consult the Department of Game and Inland Fisheries (www.dgif .virginia.gov) for more information.

Beaverdam Reservoir (804-693-2107; www.gloucesterva.info), 8687 Roaring Springs Road, Gloucester 23061. Lake on the Middle Peninsula, heavily populated by largemouth bass, hosts several tournaments annually. Boat ramps, boat rentals, bank and pier fishing; Moonlight Fishing in summer; bait and licenses for sale at the ranger station.

Chickahominy River (804-829-6715; www.dgif.virginia.gov), Department of Game and Inland Fisheries, 3801 John Tyler Highway, Charles City 23030. The upper reaches of the river offer outstanding largemouth bass fishing, while farther down the Chick, catfish reach uncommon sizes. At **Walkers Dam** in Lanexa, "dipping herring" is a tradition from early Mar. through May. Access the lower Chick at **Chickahominy Riverfront Park** (757-258-5020; www.jccegov.com/recreation; 1350 John Tyler Highway, Williamsburg 23185), where you'll find a free fishing pier open 24 hours, and Walkers Dam at **Rockahock Campgrounds** (804-966-8362; www.rockahock.com; 1428 OutPost Road/SR 649, Lanexa 23089).

Diascund Reservoir (804-829-6580; www.jccegov.com), SR 603, off US 60, Lanexa. Abundant largemouth bass and bluegill, plus some large bowfin. Free boat ramp, electric motors only, fishing pier, shore fishing near boat ramp.

James River (www.dgif.virginia.gov). The tidal James is known for its enormous blue catfish, with numerous caught fish topping 80 pounds, as well as its largemouth bass fishery and striped bass (stripers or rockfish) runs.

Little Creek Reservoir (757-566-1702; www.jccegov.com), 180 Lakeview Drive, Toano 23168. A deep, clear lake located off SR 610 has been stocked with walleye and striped bass. Boat ramp, boat rentals, fishing pier, nature trail, play and picnic areas.

Waller Mill Reservoir (757-259-3778; www.williamsburgva.gov), SR 645/Airport
Road, Williamsburg. Two sections of this reservoir joined by a navigable tunnel are
best known for striped bass, with some in the 20- to 30-pound range. A fee is
charged for fishing from a boat, but it is free to fish from the pier. Boat rentals
available all year.

York River State Park (757-566-3036; www.dcr.virginia.gov), 5526 Riverview
Road, Williamsburg 23188. Fish freshwater **Woodstock Pond** from fishing piers,
rental boat, or dam for largemouth bass and bluegill. Brackish **Taskinas Creek,**
also with rental boats, has catfish and white perch, and requires either a saltwater
or freshwater license. No license is necessary to fish or crab in the York River from
the **Croaker Landing Fishing Pier,** but a saltwater license is required to fish the
river from shore or boat.

Fishing Charters & Outfitters

Charter trips typically include all needed equipment, bait, ice, and fishing license.

Eberwien's Catfishn' (804-449-6134; www.catfishingva.com). Chris Eberwien
guarantees you'll catch a citation blue catfish, or you pay half price. All fish more
than 20 pounds are released. Rockfish charters in the spring and croaker
May–June.

Hot Spot Fishing Charters (757-867-8274 or 757-846-5546), 516 Yorktown
Road, Yorktown 23693. Saltwater charters with Capt. Danny Forrest II.

Speckulater Charters (804-693-5673 or 757-509-3522; www.speckulatercharters
.com), Gloucester. Inshore, shallow-water angling for speck (spotted sea trout), red
drum, croaker, and flounder with Capt. Ed Lawrence, a veteran of the Virginia
Institute of Marine Science.

Fishing Piers

Virginia Saltwater Fishing License required unless otherwise noted.

&. **Croaker Landing Pier at York River State Park** (757-566-3036; www.dcr
.virginia.gov), 5526 Riverview Road, Williamsburg 23188. Handicapped-accessible
360-foot pier requires no fishing license, but parking and pier fishing fee required.
A hot spot for croaker.

Gloucester Point Beach Pier (804-642-9474; www.gloucesterva.info), 1255
Greate Road, Gloucester Point 23061. Free fishing. No license required.

Powhatan Creek Park Piers (757-259-5360; www.jccegov.com), 1831 Jamestown
Road, Williamsburg 23185. Five small piers in the park. No fee to fish. Freshwater
license required.

&. **Rodgers A. Smith Landing and Fishing Pier** (757-890-3500; www.york
county.gov), Tide Mill Road, Tabb 23693. No fee to fish. Handicapped accessible.
Restrooms available.

Yorktown Fishing Pier (757-890-3500; www.yorkcounty.gov/parksandrec), Water
Street, Yorktown 23690. Free pier requires no license to fish. Open all year.

Tackle Shops

Bishop's Fishing Supply (757-591-9300; www.bishopfishingsupply.com), 1215
George Washington Memorial Highway/US 17, Yorktown 23693. Big selection of
fly-fishing supplies.

Hooker Bait and Tackle (757-566-9050; www.hookerbaitandtackle.net), 7828 Richmond Road, Toano 23168.

N Out Convenience Store (804-642-9535), 1617 George Washington Memorial Highway/US 17, Gloucester Point 23062.

GOLF As early as the 1600s, Virginia's gentry were already adopting the game of golf. The Earl of Dunmore, royal governor of the Virginia Colony in 1774, practiced his golf game on the lawn of his palace in Williamsburg.

Today the region boasts more than a dozen award-winning courses, and *Golf Digest* named it one of the Top 25 Golf Destinations in the World. Many resorts offer golf packages with special pricing. Visit www.golfwilliamsburg.com for additional information. All the courses listed here accept public play and most have rental clubs available.

The Colonial Golf Course (757-566-1600; www.golfcolonial.com), 8285 Diascund Road, Lanexa 23089. Lester George and Robert Wrenn course 10 miles west of Williamsburg, with an indoor teaching facility, video analysis, and the **Mill Creek Inn,** a full-service restaurant and bar.

Colonial Heritage Golf Course (757-645-2030; www.colonialheritageclub.com), 6500 Arthur Hills Drive, Williamsburg 23188. Arthur Hills–designed course with pro shop, driving range with grass tees, chipping and putting greens, and the **Magnolia Dining Room and Grill** (757-645-2018).

Cypress Creek Golfers' Club (757-365-4774; www.cypresscreekgolfersclub .com), 600 Cypress Creek Parkway, Smithfield 23430. A short journey via the free ferry brings you to this course by designers Tom Clark and Curtis Strange. Clark considers it one of his finest. **CC Creekside Café** on-site.

✿ **Ford's Colony Country Club** (757-258-4130; www.fordscolony.com), 1 Ford's Colony Drive, Williamsburg 23188. The picturesque **Blackheath,** the classic **Marsh Hawk,** and the challenging **Blue Heron** championship courses designed by Dan Maples are the highest ranked in the state. State-of-the-art Golf Learning Center with video swing analysis, indoor practice tees; **Harry's Tavern,** a deli-style restaurant with "golfers-to-go" window and happy hours.

✪ **Golden Horse Shoe Golf Club** (757-220-7696 or 800-648-6653; www.golden horseshoegolf.com), S. England Street, Williamsburg 23185. Williamsburg Resort Gold and Green courses, designed by the legendary Robert Trent Jones Jr. and his son Rees Jones, consistently rank among the top in the country. The senior Jones called the Gold Course his "best design ever." The nine-hole **Spotswood Executive Course** received mention as the "best short course in the country" by *Golf Magazine.*

The Golf Club at Brickshire (804-966-7888 or 866-867-7888; www.brickshire golfclub.com), 5520 Virginia Park Drive (I-64 exit 214), Providence Forge 23140. Player-friendly Curtis Strange signature course includes four "emulation holes" built to resemble the best of St. Andrews, Augusta National, Pinehurst #2, and the Riviera Country Club. Golf shop and the **Brickshire Grille** on-site.

Kingsmill Golf Club (757-253-3906 or 757-258-1623; www.kingsmill.com), 1010 Kingsmill Road, Williamsburg 23185. The **River Course** by Pete Dye, the **Plantation Course** by Arnold Palmer, the **Woods Course** by Tom Clark and Curtis Strange, and the nine-hole **Bray Links** make the most of the resort's spacious plantation.

The Tradition Golf Club at Kiskiack (757-566-2200 or 800-989-4728; www .traditionalclubs.com), 8104 Club Drive, Williamsburg 23188. Picturesque blufftop course designed by John LeFoy.

The Tradition Golf Club at Royal New Kent (804-966-7023; www.traditional clubs.com), 10100 Kentland Trail (I-64 exit 214/VA 155), Providence Forge 23140. Located between Williamsburg and Richmond, this course has been called the truest representation of an Irish links course in America.

The Tradition Golf Club at Stonehouse (757-566-1138; www.traditionalclubs .com), 9700 Mill Pond Run (I-64 exit 227/VA 30), Toano 23168. Located on steep, forested hills along the York River, with deep bunkers and exceptional vistas.

Williamsburg National Golf Club (757-258-9642 or 800-826-5732; www.wngc .com), 3700 Centerville Road, Williamsburg 23188. Two championship courses, the **Jamestown,** designed by Jack Nicklaus, and the new **Yorktown,** by Tom Clark, offer discounts to time-share guests and many specials.

HEALTH & FITNESS CLUBS Body Balance Studio (757-221-0774; www .bodybalancewilliamsburg.com), 370 McLaws Circle, Williamsburg 23185. Yoga and Pilates classes, plus massage by licensed therapists.

Core Fitness Performance Training Center (757-564-7311; www.corefitness ptc.com), 344 McLaws Circle, Williamsburg 23188. Personal trainers, endurance programs, Bikini Boot Camp, and circuit training, plus physical therapy and sports rehabilitation.

HIKING AND NATURE TRAILS Bassett Hall Woodland Trail. Three-mile trail begins at the end of S. England Street, following a ridge with great views of the Historic District, to Bassett Hall.

✪ **Greensprings Greenway Interpretive Trail** (757-259-5360; www.jccegov .com), 3751 John Tyler Highway, Williamsburg 23185. Three-mile soft-surface trail travels through wetlands with a boardwalk encircling a beaver pond. Part of the Virginia Birding and Wildlife Trail and a designated wildflower sanctuary. Trail-head and parking behind Jamestown High School.

♿ **Mid County Park** (757-229-1232; www.jccegov.com/recreation), 3793 Iron-bound Road, Williamsburg 23188. Paved ADA-accessible multiuse path circles the park.

New Quarter Park (757-890-3500; www.yorkcounty.gov), 1000 Lakeshead Drive, Williamsburg 23185. Three miles of hiking trails laid out by the **Tidewater Appalachian Trail Club** (www.tidewateratc.com) wind along ridges and through mature forest.

Quarterpath Recreation Center (757-259-3760; www.williamsburgva.gov), 202 Quarterpath Road, Williamsburg 23185. Free Walking Club program in the air-conditioned gymnasium Mon.–Fri. mornings.

Waller Mill Reservoir Park (757-259-3778; www.williamsburgva.gov), SR 645/Airport Road, Williamsburg 23188. Hiking and biking trails lead around the lake and to the Lookout Tower for views of the area.

♿ **Williamsburg City Walks** (757-259-3760 or 757-259-3777; www.williams burgva.gov), 202 Quarterpath Road, Williamsburg 23185. A *Great City Walks* brochure, available for download from the city Web site, details hikes ranging from walks in the woods to handicapped-accessible strolls along city sidewalks. Routes follow historic paths used in colonial times and explore the campus of the College of William and Mary.

✪ ♿ **Yorktown Riverwalk** (757-830-3500; www.yorkcounty.gov), Water Street, Yorktown 23690. A pleasant paved path leads along the bluff overlooking the York River from the Yorktown Victory Center to Riverwalk Landing, passing museums, shops, restaurants, and imposing statues along the way. At the other end of the village, an extension leads to the Yorktown Battlefield Visitors Center.

HORSEBACK RIDING Many miles of equestrian trails are available at **Beaverdam Park** (804-693-2107; www.gloucesterva.info; 8687 Roaring Springs Road, Gloucester 23061) and at **York River State Park** (757-566-3036; www.dcr .virginia.gov; 5526 Riverview Road, Williamsburg 23188).

Lakewood Trails at Stonehouse Stables (757-566-9633; www.stonehousestables .com), 2116 Forge Road, Toano 23168. Guided trail rides circle a private lake and explore the bridle paths in York River State Park. Lessons, boarding, and summer riding camps available.

HUNTING AND SHOOTING Chickahominy Wildlife Management Area (757-253-7072 or 804-829-6580; www.dgif.virginia.gov), SR 623, off VA 5 in Rustic. Hunting for deer, wild turkey, squirrel, rabbit, dove, and quail, plus waterfowl hunting on a first-come basis. Free boat ramp off SR 621. Free shooting range for rifles and shotguns.

Chippokes Plantation State Park (757-294-3625 or 800-933-PARK; www.dcr .virginia.gov), 695 Chippokes Park Road, Surry 23883. Hunt by reservation held in Dec., as well as the **Southern Heritage Deer Hunt,** an old-fashioned day of hunting featuring traditional meals and blessing of the hounds. Make reservations up to 11 months in advance.

Goodwin Islands National Estuarine Research Reserve (804-684-7559; www.vims.edu/cbnerr), 1208 Greate Road, Gloucester Point 23062. Managed hunt during duck season.

Hog Island Wildlife Management Area (804-829-6580; www.dgif.virginia.gov), VA 10 between Surry and Smithfield. Winter waterfowl hunts, spring bowfishing for carp, archery season for deer, managed dove fields, and general hunting for deer, quail, squirrel, rabbit, and turkey. On days without hunting, the refuge is open to the public, with a visitors center, several viewing towers near the impoundments where huge flocks of waterfowl spend the winter, and a boat ramp on the James River.

♿ **New Kent Forestry Center** (804-328-3031 or 804-966-2201; www.dof.virginia .gov), 11301 Pocahontas Trail/US 60, Providence Forge 23140. Deer hunts for handicapped hunters.

Sportsmen's Hunting Preserve (757-562-2523; www.sportsmanshuntingpreserve .com), 30304 Outland Drive, Carrsville 23315. Upland bird hunting for quail, pheasant, and partridge.

Sussex Shooting Sports (804-834-3801; www.dancessportinggoods.net), 4729 General Mahone Highway, Waverly 23890. Public shooting club with sporting clay course, plus hunting for quail, pheasant, and chukar.

York River State Park (757-566-3036 or 800-933-PARK; www.dcr.virginia.gov), 5526 Riverview Road, Williamsburg 23188. Shotgun hunting in Dec. Reservations required.

KITEBOARDING AND WINDSURFING Yorktown Beach and Gloucester Point Beach, facing each other at the Coleman/US 17 Bridge, are two of the most popular places to launch on the York River for windsurfers and kiteboarders. Farther up the York on the north side of the river, **Carmine Island** is a good spot for beginners, with shallow water and slow current. **Cooks Landing,** on Chesapeake Bay at the mouth of the Perrin River, is popular with experienced kiters.

RACQUET SPORTS & TENNIS Back Creek Park (757-890-3569; www.york county.gov/parksandrec), 3000 Goodwin Neck Road/VA 173, Seaford 23696. Award-winning USTA tennis facility with six lighted tennis courts, a backboard, lessons, and tournaments. Fees apply. Seasonal.

⊤ **James City/Williamsburg Community Center** (757-259-4200; www.jcce gov.com), 5301 Longhill Road, Williamsburg 23188. Racquetball, basketball, and volleyball courts; aquatic center; fitness center. Nonresidents must pay a daily pass fee ($4–11).

James River Community Center (757-887-5810; www.jccegov.com), 8901 Pocahontas Trail, Williamsburg 23185. Outside tennis courts, fitness center, racquetball court. $2–5.

Kiwanis Municipal Park (757-259-3776; www.williamsburgva.gov), 125 Longhill Road, Williamsburg 23185. Seven lighted all-weather tennis courts and a lighted rebound wall behind W&M's Dillard Complex dormitories.

✪ **McCormick-Nagelsen Tennis Center and ITA Women's Collegiate Hall of Fame** (757-221-7378; www.wm.edu/sites/mntc), 705 S. Henry Street, Williamsburg 23187. Facility on the W&M campus has six indoor courts; racquet and ball machine rentals; drop-in rates for clinics, lessons, drills, and league play. Admission to the **ITA Hall of Fame** (www.itahalloffame.com) is free.

Mid County Park (757-229-1232; www.jccegov.com/recreation), 3793 Ironbound Road, Williamsburg 23188. Lighted tennis courts. Free.

The Tennis Club at Kingsmill (757-253-3945; www.kingsmill.com), 1010 Kingsmill Road, Williamsburg 23185. This facility ranks among the Top 50 Tennis Resorts of the World according to www.tennisresortsonline.com.

SPAS Refresh! Center for Massage & Healing (757-345-2457; www.refresh center.com), 7151 Richmond Road, Norge Office Park, Williamsburg 23188. Licensed therapists offer massage, acupuncture, yoga, Shiatsu, Chinese herbal therapy, and aromatherapy. Yoga classes are held at the **Quarterpath Recreation Center** (757-259-3760; www.williamsburgva.gov; 202 Quarterpath Road, Williamsburg 23185). Drop-ins welcome.

The Spa at Kingsmill Resort (757-253-3919; www.kingsmill.com), 1010 Kingsmill Road, Williamsburg 23185. Full- and half-day packages, including the James River Signature Experience, with lomilomi massage.

✪ **The Spa of Colonial Williamsburg** (757-220-7720 or 800-688-6479; www .colonialwilliamsburgresort.com/spa), 307 S. England Street, Williamsburg 23185.

IN THE LAND OF POCAHONTAS: VIRGINIA'S MIDDLE PENINSULA

The story of the Indian princess who saved John Smith's life, and with him, the English colony in Virginia, spreads across southeast Virginia. Pocahontas visited Jamestown, and she lived as a captive and got married at the Citie of Henricus. However, no region is more closely associated with her than the Middle Peninsula, site of her father's major village, **Werowocomoco.**

Much of the story of John Smith's capture and rescue took place here, and a museum in Gloucester exhibits the actual stone supposedly used by Powhatan for executions—upon which John Smith is said to have laid his head. Legend holds that the massive **Powhatan's Chimney,** overlooking the York River at the end of Powhatan Drive (SR 1304), is the site of the "English-style" house Smith built for the Indian emperor. The collapse of this chimney in 1888 spurred the creation of the Association for the Preservation of Virginia Antiquities (www.apva.org), now **Preservation Virginia,** which restored the chimney in the 1930s. Archaeologists believe they have found the ruins of Powhatan's village a bit farther west on **Purtan Bay** (http://powhatan.wm.edu).

Known to locals as the Rivah, the Middle Peninsula of Virginia (sandwiched between the Virginia Peninsula and Northern Neck) remains a land set in amber, largely unchanged from the days of rural plantations, country stores, and tiny fishing villages. The region is a favorite for hunting antiques, boating, and fishing. Easily reached via the US 17 toll bridge in Yorktown, the Middle Peninsula offers a quick country getaway from the crowds that frequent Williamsburg's attractions.

Historic **Gloucester Point** lies along the York River just across the bridge. Here you'll find beaches, fishing piers, parks, seafood restaurants, and the **Virginia Institute of Marine Science** (804-684-7846; www.vims.edu; 1208 Greate Road, Gloucester Point 23062).

A few miles north on US 17 Business, the **Gloucester Courthouse Historic District** preserves the appearance of an 18th-century county seat. The **Gloucester Visitor Center** (804-693-3215 or 804-693-0014; www.visit gloucesterva.info; 6509 Main Street, Gloucester 23061), in the 1896 Roane Building, sits inside a wall that encloses historic Court Circle Green, along with several 18th-century buildings. A fine statue of the young Princess Pocahontas stands at the northern end of Main Street, at the intersection with Belroi Road. Near the southern end of town, the enormous **Pocahontas Mural** on the outside of the **Gloucester Public Library** (804-693-2998; www.gloucesterva.info/lib; 6920 Main Street, Gloucester 23061) illustrates episodes from her life. Inside the library, enjoy free Wi-Fi.

Occupying the far eastern end of the Middle Peninsula, Gwynn's Island

and **Mathews County** (www.visitmathews.com) comprise a windswept region of salt marshes, small towns, blueberry bogs, and lonely dunes. Here visitors find exceptional biking and kayaking options, as well as views of the **New Point Comfort Lighthouse** (www.newpointcomfort.com), the third-oldest light on the Chesapeake Bay. Fans of down-home music won't want to miss **Donk's Lil' Ole Opry** (804-725-7760; www.donkstheater.com).

The **River Country** (800-527-6360; www.visitrivercountry.org) contains many other charming small towns and ecotourism opportunities. Catch a passenger ferry to remote **Tangier Island** (www.tangierisland-va.com) at Reedville, explore the colonial port town of **Urbanna** (www.urbanna.com), or paddle the remote swamps of **Dragon Run** (www.dragonrun.org). The region is noted for its spring-time display of daffodils.

○ **Beaverdam Park** (804-693-2107; www.gloucesterva.info), 8687 Roaring Springs Road, Gloucester 23061. True to its name, this park offers close-up views of beaver dams and lodges, plus river otters, and many species of birds. An extensive system of uncrowded trails and loops for bikers, hikers, and horses skirt the shore of Beaverdam Reservoir. Canoes and jon boats, with or without electric motors, are available for rent. The reservoir is noted for its large-mouth bass fishery.

The Beehives of Gloucester (www .cookfoundation.info). Throughout the region you'll encounter color-fully painted beehives, part of the County of Gloucester's 350th birth-day celebration.

Bethel Beach Natural Area Pre-serve (804-445-9117; www.dcr .virginia.gov), SR 609, Mathews. This sandy finger of land on the Chesapeake Bay is home to rare birds and plants. No pets permitted.

WHILE POCAHONTAS VISITED JAMESTOWN (AS MEMORIALIZED BY THIS STATUE), LEGENDS OF THE INDIAN PRINCESS ALSO FORM PART OF THE LOCAL LORE ON THE MIDDLE PENINSULA.

Gloucester County Farmers' Market (804-693-9534 or 757-327-0051; www
.gloucestervachamber.org), Susanna Wesley United Methodist Church,
3900 George Washington Highway/US 17, Ordinary 23131. Sat. mornings.
Seasonal.

✪ **Gloucester Main Street Association** (804-695-0700; www.gloucester
-virginia.org). Gloucester Courthouse's historic downtown has a number of
interesting shops and eating places, including **Kelsick Specialty Market**
(804-693-6500; www.kelsickgardens.com; 6632 Main Street, Gloucester
23061), with gourmet foods, wines, beers, and patio dining; and the **Wild
Rabbit Cafe** (804-694-5100; 6655 Main Street, Gloucester 23061), with free
Wi-Fi, and many vegetarian options. **Twice Told Tales Booksellers** (804-693-
9209; www.tttbs.com; 6658 Main Street, Gloucester 23061) offers an excellent selection of books for adults and children.

Gloucester Museum of History (804-693-1234 or 804-693-2659; www
.gloucesterva.info), 6539 Main Street, Gloucester 23061. Exhibits in this former tavern include the history of early Native American settlements, the
Revolutionary War Battle of Hook, and artifacts from an old country store.
Free.

✪ **Gloucester Point Beach Park** (804-642-9474; www.gloucesterva.info),
1255 Greate Road, Gloucester Point 23061. Free park has a sandy beach,
with parking, free fishing pier, shady picnic area, playground, seasonal concession stand, restrooms, and outdoor shower, but no lifeguards. The **Point
Walk,** along the waterfront, tells Gloucester's history from precolonial days
and introduces local flora and fauna.

Gloucester Point Family Campground (804-642-4316 or 800-332-4316; www
.gpfcampground.com), 3149 Campground Road, Hayes 23072. Campground
on the Severn River offers full hookups, fishing and crabbing piers, kayak
rentals.

Long Bridge Ordinary (804-693-6201), US 17 Business at VA 14, Gloucester
Courthouse. Early-18th-century traveler's inn retains many of its original features. Tours by appointment.

New Point Comfort Natural Area Preserve (434-295-6106 or 804-445-9117;
www.nature.org), SR 600, southern tip of Mathews County. Managed by the
Nature Conservancy, this isolated peninsula is an important stop for
neotropical songbirds on the Atlantic Flyway. Handicapped-accessible
boardwalk and observation deck extend over the salt marsh to the best land
view available of **New Point Comfort Lighthouse.** No restrooms.

Pocahontas Museum (804-693-2795), 7339 Lewis Avenue, Gloucester 23061. Museum in downtown preserves the stone where legend says John Smith's head lay when his life was saved by Pocahontas, as well as other artifacts relating to the Powhatan Indians. Open by appointment.

The Poddery (804-725-5956; www.thepoddery.com), 177 Poddery Lane off VA 14, Foster 23056. Studio in Mathews County creates handmade, functional pottery.

✪ **River's Inn Restaurant and Crab Deck** (804-642-6161; www.riversinnrestaurant .com), 8109 Yacht Haven Road, Gloucester Point 23062. Restaurant at the York River Yacht Haven offers romantic views and regional cuisine with the emphasis on seafood, designed by award-winning chef Hans Schadler, former head of food services at Colonial Williamsburg. The casual **Crab Deck** (www.crab-deck .com) is a local favorite for steamed shrimp, oysters, clams, and blue crabs.

Rosewell (804-693-2585; www.rosewell.org), SR 664, off Aberdeen Creek Road/SR 632, Gloucester 23061. One of the largest homes ever built in colonial America is now just extremely scenic ruins overlooking the York River, but it's well worth a visit. Adults $4, children 6–12 $2.

Short Lane Ice Cream Company (804-695-2999), 6721 George Washington Memorial Highway/US 17 at Short Lane Road, Gloucester 23061. Historic old store makes ice cream and sorbets on-site.

Tyndall's Point Park (804-693-2355; www.gloucesterva.info/pr/parks/tyndall.htm), 1376 Vernon Street, off US 17 near the Coleman Bridge, Gloucester Point 23062. Small park contains an interpretive trail past the remains of Confederate earthworks.

✪ **Virginia Institute of Marine Science (VIMS)** (804-684-7846; www.vims.edu), 1208 Greate Road, Gloucester Point 23062. Research institute conducts interdisciplinary investigations in coastal ocean and estuarine science. The **VIMS Watermen's Hall Visitor Center and Aquarium** as well as the **Coastal Forested Wetland Walk** are open to the public on weekdays. Weekly tours during the summer. Call for reservations.

Walter Reed Birthplace (804-693-3992; www.apva.org/walterreed), 4021 Hickory Fork Road/SR 616 at SR 614, Gloucester 23061. Small two-room cottage, dating to before 1850, was the earliest home of the man who discovered that mosquitoes spread yellow fever. Tours by appointment.

Warner Hall Graveyard (804-693-3992; www.apva.org/warnergraveyard), 4750 Warner Hall Road, Gloucester 23061. Those buried here include ancestors of George Washington, Robert E. Lee, and Queen Elizabeth II. Free.

A timeless and peaceful retreat, this Georgian building next to the Williamsburg Inn offers treatments drawn from centuries of Native American, African, and European traditions, along with the latest technologies. Packages include a 16th-century hot stone experience, colonial herbal treatment, water cure, and more. Separate women's and men's spa areas with steam rooms, signature showers, and whirlpools, as well as salon services, fitness center, and spa boutique.

The Williamsburg Salt Spa (757-229-1022; www.williamsburgsaltspa.com), 1111 Old Colony Lane, Old Colony Professional Center, Williamsburg 23185. Spend time in a soothing salt cave, a holistic treatment believed to enhance mood and improve respiratory problems.

SPECTATOR SPORTS College of William and Mary Athletics (757-221-3340; www.tribeathletics.com), William and Mary Hall Ticket Office, 751 Ukrop Way, Williamsburg 23185. W&M's teams, nicknamed the Tribe, compete in NCAA's Division I. Tickets for home games available online.

✪ **Colonial Downs** (804-966-7223; www.colonialdowns.com), 10515 Colonial Downs Parkway (I-64 exit 214), New Kent 23124. Horse-racing facility 20 miles west of Williamsburg hosts thoroughbred racing June–Aug. and harness racing Sept.–Nov. The **Virginia Derby,** held in mid-July, attracts some 9,000 fans as well as top three-year-old turf horses. Admission to the grandstand is $2; children under 13 free.

SWIMMING POOLS James City County (www.jccegov.com/recreation) maintains outdoor pools open to the public during the summer months at **Chicka-hominy Riverfront Park** (757-258-5020; 1350 John Tyler Highway, Williamsburg 23185), **Little Creek Reservoir Park** (757-566-1702; 180 Lakeview Drive, Toano 23168), and **Upper County Park** (757-566-1451; 180 Leisure Road, Toano 23168). Pool admission $4–5; children five and under free. The **James City/Williamsburg Community Center** (757-5301; Longhill Road, Williamsburg 23188) has an indoor pool with zero depth entry and wheelchair accessibility, whirlpool, saunas, indoor track, fitness room, teen lounge, senior lounge with pool table, and an arts and crafts area with potters wheels and kiln. Nonresidents pay a daily fee.

An outdoor pool operated by the City of Williamsburg at **Quarterpath Park** (757-259-3760; www.williamsburgva.gov; 202 Quarterpath Road, Williamsburg 23185) is open to the public June–Aug.

TOURING Combination tickets to area attractions offer significant savings. The **Four-Site Combination Ticket,** available at www.historyisfun.org, gives unlimited seven-day admission to Jamestown Settlement, Historic Jamestowne, Yorktown Battlefield, and the Yorktown Victory Center ($9–29). **America's Historic Triangle Ticket** ($33–80) adds unlimited access to Colonial Williamsburg for seven days. The **Williamsburg Flex Pass** ($131–171) includes all of the above, plus seven-day access to Busch Gardens and Water Country USA, including parking. Or you can get seven days at Colonial Williamsburg, Busch Gardens, and the water park with the **Williamsburg Bounce Pass** ($102–123). Prices may vary and are

offered only as guidelines. Additional discounts may be available online at www
.history.org or www.buschgardens.com.

You can qualify for even better deals if you book your ticket package along with
your accommodations through the **Williamsburg Hotel and Motel Association**
(800-211-7165; www.gowilliamsburg.com). For additional discounts at area businesses, look for the **goWilliamsburg Discount Card** in the *Williamsburg Hotel
& Motel's Official Visitor's Guide,* or download a copy from their Web site.

In Yorktown, the **Gallery at York Hall** (757-890-4490; www.yorkcounty.gov/
tourism; 301 Main Street, Yorktown 23691) serves as the visitors center for the
town's attractions, as well as displays work by local artists. Stop by for some friendly advice and a brochure detailing a self-guided walking tour of the historic village.
Open Tues.–Sun., Apr.–Dec.

By automobile: **Battlefield Road Audio Tour** (757-898-2409; www.nps.gov/york).
CD tours of the Yorktown Battlefield are available in the Yorktown Battlefield Visitor Center bookstore.

Gloucester County Country Stores and Rural Post Offices Driving Tour
(804-693-0014; www.gloucesterva.info/tourism/tours.htm), 6467 Main Street,
Gloucester 23061. Visit charming stores and historic structures across the Middle
Peninsula.

Middle Peninsula Historical Marker Tour (www.mppdc.com/historical/choose
.htm).

1607 Captain John Smith Capture Route Driving Tour (804-843-2228;
www.twinriversrealty.com/jscr1.htm). This 350-mile, self-guided driving tour follows the route taken by John Smith and his captors who brought him, after much
journeying, before Powhatan. The tour weaves throughout the Middle Peninsula,
passing many Native American reservations and museums along the way.

By boat: **Bay Water Excursions** (804-725-2876; www.baywaterexcursions.com),
Horn Harbor Marina, Haywood 23138. Customized powerboat excursions from
Mathews County visit New Point Comfort Lighthouse, Wolftrap Light, the East
River, and New Point Island. $75/hour; two-hour minimum.

✪ **Jamestown-Scotland Ferry** (800-VA FERRY; www.virginiadot.org/travel), VA
32. Free ferry across the James runs daily, offering great views of Jamestown Settlement and Jamestown Island from the water.

Mobjack Sailing (804-815-0144; www.mobjacksailing.com), P.O. Box 162, Foster
23056. Enjoy a day sail or sunset cruise on Mobjack Bay aboard the sloop *Xanadu,*
docked in Mathews County. $65–70.

✪ ✿ **The Schooner *Alliance*** (757-639-1233; www.schooneralliance.com), Riverwalk Docks, Yorktown 23690. The 105-foot *Alliance,* a traditional gaff rigged three-
masted schooner, offers sight-seeing and sunset sails daily from the Yorktown
Waterfront, May–Oct. Tickets available online. $18–35.

By bus or limousine: **Marrow Transit** (757-564-5466; www.marrowtransit.com).
Knowledgeable chauffeurs take you on customized private tours.

Oleta Coach Lines (757-253-1008; www.oleta.com), P.O. Box 466, Williamsburg
23187. Regularly scheduled bus tours include an all-day trip around the Historic

SMITHFIELD AND SURRY: ADVENTURES IN THE LAND OF HAM

If you drive the winding roads on the south side of the James River, especially at night, you may come upon what seems to be a pocket of mist. But once you enter it, the delicious smell declares the truth: You've entered a cloud of hog fog.

The scent of hams smoking over hickory wood permeates this region, headquarters of Smithfield Foods (www.smithfieldfoods.com), the world's largest producer of pork products; Gwaltney (www.gwaltneyfoods.com), now a subsidiary of Smithfield; and S. Wallace Edwards & Sons (www .edwardsvaham.com) in Surry; as well as a number of small family operations still raising hogs and smoking them with traditional methods learned from the Native American tribes, who would smoke venison in small huts.

Besides hams, you'll find a lot more on the south side of the James. This area just across the river from Jamestown was one of the first settled by the English. Plantations lined the banks of the river, and several of the manor houses survive. Farther south, the deep cypress swamps are much as they were in colonial days, now the refuge of many endangered species of bird and plant.

Take the free ferry on VA 31 from Jamestown to Scotland Wharf (800-VA FERRY; www.virginiadot.org/travel) and you'll find yourself in **Surry County** (www.toursurryva.com), where peanuts and pork reign supreme. There's plenty of history here as well, including **Bacon's Castle** and the **Smith's Fort,** both now owned by Preservation Virginia (www.apva.org). The County Courthouse Complex, at the intersection of VA 31 and VA 10, about 5 miles from the ferry, serves as the center of town, with several restaurants and shops. Stop by the **Surry County Historical Society and Museums** (757-294-0404; www.rootsweb.ancestry.com/~vaschsm; 181 Bank Street, Surry 23883) for more information. **The Center** (757-356-5360; www.thecentersurry.com; 57 Colonial Trail E., Surry 23883), a coffeehouse across from the courthouse, offers free computers and Wi-Fi access.

Smithfield, the seat of Isle of Wight County, lies about 20 miles southeast of Surry along VA 10. Most of the region's attractions lie between the two towns, separated by rolling fields and patches of forest. From Smithfield, you can continue on VA 10 a few miles and cross over the James River Bridge (VA 32) to Newport News for a quick return to Williamsburg via I-64. The loop makes a pleasant and popular day trip.

Smithfield, established about 1750 on the banks of the Pagan River, rapidly developed as a busy river port. More than a dozen buildings survive from the 18th century, mingling with a host of ostentatious Victorians replete with turrets, stained glass, fish-scale shingles, and steamboat Gothic trim, built here after the Civil War.

Smithfield had the good fortune to escape burning in both the Revolutionary and Civil wars. Legend has it that the British were bought off with hams and whiskey, while the Union gunboat that came to take the town was met by cannon fire straight down Main Street and sank in the river. Its gilded eagle figurehead rests today in the **Isle of Wight County Museum** (757-356-1223; 103 Main Street, Smithfield 23430), next to the world's oldest peanut and Mr. Gwaltney's pet ham.

A stroll around Smithfield's walkable downtown, lined with interesting shops, historic buildings, and a half dozen life-sized bronze statues, is well worth the time. Make your first stop the **Smithfield & Isle of Wight Visitor Center** (757-301-4007 or 866-889-0688; www.smithfield-virginia.com; 319 Main Street, Smithfield 23430), where you can pick up a walking tour map, plus a card good for discounts at local shops and restaurants. For a preview, visit www.historic smithfield.com.

On weekends, free guided tours are available of the 1899 **Mansion on Main** (757-357-0006; www.mansion-on-main.net; 36 Main Street, Smithfield 23430), one of the most magnificent of the Victorians, now a bed & breakfast chock-full of museum-quality antiques. You can also tour **Christ Episcopal Church** (757-357-2826; www.christchurchsmithfield.org; 111 S. Church Street, Smithfield 23430), noted for its fine stained glass, including a Tiffany, and the Sundays at Four (www.sundaysatfour.org) concert series.

ELABORATE VICTORIAN MANSIONS LINE SMITHFIELD'S MAIN STREET.

The **Olde Towne Curb Market**, showcasing the products of the southern shore, takes place Saturday mornings, Memorial Day–Labor Day, at the Bank of Southside Virginia parking lot (115 Main Street, Smithfield 23430) Art strolls, dubbed **Smarts**, are held the second Friday evening of the month year-round.

Smithfield is a bike-friendly town, with a 5-mile off-road **Park to Park** trail leading from **Windsor Castle Park** (757-356-9939; 301 Jericho Road, Smithfield 23430), a new riverfront park downtown, to **Carrollton Nike Park**, as well as many miles of quiet country roads.

A bit farther out, history buffs will enjoy touring **Boykin's Tavern Museum** (757-365-9771; www.co.isle-of-wight.va.us or www.iwchs.com; 17130 Monument Circle, Isle of Wight 23397; free admission), on US 258/Courthouse Road. The 1632 **Historic St. Luke's Church** (757-357-3367; www.historicstlukes.org; 14477 Benns Church Boulevard/VA 10, Smithfield 23430), known as "the Old Brick," is the earliest English church in America still standing and preserves many of its Jacobean details, including an English chamber organ believed to be the oldest surviving one of its kind in the world. Tours $3–5. The excellent gift shop on-site carries American-made gifts with historical and cultural significance.

Two historic forts occupy the bluffs near Smithfield, where they defended against everything from Spanish galleons to Union ironclads. **Fort Boykin** (7410 Fort Boykin Trail, Smithfield 23430), established as early as 1632, rebuilt by the Confederacy, is still largely intact, with lush landscaping and a riverside beach. **Historic Fort Huger** (15080 Talcott Terrace, Smithfield 23430) saw heavy action during the Civil War. Walking trails lead to earthworks with cannon above the James River, where you'll get a look at the U.S. Navy's ghost fleet of "moth-balled" ships. Both sites are maintained by Isle of Wight County (757-357-0115; www.co.isle-of-wight.va.us). Get maps at www.visitsmithfieldisleofwight.com or at the visitors center in town.

Other sights of note:

✪ **Bacon's Castle** (757-357-5976; www.apva.org/baconscastle), 465 Bacon's Castle Road/SR 617 off VA 10, Surry 23883. Magnificent 1665 Jacobean home played a role in the 1676 Bacon's Rebellion. House and garden tours: $5–8. Combo ticket with Smith's Fort: $10–12. Hours vary. Closed Dec.–Feb.

Blackwater Ecological Preserve (757-683-3597; www.odu.edu/~lmusselm/blackwater), 24326 Thomas Woods Trail (off SR 614), Zuni 23898. Short nature trail leads to some of the last remaining longleaf pines in Virginia.

Blackwater River Preserve (434-295-6106; www.nature.org), Southampton County. Nature Conservancy tract preserves an eight-hundred-year-old bald cypress forest. Access by kayak or canoe only. Put in at the SR 621 bridge over the Blackwater, and take out at the SR 620 bridge. Permission required.

Captain Chuck-a-Muck's Ships Store and Grill (757-356-1005; www.captain chuck-a-mucks.com), 21088 Marina Road, Rescue 23424. Casual, out-of-the-way spot featured on the Food Network is worth finding for fresh seafood, Key lime pie, laid-back bar scene.

Carrollton Nike Park (757-357-2291; www.smithfield-virginia.com), 13036 Nike Park Road (off VA 669), Carrollton 23314. Self-guided walking tours of this former Cold War anti-aircraft Nike missile battery, plus nature trails, mountain bike trail, tennis courts, fishing and crabbing pier, playground, and free skate park.

✪ **Chippokes Plantation State Park** (757-294-3625; www.dcr.virginia.gov), 695 Chippokes Park Road, Surry 23883. Based on the oldest continuously farmed land in America, this state park on the banks of the James includes the 1854 Jones-Stewart Mansion, open for tours; formal gardens; the Farm and Forestry Museum; plus hiking, biking, and equestrian trails; a seasonal swimming pool; canoe trips; and a beach on the river where huge prehistoric fossil shells can be seen. Accommodations are available at the campground and in several restored outbuildings that once housed farm overseers. The site of the popular **Peanut, Pork and Pine Festival** (www.porkpeanutpinefestival.org) every July and **Plantation Christmas** (www.plantationchristmas.com) at the end of Oct.

Chub Sandhill Natural Area Preserve (757-925-2318; www.dcr.virginia.gov/natural_heritage), northeast side of the Nottoway River at SR 631, Sussex County. Ancient sandhills support several rare plant species. Walking trail and riverside wildlife observation platform.

Darden Country Store (757-357-6791; www.dardenscountrystore.com), 16249 Bowling Green Road, Smithfield 23431. Family store next to a smokehouse lets you have a look at meat products produced here, buy some homemade sausage, then enjoy a ham roll or a barbecue sandwich on the bench out front.

Edwards Virginia Ham Shoppe (757-294-3688; www.virginiatraditions.com), 11381 Rolfe Highway, Surry 23883. Hams here include the family's new Surryano Italian-style prosciutto (www.surryfarms.com) made from pasture-raised organic hogs.

Piney Grove Nature Preserve (804-644-5800; www.nature.org), Harrell Mill Road, Waverly 23890. Nature trail leads through the habitat of the last remaining population of red-cockaded woodpeckers in Virginia.

✪ ✎ ⟲ ⏲ **Smithfield Inn and Tavern** (757-357-1752; www.smithfieldinn.com), 112 Main Street, Smithfield 23430. Enjoy lunch or dinner in the elegant dining room, or join the locals in the tavern for ham rolls, live music, pork "wings," and microbrews.

✪ 🐾 ♿ ⟲ ⏲ ↪ **Smithfield Station Waterfront Restaurant, Inn and Marina** (757-357-7700; www.smithfieldstation .com), 415 S. Church Street, Smithfield 23430. Spend a romantic night in a Chesapeake Bay–style lighthouse, enjoy a gourmet Sun. brunch on the deck, or indulge in a sunset cocktail at the Inner Banx Bar and Grille, all accompanied by stunning views over the Pagan River. Live entertainment Wed. evenings.

EDWARDS, A FAMILY-OWNED BUSINESS IN SURRY, STILL CURES HAMS THE TRADITIONAL WAY.

Smith's Fort (757-294-3872; www.apva.org/smithsfort), 217 Smith Fort Lane, Surry 23833. Located close to the ferry landing on VA 31, this well-preserved brick plantation house, dated 1751–1765, retains much of its original interior woodwork. House tours: $5–8. Combo ticket with Bacon's Castle: $10–12.

✪ **Surry House Restaurant** (757-294-3389; www.surreyhouserestaurant .com), 11865 Rolfe Highway, Surry 23883. Popular stop on the ferry road serves creamy peanut soup, Edwards ham biscuits, homestyle vegetables, and country fried chicken.

Surry Nuclear Information Center (757-357-5410; www.dom.com), 5570 Hog Island Road, Surry 23883. Interactive exhibits explain the workings of a nuclear power plant.

Triangle with ferry ride across the James and lunch at the Surry House; a holiday lights tour of Newport News Park, Norfolk Botanical Garden, and the Virginia Beach Boardwalk; and one-day tours of Washington, D.C. On Tues., Oleta offers bus service from Williamsburg to Hampton and Newport News for $5 each way, including transfers to local transit systems.

By foot: **American Guided Tours** (757-729-2000; www.americanguidedtours.us). Lantern tours of historic Williamsburg include stories of ghosts and Blackbeard's pirate crew. Reservations required. Tickets $7–10; children six and under free.

Colonial Connections (757-258-3122 or 800-378-1571; www.colonialconnections .com). Three-hour private tours of Colonial Williamsburg for individuals or families prepare you to get the most from your visit.

Colonial Walking Tours (757-897-9600; www.williamsburgprivatetours.com). Join Williamsburg native John Sutton for private tours of Williamsburg, Yorktown, Jamestown, the Williamsburg Civil War Battlefield, or your choice of the James River plantations; treasure hunts for pirate gold; and lantern ghost tours.

Colonial Williamsburg Walking Tours (757-229-1000 or 800-447-8679; www.history.org). A wide variety of day and evening guided tours, some free with Colonial Williamsburg admission, others requiring a separate ticket. Evening tours include ghost and pirate walks, and Lanthorn tours of taverns and trade workshops. Advance reservations required.

Original Ghosts of Williamsburg Candlelight Tour (757-253-1058 or 877-62-GHOST; www.theghosttour.com). The town's most popular tour takes you through the dark streets of the Historic District revisiting tales from *The Ghosts of Williamsburg* by L. B. Taylor. Buy tickets in advance online or at the Williamsburg General Store (1656 Richmond Road, Williamsburg 23185). Tickets $11; children under seven free.

✪ **Preservation Virginia Jamestown Tours** (757-229-9973; www.historicjames towne.org), Historic Jamestowne. Senior staff offers specialty tours of the archaeological digs and Archaearium. Advanced ticketing required.

Virginia Native Plant Society (VNPS) (www.claytonvnps.org), P.O. Box 1128, Williamsburg 23187. Members of the local chapter of VNPS conduct frequent field trips and nature walks that are open to the public.

WILDLIFE- AND BIRD-WATCHING Several of the coastal loops of the **Virginia Birding and Wildlife Trail** run through the region, including the Lower Peninsula, Gloucester, Mathews, Mataponi (north side of I-64), Plantation (Charles City County), and Tidewater (south of the James) trails. Descriptions, driving directions, and maps can be found on the Virginia Department of Game and Inland Fisheries' Web site, www.dgif.virginia.gov/vbwt, or you can order a printed book of the trails by calling 804-367-1000 or by mailing 4010 W. Broad Street, Richmond 23230.

Mathews, at the tip of the Middle Peninsula, has designed its own *Mathews Birding and Nature Trails* guide, with three different driving tours. Order from the **Mathews County Visitor & Information Center** (877-725-4BAY; www.visit mathews.com; mcvic@visitmathews.com).

The **Williamsburg Bird Club** (www.williamsburgbirdclub.org) conducts public bird walks at **New Quarter Park** on the second and fourth Saturdays of every month, and a monthly field trip on third Saturdays. Visit the club's Web site for times and directions. The **Hampton Roads Birding Club** (www.hamptonroads birdclub.org) also conducts frequent field trips in the region.

✳ Wilder Places

College Landing Park (757-259-3760; www.williamsburgva.gov), S. Henry Street, Williamsburg 32185. Park adjacent to the W&M campus has a walkway crossing a marshy area, a lookout tower, and a kayak launch on College Creek.

Crawfords State Forest (804-834-2855; www.dof.virginia.gov), US 60, Providence Forge 23140. Wildlife sanctuary with large, old cypress and tupelo in Chickahominy Swamp is open for hiking, biking, and canoeing.

Cumberland Marsh Preserve (434-295-6106; www.nature.org), SR 637, New Kent 23124. Nature Conservancy preserve on the Pamunkey River in New Kent County has a handicapped-accessible boardwalk and observation deck offering views of many bird species, including bald eagles. No restrooms.

Goodwin Islands National Estuarine Research Reserve (804-684-7135; www.vims.edu/cbnerr), P.O. Box 1346, 1208 Greate Road, Gloucester Point 23062. Boaters may wade ashore at the beach on the north side of the main island for beachcombing and bird-watching.

York County Wetlands Interpretive Sanctuary for Education (WISE) at Charles E. Brown Park (757-890-4940; www.yorkcounty.gov/wise), 1950 Old Williamsburg Road/VA 238, Yorktown 23690. Informative 0.5-mile boardwalk winds through 2 acres of wetlands with many interpretive signs.

York River State Park (757-566-3036; www.dcr.virginia.gov), 5526 Riverview Road, Williamsburg 23188. Birders recommend the Taskinas Creek, Backbone, Woodstock Pond, and Majestic Oak trails, among this park's 25 miles of tracks through varied habitats.

✳ Lodging

Visitors to the Williamsburg area have a wide variety of accommodations to choose from, including upscale golf resorts, hotels from every national chain plus some fine independents, time-share resorts, bed & breakfast inns, and more modest guest houses. If you want to stay within walking distance of the Historic District, the **Colonial Williamsburg Resort** properties (www.colonial williamsburgresort.com) are a good choice and afford many special perks, including deep discounts on Colonial Williamsburg tickets. Income from Colonial Williamsburg Resort hotels and restaurants supports the Colonial Williamsburg Foundation.

The **Williamsburg Hotel and Motel Association** (800-999-4485; www.gowilliamsburg.com) offers accommodations at some three dozen different hotels, motels, and bed & breakfast inns, which can be combined with discounted tickets to Williamsburg, Jamestown, Yorktown, and other area attractions for impressive savings.

Price Categories

Inexpensive	up to $80
Moderate	$80 to $150
Expensive	$150 to $200
Very expensive	$200 and up

Williamsburg

✪ ♂ ⵏ "ɪ" ↝ **Colonial Williams-burg Resorts** (757-253-2277 or 800-HISTORY; www.colonialwilliamsburg resort.com), various sites, Williamsburg 23185. Price: Inexpensive to very expensive. Credit cards: Yes. Special features: Free Wi-Fi, day spa, championship golf courses, indoor and outdoor pools, tennis center, bicycle rentals, lawn bowling, package getaways, discount tickets. The grandest member of the Colonial Williamsburg Resort properties, the elegant **Williamsburg Inn** (136 E. Francis Street) opened in 1937, built by the Rockefellers to accommodate their friends. Since then it has housed royalty, presidents, and celebrities of every stripe. A formal lobby opens onto the wide lawns and gardens behind the hotel, with pleasant seating under the trees, while the front drive is directly adjacent to south side of the Historic District. Dining options at the inn include the **Regency Room,** with dining and dancing on weekend nights; the Rockefeller Room, with prix fixe menus; and the more casual Terrace Room and Restoration Bar. Call 757-229-2141 for reservations.

Next door, the **Providence Hall Guesthouses** (305 S. England Street) offer private, spacious accommodations, each with a balcony or patio, at slightly lower prices. Or stay at the extensive **Williamsburg Lodge** (310 S. England Street), with decor inspired by the folk art collection at the nearby Abby Aldrich Rockefeller Museum. The Lodge Restaurant serves regional cuisine, including a reasonably priced lunch buffet. Visit the Lodge Lounge for light fare and live music around the 1939 fireplace.

On the north side of the Historic District next to the visitors center, the moderately priced **Williamsburg Woodlands Hotel and Suites** (105 Visitor Center Drive) provides ideal accommodations for families, with miniature golf, bike rentals, and an outdoor pool, plus continental breakfast included in the rate. During the summer season, the nearby **Governor's Inn** (506 N. Henry Street) offers value priced, motel-style accommodations.

For a unique experience, stay in the Historic District itself, in one of 26 **colonial houses** where the Founding Fathers once lodged. Furnished in period antiques and reproductions, these range from rooms in an old tavern to former servants' quarters.

♿ "ɪ" **Fife & Drum Inn** (888-838-1783; www.fifeanddruminn.com), 441 Prince George Street, Williamsburg 23185. Innkeepers: Billy and Sharon Scruggs. Price: Moderate to expensive. Credit cards: Yes. Special features: Free Wi-Fi in the common room. Inn operated by members of an old Williamsburg family enjoys a hugely convenient location adjacent to Merchants Square, steps from the Historic District, and just two blocks from the AMTRAK train station. Seven spacious rooms and two suites, decorated with historic memorabilia, are located upstairs above the shops and restaurants on Prince George Street. Daily breakfast, with savory casseroles, ham biscuits, granola, and fresh fruit, is included. The common room contains a TV, plus fireplace, library, and colonial games. The private, handicapped-accessible **Drummers Cottage,** which sleeps six, is located across Boundary Street.

♿ ♂ ⵏ "ɪ" ↝ **Williamsburg Hospitality House** (757-229-4020 or 800-932-9192; www.williamsburghosp house.com), 415 Richmond Road, Williamsburg 23185. Price: Moderate to expensive. Credit cards: Yes. Special features: Safe deposit boxes, fax service, laundry service, Wi-Fi (fee), concierge and bellman, on-site gift shop, fitness center, free underground parking, outdoor pool. Two blocks from Merchants Square and right across the street from the W&M campus, this independent hotel was recently renovated with nicely appointed guest rooms and suites, a welcoming lobby with fireplace, and a garden courtyard. Two restaurants are located on-site: the casual **415 Grill,** serving lunch and dinner, with a lounge that hosts dancing and karaoke, and **Papillon,** a garden bistro serving breakfast daily plus holiday buffets.

Yorktown

& "1" **Duke of York Hotel** (757-898-3232; www.dukeofyorkmotel.com), 508 Water Street, Yorktown 23690. Price: Moderate. Credit cards: Yes. Special features: Jacuzzi and kitchenette rooms available, free trolley to Yorktown attractions, outdoor seasonal pool, free parking, free Wi-Fi in public areas. Located across the street from Yorktown Beach, this well-kept older property with a 1950s vibe enjoys an excellent location and superb views across the York River, at prices far lower than you'll pay at beachfront establishments elsewhere. Most rooms have balconies overlooking the water. The hotel's **Duke of York Cafe** (757-898-5270) serves breakfast and lunch, seven days a week, and dinner Wed.–Sun., with a seafood kabob and other local specialties on the menu.

♪ ✿ **Marl Inn Bed and Breakfast** (757-898-3859 or 800-799-6207; www.marlinnbandb.com), 220 Church Street, Yorktown 23690. Innkeepers: Seldon and Marcia Plumley. Price: Moderate. Credit cards: Yes. Special features: Children and pets welcome; two-night minimum on weekends, Mar.–Oct., and holidays. Located in Yorktown's historic district just two blocks from the Riverwalk, this rambling Colonial set amid gardens rents two rooms and two suites, all with private outside entrances; private baths; microwaves, refrigerators, coffeemakers, and dishes; TVs; and VCRs with a movie library. Enjoy a full breakfast of crab quiche or eggs Benedict in the dining room or on the garden patio, or opt for the value package with cereal, juice, oatmeal, and fresh banana cinnamon bread in your room.

↝ **York River Inn Bed and Breakfast** (757-887-8800 or 800-884-7003; www.yorkriverinn.com), 209 Ambler Street, Yorktown 23690. Innkeeper: Bill Cole. Price: Moderate. Credit cards: Yes. Special features: Wi-Fi access, iPods, bidets, fax service, washer and dryer. Set high on a bluff with wonderful views of the York River and close to the historic district, this brick Colonial has three spacious guest rooms available for visitors. The three-story house is surrounded by gardens, and a large deck overlooks the river. Gourmet breakfasts feature many unusual family recipes, such as Clam-a-lama-Ding-Dongs and Wild Rice, Sausage, and Mushroom Pie. Guests can help themselves to freshly baked sweets and a refrigerator full of beverages all day. Besides being an expert chef, innkeeper Bill Cole comes from a family of collectors and displays an impressive set of maps, prints, books, and other memorabilia related to early Virginia.

SMALL INNS, COTTAGES, AND GUEST HOUSES Williamsburg has many bed & breakfast inns, as well as some private homes that take in guests, an old local tradition. The **Williamsburg Bed and Breakfast Network** (www.bandbwilliamsburg.com) lists more than two dozen inns around the region, from modest homes close to the Historic District to country manor houses. Many of the B&Bs are noted for their excellent, colonial-inspired morning fare. Breakfast is usually not served at guest houses, but rates are considerably lower.

Country Cottage (757-715-2332; www.countrycottagebnb.com), 325 Ewell Road, Williamsburg 23188. Two-bedroom cottage with full kitchen just off the Richmond Road. Moderate.

Forest Hill Guest Home (757-229-1444), 15 Forest Hill Drive, Williamsburg 23185. For a romantic getaway, reserve the only room at this hideaway, next to a duck pond in the heart of Williamsburg. Inexpensive.

Hughes' Guest Home (757-229-3493), 106 Newport Avenue, Williamsburg 23185. First-floor rooms a block from the Historic District. Inexpensive.

Johnson's Guest Home (757-229-3909), 101 Thomas Nelson Lane, Williamsburg 23185. Rooms with canopy beds. Inexpensive.

Moss Guest Cottage (757-715-2007; www.mossguestcottage.com), 224 Nelson Street, Yorktown 23690. One-bedroom cottage in Yorktown's historic district is perfect for romantic getaways. No smoking, children, or pets. Moderate.

✪ ✎ ❀ **Newport House Bed and Breakfast** (757-229-1775 or 877-565-1775; www.newporthousebb.com), 710 S. Henry Street, Williamsburg 23185. A former museum director, owner of this authentic re-creation of a 1756 design by the architect of the Williamsburg Capitol, hosts Tues.-night colonial dancing parties and rents period costumes to guests.

🍴 **The Pineapple Inn and Housing** (757-259-9670 or 866-538-6194; www.pineapplehousing.com), 5437 Richmond Road, Williamsburg 23188. Inexpensive hostel-style rooms available at weekly rates. Caters to international students and visitors.

✎ **Simpson House Cottage** (757-220-3575; www.aviewofamerica.com), 10 Bayberry Lane, Williamsburg 23185. Small cottage with upstairs master bedroom overlooks a wooded ravine near the W&M campus. Children under 12 welcome. Continental breakfast included. Moderate.

Williamsburg Sampler (757-253-0398 or 800-722-1169; www.williamsburgsampler.com), 922 Jamestown Road, Williamsburg 23185. Decorated with antique samplers throughout, this inn across from W&M is noted for its bounteous Skip Lunch breakfast, on-site billiards parlor, and fitness center with sauna. Expensive.

RV AND CAMPING RESORTS 🍴

American Heritage RV Park (757-566-2133 or 800-530-2267; www.americanheritagervpark.com), 146 Maxton Lane, Williamsburg 23185. Big-rig-friendly Good Sam park includes free Wi-Fi and cable TV at every site. Park models and cabins available.

Anvil Campground (757-565-2300 or 800-633-4442; www.anvilcampground.com), 5243 Mooretown Road, Williamsburg 23188. Operated by a family of blacksmiths, this campground offers shuttle service via Williamsburg Area Transit to local attractions, rental cottages, and more.

✪ ✎ **Chickahominy Riverfront Park** (757-258-5020; www.jccegov.com), 1350 John Tyler Highway, Williamsburg 23185. County park on the Chickahominy, with tents and RV sites, two seasonal swimming pools, boat ramp, free fishing pier, driving range, and rental boats. Served as the backdrop for the film *The New World*, starring Colin Farrell.

Ed Allen's Chickahominy Recreational Park (804-966-2582; www.edallens.com), 13501 Campground Road, Lanexa 23089. Family-friendly resort on Chickahominy Lake, with full-service campground, rental cabins, stocked fishing pond, lakeside restaurant, and the world's largest bass-shaped swimming pool. **Ed Allen's Boats and Baits** (804-966-5368) next door.

Riverside Camp II Campground (804-966-5536; www.riversidecamp2 .com), 715 Riverside Drive, Lanexa 23089. Small fish camp on the Chickahominy with riverfront cabins and sites for tents and RVs, fishing boat and kayak rentals, bait and tackle shop, boat ramp and pier. Open Mar. 1–Nov. 15.

Ψ **Rockahock Campgrounds** (804-966-8362; www.rockahock.com), 1428 OutPost Road, Lanexa 23089. Resort on the Chickahominy offers RV sites; rental cottages, park models, and yurts; marina; **Rock's River Roadhouse,** with live bands year-round; and amphitheater hosting outdoor music festivals.

White Tail Resort (757-859-6123 or 800-987-6833; www.whitetailresort .org), 39033 White Tail Drive, Ivor 23866. Virginia's only year-round nudist resort, with RV and tent sites, indoor and outdoor pools, children's activities, rental units, and more. Day passes available.

⚘ "¶" **Williamsburg KOA Campground** (757-565-2734 or 800-562-1733; www.williamsburgkoa.com), 4000 Newman Road, Williamsburg 23188. Large 390-site campground with heated pools; Jumping Pillow; free cable, bicycle use, and Wi-Fi; K9 dog park; lodges and Kamping Kabins; golf-cart rentals. Open all year.

Williamsburg Pottery Campground (757-565-2101 or 800-892-0320; www .williamsburgpottery.com), 6692 Richmond Road, Williamsburg 23188. Campground next to the famous pottery factory has 550 sites with hookups, including 50 amp sites and tent sites, plus a large swimming pool.

TIME-SHARE AND CONDOMINIUM RENTALS Williamsburg is one of the nation's top destinations for time-share exchanges, with more than four thousand units available for weekly exchange through RCI and Interval International. Most of these resorts also rent to nonmembers by the night or week, with some attractive packages available. With complete kitchens, washer/dryers, and many recreational options, these are often a good choice for families.

Contact the individual resorts for reservations or use a company that books condominium rentals, such as **Resort Rentals International** (757-259-9294 or 800-910-9294; www.resort rentalsintl.com).

Ψ "¶" **Diamond Resorts** (www .diamondresorts.com). Prestigious international company with two resorts occupying old plantation sites on the east side of Williamsburg: **Greensprings Plantation** (757-253-1177 or 800-438-2929; www.greensprings plantation.com; 3500 Ludwell Parkway, Williamsburg 23188), adjacent to the Jack Nicklaus–designed National Golf Course; and **Powhatan Plantation** (757-220-1200 or 800-438-2929; www .powhatanplantation.com; 3601 Ironbound Road, Williamsburg 23188), with a historic restored manor house, cocktail lounge, two restaurants, and free racquetball court.

King's Creek Plantation (757-221-6766 or 877-557-3529; www.kings creekplantation.com), 191 Cottage Cove Lane, Williamsburg 23185. Cottages and town houses next to Water Country USA.

⤵ **Marriott's Manor Club at Ford's Colony** (757-258-1120; www.marriott .com), 101 St. Andrew's Drive, Williamsburg 23188. Enjoy world-class golf and AAA five diamond dining at the country's most acclaimed planned community, **Ford's Colony** (800-334-6033; www.fordscolony.com).

➤ **Wyndham Vacation Resorts** (800-438-6493; www.wyndhamvacation resorts.com). Three resorts, formerly Fairfield, in Williamsburg: **Wyndham Governor's Green** (757-564-2420; 4600 Mooretown Road, Williamsburg 23188), **Wyndham Kingsgate** (757-220-5702; 619 Georgetown Crescent, Williamsburg 23185), and **Wyndham Patriots' Place** (757-220-5300; 725 Bypass Road, Williamsburg 23185).

✳ Where to Eat

The Historic Triangle is one of the best places in the country to sample foods and recipes popular in the 18th century. Numerous chefs at area restaurants take their inspiration from the regional produce that made up the colonial diet, from crabs to corn bread. Sweet potato biscuits with country ham, Brunswick stew, and johnnycakes are just a few of the local dishes you'll find on menus.

This is the land of pork, with Smithfield, the world's largest producer of hams, and Edwards, a local contender, headquartered just across the James. Local stores carry a wide range of bacons, hams, and other pork products. One rather unusual local item to look for is the Dandoodle or Tom Thumb sausage, made by stuffing a spicy mix of ground pork, sage, red pepper, and other spices into a clean pork intestine or stomach, then dry-curing and smoking the haggis-shaped delicacy. To serve, the Dandoodle is boiled, then slipped from its casing, sliced, and accompanied with deviled eggs.

Dandoodles can be found in small markets all across the region, such as **Grayson & Emma's Gardenspot** on US 58 in Courtland. **Edwards of Surry** (www.virginiatraditions.com) makes its own version that you can order online.

Colonial Williamsburg's Historic Foodways program preserves and demonstrates period food-preparation techniques. Members of the Foodways team keep busy in the restored kitchens of the Governor's Palace and the Peyton Randolph House cooking dishes typical of the day, using reproduction utensils. A Foodways conference is held in November (www .history.org/conted), and special programs are offered seasonally, including Hogs to Ham in December, the Art and Mysteries of Brewing in spring and fall, and the popular Secrets of the Chocolate Maker, where cocoa beans are ground by hand into liquid chocolate, during the fall, winter, and spring.

Chocolate company Mars Inc. sponsors the chocolate program and produces a line of American Heritage Chocolates based on traditional techniques, available at stores in the Historic District, the Craft House, and museum shops.

Foodies may want to plan their visit in late January to coincide with the annual **Williamsburg Restaurant Week** (www.williamsburgarea restaurants.com), when more than a dozen of the best local restaurants offer bargain-priced lunch and dinner menus.

Price Categories

Inexpensive	under $10
Moderate	$10 to $20
Expensive	$20 to $25
Very expensive	$25 and up

The listings in this section also include information on what meals are served, using the following abbreviations:

B	Breakfast
L	Lunch
D	Dinner
SB	Sunday brunch

Williamsburg

🎣 ♿ 🍷 **Berret's Seafood Restaurant and Taphouse Grill** (757-253-1847; www.berrets.com), 199 S. Boundary Street, Williamsburg 23185. Open: Tues.–Sun., Jan.–Feb.; grill closed Nov.–Mar. Credit cards: Yes. Serving: L, D, SB. Price: Expensive (restaurant); moderate (grill). Cuisine: Seafood. Handicapped access: Yes. Special features: Live music in the Taphouse on weekends, nightly specials, children's menu, online reservations for the dining room, no reservations in the grill. Popular spot in Merchants Square receives the locals' award for Best Seafood nearly every year. Specializing in fresh Chesapeake Bay seafood, including blue crab feasts, fish baked in parchment, bouillabaisse, and crabcakes topped with Virginia ham, the inside restaurant also serves an excellent steak topped with Brie and a vegetarian polenta lasagna. Outside in the open-air Taphouse Grill, the action is livelier and the prices lower, with a menu of steamed seafood favorites, sandwiches, and specialties from the rotisserie, including Cornish game hens and dry-rubbed pork. Much of the food and wine here is from local Virginia sources, with several local microbrews on tap.

🎣 ♿ **Food for Thought** (757-645-4665; www.foodforthoughtrestaurant .com), 1647 Richmond Road, Williamsburg 23185. Open: Daily. Credit cards: Yes. Serving: L, D. Price: Moderate. Cuisine: American. Handicapped access: Yes. Special features: Call ahead for priority seating, children's menu, full bar, local microbrews. Eat surrounded by quotations from Ben Franklin and other Founding Fathers at this restaurant that urges you to: "Eat! Drink! Think!" Puzzles and games are fun for the whole family, as is the menu, stacked with popular comfort food such as pot roast, ribs, and meat loaf; some healthy chicken and seafood dishes; plus several creative vegetarian offerings featuring spaghetti squash, eggplant, and portobello mushrooms. The "All In One" grilled steak salad also comes in a vegetarian version, and the roasted veggie bisque takes the edge off a chilly day. Top off your meal with bread pudding laced with cherries.

♿ **The Kitchen at Powhatan Plantation** (757-253-7893 or 757-220-1200; www.kitchenatpowhatan.com), 3601 Ironbound Road, Williamsburg 23188. Open: Fri. and Sat. evenings and holidays. Credit cards: Yes. Serving: D. Price: Very expensive. Cuisine: American. Handicapped access: Yes. Special features: Reservations highly recommended; wine, beer, sherry, cognacs, and cordials available. In this little white frame building next to the imposing brick manor house built by architect Robert Taliaferro in 1736, Chef Julia Fitchett brings the lavish dishes that once graced the tables of Williamsburg's gentry to life. Relying largely on foods produced by local Virginia farmers, and herbs and vegetables from the plantation garden, the menu changes often, featuring seafood and wild game, quail stuffed with sausage and corn bread, a creamless wild mushroom soup laced with white truffle oil, and, for dessert, warm pecan pie. The atmosphere is reminiscent of a fine colonial tavern, lit by candlelight and the glow from a fire in the large fireplace, with servers dressed in period costumes, and pewter serving dishes. Today part of the Historic Powhatan Plantation resort, this restaurant transports you to another time and is well worth the journey.

The Trellis (757-229-8610; www.the trellis.com), 403 Duke of Gloucester Street, Williamsburg 23185. Open: Daily. Credit cards: Yes. Serving: L, D, SB. Price: Expensive. Cuisine: Locavore. Handicapped access: Yes. Special features: Daily specials, small-plate bar menu, vegan or lacto-ovo vegetarian entrées available, prix fixe dinners, outdoor dining, lounge. An island of serenity in the midst of Merchants Square, this freshly renovated restaurant brings the garden indoors, featuring locally produced seasonal foods in innovative combinations. Now owned by chef David Everett, who also operates the nearby highly rated **Blue Talon Bistro** (757-476-2583; www.bluetalonbistro.com; 420 Prince George Street, Williamsburg 23185), the Trellis has a new focus on American foods, wines, and beers, many produced in the region. The restaurant is known for its desserts, designed by former owner Marcel Desaulniers, author of *Desserts to Die For.* His masterpiece, the original Death by Chocolate, seven luscious layers of chocolate cake, mousse, and cocoa meringue, remains on the menu.

Yorktown

Carrot Tree Kitchen at Yorktown (757-988-1999; www.carrottreekitchens.com), 411 Main Street, Yorktown 23690. Open: Daily for lunch, Thurs.–Sat. for dinner. Credit cards: Yes. Serving: L, D, high tea. Price: Moderate. Cuisine: Locavore. Handicapped access: Yes. Special features: Historical meals with entertainment and reenactors, children's menu, literary teas, reservations recommended. Occupying one of the oldest buildings in town, the circa 1720 Cole Digges House, this restaurant offers authentic colonial recipes with some modern twists, including Old Dominion ham

biscuits, Brunswick stew, crabcakes laced with country ham, and the President's Fruit Salad, combining the favorite fruits of Washington, Jefferson, and Monroe. Lunch here is a real bargain and the foodie highlight of a day in Yorktown. Don't miss the famous carrot cake and other baked goods, also available at the Carrot Tree's Williamsburg locations near the Jamestown ferry dock (1782 Jamestown Road) and inside Yankee Candle (2200 Richmond Road).

Nicks Riverwalk Restaurant and the Rivah Cafe (757-875-1522; www.riverwalkrestaurant.net), 323 Water Street, Yorktown 23690. Open: Daily. Credit cards: Yes. Serving: L, D, SB. Price: Expensive; Rivah Cafe moderate. Cuisine: Seafood. Handicapped access: Yes. Special features: Children's menu; outdoor dining; lounge with full bar and happy hour specials; dinner and a sunset sail package; live music on the patio; wine and beer dinners; comedy and poker nights. Enjoying spectacular views of the York River and

COLONIAL WILLIAMSBURG'S HISTORIC FOODWAYS PROGRAM RE-CREATES AUTHENTIC DISHES TYPICAL OF THE 18TH CENTURY.

REENACTORS IN PERIOD COSTUMES FREQUENT COLONIAL WILLIAMSBURG'S TAVERNS.

COLONIAL DINING

Due to health regulations, the dishes produced by the Historic Foodways chefs can't be served to visitors, but Colonial Williamsburg has several taverns and shops where you can sample authentic 18th-century fare. Besides period dishes, the taverns offer ales made using traditional methods and an array of colonial-style rum punches, as well as nonalcoholic root beer and ginger ale made from old recipes. The taverns usually close during January for refurbishment.

Coleman Bridge, these swank spots on the Riverwalk provide a variety of dining choices. The restaurant serves seafood, steaks, lamb, pastas, and poultry, including several surf and turf combinations and the signature Baked Oysters Riverwalk, topped with crabmeat and garlic butter. Or opt for the more casual Rivah Cafe and Courtyard for a menu of sandwiches and salads. Locals like this spot for Sun. brunch, attracted by the creative treatments of eggs, crab, and local pork, and the bottomless mimosas.

& ⵕ **Yorktown Pub** (757-886-9964; www.myspace.com/yorktownpub), 112 Water Street, Yorktown 23690. Open: Daily. Credit cards: Yes. Serving: L, D. Price: Inexpensive. Cuisine: American. Handicapped access: Yes (dining room). Special features: Happy hour, nightly dinner specials, full bar. Local watering hole across the street from Yorktown Beach serves a pub menu featuring fresh local seafood, Boar's Head deli sandwiches, and Carrot Tree desserts, plus a nice list of brews, in a casual, friendly atmosphere. Prime rib

Call 757-229-2141 or 1-800-HISTORY for reservations, or visit www.history.org for information and menus.

Charlton's Coffeehouse, Duke of Gloucester Street. New reconstruction near the capitol building serves traditional chocolate, tea, and coffee drinks.

↪ **Christiana Campbell's Tavern,** 101 S. Waller Street. George Washington's journals reveal that he often supped on oysters at this tavern behind the Colonial Capitol building. Seafood is still the specialty, along with a macaroni dish based on a 1769 recipe. Reservations required.

Chowning's Tavern, 109 E. Duke of Gloucester Street. An establishment appealing to the common man, this tavern serves Brunswick stew, barbecue, and sandwiches (an 18th-century invention), as well as a long list of ales on tap and rum drinks. No reservations.

↪ **King's Arms Tavern,** 416 E. Duke of Gloucester Street. Williamsburg's most elegant tavern serves lunch and candlelight dinner by reservation only.

M. Dubois Grocer, 424 Duke of Gloucester Street. Reconstruction of a 1779 store carries smoked hams, ales, root beer, ciders, preserved fruits, and American Heritage Chocolates.

Raleigh Tavern Bakeshop, 410 Duke of Gloucester Street. Colonial bake shop serves ginger cakes, cookies, cider, and cheese to tourists, but locals stop by for a dozen sweet potato muffins, a loaf of authentic Sally Lunn Bread, or a currant-laden Queen's Cake.

↪ **Shields Tavern,** 422 E. Duke of Gloucester Street. Specialties include crayfish chowder, Welsh rarebit, and peanut butter pie. Reservations required.

sandwiches are a specialty. Live music by local bands for ages 21 and older most weekend nights.

BAKERIES AND COFFEE SHOPS

✪ 🐾 ♿ "♍" **Aromas Coffeehouse, Bakeshop & Cafe** (757-221-6676; www.aromasworld.com), Merchants Square, 431 Prince George Street, Williamsburg 23185. Great location close to the Historic District; coffee and tea, beer and wine; live music; dog-friendly sidewalk tables; DIY s'mores; and free Wi-Fi—all crucial for a day of touring.

♿ "♍" **Ben & Jerry's/Green Mountain Coffee Cafe** (757-969-1990; www.benjerry.com/yorktown), 332 Water Street, Yorktown 23690. Organic, fair trade coffee; ice cream; and free Wi-Fi on the Yorktown waterfront.

Carrot Tree Kitchens (757-229-0957; www.carrottreekitchens.com), 1782 Jamestown Road, Williamsburg 23185. Wonderful baked goods, including a famous carrot cake, at this little lunchroom in a motel just north of the ferry landing.

The Coffeehouse (757-229-9791; www.gocoffeehouse.com), 5251 John Tyler Highway, Williamsburg Crossing Shopping Center, Williamsburg 23185. Gourmet teas and coffees, including a signature Williamsburg blend made with beans roasted on-site.

&. "T" **Harbour Coffee** (757-220-2334; www.harbourcoffee.com), 4260 Casey Boulevard, Williamsburg 23188. House-roasted beans and free Wi-Fi in New Town.

BARBECUE AND FAST FOOD

Hog Wild Smokehouse (757-741-2515; www.hogwildsmokehouse.com), 8864 Richmond Road, Toano 23168. Barbecue meets the bayou at this restaurant serving pulled pork and ribs, plus Louisiana favorites such as muf-fulettas and shrimp Creole. New Orleans–style Sun. brunch.

❂ **Pierce's Pitt Bar-B-Que** (757-565-2955; www.pierces.com), 447 E. Rochambeau Drive, Williamsburg 23188. Tennessee-style barbecue pork, voted Best of the South by the readers of *Southern Living*, marinated in "Doc" Pierce's special sauce.

Retro's Good Eats (757-253-8816; www.retrosgoodeats.com), Merchants Square, 435 Prince George Street, Williamsburg 23185. Cool, '50s soda shop serves burgers, barbecue, and hot dogs, plus frozen custard ice cream. Summer movie series.

BREAKFAST AND CASUAL

MEALS Pancakes and waffles are the name of the game at breakfast time in Williamsburg. Over a dozen local and chain pancake houses offer very similar menus: fruit-topped and chocolate chip pancakes and waffles, plus "plan-tation" breakfasts with eggs, Virginia country ham or bacon, grits, and bis-cuits. Most open early and close at 2 PM. We list a couple of the most popu-lar below, but all are similar in food

and price, and many are showing their age a bit. Usually the best plan is to patronize a spot between your hotel and your day's destination.

Candle Light Kitchen (757-564-0803), 7521 Richmond Road, Williamsburg 23188. Local favorite serves breakfast and lunch next to the former Williamsburg Candle Factory.

✐ "T" **Capitol Pancake & Waffle House** (757-564-1238; www.pancake houses.com), 802 Capitol Landing Road, Williamsburg 23185. A couple of unusual items join the menu here, including breakfast burritos and pigs in a blanket, both available in kid-sized portions. Free Wi-Fi.

The Gazebo Pancake and Waffle House (757-220-0883; www.thegazebo restaurant.com), 409 Bypass Road, Williamsburg 23185. One of the high-est rated pancake houses has all the usual items, generally priced under $6, plus friendly service.

❂ **Old Chickahominy House** (757-229-4689; www.oldchickahominy.com), 1211 Jamestown Road, Williamsburg 23185. One of the town's highest rated restaurants, but it's only open for breakfast and lunch. The Virginia ham biscuits, blueberry pancakes, Bruns-wick stew, chicken and dumplings, and Rebel cocktails all live up to their rep-utations. The historic plantation house also displays three stories of antiques and gifts. Open seasonally.

CANDY AND SWEETS ✐ ✿ The

Candy Store Factory Warehouse Outlet (757-565-1151; www.wythewill .com), 6623 Richmond Road/US 60, Lightfoot 23090. Candies from all over the world at discount prices.

CoCo Chocolatier and Creperie (757-258-0808; www.cocochocolatier .com), 4904 Courthouse St., New Town, Williamsburg 23188. Chocolate fondue, sweet and savory crêpes, plus

AFTERNOON TEA

Taking tea was an important part of colonial society. Several spots in the region offer traditional afternoon tea to put you in that historical mood.

Carrot Tree Kitchen at Yorktown's Cole Digges House (757-988-1999; www.carrottreekitchens.com), 411 Main Street, Yorktown 23690. Literary and musical teas weekly. Call for schedule.

First Ladies Tea Parlor at Presidents Park (757-259-1121; www.presidentspark.org or www.firstladiesteaparlor.com), 211 Water Country Parkway, Williamsburg 23185. Afternoon tea on weekends by reservation. Second location at Port Warwick (757-725-3111; The Melville, 2312 William Styron Square, Suite 2170, Newport News 23606).

La Petite Tea Room (757-565-3422; www.antiqueswilliamsburg.com), 500 Lightfoot Road/SR 646, Williamsburg 23188. Scottish-style tearoom inside the Williamsburg Antique Mall.

⁰ı⁰ **New Town Avenue Coffee and Tea at Parlett's** (757-564-7000; www.parletts.com), 5000 Foundation Street, Williamsburg 23188. Free Wi-Fi.

Olde World Tea Company (757-3560-TEA; www.oldeworldtea.com), 327 Main Street, Smithfield 23430. Free tea samples next to the Smithfield Visitor Center.

Taste Tea Salon and Gifts (757-221-9550; www.tasteteasalon.com), 1915 Pocahontas Trail/US 60, the Village Shops at Kingsmill, Williamsburg 23185. Afternoon and children's tea by reservation.

⇔ **Williamsburg Inn** (757-229-2141), 136 E. Francis Street, Williamsburg 23185. Call for schedule.

---

artisanal chocolates from around the world.

Virginia's Finest Chocolates (757-258-5465 or 888-821-2462; www.chocolategifts.com), 233 Jones Mill Road, Williamsburg 23188. Handmade chocolates, plus unique chocolate camps for children and adults.

Wythe Candy & Gourmet Shop (757-229-4406; www.wythecandy.com), 414 W. Duke of Gloucester Street, Williamsburg 23185. Huge selection of candies, plus fudge, candy apples, and chocolates, in Merchants Square.

DELIS & SANDWICHES The Cheese Shop (757-220-0298; www.cheeseshopwilliamsburg.com), 410 W. Duke of Gloucester Street, Williamsburg 23185. Popular with locals and tourists alike, this Merchants Square sandwich shop can be chaotic at lunchtime. Regulars suggest you call in your order and pick it up at the outside window. Extensive basement wine cellar. Most seating is outdoors. Sister restaurant **Fat Canary** (757-229-3333; www.fatcanarywilliamsburg.com; 410 W. Duke of Gloucester Street,

Williamsburg 23185) is a consistent winner of AAA four-diamond awards.

⁰Ⱡ⁰ College Delly & Pizza (757-220-0353; www.collegedelly.com), 336 Richmond Road, Williamsburg 23185. College hangout with a big, covered patio and full bar serves New York–style pizza, gyros, and several vegetarian subs, including the popular Three Way, with three cheeses and dill pickles. Free Wi-Fi.

Florimonte's Fine Foods and Deli (757-253-2266; www.florimontes.com), 5251 John Tyler Highway, Williamsburg 23185. Culinary Institute of America grad creates fresh pasta, New York–style pizza, prepared salads, and ready-to-eat meals.

Sweet Madeleine's (www.sweet madeleines.com), two locations: Monticello Market Place, 4680 Monticello Avenue, Williamsburg 23288 (757-220-3131); and 2091 George Washington Memorial Highway/US 17, Gloucester 23062 (804-642-1780). Lunch spots, famous for desserts, run by a top area cater.

Ⱡ Paul's Deli Restaurant (757-229-8976; www.paulsdelirestaurant.com), 761 Scotland Street, Williamsburg 23185. Located across from the W&M campus, this casual spot, named one of the best delis in the country by *Rolling Stone* magazine, serves Greek and Italian dishes, and New England–style pizza and subs, with a full bar, until 2 AM.

FARMS, FARMER'S MARKETS, AND COOKING SCHOOLS

A Chef's Kitchen (757-564-8500; www.achefskitchen.biz), 501 Prince George Street, Williamsburg 23185. Enjoy a five-course meal, accompanied by paired wines and champagne, prepared by Chef John Gonzales, author of two books for the Colonial Williamsburg Foundation, in his demonstration

kitchen.

⌀ Bush Neck Farm (757-258-0114), 1502 Bush Neck Road, Williamsburg 23188. Pick-your-own strawberries, apples, blueberries, asparagus, sweet corn, peaches, and pumpkins just a few miles from the Historic District. Picnic area.

College Run Farms (757-294-3970; www.collegerunfarms.com), Alliance Road, Surry 23883. Pick-your-own or fresh-picked strawberries (Apr.–May), sweet corn (June–July), and pumpkins (Sept.–Oct.), across the ferry in Surry County.

⌀ Hidden Brook Farm (757-561-1477; www.hiddenbrookfarm.us), 100 Skillman Drive, Toano 23168. Pick-your-own strawberries and blackberries.

Toano Farmers Market (757-508-3352), 3135 Forge Road, Toano 23168. Market run by the Toano Volunteer Fire Department is open all year, Tues.–Sat. dawn–dusk.

⁰Ⱡ⁰ Williamsburg Farmers Market (757-259-3768; www.williamsburg farmersmarket.com), Duke of Gloucester Street, Merchants Square, Williamsburg 23185. Recently voted the best midsized farmer's market in the United States, with local organic produce, soft-shell crabs, chocolates, and goat cheese, plus live music, and cooking and gardening demonstrations. Sat. mornings. Seasonal.

Yorktown Market Days at the River (757-890-3500; www.york county.gov/riverwalk), Riverwalk Landing, Yorktown. Sat.-morning markets on the Riverwalk feature local produce and seafood, baked goods, herbs, and crafts, plus live music. Seasonal.

ICE CREAM AND FROZEN YOGURT **Berry Body Frozen Yogurt** (www.berrybody.com). Healthy frozen treats with active probiotics at

three regional locations: Williamsburg, in Five Forks (757-221-0505; 4511 John Tyler Highway, Williamsburg 23185); Yorktown, next to the County Grill (757-594-9393; 1213 H George Washington Highway, Yorktown 23693); and in Port Warwick (757-595-6110; 4181 William Styron Square, Newport News 23606).

Handel's Homemade Ice Cream & Yogurt (757-565-3003; www.handels icecream.com), 6601 Richmond Road, Williamsburg 23188. Quality frozen treats made fresh daily on-site.

⌀ **Sno-To-Go** (757-229-0017; www .sno-to-go.com), 2229 Richmond Road, Williamsburg 23185. Refreshing shaved ice snow cones come filled with ice cream, New Orleans style, in 40 flavors. Seasonal.

NATURAL FOODS AND VEGE-TARIAN MENUS
Dudley's Farmhouse Grille (757-577-1157; www .dudleysfarmhousegrille.com), 7816 Richmond Road/US 60, Toano 23168. Lunch, dinner, and Sun. brunch served in this 1905 farmhouse, or in the organic herb garden outside, feature local produce and organic meats.

Farm Fresh Foods (www.farmfresh supermarkets.com), several locations. Full-service supermarkets have extensive Natural Connection departments stocking organic, vegetarian, and natural foods and products, plus salad bars and delis.

Martin's (757-564-0455; www.martins foods.com), 4660 Monticello Avenue, Williamsburg 23188. Former Ukrop's supermarket in Monticello Marketplace has an expanded organic and natural foods section, wine and beer tastings, plus 60-item salad bar and café with vegetarian options.

Nawab Indian Cuisine (757-565-3200; www.nawabonline.com), 204 Monticello Avenue, Williamsburg 23185. Special menu section of vegetarian dishes, with several vegan choices. Additional locations in Virginia Beach, Norfolk, and Newport News.

PIZZA AND TAKE-OUT
Jamestown Pie Company (757-229-7775; www.buyapie.com), 1804 Jamestown Road, Williamsburg 23185. Devoted to all food round, this little take-out-only spot tucked into the trees serves gourmet pizzas, deep-dish potpies, and famous pecan pie. Call ahead if you don't want to wait.

⌀ **Sal's by Victor Restaurant and Pizzeria** (757-220-2641; www.salsby victor.com), 1242 Richmond Road, Williamsburg 23185. Voted Best Pizzeria for more than a decade, this spot in Williamsburg Shopping Center offers thin-crust and Sicilian square pizzas, plus Italian specialties, to eat in or take out. Free delivery.

⌀ **Stephanos Pizza and Subs** (757-476-8999; www.stephanosofwilliams burg.com), 110 S. Henry Street, Williamsburg 23185. Good stop in Merchants Square for young tourists in need of a pizza fix.

SPECIALTY FOODS
Think you know your hams? A tour of Williamsburg's specialty-food shops may reveal a thing or two.

Edwards Virginia Ham Shoppe of Williamsburg (757-220-6618; www .virginiatraditions.com), 1814 Richmond Road, Williamsburg 23185. The Edwards family has been smoking hams over hickory logs since 1926. Drop by for a free sample or a ham roll, plus peanuts, sweet potato biscuit mix, and Ugly cakes.

❧ **The Genuine Smithfield Ham Shoppe** (757-258-8604; www.smith field.com), 421 Prince George Street, Williamsburg 23185. Merchants Square shop sells world-famous Genuine Smithfield Hams, the Paula Deen Collection of gourmet foods, and pig collectibles.

German Store & Cafe (757-591-1001), 1900 George Washington Memorial Highway, Yorktown 23693. Yorktown shop sells German groceries, beers, and music, along with a menu of authentic German sausages and other specialties.

Kielbasa Euro Deli (757-220-0223; www.kielbasava.com), 113 Palace Lane, Williamsburg 23185. Authentic Polish kielbasa, golabki, and pierogi; Polish rye bread; and other imported groceries.

La Tienda (888-331-4362; www .tienda.com), 1325 Jamestown Road, Williamsburg 23185. Gourmet foods and accessories from Spain, including Jamon Serrano country ham, olives, cheeses, wines, sangria pitchers, and paella kits.

The Peanut Shop of Williamsburg (757-229-3908; www.thepeanutshop .com), 414 Prince George Street, Williamsburg 23185. Hand-roasted peanuts, all-natural Virginia peanut butter, and gourmet treats.

Whitley's Peanut Factory (757-229-4056; www.whitleyspeanut.com), 1351 Richmond Road, Williamsburg 23185. Hand-roasted jumbo Virginia peanuts cooked in the shell, peanut candies, and boiled peanuts. Additional location in Gloucester (804-642-1975; 1977 George Washington Highway), 1 mile north of the US 17 bridge.

WINE SHOPS, WINE BARS, AND TASTINGS The Cheese Shop (757-220-0298; www.cheeseshopwilliams burg.com), 410 W. Duke of Gloucester Street, Williamsburg 23185. Surprisingly extensive wine cellar lurks below this popular Merchants Square deli.

Cities Grille (757-564-3955; www .citiesgrilles.com), 4511-C John Tyler Highway, Williamsburg 23185. This restaurant, recipient of the *Wine Spectator* Award of Excellence, offers wine classes several times a month.

Terra Coffee and Wine (757-645-5041; www.terracoffeewine.com), 1430 High Street, Suite 803, Williamsburg 23185. Espresso bar by day, wine bar by night, this spot next to the **Movie Tavern** (www.movietavern.com) at High Street also offers small plates of food, and a unique "automat" wine-dispensing system that uses gift cards.

The Wine and Cheese Shop at Kingsmill (757-229-6754; www .potterywineandcheese.com), 1915 Pocahontas Trail, Shops at Kingsmill, Williamsburg 23185. Cheeses and wines from around the world, plus deli sandwiches; monthly wine tastings and wine dinners. Patio seating.

The Wine Seller (757-564-4400; www.grapesbythecrate.com), 4680-15 Monticello Avenue, Monticello Marketplace, Williamsburg 23188. Free wine and beer tastings every weekend.

WINERIES, BREWPUBS, AND BREWERIES ✪ ⲩ ⁍ᴵᵀ⁍ **Green Leafe Café** (757-220-3405; www.greenleafe .com), 765 Scotland Street, Williamsburg 23185. Three dozen beers on tap, including many local brews, plus a hand-pulled cask and one hundred beers in the bottle, make this pub, named one of the 10 best bars in the country by *USA Today*, a prime hangout for hops enthusiasts. A second location in **New Town** (757-221-9582; 4345 New Town Avenue) has more than 60 beers on tap. Free Wi-Fi at both locations. Tues. is Virginia Draft Day.

○ **Williamsburg Alewerks** (757-220-3670; www.williamsburgalewerks.com), 189 Ewell Road, Williamsburg 23188. Take a tour of Williamsburg's only microbrewery, then sample its excellent beers, including several made in traditional colonial styles, in the tasting room and retail store. Growlers available.

○ **Williamsburg Winery** (757-258-0999; www.williamsburgwinery.com), 5800 Wessex Hundred, Williamsburg 23185. Virginia's largest winery produces the award-winning Governor's White and Bordeaux-style Gabriel Archer Reserve, as well as a seasonal spiced wine. Tours and tastings daily (fee). The **Gabriel Archer Tavern,** next door, serves light lunches daily and dinner Thurs.–Mon. **Wedmore Place** (757-941-0310 or 866-933-6673; www.wedmoreplace.com), also in the winery village, is a European-style country inn, member of Small Luxury Hotels of the World and Relais & Chateaux. Amenities include the **Cafe Provencal,** serving dinner; on-site spa; and a swimming pool with wine bar.

✱ Selective Shopping

If you like to shop, you'll love the Historic Triangle. Within barely 20 miles, you can have your choice of stepping into an 18th-century store, complete with all its period merchandise, or strolling one of the world's largest outlet malls in pursuit of bargains.

Often overlooked as a shopping destination, the **Colonial Williamsburg Shops** (757-229-1000; www.history.org), along Duke of Gloucester Street in Williamsburg's Historic District and staffed by costumed reenactors, offer a wide variety of goods, including pottery, leather items, clothing, pewter and sterling tableware, tinware, wrought iron, and baskets, most made by hand using 18th-century techniques. These shops, including the Golden Ball, the Prentis Store, the John Greenhow Store, the Mary Dickinson Shop, and Tarpley's Store, are open to all; a Colonial Williamsburg admission pass is not required to shop. As an added benefit, you may also see craftspeople at work.

CHESAPEAKE BAY WINE TRAIL: THE WINERIES OF NORTHERN NECK
The closest Virginia wine trail to the Historic Triangle region, the **Chesapeake Bay Wine Trail** (www.chesapeakebaywinetrail.com) visits seven wineries in the Northern Neck George Washington Birthplace American Viticultural Area, where sandy loam soil and a temperate climate year-round encourage vine growth, before returning to I-95 just outside Washington, D.C.

The closest Northern Neck winery to the Yorktown bridge is **White Fences Vineyard & Winery** (804-438-5559; www.whitefencesvineyard.com; 170 White Fences Drive, Irvington 22480), where dining and lodging are available at the romantic **Hope and Glory Inn** (www.hopeandglory.com) and unique "tent" cottages. Or spend the night in rustic cabins at **Belle Mount Vineyards** (804-333-4700; www.bellemount.com; 2570 Newland Road, Warsaw 22572). The **Chesapeake Bay Wine Festival** (www.chesapeakebaywinefestival.com) is held each June at **Ingleside Vineyards** (804-224-8687; www.inglesidevineyards.com; 5872 Leedstown Road, Oak Grove 22443).

Rentals of 18th-century costumes for boys and girls, as well as toys, hats, pottery, baskets, and discount items, are available at the open-air **Market Square Stands.**

Many craftspeople have settled in the Williamsburg area, creating everything from pewter to floorcloths in fine reproductions of colonial designs. Colonial Williamsburg itself has licensed many of the items found in its museums. The shops of Merchants Square, as well as the museum stores, offer reproduction furniture, textiles, and folk art.

If you prefer the real thing, the area is rich in antiques shops as well, with stores specializing in everything from leatherbound books to ancient Chinese bronzes.

SHOPPING CENTERS Candle Factory Shopping Complex, 7521 Richmond Road, Williamsburg 23188. Site of the old Williamsburg Soap & Candle Factory is home to a variety of stores, including **Amish Country Products** (800-786-0407; www.amishcountryproducts.com), carrying furniture and homemade Amish foods; **DoveTail Antiques** (757-565-3553; www.dovetailantiquesatnorge .com); and the budget **Candle Light Kitchen** (757-564-0803), a popular breakfast spot.

OUTLET SHOPPING ON THE RICHMOND ROAD

Williamsburg's true claim to a place in the shopping hall of fame lies in its outlet shopping. The idea was virtually born here, when potter James E. Maloney opened a shop next to his pottery factory to sell seconds and over-stocks at discount prices back in the 1930s. Since then the concept has taken flight, with outlet malls blossoming across the nation, including one of the largest, Prime Outlets, with some 120 stores, right here in Williamsburg.

The majority of these outlets can be found along the **Richmond Road,** US 60, heading west from Williamsburg's Historic District. Strung along this old road are a series of little unincorporated towns—Lightfoot, Norge, Toano. The **Williamsburg Pottery Factory,** now grown to a huge complex, is in Lightfoot, while Norge is home to the Doll Factory and the popular and unique **Tumblerstore** (757-220-9504 or 800-979-3135; www.tumblerstore.com), 7463 Richmond Road, Williamsburg 23188.

Patriot Plaza Premium Outlets (757-258-0767), 3040 Richmond Road, Williamsburg 23185. Outlets close to the Historic District include Dansk, Lenox, Polo Ralph Lauren, SAS Shoes, Villeroy & Boch, West Point Stevens, and more with discount prices.

Prime Outlets Williamsburg (757-565-0702; www.primeoutlets.com), 5715-62A Richmond Road, Williamsburg 23188. Named one of the top 10 outlet malls in the nation, this recently expanded center houses 120 name brand outlets offering discounts of 25 to 70 percent, including Coach, J.Crew, Brooks

Colony Square Shopping Center, 1200 and 1300 blocks of Jamestown Rd., Williamsburg 23185. Bookstores, galleries, and service shops group around a Fresh Market grocery. Eating options here include a casual tavern, the **Polo Club** (757-220-1122; www.poloclubrestaurant.com; 1303 Jamestown Road).

High Street Williamsburg (www .highstreetwilliamsburg.com), 1424 Richmond Road, Williamsburg 23185. New mixed-use development centers on the **Movie Tavern at High Street** (757-941-5362; www.movietavern.com; 1430 Richmond Road), an eight-screen first-run cinema, serving pizzas, burgers, beer, wine, and margaritas.

EVEN THE YOUNGEST TOURISTS ENJOY DRESSING IN PERIOD COSTUMES.

Brothers, Nike, Polo Ralph Lauren, and Burberry. Visit the food court or stop by **Harry & David** (757-221-7089; www.harryanddavid.com) for its trademark Moose Munch or some free samples of gourmet gifts. Complimentary wheelchairs available. Join the free 1Club for additional savings. Free RV parking behind L. L. Bean.

The Shops at Carolina Furniture of Williamsburg (757-565-3000; www.carolina -furniture.com), 5425 Richmond Road, Williamsburg 23188. Discounts of 30–60 percent on furniture, carpets, and lighting. Martha Stewart and Ralph Lauren signature galleries, plus the Carolina Kids Room.

Williamsburg Outlet Mall (757-565-3378; www.williamsburgoutletmall.com), 6401 Richmond Road, Lightfoot 23090. Enclosed mall houses more than 40 brand name stores offering discounts of 20–70 percent on men's and women's apparel, jewelry, toys, vitamins, and housewares. Refreshments are available at **Hershey's Malt Shoppe** (757-645-2958) and **Los Tres Gallos** (757-565-1149), an authentic Mexican food stand.

Williamsburg Pottery Factory and Outlets (757-564-3326; www.williamsburg pottery.com), 6692 Richmond Road, Williamsburg 23188. In addition to hand-turned, salt-glazed 18th-century-style pottery made on-site, items from more than 20 countries, and more than a dozen factory outlets, now crowd this 32-building shopping mecca, known for its custom framing and lamps, silk flower arrangements, Christmas shop, and bargain prices. The **Ceramic Factory** is open for tours on weekdays.

The Marquis, VA 199 at I-64 exit 242B, Williamsburg 23185. National retailers including JCPenney, Kohl's, Dick's Sporting Goods, Target, and Best Buy, next to Water Country USA.

ⁱ¹ Merchants Square (757-229-1000; www.merchantssquare.org), S. Boundary Street, Williamsburg 23185. Reproduction retail village dating to the 1930s at the west end of Duke of Gloucester Street was one of America's first shopping centers. Today it contains more than 40 fine shops and restaurants, including the legendary **Williamsburg Craft House** (757-220-7747; www.williamsburgmarket place.com; 402 W. Duke of Gloucester Street), carrying the full line of Williamsburg-brand reproduction tableware, pewter, Delft, and more. Downstairs, the **Sign of the Rooster** sells folk art reproductions from the Rockefeller collection. Parking is available at a deck on N. Henry Street and several lots. The Square hosts frequent live entertainment and a Sat. farmer's market. Free Wi-Fi access (www .williamsburgwifi.com) throughout Merchant's Square and along Prince George Street.

Monticello Marketplace (757-565-0845), 4600 block Monticello Avenue, Williamsburg 23188. One of the newer shopping centers has a Martin's grocery, plus fast food, a wine store, and **Wild Birds Unlimited** (757-253-0873; www.williamsburg.wbu.com; 4640 Monticello Avenue).

New Town (757-565-6200; www.new townwilliamsburg.com), 4801 Court-house Street, Williamsburg 23188. Bounded by Monticello Avenue and Ironbound Road, this mixed-use development includes residential, office, and retail districts, linked by sidewalks and biking trails. Shops, restaurants, and sidewalk cafés line Main and Center streets. Tenants include **Regal New Town Cinemas 12** (757-645-

0440; www.regmovies.com; 4911 Courthouse Street), Panera Bread, White House Black Market, Barnes & Noble, and Chico's. Popular jazz buffet brunch at **Opus 9 Steakhouse** (757-645-4779; www.opus9steakhouse.com; 5143 Main Street). Summer concert series in Sullivan Square.

🦆 **Riverwalk Landing** (757-890-3300; www.riverwalklanding.com), Water Street, Yorktown 23690. New shops with colonial style along the riverbank in historic Yorktown are a nice mix of upscale national specialty shops and local one-of-a-kind craft and gift stores. Frequent concerts and other events.

The Village Shops at Kingsmill, 1915 Pocahontas Trail (US 60 E), Williamsburg 23185. Courtyard-style center houses upscale shops, galleries, and restaurants, including unique **Le Yaca French Restaurant** (757-220-3616; www.leyacawilliamsburg.com).

Williamsburg Shopping Center, 1200 block, Richmond Road at Monticello Avenue, Williamsburg 23185. Built in the 1960s on what was then the edge of town, this shopping plaza contains a Food Lion grocery, Books-A-Million, Blue Ridge Mountain Sports, Kinkos, and several specialty food stores.

ANTIQUES *Williamsburg:* **Antiques in the Old Store** (757-220-0562; www.tias.com/stores/oldstoreantiques), 7421 Richmond Road, Williamsburg 23185. Specializing in early American antiques, Victorian majolica and other ceramics, folk art, and antique dolls.

Charlie's Antiques and Repairs (757-566-8300), 7766 Richmond Road, Williamsburg 23185. A great place for those who like to dig through piles of stuff in search of treasures.

DoveTail Antiques (757-565-3553; www.dovetailantiquesatnorge.com), 7521 Richmond Road, Williamsburg

23188. Shop in the former Williamsburg Soap & Candle Factory building features antique clocks, American and European antique furniture, ceramics, antique tools, and some candles from the previous tenant.

TK Asian Antiquities (757-229-7720; www.tkasianantiquities.com), 1654 Jamestown Road, Williamsburg 23185. Virginia branch of a New York City gallery showcases ancient Chinese bronzes and pottery.

⬆ **Williamsburg Antiques Mall** (757-565-3422; www.antiqueswilliamsburg.com), 500 Lightfoot Road, Williamsburg 23188. More than four hundred dealers make for hours of browsing. **La Petite Tea Room** on-site serves pots of hot tea,

Scottish iced tea, sangria, scones, and chowders.

Yorktown: **House Key** (757-968-5266), 7628 George Washington Memorial Highway, Yorktown 23692. Huge showroom offers 40,000 square feet of antiques, fine reproductions, collectibles, and more.

Yorktown antiques shops (www.yorkcounty.gov/tourism). Several shops cluster close together in Yorktown's historic district, making this a great stop for antiques hunters. **Black Dog Gallery** (757-989-1700; www.blackdoggallery.net; 114 Ballard Street, Yorktown 23690) specializes in 18th-century prints and maps, as well as period reproduction floorcloths. **Redcoat Antiques** (757-890-1409;

ANTIQUING ON THE MIDDLE PENINSULA

Antiques shops and flea markets line US 17 between Gloucester Point and Gloucester Courthouse, just over the US 17 bridge linking Yorktown with the Middle Peninsula.

Holly Hill Antiques Farm (804-695-1146; www.hollyhill.biz), 9162 John Clayton Memorial Highway/VA 14, Gloucester 23061. This 1880s Victorian farmhouse and some dozen outbuildings are stuffed with country primitives, fine glassware, antique farm implements from Virginia and Pennsylvania, and much more. Free guided tours available.

Marketplace Antiques (804-694-0544; www.marketplaceantiques.com), 4872 George Washington Memorial Highway/US 17, White Marsh Shopping Center, Gloucester County 23061. Informal market promises "something for everyone."

Mathews Community Yard Sale (804-725-4BAY), Main Street, Mathews 23109. Last Sat. morning of each month, May–Oct.

Stagecoach Markets and Antique Village (804-693-3951), 6049 George Washington Memorial Highway, Gloucester 23061. Weekend flea market attracts a hundred or so vendors, plus 50 antiques dealers.

Urbanna Flea Market & Antiques (804-758-4042), 165 Urbanna Road, Saluda 23149.

Wisteria Lane Antiques and Collectibles (804-413-1926; www.gloucester -virginia.org), 6568 Main Street, Gloucester Courthouse 23061.

121 Alexander Hamilton Boulevard, Yorktown 23692) carries furniture, silver, and oil paintings from the 17th to 19th centuries, as well as discounted Waterford lighting. **Swan Tavern Antiques** (757-898-3033; www.antiquesatswantavern.com; 300 Main Street, Yorktown 23690) displays 18th-century furniture and accessories in a rebuilt tavern, creating a museum-like experience.

BOOKS, GAMES & MUSIC
Barnes & Noble @ the College of William and Mary Bookstore (757-253-4900; http://wm.bkstore.com), 345 Duke of Gloucester Street, Merchants Square, Williamsburg 23185. Many titles on Williamsburg history, plus W&M logo souvenirs. Upstairs café serves Starbucks coffee and hosts frequent live music.

Bertram & Williams Books & Fine Art (757-564-9670; www.bertbook.com), 1459 Richmond Road, Williamsburg 23185. Rare and used books, antique maps and prints. Appraisals available.

Book Exchange of Williamsburg (757-220-3778), 1303 Jamestown Road, Colony Square Shopping Center, Williamsburg 23185. Huge selection of secondhand paperbacks, well organized and easy to browse.

The Bookpress, Ltd. (757-229-1260; www.bookpress.com), 1304 Jamestown Road, Williamsburg 23185. Rare volumes on architecture, the history of printing, colonial Americana and Virginiana, wine, and horticulture.

Byrd Aviation Books (757-565-4814; www.byrdaviationbooks.com), 114 Deer Path Road, Williamsburg 23188. More than a thousand new and out of print aviation titles, plus back issues of aviation magazines. Open by appointment.

Groovy Geckos Comics & Games (757-258-4464;www.groovygeckos games.com), 1505 Richmond Road, Williamsburg 23185. Family-oriented gaming store sponsors tournaments of card, board, and fantasy battle games.

Mermaid Books (757-229-3603; www.mermaidbookswilliamsburg.com), 421-A Prince George Street, Williamsburg 23185. Fun shop in the Historic District stocks old and rare books, including many history volumes, plus antiques, old postcards, and mermaid-themed gifts.

Williamsburg Booksellers (757-229-1000; www.williamsburgmarketplace .com), 100 Visitor Center Drive, Williamsburg 23185. Bookstore in the visitors center carries many books about Williamsburg's history, gardens, and decor, as well as music and cookbooks.

CLOTHING
Kyrie Designs (757-220-0008; www.kyriedesigns.com), 1490 Quarterpath Road, Williamsburg 23185. Clothing and accessories made of all-natural fibers.

Magnolia's Boutique (757-229-4005), 1915 Pocahontas Trail, Village Shops at Kingsmill, Williamsburg 23185. Women's boutique excels at the pulled-together look.

Quilts Unlimited (757-253-8700; www.quiltsunlimited.com), 110 S. Henry Street, Henry Street Shops, Williamsburg 23185. Get 18th-century-style clothing for the entire family at this shop, which displays more than 80 new and antique quilts.

CONSIGNMENT AND THRIFT STORES
The Bottom Line (757-258-9051), 6401 Richmond Road, Lightfoot 23090. Locally owned thrift shop in the Williamsburg Outlet Mall carries factory close-outs and odd lots at great prices.

Classic Consignments (757-220-1790; www.classiconsignments.com), 1915 Pocahontas Trail, Williamsburg 23185. Boutique shop in the Village Shops at Kingsmill offers upscale furniture and accessories.

CHKD Thrift Store (757-220-KIDS; www.chkd.org/giving), 222C Monticello Avenue, Monticello Shopping Center, Williamsburg 23185. Proceeds benefit the Children's Hospital of the King's Daughters.

The Clothes Tree (757-220-2119), 170 Second Street, Williamsburg 23185. Designer-label ladies' clothes sold on consignment.

The Wardrobe Upscale Resale Consignment (757-220-0778), 1915 Pocahontas Trail, Village Shops at Kingsmill, Williamsburg 23185. Designer-label women's clothing, bags, and jewelry at great prices.

Williamsburg Consignment Shop (757-206-1058; www.williamsburg consignment.com); 6963 Richmond Road, Williamsburg 23188. Wide variety of merchandise includes collectible model railroad trains.

CRAFTS ✪ 🍴 **Jamestown Glasshouse** (757-229-2437; www.jamestown glasshouse.com), Historic Jamestowne. Craftsmen hand-blow glass using 17th-century techniques in a reproduction of the first glass furnace in the English colony.

Knitting Sisters (757-258-5005; www.knittingsisters.com), 1915 Pocahontas Trail, Village Shops at Kingsmill, Williamsburg 23185. Hand-dyed yarns, plus knitting supplies, lots of classes, yarn swaps.

Love 2 Quilt & More (757-565-0978; www.love2quilt.com), 1915 Pocahontas Trail, Williamsburg 23185. Quilting supplies and classes in the Village Shops at Kingsmill.

More Than Just Beads (757-229-7499; www.morethanjustbeads.com), 4917 A Courthouse Street, New Town, Williamsburg 23188. Freshwater pearls, semiprecious stones, crystal, bone, horn, and nut beads. Classes in beading and hemp knotting.

🍴 **Shirley Metalcraft and Pewter Shop** (757-229-3668 or 800-550-5356; www.shirleypewter.com), 1209 Jamestown Road, Williamsburg 23185. Pewter factory welcomes visitors. Handcrafted pewterware, including the famous Jefferson cup, available here and at the **Shirley Pewter Shop** at 417 Duke of Gloucester Street in Merchants Square.

Studio Foray (757-969-1094; www.studioforay.com), 323 Water Street, Riverwalk Landing, Yorktown 23690. Wide selection of beads, crystals, semiprecious stones, and other jewelry supplies, plus classes in the art of beading.

GIFTS Camelot Bears (757-565-9060 or 866-379-2101; www.camelot bears.com), 6401 Richmond Road, Williamsburg Outlet Mall, Lightfoot 23090. Locally owned store, dedicated to educating the public on the plight of bears around the world, carries collectible bears and a make-your-own bear machine.

Cooke's Christmas Gifts and Collectibles (757-220-0099; www.cookes gardens.com), 1820 Jamestown Road, Williamsburg 23185. Christmas store with more than 30 decorated trees; open all year.

Lightfoot Manor Shoppe (757-220-1805; www.lightfootmanor.com), 3044 Richmond Road, Williamsburg 23185. All kinds of collectibles, including Delft, pewter, dolls, and Christmas figurines.

Williamsburg Souvenir Company (800-283-8630; www.williamsburg souvenirco.com). Locations include the **Williamsburg General Store** (757-564-5800; 1656 Richmond Road, Williamsburg 23185), with Häagen-Dazs ice cream on-site; and **Wallace's Trading Post** (757-564-6101; 1851 Richmond Road, Williamsburg 23185), with homemade fudge. Both locations have fife and drum performances during the summer.

✪ ✎ ⍨ **Yankee Candle Co.** (757-258-1002; www.yankeecandle.com), 2200 Richmond Road, Williamsburg 23185. Fascinating store has an animated clock, toy store with life-sized stuffed animals, a Christmas shop where it snows all the time, a snack bar, and lots of candles. You can even dip your own.

HOME DECOR **Early American Floorcloths** (757-695-3282; www .earlyamericanfloorcloths.com), 307-B Ewell Road, Williamsburg 23188. Reproduction floorcloths created using 18th-century designs. Classes available.

Gerald H. Felix, Chairmaker (757-220-0662; www.geraldfelixchair maker.com), 101 Elizabeth Page, Williamsburg 23185. Handmade wood furniture in the Windsor tradition. Open by appointment.

Period Designs (757-886-9482 or 757-727-9139; www.perioddesigns.com), 401 Main Street, Yorktown 23690. Specializing in 17th- to 19th-century decorative arts, including antique porcelain, museum-quality framed maps and prints, floorcloths, and English Delft.

Suter's (757-564-8812; www.suters .com), 800 Richmond Road, Williamsburg 23185. Classic, made-in-Virginia furniture of solid cherry, mahogany, and walnut hardwoods, finished by hand.

JEWELRY **Boyer's Diamond and Gold Source** (757-565-0747; www .boyersjewelry.com), 6564 Richmond Road, Lightfoot 23090. Home of the Williamsburg, Jamestown, and Yorktown hook bracelets.

Master Craftsmen Shop (757-253-2993 or 800-866-7458; www.mastercraftsmen shop.com), 221 N. Boundary Street, Williamsburg 23185. Gold, silver, and pewter jewelry and gifts; Christmas angels; and Peaceful Kingdom animal ornaments, made on-site.

Viccellio Goldsmith (757-890-2162; www.viccelliogoldsmith.com), 325

HAND-BLOWN GLASS FROM HISTORIC JAMESTOWNE'S GLASSHOUSE IS ONE OF THE AREA'S TOP SOUVENIRS.

Water Street, Riverwalk Landing, Yorktown 23690. Master goldsmith and Yorktown native "Hank" Viccellio handcrafts unique jewelry in precious metals, including his signature Yorktown Bracelet.

✳ Special Events

For many more events in Williamsburg, Yorktown, and the Virginia Peninsula, visit www.villageevents.org, www.yorkcounty.gov, www.colonial williamsburg.com, www.williamsburgcc .com, www.wydaily.com, www.busch gardens.com, www.williamsburgweek ends.com, and www.williamsburg winery.com.

February: **The Chocolate Affair** (www.thechocolateaffair.org), Williamsburg Community Building, 401 N. Boundary Street, Williamsburg.

March: ❂ **Daffodil Festival & Show** (804-693-2355; www.gloucesterva .info), Main Street, Gloucester

April: **Art on the Square** (www .williamsburgjuniors.org), Merchants Square, Williamsburg. Junior Woman's Club of Williamsburg's annual free spring art show.

Colonial Market Fair and Militia Muster (757-887-2641; www.water mens.org), Watermen's Museum, Historic Yorktown.

Taste of Williamsburg (757-229-6511; www.williamsburgcc.com).

May: **Drummer's Call Weekend** (800-HISTORY; www.colonialwilliams burg.com), Colonial Williamsburg. Performances by fife and drum corps from around the country.

Pedal the Parkway (www.wabonline .org), Colonial Parkway. Annual family event closes the parkway to motorized vehicles.

Spring Antique Show & Flea Market (757-253-8126; www.vagazette .com), New Town, Williamsburg. Sponsored by the *Virginia Gazette*.

❂ **Strawberry Hills Steeplechase Races** (804-966-7223; www.strawberry hillraces.com), Colonial Downs Racetrack, New Kent.

Tour de Chesapeake Bicycling Festival (757-229-0507; www.bikechesa peake.org), Mathews.

Upper Mattaponi Spring Festival & Tribal Pow Wow (804-769-3378; www.uppermattaponi.org), 13383 King William Road, King William.

Vines and Wines Garden Party (www.williamsburgbotanicalgarden.org), Rockefeller/Spa Garden, Colonial Williamsburg. Benefit for the Williamsburg Botanical Garden.

Williamsburg Wine and Food Festival (757-645-4100; www.williams burgwineandfoodfestival.com), Colonial Heritage Club, Williamsburg.

June: **Foodapalooza Wine and Food Festival** (757-221-0278; www.food apaloozava.com), Sullivan's Square in New Town and other venues. A weekend of wine, gourmet food, live music, and dancing.

Gwynn's Island Festival (804-725-5777; www.gwynnsisland.com or www .visitmathews.com), Gwynn's Island Civic Center, Old Ferry Road.

Paddle Jam (804-693-2355; www .gloucesterva.info), Beaverdam Park, Gloucester.

July: **Gloucester Renaissance Festival** (804-693-2355; www.gloucesterva .info), Courthouse Circle, downtown Gloucester.

Independence Day Celebration (757-890-3500), Yorktown.

VIRGINIA GARDEN WEEK

For more than 75 years the good people of Virginia have opened their houses and gardens every April during Virginia Garden Week. The oldest and largest home and garden extravaganza in the United States, this unprecedented event involves more than three dozen separate, self-guided tours all across the state. About half of these take place in the Tidewater region.

In addition to tours of outstanding private mansions and gardens, many historic houses, including some of the James River plantations, open their interiors only for this special event. Colonial Williamsburg also offers guided tours of houses not normally open to the public. Admission to area museums and other attractions is often included in the ticket price.

For more information, call 804-644-7776 or visit www.vagardenweek.org.

July 4 Ice Cream Social (757-221-4000; www.wm.edu), Wren Courtyard, College of William and Mary, Williamsburg.

❂ Pork, Peanut and Pine Festival (757-294-3625; www.porkpeanutpine festival.org), Chippokes Plantation State Park, Surry.

Racing to the Stars & Stripes Festival (804-966-7223; www.colonial downs.com), Colonial Downs Racetrack, New Kent.

❂ Virginia Derby (804-966-7223; www.colonialdowns.com), Colonial Downs Racetrack, New Kent.

Watermen's Heritage Celebration (757-887-2641; www.watermens.org), Watermen's Museum, Yorktown.

August: **1863—A Step Back in Time Civil War Encampment** (804-693-0014; www.gloucesterva.info), Courthouse Circle, downtown Gloucester.

Gloucester County Fair (804-693-2355; www.gloucesterva.info), Ark

COLONIAL WILLIAMSBURG'S FIFES AND DRUMS PERFORM AT MANY AREA EVENTS.

Park, US 17 at Number Nine Road, Gloucester.

September: **Chalk Fest** (804-695-0700; www.gloucesterchalkfest.com), Main Street, downtown Gloucester.

✪ **Chickahominy Fall Festival & Pow-wow** (804-829-2027; www.chicka hominytribe.org), Chickahominy Tribal Grounds, Charles City.

Mathews Market Days (804-725-7196; www.visitmathews.com), Courthouse Green, Mathews.

New Kent County Fair (804-966-7223; www.colonialdowns.com), Colonial Downs Racetrack, New Kent. Opening weekend of harness racing.

Nottoway Indian Tribe of Virginia Annual Powwow (757-654-9301; www.nottowayindians.org), Surry Parks and Recreation Center, 205 Enos Farm Drive/VA 10 at VA 31, Surry.

October: **An Occasion for the Arts** (www.aofta.org), Williamsburg. Annual outdoor juried art show is ranked among the top one hundred in the country.

Haunted Trail (804-693-2355; www .gloucesterva.info), Beaverdam Park, Gloucester.

Main Street Trick or Treat (804-695-0700; www.gloucester-virginia .org), downtown Gloucester.

Old Virginia Christmas Fair (757-294-3872; www.oldvirginiachristmas .com), Smith's Fort Plantation, Surry.

Rappahannock Tribal Pow Wow (804-769-0260; www.rappahannock tribe.org), 5036 Indian Neck Road/VA 623, Indian Neck.

Roswell's Barbecue in the Ruins (804-693-2585; www.rosewell.org), SR 664, off Aberdeen Creek Road/SR 632, Gloucester.

Tidewater Mountain Bike Challenge (www.tidewaterchallenge.blog spot.com or www.evma.org), Williamsburg.

West Point Crab Carnival (804-843-4620; www.westpointvachamber.com).

221

HISTORY COMES TO LIFE—WILLIAMSBURG, JAMESTOWN, AND YORKTOWN

Yorktown Victory Celebration (757-890-3500; www.yorkcounty.gov), downtown Yorktown.

November: ✪ **Foods & Feasts of Colonial Virginia** (888-593-4682; www.historyisfun.org), Yorktown Victory Center.

✪ **Made in Matthews Open Studio Tour** (804-725-7196; www.visit mathews.com), Mathews.

Urbanna Oyster Festival (www .urbannaoysterfestival.com).

Veterans Day Ceremony (757-890-3500), York Hall, 301 Main Street, Yorktown.

Yorktown Tea Party (757-887-2641; www.watermens.org), Watermen's Museum, Yorktown.

December: **A Colonial Christmas** (888-593-4682; www.historyisfun.org), Yorktown Victory Center.

Christmas Market on Main Street (757-890-3500), Historic Main Street, Yorktown.

Christmas Town (800-343-7946; www.christmastown.com), Busch Gardens, Williamsburg.

Colonial Christmas Antiques and Artisans Show (www.colonial christmasshow.com), George Washington Inn & Conference Center, Williamsburg.

✪ **First Night Williamsburg** (757-258-5153; www.firstnightwilliamsburg .org). Alcohol-free New Year's Eve celebration of the arts.

Williamsburg Community Christmas Parade (757-229-6511 or 800-368-6511; www.williamsburgcc.com).

Yorktown Illumination and Christmas Tree Lighting (757-890-3500), Victory Monument to Riverwalk Landing.

Yorktown Lighted Boat Parade (757-890-3500; www.wormleycreek marina.com), Yorktown waterfront.

Yule Log Ceremony (757-221-4000; www.wm.edu), Wren Courtyard, College of William and Mary, Williamsburg.

CROSSROADS OF THE WORLD—
HAMPTON AND NEWPORT NEWS

We were never more merry, nor fed on more plenty of good oysters, fish, flesh, wildfowl, and good bread . . . than in the dry, warm, smoky houses of the Kecoughtan. —Capt. John Smith, 1608

At the tip of the Virginia Peninsula lie two cities that witnessed much of our nation's history. On April 28, 1607, just two days after planting the First Landing Cross at Cape Henry in what is now Virginia Beach, Capt. Christopher Newport's flagship, the *Susan Constant*, made landfall on a welcoming coast rich in wild strawberries. The local Native Americans, members of the Kecoughtan tribe, living along the banks of a wide and deep river, made the explorers welcome, on this and subsequent visits. The sailors, impressed by the protected anchorage, named the area Point Comfort.

By 1609, the English had fortified Point Comfort (soon dubbed Old Point Comfort to distinguish it from New Point Comfort in today's Mathews County). Wooden Fort Algernourne was the first fortification to occupy the spot where Fort Monroe, the largest moated masonry fort ever built in the United States, grew up beginning in 1819. The young army engineer Lt. Robert E. Lee was stationed here and helped design the fortifications at nearby Fort Calhoun, now Fort Wool.

Fort Monroe, today the headquarters of the U.S. Training and Doctrine Command (TRADOC), is scheduled to be decommissioned in 2011 and will most likely become our nation's newest national park. You can check on the ongoing negotiations toward that end at www.createfortmonroenationalpark.org and www.fmfada .com. In the meantime, to visit the fort, you'll need photo IDs for all visitors 16 and older, and cars are subject to search.

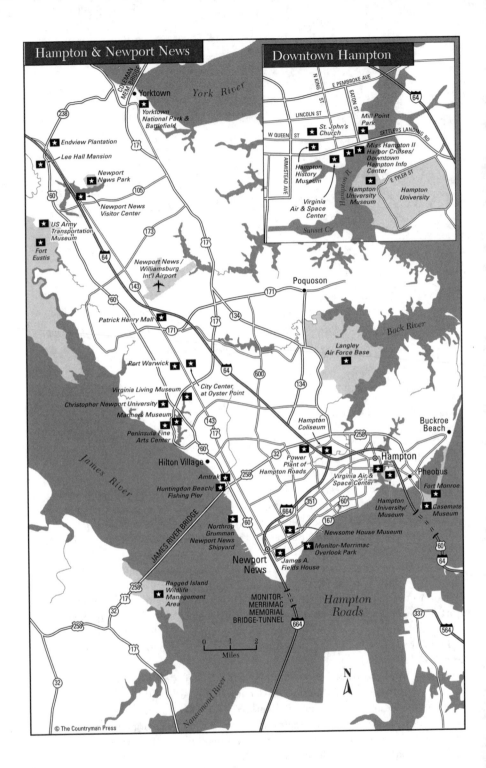

Hampton & Newport News

York River

Coleman Mem. Bridge

Yorktown
★ Yorktown National Park & Battlefield

238

17

★ Endview Plantation

★ Lee Hall Mansion

★ Newport News Park

60

105

★ Newport News Visitor Center

★ US Army Transportation Museum

★ Fort Eustis

64

60

173

17

Newport News / Williamsburg Int'l Airport

143

60

Patrick Henry Mall ★

171

17

134

Poquoson

171

Back River

134

600

Langley Air Force Base ★

Port Warwick ★

64

Virginia Living Museum ★

City Center at Oyster Point ★

Christopher Newport University ★

Mariners Museum ★

143

17

Peninsula Fine Arts Center ★

60

Hilton Village ●

Amtrak ★

258

32

Hampton Coliseum

Power Plant of Hampton Roads

Buckroe Beach

Hampton ★

Pheobus

Virginia Air & Space Center ★

258

Fort Monroe ★

Huntingdon Beach/ Fishing Pier ★

James River

James River Bridge

Northrop Grumman Newport News Shipyard ★

60

664

351

167

60

Hampton University/ Museum ★

Casemate Museum ★

60

64

Newsome House Museum

Newport News

James A. Fields House ★

Monitor-Merrimac Overlook Park ★

337

564

Ragged Island Wildlife Management Area ★

258

17

32

258

17

32

MONITOR-MERRIMAC MEMORIAL BRIDGE-TUNNEL

664

Hampton Roads

0   1   2
Miles

N

Nansemond River

© The Countryman Press

Downtown Hampton

N King St

E Pembroke Ave

Eaton St

64

Lincoln St

Mill Point Park

W Queen St

St. John's Church ★

Settlers Landing Rd

Miss Hampton II Harbor Cruises/ Downtown Hampton Info Center ★★

E Tyler St

Armistead Ave

Hampton History Museum ★

Hampton R.

Hampton University Museum ★

Hampton University

Virginia Air & Space Center ★

Sunset Cr.

HAMPTON

The city of Hampton grew up on the lands of the Kecoughtan, after the English drove the tribe off in 1610. The Elizabeth City Parish Church, today St. John's Episcopal, was founded that same year, making Hampton village the oldest continuously occupied English settlement in the United States. (Jamestown was deserted after 1699.)

Because of the deep water anchorage on both sides of the Hampton River, the town served for many years as the seat of royal naval authority. It is here that Lt. Robert Maynard, commander of the sloop *Adventure,* returned with Blackbeard's severed head after defeating the pirate off Ocracoke Island on North Carolina's Outer Banks. The head was set on a pole at what is still called Blackbeard's Point, at the entrance to the Hampton River, as a warning to other pirates.

The naval battle between the British and Blackbeard's crew, as well as the parade through town with a model of the severed head, are re-created every year during the **Blackbeard Pirate Festival** (www.blackbeardpiratefestival.com), held in June.

Fort Monroe remained in Union hands throughout the Civil War, serving as a launching point for the 1862 and 1864 Peninsula campaigns. Many people fleeing slavery gathered around the fort after its commander, Gen. Benjamin Butler, declared them "contraband of war," thus ensuring they would never be turned over to the Confederates. In 1868, army officers founded a school to train these newly freed people, today's **Hampton University** (www.hamptonu.edu), on the north bank of the Hampton River, across from downtown. Among its many notable graduates are Booker T. Washington, Alberta Williams King, and artist John Biggers.

The town of **Phoebus** (www.phoebus.info) grew up outside the fort after the war, and today the charming historic district of Victorian houses and storefronts is part of the city of Hampton. During the early years of the 20th century, railroads brought many travelers to nearby Buckroe Beach Amusement Park and several big resort hotels on Point Comfort. The **Hotel Chamberlin** (www.historicchamberlin.com), today a rental community open to the public for dining, is the last of these grand old buildings.

The walkable streets of **downtown Hampton** (www.downtownhampton.com) provide one of the best shopping and strolling experiences on the Peninsula. By day, antiques shops, art galleries, historic landmarks, and the nearby docks combine in a rich mix, laced with a variety of food options from spicy Thai curries to traditional Southern tea. By night, a string of pubs and restaurants come to life along Queens Way. And wherever you go in downtown Hampton, you'll enjoy free Wi-Fi.

Just north of downtown off I-64, the **Coliseum Central business district** (www.coliseumcentral.com) includes several new attractions, including **Peninsula Town Center** (www.peninsulatowncenter.com) and the **Power Plant** (www.powerplanthamptonroads.com), both with many shopping, dining, and entertainment options.

NEWPORT NEWS

Originally called Warwick County, the banks of the River James in what is today Newport News, the largest municipality on the Virginia Peninsula, were once lined with plantations. This rural character changed dramatically in 1881, when industrialist Collis P. Huntington extended the Chesapeake & Ohio Railroad to Newport News Point and established a deep water port there to carry West Virginia coal around the world.

Ten years later, Huntington founded a shipyard next to the coal docks. In time, it grew into today's **Northrop Grumman Shipbuilding** (www.northropgrumman .com), where *Nimitz*-class nuclear aircraft carriers and *Los Angeles*–class nuclear submarines are built. Drive down Washington Avenue alongside the waterfront to see the 1891 tugboat *Dorothy,* the first craft built at these historic yards.

Warwick Boulevard/US 60 remains a major thoroughfare running through Newport News, as it has since colonial days. Much of the modern city, however, is located along Jefferson Avenue/VA 143, running parallel to Warwick but slightly farther inland. Two impressive mixed-use developments, **City Center at Oyster Point** (www.citycenteratoysterpoint.com) and Port Warwick, both with many upscale shops, restaurants, and galleries, as well as offices and residential units, lie on either side of Jefferson as it approaches the Newport News/Williamsburg International Airport.

The arts-friendly **Port Warwick** (www.portwarwick.com) centers on the 3-acre William Styron Square, named for the Pulitzer Prize–winning author born in Newport News who wrote *Lie Down in Darkness, The Long March, The Confessions of Nat Turner,* and *Sophie's Choice.* At Styron's request, many of the streets in Port Warwick are named for famous authors.

GUIDANCE Downtown Hampton Development Partnership (757-727-1271; www.downtownhampton.com), 710 Settlers Landing Road, Hampton 23669. Offers information on attractions, restaurants, cruises, events, and shops in the downtown area.

Hampton (757-727-8311; www.hampton.va.us), 22 Lincoln Street, Hampton 23669.

Hampton Visitor Center (757-315-1610 or 866-484-HRCC; www.hamptoncvb .com), 120 Old Hampton Lane, Hampton 23669. Occupying the lobby of the Hampton History Museum in downtown, this is the spot to gather information on this harbor city and find local souvenirs. Free parking is available across the street in the garage at 555 Settlers Landing Road. Open daily 9–5.

Newport News (757-926-8000; www.nngov.com), 2400 Washington Avenue, Newport News 23607.

✧ **Newport News Visitor Center** (757-886-7777 or 888-493-7386; www.newport -news.org), 13560 Jefferson Avenue, Newport News 23603. Conveniently located off I-64 exit 250, at the entrance to enormous Newport News Park, with hiking and biking trails, Civil War sites, gardens, disc golf, and a campground. Open daily 9–5.

Poquoson (757-868-3000; www.poquoson-va.gov), 500 City Hall Avenue, Poquoson 23662.

Virginia Peninsula Chamber of Commerce (757-262-2000 or 800-556-1822; www.vpcc.org), 21 Enterprise Parkway, Hampton 23666. Includes Newport News, Hampton, Poquoson, James City County, and York County on the Virginia Peninsula.

MEDICAL EMERGENCY Mary Immaculate Hospital (757-886-6000; www .bshr.com), 2 Bernardine Drive, Newport News 23602.

Med Express (757-369-9446; www.medx-online.com), 12997 Warwick Boulevard at Oyster Point, Newport News 23602.

Riverside Regional Medical Center (757-597-2000; www.riversideonline.com), 500 J. Clyde Morris Boulevard/US 17 at Warwick Boulevard, Newport News 23601.

Sentara Port Warwick Outpatient Center (757-736-9898; www.sentara.com), 11803 Jefferson Avenue, Newport News 23606.

Veterans Affairs Medical Center (757-722-9961; www.hampton.va.gov), 100 Emancipation Drive, Hampton 23667.

✳ To See

With more than four hundred years of documented history, Hampton and Newport News each developed rich cultural traditions, with numerous historic buildings, museums, and cultural activities throughout the region. The area is particularly rich in African American Heritage sites.

To make its attractions easier for visitors to find, Newport News established a **Cultural Corridor** along the Avenue of the Arts, an extension of J. Clyde Morris Boulevard S. (US 17) off I-64, exit 258A. Heading south, within 1 mile you'll find the Virginia Living Museum, the SPCA Petting Zoo, Abernathy Gardens, Mariners' Museum Park and the USS *Monitor* Center, the Peninsula Fine Arts Center, and the Ferguson Center for the Performing Arts on the Christopher Newport University campus. Along the way, look for several impressive pieces of public art, including a statue of Leif Erickson at the entrance to **Museum Drive,** and a colossal 24-foot bronze likeness of Capt. Christopher Newport by sculptor Jon Hair (www .jonhair.com) at the entrance to the university.

ARCHITECTURE Thanks to frequent burnings in both the Revolutionary and Civil wars, Hampton and Newport News have few buildings dating from the antebellum period. Lee Hall and Endview Plantation, both in Newport News, remain the exceptions, along with the 1828 president's mansion on the campus of Hampton University.

The historic campus of **Hampton University** (www.hamptonu.edu) is home to several other notable buildings, including the 1874 Virginia-Cleveland Hall and 1881 Academy Building, both designed by well-known New York architect Richard Morris Hunt. The campus's Italian Romanesque Revival–style **Memorial Chapel** (1886) is the work of J. Cleveland Cady.

Several late-19th- and early-20th-century historic districts have notable architecture. The oldest in Newport News is the **East End,** an early community of affluent African Americans, some of them graduates of nearby Hampton University. Many of the homes here are Queen Annes from the late 1800s, including the Newsome House Museum and the James A. Field House, both open to the public.

Many early commercial buildings are preserved in the East End as well, including **Historic Smith's Pharmacy** (3114 Chestnut Street) and the shops in **JAMA (Jefferson Avenue Merchants Association) Square** at 25th and Jefferson, also the site of the **Dr. Martin Luther King Jr. Memorial Park.**

Newport News' **Historic Hilton Village** (www.historichamptonroads.com), the first Federal War Housing project, contains about three hundred cottages constructed in 1918 as housing for workers at the nearby Newport News Shipbuilding and Dry Dock Company (now Northrup Grumman). Built to resemble the villages of Tudor England, the houses in this planned community are mostly of Jacobean design with Dutch Colonial and Georgian Colonial styles mixed in. One interesting stop is the Newport News Police Department's **Community Education and Outreach Center** (757-597-2847; 10188 Warwick Boulevard, Newport News 23601), housed in a historic building that was one of the area's earliest service stations.

Several other communities, today historic districts, grew up to house the shipyard workers. The **North End/Huntington Heights Historic District,** located between Huntington Avenue and Warwick Boulevard from 46th to 73rd streets, contains numerous bungalow-style 1920s homes.

Hampton also has several neighborhoods of notable architecture, primarily of the late Victorian Queen Anne style. Just west of downtown, S. Armistead Avenue is lined with some of the finest homes of the period, among them the 1899 Scott mansion at 232 S. Armistead, now the **Magnolia House Bed and Breakfast** (757-722-2888; www.maghousehampton.com).

The **Phoebus Historic District** (www.phoebus.info), an independent town annexed by the city of Hampton in 1952, includes a commercial corridor and its surrounding neighborhoods, with architectural styles ranging from late Victorian to art deco. The oldest property is the 1854 **Reuben Clark House** (125 S. Willard Avenue), the area's sole representative of the Picturesque style. Houses in the Queen Anne and Bungalow/Craftsman style can be found along Willard, Mellen, and Mallory streets, the main commercial corridors. Among them is **Victoria Station** (36 N. Mallory), a circa1905 Queen Anne, now an antiques and tea shop. The Beaux-Arts–style **American Theatre** (125 E. Mellen Street) was recently restored.

Visitors with a particular interest in Colonial architecture can visit the **Matthew Jones House,** located on the Fort Eustis Army Base in Newport News. Constructed between 1660 and 1727 in glazed-header Flemish bond brickwork, this is one of four surviving colonial Virginia homes incorporating a projecting entrance and cruciform plan drawn from post-Medieval traditions. Now a museum house exposing three periods of construction, it contains 90 labeled architectural features. Call the **Fort Eustis Historical and Archaeological Association** at 757-898-5090 or 757-872-8283 to arrange a free tour.

ART MUSEUMS & VISUAL ARTS CENTERS **Anderson Johnson Gallery** (757-247-8950; www.downinggross.org), 2410 Wickham Avenue, Newport News 23607. Open: Tues.–Sat. Admission: Adults $5, children 12 and under $3. Gallery in the Downing-Gross Cultural Arts Center exhibits murals and other works by folk artist Elder Anderson Johnson, as well as changing exhibits of African American art. In the same building, the free Newport News Community Gallery is open Mon.–Sat.

Charles H. Taylor Arts Center (757-727-1490; www.hamptonarts.net), 4205 Victoria Boulevard, Hampton 23669. Open: Tues.–Sun. Admission: Free. This distinguished neoclassical building, former home of the Hampton public library, houses art exhibitions as well as a varied program of classes, lectures, and workshops. The downstairs galleries present changing exhibitions, many sponsored by local art organizations, while on the second floor the art center's permanent collections are on display.

✪ ✝ **Hampton University Museum** (757-727-5308; http://museum.hamptonu .edu), Huntington Building, Ogden Circle, Hampton University campus, Hampton 23668. Open: Mon.–Sat. Admission: Free. The oldest African American museum in the United States, established in 1868, boasts a collection of more than nine thousand items, including many remarkable works and treasures from cultures around the world. The African galleries display the world's first and largest collection of Kuba art, donated by an alumnus. The superb Native American collection represents the artistry of many tribes collected in association with the school's historic American Indian education program. Other galleries display Asian and Pacific Islander artifacts, one of the world's best collections of Harlem Renaissance art, and a fine selection of works by Henry O. Tanner, including his famous 1893 painting, *The Banjo Lesson*. Also on exhibit: items relating to the university's history, including a pen used by Abraham Lincoln in signing the emancipation legislation. Special children's activities available.

✎ ✝ **Peninsula Fine Arts Center** (757-596-8175; www.pfac-va.org), 101 Museum Drive, Mariners' Museum Park, Newport News 23606. Open: Tues.–Sat. 10–5, Sun. 1–5, Tues. 5:30–8 PM. Admission: Adults $7.50; seniors, military, and students $6; children (6–12) $4; under six free; free on Tues. evenings; tickets valid for seven days. Located next to the Mariners' Museum, the PFAC presents constantly changing exhibitions of intriguing contemporary art and juried shows. An interactive Hands On for Kids gallery features Paint Day on Tues. and Thurs., free with admission. Adults enjoy the monthly Thurs.-evening **Art Cafés,** with live music and refreshments ($7.50). The **Gallery Shop** sells original works by regional artists on consignment.

Port Warwick Outdoor Sculpture Trail (757-369-3014; www.portwarwick.com/ public_art.html), Port Warwick, Newport News 23606. Open: Daily. Admission: Free. Permanent works of contemporary sculpture by internationally recognized artists Masaru Bando, Emanuele de Reggi, Rodney Carroll, Harry Gordon, and Romolo Del Deo line the streets and squares of Port Warwick, joined each year by six to eight new works debuting each Oct. at the **Port Warwick Art and Sculpture Festival** (www.pwartfest.org).

GALLERIES Blue Skies Gallery (757-727-0028; www.blueskiesart.com), 26 S. King Street, Hampton 23669. Juried membership gallery in downtown Hampton displays the works of more than 70 local artists who work in the shop. Monthly gallery openings.

JSL Fine Art (757-327-0425; www.jsl-fine-art.com), 1105 William Styron Square S., Port Warwick, Newport News 23606. Works by many well-known artists for sale or rent.

GARDENS Abernathy Gardens, 11700 Warwick Boulevard at Avenue of the Arts, Newport News 23601. A brick labyrinth and shady paths lined with flowers on the shores of Lake Maury, next to the Riverside Regional Medical Center and historic Causey's Mill.

Bluebird Gap Farm (757-827-2765; www.hampton.gov/bbgf), 60 Pine Chapel Road, Hampton 23666. Home of the Hampton Master Gardeners' Display Garden and Arboretum, including the Azalea Trail, with many rare species.

⚘ **The Rose Garden at Huntington Park** (757-886-7912; www.nnparks.com), Warwick and Mercury boulevards, Newport News 23607. More than a thousand rose bushes in 74 varieties surround a pleasant gazebo.

HISTORIC SITES

Hampton

Aberdeen Gardens Historic Museum (757-722-1183; www.hfag.org/museum), 57 N. Mary Peake Boulevard, Hampton 23666. Built by and for African Americans in 1935 as part of the New Deal Subsistence Homestead Project, this neighborhood of brick houses is one of the last of its kind, still occupied by many of the original families. One house, restored to its original state, contains a museum with exhibits about the community, listed on the National Register of Historic Places.

⚘ **Air Power Park** (757-727-1163; www.hampton.gov/parks), 413 W. Mercury Boulevard, Hampton 23669. Outdoor exhibits include aircraft, missiles, and rockets from the Air Force, Army, Navy, Marine Corps, and NASA. A playground and canoe/kayak launch are located on the grounds. Free.

ROCKETS AT AIR POWER PARK RECALL THE REGION'S IMPORTANT ROLE IN THE HISTORY OF AVIATION.

Fort Wool (757-722-9102 or 888-757-2628; www.misshamptoncruises.com), Hampton Roads Harbor, Hampton. This island fortress, designed in part by Lt. Robert E. Lee, dates to 1819 and saw extensive action during the Civil War. The fort can only be reached by boat; the *Miss Hampton II* stops here for a guided tour during its harbor cruise.

⚘ **Hampton Carousel Park** (757-727-0900; www.vasc.org), 602 Settlers Landing Road, Hampton 23669. Built in 1920 by the Philadelphia Toboggan Company, this rare handcrafted wooden carousel, originally part of the Buckroe Beach Amusement Park, today delights the young at heart in a pavilion on the Hampton waterfront. Open seasonally. $2 per ride; 10 rides for $12.

Hampton University Campus (757-727-5000; www.hamptonu.edu), 100 Cemetery Road, Hampton 23668. Founded in 1868 as the Hampton Normal and Agricultural Institute to educate newly freed African Americans, the university has six National Historic

Landmarks on its campus, among them the **Booker T. Washington Memorial**

Garden and Statue and the **Emancipation Oak,** site of the first Southern reading of Lincoln's Emancipation Proclamation in 1863. The National Geographic Society designated the oak, now 98 feet in diameter, one of the Ten Great Trees of the World. The **Harvey Library** (130 E. Tyler Street) houses murals by another alumnus, John Biggers. Pick up a self-guided walking-tour brochure at the **Hampton University Museum** (757-727-5308) or download a map from the Web site. Meals are available at the food court in the new **Student Center** (Marshall Avenue at Soldier's Home Road), or with advance reservations (757-727-5218) at the historic cafeteria in Virginia-Cleveland Hall.

Little England Chapel (757-722-4249), 4100 Kecoughtan Road, Hampton 23661. Built circa 1879, this historic chapel, listed on the National Register of Historic Places, contains exhibits illustrating the religious lives of post–Civil War African Americans, including handwritten Sun.-school lessons, photographs, and a video. Open Mon.–Thurs. 9–3 or by appointment. Free; donations requested.

St. John's Episcopal Church (757-722-2567; www.stjohnshampton.org), 100 W. Queens Way, Hampton 23669. This 1728 brick church is the only colonial building in downtown Hampton that survived the town's burning during the Civil War. A recorded message and small museum in the parish house tell its history. Highlights include an 1879 stained-glass window depicting the baptism of Pocahontas, a gift from Native American students at Hampton University. Open Mon.–Sat. Guided tours available. Free.

Newport News

Civil War Trail Sites (757-247-8523; www.nnparks.com). Many significant Civil War sites dating to the Peninsula Campaign of 1862 lie within the city limits of Newport News, including miles of well-preserved earthworks created by General Magruder's Confederate forces. The Union army advanced down the Warwick Road, now Warwick Boulevard/US 60, and most of the sites lie close to it. The City of Newport News publishes an excellent brochure, *Echoes of Gunfire,* with a map and directions to the various locations, available at the Newport News Visitors Center.

Lee Hall Train Depot (757-886-2715; www.leehalldepot.org), Elmhurst Street and Warwick Boulevard, Newport News 23603. The last remaining train station on the Lower Peninsula built by the C&O Railroad in 1881 is under restoration and will house exhibits on the role of the railroad in the region and historic village of Lee Hall.

Victory Landing Park and Victory Arch (757-247-8523; www.nnparks.com), West Avenue at 25th Street, Newport News 23607. A permanent stone arch and eternal flame, replacing the hurriedly built 1919 originals, lie in a pleasant park overlooking the James River.

HOUSE MUSEUMS ♂ **Endview Plantation** (757-887-1862; www.endview.org), 362 Yorktown Road, Newport News 23603. Open: Mon. and Wed.–Sun.; closed Wed. Jan.–Mar. Admission: Adults $6, seniors (62-plus) $5, children (7–18) $4, under seven free. This 1769 Georgian home served as a Confederate hospital during the Civil War before being occupied by Union forces. Restored to its 1862 appearance by the City of Newport News, it interprets the African American experience before and during the war, as well as medical practices of the era. In the

THE JAMES A. FIELDS HOUSE IN NEWPORT NEWS WAS THE HOME OF A PROMINENT AFRICAN AMERICAN LAWYER WHO ESCAPED SLAVERY AT FORT MONROE.

basement, a museum exhibits artifacts found during archaeological digs on the grounds. Four-day **Civil War Children's Camps,** covering camp life for boys and girls ages 8–12, and **Miss Sallie's Academy,** teaching needlework, etiquette, games, and dancing to girls 8–12, are offered during July. A Civil War reenactment is held annually in Mar.

James A. Fields House (757-245-1991; http://jamesafieldhouse.blogspot.com), 617 27th Street, Newport News 23607. Open: Tues.–Sat. 11–4. Admission: Adults $3; children (13–17), military, and seniors $2; 12 and under free. This impressive town house was the law office and primary residence of James Apostle Fields, one of the slaves who found refuge at Fort Monroe as "contraband of war." In 1871, he was among the first graduates of the Hampton Normal and Agricultural Institute and went on to become a delegate to the Virginia Legislature. Guided tours provide insight into the social and civic life of the African American community during the early 1900s.

✪ **Lee Hall Mansion** (757-888-3371; www.leehall.org), 3 Yorktown Road, Newport News 23603. Open: Mon. and Wed.–Sun.; guided tours every half hour. Admission: Adults $6, seniors (62-plus) $5, children (7–18) $4, under seven free. This 1859 mansion, home of affluent planter Richard Decauter Lee, sits on a hill with a commanding view of the surrounding countryside, making it an ideal spot for Confederate generals Magruder and Johnston to use as headquarters during the 1862 Peninsula Campaign. Confederate earthworks still surround the imposing brick house. Today, restored to its antebellum appearance, it contains several unusual features from the period, including wall-to-wall carpeting. In the English basement, an extensive Civil War museum recounts events on the Peninsula in 1861 and 1862.

Newsome House Museum and Cultural Center (757-247-2360 or 757-247-2380; www.newsomehouse.org), 2803 Oak Avenue, Newport News 23607. Open: Mon.–Sat. Admission: Suggested $2 donation. Elegant 1899 Queen Anne residence was the home of Joseph Thomas Newsome, a prominent African American attorney, journalist, and civil rights pioneer. Today restored, it continues to serve as an important hub of the local black community, hosting art exhibits and special events. Free parking.

Hampton

✪ Casemate Museum at Fort Monroe (757-788-3391; www.monroe.army.mil), Casemate 20, Bernard Road, Fort Monroe 23651. Open: Daily. Admission: Free. Located within the moated walls of Fort Monroe, the largest stone fort ever built in the United States, the Casemate Museum contains extensive exhibits detailing the early settlement of the region, the fort's history, and its time as "Freedom's Fortress" during the Civil War when escaping slaves found refuge here. Exhibits include uniforms, artillery, and other weapons, and a special section on the Coast Artillery Corps. Mementos of famous prisoners held at the fort are also on display, including Black Hawk's peace pipe and the prison cell where Jefferson Davis spent the first weeks of his confinement after the Civil War. A self-guided walking tour leads past other sites on the fort grounds, including the 1802 **Old Point Comfort Lighthouse** (www.cheslights.org/heritage.htm), the 1858 Chapel of the Centurion, Lt. Robert E. Lee's quarters, and the historic **Hotel Chamberlin** (757-637-7200; www.historicchamberlin.com). Stupendous views of Hampton Roads can be seen from atop the fort's walls. Fort Monroe is scheduled to be decommissioned in 2011. Until then you need picture ID for everyone over 16 and your car registration and insurance to enter the gates.

✪ ⛱ Hampton History Museum (757-727-1610 or 800-800-2202; www .hampton.gov/history_museum), 120 Old Hampton Lane, Hampton 23669. Open: Daily. Admission: Adults $5; children (4–12); NASA, active military, and seniors $4. Nine permanent galleries trace the region's history through more than four hundred years, from the early villages of the Kecoughtan tribe to the founding of the U.S. space program at Langley Field. Evocative exhibits recount the growth of the tobacco and slave trades, the capture of Blackbeard the pirate, the smoking ruins left in the wake of Civil War battles, and the town's reemergence as "Crabtown, USA." The slide show of superb, natural-light post–Civil War photos from the Cheyne Collection, now part of the Historical Collection of the **Hampton Public Library** (757-727-1154; www.hamptonpublic library.org; 4207 Victoria Boulevard, Hampton 23669), should not be missed. A gallery on the second floor houses changing exhibits. Free monthly lunchtime lecture series. Free parking in the garage across the street.

THE OLD POINT COMFORT LIGHTHOUSE STANDS GUARD AT FORT MONROE.

THE SWOOPING ROOFLINE OF THE VIRGINIA AIR AND SPACE CENTER EVOKES THE SPIRIT OF FLIGHT.

✪ ⬆ ⇲ **Virginia Air and Space Center** (757-727-0900 or 800-296-0800; www .vasc.org), 600 Settlers Landing Road, Hampton 23669. Open: Daily. Admission: Adults $10.50; military, NASA, and seniors $9.50; children (3–11) $8.50; IMAX combo tickets available. More than 30 aircraft and numerous hands-on exhibits, well maintained by the museum staff, make this a fascinating stop for all ages. You can wing walk on a Jenny biplane, ride aboard a World War II bomber, try your hand at air traffic control, or fly an F/A-22 fighter jet. In the new Space Quest galleries, visitors drive a Mars Rover, operate a Lunar Landing Simulator, take the controls of a space shuttle, and enter a time machine. The **Riverside IMAX Theatre** shows short science films as well as full-length features, some in 3-D, on its five-story screen. The **Cosmic Café** stocks sandwiches, snacks, and beverages.

THE VIRGINIA AIR AND SPACE CENTER ON HAMPTON'S WATERFRONT IS THE OFFICIAL VISITOR CENTER FOR LANGLEY AIR FORCE BASE, WITH MORE THAN 30 AIRCRAFT ON DISPLAY.

Newport News

✪ ⬆ **The Mariners' Museum and USS** *Monitor* **Center** (757-596-2222 or 800-581-7245; www.mariner.org), 100 Museum Drive, Newport News 23606. Open: Wed.–Sun. Admission: Adults $12; military, students, and seniors $11; children 6–12 $7. Really several museums in one, this enormous facility dedicated to all things nautical is one of the finest museums of its kind in the world. Star of the show is the ironclad USS *Monitor,* whose gun turret—rescued from the ocean floor—is undergoing preservation here. Exhibits re-create the surprisingly luxurious interior of the *Monitor,* while the Battle Theater brings the fateful encounter between the ironclads to life in an excellent 13-minute sound and light show.

Other exhibits include the International Small Craft Center, containing 150 watercraft from 36 countries, and the Crabtree collection of more than 300 miniature ships, plus galleries on the Age of Exploration, the Age of Steam, the lighthouses of Chesapeake Bay, and the evolution of the U.S. Navy.

The **Mariners' Museum Library** (757-591-7782; www.mariner.org/library) contains the largest maritime history collection in the Western Hemisphere, including the archives of the Chris-Craft company. Located within the Trible Library on the campus of Christopher Newport University, the library features changing exhibitions and a boat-themed play area for children. Open weekdays. Free.

✪ **U.S. Army Transportation Museum** (757-878-1115; www.transchool.eustis.army.mil), 300 Washington Boulevard, Fort Eustis 23604. Open: Tues.–Sun.; closed federal holidays. Admission: Free; free parking; photo ID for visitors over 16 and vehicle registration may be required. This fascinating museum takes a fresh look at combat from the perspective of the U.S. Transportation Corps, charged with the duty of getting there "first with the most." From the Conestoga wagons and bateaux used to move supplies during the Revolutionary War to the Humvees of today, detailed dioramas re-create the realities of logistical support in every theater of war, with special exhibits on the famed U.S. Camel Corps, the Berlin Airlift, and much more. Full-scale vehicles are included in the exhibits, along with uniforms, tents, and equipment typical of each engagement—even music of the era.

Once you've explored the indoor exhibits, step outside, where 6 acres of pavilions contain a comprehensive collection of actual Army vehicles, including trucks, railroad engines and rolling stock, tugboats, and landing craft. There are also aircraft, including some rare experimental machines such as a flying saucer that almost worked.

✪ ✐ ⚓ ↝ **Virginia Living Museum** (757-595-1900; www.thevlm.org), 524 J. Clyde Morris Boulevard, Newport News 23601. Open: Daily. Admission: Adults $15, children 3–12 $12, under three free. At this unique facility, which combines the elements of a native wildlife park, science museum, aquarium, botanical preserve, and planetarium, living exhibits depict Virginia's natural heritage with more than two hundred species on display. Indoor galleries explore the state's ecology, with special exhibits on the James River fall line, and the Underground Gallery, illustrating Virginia's geological history.

LION CARVED BY ANNA HYATT HUNTINGTON GRACES A BRIDGE LEADING TO THE MARINERS' MUSEUM, AN INSTITUTION BEGUN BY THE HUNTINGTON FAMILY, FOUNDERS OF THE NEWPORT NEWS SHIPBUILDING AND DRYDOCK COMPANY, TODAY NORTHROP GRUMMAN.

Outside, an enormous aviary showcases birds that frequent the Coastal Plain, and gardens introduce the state's botanical history, including plants used by the Native Americans. A boardwalk stretches across a lake and wetlands area, interspersed with close-up looks at animals native to Virginia, including red wolves, bald eagles, bobcats, foxes, and river otters, all living in natural habitats.

The recently renovated **Abbitt Planetarium** (757-595-1900, ext. 256) presents star shows for a small additional fee. The observatory is open daily for safe viewing of the sun, for monthly evening star parties, and for **Laser Light Nights.** The museum's **Wild Side Café** (757-534-7477) offers indoor and outdoor seating, and free Wi-Fi access.

GET AN UP-CLOSE VIEW OF THE NATURAL WORLD AT THE VIRGINIA LIVING MUSEUM IN NEWPORT NEWS.

⊤ **Virginia War Museum** (757-247-8523; www.warmuseum.org), 9285 Warwick Boulevard, Huntington Park, Newport News 23607. Open: Daily. Admission: Adults $6, seniors (62 and over) $5, children 7–18 $4, under seven free. Surrounded by tanks and cannons, this museum in Huntington Park follows the history of American combat from the Revolution to Vietnam. Outstanding collections of uniforms, weapons, Civil War presentation swords, photographs, and newspaper illustrations from every era are on display. A corridor of SS and other Axis memorabilia will give you the shivers. The Propaganda Poster Gallery, with recruiting and war bond broadsides from around the world, is particularly interesting from both artistic and historic perspectives.

ANTI–AIRCRAFT GUN ON DISPLAY OUTSIDE THE VIRGINIA WAR MUSEUM

MUSIC & DANCE SERIES First Presbyterian Church Memorial Concert Series (757-722-0006; www.firstpreshampton.com), 514 S. Armistead Avenue, Hampton 23669. Free musical series includes the annual Young Performing Artists Competition in Feb.

Fridays @ The Fountain Concert Series (757-873-2020; www.citycenterat oysterpoint.com), City Center Fountain Plaza, Newport News 23606. Free concerts, May–Sept., at Oyster Point.

Music Under the Stars (www.tradoc.army.mil/band), Continental Park Gazebo, Fort Monroe, Hampton. Thurs.-evening summer concerts by the U.S. Army Training and Doctrine Command Band. ID required for 16 and up. Free.

Roberto's Dances (757-877-0610; www.robertoinc.net). Latin and ballroom DJ hosts public dances at various venues.

✍ **Saturday Summer Street Fest** (757-727-0900; www.vasc.org/celebrations bythebay), Queens Way, downtown Hampton. Free block parties every Sat. night, late Apr.–Sept., feature regional and national bands, wine and beer gardens, street performers, and children's activities.

Summer Sounds on Styron Square (757-875-9351; www.theportwarwick conservancy.com), Port Warwick, Newport News. Free concerts in Styron Square Wed. evenings June–Sept.

TFFM Coffee House Series (757-626-3655; www.myspace.com/tffmcoffee houseseries), First United Methodist Church, 10246 Warwick Boulevard at Main Street, Newport News 23601. Acoustic coffeehouse, 1960s-style, in Hilton Village presented by the Tidewater Friends of Folk Music.

York River Symphony Orchestra (757-867-7115; www.yrso.org), Dr. Mary T. Christian Auditorium, Thomas Nelson Community College, 99 Thomas Nelson Drive, Hampton 23670. All-volunteer symphony presents four to five concerts annually.

NIGHTLIFE

Hampton

🐾 ⅄ **Goodfellas Restaurant & Bar** (757-723-4979; www.myspace.com/good fellashamptonva), 13 E. Queens Way, Hampton 23669. The sign out front calls it the HOME OF THE BLUES, but bands here play a wide range of musical styles, plus karaoke, open mics, and the Monday Mutt Mixer for dogs and their dates on the outdoor patio.

⅄ **Goody's Deli and Pub** (757-722-3662; www.goodysdeliandpub.net), 11 E. Queens Way, Hampton 23669. Late-night menu, billiards, frequent live music.

The Grey Goose (757-723-7978; www.greygooserestaurant.com), 101-A W. Queens Way, Hampton 23669. Special "dinnertainment" shows. Call for schedule.

⅄ **Luckies Dueling Pianos** (757-224-5968; www.luckiesduelingpianoshampton .com), 1990 Power Plant Parkway, Hampton 23666. Saloon in Hampton's Power Plant complex with two pianists playing songs by request, happy hour specials, deck parties, theme nights.

⅄ **Marker 20** (757-726-9410; www.marker20.com), 21 E. Queens Way, Hampton 23669. Live music on the outdoor covered deck all summer, plus open mic, microbrews, NFL Sunday Ticket, Green Drinks night.

⅄ **Mary Helen's Southern and Creole Cuisine** (757-728-9050; www.mary helens.com), 87 Lincoln Street, Hampton 23669. Cool spot close to downtown Hampton serves up jazz on Thurs. and blues on Fri., along with a menu of Southern specialties.

✪ ♈ **Saddle Ridge Rock and Country Saloon and Cheyenne Supper Club** (757-827-8100; www.saddleridgeva.com), 1976 Power Plant Parkway, Hampton 23666. Two stages present live music, karaoke, country dancing, bull riding, barbecues on the outdoor deck, Western-style menu. Closed Sun.

Newport News

♈ **Blurr Bistro and Ultra Lounge** (757-240-2382; www.gotoblurr.com), 605 Pilot House Drive, Newport News 23606. Sophisticated dining and late-night dancing in Oyster Point.

♈ **Cozzy's Comedy Club and Tavern** (757-595-2800; www.cozzys.com), 9700 Warwick Boulevard, Newport News 23601. Local favorite in Hilton Shopping Center hosts national comedians, live music, karaoke, comedy open mic, and happy hours.

♈ **Firkin & Frigate Pub** (757-223-5857; www.firkinandfrigate.com), 711 Thimble Shoals Boulevard, Oyster Point, Newport News 23606. Traditional English pub grub, plus live music, darts, billiards, Sun. jazz brunch.

♈ **Keagan's Irish Pub and Restaurant** (757-890-4560; www.keagans.com), 12551 Jefferson Avenue, Jefferson Commons, Newport News 23602. Gorgeous Irish pub with an interior imported from Ireland books daily live entertainment.

✪ ♈ **Manhattan's New York Deli and Pub** (757-873-0555; www.manhattans deli.com), 601 Thimble Shoals Boulevard at Jefferson Avenue, Newport News 23601. Live entertainment every evening, indoor and outdoor dining, happy hour specials.

♈ **Schooners Grill at CNU Village** (757-599-4144; www.myspace.com/schooners grill or www.schoonersgrill.com), 12368 Warwick Boulevard, Newport News 23606. Popular sports bar on the CNU campus offers live music on weekends, daily happy hour.

♈ **Tribeca Night Club** (757-873-6664; www.tribecann.com), 1000 Omni Boulevard/I-64 exit 258, Newport News 23606. Two-level lounge in the Omni Hotel hosts live bands and DJ dance parties, plus Sat. early-evening socials and lessons with the **Colonial Shag Club** (www.colonialshagclub.com).

PERFORMING ARTS VENUES ✪ **The American Theatre** (757-722-2787; www.hamptonarts.net), 125 E. Mellen Street, Hampton 23663. Beautifully restored 1908 vaudeville house in historic Phoebus features folk culture groups from around the world.

Downing-Gross Cultural Arts Center (757-247-8950), 2410 Wickham Avenue, Newport News 23607. In addition to the Anderson Johnson and Newport News Community galleries, this arts center houses the **Ella Fitzgerald Theater,** named for the First Lady of Song, born nearby. Next door is the **Pearl Bailey Library** (757-247-8677), dedicated to another native daughter.

Ferguson Center for the Arts (757-594-8752; http://fergusoncenter.cnu.edu), 1 University Place, Christopher Newport University, Newport News 23606. Acoustically engineered concert hall designed by Pei Cobb Freed & Partners hosts a full schedule of national and international artists and top touring productions.

↪ **Hampton Coliseum** (757-671-8100; www.hamptoncoliseum.org), 1000 Coliseum Drive, Hampton 23666. Easily spotted from I-64, thanks to unique architecture that earned its nickname "the mother ship," Hampton's Coliseum seats 13,800 for concerts, nearly 10,000 for basketball games, and hosts many events, including the Hampton Jazz Festival every June.

Mill Point Park (www.hampton.va.us/parks), 100 Eaton Street, Hampton 23669. Waterfront park at the end of Queens Way hosts many annual concerts and festivals, including the **Blackbeard Pirate Festival** (www.blackbeardpiratefestival .com) held every summer.

THEATER Iron Street Productions (757-224-8937; www.ironstreetproductions .com), Dr. Mary T. Christian Auditorium, Thomas Nelson Community College, 99 Thomas Nelson Drive, Hampton 23670. Well-reviewed company specializes in multicultural casting and programming.

✐ **Peninsula Community Theatre** (757-595-5728; www.peninsulacommunity theatre.org), 10251 Warwick Boulevard, Newport News 23601. Family-oriented amateur theatrical troop presents main stage and children's shows at the **Village Theatre,** a converted art deco movie house in Historic Hilton Village.

Poquoson Island Players (757-881-9797; www.pipstheatre.com), P.O. Box 2111, Poquoson 23662. Community theater group performs at several venues.

❂ **Virginia Premiere Theatre** (866-430-1630; www.vptheatre.com), Yoder Barn Theatre, 660 Hamilton Drive, Newport News 23602. Professional theater company, specializing in new play development and world premieres, stages shows in a former dairy barn turned unique 290-seat theater.

✳ To Do

BEACHES The beaches of Hampton and Newport News don't have the glossy reputation of Virginia Beach, but they also don't have the same crowds and traffic. Families will enjoy the uncrowded sands, salty water, and gentle waves of Chesapeake Bay and the Tidewater rivers, perfect for young sand castle builders.

✐ **Buckroe Beach and Park** (757-850-5134; www.buckroebeach.net or www .hampton.va.us/parks), N. First Street, Hampton 23664. Hampton's mile-long public beach and boardwalk invites visitors to swim, stroll, bike, windsurf, or sail. The park, at the end of Pembroke Avenue, includes an enclosed playground, picnic tables and grills, restrooms with outdoor showers (May 15–Sept. 15), new fishing pier, and a waterfront pavilion hosting beach music concerts on Sun. during summer. Kayaks and paddleboats, fishing tackle, beach umbrellas and chairs available for rent. Lifeguards are on duty during the summer, and park rangers patrol all year. Open 7 AM–sunset daily. Dogs are not allowed in the park May 15–Sept. 15, and this is strictly enforced. Fee for parking.

Fort Monroe (757-788-3151 or 800-800-2202; www.monroemwr.com), 490 Fenwick Road, Hampton 23651. Fort Monroe, currently a military base, also has fine bayfront beaches usually closed to the general public, although this may change by 2011 as the post is decommissioned. The public is invited to visit the Fort on Fri. evenings from Memorial Day to Labor Day for **Summerfest by the Bay,** with music, games, and fun at the Fort Monroe Outdoor Pool, Beach and Boardwalk. Free and open to the public, although you will need valid picture ID for everyone over 16 to enter the base.

Grandview Nature Preserve (757-850-5134; www.hampton.va.us/parks), State Park Drive, Hampton 23664. Two miles of sandy beach fronting a wide expanse of salt marsh provide a wilder experience than Buckroe, with no lifeguards, but excellent beachcombing. Open daily sunrise–sunset. Free.

✔ **Huntington Park Beach** (757-886-7912; www.nnparks.com), 5500 W. Mercury Boulevard, Newport News 23607. Newport News' public beach is located off Warwick Boulevard at the base of the James River Bridge. Lifeguards on duty Memorial Day–Labor Day. Fishing pier; playground; picnic shelters; snack bar; restrooms; public boat ramp; tennis, basketball, and sand volleyball courts. Free.

Newport News has other small beaches with no lifeguards fronting on the Chesapeake Bay at **Anderson Park** (16th Street and Oak Avenue) and **King-Lincoln Park** (600 Jefferson Avenue), plus a small beach suitable for wading in the James River at the **Hilton Beach and Pier** at the north end of Main Street.

BICYCLING AND BMX In Newport News, the huge **Newport News Park** (757-886-7912 or 800-203-8322; www.nnparks.com), 13564 Jefferson Avenue/I-64 exit 250B, Newport News 23603, offers exceptional biking opportunities, including an easy 5-mile unpaved bike path, and bike and helmet rentals. Another bikeway connects with Yorktown Battlefield Park.

Gosnold's Hope Park, 901 E. Little Back River Road, Hampton 23669, is home to the **Hampton Supertrack,** sponsoring BMX races. For more information and directions for Hampton city parks, call 757-850-5116 or visit www.hampton.va.us/parks.

For off-road biking, visit **Harwood's Mill Mountain Bike Trail** (757-888-3333), where three loops, rated from novice to expert, create some 5 miles of single-track. The entrance to the trails is located across from the Harwood's Mill Fishing Facility, on Oriana Road in Newport News.

The **Peninsula Bicycling Association** (757-356-1451; www.pbabicycling.org), P.O. Box 12115, Newport News 23612, conducts on- and off-road rides for all abilities on the Peninsula and beyond. Check Web site for schedule and suggested routes.

Bike Shops and Rentals
BikeBeat (757-833-0096; www.bikebeatonline.com), 120 Ottis Street, Suite 118, Newport News 23602. "Get to Know Your Bike" nights; free weekly group rides.

Conte's of Newport News (757-595-1333; www.contebikes.com), 9913 Warwick Boulevard, Newport News 23601. Hilton Village shop sponsors group road rides on Sat. mornings.

Newport News Park (757-886-7912 or 800-203-8322; www.nnparks.com), 13564 Jefferson Avenue (I-64 exit 250B), Newport News 23603. Rent bikes and helmets at the campsite office to use on the park's trails or the nearby Yorktown Battlefield tour roads.

BOATS & BOATING With many miles of bayfront beaches, saltwater and brackish marshes, freshwater lakes, and rivers, the lower end of the Virginia Peninsula offers a wealth of water activities.

Boat Rentals
In Hampton, rent kayaks and paddleboats at **Buckroe Beach Park** during the summer months. Canoes and jon boats are for rent by the hour or day at the

Nature Center (757-825-4657) in **Sandy Bottom Nature Park,** located off I-64 at exit 261A. For information and directions, call 757-850-5116 or visit www .hampton.va.us/parks.

In Newport News, canoes, jon boats, and paddleboats can be rented at two locations in **Newport News Park** (757-886-7912 or 800-203-8322; www.nnparks.com) for use on Lee Hall Reservoir. **Harwood's Mill Reservoir,** to the southwest of Newport News Park, also rents jon boats on weekends, May–October.

The restored Lake Maury boathouse (757-591-7799), in **Mariners' Museum Park** (757-596-2222; www.mariner.org), 100 Museum Drive, Newport News 23606, rents canoes and jon boats by the hour or day during the summer. Children will enjoy a cruise in one of the museum's unique paddleboats, shaped like dragons, pirate ships, and birds, which rent by the hour or half hour at the museum shop.

Canoeing & Kayaking

With many miles of shoreline and salt marsh, winding rivers, and many freshwater lakes, the end of the Virginia Peninsula offers paddlers a wide variety of trip options. Hampton Parks and Rec offers guided paddling tours that include equipment rental. Call 757-850-5134 for a current schedule. The routes can also be followed independently. Download a **Hampton Paddling Guide** at www.hampton .va.us/parks.

The **Long Creek Trail** puts in at the entrance of Grandview Nature Preserve and continues to the northern tip of the preserve at Back River. Boat ramps at Dandy Haven Point and **Gosnold's Point Park** launch directly into the Back River.

The **Newmarket Paddle Trail** will eventually extend as far as Bluebird Gap Farm. A floating dock on Newmarket Creek at **Air Power Park** (757-727-1163), 413 W. Mercury Boulevard, Hampton 23669, gives access to streams leading to the Hampton Coliseum, as well as Back River.

The **Powhatan Paddle Trail** travels up the Hampton River as far as Ridgeway Park. Spots to launch near downtown are **River Street Park,** on Pembroke Avenue under I-64; **Mill Point Park,** in downtown; and at the Sunset Creek boat ramp, on the far side of the Hampton River.

In Newport News, nonmotorized boats can launch into **Lee Hall Reservoir,** in Newport News Park; into **Harwood's Mill Reservoir;** and into **Little Creek Reservoir,** after paying a small fee. Details and directions at www.dgif.virginia.gov.

More good paddling can be found on the upper Warwick River near the **Denbigh Park** (www.nnparks.com; Denbigh Avenue) boat ramp. Several restaurants with spots to tie up can be found at marinas farther down the Warwick along Deep Creek. (See *Marinas.*)

For the adventurous, cross the James River Bridge to the **Ragged Island Wildlife Management Area** (757-253-7072; www.dgif.virginia.gov), US 17/US 258, Isle of Wight. Launch sites next to a large parking lot at the southern end of the bridge access an extensive system of untamed marsh and streams. A boardwalk, interpretive trails, and a public fishing pier provide additional opportunities to explore.

Marinas

Hampton: Marinas form an important part of Hampton's downtown. The deep, calm waters of the Hampton River and its tributary Sunset Creek attract numerous boaters traveling the Intracoastal Waterway. The Hampton waterfront is lined with docks, including the Hampton Public Piers, stretching from the Crown Plaza hotel to the Virginia Air and Space Museum. Many of the city's attractions are within walking distance. Free public Wi-Fi service is available on the docks and throughout downtown Hampton.

⚓ **Bluewater Yachting Center** (757-723-6774; www.bluewateryachtingcenter .com), 15 Marina Road, Hampton 23669. Located on the west side of the Hampton River, this marina accommodates larger boats, with complete repair services, travel lifts, and complimentary water taxi service, plus a pool, laundry, ships store, and Wi-Fi. The **Surf Rider Restaurant** (757-723-9366; www.surfridergroup.com; 1 Marina Road), a family-owned spot locally famous for its crabcakes, is on-site.

Customs House Marina (757-868-9375; www.downtownhampton.com), 714 Settlers Landing Road, Hampton 23669. Marina in front of the Crown Plaza hotel offers convenient downtown slips for transients and is the dock for the *Miss Hampton II* sight-seeing boat.

Dandy Haven Marina (757-851-1573; www.dandyhavenmarina.com), 374 Dandy Haven Road, Hampton 23664. Secluded spot on the Back River.

⚓ **Downtown Hampton Public Piers** (757-727-1276 or 866-556-9631; www .downtownhampton.com/marinas), 756 Settlers Landing Road, Hampton 23669. Slip rentals include use of the Crown Plaza's pool, spa, and fitness center, and free loaner bicycles. Boater's business center with phone, fax and Wi-Fi; bathhouse with public showers; ships store; book exchange; and discounted car rentals. Free dinghy mooring.

⚓ **Joy's Marina** (757-723-1022; www.joysmarina.com), 424 E. Queen Street, Hampton 23669. Located across from the historic downtown, this quiet marina includes dockside parking and free Wi-Fi. A walkway across the Settlers Landing Bridge joins Joy's with downtown.

Salt Ponds Marina Resort (757-850-4300; www.saltpondsmarinaresort.com), 11 Ivory Gull Crescent, Hampton 23664. Located just north of Buckroe Beach, with transient dockage, swimming pool, tennis courts, and sandy beach. **Waters Edge Restaurant and Cabana Bar** (757-864-0336) with live entertainment on weekends, **Down Under Diving** (757-592-4913), and **Salt Ponds Massage Studio** (757-851-2768) on-site.

⚓ **Southall Landings Marina** (757-850-9929; www.southallmarina.com), 333 Mainsail Drive, Hampton 23664. Marina popular with the sailing crowd offers swimming pool, saunas, tennis courts, and free Wi-Fi, plus kayaking through a nearby salt marsh.

Wallace's Marina and Bait and Tackle Shop (757-851-5451), 356 Dandy Point Road, Hampton 23664. Located next to the public boat ramp on the Back River; renowned for citation-sized cobia. Boat slips, fuel dock, retail bait and tackle, and restaurant on-site.

Newport News: **Deep Creek Landing** (757-877-9555; www.deepcreeklanding .com), 200 Old Marina Lane, Newport News 23602. Modern marina in a secluded setting.

James River Marina (757-930-1909; www.jamesrivermarina.com), 665 Deep

Creek Road, Newport News 23606. Full-service marina with 250 slips. Restaurant on-site.

Leeward Municipal Marina (757-247-2376; www.leewardmarina.com), 7499 River Road, Newport News 23607. City-owned facility conveniently located at the base of the James River Bridge, available for daily, weekly, monthly, or annual rental.

✍ **Warwick Yacht & Country Club** (757-930-0561; www.wycc.biz), 400 Maxwell Lane, Newport News 23606. Friendly family club located on Deep Creek, with pool, tennis courts, and a junior sailing program, welcomes transient boaters. The **Yacht Pub,** a casual raw bar located on the water, is open to the public seasonally.

Poquoson: **Messick Point Boat Ramps and Waterman's Park** (757-868-3000; www.ci.poquoson.va.us/parks), Messick Road, Poquoson 23662. Municipal boat ramps with rental slips, comfort station, ample parking, and handicapped-accessible pier.

Public Boat Ramps

The city of Hampton maintains public boat ramps for motorized craft on the Back River at **Dandy Point** (757-247-8155; 356 Dandy Point Road, Hampton 23664), an area known as the Cobia Capital of the World; at **Gosnold's Hope Park** (901 E. Little Back River Road, Hampton 23669); and on Sunset Creek, next to Bluewater Yachts near downtown. Visit www.hampton.gov/parks or call 757-727-6348.

In Newport News, public ramps are located at the **Peterson Yacht Basin/ Anderson Park,** on the Chesapeake Bay; in **Huntington Park,** at the base of the James River Bridge; and at **Denbigh Park,** with access to the Warwick River. Details and directions are at www.nnparks.com, or call 757-926-1400.

The Virginia Department of Game and Inland Fisheries maintains free boat ramps at **Fox Hill,** at the end of Dandy Point Road in Hampton, and at **Messick Point** in Poquoson. Both have access to the Back River. Visit www.dgif.virginia.gov for directions and maps, or call 757-253-7072.

FAMILY FUN ✍ ⊤ **Bass Pro Shops Outdoor World** (757-262-5200; www.bass pro.com), 1972 Power Plant Parkway, Hampton 23666. Massive store features a cascading waterfall emptying into a huge aquarium stocked with stripers, large-mouth bass, catfish, and crappie. Climb the 30-foot indoor rock wall, visit the archery range or the virtual shooting gallery, learn to tie flies, or take a course in nature photography or outdoor cooking.

✍ **Bluebird Gap Farm** (757-827-2765; www.hampton.gov/bbgf), 60 Pine Chapel Road, Hampton 23666. Park across the interstate from the Hampton Convention Center is home to more than 250 domestic and wild animals in a unique farm setting, plus nature trails, playground, the Hampton Master Gardeners' Display Garden and Arboretum, hayrides, and pony rides. Open Wed.–Sun. Free.

Newport News Park Disc Golf Course (757-886-7912 or 800-203-8322; www .nnparks.com), 13564 Jefferson Avenue (I-64 exit 250B), Newport News 23603. $2; seniors and under 12 play free. Rental discs available at the campsite office.

✍ **SPCA Exotic Animal Sanctuary and Petting Zoo** (757-595-1399; www .peninsulaspca.com), 523 J. Clyde Morris Boulevard, Newport News 23601. Friendly deer, emu, sheep, chickens, peacocks, and goats occupy the petting zoo, while the sanctuary contains more exotic rescued animals, including river otters and a Siberian tiger. Adults $2, children (3–12) $1. Proceeds help support homeless animals.

☂ **West Hampton Community Center** (757-896-4687; www.hampton.gov/parks), 1638 Briarfield Road, Hampton 23661. A 30-foot climbing wall has routes suitable for all abilities. Visitors pass $5.

Playgrounds

✍ ♿ **Boundless Playground at Deer Park** (757-886-7912; www.nnparks.com), 11523 Jefferson Avenue, Newport News 23601. Newport News' first barrier-free playground provides wheelchair access to a variety of play equipment.

✍ **Fort Fun at Huntington Park** (757-886-7912; www.nnparks.com), 361 Hornet Circle, Newport News 23607. Wooden playground on a bluff overlooking the James River, plus a children's fishing pier on pocket-sized Lake Biggins, public beach, and summer snack bar.

✍ **Riverview Farm Park** (757-886-7912; www.nnparks.com), 105 City Farm Road, Newport News 23602. The **Fantasy Farm Playground,** plus a **skate park** (757-926-1400 or 757-888-333), 2 miles of paved multiuse trails suitable for skating or biking, a dog park, sledding hill, and a scenic hiking trail to the shore of the Warwick River, make this a family favorite. A concession stand sells snacks on summer weekends.

Skateboard Parks

Also see Riverview Farm Park under *Playgrounds.*

☂ **Mekos Surf, Skate and More** (757-826-7873; www.mekosskate.com), 3420 Von Schilling Drive, Peninsula Town Center, Hampton 23666. The only indoor bowl in southeast Virginia hosts sessions for skateboards, in-line skates, and BMX bikes. Devotional skate on Sun.

Woodland Skateboard Park (757-727-6348; www.hampton.gov/parks), 9 Woodland Road, Hampton 23663. Free outdoor park open from sunrise to sunset.

FISHING The rich waters of the Lower Chesapeake, just a short ride from the marinas of Hampton, offer exceptional fishing year-round. Beginning in March, tautog and flounder are common. In May, trout, sea bass, and black and red drum join the catch. Cobia and spadefish arrive in June. By August, charters are bringing in Spanish mackerel, bluefish, spot, croaker, and triggerfish. Winter features the great rockfish run, largest in the United States, from October to January.

OSPREYS, OTHERWISE KNOWN AS SEA EAGLES, FREQUENTLY NEST ON PILINGS IN HAMPTON HARBOR.

The underwater geography of the lower bay, with its mix of drop-offs, rips, and open water, create unique fishing opportunities. The Hampton Bar, a few hundred yards outside of Hampton Harbor, is a hot spot for flounder in late summer and early fall.

Great shallow-water fishing is found along the north shore of the Peninsula at Poquoson and Drum Island Flats, York Spit and the Goodwin Islands, and the Back River and Poquoson reefs.

Fishing Charters & Outfitters

Captain Hogg's Charter Fishing and Bait and Tackle (757-876-1590; www.captainhoggscharters.com), Downtown Hampton Docks. Sportfishing in the Lower Chesapeake Bay, whale- and bird-watching tours, sight-seeing cruises.

Jerry's Charter Fishing (757-288-1081; www.jerryscharterfishing.com), Downtown Hampton Docks. Fourth-generation Hampton fisherman offers trips year-round.

⚓ **Matty J Fly & Light Tackle Charters** (757-728-1600; www.matty-j.com), operating out of **Sunset Boating Center** (757-722-3325; 800 S. Armistead Avenue, Hampton 23669). Light tackle and fly-fishing trips feature custom hand-tied saltwater flies and flounder rigs. Special parent/child instructional trips, and Half and Half packages, with fly-fishing at the CBBT in the morning and drifting for flounder in the afternoon.

Pride Charter Service (757-675-5010 or 757-595-6944; www.fishwithpride.com), 11 Rivercrest Drive, Poquoson 23662. Light-tackle and shallow-water fishing on the Poquoson flats and reefs. Kayak fishing also available.

Fishing Piers

The shores of the Chesapeake Bay and Tidewater rivers have numerous public saltwater fishing piers where you can try your luck.

In Hampton, the newly completed **Buckroe Fishing Pier** (757-727-1486; www.hampton.gov/buckroe) replaces a wooden pier destroyed by Hurricane Isabel in 2003. The lighted, city-operated 709-foot pier, with bait and tackle shop, tackle rentals, snack bar, parking lot, and fish cleaning tables, is open 24/7 during the fishing season, April–October. Fishing license not required. Admission $4–8; sight-seers $1.

In Newport News, saltwater fishing piers are located at **Denbigh Park** (open 5 AM–10 PM daily); **Monitor-Merrimack Overlook Park/Peterson's Yacht Basin** (open 24 hours); the **Hilton Fishing Pier,** at the end of Main Street in Hilton Village; and **King-Lincoln Park** (open 7 AM–10 PM daily). The new 1,600-foot, lighted King-Lincoln pier is fully accessible and specially designed for children and the handicapped. Fishing is free at these piers, but a Virginia Saltwater License is required.

The **James River Bridge Fishing Pier** (757-247-0364; www.crabshackonthe james.com), 6701 River Road, Newport News 23607, nearly a mile long, provides exceptional catches of striped bass, flounder, gray trout, red drum, sea bass, croaker, and spot. Located in Huntington Park, the pier has a bait shop with limited tackle and is handicapped accessible. The **Crabshack Seafood Restaurant** (757-245-CRAB), with full bar and free Wi-Fi, is next door. The pier is open most of the year, with overnight fishing during the summer. Call for current hours. No license required. Adults $8.50, seniors and juniors (6–12) $6.50.

Freshwater Fishing Lakes

Numerous freshwater lakes in the region provide fishing opportunities from bank, pier, or boat. A Virginia Freshwater Fishing License is required. Special permits may be required at some locations.

In Hampton, fish from the pier or a rental boat at **Sandy Bottom Nature Park** (757-825-4657; www.hampton.gov/sandybottom), just off I-64 at exit 261.

In Newport News (757-886-7912; www.nnparks.com), you can fish from the banks of fishing ponds at **Beechlake Park** (end of Longmeadow Drive) and **Deer Park** (11523 Jefferson Avenue). In Huntington Park, try your luck at the fishing pier on little **Lake Biggins,** stocked with rainbow trout. Anglers need both a valid Virginia Freshwater License and a trout license to fish here from November 1 to April 30.

On **Lake Maury,** in the Mariners' Museum Park (757-596-2222; www.mariner .org; 100 Museum Drive, Newport News 23606), catch-and-release fishing is permitted from the shoreline close to the boathouse and from rental boats available Friday–Sunday. Electric trolling motors are available for rent. No gasoline motors or private boats.

The 230-acre **Lee Hall Reservoir** is the centerpiece of Newport News Park. I-64 and VA 143 cross the reservoir, dividing it into three basins. The middle basin produces largemouth bass, while black crappie are prevalent in the upper basin. Boats can be rented year-round. Private boats without gasoline engines can be launched for a fee into either area. Shore anglers can fish from the bank or pier with a permit ($1.50).

Similar rules apply at 265-acre **Harwood's Mill Reservoir.** Oriana Road (SR 620) divides the lake in half. The cypress trees in the northern section harbor many bass, while the southern section is good for yellow and white perch. Concessions on both sides of the reservoir rent boats May–October. A boat launch (no gasoline motors) is located at the reservoir's southern end. Get permits at the Newport News Park campsite store when the concessions aren't open.

Party or Head Boats
Ocean Eagle Hampton (757-866-FISH; www.hamptonroadscharter.com), Downtown Hampton Public Piers. This 73-passenger head boat cruises the Lower

THE JAMES RIVER BRIDGE FISHING PIER IN NEWPORT NEWS IS NEARLY A MILE LONG.

Chesapeake for some of the best bottom fishing on the East Coast. Winter striper trips and summer night trips. Rod, reel, bait, and license included. $35.

Tackle Shops

Bass Pro Shops Outdoor World (757-262-5200; www.basspro.com), 1972 Power Plant Parkway, Hampton 23666. Equipment for freshwater, saltwater, and fly-fishing. Classes available.

Wilcox Bait & Tackle (757-595-5537; www.wilcoxoutdoorsports.com), 9501 Jefferson Avenue, Newport News 23605. Family-owned store carries boats, canoes, fishing equipment, live and frozen bait, and hunting equipment from guns to crossbows.

GOLF

Golf Centers

Northampton Driving Range (757-766-7550), 223 N. Park Lane, Hampton 23666. Featuring a lighted par 3.

Peninsula Golf Center (757-723-9220), 100 S. Seldendale Drive, Hampton 23669. Convenient location with 60 practice tees.

Public and Semiprivate Golf Courses

The Hamptons Golf Course (757-766-9148; www.hampton.va.us/parks), 320 Butler Farm Road, Hampton 23666. Three distinctive nine-hole courses—the Woods, the Lakes, and the Links—designed by Dr. Michael Hurdzan and operated by the City of Hampton. Clubhouse with full-service restaurant overlooks the signature 10th hole.

Kiln Creek Golf Club and Resort (757-874-2600; www.kilncreekgolf.com), 1003 Brick Kiln Boulevard, Newport News 23602. Tom Clark designed this course, named one of the five best courses in Virginia by *Golf Digest*. Pro shop, the **Manchester Grill,** a day spa, and an inn are part of the resort complex.

✍ **Newport News Golf Club at Deer Run** (757-886-7925; www.nngolfclub .com), 901 Clubhouse Way, Newport News 23608. The Ed Ault–designed Championship Course and the Cardinal Course make up the 36 holes at Newport News Park. Golf lessons, pro shop, driving range, and the **Legends Grille** (757-833-1616) on-site. Juniors 16 and under play free with a paying adult.

The Woodlands Golf Course (757-727-1195; www.hampton.va.us/parks), 9 Woodland Road, Hampton 23663. City of Hampton's inexpensive 18-hole Donald Ross course offers rental clubs; senior and student rates.

HEALTH & FITNESS CLUBS ✝ Riverside Wellness and Fitness Center

(757-875-7525; www.riversideonline.com/rwfc/peninsula), 12650 Jefferson Avenue, Newport News 23602. Daily guest passes are available at this center, which offers tennis and racquetball courts, an indoor heated pool, and a whirlpool, as well as five-day stop-smoking classes, and summer fitness camps for youths 5–15.

✍ ✝ **Sentara Center for Health & Fitness** (757-766-2658; www.sentarafitness .com), 4001 Coliseum Drive, Hampton 23666. Hospital-associated wellness campus offers aqua exercise and lap pool; whirlpool, steam, and sauna; indoor track; Kidz In Motion exercise program; full spa services; healthy cafeteria. Daily and weekly guest passes available.

Zenya Yoga and Massage Studio (757-643-6900; www.zenyayoga.com), 101 Herman Melville Avenue, Port Warwick, Newport News 23606. Elegant Port Warwick studio with body fusion, Pilates, and hot yoga, for all abilities, plus facials and massages.

HIKING, JOGGING, AND FITNESS TRAILS Briarfield Park Fitness Trail (757-850-5116; www.hampton.va.us/parks), 1560 Briarfield Road, Hampton 23661.

Darling Stadium (757-727-8311; www.hampton.va.us/parks), 4111 Victoria Boulevard, Hampton 23669. Municipal stadium open for public jogging year-round, 7–3 Mon.–Fri.

Deer Park (757-886-7912; www.nnparks.com), 11523 Jefferson Avenue, Newport News 23601. Hiking trails lined with camellias, azaleas, and rhododendron lace the 13 wooded acres of this former deer-breeding preserve.

Matteson Trail (757-766-9148; www.hampton.va.us/parks), 320 Butler Farm Road, Hampton 23666. Three-mile nature and fitness trail circles the Hamptons Golf Course, a sanctuary for bluebirds and other songbirds. Trail begins and ends at the Sentara Health & Fitness Center (4001 Coliseum Drive).

&. **Noland Trail in Mariners' Museum Park** (757-596-2222; www.mariner.org), 100 Museum Drive, Newport News 23606. Clay-surfaced 5-mile trail circles Lake Maury, through a nature preserve with stands of rare Virginia pine, tall tulip poplar, and an understory of holly, dogwood, and azalea. The shady, 6-foot-wide path is handicapped accessible. A good place to park is at the **Lion's Bridge,** with sculptures by Anna Hyatt Huntington, wife of the museum's founder.

The Peninsula Pathfinders of Virginia (www.peninsulapathfinder.org), P.O. Box 7100, Hampton 23666. Local Volkssporting association awards patches to walkers who complete mapped routes throughout the Lower Peninsula.

RACQUET SPORTS & TENNIS An Achievable Dream Tennis Center (757-247-2428; www.nnparks.com), 1300 Ivy Avenue, Newport News 23607. Facility with four indoor tennis courts offers hourly court rentals, as well as ball machine rental.

Hampton Tennis Center (757-727-1193; www.hampton.va.us/parks), 9 Woodland Road, Hampton 23663. City-operated facility with seven clay courts, individual and group lessons, summer camps, ball machine rentals, and racquet demos.

Huntington Park Tennis Center (757-247-8587; www.nnparks.com), 361 Hornet Circle, Newport News 23607. Twenty lighted hard-surface courts rent for day and night play ($2–3). Clinics and summer camps; ball machine and backboard rentals. Open seasonally.

SPAS Center 4 Massage Therapy (757-723-3829; www.center4massage therapy.com), two locations: 66 W. Mercury Boulevard, Hampton 23669; and 11010 Warwick Boulevard, Newport News 23601. Certified massage therapists administer treatments in a variety of modalities.

Naya Spa Sanctuary (757-271-8813; www.nayaspasanctuary.com), 707 Mariners Row, Oyster Point, Newport News 23606. Asian-inspired holistic spa offers its signature Green Tea Infusion bathing ritual and French manicures.

Salters Creek Retreat Day Spa (757-723-1934; www.salterscreek.com), 100 Bridge Street, Hampton 23669. Full spa services close to the Virginia Air and Space Center in downtown Hampton. The **Hampton Yoga Center and Fitness Studio** (757-741-8507; www.hamptonyogacenter.com), upstairs, offers a full schedule of classes.

Spa Botanica (757-827-8200; www.spabotanicahampton.com), 1700 Coliseum Drive, Hampton 23666. Spa inside the Embassy Suites features the signature Caviar and Pearl facial.

SPECTATOR SPORTS Arena Racing USA (757-671-8100; www.arenaracingusa .com), 1000 Coliseum Drive, Hampton 23666. Half-scale stock cars race around a high-banked indoor oval in Hampton Coliseum. Weekend nights, Oct.–Mar.

Boo Williams Sportsplex (757-637-7300; www.boowilliamssportsplex.com), 5 Armistead Pointe Parkway, Hampton 23666. New indoor sports and event center hosts tournaments and classes in many sports.

Christopher Newport University Captains (757-594-7880; www.cnusports .com), 1 University Place, Newport News 23606.

Hampton University Pirates (757-728-5315; www.hamptonpirates.com), Hampton University Ticket Office, 121 Holland Hall, Hampton 23668.

Langley Speedway (757-865-7223; www.langley-speedway.com), 3165 N. Armistead Avenue, Hampton 23666. Asphalt oval hosts NASCAR races, including Super Truck and Legends divisions, Sat. nights, Apr.–Oct. Events include the two-hundred-lap Hampton Heat NASCAR Late Model Stock race in July, the popular season-ender **Night of Destruction,** and Wacky Wednesdays. The **Hampton Roads Kart Club** (757-249-KART; www.hrkc.com) sponsors races here as well.

✪ ✐ ♞ **Peninsula Pilots** (757-245-2222; www.peninsulapilots.com), War Memorial Stadium, 1889 W. Pembroke Avenue, Hampton 23661. Baseball's stars of tomorrow play ball all summer, battling teams in the collegiate **Coastal Plain League** (www.coastalplain.com) at historic **War Memorial Stadium,** a classic wooden ballfield—one of the largest in the world—built in 1947, recently updated with video scoreboard, field lighting, food court, and full-service tiki bar. Adults $5, seniors (60-plus) and children under 12 $3.

TOURING The **Newport News Visitor Center** (757-886-7777 or 888-493-7386; www.newport-news.org; 13560 Jefferson Avenue, Newport News 23603) sells combination tickets that represent a considerable savings over individual admissions. One combination includes seven different attractions, including the Mariners' Museum and USS *Monitor* Center, and the Virginia Living Museum, priced $45 for adults, $30 for children 6–12, $12 for children 3–5. A less-expensive combo ticket designed for history buffs includes admission to Lee Hall Mansion, Endview Plantation, and the Virginia War Museum (adults $15, seniors $12, children 7–17 $9). Combination tickets are also sold at the individual attractions.

Buy a **Hampton Day Pass** at the **Hampton Visitor Center** (757-315-1610 or 866-484-HRCC; www.hamptoncvb.com; 120 Old Hampton Lane, Hampton 23669) for very significant savings at five local attractions. Ask also for a free **Hampton Day Pass Value Card** for discounts at local restaurants and shops. Day passes are also available at the Virginia Air and Space Center.

By automobile: **Newport News CD Driving Tour** (757-886-7777 or 888-493-7386; www.newport-news.org), 13560 Jefferson Avenue, Newport News 23603. Audio tour of the region contains turn-by-turn directions to 23 different historic sites and shopping districts, interspersed with engaging stories and music. Available at the Newport News Visitor Center or by mail for $12.95.

By bicycle or on foot: ✪ **Hampton iPod Tours** (757-315-1610 or 866-484-HRCC; www.hamptoncvb.com). Several tours through the historic neighborhoods of Hampton are available for download from the Hampton Convention and Visitors Bureau Web site in both audio and video formats. If you don't have an iPod or similar MP3 device, you can rent one at the **Hampton Visitor Center** (757-315-1610; 120 Old Hampton Lane) or **Virginia Air and Space Center** (757-727-0900; 600 Settlers Landing Road) for $10. The tours are suitable for walking, biking, or driving.

Thomas Jefferson National Accelerator Facility (757-269-7100; www.jlab.org), 12000 Jefferson Avenue, Newport News 23606. Groups of five or more can arrange guided tours of the famous Jefferson Lab through its Public Affairs Office. Visitors must be 18 or over and have photo ID. Jefferson Lab schedules an open house on alternate years.

By boat: ✪ **Miss Hampton II** **Harbor Cruises** (757-722-9102 or 888-757-2628; www.misshamptoncruises.com), 710 Settlers Landing Road, Hampton 23669. Comfortable tour boat departs from the downtown Hampton waterfront for tours of Hampton Roads Harbor, the Chesapeake Bay, and the Atlantic Fleet docked at Norfolk Naval Base. A half-hour walking tour of Fort Wool, accessible only by boat, is included. An all-day cruise up the Elizabeth River passing through the locks at Great Bridge is also available. Snack bar with full-service bar onboard. Seasonal.

By bus or minivan: **Lee Hall Mansion Civil War Bus Tours** (757-888-3371; www.leehall.org), 163 Yorktown Road, Newport News 23603. Historian-led tours explore regional Civil War sites. Advance reservations required.

THE *MISS HAMPTON II* OFFERS DAILY CRUISES OF HAMPTON ROADS AND THE NORFOLK NAVAL BASE, INCLUDING A STOP AT FORT WOOL.

VMW Guided Tours (757-988-0015; www.vmwguidedtours.com). Groups can arrange tours of local and regional African American Heritage sites, led by professional guides.

WATER SPORTS Surrounded on three sides by water, the Virginia Peninsula offers excellent opportunities for aquatic fun. Jet Skis and personal watercraft are very popular in these shallow waters. Launch your craft from the north end of Buckroe Beach at Pilot Avenue in Hampton or at Huntington Park in Newport News.

Popular launch sites for windsurfing include Messick Point and Factory Point on Back River; Buckroe Beach in Hampton; and Anderson Park, Huntington Park, and the Hilton Ridge Beach and Pier in Newport News. **Mill Creek,** a small bay adjacent to Buckroe Beach, is one of the most popular spots for windsurfing in the area, with good sailing conditions even in strong winds. The launch site is inside Fort Monroe. Visit www.windvisions.com for more information.

Beach Sports Windsurfing (757-851-3224; www.beachsports.net), 203 Buckroe Avenue, Hampton 23664. Rentals, lessons, and sales of top brand windsurfing equipment; repairs; and used and demo equipment near Buckroe Beach.

Scuba Diving Shops & Charters

Deep Dream Diving (757-713-0168; www.deepdreamdiving.com), 13673 Warwick Boulevard, Newport News 23601. Dive courses include online training, and private and semiprivate classes.

Shark Bites Scuba Club (www.divealot.com). Scuba club meets on the first Thurs. of the month. Guests welcome.

Underwater Adventures (757-826-3945; www.underwateradventures.com), 3300-G W. Mercury Boulevard, Hampton 23666. Full range of services, including Nitrox fills and oxygen cleaning. Courses include a one-day spearfishing course with lobster taking.

WILDERNESS CAMPING Sandy Bottom Nature Park (757-896-4657; www.hampton.gov/sandybottom), 1255 Big Bethel Road, Hampton 23666. Nine primitive campsites that each accommodate two four-person tents are available on a first-come, first-served basis. Four permanent tent cabins with six cots each are located on platforms overlooking Crystal Lake. None of the campsites have electricity, running water, or adjacent parking. Open all year. $10–40.

WILDLIFE- AND BIRD-WATCHING The Lower Peninsula loop in the Coastal Section of the **Virginia Birding and Wildlife Trail** runs through this region. Visit www.dgif.virginia.gov/vbwt or call 866-VABIRDS for more information. For additional birding opportunities, see our listings under *Hiking* and *Wilder Places.*

Chesapeake Avenue Waterfront Drive (757-727-1102), Newport News. Seven parking areas and scenic overlooks provide opportunities during the winter to sight migrating waterfowl, including common and red-throated loons, tundra swans, and red-breasted mergansers.

Hampton Roads Bird Club Sunday Morning Walks (757-877-9415; www.hamptonroadsbirdclub.org). Local birders conduct free expeditions through Newport News Park on the first and third Sun. of each month. Meet at 7 AM in the parking lot behind the ranger station. The club also plans many field trips open to visitors.

Wild Wings Nature Store (757-595-3060; www.wildwingsnnva.com), 27 Hidenwood Shopping Center, Newport News 23606. The Tidewater's largest bird and nature store maintains the Bluebird Trail in the Newport News Park Arboretum and organizes birding events.

POQUOSON: OFF THE BEATEN TRACK

The waterside village of **Poquoson** (www.ci.poquoson.va.us), founded in 1628, is a great place to browse, with some 20 unique stores (www.bull -island.com/uniqueshoppes) and a number of fine seafood restaurants. Gift shops with intriguing names such as **Betsy's Items of Interest** (757-342-6568; 891 Yorktown Road) and **Joanne's This, That & The Other** (757-868-4770; 798 Poquoson Avenue), as well as several antiques stores, galleries, delis, a tearoom, and a wine shop, can be found along Wythe Creek Road and nearby streets. Special events include the annual Holiday Open House the first weekend in November and the **Poquoson Seafood Festival** (www.poquoson seafoodfestival.com) in October.

Poquoson is located 6 miles north of I-64 exit 256B (Victory Boulevard/VA 171). The shops and attractions listed here are all in Poquoson, at zip code 23662.

Briar Patch Tea Room (757-868-6843; www.briarpatchtearoom.com), 475-I Wythe Creek Plaza (at Victory Boulevard). Lunch spot serves soups, salads, and quiche, as well as beer and wine.

Linville's Wine & Deli (757-868-5051), 477-A Wythe Creek Road. Deli items, as well as wines from around the world. Wine tastings on Sat.

Oxford Run Canal Trail (757-868-3580; www.ci.poquoson.va.us/parks), 830 Poquoson Avenue. Scenic trail circles Poquoson City Hall.

✐ **Poquoson Municipal Pool** (757-868-3580; www.ci.poquoson.va.us/parks), 830 Poquoson Avenue. Outdoor pool at Poquoson Municipal Park is open Memorial Day–Labor Day.

✳ Wilder Places

For additional nature walks, see our listings under *To Do—Hiking.*

Grandview Nature Preserve (757-825-4657; www.hampton.gov/parks), State Park Drive, Hampton 23664. Birding is good all year at this 500-acre preserve, which can be explored on foot, by bicycle, or by kayak. The dunes are home every spring to the largest colony of least terns on the Atlantic Coast. Kayakers can paddle Long Creek through the cordgrass marsh out to the Back River. Free.

King-Lincoln Park Interpretive Center (757-888-3333 or 757-886-7912; www .nnparks.com), 600 Jefferson Avenue, Newport News 23607. Exhibits highlight native wildlife and ecosystems along the bay shore at this city park with a natural beach at the end of Jefferson Avenue. Open weekends, Memorial Day–Labor Day. Free.

✐ **Newport News Park and Discovery Center** (757-886-7912 or 800-203-8322; www.nnparks.com), 13564 Jefferson Avenue/I-64 exit 250B, Newport News 23603. This 8,330-acre municipal park, the largest east of the Mississippi River, wraps around two reservoirs. Activities include RV camping, rental boats and bikes, fishing, Civil War trail sites, golf and disc golf courses, an archery range, orienteering course, the **Aeromodel Flying Field** (757-591-4848), and more than 35 miles of trails for biking and hiking. The Bluebird Trail runs through the park's arboretum. Extensive gardens include a **Japanese Peace Garden** with teahouse and stands of dogwoods, azaleas, and camellias. The **Discovery Center** features nature and history exhibits. Open all year. Free.

Sandy Bottom Nature Park (757-896-4687; www.hampton.gov/parks), 1255 Big Bethel Road, Hampton 23666. Six miles of interpreted trails wind through forest, wetlands, and along the shores of two lakes. Nature center exhibits, with many living creatures; interpretive walks; rental canoes; fishing pier; primitive campsites and tent cabins; and a garden of native plants are among the attractions. Flocks of migrating bufflehead and other waterfowl are abundant in the winter months. Open all year. Free.

✳ Lodging

Price Categories

Inexpensive	up to $80
Moderate	$80 to $150
Expensive	$150 to $200
Very expensive	$200 and up

HOTELS & RESORTS Thanks to the area's strategic position between Williamsburg and Virginia Beach, the I-64 corridor has representatives of nearly every national chain hotel, most located close to the exit ramps. You'll find clusters of hotels at exit 255 near the Williamsburg/Newport News Airport, at exit 258 near City Center at Oyster Point, and at exit 263 in the Coliseum Central/Power Plant hotel district in Hampton.

Hampton

✪ ⬦ ♿ 🐾 ⚲ ⅋ ❞❜❞ ⊸ **Crowne Plaza Hampton Marina** (757-727-9700 or 866-727-9990; www.hamptonmarina hotel.com), 700 Settlers Landing Road, Hampton 23669. Price: Moderate. Credit cards: Yes. Special features: Free Wi-Fi access, covered self parking, on-site salon and shops, concierge and rental car service, rooftop pool and spa, 24-hour business and fitness centers. Hampton's only year-round waterfront hotel recently enjoyed a complete renovation as it joined the Crowne Plaza family, with both rooms and public areas decorated in striking

blue and white nautical decor. Each of the 173 nonsmoking rooms and suites enjoys magnificent floor-to-ceiling views of Hampton and its harbor. Request a corner king for the best views of all. The Crowne Plaza occupies Hampton's most convenient location, just steps from the marina and its sight-seeing cruises, the Virginia Air and Space Center, and Queens Way, home to many restaurants and festivals. The hotel guarantees a good night's sleep with its complimentary Sleep Advantage Program. Dining options include the Latitude 37 lounge, the Regatta Grill, Oyster Alley waterfront dining, and room service.

⬦ ⊸ **Embassy Suites Hotel, Spa and Convention Center** (757-827-8200; www.embassysuiteshampton .com), 1700 Coliseum Drive, Hampton 23666. Price: Expensive. Credit cards: Yes. Special features: Free self parking, on-site day spa, coffee shop, 24-hour business center, valet and concierge services. The two-room suites at this 10-story hotel adjacent to the Hampton Coliseum are arranged around a lofty interior atrium. Accommodating up to four people and ideal for a family, the suites include a bedroom with king bed or two queens, separate living room with pull-out sleeper sofa, two TVs, microwave, refrigerator, dining/work table, wet bar, coffeemaker, and phones. Internet access is available for an additional fee. Guests enjoy a complimentary made-to-order breakfast with omelet station each morning, and a free manager's reception with cocktails and appetizers every evening. Amenities include an indoor pool and whirlpool, fitness center with sauna, laundry, room service, and the on-site Cypress Grille and lounge.

♂ "ᵀ" ⇒ **Magnolia House Bed and Breakfast** (757-722-2888 or 800-398-1662; www.maghousehampton.com), 232 S. Armistead Avenue, Hampton 23669. Innkeepers: Joyce and Lankford Blair. Price: Expensive. Credit cards: Yes. Special features: Free Wi-Fi, free off-street parking, therapeutic massage available; no pets or children under 13. Lovely restored Queen Anne surrounded by old magnolias situated not far from the downtown waterfront offers two queen bedrooms, plus a king bed suite with spa tub. The friendly innkeepers are happy to help with suggestions and directions to area attractions and are expert hosts, constantly surprising guests with little extras and special treats. Each room has a private bath, cable TV, CD player, luxury linens, terry-cloth robes, and slippers. Downstairs, guests enjoy the use of shady porches; several parlors for reading, viewing TV, or listening to the hosts' large jazz collection; and a guest kitchen with complimentary drinks and snacks. A gourmet breakfast of regional specialties is served daily in the elegant dining room. Elopement and special-occasion packages available.

Newport News

♂ "ᵀ" **The Boxwood Inn Bed and Breakfast** (757-888-8854; www.boxwood-inn.com), 10 Elmhurst Street, Newport News 23603. Innkeepers: Kathy and Derek Hulick. Price: Moderate. Credit cards: Yes. Special features: Lunch and Fri.-night dinner served by reservation only; monthly special events; free Wi-Fi; no smoking, children, or pets. This gracious Southern inn, which has been standing next to the train tracks in Historic Lee Hall Village since 1896, now offers accommodations in four rooms and suites decorated with antiques of a bygone day, including one frequented by Gen. "Black Jack" Pershing when he was stationed in the area. One room has its own chamber pot, but all have private baths. The innkeepers serve breakfast daily in the dining room but will provide a breakfast basket on request. Popular for romantic getaways and weddings, the inn is located close to Endview and Lee Hall Mansion, at the intersection of Warwick Boulevard (US 60) and VA 238. Special brunches are offered on holidays.

"ᵀ" **Courtyard by Marriott Newport News Airport** (757-842-6212 or 800-321-2211; www.marriott.com), 530 St. Johns Road, Newport News 23602. Price: Moderate to expensive. Credit cards: Yes. Special features: Smoke-free, complimentary shuttle service to Newport News/Williamsburg International Airport, free Wi-Fi, indoor pool and whirlpool, fitness center, guest laundry, 24/7 market, in-room coffeemakers. Stylish, state-of-the-art hotel is the first built in Marriott's new contemporary design featuring the Lobby Experience: a large open first floor with comfortable seating; business center with complimentary computers and free wired and wireless Internet access; media pods with LCD TVs; the GoBoard, with local weather and area maps; complimentary coffee service; and the Bistro, selling breakfast items, snacks, and in the evening, dinner entrées and cocktails. Just outside, a patio area with a cozy fire pit and Wi-Fi access is a great place to relax. The five-floor hotel, located off

Jefferson Avenue (VA 143) at I-64 exit 255, is across the street from the Patrick Henry Mall.

 ✰ **The Mulberry Inn** (757-887-3000 or 800-223-0404; www.mulberryinnva.com), 16890 Warwick Boulevard (US 60), Newport News 23603. Price: Moderate. Credit cards: Yes. Special features: Free Wi-Fi access and local phone calls, free parking, smoking and nonsmoking rooms available, free shuttle to Newport News/Williamsburg International Airport. This 102-room inn shares amenities and the Beck Hotel Group (www.funinva.com) commitment to excellence with sister hotel, the 57-room **Holiday Inn Express,** next door. Conveniently located off I-64 at exit 250A, close to Fort Eustis, Newport News Park, and Busch Gardens, the Mulberry's newly upgraded doubles, kings, efficiencies, and studios offer granite vanities, satellite television, coffeemakers, microwaves, refrigerators, free Wi-Fi, and other amenities that make this a good home base for families. A seasonal outdoor pool, fitness center, laundry, and business center with complimentary computers and Internet access. The free continental breakfast includes the Mulberry's famous sausage gravy and biscuits.

RV RESORTS AND CAMPGROUNDS **Gosnold's Hope Park**
(757-850-5116; www.hampton.va.us/parks), 901 E. Little Back River Road, Hampton 23669. Small campground offers water and electric hookups, with grills and picnic tables, showers, dump station, boat ramp, fitness trail, BMX track. RVs only. Tent camping available at **Sandy Bottom Nature Park** (see *To Do—Wilderness Camping*).

Newport News Park Campsites (757-888-3333 or 800-203-8322; www.nnparks.com/parks_nn.php), 13564 Jefferson Avenue, Newport News 23603. Enjoy camping at one of the country's largest municipal parks, with biking and hiking trails, Civil War sites, excellent birding, disc golf, archery, and rental boats and bikes, all on-site. Campsites have water and electric, paved parking pads, modern restrooms, laundry, dump station, and camp store. Pets welcome with current rabies certificate. Senior rates available. Credit cards accepted.

✳ Where to Eat

Here at the end of the Virginia Peninsula, seafood rules, with numerous restaurants competing to bring you the freshest catch. Fine dining has seen an upturn recently in Newport News, with Port Warwick and Oyster Point attracting upscale eateries. In downtown Hampton, Queens Way is a veritable restaurant row, with one eatery after another lining the sidewalks. But don't overlook the restaurants around the lake at the Power Plant, where another entertainment complex is taking shape.

Price Categories

Inexpensive	under $10
Moderate	$10 to $20
Expensive	$20 to $25
Very expensive	$25 and up

The listings in this section also include information on what meals are served, using the following abbreviations:

B	Breakfast
L	Lunch
D	Dinner
SB	Sunday brunch

DINING OUT

Hampton

✪ ♿ **Chesapeake Dining Room at the Chamberlin** (757-637-7200;

www.historicchamberlin.com), 2 Fenwick Road, Fort Monroe, Hampton 23651. Open: Sun.–Fri. Credit cards: Yes. Serving: L (Mon.), D (Mon.–Fri.), SB. Price: Expensive. Cuisine: American. Handicapped access: Yes. Don't miss the opportunity of a meal in the magnificently restored Chamberlin Hotel's famous Chesapeake Dining Room, with its original hardwood dance floor and exquisite windows looking out on the waters where so much history took place. Although now a private retirement apartment complex, the Chamberlin, a Beaux-Arts beauty built in the 1920s and renovated at the cost of $54 million, is open to the public for a grand Sun. brunch, buffet lunch on Mon., and dinner on weeknights. Reservations are a must, and while you have them on the phone, arrange a visit to the Chamberlin Museum for a peek at various historic memorabilia. The Channel Bistro serves more casual lunches (Tues.–Sat.), or just opt for tapas and cocktails in the Chamberlin Bar (evenings, Thurs.–Sat.). Since the hotel is located within the gates of Fort Monroe, a photo ID for visitors over 16 and car registration may be required.

⚹ ⚹ **Kelly's Tavern** (757-313-9555; www.kellystavern.com), 1934 Coliseum Drive, Hampton 23666. Open: Daily. Credit cards: Yes. Serving: L, D. Price: Moderate. Cuisine: American. Handicapped access: Yes. Special features: Kelly's Curbside to Go, full bar, patio dining. The Hampton Kelly's on Coliseum Drive is the newest in this locally owned chain with 11 locations around Hampton Roads, and it serves the same award-winning menu that has earned "best of" awards for more than a decade. Burgers—available in ground beef, bison, turkey, or garden vegetable—dressed more than a dozen

different ways are the most popular menu items, but the wings, crab soup, crabcakes, and hot dogs earn rave reviews as well. Dining here is a casual affair, with lots of sandwiches, wraps, and appetizers. The huge brownie à la mode is such a hit that it's the only dessert offered.

In Newport News, another **Kelly's Tavern** (757-246-0080; 1010 Loftis Boulevard, Newport News 23606) is located at the entrance to Port Warwick.

⚹ ⚹ **Oyster Alley** (757-727-9700; www.hamptonmarinahotel.com), 700 Settlers Landing Road, Crown Plaza Hampton Marina, Hampton 23669. Open: Daily, late Apr.–Oct. Credit cards: Yes. Serving: L, D. Price: Moderate. Cuisine: Seafood. Handicapped access: Yes. Special features: Patio dining, live music on Sat. Known for its superb location and fresh seafood, this seasonal café on the waterfront side of the Crown Plaza faces the marina and Hampton River. Dine inside or outside on a menu long on seafood, especially oysters, and American standards, including some very reasonably priced steaks. Oyster Alley can get crowded in the summer, so if the wait seems too long, step around to **Latitude 37,** the hotel's lounge, where you'll find daily specials, big-screen TVs, and happy hour prices, or the **Regatta Grill,** serving everything from fish tacos to T-bone steaks.

⚹ ⚹ ⚹ **Six** (757-722-1466; www.little barbistro.com), 6 E. Mellon Street, Hampton 23663. Open: Daily. Credit cards: Yes. Serving: D. Price: Moderate. Cuisine: Tapas. Handicapped access: Yes. Special features: Late-night service, cocktail menu. The sister restaurant of **Crackers** (757-640-0200; 4226 Granby Street in Ghent, Norfolk 23504), **Empire** (757-626-3100; 245 Granby Street, downtown, Norfolk 23510), and **Pacifica** (757-422-5770;

214 40th Street, Virginia Beach 23451), this sweet spot in Phoebus follows the same recipe: lots of hot and cold tapas priced $10 or less, teamed with a long menu of martinis and other creative drinks, served until the wee hours of the morning. Order up a mix of small plates from lemongrass shrimp to grilled lobster claws, or upgrade any tapa to an entrée with bread and house salad for an additional $10. Try the S'mores Pu-Pu Platter for a fun dessert. Great spot for a bite before shows at the American Theatre or for lingering long into the evening.

Newport News

🐟 ⅃ **Al Fresco Italian Restaurant** (757-873-0644; www.alfrescoitalian restaurant.com), 11710 Jefferson Avenue, Newport News 23606. Open: Mon.–Sat. Credit cards: Yes. Serving: L, D. Price: Moderate. Cuisine: Italian. Special features: Full bar, patio dining, children's menu, take-out available. Award-winning local favorite overcomes its strip mall location with an elegant candlelit interior, white tablecloths, attentive service, and secluded patio. The cuisine is authentically Italian, featuring classic seafood, veal, chicken, and pasta dishes. Seafood lovers swoon over the salmon with artichoke hearts and mushrooms sautéed in white wine. Nice wine cellar includes some unique wines by the glass. Desserts, pastas, and sauces are all made in-house.

✪ ⅃ ⁗ᴵ⁗ **The Crabshack Seafood Restaurant** (757-245-CRAB; www.crabshackonthejames.com), 7601 River Road, Newport News 23607. Open: Daily. Credit cards: Yes. Serving: L, D. Price: Moderate. Cuisine: Seafood. Handicapped access: Yes. Special features: Free Wi-Fi access, free parking, full bar. Located next to the James River Fishing Pier in Hunt-

ington Park, this restaurant delivers superb views and sunsets from its wall of windows overlooking the river. The menu here, served all day and night, includes many inexpensive appetizers, salads, and sandwiches, plus slightly higher fresh-fish entrées. Burgers and chicken sandwiches are available for those who don't do seafood, and the kids will love the bacon cheese fries. Don't miss the fresh soft-shell crabs served all summer or the homemade Key lime pie for dessert. At sunset, join the local folks at the bar for raw or steamed oysters, clams, and shrimp.

⅃ **Schlesinger's Chop House at Port Warwick** (757-599-4700; www.schlesingerssteaks.com), 1106 William Styron Square S., Newport News 23606. Open: Daily. Credit cards: Yes. Serving: L, D, SB. Price: Very expensive. Cuisine: Steaks and seafood. Special features: Reservations recommended, online reservations, patio dining, cigar bar. Like many of the features in Port Warwick, this elegant chop house is named for a Pulitzer Prize–winning author, Arthur Schlesinger Jr., historian and JFK speechwriter. Definitely in the "splurge" category, the menu here is famous for its prime steaks, including bone-in filet mignon and rib eyes; lump crabcakes; tuna mignon; and Steak Schlesinger—an 8 ounce filet on a portobello mushroom cap topped with lump crabmeat, asparagus, and béarnaise. To avoid sticker shock, be aware that this is an à la carte restaurant with salads and other add-ons priced separately, although entrées do include one side item. The wine cellar, with 150 different vintages, received *Wine Spectator*'s Award of Excellence. Order the signature dessert, Chocolate Punctuation—a baked-to-order cake with a gooey chocolate center—early to avoid a long wait.

BAKERIES, TEAROOMS & COFFEE SHOPS

"ı" Aromas CoffeeHouse & Bakeshop Cafe (757-240-4650; www.aromasworld.com), 706 Town Center Drive, Newport News 23606. Beer, wine, coffee, and fresh baked goods, including the famous Chocolate Vacation Cookie, near the Oyster Point fountain.

Florimonte's Bakery (757-877-6668; www.florimontes.com), 533 Denbigh Boulevard, Newport News 23608. Breakfast pastries, breads, pies, and cakes by a Swiss pastry chef.

Ÿ "ı" Java Junkies (757-722-6300), 768 Settlers Landing Road, Hampton 23669. Colorful coffee shop next door to the Crowne Plaza. Jam sessions on Fri. evenings; full bar; free Wi-Fi.

"ı" Java on the James (757-596-5282; www.evertize.com/coffee/java.htm), 10234 Warwick Boulevard, Newport News 23601. Eat inside or on the deck at this Historic Hilton Village coffeehouse. Free Wi-Fi.

Victorian Station Restaurant, Tea Room, and Gift Shop (757-723-5663; www.victorianstation.net), 36 N. Mallory Street, Hampton 23663. Victorian mansion in the Phoebus serves lunch and afternoon tea Wed.–Sat. Reservations required.

BREAKFAST AND CASUAL MEALS

ℰ Belgian Waffle and Steak House (757-874-3562; www.belgianwaffleandsteakhouse.com), 14700 Warwick Boulevard, Newport News 23608. Southern breakfast served all day.

✪ The Grey Goose (757-723-7978; www.greygooserestaurant.com), 101 W. Queens Way, Hampton 23669. Downtown Hampton lunchroom serves creative dishes featuring Virginia ham, blue crab, and homemade buttermilk biscuits.

Tommy's Restaurant (757-825-1644), 3406 W. Mercury Boulevard, Hampton 23666. No-frills spot is beloved by locals for its bargain-priced breakfast combo (under $5).

CANDY & ICE CREAM

"ı" Belgian Chocolatier and Beanery (757-272-1125; www.belgianchocolatierandbeanery.com), 675 Town Center Drive, Newport News 23606. Imported Leonidas chocolates, plus sweet and savory baked goods. Free Wi-Fi.

Hilton Village Parlor and Restaurant (757-595-6708), 10359 Warwick Boulevard, Newport News 23601. Hershey's old-fashioned ice cream served at this Historic Hilton Village landmark.

ℰ Portside Pharmacy & Olde Fashioned Soda Fountain (757-327-0780; www.portsidepharmacy.com), 1101 William Styron Square S., Port Warwick, Newport News 23606. Milk shakes, sundaes, banana splits, and cherry Cokes from an old fashioned BobCat Soda Fountain.

DELIS & SPECIALTY FOODS

Best of British (757-723-7480), 50 Old Hampton Lane, Hampton 23669. Imported British and Scottish foods, sausage rolls, and Cornish pasties in downtown Hampton.

The Virginia Store (757-727-0600 or 800-633-2203; www.hamptonva.com/vastore), 555 Settlers Landing Road, Hampton 23669. Virginia wines, hams, peanuts, and gifts.

Warwick Cheese Shoppe (757-599-3985; www.warwickcheese.com), 53 Hidenwood Shopping Center, Newport News 23606. Deli serves sandwiches stuffed with sliced meats, pâté, Brie, or blue cheese; estate bottled wines; and the area's largest selection of cheeses.

FARMS, FARMER'S MARKETS & VEGETABLE STANDS Dean and Don's Farm Markets, two locations: 12601 Warwick Boulevard, Newport News 23606 (757-930-2707), and 600 LaSalle Avenue, Hampton 23669 (757-722-3161). Join area chefs browsing the excellent selection.

✔ **Downtown Hampton Market Place** (757-727-0900; www.vasc.org/celebrationsbythebay), 756 Settlers Landing Road, Hampton 23669. Sat. mornings on Queens Way, with live entertainment, cooking and gardening demonstrations, and children's activities. Seasonal.

Newport News Farmers Market (757-247-2351; www.nnparks.com), 2801 Jefferson Avenue at 28th Street, Newport News 23607. Open-air market with many special events is open year-round, Wed.–Sat. in the summer, Fri.–Sat. in the winter.

NATURAL FOODS Granma T's Health Foods (757-594-9868; www.mygranmat.com), 4161 William Styron Square N., Newport News 23606. Port Warwick store stocks organic groceries and dairy products.

Health Trail Natural Foods (757-596-8018; www.healthtrailnatural foods.com), 10848 Warwick Boulevard, Newport News 23601. Large selection of vegetarian and vegan foods, organic produce, dried herbs.

PIZZA Chanello's Pizza (www.chanellospizza.com). Locally owned chain with seven locations in Newport News and Hampton serves pizzas, subs, and wings, plus apple and cherry dessert pizzas. Pick up or delivery.

Ⓨ **Mitty's Ristorante** (757-873-6664; www.omninn.com), 1000 Omni Boulevard, Newport News 23606. Omni Newport News Hotel restaurant serves brick-oven-baked pizza. Happy hour.

✎ **Vinny's Pizza and Pasta** (757-594-3354; www.vinnyspizzaandpasta.com), 748 J. Clyde Morris Boulevard, Newport News 23601. Big menu of slices, gourmet pies, pastas, subs, and Philly cheesesteaks. Drive-through window for take-out.

SANDWICHES & TAKE-OUT Jamestown Pie Company (757-596-3888; www.buyapie.com), 11800 Mariners Row, Oyster Point, Newport News 23606. Drop by for a potpie, pizza pie, dessert pie, sandwich, or pasta entrée, or try one of the Mediterranean specialties.

Old Hampton Seafood Kitchen (757-723-5777), 124 S. Armistead Avenue at Settlers Landing Road, Hampton 23669. Fast-food-style restaurant serves fried seafood dinners to eat in or take out.

Rocky Mount Bar-B-Que House (757-596-0243; www.rockymount bbq.com), 10113 Jefferson Avenue, Newport News 23605. Eastern North Carolina–style barbecue, seafood, fried chicken, pies, and banana pudding to eat in or take out. Delivery available.

WINE SHOPS, BREWERIES, AND BREWPUBS Ⓨ County Grill and Smokehouse (757-723-0600; www.countygrill.net), 26 E. Mercury Boulevard, Hampton 23669. Meats, from St. Louis ribs to tuna, smoked and grilled on an open pit, accompanied by six sauces; live entertainment and 13 microbrews on tap.

❂ **La Bodega Hampton** (757-722-VINO; www.labodegahampton.com), 22 Wine Street, Hampton 23669. Relaxing spot in downtown Hampton stocks hundreds of wines, imported beers, cheeses, pâtés, and French bread baked daily in-house. Deli sandwiches and wines by the glass are served at tables amid the wine racks.

⦿ **St. George Brewing Company**
(757-865-BEER; www.stgeorge
brewingco.com), 204 Challenger Way,
Hampton 23666. Craft microbrewery
combines traditional English and German recipes with modern techniques
to create award-winning brews. Tours
are followed by tastings in the hospitality room, where the taps are topped
with dragons.

⦿ ⵖ **The Taphouse on Queens Way**
(757-224-5829; www.facebook.com/
hamptontaphouse), 17 E. Queens Way,
Hampton 23669. More than three
dozen beers on tap and a hundred bottled brews pair with some very fine
tavern fare and live music in downtown Hampton.

Taste Unlimited (757-596-8651; www
.tasteunlimited.com), 702 Mariners
Row, Oyster Point, Newport News
23606. Specialty food and wine retailer
offers weekly wine tastings.

✴ Shopping

The cities at the tip of the Virginia
Peninsula experienced a retail boom in
recent years, with numerous new shopping destinations along the I-64 corridor. Exits at Jefferson Avenue (VA 143)
in Newport News and Mercury Boulevard (US 258) in Hampton offer all the
major national retail and restaurant
brands, as well as some unique local
venues.

Venture a bit beyond the interstate, and
you'll find several lovely shopping destinations where you can walk from store
to store amid historic surroundings.
Nearly all the shops and restaurants
you'll encounter in these downtown
areas are locally owned.

The walkable streets of **downtown
Hampton** (www.downtownhampton
.com) are lined with antiques stores,
art galleries, and charming shops,
mixed with numerous restaurants and
pubs along Queens Way.

Mellen Street, the main shopping drag
of the historic neighborhood of **Phoebus** (www.phoebus.info), makes for a
pleasant stroll past unusual shops,
bookstores, thrift shops, antiques
stores, restaurants, pubs, and the venerable **American Theater.**

Several of the English-style cottages in
Historic Hilton Village (www.shop
hiltonvillage.com) in Newport News
today house unique shops, galleries,
and coffee shops. The Peninsula Community Theatre, the Main Street
Library, and the **Hilton Village Parlor & Restaurant** (757-595-6708;
10359 Warwick Boulevard), a local
landmark, as well as the Hilton Pier at
the end of Main Street, are part of the
eclectic mix.

SHOPPING CENTERS & MALLS
⦿ **City Center at Oyster Point** (757-
873-2020; www.oysterpointonline
.com), 701 Town Center Drive, Newport News 23606. Newport News'
vibrant new heart is full of retail,
restaurants, and residences. Shops are
upscale and mostly national, among
them Banana Republic, Coldwater
Creek, and Talbots. The streets of the
mixed-use project center on a 5-acre
fountain, the scene of free summer
concerts and outdoor films. The 11-
story **Marriott Hotel at Oyster Point**
(757-873-9299; www.marriott.com/
phfoy; 740 Town Center Drive, Newport News 23606), overlooking the
fountain, has Rockefeller's Seafood
Restaurant and the Oyster Point
Lounge on-site. Plenty of free street
and deck parking. Look for the impressive entrance to City Center on Jefferson Avenue just south of I-64.

Jefferson Commons, 12551 Jefferson
Avenue, Newport News 23602.
Stretching along Jefferson Avenue (VA
143) north of I-64, across from the
Newport News/Williamsburg Interna-
tional Airport, lie numerous shopping

and restaurant destinations, as well as big-box stores such as Walmart and Home Depot.

Patrick Henry Mall (757-249-4305; www.shoppatrickhenrymall.com), 12300 Jefferson Avenue, Newport News 23602. Off I-64 at exit 255B, Newport News' largest enclosed mall hosts more than a hundred specialty stores; a large, comfortable food court; and numerous special events.

Peninsula Town Center (757-838-1505; www.peninsulatowncenter.com), 1800 W. Mercury Boulevard (US 258), Hampton 23666. Off I-64 at exit 263, the former Coliseum Mall has been transformed into a mixed-use community featuring national retail stores, specialty shops, restaurants, and many special events. Major tenants include Macy's, Barnes & Noble, and **CinéBistro** (www.cobbcinebistro.com), a cross between a cinema and a nightclub exclusively for the 21-and-over set.

Port Warwick (757-875-9351; www.portwarwick.com), Loftis Boulevard off Jefferson Avenue, Newport News 23606. Award-winning mixed-use community centers on Stryon Square, a 3-acre green space surrounded by upscale shops and restaurants. Special events include a free summer concert series and the annual **Port Warwick Art and Sculpture Festival** (www.pwartfest.org), in Oct.

✪ **Power Plant of Hampton Roads** (757-826-6351; www.powerplanthampton.com), 1972 Power Plant Parkway, Hampton 23666. Off Mercury Boulevard (US 258) at I-64, this entertainment, dining, and retail district enjoys a scenic lakeside location. Bass Pro Shops, Lowe's, and BJ's Wholesale Club are anchor tenants, alongside several entertainment and dining venues with decks overlooking the lake.

BOOKS & MUSIC Bender's Books & Comics (757-723-3741), 22 S. Mallory Street, Hampton 23663. Bookstore in historic Phoebus.

Friends of the Newport News Public Library Bookstore (757-926-1350 or 757-591-4858; www.nngov.com/library), 110 Main Street, Newport News 23601. Main Street Library in Hilton Village sells gently used books, classics, and collectibles, as well as books and music on tape, videos, CDs, and cross-stitch patterns.

Paperbacks, Ink (757-873-1211), 11710-O Jefferson Avenue, Oyster Point, Newport News 23606. Stocks new and used books.

The Way We Were Bookstore (757-726-2300), 32 E. Mellen Street, Phoebus, Hampton 23663.

CLOTHING Benton-Knight Ltd. (757-723-0521 or 800-291-2219; www.bentonknight.com), 28 S. King Street, Hampton 23669. Founded in 1945, this men's clothier sells top-quality suits, blazers, nautical wear, and collegiate apparel.

Ignatius Ladies' Specialty Shop (757-596-6919; www.ignatiusladies.net), 2110 William Styron Square S., Newport News 23606. Owner-operated shop in Port Warwick carries handcrafted Murano jewelry, the Brighton Collection, and top European fashion lines.

CRAFTS ⏛ The Bead Store (757-591-0593; www.beadstore-va.com), 10375 Warwick Boulevard, Hilton Village, Newport News 23601. Huge selection of beads, semiprecious stones, sterling silver, and Venetian glass. Free beading classes.

Nancy's Calico Patch (757-596-7397; www.ncpquilting.com), 21 Hidenwood Shopping Center, Newport News 23606. Quilt shop offers classes in "scrap therapy."

Olde Hampton Quilt Shoppe (757-722-5014), 47 E. Queens Way, Hampton 23669.

✂ 🧵 **Phoebus Needlework, Crafts & Miniatures** (757-723-1558; www.phoebuscrafts.com), 13 E. Mellen Street, Phoebus, Hampton 23663. Dollhouse and village kits, needlework and crafts supplies, and more.

✂ 🧵 **Starving Artist Studio** (757-594-0518; www.starartiststudio.com), 157 Herman Melville Avenue, Port Warwick, Newport News 23606. Paint-it-yourself pottery studio also displays Polish pottery and original works by regional artists.

Village Stitchery (757-599-0101; http://villagestitchery.tripod.com), 97 Main Street, Newport News 23601. Needlepoint and cross-stitch supplies, and free classes, in Historic Hilton Village.

FLEA MARKETS, CONSIGN-MENT, AND THRIFT STORES
Act II (757-595-0507), 10253 Warwick Boulevard, Hilton Village, Newport News 23601. Fashion-forward stock from some eight thousand consignors, plus a special bargain room with deep discounts.

CHKD Thrift Stores (www.chkd.org/Giving/Thrift), three locations: 4111 W. Mercury Boulevard, Hampton 23666 (757-827-5437); 11049 Warwick Boulevard, Newport News 23601 (757-599-KIDS); and 14346 Warwick Boulevard, Newport News 23602 (757-877-KIDS). Proceeds benefit the Children's Hospital of the King's Daughters.

🧵 **Jefferson Flea Market** (757-594-9035), 10171 Jefferson Avenue, Newport News 23605. More than 85 indoor shops, plus weekend outdoor booths, Thurs.–Sun.

Phoebus Auction Gallery (757-722-9210; www.phoebusauction.com), 16 E. Mellen Street, Phoebus, Hampton 23663. Top-quality antiques, collectibles, and biweekly charity auctions, plus specialty auctions and gallery sales. On-site appraisers.

GIFTS Bo Essentials (757-240-5644; www.boessentials.com), 707 Mariners Row, Oyster Point, Newport News 23606. Blend your own fragrance using a hundred different essences, from frankincense to fudge brownie.

Countryside Gardens (757-722-9909; www.countrysidegardens.biz), 220 E. Mercury Boulevard, Hampton 23669. Boutique with many limited-edition and exclusive products displayed in a fragrant, relaxing setting.

Soapalooza (757-224-2670; www.soapalooza.com), 3411 Old Armistead Avenue, Hampton 23666. Make your own soaps, bath salts, and body butters.

HOME DECOR The Perfect Setting (757-594-9415), 11850 Merchants Walk, Oyster Point, Newport News 23606. Tableware and unique gifts, including a large selection of Christmas ornaments and Irish Waterford crystal.

Shabby Chic (757-727-0100), 47 E. Queens Way, Hampton 23669. Cottage furniture, dried flowers, baskets, and other country-style decor in a pleasant shop in downtown Hampton.

Sisters Unique (757-595-9355; www.sistersunique.com), 701 Mariners Row, Oyster Point, Newport News 23606. Eclectic collection of home furnishings and accessories.

JEWELRY The Fine Arts Shop (757-595-7754; www.fineartsshop.com), 10178 Warwick Boulevard, Newport News 23601. Nationally known Historic Hilton Village shop stocks top-name designer jewelry and brokers estate jewelry. A top jewelry designer, **Hilton Village Goldsmith Shop** (757-599-6300 or 800-299-3079; www.ontheline.com; 10345 Warwick Boulevard), is just down the street.

Goodman & Sons Jewelers (757-838-2328; www.goodmanandsons.com), 2018 Coliseum Drive, Hampton 23666. Named Best Place for Jewelry in local polls. Additional location in Williamsburg's Monticello Marketplace (757-229-5388).

Hauser's Jewelers (757-595-6006; www.hausersjewelers.com), 701 Mariners Row, Oyster Point, Newport News 23606. Fifth-generation family business selling designer jewelry and Swiss watches since 1898.

✻ Special Events

For a general listing of events in Hampton Roads, visit www.your757 .com. For blues and other concerts in the Hampton Roads region, visit the Web site of the Natchel' Blues Network: www.natchelblues.org.

January: **◉ Hampton Blues Festival** (757-838-4203; www.natchelblues.org), Hampton Coliseum.

February: **Civil War Reenactment at Endview Plantation** (757-887-1862; www.endview.org), Newport News.

Mid-Atlantic Quilt Festival (757-315-1610; www.mancusoshows.com), Hampton Roads Convention Center, Hampton.

March: **Shamrock Party on O'Plaza** (757-926-1400; www.nnparks.com), City Center at Oyster Point Fountain Plaza, Newport News.

Tidewater Boat Show (804-425-6556; www.agievents.com), Hampton Roads Convention Center, Hampton.

April: **◉ Downtown Hampton In-Water Boat Show** (757-727-1276; www.downtownhampton.com), Down-

town Hampton Public Piers. The only in-water boat show on the Peninsula.

◈ Hampton Acoustic Blues Revival (757-456-1675; www.natchelblues.org), Thomas Nelson Community College, Mary T. Christian Auditorium, Hampton. Free.

May: **Armed Forces Day Toy Soldier Show** (757-247-8523; www.war museum.org), Virginia War Museum, Newport News.

Colonial Craftsman's Faire at Endview Plantation (757-887-1862; www.colonialfaire.com), Newport News.

Memorial Day Celebration at the Victory Arch (757-926-1400; www .nnparks.com), 25th Street and West Avenue, downtown Newport News.

✎ Newport News Children's Festival of Friends (757-926-1400; www.nnparks.com), Newport News Park.

June: **Afrikan American Festival** (757-850-4721), Mill Point Park, Hampton.

◉ Hampton Jazz Festival (757-838-4203; www.hamptonjazzfestival.com), Hampton Coliseum.

July: **◉ Blackbeard Pirate Festival** (757-727-0900; www.blackbeardfestival .com), downtown Hampton.

4th of July Stars in the Sky (757-926-1400; www.nnparks.com), Victory Landing Park, Newport News. The region's largest fireworks display.

August: **Hampton Cup Regatta** (757-265-0964; www.hamptoncupregatta .org), East Mercury Bridge at Fort Monroe. North America's oldest continuously running hydroplane boat race.

September: **⟿ Hampton Bay Days** (757-727-1641; www.baydays.com). Free street festival in downtown Hampton blends national music acts, art show, children's activities, and environmental education.

Military Vehicle Show (757-247-8523; www.warmuseum.org), Virginia War Museum, Newport News. Free

October: **Mariners' Museum 10K on the Noland Trail** (757-591-7739;

EVERY YEAR, PIRATES AND ROYAL NAVY SHIPS FIGHT IT OUT IN HAMPTON HARBOR—AND BLACKBEARD ONCE AGAIN LOSES HIS HEAD.

www.mariner.org), Newport News.

Newport News Fall Festival of Folklife (757-926-1400; www.nnparks .com), Newport News Park. Southeast Virginia's biggest traditional craft show.

Oyster Point Oyster Roast (757-926-1408; www.citycenteratoysterpoint .com), City Center at Oyster Point, Newport News.

Phoebus Days (757-722-1575; www .phoebusdays.com), Mellen Street, Hampton. Includes parade and beer festival.

✪ **Poquoson Seafood Festival** (www.poquosonseafoodfestival.com), Poquoson Municipal Park.

Port Warwick Art & Sculpture Festival (757-369-3014; www.pwartfest .org), Newport News.

November: **Get Hooked On Hampton Rockfish Tournament, Oyster Bash and Pig Pickin'** (800-800-2202; www.jimbaughoutdoors.com), downtown Hampton waterfront.

December: **Celebration in Lights** (757-926-1400; www.nnparks.com), Newport News Park. Begins Thanksgiving weekend.

Downtown Hampton Lighted Boat Parade (www.downtownhampton .com).

Pearl Harbor Day Memorial Ceremony (757-247-8523; www.war museum.org), Virginia War Museum, Newport News.

Southside

3

HISTORY ALONG THE ELIZABETH
RIVER—NORFOLK, PORTSMOUTH,
AND CHESAPEAKE

THE OLD DOMINION'S SEASIDE
PLAYGROUND—VIRGINIA BEACH

HISTORY ALONG THE ELIZABETH RIVER—NORFOLK, PORTSMOUTH, AND CHESAPEAKE

Home to the world's largest naval base, the U.S. Navy's oldest and largest shipyard, as well as the Navy's oldest and largest hospital, the deepwater ports of Norfolk and Portsmouth on either side of the Elizabeth River are deeply involved our country's defense and military history. A visit to this busy harbor ensures views of ships large and small, cargo vessels being loaded with containers, cruise liners headed for the Caribbean, and naval ships of the great Atlantic Fleet, from aircraft carriers to submarines, at berth, in dry dock, or embarking for the high seas.

You'll find pleasure craft here, too, gathering at Mile Zero of the great interior water highway called the **Atlantic Intracoastal Waterway** (ICW). South of Norfolk lies the **Great Dismal Swamp,** never tamed by man, one of the largest wild areas remaining along the East Coast. Two canals, alternate routes of the ICW, lead from the South Branch of the Elizabeth River across this watery wilderness: the **Albemarle and Chesapeake Canal,** and the historic **Dismal Swamp Canal,** begun by a group of investors that included George Washington, running due south toward Elizabeth City, North Carolina.

Downtown Norfolk lies along the East Branch of the Elizabeth River, while Portsmouth faces it across the harbor, along the West Branch. Two tunnels connect the cities, the Downtown Tunnel (I-264) and the Midtown Tunnel (US 58), but the best way to cross is aboard the low-cost, pedestrian **Paddlewheel Ferry,** running daily from early morning until late at night. Most of the main attractions of both cities are within easy walking distance of the ferry landings.

NORFOLK

Crossing from Hampton on the I-64 Hampton Roads Bridge-Tunnel, you make landfall on **Willoughby Spit** (www.willoughbyontheweb.com), a narrow finger of sand thrown up by a hurricane in 1749. Along its northern edge lie the Chesapeake Bay beaches of **Ocean View** along US 60 running toward Virginia Beach. Nearby: **Naval Station Norfolk,** the largest naval base in the world.

By the early years of the 20th century, electric trolleys ran from downtown Norfolk to Ocean View. At the spot where the trolleys, running up Granby Street, met

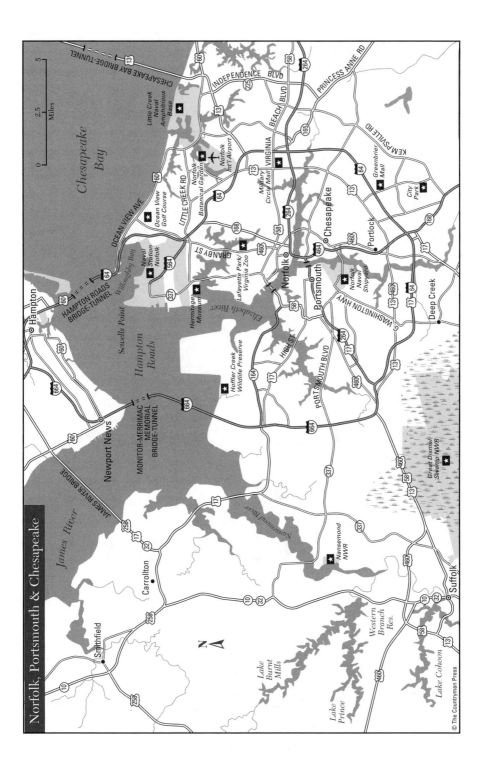

Norfolk, Portsmouth & Chesapeake

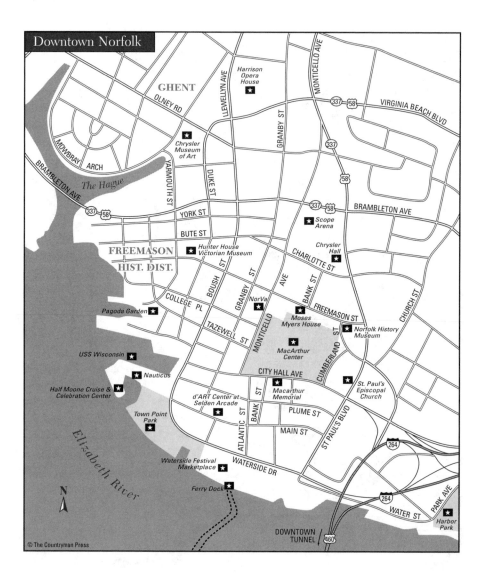

Downtown Norfolk

GHENT

Harrison Opera House ★

OLNEY RD

LLEWELLYN AVE

MONTICELLO AVE

GRANBY ST

VIRGINIA BEACH BLVD

337 58

Chrysler Museum of Art ★

MOWBRAY ARCH

BRAMBLETON AVE

The Hague

YARMOUTH ST

DUKE ST

337 58

337

58

BRAMBLETON AVE

Scope Arena ★

337 58

YORK ST

BUTE ST

FREEMASON HIST. DIST.

Hunter House Victorian Museum ★

Chrysler Hall ★

CHARLOTTE ST

BOUSH ST

GRANBY ST

AVE

BANK ST

FREEMASON ST

CHURCH ST

COLLEGE PL

Pagoda Garden ★

NorVa ★

Moses Myers House ★

Norfolk History Museum ★

TAZEWELL ST

MONTICELLO ST

CUMBERLAND ST

MacArthur Center ★

USS Wisconsin ★

Nauticus ★

CITY HALL AVE

St. Paul's Episcopal Church ★

Half Moone Cruise & Celebration Center ★

d'ART Center at Selden Arcade ★

Macarthur Memorial ★

BANK ST

ATLANTIC ST

PLUME ST

ST PAUL'S BLVD

Town Point Park ★

MAIN ST

Waterside Festival Marketplace ★

WATERSIDE DR

264

Elizabeth River

N

Ferry Dock ★

DOWNTOWN TUNNEL 460

264

WATER ST

PARK AVE

Harbor Park ★

the water, the famous Ocean View Amusement Park provided fun for generations of vacationers. Its legendary wooden coaster, the Skyrocket, finally succumbed to 88 sticks of dynamite, an event captured by film crews for the movie *Death of Ocean View Park* in 1979. Today, the **Ocean View Beach Park** occupies this spot, and the only remaining car from the Rocket sits in the Pretlow Library across the street.

Follow Granby Street (US 460) due south, and you'll soon reach the **Downtown Waterfront District,** once a rowdy area full of sailors on leave, now transformed to a trendy urban playground with three-quarters of a billion dollars of further construction under way or planned. Here Nauticus, the Battleship *Wiscon-sin,* the MacArthur Memorial, the historic Freemason District, docks lined with sight-seeing boats, and **Town Point Park,** site of numerous annual festivals, all lie within a few blocks, along with a wealth of restaurants, theaters, shops, and galleries. The last few blocks of Granby Street itself boast so many upscale nightclubs and sports bars that locals call it Martini Row.

By 2011, a new light rail line, dubbed the **Tide** (www.ridethetide.com), running through downtown will make it even easier to see the sights. Plans will eventually extend it all the way to Virginia Beach.

Just north of downtown, Norfolk's first streetcar suburb, called **Ghent** (www .destinationghent.com), lays down a funky, eclectic vibe with numerous shops and cafés grouped around the historic Naro Cinema. South of downtown on the city of Chesapeake border, the old factories of the industrial South Norfolk neighborhood are being transformed into a new arts district, dubbed **SoNo** (www.historicsouth norfolk.com).

Naval Station Norfolk, the largest naval base in the world, occupies the entire northwest quadrant of Norfolk. Its presence is due not just to the city's exceptional location on one of the world's great harbors but also to a successful bit of self-promotion on the part of Norfolk's city fathers. In celebration of the 300th anniversary of English settlement, local businessmen went all out to host the spectacular **1907 Jamestown Exposition** (www.hrnm.navy.mil/1907exposition) on Sewell's Point, the site of old Civil War batteries. They attracted 21 states to the event, each of which built a reception house to represent its history, as well as exhibits by numerous railroads and other industries. President Theodore Roosevelt attended twice and sent 16 U.S. battleships to anchor in Hampton Roads within sight of the spectators. After the seven-month exposition closed, Roosevelt dispatched these ships, designated the **Great White Fleet** (www.greatwhitefleet.info), on the first around-the-world cruise by steam-powered steel battleships. Ten years later, the U.S. Navy, impressed by the location and infrastructure, established Naval Station Norfolk on the exposition grounds.

Today, the Navy forms the backbone of Norfolk's identity. Don't miss a chance to cruise down the impressive line of berthed Navy ships aboard one of the city's many sight-seeing boats, or, for a sailor's perspective, take the base bus tour.

PORTSMOUTH

A quick ferry ride across the Elizabeth River brings you to Portsmouth, one of the world's great shipbuilding and refitting centers. The Gosport Ship-

A NOTE ON NAMES

A considerable controversy rages around the correct pronunciation of the name *Norfolk.* Most long-term residents and natives say *NOR-fik.* Others swear it should be *NAW-fuk,* a pronunciation that seems particularly popular among former and current Navy folk.

Further confusion surrounds the name of the Norfolk Naval Shipyard, actually located completely in Portsmouth. To avoid mixing it up with the Navy Shipyard in Portsmouth, New Hampshire (actually located across the river in Kittery, Maine), the military named the shipyard Norfolk instead.

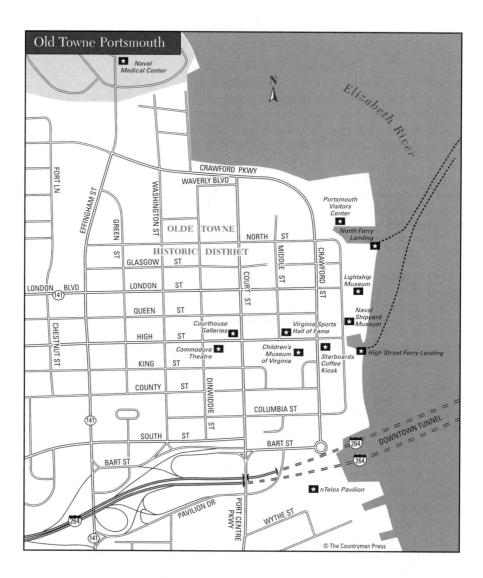

Old Towne Portsmouth

yard, established in 1767, was renamed the **Norfolk Naval Shipyard** (www.navsea.navy.mil/shipyards/norfolk) in 1862.

The shipyard's dry docks, usually occupied by a variety of Navy vessels, can be seen during the ferry crossing. Near the ferry dock at High Street Landing, the **Naval Shipyard Museum** (www.portsnavalmuseums.com) tells of the many ships built or refitted here, including the CSS *Virginia,* and the USS *Langley,* the Navy's first aircraft carrier.

Although the shipyard was destroyed by fire in both the Revolutionary and Civil wars, the town of Portsmouth was more fortunate, escaping major destruction. As a result, the Historic Olde Towne contains the best collection of antique buildings between Alexandria, Virginia, and Charleston, South Carolina.

Most of Portsmouth's museums, restaurants, and galleries lie on either side of High Street, within easy walking distance from the ferry landing. Marinas, hotels, and the nTelos Pavilion border the scenic waterfront within just a few blocks.

Many of the original merchants who settled the seaport in 1752 were Scots, and today, bagpipes and kilts frequently figure in area celebrations, such as the Olde Towne Scottish Walk, held annually on New Year's Eve.

CHESAPEAKE

Composed originally of farm lands and swamp stretching all the way to the North Carolina border, the City of Chesapeake experienced rapid growth in recent years thanks to the I-64/I-664 Beltway, which opened access to many new areas.

The region has always been an important crossroads. The Dismal Swamp Canal, dug by hand beginning in the 1790s and still in use, connects the Elizabeth River with the ports and river traffic of North Carolina. Today, the Chesapeake Expressway/VA 168, a toll road, provides the fastest route to North Carolina's Outer Banks.

At **Great Bridge Lock Park** (www.cityofchesapeake.net), on Battlefield Boulevard, you can watch yachts passing through the locks on the Albemarle and Chesapeake Canal, launch a boat, or go fishing and crabbing. This is also the location, every December, of the reenactment of the **Battle of Great Bridge** (www.gbbattlefield.org), when Virginia militiamen defeated the forces of Royal Governor Dunmore in 1775, causing him to abandon his occupation of Norfolk. Informational signs and a new visitors center at the park give the details.

GUIDANCE Chesapeake (757-382-2489; www.cityofchesapeake.net), 306 Cedar Road, Chesapeake 23322.

Chesapeake Conventions and Tourism (757-502-4898 or 888-889-5551; www

A TRIP ABOARD THE PADDLEWHEEL FERRY PROVIDES AN UP-CLOSE VIEW OF NORFOLK NAVAL SHIPYARD.

.visitchesapeake.com), 860 Greenbrier Circle, Suite 101, Chesapeake 23320.

Downtown Norfolk (757-623-1757; www.downtownnorfolk.org). Get information on Norfolk's dynamic downtown, including parking, dining, attractions, hotels, and more, at this Web site or by calling. The Web site features an excellent interactive map.

Elizabeth City Info Center (252-335-5330 or 866-324-8948; www.discoverec .org), 400 S. Water Street, Elizabeth City, NC 27909.

Emporia-Greensville Chamber of Commerce (434-634-9441; www.emporia -greensvillechamber.com), 400 Halifax Street, Emporia 23847.

Franklin-Southampton Area Chamber of Commerce (757-562-4900; www .fsachamber.com), 108 W. Third Avenue, Franklin 23851.

Greater Hampton Roads Black Chamber of Commerce (757-628-5300; www.ghrbcc.org), Norfolk.

Hampton Roads—America's First Region (www.americasfirstregion.com).

Hampton Roads Chamber of Commerce (757-622-2312; www.hamptonroads chamber.com), 420 Bank Street, Norfolk 23510. Includes Chesapeake, Norfolk, Portsmouth, Suffolk, and Virginia Beach.

Hampton Roads Hispanic Chamber of Commerce (www.hamptonroads hispanic.org).

Isle of Wight County (757-357-3191; www.co.isle-of-wight.va.us), P.O. Box 80, Isle of Wight 23397.

Isle of Wight–Smithfield–Windsor Chamber of Commerce (757-357-3502 or 888-2-THE-ISLE; www.theisle.org), 100 Main Street, Smithfield 23431.

Norfolk (757-664-4000; www.norfolk.gov), 810 Union Street, Norfolk 23510.

✧ **Norfolk Convention and Visitors Bureau** (757-664-6620 or 800-368-3097; www.visitnorfolktoday.com), 232 E. Main Street, Norfolk 23510. The main office at 232 E. Main Street in Norfolk is open weekdays. Nearby, a satellite office in the **Selden Arcade** (757-664-6880; www.theselden.com; 208 E. Main Street, Norfolk 23510) offers Norfolk- and mermaid-themed merchandise, as well as art exhibits, free Wi-Fi, and travel information daily. Additional downtown information kiosks can be found at the **MacArthur Center** (300 Monticello Avenue) and **Nauticus** (1 Waterside Drive).

Norfolk/Ocean View Visitors Information Center (757-441-1852), 9401 Fourth View Street, Norfolk 23503. Located at I-64, exit 273, just south of the Hampton Roads Bridge-Tunnel. Open daily.

Portsmouth (757-393-8000; www.portsmouthva.gov), 801 Crawford Street, Portsmouth 23704.

Portsmouth Convention and Visitors Bureau (757-393-5111 or 800-PORTS-VA; www.visitportsva.com), 6 Crawford Parkway, Portsmouth 23704. Conveniently located between the North Landing dock of the Elizabeth River Ferry and a large parking deck. Additional maps and information can be found at the **Starboards Coffee Kiosk** (757-478-0056; www.starboards.biz) at the High Street Ferry Landing. Visit www.oldetowneportsmouth.com for more about the historic district.

Smithfield (757-365-4200; www.smithfieldva.gov), P.O. Box 246, Smithfield 23431.

Smithfield & Isle of Wight Convention and Visitors Bureau (757-357-5182 or 800-365-9339; www.smithfield-virginia.com), 319 Main Street, Smithfield 23430.

Southampton County (757-653-3015; www.southamptoncounty.org), P.O. Box 400, Courtland 23837.

Suffolk (757-514-4000; www.suffolk.va.us), 41 Market Street, Suffolk 23434.

✧ **Suffolk Visitor Center** (757-923-3880; www.suffolk-fun.com), 321 N. Main Street, Suffolk 23434.

Windsor (757-242-4288; www.windsor-va.gov), 8 E. Windsor Boulevard, Windsor 23487.

GETTING AROUND ✪ **Elizabeth River Paddlewheel Ferry** (757-222-6100 or 800-767-8782; www.hrtransit.org). Three paddle-wheel ferries, carrying pedestrians and bicyclists between Norfolk and Portsmouth all year, offer scenic views of the waterfronts of Portsmouth and Norfolk, at minimal cost. Ferries dock at **High Street Landing** (1 High Street) and **North Landing** (6 Crawford Parkway) in Portsmouth and at the **Waterside** in Norfolk, running every half hour until nearly midnight in summer, shorter hours in winter. During baseball season, the ferries also run directly from North Landing to Harbor Park. Round-trip fare $3; one-way and multiride passes available. Handicapped accessible.

✧ **Portsmouth Downtown Loop Shuttle** (757-222-6100; www.gohrt.com/services/portsmouth-loop), Portsmouth. Low-emission hybrid buses circle downtown Portsmouth Mon.–Sat. 7 AM–midnight, with stops at the ferry landings, hotels, museums, and other attractions. Free.

✧ **Norfolk Electric Transit (NET)** (757-222-6100 or 800-767-8782; www.hrtransit.org). Complimentary downtown Norfolk bus runs along Granby Street from the waterfront as far as Harrison Opera House. Weekend routes connect to Nauticus and the Chrysler Museum. Free.

The Tide (757-222-6100 or 877-456-8433 [24-hour hotline]; www.ridethetide.com). In 2011, Norfolk's new light rail line begins service, running 7.4 miles from the Eastern Virginia Medical Center through downtown to Newtown Road, on the Virginia Beach border. Eleven stations, including four park-and-ride locations, provide access to numerous attractions.

Water taxi (757-439-8294). Convenient water taxi delivers you to any destination on the waterfront in Portsmouth or Norfolk, especially nice after big events when the Paddlewheel Ferry lines are long. The water taxi also offers 20-minute tours of the Portsmouth waterfront.

MEDICAL EMERGENCY **Bon Secours at Harbour View** (757-673-5800; www.bshr.com), 5818 Harbour View Boulevard, Suffolk 23435.

Bon Secours DePaul (757-889-5000; www.bshr.com), 150 Kingsley Lane, Norfolk 23505.

Chesapeake General Hospital (757-312-8121; www.chesapeakeregional.com), 736 Battlefield Boulevard N., Chesapeake 23320.

Children's Hospital of the King's Daughters (757-0668-7000; www.chkd.org), 601 Children's Lane, Norfolk 23507.

HOP A WATER TAXI FOR A QUICK TRIP ACROSS THE HARBOR, ESPECIALLY DURING BUSY FESTIVALS.

Eastern Virginia Medical School Health Services (757-446-5955; www.evms .edu), 825 Fairfax Avenue, Norfolk 23507.

Maryview Medical Center (757-398-2449; www.bshr.com), 3636 High Street, Portsmouth 23707.

Naval Medical Center Portsmouth (757-953-5000; www-nmcp.med.navy.mil), 620 John Paul Jones Circle, Portsmouth 23708.

Portsmouth Family Medicine (757-397-6344; www.evms.edu), 600 Crawford Street, Portsmouth 23704.

Sentara Norfolk General Hospital (757-388-3000; www.sentara.com), 600 Gresham Drive, Norfolk 23507.

Sentara Obici Hospital (757-934-4000; www.sentara.com), 2800 Godwin Boulevard, Suffolk 23434.

Sentara St. Luke's Outpatient Center (757-542-1000; www.sentara.com), 20209 Sentara Way, off US 258, Isle of Wight County, Carrollton 23314.

Southampton Memorial Hospital (757-569-6100; www.smhfranklin.com), 100 Fairview Drive, Franklin 23851.

✳ To See

Long somewhat notorious as a Navy town full of sailors looking for fun, Norfolk today is undergoing a cultural renaissance, with a revitalized downtown full of restored buildings housing upscale dining and nightlife, and many fine museums lining the waterfront. The area is especially rich in the performing arts, with numerous theater, music, and dance organizations performing throughout the region.

Across the harbor, Portsmouth, now a favorite stop for visiting boaters, provides many attractions within just a few blocks in its historic Old Towne.

ARCHITECTURE

Norfolk

Although only one structure, St. Paul's Church, survived the British bombardment of 1776 and the subsequent fire, residents quickly rebuilt after the war, and some of those houses remain in the **East Freemason District,** including the 1792 brick **Moses Myers House** (E. Freemason Street at Bank), with a unique octagonal-end dining room, considered one of the finest rooms of Federal design in the country. The nearby 1794 **Willoughby-Baylor House** (601 E. Freemason Street) combines Federal and Greek Revival features, and retains much of its original interior trim. Both are open to the public.

Other significant structures in the East Freemason District include the 1840 **Old Norfolk Academy** (420 Bank Street), a Greek Revival structure with Doric portico based on the Temple of Thesis in Athens; and the 1848 **Freemason Street Baptist Church** (E. Freemason and Bank), a magnificent Gothic Revival that was once the tallest building in Norfolk. Both were designed by Thomas U. Walter, architect of the Capital dome in Washington, D.C. A walking tour of the Freemason District is available online at www.chrysler.org/historyatyourfeet.

The **Ghent Historic District,** Norfolk's best-preserved turn-of-the-20th-century neighborhood, developed between 1880 and 1907 as streetcars reached into the suburbs. Mowbray Arch, following the shoreline of Smith's Creek, renamed the Hague in 1897, saw the earliest and most lavish homes, easily viewed today from the bridge on W. Brambleton Avenue. Late Queen Anne, Colonial Revival, and Shingle styles dominate, with examples of English Tudor and Half Timber, Italianate town house, and gambrel-roofed Dutch Colonials adding to the mix.

The Downtown Historic District is especially rich in restored vaudeville theaters and movie palaces, now housing performance and entertainment venues, including the 1913 Beaux-Arts **Wells Theatre** (110 E. Tazewell Street), the 1919 **Attucks Theatre** (1010 Church Street), the 1926 **Loew's State Theater** (340 Granby Street), the 1922 **NorVa** (317 Monticello Avenue), and the 1915 **Granby Theater** (421 Granby Street).

Two unusual survivors close to the waterfront are the 1931 **Selden Arcade,** between Main and Plume streets, and the 1907 **Monticello Arcade,** between Plume and City Hall Avenue. Together, the two arcades, home of numerous art galleries, line up to provide a covered walkway most of the way from MacArthur Center to the Waterside.

Another group of architecturally significant buildings is found on the **Norfolk Naval Base,** including houses built by 21 states for the 1907 Jamestown Exposition. Today, they line **Admiral's Row,** occupied by senior officers. Pictures of the buildings in their original forms can be found at www.hrnm.navy.mil/1907 exposition; you can see the present-day structures on the bus tour of the naval base.

For more information on Norfolk's historic neighborhoods and buildings, visit the City of Norfolk Web site, www.norfolk.gov, and the Norfolk Historical Society's

THE MERMAIDS OF NORFOLK

You see them everywhere—swimming through fountains, adorning city streets, hanging out in private yards. The mermaids, Norfolk's official symbol, are nearly four hundred strong in the city and have inspired their own series of children's books, jewelry, collectibles, posters, and artwork of all kinds.

Each individually decorated by local artists, the mermaids first swam onto the scene in 2000, part of a project to raise funds for local arts organizations and children's charities. They proved so popular that they stayed and multiplied.

While no one has mapped the location of every mermaid, many congregate in the downtown area, around the Waterside, hiding beneath Nauticus, and along Granby. Three heart-healthy walking routes, the **Heart and Art Mermaid Story Trails,** encourage families to find the mermaids while enjoying pages from new mermaid stories by Lisa Suhay, author of *There Goes a Mermaid! A NorfolkTale.* All the trails begin at the Nauticus Naval Museum. Maps can be found at www.mermaidsonparade.com and www.mermaid watch.blogspot.com, or at city visitors centers.

HUNDREDS OF MERMAIDS GREET NORFOLK VISITORS.

Web site, www.norfolkhistorical.org. You can download a pattern book of Norfolk's architectural styles at www.norfolk.gov/Planning/comehome/Norfolk_Pattern_Book or receive a copy by calling 757-664-6770.

Portsmouth

Portsmouth founder William Crawford laid out his new town in 1732, centering it on the Towne Square at Court and High streets. A walk along nearby sidewalks passes numerous examples of Colonial, Federal, Greek Revival, Georgian, and Victorian architecture, said to be the largest collections of antique buildings between

Alexandria, Virginia, and Charleston, South Carolina. Among them are the Classic Revival house at 315 Court Street, based on plans by Pierre L'Enfant, designer of Washington, D.C.; the circa 1790 **Hart House** (320 Court Street), one of the oldest in the city; and English basement–style houses at 355 Middle Street and 218 Glasgow Street, which retain their 1795 exteriors. The 1780 **Ball Nivison House** (417 Middle Street), with its gambrel roof coming down to the first floor, is an example of the so-called tax dodger house popular in the Virginia colony, built to avoid the crown's tax on two-story homes.

Many of Portsmouth's historic houses line North Street, the city's original waterfront, including the 1820 **Grice-Neely House** (202 North Street), with ornamental New Orleans–style ironwork; the four-story **Hill House** (221 North Street); and the 1799 **Watts House** (517 North Street), an excellent example of the Federal style.

For a walking tour of Portsmouth's historic merchant squares, visit the Web site of the Olde Towne Business Association (www.oldetowneportsmouth.com).

ART MUSEUMS & VISUAL ARTS CENTERS ⁰ʇ⁰ The **Selden Arcade** (757-664-6880; www.theselden.com; 208 E. Main Street, Norfolk 23510), a unique building dating from 1931 with an interior row of shops, serves as the City of Norfolk's Cultural Arts Center. In addition to the galleries and studios of the **d'Art Center** (www.d-artcenter.org), the arcade houses two city-operated galleries of local works; two of Norfolk's most popular eateries, d'Egg and Yorgo's; a visitor's information center; and gift shop. Visitors enjoy free Wi-Fi and Wednesday Brown Bag lunchtime concerts.

The quarterly **Downtown ArtSeen Norfolk** (757-664-6880) stroll begins at the Selden Arcade and tours the galleries and restaurants of the historic downtown.

In Olde Towne Portsmouth (www.oldetowneportsmouth.com), the first weekend of every month features a series of special events: a **First Friday Art Walk** along High Street, a **First Saturday Antiques to Flea Market,** and First Sunday free admission to the Courthouse Galleries.

Baron and Ellin Gordon Art Galleries (757-683-6271; www.al.odu.edu/art/gallery), 4509 Monarch Way at 45th Street, University Village, Norfolk 23508. Open: Tues.–Sun. Admission: Free. Gallery on the Old Dominion University campus showcases the Gordon collection of folk art by self-taught artists, including paintings, sculptures, jugs, canes, and carvings. A second gallery houses changing exhibits of works by contemporary artists, with monthly opening receptions.

Courthouse Galleries (757-393-8393 or 757-393-8543; www.courthousegalleries .com), 420 High Street, Portsmouth 23704. Open: Tues.–Sun. Admission: $5; free on First Friday evenings and First Sunday afternoons. The city of Portsmouth's art gallery is housed in the 1846 courthouse in the heart of Olde Towne. Frequent rotating exhibits feature local and regional artists working in a variety of media. A pleasant, tree-shaded courtyard hosts sculpture shows. During Dec., the popular Coleman Collection of more than a hundred animated figures creates a winter wonderland.

✪ ʇ **Chrysler Museum of Art** (757-664-6200; www.chrysler.org), 245 W. Olney Road, Norfolk 23507. Open: Wed.–Sun. Admission: Free, except for special exhibitions; free parking. Considered one of the finest art museums in America, the

Chrysler houses some forty thousand objects, including many donated by patron Walter P. Chrysler Jr., one of the great private art collectors of all time. The 60 galleries in the Italianate building facing Hague Inlet contain extensive displays of colonial and American folk art, one of the world's finest collections of European paintings, marble sculptures from the James H. Ricau collection, plus 18th-century Worcester porcelain, art nouveau furniture, and an impressive collection of photographs, including many related to the Civil War and the civil rights movement. The stunning eight-thousand-piece glass collection, one of America's best, contains a wealth of Tiffany blown glass, windows, and lamps; French glass by Baccarat and Cie; and English cameo glass, including John Northwood's famous Milton Vase. Audio guides available. The **Jean Outland Chrysler Library,** open to the public, contains eighty thousand volumes on art history. The Museum Shop, Museum Café, and galleries are grouped around an expansive sky-lit courtyard, which hosts free jazz concerts every Wed. evening.

✪ ✈ **Hermitage Museum & Gardens** (757-423-2052; www.hermitage foundation.org), 7637 North Shore Rd., Norfolk 23505. Open: Daily, except Wed. and Thurs. Admission: Adults $5, college students with ID $4, children 6–18 $2, under six and active military free. This 42-room Arts and Crafts gem on the banks of the Lafayette River is a must-stop for those who delight in fine handcrafted wood. Several noted woodcarvers collaborated on the project, begun in 1908, including Charles J. Woodsend, creating a wealth of elaborate woodwork, both inside and out. Docents lead tours through the downstairs, pointing out many unique features and hidden rooms. Upstairs, a remarkable collection of art objects on display ranges from Spanish religious icons to a rare Neolithic jade cong. Paths lead through gardens dotted with sculpture and across a boardwalk over restored wetlands. An excellent playground on North Shore Road is open to the public.

THE TORCH BEARERS, A SCULPTURE BY LOCAL ARTIST ANNA HYATT HUNTINGTON, GREETS VISITORS TO THE CHRYSLER MUSEUM OF ART.

Lois E. Woods Museum and Harrison B. Wilson Archives (757-823-2006 or 757-823-2002; www.highervision.biz/museum or www.nsu.edu/archives/gallery), Norfolk State University, 700 Park Avenue, Norfolk 23504. Open: Mon.–Fri. Admission: Free; parking passes available. Located in the east wing of the Lyman B. Brooks Library on the Norfolk State University campus, this museum houses more than 300 pieces of African art from 14 countries and 46 cultures; a reference library of more than 400 volumes on the art, folklore, and history of Africa; and historical records of African Americans in Virginia.

Tidewater Community College Visual Arts Center (757-822-1888; www.tcc .edu/visarts), 340 High Street, Portsmouth 23704. Open: Daily; closed holidays. Admission: Free. Rotating exhibits, student and faculty exhibitions, and selections from the college's permanent collection hang in this unique TCC facility in Historic Olde Towne Portsmouth. The three-story arts center contains three exhibit galleries, plus classrooms, a Books and Images library, and a glass rooftop studio.

CINEMA ✨ 🌳 **Cinema Café** (757-523-7469; www.cinema-cafe.com), 1401 Greenbrier Parkway, Chesapeake 23320. Family dining and discount movies inside Greenbrier Mall. Additional locations in Virginia Beach and Hampton.

✪ 🍴 **Commodore Theatre** (757-393-6962; www.commodoretheatre.com), 421 High Street, Portsmouth 23704. Enjoy first-run films on a 42-foot screen in this beautifully restored 1945 art deco theater. Table service, with a menu of sandwiches, pizza, desserts, beer, wine, and soft drinks, is available, as well as traditional theater seating. Children under eight not admitted.

Naro Expanded Cinema (757-625-6276; www.narocinema.com), 1507 Colley Avenue, Norfolk 23517. Old-fashioned movie theater in the heart of Ghent shows first-run films, classics, documentaries, indies, film series, and the *Rocky Horror Picture Show*. A video-rental store next door stocks new and classic titles.

🍴 **DANCE Attucks Swing Night** (757-622-4763; www.swingvirginia.com), 1010 Church Street, Norfolk 23510. Enjoy an evening of jitterbug lessons in this historic hall, or just come to dance, Thurs. 7–11 PM. Free parking.

Ballet Virginia International (757-446-1401; www.balletvirginia.org), 700 21st Street, Norfolk 23517. Talented young company presents an annual *Nutcracker* at the Harrison Opera House, plus other classic ballets.

THE NARO CINEMA IS A LANDMARK IN NORFOLK'S GHENT NEIGHBORHOOD.

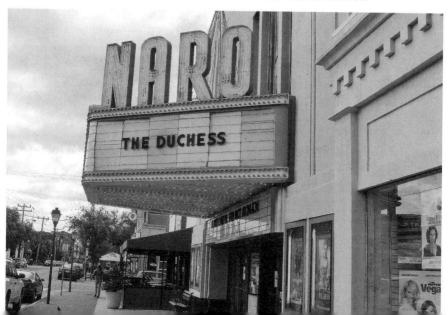

Boogie on the Bay Shag Club (www.boogieonthebay.com). Shagging to beach music Sun. and Mon. at **Roger's Sports Pub** (757-200-9069; 2002 Bainbridge Boulevard, Chesapeake 23324).

The Mambo Room (757-351-6092; www.mamboroomdance.com), 2200 Colonial Avenue, Norfolk 23517. Classes in salsa, Zumba, and Pilates; latin and swing dance socials.

Todd Rosenlieb Dance (757-626-3262; www.trdance.org), 325 Granby Street, Norfolk 23510. Company headed by acclaimed choreographer Todd Rosenlieb performs cutting-edge contemporary works at its Granby Street studio theater and other venues. Summer camps, workshops, and Pilates sessions are open to the public.

USA Dance Tidewater Chapter (757-587-3548; www.twcusabda.org), Knights of Columbus Hall, 211 W. Government Avenue, Norfolk 23503. Ballroom dances on the fourth Sat. of the month are open to the public.

FAMILY ATTRACTIONS ♂ ⊤ **Children's Museum of Virginia** (757-393-5258; www.childrensmuseumva.com), 221 High Street, Portsmouth 23704. Fun for all ages in Olde Towne, this newly renovated museum has interactive play spaces, giant musical instruments, art room with Harmonograph, walk-in kaleidoscope, and much more. Model-train buffs shouldn't miss the million-dollar **Lancaster Toy and Train Collection,** one of the world's largest. Summer art and history camps. Closed Mon. Admission $5; children under two free.

♂ ↬ **Virginia Zoo** (757-441-5227; www.virginiazoo.org), 3500 Granby Street, Norfolk 23504. Begun in 1892, this zoo contains more than 350 animals from around the world in natural habitats, interspersed with gardens. The Zoo Train ($2) circles the red panda and new Trail of the Tiger exhibits. Open daily. Adults $8, seniors 62-plus $7, children 2–11 $6.

GALLERIES

Norfolk and SoNo
Art Works Gallery and Frame Shop (757-625-3004; www.artworksva.com), 321 W. Bute Street, Norfolk 23510. Enormous gallery in the Freemason District exhibits oil and watercolor paintings, etchings, engravings, and prints.

✪ **d'Art Center** (757-625-4211; www.d-artcenter.org), 208 E. Main Street, Selden Arcade, Norfolk 23510. Unique artist colony in the renovated 1931 Selden Arcade houses galleries and the open studios of 50 artists.

Charles Kello Galleries (757-622-3808; www.charleskellogalleries.com), 1107 Colonial Avenue, Norfolk 23507. Ghent gallery displays local artist Kello's oil landscapes and portraits in the style of the old masters.

Glen McClure Studio (757-623-4046; www.glenmcclure.com), 117 W. City Hall Avenue, Norfolk 23510. Nationally recognized photographer creates color landscapes of Virginia and black-and-white portraits.

Harbor Gallery (757-627-2787; www.harbor-gallery.com), 1508 Colley Avenue, Norfolk 23517. Friendly gallery in Ghent showcases fun artworks by regional artists.

Portlock Galleries at SoNo (757-502-4901; www.portlockgalleries.com), 3815 Bainbridge Boulevard, Chesapeake 23324. Located in Historic South Norfolk (SoNo), these galleries in a refurbished school exhibit artworks by regional artists.

The Studios at Monticello (757-286 6210; www.studiosatmonticello.com) and **Walls Fine Art Gallery** (757-472-6531; www.wallsva.com), 208 E. Plume Street, Norfolk 23510. Galleries in the historic 1907 Monticello Arcade, between Plume and City Hall Avenue.

Portsmouth

Olde Towne Art (757-673-2667; www.oldetowneart.com), 525 High Street, Portsmouth 23704. Unique sidewalk gallery displays the work of a dozen artists with studios in this historic bank building. Weekly life drawing sessions.

Riverview Gallery (757-397-3207; www.riverviewgallery.biz), 1 High Street, Portsmouth 23704. Upscale gallery located within the distinctive round facade of the 1894 Seaboard Air Line Railroad terminal at High Street Landing.

Skipjack Nautical Wares and Marine Gallery (757-399-5012; www.skipjack marinegallery.com), 1 High Street, Portsmouth 23704. Waterfront shop carries superb nautical antiques, including ship models and figureheads, as well as maritime art, sailboat pendants, and souvenirs of the Schooner *Virginia*.

GARDENS ✧ **Ernie Morgan Environmental Action Center** (757-441-1347; www.norfolkbeautiful.org), 3500-A Granby Street, Norfolk 23504. Headquarters of Keep Norfolk Beautiful in historic Lafayette Park has exhibits in a platinum-level LEED Green building, outside EcoGarden, and restored wetlands. Open weekdays.

The Fred Heutte Center (757-441-2513; www.fredheutte.org), 1000 Botetourt Gardens, Norfolk 23507. Dedicated to the founder of the botanical gardens, this center in the heart of Ghent includes a beautifully restored, historic ferry terminal; an English knot herb garden; heirloom vegetable garden; and a water garden.

✪ ✐ ⓖ ✧ **Norfolk Botanical Garden** (757-441-5830; www.norfolkbotanical garden.org), 6700 Azalea Garden Road, Norfolk 23518. Located on the shores of Lake Whitehurst, this lovely spot offers blooming gardens in each season for touring by foot, tram, or boat. The free tram tour whisks you through the Rhododendron Glade and past more than three dozen gardens. The **World of Wonders Adventure Garden,** dedicated to children, includes a Dirt Factory, tree house, and fountains designed for getting wet. Also on the grounds: the excellent **Garden Cafe,** boat tours ($2–4), bonsai garden, Eagle Observation site, and—a favorite with the kids—an overlook where you can watch airplanes take off and land at Norfolk International Airport next door. Adults $9, seniors $8, children (3–18) $7.

✪ ⓖ **Pagoda Oriental Garden** (757-623-1949; www.pagodagarden.org), 265 W. Tazewell Street, Norfolk 23510. A short walk from Nauticus, an authentic Chinese pagoda, a gift to Norfolk from Taiwan, sits in an Asian garden containing more than 130 species of Asian plants, plus a waterfall, crooked bridge, and large koi pond. The pagoda itself, actually an observation tower, houses the **Pagoda Garden Tea House and Gallery** (757-622-0506), exhibiting Chinese brush paintings and artifacts, and serving Pacific Rim cuisine at lunch and dinner.

Norfolk

Elmwood and West Point Cemeteries (757-441-2653; www.norfolk.gov/ Cemeteries), 238 Princess Anne Road, Norfolk 23510. Opened in 1858, Elmwood contains many examples of Victorian funerary sculpture. Nearly a hundred African American soldiers who fought for the Union lie nearby in West Point Cemetery. A statue of Norfolk native James Carney, inspiration of the movie *Glory* and the first black recipient of the Medal of Honor, stands atop a monument, one of the few in the country dedicated to African American servicemen of the Civil War era.

Epworth United Methodist Church (757-622-2970; www.gbgm-umc.org/ epworthumc), 124 W. Freemason Street, Norfolk 23510. Completed in 1896, this landmark sanctuary contains 22 original stained-glass windows, and a stained glass dome. Tours available weekdays.

Fort Norfolk (757-640-1720; www.norfolkhistorical.org), 801 Front Street, Norfolk 23510. Authorized by President George Washington in 1794, this restored masonry fort saw action in the War of 1812 and the Civil War. Self-guided tours available weekdays. Enter through the Southampton Avenue gate. Free.

Hunter House Victorian Museum (757-623-9814; www.hunterhousemuseum .org), 240 W. Freemason Street, Norfolk 23510. Built in 1894 in the Richardsonian Romanesque style, this home contains the original late Victorian furniture, decor, paintings, and other possessions of its first owners. Open Wed.–Sun., Apr.–Dec. Adults $5, seniors $4, children $1. Special monthly teas.

☻ Moses Myers House (757-333-1087; www.chrysler.org), 323 E. Freemason Street, Norfolk 23510. Elegant Federal town house built circa 1797 by one of Norfolk's first Jewish families contains many original furnishings showing the strong French influence of the period, as well as family portraits by Gilbert Stuart. The gardens outside re-create late-18th-century design. Open Wed.–Sun. Free.

The Norfolk History Museum at the Willoughby-Baylor House (757-333-1087; www.chrysler.org), 601 E. Freemason Street, Norfolk 23510. Brick house dating to 1794 contains exhibits on the city's history, including the yellow fever epidemic.

Norfolk Southern Museum (757-823-5555; www.nscorp.com or www.norfolk southernhs.org), 3 Commercial Place, Norfolk 23510. Museum on the ground floor of the Norfolk Southern Railroad Corporate Headquarters contains sections of Civil War–era track, uniforms, photographs, and other mementos from the early days of rail. Open weekdays. Free.

Ocean View Station Museum (757-531-0445; www.ovsm.org), 111 W. Ocean View Avenue (at Granby Street, inside the Pretlow Library), Norfolk 23503. Pictures, maps, and memorabilia of days gone by in Ocean View, including the famous amusement park that once stood across the street. Free.

Ohef Sholom Temple Archives (757-625-4295; www.ohefsholom.org), 530 Raleigh Avenue, Norfolk 23507. More than 2,500 objects relating to the 150-year history of Jews in Norfolk. Open weekdays. Free.

☻ St. Paul's Episcopal Church (757-627-4353; www.saintpaulsnorfolk.com), 201 St. Paul's Boulevard, Norfolk 23510. Built in 1739, St. Paul's was the only building in Norfolk to survive the British destruction of the city in 1776 and has a cannonball in its wall to prove it. The interior, with several stained-glass windows, including a Tiffany, and the shady graveyard dating to the 17th century are open daily.

Windows on History (757-664-6620), City Hall Avenue, Norfolk 23510. Sixteen window displays along one exterior side of the MacArthur Center detail four hundred years of Norfolk history.

Portsmouth

Cedar Grove Cemetery (757-488-1397), London Boulevard between Effingham Street and Fort Lane, Portsmouth 23704. Oldest city-owned cemetery, established 1832, contains impressive funerary art. Enter through the south gate behind Hardee's on London Boulevard.

Fort Nelson Park, Crawford Parkway at Effingham Street, Portsmouth 23704. Pleasant park at the entrance of the Naval Medical Center Portsmouth contains informational signs and artifacts about the nation's first naval hospital. The **Naval Medical Center** (757-953-6950; www.med.navy.mil/sites/nmcp) is not open without advance clearance.

Hill House (757-393-0241), 221 North Street, Portsmouth 23704. Four-story beauty is furnished throughout with original possessions collected by the Hill family over a period of 150 years. Open weekends only, Apr.–Dec. Admission.

Hog Island Fresnel Lens Pavilion (757-393-8591), High Street Landing, Portsmouth 23704. The only Fresnel lens on display outside of a museum setting, this 1896 first-order lens occupies a pavilion along the Portsmouth Seawall, south of High Street Landing. Free.

Jewish Museum & Cultural Center (757-391-9266; www.jewishmuseumports mouth.org), 607 Effingham Street, Portsmouth 23707. Museum in the 1918 Colonial Revival–style Chevra T'helim Synagogue contains artifacts detailing the history of the Eastern European Jewish community of Hampton Roads, including a rare 18th-century Torah rescued from the Holocaust. Tours and lectures Sat.–Sun. Adults $3, children $1. Summer music series.

St. Paul's Catholic Church (757-484-1921 or 757-397-7066; www.stpauls-ports mouth.org), 518 High Street, Portsmouth 23704. Docents lead free tours of this magnificent 1905 Gothic Revival cathedral, with stone bell tower, copper steeple, 28 stained-glass windows, and many Gothic details.

MUSEUMS

Norfolk

✪ ⊤ **Hampton Roads Naval Museum** (757-322-2987; www.hrnm.navy.mil), 1 Waterside Drive, Norfolk 23510. Open: Daily, Memorial Day–Labor Day; closed Mon. Sept.–May; battleship open limited hours Jan.–Mar. Admission: Free. Operated by the U.S. Navy, this museum on the second floor of the Nauticus building tells Hampton Roads' naval history, including the Battle of the Ironclads, the USS *Maine* and the Spanish-American War, the 1907 Jamestown Exposition, and the establishment of Naval Station Norfolk.

⊤ **MacArthur Memorial Museum** (757-441-2965; www.macarthurmemorial .org), MacArthur Square, City Hall Avenue, Norfolk 23510. Open: Daily. Admission: Free; parking at MacArthur Center South Parking Garage validated. Located in Norfolk's former city hall and courthouse, circa 1850, the four buildings of this

GEN. DOUGLAS MACARTHUR AND HIS WIFE ARE BURIED WITHIN THIS MEMORIAL AND MUSEUM IN DOWNTOWN NORFOLK.

monument portray the life and times of General of the Army Douglas MacArthur, from his early days as the son of a Norfolk belle to his final command in the Korean War. View a short film on his life before touring chronological galleries displaying medals, flags, weapons, and military equipment; wartime art and photographs; as well as MacArthur's trademark military cap, corncob pipe, and sunglasses. His 1950 Chrysler Crown Imperial limousine is on display in the gift shop. The memorial's rotunda is the final resting place of the general and his wife.

✪ ✧ ♿ ⛵ **Nauticus National Maritime Center and the Battleship *Wisconsin*** (757-664-1000; www .nauticus.org), 1 Waterside Drive, Norfolk 23510. Open: Daily, Memorial Day–Labor Day; closed Mon. Sept.–May. Admission: Adults $11.95, children 4–12 $9.50. Occupying the upper story of the landmark Nauticus building on the Norfolk waterfront, this museum divides its space between the U.S. Navy and the National Oceanic and Atmospheric Administration (NOAA). Interactive exhibits and hi-tech shows allow visitors to take control of a ship's guns in the heat of battle, design a battleship, hunt subs, and explore the wreck of the USS *Monitor*. Artifacts and a movie about the 1907 Jamestown Exposition trace the route of the Great White Fleet after it departed from Hampton Roads. Admission to Nauticus includes access to the Battleship *Wisconsin*, moored next door. Self-guided and

BATTLESHIP *WISCONSIN*

audio tours of its deck are available. The interior of the *Wisconsin* is sealed since it is officially still "mothballed" until needed.

Norfolk Police and Fire Museum (757-441-1526; www.norfolk.gov/police/museum.asp), 401 E. Freemason Street, Norfolk 23510. Open Wed.–Sun. Admission: Free. Recently relocated, this museum contains early photographs, uniforms, badges, firearms, and handcuffs used by the Norfolk Police Department since its founding in 1797, as well as memorabilia collected by the Norfolk Fire Department since before the Civil War.

Portsmouth

Naval Shipyard Museum and Lightship *Portsmouth* Museum (757-393-8591; www.portsnavalmuseums.com), 2 High Street, High Street Landing, Portsmouth 23704. Open: Tues.–Sun. Admission: $3 for both museums, $1 for children 2–17. Museum exhibits tell of the many craft built at Portsmouth's shipyard, including the CSS *Virginia* (otherwise known as the ironclad *Merrimack*); USS *Texas*, the nation's first battleship; and the world's first aircraft carrier, the USS *Langley;* as well as the first dry dock in the United States, still in use. Tours of the 1915 Lightship *Portsmouth,* moored a block away at the foot of London Street, include the completely equipped quarters below deck, as well as exhibits on the U.S. Lightship Service. Daylong summer history camps focus on Revolutionary War, Civil War, and pirate seamanship, for ages 8–12.

✔ ૯ ↑ **Virginia Sports Hall of Fame & Museum** (757-393-8031; www.vshfm .com), 206 High Street, Portsmouth 23704. Open: Daily; closed winter Mon. Admission: $7, seniors and military $6, children two and under free. This 35,000-square-foot museum honors outstanding Virginia athletes from high school champions to Olympic and pro team stars with an introductory film; hands-on baseball, basketball, football, soccer, and auto-racing activities; plus exhibits on golf, Redskins football, Virginia's collegiate teams, and the greatest moments of Virginia sports.

MUSIC AND CONCERT SERIES Arts Within Reach (757-664-4321; www .norfolkarts.net). Free concerts, performances, and workshops by local art groups in neighborhoods throughout Norfolk.

Bellissima! (www.bellissimachorale.org). Women's choral ensemble presents two free concert series each year.

✪ **Big Bands on the Bay** and **Thank Goodness Its Ocean View Concerts** (757-441-2345; www.festeventsva.org), 100 W. Ocean View Avenue, Norfolk 23503. Free summer evening concerts and dancing at the Ocean View Beach Park gazebo. Big Bands on the Bay runs Sun. evenings Memorial Day–Labor Day. Thank Goodness Its Ocean View takes place Fri. evenings July–Aug. Free.

Cantata Chorus (757-397-8390; www.cantatachorus.org). Performing choral master works for more than 50 years.

The Feldman Chamber Music Society Series (757-552-1630; www.feldman chambermusic.org), P.O. Box 6144, Norfolk 23508. Nationally and internationally acclaimed chamber groups perform at the Chrysler Museum Theater.

Governor's School for the Arts (757-451-4711; www.gsarts.net). Talented student performances of dance, theater, vocal music, and instrumental music at area venues.

Great Bridge Presbyterian Church Candlelight Concert Series (757-547-4706; www.gbpres.org), 333 Cedar Road, Chesapeake 23322. Free series features classical works.

Norfolk Chamber Consort (757-622-4542 or 757-852-9072; www.ncconsort.org). Emphasizes lesser-known works and neglected masterpieces.

Portsmouth Community Concert Association (757-686-5447; www.portsmouth communityconcerts.com), Willett Hall, 3710 Willett Drive, Portsmouth 23707. Concerts by nationally and internationally known musical artists.

Schola Cantorum (757-683-4071; www.scholacantorumofva.org), P.O. Box 1110, Norfolk 23501. Auditioned group presents choral concerts and the annual **Summer Sing** community sing-along at venues throughout Hampton Roads.

Tapestry Bells (www.tapestrybells.com). Handbell quartet, sponsored by **Monumental United Methodist Church** (757-397-1297; www.monumentalumc.org; 450 Dinwiddie Street, Portsmouth 23704), performs frequently at the church's free Noonday Concert Series, plus other venues.

Tidewater Bluegrass Music Association (www.tidewaterbluegrass.org). Listings of concerts and jam sessions throughout the region.

Tidewater Classical Guitar Society (757-627-6229; www.tcgs.cx). One of the few guitar orchestras in North America also sponsors appearances by visiting guitar masters.

Tidewater Winds (757-480-0953; www.tidewaterwinds.org). Orchestra dedicated to preserving John Philip Sousa's American concert band tradition performs free concerts throughout the region.

U.S. Fleet Forces Band (757-444-6777 or 757-445-0899; www.usfleetforcesband .navy.mil). The largest of the U.S. Navy's Fleet Bands and its various ensembles play at many events and venues annually. See schedule online.

Virginia Chorale (757-627-8375; www.vachorale.org). Virginia's only fully professional choral ensemble performs many concerts, most a capella, at venues throughout the region.

Virginia Opera Company (757-627-9545 or 866-673-7282; www.vaopera.org). Virginia's official opera company produces four operas a year at the **Harrison Opera House** (160 E. Virginia Beach Boulevard, Norfolk 23510).

Virginia Symphony Orchestra (757-892-6366; www.virginiasymphony.org). One of the country's top orchestras travels widely throughout the region.

Virginia Wesleyan College Center for Sacred Music (757-455-3376; www .vwc.edu/academics/csm), Monumental Chapel, 1584 Wesleyan Drive, Norfolk 23455. Hymn festivals, choir services, and an annual Sacred Music Conference each July include many free events open to the public.

NIGHTLIFE

Norfolk and Chesapeake

Y **The Banque** (757-480-3600; www.thebanque.com), 1849 E. Little Creek Road, Norfolk 23518. Country-western nightclub is out a ways but offers free dance lessons on the area's largest dance floor, restaurant, ladies' night with male stage show, happy hour, pool, and poker.

✪ ɤ ↝ **The Boot** (757-627-2668; www.insidetheboot.com), 123 W. 21st Street at Omohundro, Norfolk 23517. Live music, including a jazz series, in Ghent, plus late-night menu served until 2 AM on weekends.

ɤ **Cap'n Ron's Bar and Grill** (757-587-0547; www.capnronsbarandgrill.com), 9300 Chesapeake Boulevard, Norfolk 23503. Live music, happy hour, and karaoke at this club near Ocean View.

Granby Theater (757-961-7208; www.granbytheater.com), 421 Granby Street, Norfolk 23510. Magnificent restored 1915 downtown theater hosts dance parties on weekend nights and many special events.

✪ ɤ **The NorVa** (757-627-4500 or 800-745-3000; www.thenorva.com), 317 Monticello Avenue, Norfolk 23510. Midsize performance venue boasts state-of-the-art V-DOSC sound equipment and a roster of top national and local alternative music acts. Plenty of bars, but not many seats. Get in early by eating before the show at **Kelly's Backstage Tavern** (757-622-5915; 320 Granby Street).

ɤ **O'Sullivan's Wharf** (757-423-3753; www.osullivanswharf.com), 4300 Colley Avenue, Norfolk 23508. Live music, seafood, and happy hour on the shores of the Lafayette River.

ɤ **Scotty Quixx** (757-625-0008; www.scottyquixx.com or www.myspace.com/scotty quixx), 436 Granby Street, Norfolk 23510. Something for everyone at this downtown nightclub: live bands, DJs, Texas Hold 'em, hookahs, happy hour, late-night menu.

ɤ **Time Lounge** (757-623-8463; www.timelounge.com or www.myspace.com/ timenorfolk), 271 Granby Street, Norfolk 23510. Classy club in downtown has live music and dancing, elegant decor, tapas menu.

❋ ɤ **The Venue On 35th** (757-469-0337; www.venue-35.com), 631 35th Street, Norfolk 23508. Unique club provides a stage for all the arts, from poetry and play readings to jazz, dance, and classic cinema, inside or on the outdoor stage.

Portsmouth

ɤ **Baron's Pub and Restaurant** (757-399-4840; www.baronspubva.com), 500 High Street, Portsmouth 23704. Olde Towne nightspot hosts frequent live music, happy hour, patio dining.

ɤ **Flagship Restaurant and Raw Bar** (757-398-1600; http://flagshipportsmouth .blogspot.com), 103 Constitution Avenue, Portsmouth 23704. After-work and weekend deck parties with live music; Sun. brunch. Tie up at the dock if you arrive by boat.

ɤ **Foggy Point Bar & Grill** (757-673-3032; www.marriott.com), 425 Water Street, Portsmouth 23704. Lounge in the Renaissance Portsmouth Hotel schedules occasional live music.

ɤ **Gosport Tavern** (757-337-0637; www.gosport702.com), 702 High Street, Portsmouth 23704. Live music, happy hour, fish tacos, and lots of beer on tap in Olde Towne.

ɤ **Longboards Lounge** (757-399-4010; www.longboardslounge.com), 440 High Street, Portsmouth 23704. Hawaiian-themed hangout in Olde Towne serves island-inspired cuisine from Loco Moco and Teriyaki plate lunches to grinders; live music and DJs on weekends, TVs tuned to sports, happy hour, outdoor patio.

Olde Towne Coffee-House (757-391-9220; www.portsmouthcoffee.com), 600

Crawford Street, Portsmouth 23704. Located in the lobby of the Portsmouth Family Medicine Building, this alcohol-free coffee shop hosts live music and open mic nights, sponsored by **The Bridge Christian Community** (757-397-1297; www.cometothebridge.org).

PERFORMING ARTS VENUES Chandler Recital Hall at Diehn Fine and Performing Arts Center (757-683-5035; www.al.odu.edu), 49th Street and Elkhorn Avenue, Norfolk 23508. Old Dominion University hosts a variety of events, including a concert series of significant classical and jazz musicians.

L. Douglas Wilder Performing Arts Center (757-823-2063; www.nsu.edu/wilder), 700 Park Avenue, Norfolk 23504. New performing-arts center at Norfolk State University offers classical and jazz performances by national and international artists.

✧ **Ntelos Wireless Pavilion** (757-393-8181; www.pavilionconcerts.com), 901 Crawford Street, Portsmouth 23704. Outdoor concert pavilion, on the riverfront three blocks from High Street Landing, hosts top national touring groups and music festivals.

Roper Performing Arts Center (757-822-1450; www.tcc.edu/roper), 340 Granby Street, Norfolk 23510. The 1926 Loew's State Theater, an ornate restored vaudeville hall in downtown Norfolk, hosts Tidewater Community College performing-arts groups, plus the Jazz on Granby series (www.jazzongranby.com).

✧ **Seven Venues** (757-664-6464; www.sevenvenues.com). Much of the live entertainment in Norfolk goes on at seven venues with consolidated booking and ticket services. Schedules for all venues can be found at the Seven Venues Web site; tickets to all shows can be purchased at the **Scope Arena Box Office** (757-664-6980; 201 E. Brambleton Avenue, Norfolk 23510) or from Ticketmaster (800-745-3000; www.ticketmaster.com). The Seven Venues are:

1. **Attucks Theatre** (www.attuckstheatre.org; 1010 Church Street, Norfolk 23504), built in 1919 and now restored, was once known as the Apollo Theater of the South. Today it schedules jazz, blues, and heritage music.

2. **Chrysler Hall** (215 St. Paul's Boulevard, Norfolk 23510), the city's premiere performing-arts center, hosts several resident companies, including the state symphony and ballet, plus **Broadway Across America** (www.broadwayacrossamerica.com), **Norfolk Forum** speaker series (757-627-8672; www.thenorfolkforum.org), and the **Virginia Arts Festival** (757-282-2800; www.virginiaartsfest.com).

3. **Harbor Park** (757-622-2222; 150 Park Avenue, Norfolk 23504) is home of the **Norfolk Tides** AAA baseball team (www.norfolktides.com), as well as a venue for large concerts.

4. The **Harrison Opera House** (160 Virginia Beach Boulevard, Norfolk 23510) is home of the **Virginia Opera Company** (www.vaopera.org).

5. The **Wells Theatre** (757-627-1234; 110 E. Tazewell Street, Norfolk 23510), a restored 1913 Beaux-Arts vaudeville hall, is home of the professional nonprofit **Virginia Stage Company** (www.vastage.com).

6. **Norfolk Scope Arena** (201 E. Brambleton Avenue, Norfolk 23510), the city's largest venue, hosts **Norfolk Admirals** ice hockey games (www.norfolk

admirals.com), as well as concerts and family shows. Within Scope is the
Showcase Restaurant (757-605-0208), which serves preshow meals.

7. The **Prism Theatre at Scope Arena** is a large theatrical venue that hosts national acts.

Ted Constant Convocation Center (757-683-5762; www.constantcenter.com), 4320 Hampton Boulevard, Norfolk 23508. With ten thousand seats, "The Ted," in Old Dominion's University Village, is a popular venue for large concerts and shows.

✪ **Town Point Park, Waterside, and TowneBank Fountain Park** (757-441-2345; www.festeventsva.org), Waterside Drive, Norfolk 23510. Newly refurbished parks on the Norfolk waterfront host hundreds of concerts, festivals, films, live music, and special events each year, with boater packages available. Special features include the **Armed Forces Memorial,** inscribed with letters written home by U.S. servicepeople, and **Omar's Fountain Café,** wih live music and alfresco dining.

Willett Hall (757-393-5460; www.willetthall.com), 3701 Willett Drive, Portsmouth 23707. Intimate two-thousand-seat facility hosts concerts, lectures, and theater.

THEATER The Foggy Point Murder Mystery Dinner Theater (757-673-3000; www.maverickmurdermystery.com), Renaissance Portsmouth Hotel, 425 Water Street, Portsmouth 23704. Whodunit comes with all-you-can-eat buffet.

✎ **40th Street Stage** (757-423-4084; www.40thstreetstage.com), 809 W. 40th Street, Norfolk 23508. This community stage is home to a number of adult and children's theater groups, including Bucket of Monkeys youth improv and the Children's Theatre of Hampton Roads.

Generic Theater (757-441-2160; www.generictheater.org), Downunder Chrysler Hall, 215 St. Paul's Boulevard, Norfolk 23510. Norfolk's "off-Broadway" company stages innovative new plays and offbeat productions.

✪ ✎ **Hurrah Players** (757-627-5437; www.hurrahplayers.com), 20 Bank Street, Norfolk 23510. Professionally produced children's productions showcase talented young actors.

Little Theatre of Norfolk (757-627-8551; www.ltnonline.org), 801 Claremont Avenue, Norfolk 23507. One of the country's oldest continually running community theater groups presents a full season of plays.

Little Theatre of Portsmouth (757-488-7866; www.portsmouthlittletheatre.org), 1401 Elmhurst Lane, Portsmouth 23701. Community-based theater group presents four productions a year using local talent.

✪ **Virginia Stage Company** (757-627-1234; www.vastage.com), Wells Theatre, 110 E. Tazewell Street, Norfolk 23510. The region's only professional resident theater company is a favorite with playwrights and directors trying out new plays and musicals with Broadway in mind.

✳ To Do

The same deepwater harbor that attracted the U.S. Navy to Hampton Roads provides exceptional recreational opportunities, most centered on the water.

BEACHES Although almost no one thinks of Norfolk as a beach destination, the city, in fact, has 7.5 miles of sandy beach fronting on Chesapeake Bay. The entire strand is open to the public, and the city grooms the sand daily during the summer months. Three beachfront parks, all located along Ocean View Avenue, have restrooms, showers, and lifeguards in season: **Community Beach Park** (600 E. Ocean View at Chesapeake Boulevard), **Ocean View Beach Park** (100 W. Ocean View), and **Sarah Constance Beach Park** (300 W. Ocean View at Tidewater Drive). In addition, 36 pedestrian accesses are located at the foot of nearly every street ending on the bay. The Ocean View beaches provide a nice, laid-back beach experience for those burned out on the Virginia Beach crowds.

BICYCLING Despite its busy streets, Norfolk has several nice dedicated bike paths. The **Elizabeth River Bike Trail** (757-664-4769; www.baygateways.net), an off-road path following an old railroad right-of-way, runs along the waterfront from the USS *Wisconsin* into the Freemason District and beyond to Fort Norfolk and several city parks. The route is marked with pelican signs. Another good ride is along **Ocean View Avenue,** where a bike lane extends all the way to the tip of Willoughby Spit.

In Chesapeake, **Indian River Park,** located between Paramont Avenue and Rokeby Avenue, has mountain-bike and BMX trails and jumps.

In Portsmouth's **Reflection Park** on Bayview Avenue, pleasant walking and bike paths follow the shore of the Elizabeth River.

BIKE SHOPS **All About Bikes** (757-382-7878; www.allaboutbikes.org), 109-B Gainsborough Square, Battlefield Boulevard, Chesapeake 23320. Rides range from single-track trips on mountain bikes at night to road rides of up to 40 miles.

THE BIKE PATH ALONG THE SHORE IN OCEAN VIEW PROVIDES PEACEFUL VIEWS OF CHESAPEAKE BAY.

Conte's of Norfolk (757-962-6766; www.contesbikestores.com), 314 W. 21st Street, Norfolk 23517. Sat.-morning group rides around the airport and out to Ocean View, as well as shorter rides through the Ghent neighborhood.

Cycle Classics (757-393-4498; http://cycleclassicsva.tripod.com), 427 High Street, Portsmouth 23704. Several rides every weekend, including a fun ride out to City Park, from this shop that restores classic bikes.

East Coast Bicycles (www.eastcoastbicycles.com), two Norfolk locations. Ghent: 1910 Colley Avenue, Norfolk 23517 (757-622-0446); Ocean View: 9605 Granby Street, Norfolk 23503 (757-351-2112). Weekly group rides for all abilities, plus clinics and workshops on bike maintenance. Test rides available.

Canoeing & Kayaking

With so many lakes and rivers to choose from, the Hampton Roads region is a hot spot for paddlers. Two highly recommended places to put in are Bennett's Creek Park in Suffolk, where you can access the extensive **Suffolk Canoe Trail** (757-514-7250; www.suffolk.va.us/parks) system, and Chesapeake's popular **Great Bridge Lock Park** (757-382-6411; www.chesapeake.va.us), providing access to the Southern Branch of the Elizabeth River, as well as the Albermarle and Chesapeake Canal.

At **Northwest River Park** in Chesapeake, you can rent canoes, kayaks, jon boats, and paddleboats by the hour or day for use on the lake or river. The rangers at this park lead low-cost canoe and kayak trips on the Northwest River and to Lake Drummond, as well as easy evening paddles. All equipment is provided. Reservations are required; call 757-421-7151.

For additional paddling options, see our listings under *Fishing*.

Several outfitters lead kayak trips in the area, especially to Lake Drummond in the Dismal Swamp National Wildlife Refuge. **Wild River Outfitters** (757-431-8566 or 877-431-8566; www.wildriveroutfitters.com) offers full-day paddles in Lake Drummond led by a naturalist. **Kayak Nature Tours** (757-480-1999 or 888-669-8368; www.tidewateradventures.com) conducts trips up the Northwest River, through the four-hundred-year-old cypress stands on the Blackwater River in Zuni, plus all-day trips on Lake Drummond. They also have daily and weekly car-top kayak rentals with racks from their office in Norfolk.

Marinas

Norfolk's waterfront is mile marker 0 on the Atlantic Intracoastal Waterway, and many pleasure craft pass this way. The traditions of boat building and service run deep here, so if you need repairs or refitting, this may be the place to stop a while.

Marinas in the Little Creek area are especially convenient to the lower Chesapeake Bay, while others offer dockage in the heart of Olde Towne Portsmouth and downtown Norfolk, close to many attractions.

Chesapeake: **Top Rack Marina** (757-227-3041 or 888-784-6708; www.toprack marina.com), 5532 Bainbridge Boulevard, Chesapeake 23320. Marina with new and used boat sales offers wet slips and dry storage. Overnight mooring vouchers available for guests at the on-site **Amber Lantern Restaurant** (757-227-3057), a fine-dining spot specializing in steak and seafood.

Norfolk: **Bay Point Marina** (757-362-8432; www.littlecreekmarina.com), 9500 30th Bay Avenue, Norfolk 23518. A favorite with the sailing and live-aboard crowd, Bay Point sponsors weekly sail races and the Little Creek Cup in Aug. The on-site **Bay Point Grille** serves meals and drinks inside or on the patio.

⚓ **Cobb's Marina** (757-588-5401; www.cobbsmarina.com), 4524 Dunning Road, Norfolk 23518. Family-owned marina in Little Creek offers a boatyard with repair service, marine store, boat ramp, Wi-Fi, free coffee, and friendly advice.

Little Creek Marina (757-362-3600; www.littlecreekmarina.com), 4801 Pretty Lake Avenue, Norfolk 23518. Catering to the fishing and powerboat crowd, this marina offers gas and diesel fuel, a bait and tackle store, and a swimming pool.

Vinings Landing Marine Center (757-587-8000; www.viningslanding.com), 8166 Shore Drive, Norfolk 23518. Transients are welcome at this large facility in Little Creek, with 220 wet slips, a boatel, swimming pool, fish cleaning stations, ships store, and fishing charters. The **Surf Rider Restaurant and Tiki Bar** (757-480-5000; www.surfridergroup.com) keeps the party going.

⚓ ⓣ **Waterside Marina and Nauticus Marina** (757-625-36251; www.waterside marina.com), 333 Waterside Drive, Norfolk 23510. Dock in the heart of downtown Norfolk within walking distance of many attractions and more than 50 restaurants. Free Wi-Fi, showers, laundry, athletic club, and grocery van service. The Nauticus Marina, nearby, has 16 slips next to the Halfe Moone Cruise and Celebration Center.

ⓣ **Willoughby Harbor Marina** (757-583-4150; www.willoughbyharbormarina .com), 1525 Bayville Street, Norfolk 23503. Facility just off I-64 offers valet boat service, on-site pump out, showers, Wi-Fi, marine store, and the **Sunset Restaurant** (757-588-1255), noted for its soft-shell crabs.

Portsmouth: ⓣ **Ocean Marine Yacht Center** (757-399-2920; www.ocean marinellc.com), 1 Crawford Court, Portsmouth 23704. Yacht repair and refit yard and marina within walking distance of Olde Towne offers cable TV, Wi-Fi, a courtesy car, and ships store.

⚓ ⓣ **Tidewater Yacht Marina** (757-393-2525 or 888-390-0080; www.tyamarina .com), 10 Crawford Parkway, Portsmouth 23704. Located next to the ferry landing, this is Virginia's largest marina and a terrific base from which to explore the area. Facilities include air-conditioned bathhouses, satellite TV, ships store, Wi-Fi, and a floating swimming pool with party deck. The **Deck Restaurant** is on-site.

Suffolk: **Bennett's Creek Restaurant and Marina** (757-484-8700; www.bennetts creekmarina.com), 3305 Ferry Road, Suffolk 23434. Small marina on Bennett's Creek offers slips, a boat ramp, and waterfront dining.

Constant's Wharf Marina (757-514-7250; www.suffolk.va.us/parks), 100 E. Constance Road, Suffolk 23434. Owned by the City of Suffolk, this 25-slip marina on the Nansemond River is adjacent to a park with frequent free festivals and concerts, and a **Hilton Garden Inn** (757-925-1300; www.suffolk.gardeninn.com), where the **Constant's Wharf Grill** serves meals overlooking the marina.

Public Boat Ramps

In Norfolk, the city maintains several public boat ramps. The largest, **Willoughby Boat Ramp,** at 13th View and Bayville Street in Ocean View, has two ramps, 80 parking spaces, and restrooms. The much smaller **Haven Creek Boat Ramp,** at the corner of Llewellyn and Delaware avenues, has two ramps launching into the Lafayette River. For additional information, visit www.norfolk.gov/rpos.

Public boat ramps in Chesapeake include: **Elizabeth River Boat Landing and Park** (103 Poindexter Street, Chesapeake 23324), with a fishing and crabbing pier and playground; the **Ballahack Road/Great Dismal Swamp Boat Ramp** (1200 Dismal Swamp Canal Trail, Chesapeake 23322); and **Great Bridge Lock Park** (757-382-6411; 100 Lock Road, Chesapeake 23320), with access to the Southern Branch of the Elizabeth River and the Albermarle and Chesapeake Canal. A canoe and kayak launch with access to the Dismal Swamp Canal and the Elizabeth River is located at **Deep Creek Lock Park** (300 Luray Street, Chesapeake 23323). All

Chesapeake city boat ramps are free. Call 757-382-6411 or visit www.cityofchesa peake.net/parks for maps and more information.

In Portsmouth, **City Park** (757-465-2937; www.portsmouthva.gov; 140 City Park Avenue, Portsmouth 23701) offers boat ramps, a sailboat launch area, and a small watercraft beach with access to the Western Branch of the Elizabeth River.

In Suffolk, **Bennett's Creek Park and Boat Ramp** (757-514-7250; www.suffolk .va.us/parks; Bennett's Creek Park Road, off SR 626) has two free ramps giving access to the Nansemond River, plus a handicapped-accessible fishing and crab-bing pier, playground, nature trail, and disc golf course. This is a good spot to access the **Suffolk Canoe Trail.**

For additional boat ramps, see our *Marinas* and *Fishing* listings.

Sailboat Charters, Cruises, and Rentals

American Rover (757-627-7245; www.americanrover.com), 333 Waterside Drive, Norfolk 23510. Distinctive red sails identify this three-masted topsail schooner modeled after 19th-century cargo ships. Daily harbor cruises Apr.–Oct.; private charters available.

Capt. Tom's Marine and Charter Service (757-408-2105; www.ctm-cs.com), Vinings Landing Marina, Norfolk. Day and evening charters aboard the *Raven,* a 35-foot sloop, and boat orientation training.

Carrie B Showboat (757-393-4735 or 954-609-4735; www.carrieb.com), 1238 Bay Street, Portsmouth 23704. Private charters are available aboard this 19th-century replica Mississippi paddle-wheeler.

SailTime (757-480-7245; www.sailtime.com), 1525 Bayville Street, Norfolk 23503. Sailboat charters, rentals, and instruction, plus fractional ownerships, based at the Willoughby Harbor Marina.

Schooner Virginia (757-627-7400; www.schoonervirginia.org), 500 E. Main Street, Norfolk 23510. Board the Schooner *Virginia,* a wooden hull, gaff topsail replica of a 1917 pilot schooner, for a relaxing weekend cruise on the bay or a week of sailing instruction. Adult and youth programs available.

Spirit of Independence (757-971-1865; www.spiritofindependence.net), Tidewa-ter Yacht Marina, 10 Crawford Parkway, Portsmouth 23704. Two-masted schooner available for private charter sails from Olde Towne Portsmouth. Live-aboard "boat and breakfast" accommodations available.

FAMILY FUN ⵝ **American Indoor Karting** (757-405-9715; www.american indoorkarting.com), 2884 Airline Boulevard, Portsmouth 23701. Fastest indoor karting on the East Coast. New location in Virginia Beach.

Bennett's Creek Park Disc Golf Course (757-484-3984; www.suffolk.va.us/parks), Bennett's Creek Park Road, off SR 626, Suffolk 23435. State-of-the-art 18-hole course, with rolling fairways and water hazards. Free.

Chesapeake Planetarium (757-547-STAR or 757-547-0153; www.cpschools.com/departments/planetarium), 312 Cedar Road, Chesapeake 23322. Free public programs Thurs. at 8 PM. Reservations required.

Chesapeake Skate Park (757-382-8878 or 800-828-1120; www.cityofchesapeake .net), Chesapeake City Park, 900 Greenbrier Parkway, Chesapeake 23320. Park for skateboarders and in-line skaters. Safety equipment required. Visitor pass ($5) is available at the City Park Ranger Station (757-312-0243).

☂ **Chilled Ponds Ice Sports Complex** (757-420-4488; www.chilledponds.point streaksites.com), 1416 Stephanie Way, Chesapeake 23320. Dual-rink facility with open skating sessions, fitness center, and café.

Dog parks (757-441-2400; www.norfolk.gov/rpos). The city of Norfolk is dog friendly, with a dozen parks where your pooch can run free; no fees or registration required.

✎ ♿ **Fun Forest at Chesapeake City Park** (757-312-0243; www.cityofchesa peake.net), 900 Greenbrier Parkway, Chesapeake 23320. Three-acre playground combines fun and education, with a free fossil dig, science learning area, and special sections for toddlers and older children. Much of the Fun Forest is handicapped accessible.

☂ **Greenbrier Family Skating Center** (757-420-0258; http://users.erols.com/ gfskate), 1409 Stephanie Way, Chesapeake 23320. Roller skating on a large floor, arcade room, snack bar.

☂ **Hi Score Gaming** (757-410-9494; www.hiscoregaming.com), 1200 N. Battlefield Drive, Chesapeake 23320. All-console gaming center with Xbox, Wii, and retro games sponsors tournaments, lock-ins, and summer camps.

Skydive Suffolk (757-539-3531 or 866-465-2779; www.skydivesuffolk.com). Full-service jump facility offers tandem, accelerated free fall, and packages for experienced jumpers at **Suffolk Executive Airport,** 1200 Gene Bolton Drive, Suffolk 23434.

FISHING All of the freshwater fishing spots listed below require a Virginia Freshwater Fishing License (www.dgif.virginia.gov), unless otherwise noted.

Lake Kilby, Lake Meade, and Lake Cahoon (757-539-6216; www.dgif.virginia .gov), SR 668, Suffolk. Popular local spots for largemouth bass, crappie, chain pickerel, and redear sunfish. Lake Kilby is noted for its unusual black bream. Fishing and boating permits required (757-539-2201).

Lone Star Lakes (757-255-4308; www.suffolk.va.us/parks), 1 Bob House Parkway, off VA 125, Suffolk 23432. A unique series of 11 lakes, some interconnected, provide a wide range of fishing opportunities. **Crane Lake,** opening onto Chuckatuck Creek, is a favorite with locals. Facilities include boat ramps ($4; no gas motors), nature trails, fishing and crabbing pier, archery range, and a model-airplane flying field.

Northwest River Park (757-421-7151 or 757-421-3145; www.cityofchesapeake .net), 1733 Indian Creek Road, Chesapeake 23322. Fish the stocked lake, a good family spot for bluegill, crappie, catfish, and largemouth bass, or from the fishing pier on the river.

Oak Grove Lake Park (757-382-6411; www.cityofchesapeake.net), 409 Byron Street, Chesapeake 23320. Hiking trail and five ADA-accessible fishing platforms surround the 65-acre lake.

Western Branch Reservoir (757-441-5678; www.norfolk.gov/utilities or www .dgif.virginia.gov/fishing), 4601 Girl Scout Road, off SR 605, Suffolk 23434. The largest and deepest reservoir in the region, stocked annually with striped bass, yields citation-sized fish of several species. Boat ramp and restrooms on-site. Norfolk boat permit required. Get a daily pass ($5) in person or by mail from the **City**

of **Norfolk, Department of Utilities** (757-664-6701; www.norfolk.gov/utilities), 400 Granby Street, Norfolk 23510.

Fishing Charters & Outfitters

Chesapeake Fishing Charters (757-548-6991 or 757-373-8530; www.captainkenny.com), Bay Point Marina, Little Creek Inlet, 30th Bay Street, Norfolk 23518. Full- and half-day trips to the lower Chesapeake Bay. All equipment, license, and fish cleaning included.

His Doghouse Charters (757-572-9236; www.shipdriver.net), Bay Point Marina, 9500 Pretty Lake Avenue, Norfolk 23518. Join Captain Joe, a retired Navy officer, for fishing in the bay or offshore trips after tuna.

ReelTime Sportfishing (757-292-7702; www.teamreeltime.com), Vinings Landing, 8166 Shore Drive, Norfolk 23518. Shared and private charters from Little Creek. Four anglers maximum.

Party or Head Boats

Harrison Charters (757-587-9630; www.harrisonspier.com), 4801 Pretty Lake Avenue, Norfolk 23518. Five-hour fishing trips depart from Little Creek Marina. Rod and reel rentals available. Squid bait and license provided. $35.

✍ **Judith Ann** (757-583-6000; www.norfolkcharters.com), Ocean View Fishing Pier, 400 W. Ocean View Avenue, Norfolk 23503. Daily four-hour fishing trips visit some of the area's most productive waters. Fishing tackle, bait, ice, fish cleaning, and license included. $20–35.

Saltwater Fishing Piers

&. **East Ocean View Community Center Pier** (757-441-1785; www.norfolk.gov/rpos), 9520 20th Bay Street, Norfolk 23518. New 134-foot U-shaped pier is handicapped accessible.

Elizabeth River Park (757-382-6411; www.cityofchesapeake.net), 103 Poindexter Street, Chesapeake 23324. This 144-foot pier on the Elizabeth River is great for fishing and crabbing.

✪ **Ocean View Fishing Pier** (757-583-6000; www.oceanviewfishingpier.com), 400 W. Ocean View Avenue, Norfolk 23503. Extending 1,690 feet into the bay, this pier has a tackle and bait shop, restaurant serving breakfast from 6 AM and seafood all day, game room, and the **Upper Deck**, where you can enjoy music, superb views, and your favorite beverage. Rod and reel rentals $6. Adults $8, seniors over 64 and children under 10 $6. Sightseers $1.

Willoughby Fishing Pier (757-583-4150 or 757-587-2270), 1631 Bayville Street, Norfolk 23503. Pier at the end of Willoughby Spit has a full-service bait and tackle shop.

GOLF If you'd like to sample the courses at a variety of area clubs, the **Hampton Roads Golf Players Pass** (757-490-8822; www.golfhamptonroads.net) is a good investment. For $55 you get more than 20 rounds of golf at seven local municipal courses.

Chesapeake

Battlefield Golf Club at Centerville (757-482-4779; www.playthebattlefield.com), 1001 S. Centerville Turnpike, Chesapeake 23322. New course by Bobby Holcomb has a rolling links design built around seven lakes.

Cahoon Plantation (757-436-2775; www.cahoonplantation.com), 1501 Cahoon Parkway, Chesapeake 23322. Links-style course, by Brian Ault and Tom Clark, is the first and only course in the region to have bent grass throughout. The **Caddy Shack** serves refreshments on and off the course. Club rentals available.

Chesapeake Golf Course (757-547-1122; www.hamptonroadsgolf.net), 1201 Clubhouse Drive, Chesapeake 23322. Challenging course has some tricky layups and blind water hazards, but greens fees are a bargain on weekends.

Norfolk
Lake Wright Golf Course (757-459-2255; www.hamptonroadsgolf.net), 6280 Northampton Boulevard, Norfolk 23502. Municipal course is a friendly spot for beginning golfers.

🍴 **Lambert's Point Golf Club** (757-489-1677; www.lambertspointgolf.com), 4301 Powhatan Avenue, Norfolk 23508. Designed by Lester George, this nine-hole executive course, located along the waterfront, was built to improve your game, with educational holes, one of the largest chipping areas in the country, a huge putting green, and a covered and heated year-round driving range.

♿ **Ocean View Golf Course** (757-480-2094; www.oceanviewgc.com), 9610 Norfolk Avenue, Norfolk 23503. Reasonably priced public course, voted best by locals, welcomes golfers with disabilities. Early-bird specials.

Portsmouth
✪ **Bide-A-Wee Golf Course** (757-393-8600; www.bideaweegolf.com), 1 Bide-A-Wee Lane, Portsmouth 23701. An $8 million renovation reshaped this municipal chestnut into a Curtis Strange signature course rated the best municipal play in Virginia. Rental clubs available.

⛳ **The Links at City Park** (757-465-1500 or 757-465-2937; www.portsmouth va.gov), 140 City Park Avenue, Portsmouth 23701. City-run golf practice center has a nine-hole course, lighted driving range, and natural putting course.

Suffolk
Nansemond River Golf Club (757-539-4356; www.nansemondrivergolfclub .com), 1000 Hillpoint Boulevard, Suffolk 23434. The 17th hole of this riverfront course sits on a natural island that reminds many golfers of TPC Sawgrass.

Riverfront Golf Club (757-484-2200; www.riverfrontgolf.com), 5200 River Club Drive, Suffolk 23435. Course architect Tom Doak designed this course on the Nansemond River. *Golf Digest* rates it a 4.5.

Sleepy Hole Golf Course (757-538-4100; www.sleepyholegolfcourse.com), 4700 Sleepy Hole Road, Suffolk 23435. Recently refurbished under the direction of Tom Clark, this course has hosted eight LPGA events. The 18th hole is ranked the toughest in Hampton Roads.

Suffolk Golf Course (757-539-6298), 1227 Holland Road, Suffolk 23434. Public course near downtown Suffolk borders Lake Kilby.

HEALTH & FITNESS CLUBS Fitness Evolution Gym (757-410-5099; www .fitnessevolutiongym.com), 800 S. Battlefield Boulevard, Chesapeake 23322. Guest passes and short-term memberships available.

🏋 **Norfolk Fitness and Wellness Center** (757-823-4300; www.norfolk.gov/ wellness), 7300 Newport Avenue, Norfolk 23505. City facility with indoor and outdoor pools; basketball, tennis, and racquetball courts; fitness room; treadmill and circuit room; cardio bike room; locker rooms with showers and saunas. Single-day pass $10; weekly pass $25.

HORSEBACK RIDING Several parks in the area have dedicated equestrian trails, including **Northwest River Park** (757-421-7151) in Chesapeake and **Lone Star Lakes** (757-255-4308) in Suffolk. Horses are also permitted on the multiuse Dismal Swamp Canal Trail.

HUNTING The **Great Dismal Swamp National Wildlife Refuge** (757-986-3705; www.fws.gov/northeast/greatdismalswamp; 3100 Desert Road, Suffolk 23434) hosts annual hunts for black bear, usually in Dec. Deer and other game, including dove, quail, turkey, raccoon, and rabbit, are hunted at the nearby **Cavalier Wildlife Management Area** (804-843-5966; www.dgif.virginia.gov/wmas) during the General Deer Firearm Season. Permits required. Contact the ranger station for regulations and fees.

RACQUET SPORTS & TENNIS Racquetball and tennis courts are among the amenities at the **Norfolk Fitness and Wellness Center** (757-823-4300; www .norfolk.gov/wellness; 7300 Newport Avenue, Norfolk 23505). Single-day passes to the center are $10; weekly visitor passes are $25.

Public tennis courts operated by the City of Norfolk include **Lafayette Park** (35th and Granby streets), **Lakewood Park Tennis Center** (1612 Willow Wood Drive), and **Northside Park** (8445 Tidewater Drive). Lighted tennis courts can be found at **Tarrallton Park and Community Center** (2100 Tarrallton Drive).

In Chesapeake, lighted courts can be found at the **Western Branch Park and Sport Complex** (4437 Portsmouth Boulevard).

In Portsmouth, lighted tennis courts can be found in **City Park** (757-465-2937; www.portsmouthva.gov; 140 City Park Avenue, Portsmouth 23701), along with new playground equipment, a golf learning center, Friendship Gardens, and, coming soon, the Pokey Smokey train.

SPAS **Inner Harmony Center for the Healing Arts** (757-547-1100; www .innerharmony.net), 505 Cedar Road, Chesapeake 23322. Organic facials and peels, raindrop aromatherapy, and other natural beauty treatments.

Totally Pampered Day Spa (757-399-1578; www.totallypampereddayspa.net), 604½ High Street, Portsmouth 23704. Small, holistic day spa in Olde Towne offers Ayurveda nutrition counseling, Reiki, and other natural treatments.

Tranquilities Day Spa & Wellness Center (757-583-7721; www.tranquilities dayspa.com), 9649 First View Street, Norfolk 23503. Day spa in Ocean View also offers drop-in classes in yoga, Pilates, and aerobics, plus a juice bar and café.

SPECTATOR SPORTS **Norfolk Admirals Hockey** (757-664-6464 [Scope box office] or 757-640-1212; www.norfolkadmirals.com), 201 E. Brambleton Avenue, Norfolk 23510. Professional AHL hockey team plays 40 home games a year, Oct.–Apr.

Norfolk City Blues Rugby Football Club (www.bluesrugby.org). Men's rugby organization plays in the spring and fall.

Norfolk State University Spartans (757-823-9009; www.nsuspartans.com), 700 Park Avenue, Norfolk 23504. Men's and women's teams in baseball, basketball, football, and more compete in the Mid-Eastern Atlantic Conference.

Norfolk Storm Women's Rugby Football Club (www.norfolkrugby.com). Spring and fall schedule.

Norfolk Tides Baseball (757-622-2222; www.norfolktides.com), Harbor Park, 150 Park Avenue, Norfolk 23510. Triple-A affiliate of the Baltimore Orioles plays 72 home games, Apr.–Sept., at **Harbor Park,** on the Norfolk waterfront. **Hits at the Park Restaurant** (✆ 757-624-9000) serves buffets and full bar overlooking the on-field action.

Old Dominion University Monarchs (757-683-4444 [ticket office]; www.odu sports.com), Third Street and Hampton Boulevard, Norfolk 23529. Men's football returned to the Old Dominion's newly renovated **Foreman Field Football Complex,** complete with luxury suites, in 2009. Men's and women's basketball and wrestling matches are held in the **Ted Constant Convocation Center**. Men's and women's soccer and baseball game tickets are available at the Old Dominion Soccer Complex and Bud Metheny Baseball Complex on game day.

Virginia Wesleyan College Marlins (757-455-3303; www.vwc.edu/athletics), Batten Student Center, 1584 Wesleyan Drive, Norfolk 23502. The Marlins men's basketball team recently won the NCAA Division III national title.

TOURING The **Portsmouth Museums Key Pass,** providing admission to the Children's Museum of Virginia, the Naval Shipyard Museum, the Lightship *Portsmouth,* and the Courthouse Galleries for just $9, is available at each of the museums.

By bicycle or on foot: **Freemason Historic District Walking Tour** (757-623-9814; www.hunterhousemuseum.org), 240 W. Freemason Street, Norfolk 23510. Pick up a brochure guide to this unique Victorian neighborhood at the Hunter House Victorian Museum.

The Cannonball Trail (www.downtownnorfolk.org). Sidewalk inlays and narrative signs guide visitors past more than 40 heritage sites in downtown Norfolk and the Freemason District.

Heart and Art Mermaid Story Trails (www.mermaidsonparade.com). Three family-friendly walking routes visiting Norfolk's many mermaid statues begin at Nauticus.

Legends of Music Walk of Fame (www.norfolk.gov/WalkofFame), Norfolk. Bronze stars set in the sidewalk along the 300 block of Granby Street, beginning at the TCC Roper Performing Arts Center, honor Hampton Roads natives who have made significant contributions to the world of music, including Pearl Bailey, Gary "U.S." Bonds, Charlie Byrd, and Ella Fitzgerald.

✪ **Olde Towne Portsmouth Lantern Tour** (757-393-5111 or 757-391-0155; www.oldetownetheatricals.com). Stroll the historic district with a costumed interpreter, learning about the city's history, legends, and architectural styles. $5, May–Oct. High Tea & History programs also available.

The Path of History (757-393-5111; www.visitportsva.com), Portsmouth. One-mile self-guided walking tour connects two of the Navy's oldest facilities, the Naval Medical Center and the Naval Shipyard, visiting 45 historic stops along the way.

CRUISING FROM NORFOLK

Norfolk's **Half Moone Cruise and Celebration Center** wins rave reviews from passengers impressed with the ease of embarking, convenient parking, and many attractions located close at hand, not to mention the scenic views of historic Hampton Roads and exciting encounters with Navy ships and subs while under way.

Situated next door to Nauticus and the Battleship *Wisconsin,* in the heart of the downtown Waterside district, the futuristic cruise center displays one of the nation's largest ocean-liner memorabilia collections, including original deck chairs from the R.M.S. *Queen Mary* and the R.M.S. *Queen Elizabeth,* ship models, and boarding passes, as well as four-hundred—year-old artifacts on loan from Jamestown.

Several cruise lines, including Carnival and Royal Caribbean, offer trips originating in Norfolk. Pre- and post-cruise packages, as well as shore excursions, are available.

For more information on cruises from Norfolk, visit www.cruisenorfolk .org or call 757-664-6620.

CRUISE SHIPS DOCKED AT THE HALF MOONE CRUISE AND CELEBRATION CENTER DOMINATE NORFOLK'S HARBORFRONT.

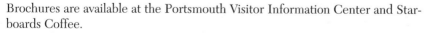

Brochures are available at the Portsmouth Visitor Information Center and Starboards Coffee.

By boat: ✪ *American Rover* **Tall Ship Cruises** (757-627-7245; www.americanrover.com), 333 Waterside Drive, Norfolk 23510. See Hampton Roads under canvas aboard this three-masted topsail schooner with distinctive red sails. Daily Apr.–Oct.

SUFFOLK: MR. PEANUT'S HOMETOWN

To the west of the Great Dismal Swamp, another major river makes its lazy way to the James—the Nansemond, discovered in 1608 by John Smith, and by the 1640s, the site of Constant's Wharf and tobacco warehouse. A quiet country town grew up around the wharf, taking the name of Suffolk in 1742.

MR. PEANUT, HOMETOWN MASCOT OF SUFFOLK, HOSTS A PEANUT FESTIVAL EVERY OCTOBER.

Italian immigrant Amadeo Obici moved his Planters Peanut company to Suffolk in 1912, and **Mr. Peanut** (www.planters.com or www.peanut pals.org) became the town's icon. A peanut-sized statue of the dapper legume occupies the center of town, at the intersection of Main and Washington streets. Real fans will also want to check out the fence around the Planters factory (245 Culloden Street), now owned by Kraft, with fenceposts topped by miniature Mr. Peanuts, or visit during the annual **Peanut Festival** (www.suffolkfest.org) in October.

In 1974, Suffolk merged with the nearby town of Nansemond to form the independent City of Suffolk, the largest municipality in land area in Virginia. Today, with growth spurred by new golf communities going up on the shores of the Nansemond River, and an active biotech corridor, Suffolk is the fastest growing city in the state. Major highways US 13, US 460, and US 58 converge here.

Stop at the **Suffolk Visitor Center** (757-923-3880; www.suffolk-fun.com; 321 N. Main Street, Suffolk 23434) for information on the rich historical and natural resources of the region. The center is open daily 9–5 and occupies the restored **Historic Prentis House,** circa 1800, one of the oldest houses in town and available for tours. Pick up self-guided walking tour maps here of the historic downtown, with many buildings of architectural interest and several antiques shops, or of the nearby **Cedar Hill Cemetery** (757-923-3880; 326 N. Main Street), a beautifully landscaped sanctuary established in 1802. The visitors center also offers a variety of area tours, including lantern tours of Cedar Hill Cemetery, bus tours of the Great Dismal Swamp and Suffolk's historic downtown, and canoe trips on Lone Star Lakes.

Attractions, located within a few blocks and sharing the Suffolk 23434 zip code, include:

Constant's Wharf Park and Marina (757-925-1300; www.suffolk.va.us/parks), 100 E. Constance Road. City park on the banks of the Nansemond hosts frequent festivals and free TGIF summer concerts. Next door, the **Hilton Garden Inn** (757-925-1300; www.suffolk.gardeninn.com) serves meals overlooking the marina in the **Constant's Wharf Grill.**

Holland Produce and Country Gourmet (757-934-1787; www.hollandsproduce .com), 100 S. Commerce Street. Country hams cooked on-site, plus homemade chicken salad, collard greens, fried chicken, and deviled eggs made from scratch. Dine in or take out. Closed Sun.

Planters Peanut Center (757-539-4411; www.suffolkpeanuts.com), 308 W. Washington Street. Burlap bags of peanuts roasted in an original 1936 roaster, plus many other nuts and candies, for sale in this museum of peanut memorabilia.

Producers Peanut Company Store (757-539-7496 or 800-847-5491; www.producers peanut.com), 337 Moore Avenue. Factory store carries the popular Peanut Kids (www.thepeanutkids.com) line of natural peanut butters.

Red Thread Studio (757-923-9832; www.theredthreadstudio.com), 153 W. Washington Street. Fabric and fiber arts and supplies, plus local crafts, vintage clothing, and antiques. Open knitting sessions weekly.

✪ **Riddick's Folly House Museum** (757-934-0822; www.riddicksfolly.org), 510 N. Main Street. Beautifully preserved 1837 Greek Revival home in Suffolk's downtown, with 21 rooms and four floors open to visitors, still retains graffiti drawn by Union soldiers during the Civil War. Open Thurs.–Sun. $2–4.

Shooting Star Gallery (757-934-0855; www.shootingstargallery.net), 118 N. Main Street. Photography, fine arts, and crafts by regional and national artists.

Southern Gun Works and Museum (757-934-1423), 167 S. Main Street. Limited-edition military art, war souvenirs, military weapons, uniforms, and war photos on display. Reproduction weapons suitable for reenactors for sale.

Suffolk Center for Cultural Arts (757-923-0003; www.suffolkcenter.org), 110 W. Finney Avenue. The former 1922 Suffolk High School now houses the Birdsong Theatre, with performances for the whole family; art galleries; **Jester's Gallery Shop,** showcasing locally made art and crafts; and the **Mosaic Cafe** (757-538-5090; www.mosaicedibles.com).

Suffolk Museum (757-923-2371; www.suffolkmuseumva.com), 118 Bosley Avenue. Changing exhibits of contemporary and mixed-media artworks. Free.

✪ **Suffolk Seaboard Station Museum** (757-923-4750; www.suffolktrainstation .org), 326 N. Main Street. The restored 1885 Main Street Railroad Station displays a model of Suffolk in 1907 when six railroads met here. Open Thurs.–Sun. Donation $2.

THE LOW–COST PADDLEWHEEL FERRY OPERATES DAILY BETWEEN THE WATERFRONTS OF NORFOLK AND PORTSMOUTH.

Spirit of Independence (757-971-1865; www.spiritofindependence.net), Tidewater Yacht Marina, 10 Crawford Parkway, Portsmouth 23704. Two-masted schooner sails from Olde Towne Portsmouth on daily sight-seeing and sunset cruises. Seasonal.

Spirit of Norfolk **Harbor Cruise** (757-625-3866 or 866-304-2469; www.spiritof norfolk.com), Waterside Marina, Norfolk. Cruise Hampton Roads aboard this modern, climate-controlled ship with lavish buffets, dancing, and live entertainment on lunch, dinner, moonlight, and specialty cruises all year.

✿ **Victory Rover Naval Base Cruises** (757-627-7406; www.navalbasecruises .com), 1 Waterside Drive, Norfolk 23510. Narrated year-round cruises aboard a motor launch departing from Nauticus offer the most comprehensive tour available of the Atlantic Fleet.

By bus, minivan, or trolley: **Olde Towne Trolley Tours** (757-393-5111; www.oldetownetheatricals.com). Costumed interpreters narrate tours departing from the Portsmouth Visitor Center.

Norfolk Naval Base Tour (757-444-7955; www.cnic.navy.mil/Norfolk). Daily bus tours conducted by Navy personnel take visitors past aircraft carriers, destroyers, and other ships in port; the USS *Cole* Memorial; and one of the busiest airfields in the country, as well as historic homes from the 1907 Jamestown Exposition. Buses depart from the **Naval Tour and Information Center** (9079 Hampton Boulevard, Norfolk 23505), next to gate 5, and are not handicapped accessible. Photo ID required for adults. Adults $10, children 3–11 and seniors over 60 $5.

Other tours: **Decker Aviation Helicopter Tours** (757-925-0040 or 757-532-6914; www.deckeraviation.com), 1200 Gene Bolton Drive, Suffolk 23434. Pilots with more than 35 years of military and civilian experience conduct flightseeing tours from Suffolk Executive Airport.

Olde Towne Carriage Company (757-636-5315, 757-635-9963, or 888-842-4407; www.portsmouthhorsecarriage.com), carriage stop at the **Renaissance**

Hotel, 425 Water Street, Portsmouth 23704. Enjoy an informative carriage ride through the streets of Olde Towne on weekends. Adults $15, children 10 and under are $10. Reservations suggested.

↠ **Segway Tour of the Freemason District** (757-412-9734; www.segwayhr .com). Follow Norfolk's Cannonball Trail aboard a fun, green Segway.

WATER SPORTS

Kiteboarding & Sailboarding
Kiters and boarders launch from the beach in **Ocean View,** especially the eastern end where breakwaters diminish the shore break. Other popular spots are the **Willoughby Boat Ramp** in Norfolk and **City Park** in Portsmouth.

Snorkeling & Scuba Shops and Charters
Chesapeake Bay Diving Center (757-397-3483; www.chesapeakebaydiving .com), 655 Mt. Vernon Avenue, Portsmouth 23707. Classes in scuba and snorkeling, equipment rentals, service, and sales.

Divers Unlimited of Norfolk (757-480-DIVE [3483]; www.diversunlimited.us), 4247 E. Little Creek Road, Norfolk 23518. Scuba equipment rentals, plus skateboard and surfing items, spearfishing supplies, classes, and a full schedule of inshore and offshore dive trips.

Grimsley Scuba Services (757-539-8709; www.scubagss.com), 200A Byrd Street, Suffolk 23434. Snorkeling and scuba classes at Davis Lakes Campground.

WILDLIFE- AND BIRD-WATCHING The South Chesapeake and Suffolk loops in the Coastal Section of the **Virginia Birding and Wildlife Trail** run through this region. Visit www.dgif.virginia.gov/vbwt or call 866-VABIRDS for more information. For additional birding opportunities, see our listings under *Fishing* and *Wilder Places.*

✳ Wilder Places

NORFOLK AND CHESAPEAKE The Outback at A Place for Girls—Nellie Hayse Site (757-547-4405, ext. 255; www.gsccc.org/Funding_Tribute.asp), 912 Cedar Road, Chesapeake 23322. Excellent birding along Bells Mill Creek, plus canoe launch, picnic areas, and fitness trail.

Bells Mill Park (757-382-6411; www.cityofchesapeake.net/parks), 424 Albemarle Drive, Chesapeake 23322. Pleasant footpath passes tidal marsh to a scenic overlook on the Elizabeth River. Free parking across the street in the Civic Center–West lot.

↠ **Chesapeake Arboretum** (757-382-7060; www.chesapeakearboretum.com), 624 Oak Grove Road, Chesapeake 23320. Attractive mulched trails wander through mature hardwood forest, and fragrance and antique rose gardens. Free.

✪ ♿ **Northwest River Park** (757-421-7151 or 757-421-3145; www.cityofchesapeake.net/parks), 1733 Indian Creek Road, Chesapeake 23322. Seven miles of nature trails wind through bald eagle habitat. The handicapped-accessible **Marjorie Rein Memorial Walkway** crosses a bald cypress swamp to a pier on the Northwest River. Year-round rental boats, fishing, fragrance garden, minigolf, and an RV campground and camping cabins. The **Back Bay Amateur Astronomers** (www.backbayastro.org) host free Sky Watch events monthly.

Weyanoke Wildlife Sanctuary (757-423-8868 or 757-625-1907; www.chasnor folk.org), 1501 Armistead Bridge Road, Norfolk 23507. Small sanctuary administered by the Cape Henry Audubon Society in West Ghent is a popular stopover for migrating birds. Open on weekends. Free nature walk and field trips.

PORTSMOUTH AND SUFFOLK ✧ **The Elizabeth River Project Information Center** (757-399-7487; www.elizabethriver.org), High Street Ferry Landing, 475 Water Street, Portsmouth 23704. Learn about successful public-private efforts

EXPLORING THE GREAT DISMAL SWAMP AND LAKE DRUMMOND: PADDLING, HIKING, AND BIKING THE PRIMEVAL FOREST

One of the last true wildernesses remaining on the East Coast, **Great Dismal Swamp National Wildlife Refuge** (757-986-3705; www.fws.gov/northeast/greatdismalswamp; 3100 Desert Road, Suffolk 23434) contains more than 100,000 acres of forested wetlands, with round Lake Drummond, the largest of Virginia's natural freshwater lakes, at its heart.

The historic **Dismal Swamp Canal,** begun in 1793 by a consortium of businessmen that included George Washington, is a great place to paddle kayaks or canoes. Running about 23 miles between Deep Creek Lock in Chesapeake, Virginia, and South Mills Lock in North Carolina, the canal is the site of the popular **Paddle for the Border** event held every May. The new US 17, now four lanes, parallels the canal for most of its length, while old US 17 is now the **Dismal Swamp Canal Trail** (757-382-6411; www.cityofchesa peake.net), restricted to hikers, bikers, and horses. This multiuse path runs south 8.5 miles along the canal and the eastern edge of the wildlife refuge, from the intersection of Dominion Boulevard and Old US 17 in Chesapeake to the North Carolina border.

To paddle the canal, put in at Deep Creek Lock or head farther south to the boat ramp off US 17 at Ballahack Road. From here you can paddle south about 7 miles down the canal to the **Dismal Swamp Canal Welcome Center and State Park** (252-771-8333, 252-771-6593, or 877-771-8333; www.dismal swamp.com or www.ncparks.gov; 2356 US 17 N., South Mills, NC 27976) just over the North Carolina line, where you'll find a dock, a canoe and kayak launch, a new museum with exhibits on the history and ecology of the canal and swamp, restrooms, and trails for hiking and mountain biking.

Alternatively, you can paddle south from Ballahack about a mile and enter the narrow Feeder Ditch leading to **Lake Drummond.** After about 3 miles, you'll come to a portage to the lake. An Army Corps of Engineers campground with restrooms is located here, so it's a good place to eat lunch, or to set up a tent if you decide to stay several days.

The lake itself is almost perfectly round, more than 2 miles across, and to restore one of the most environmentally degraded rivers in the United States. Open weekdays. Free. The center's **Learning Barge,** an award-winning, green floating classroom powered by sun and wind, with a living wetland onboard, conducts family field trips that are open to the public. Registration required.

✪ ♿ ⏵ **Hoffler Creek Wildlife Preserve** (757-686-8684; www.hofflercreek.org), 4510 Twin Pines Road, Portsmouth 23703. Pocket-sized preserve located near the I-664 Bridge-Tunnel has a 1-mile loop trail circling Lake Ballard, with shorter

just 6 feet deep. Make a careful note of the ditch entrance, since it's easy to become disoriented among the cypress trees that line the shore. The peace and timeless quality you'll encounter on the dark waters of Lake Drummond make it one of the finest spots to paddle on the East Coast.

An estimated 300 black bears, along with deer, mink, bobcats, and foxes, make the refuge their home, as well as some 200 species of birds, including 35 different warblers. Birding is good all year, but it's best during the spring migration, mid-Apr.–mid-May, when the annual **Great Dismal Swamp Birding Festival** is held. Swainson's and Wayne's warblers, two of the most secretive and least-observed North American birds, have been spotted here.

More than 40 miles of unpaved roads, open year-round for biking and hiking, crisscross the refuge. Birders recommend the South Jericho Ditch Trail and **Lynn Ditch Trail** accessed at the Jericho Lane entrance, off White Marsh Road (SR 642) in Suffolk on the west side of the refuge. The Washington Ditch entrance nearby provides the most direct land access to Lake Drummond via the 4.5-mile **Washington Ditch Trail,** leading to a pier with mounted scope. The **Dismal Town Boardwalk Trail,** adjacent to the Washington Ditch parking area on White Marsh Road, provides a good view of swamp habitats with a minimum of walking.

Motor vehicle access to the refuge is limited. On weekdays, apply for a vehicle pass, 8–3, at the Railroad Ditch entrance ranger station, located off Desert Road (SR 604) in Suffolk. This permits you to drive on gravel roads 6 miles to the Interior Ditch pier for an excellent view of Lake Drummond and to access to the **West Ditch Boardwalk Trail,** with views of centuries-old bald cypress trees. A boat ramp located at the Interior Ditch pier can only be used by special permit, usually Apr. 1–June 15, during fishing season.

Rangers offer several activities, including guided bus tours to Lake Drummond, bird banding, and butterfly counts. Special programs explore the role of the Great Dismal in the **Underground Railway Network to Freedom** (www.nps .gov/ugrr), when enslaved persons escaped to the swamp before and during the Civil War. The refuge is closed during annual hunts for black bear and white-tailed deer held in the fall.

trails leading to several bird blinds. A pier on Hoffler Creek offers views of a demonstration oyster garden. Golf cart tours for those unable to walk can be arranged in advance. Kayak rentals and tours, geocaching, free birding walks. Open Tues.–Sun. Free.

↪ **Paradise Creek Nature Park** (757-399-7487; www.paradisecreekpark.org), Victory Boulevard, Portsmouth 23702. New park on Paradise Creek, part of the Elizabeth River Project, will have restored tidal wetlands, boardwalks, nature trails, canoe/kayak ramps and trails, tidal and rain gardens, and a unique green interpretive center run completely on natural energy. PhaseOne opens in 2012.

Sleepy Hole Park (757-514-7250 or 757-923-2360; www.suffolk.va.us/parks), Sleepy Hole Road/SR 629, Suffolk 23435. Nature trails lead through an upland forest to the edge of a bluff overlooking the Nansemond River, where wintering waterfowl are often visible.

✳ Lodging

Norfolk finds itself in the midst of a building boom, with several new downtown high-rise hotels set to open within the next few years close to the new light rail line.

A 23-story Westin, under way at Main and Granby streets, will feature a large convention center, parking garage, and two restaurants. The new nine-story **Residence Inn by Marriott** (↪ 757-842-6216; www.marriott.com), at 227 W. Brambleton Avenue, has 160 guest rooms and spacious meeting facilities.

Among the existing downtown hotels associated with national chains are the **Sheraton Norfolk Waterside Hotel** (757-622-6664; www.sheraton norfolkwaterside.com; 777 Waterside Drive, Norfolk 23510), the only downtown hotel actually on the waterfront; and the **Norfolk Waterside Marriott Hotel** (757-627-4200; www.marriott.com; 235 E. Main Street, Norfolk 23510), a block or so away.

In Portsmouth, the **Renaissance Portsmouth Hotel and Conference Center** (↪ 757-673-3000 or 888-839-1775; www.marriott.com; 425 Water Street, Portsmouth 23704) sits on the waterfront, offering terrific views of the harbor and the Norfolk skyline.

The town of Chesapeake also has several fine hotels, including the stylish new **Aloft** (↪ 757-410-9562; www.starwoodhotels.com; 1454 Crossways Boulevard, Chesapeake 23320), close to Greenbrier Mall and Regent University.

Price Categories

Inexpensive	up to $80
Moderate	$80 to $150
Expensive	$150 to $200
Very expensive	$200 and up

HOTELS & INNS

Norfolk

✪ ♂ "♥" **Freemason Inn Bed and Breakfast** (757-963-7000 or 866-388-1897; www.freemasoninn.com), 411 W. York Street, Norfolk 23510. Innkeepers: Robert Epstein and Ke Jing Jang. Price: Expensive to very expensive. Credit cards: Yes. Special features: Free Wi-Fi, free parking, TVs, complimentary robes and snacks. Located in the historic Freemason District just steps from a station on Norfolk's new light rail line and several restaurants, this 1897 vintage Victorian provides three stories of elegant accommodations furnished with antiques and working gas fireplaces, along with some very modern amenities, such as free Wi-Fi and Jacuzzi tubs big enough for two. Guests gather in the dining room for three-course gourmet breakfasts and afternoon wine and cheese socials. Private dinners can also be arranged. The inn is a favorite for honeymoons and romantic getaways, and weddings often take place on the outdoor terrace.

☙ ⁕ "I" **The Page House Inn Bed and Breakfast** (757-625-5033 or 800-599-7659; www.pagehouseinn .com), 323 Fairfax Avenue, Norfolk 23507. Innkeeper: Carl Albero. Price: Expensive to very expensive. Credit cards: Yes. Special features: Free Wi-Fi, fitness room, complimentary bikes, guest computer, free parking. Distinguished 1899 mansion turned bed & breakfast inn enjoys a fine location next door to the Chrysler Museum of Art. Four guest rooms and three suites, furnished with antiques, TVs, VCRs, and CD players; gas log fireplaces; canopy beds; and Jacuzzi tubs. The front porch and spacious deck look out on the historic neighborhood, and an entertainment room features billiards and a large-screen TV. Rates include a full breakfast, afternoon tea or sherry, and complimentary snacks. In-room champagne and candlelight breakfasts available. Small dogs are welcome with additional fee.

❂ ⁕ ♂ "I" **The Tazewell Hotel and Suites** (757-623-6200; www.the tazewell.com), 245 Granby Street, Norfolk 23510. Price: Moderate. Credit cards: Yes. Special features: Free Wi-Fi, continental breakfast included, in-room coffeemakers, free daily local paper. Located in the heart of Granby Street's Martini Row, with restaurants, theaters, and nightclubs just steps away and many area museums and the MacArthur Mall within a few blocks, the Tazewell enjoys one of the best locations in the city for seeing the sights. Built in 1906 as one of the city's

showplaces, with a spacious two-story lobby, the hotel enjoyed a complete renovation not too many years ago. King-bed suites feature refrigerators, microwaves, and wet bars. Parking is available in a nearby deck ($15/day) or on the street. Guests receive complimentary passes to a gym three doors away and breakfast daily. The popular **Empire** (757-626-3100; www.little barbistro.com), one of the Little Bar Bistros, serving great cocktails and tapas, is located on the street level.

Portsmouth

"I" **The Glencoe Inn** (757-397-8128; www.glencoeinn.com), 222 North Street, Portsmouth 23704. Innkeeper: Anne McGowan McGlynn. Price: Moderate. Credit cards: Yes. Special features: Free Wi-Fi, robes, coffee/tea makers. Restored Victorian, built in 1890 on the Portsmouth waterfront, enjoys new life as a bed & breakfast inn, reflecting the Scottish heritage of its innkeeper. Breakfasts of fresh baked scones and breads, jams, and marmalades, plus porridge on request, are included in the nightly rate. Four guest rooms decorated with antiques occupy three floors, with decks overlooking the Elizabeth River. Rooms with Jacuzzi tubs, kitchenettes, and balconies available. The city's attractions and the ferry to Norfolk are close by.

❂ ♿ ⁕ ♀ "I" **The Governor Dinwiddie Hotel and Suites** (757-392-1330; www.governordinwiddiehotel .com), 506 Dinwiddie Street at High Street, Portsmouth 23704. Price: Moderate. Credit cards: Yes. Special features: Free Wi-Fi, fitness center with sauna, valet, laundry, free parking, free local calls and daily paper. A member of the Historic Hotels of America, this seven-story brick hotel occupies a central corner on Portsmouth's High Street, just steps from restaurants, antiques shops, art galleries, and the

Commodore Theatre. Built in 1945, the building was totally renovated in 2005 into an all-suite hotel. The on-site **Revolutions Restaurant and Bar** (757-966-5385; www.myspace.com/revolutionrestaurant) serves a complimentary hot buffet breakfast to hotel guests and is open to the public for weekday lunch, offering specials such as Voodoo Oysters, ahi tuna sliders, and prime rib sandwiches.

⁰ı⁰ The Patriot Inn Bed and Breakfast (757-391-0157; www.bbonline.com/va/patriot), 201 North Street, Portsmouth 23704. Innkeepers: Ron and Verle Weiss. Price: Moderate. Credit cards: Yes. Special features: Wi-Fi, smoke-free, cable TV, breakfast included. Colonial built in 1784 retains its handblown-glass windowpanes, heart pine floors, and handcarved mantels. Four rooms furnished with antiques and period reproductions, some with working, wood-burning fireplaces and whirlpool tubs, welcome guests with down comforters and pillows. A pleasant veranda offers views of the Elizabeth River. Full English-style breakfast and afternoon tea included in nightly rate. No pets or children under 12.

RV RESORTS ⌀ **Chesapeake Campground** (757-485-0149 or 888-584-2267), 693 S. George Washington Parkway/US 17 Business, Chesapeake 23323. RV hookups, cabins, and tent camping on a 100-acre farm with swimming pool, bike and canoe rentals, fishing, tennis, hiking trails, hayrides, minigolf, driving range, chapel, a chicken house, pony rides, and a petting zoo. Located near the Great Dismal Swamp Canal.

Davis Lakes and Campground (757-539-1191), 200 Byrd Street, Suffolk 23435. Good Sam park with 275 sites situated around several lakes; rental cabins, nature trail, swimming and fishing lakes; boating; camp store; LP gas.

Northwest River Park Campground (757-421-7151 or 757-421-3145; www.chesapeake.va.us/nwrp), 1733 Indian Creek Road, Chesapeake 23322. Chesapeake's finest city park offers boating and fishing on the lake or river; hiking and biking trails; minigolf; rental kayaks, canoes, jon boats, and paddleboats; camping cabins; and 70 sites with electric hookups for RVs or tents. Campground open Apr. 1–Nov. 30.

✳ Where to Eat

Norfolk's increasingly sophisticated dining scene is concentrated in the downtown area, known for its tapas bars, and the Ghent neighborhood, known for its wine bars. Granby Street downtown is popularly known as Martini Row, with numerous establishments offering tapas and cocktails, and entertainment lining both sides of the street.

Foodies may want to plan their visit to coincide with Norfolk's Summer or Winter **Restaurant Weeks** (www.norfolkrestaurantweek.com), held in January and July, when some of the city's finest eateries offer their specialties at special prices. Portsmouth schedules its **Restaurant Week** (www.eatinportsmouthva.com) in April.

Another new dining event in Hampton Roads is of particular interest to locavores. Every October, local foods and seasonal menus are featured at special prices during **Farm to Feast Week.** Local restaurants where you'll find a continuing commitment to local foods include the **Boot** (✆ 757-627-2668; www.insidetheboot.com), **Vintage Kitchen** (757-625-3370; www.vintage-kitchen.com), and **Todd Jurich's Bistro** (757-622-3210; www

.toddjurichsbistro.com) in Norfolk; **Stove** (757-397-0900; www.stove restaurant.com) in Portsmouth; **99 Main** (757-599-9885; www.99main restaurant.com) in Newport News; and **Cro's Eco Bistro** (↷ 757-428-5444; www.crocsecobistro.com), **Zoe's** (↷ 757-437-3636; www.zoesvb.com), and the **Cellars at Churchpoint** (757-460-2210; www.churchpoint manor.com) in Virginia Beach.

As the home of the international headquarters of People for the Ethical Treatment of Animals (PETA), Norfolk is a mecca for vegetarian and vegan fare. See our listings below, or visit the Web sites www.happycow.net or www.vegguide.org for more suggestions.

Price Categories

Inexpensive	under $10
Moderate	$10 to $20
Expensive	$20 to $25
Very expensive	$25 and up

The listings in this section also include information on what meals are served, using the following abbreviations:

B	Breakfast
L	Lunch
D	Dinner
SB	Sunday brunch

DINING OUT

Norfolk

& Ⴤ ↷ **Bodega** (757-622-8527; www.bodegaongranby.com), 442 Granby Street, Norfolk 23510. Open: Daily. Credit cards: Yes. Serving: D. Price: Inexpensive. Cuisine: Tapas. Handicapped access: Yes. Special features: Chalkboard specials, fondue of the day. With an extensive menu of hot and cold tapas, plus Mediterranean specialties such as paella and crab and spinach gnocchi, this stylish café, with

dark wood, exposed brick, and a copper-top bar, serves only small plates. A nice list of cocktails, beers, and wines, including flights and house sangria, complements the menu. Several items will appeal to vegetarians, including eggplant fries and spinach with cherries and pine nuts. If you are looking for a more substantial meal, visit one of the other fine restaurants owned by the same investors, all located within few blocks: **Byrd & Baldwin Brothers Steak House** (↷ 757-222-9191; www.byrdbaldwin.com; 116 Brooke Avenue), a fine-dining steak and chop eatery, tucked behind an impressive 1906 Beaux-Arts Italianate facade; **456 Fish** (↷ 757-625-4444; www.456fish.com; 456 Granby Street), serving seafood with Caribbean accents; and the **Big Easy Grill & Oyster Bar** (↷ 757-227-6222; www.bigeasygrillandoysterbar.com; 111 W. Tazewell Street), with a downstairs oyster-shucking bar, New Orleans–style menu, and live jazz. All serve dinner only.

& **Espeto na Brasa—A Brazilian Restaurant** (757-313-4363; www.espetonabrasa.com), 233 Granby Street, Norfolk 23510. Open: Tues.–Sun. Credit cards: Yes. Serving: L, D. Price: Very expensive. Cuisine: Brazilian. Handicapped access: Yes. Special features: Full bar, reservations suggested, happy hour. Former grand 1908 department store with marble floors, towering columns, double mezzanines, and chandelier lighting provides a stunning setting for this excursion into the world of Brazilian dining. Waiters circulate through the room, slicing off pieces of more than a dozen different meats—from chicken and beef to pork and lamb—threaded on long skewers. Diners help themselves to an extensive salad bar, and a buffet of hot items with several soups and Brazilian specialties such as shrimp in coconut milk.

NORFOLK'S WAFFLE CONNECTION

Thomas Jefferson reputedly brought back America's first waffle iron from France, and the Tidewater has been enjoying—and experimenting with—the crispy delicacies ever since.

Abe Doumar, founder of **Doumar's Cones and Barbecue** (757-627-4163; www.doumars.com; 1919 Monticello Avenue, Norfolk 23517), claimed to have rolled a waffle into a cone and filled it with ice cream during the steamy summer of 1904 at the St. Louis World's Fair (where iced tea was also popularized). While many have disputed his claim to the first cone, there is no question that Doumar opened the first ice cream cone stand in Norfolk in 1907 at the Ocean View Amusement Park and patented his waffle cone maker. The Smithsonian displays one of his machines, and his family continues to hand-roll cones on another of the antiques today.

Another waffle-based Tidewater delicacy has been traced back to Jefferson's time. Chicken and waffles, crispy fried chicken atop a waffle dressed in butter and syrup, was a celebration supper in the Old South, especially among African American families. You can try a modernized, lower-fat version at **The Wing Spot Chicken and Waffles** (757-543-0278; www.myspace.com/thewingspotva; 1924 N. Battlefield Boulevard, Chesapeake 23324).

A lengthy cocktail menu features the Caipirinha, national drink of Brazil, available in several flavors. This all-you-can-eat meal falls into the splurge category, although you can pass on the meat and just have the salad and hot buffet for less. For those with smaller appetites, or lighter wallets, consider stopping by at lunchtime for a far less hefty tab. Second location in Virginia Beach (757-351-0598; 1069 Laskin Road).

♂ & ⅄ **Freemason Abbey Restaurant and Tavern** (757-622-3966; www.freemasonabbey.com), 209 W. Freemason Street at Boush, Norfolk 23510. Open: Daily. Credit cards: Yes. Serving: L, D, SB. Price: Moderate to expensive. Cuisine: American. Handicapped access: Yes. Special features: Separate lounge, children's menu, vegetarian menu, weekday Lunch in a Flash menu, reservations recommend-

ed, free parking. This steepled building, dedicated as a church in 1873, now houses one of Norfolk's most popular restaurants. Locals make weekly pilgrimages for the Wednesday Lobster, Thursday Prime Rib, and other nightly specials. Eat in the main sanctuary under the soaring vault, or in the cozy lounge, where you can drink local beer and order appetizers till late. A regular on "Best of" lists, the Abbey is known for its she-crab and French onion soups, salmon Oscar, pasta dishes, and Sun. brunch served with brandy bread pudding. For lighter appetites, a sandwich menu is offered every afternoon.

✪ ♂ & ⅄ ⊹ **No Frill Bar and Grill** (757-627-4262; www.nofrillgrill.com), 806 Spotswood Avenue, Norfolk 23517. Open: Daily. Credit cards: Yes. Serving: L, D, SB. Price: Moderate. Cuisine: American. Handicapped access: Yes. Special features: Full bar, children's menu, daily specials, martini menu. Located in the heart of the historic Ghent neighborhood just down the block from the Naro Theatre, this popular spot serves greats salads, soups, stuffed pitas, sandwiches, and burgers, as well as heartier entrées ranging from grilled catfish to locally famous meat loaf, and portions are generally huge. The Spotswood Salad, laced with apples, blue cheese, and caramelized almonds, is one of the best in town. Several dishes, including the tasty Portabella Pasta, cater to the vegetarian crowd. Second location in Virginia Beach (757-425-2900; 1620 Laskin Road).

✐ ♿ ⚲ ☂ **Ship's Cabin Restaurant** (757-362-0060; www.shipscabin restaurant.com), 4110 E. Ocean View Avenue at Shore Dr., Norfolk 23518. Open: Daily. Credit cards: Yes. Serving: L, D. Price: Moderate. Cuisine: Seafood and Italian. Handicapped access: Yes. Special features: Outside dining, covered deck, weeknight happy hour, separate lounge, free parking. Huge restaurant in Ocean View offers expansive views of Chesapeake Bay from the nautically decorated dining room or from outside on the covered deck. A local favorite that wins many "Best of" awards, its menu is a mix of steaks cooked on a charcoal grill, seafood, and Italian specialties. For the best of both worlds, order one of the dozen different seafood pastas, such as the Zupe di Mare, shrimp, scallops, and clams sautéed in olive oil over linguine. The inexpensive lunch menu offers smaller portions of some of the Italian dishes, plus a long list of salads, burgers, Italian-style grinders, and Greek gyros. A spacious lounge holds seven TVs, two pool tables, and occasional live entertainment.

✪ ♿ **Voila** (757-640-0343   ), 509 Botetourt Street at W. York, Norfolk

23510. Open: Daily, except Mon. dinner. Credit cards: Yes. Serving: L (Mon.–Fri.), D (Tues.–Sun.). Price: Moderate. Cuisine: French. Handicapped access: Yes. Special features: Seasonal menus, full bar, late-night hours on weekends, free parking. Like its nearby sister restaurants, **Omar's Carriage House** (757-622-4990; www.omarscarriagehouseva.com; 313 W. Bute Street) and the **Pagoda Garden Tea House** (757-622-0506; www .pagodagarden.org; 265 W. Tazewell Street), this French jewel adds diversity to dining in the Freemason District. Small, colorful, and quite romantic, Voila is the perfect spot for an intimate dinner, especially for those fond of French cuisine. While the large entrées, such as sole meunière and steak au poivre, command big splurge status, the majority of the menu is made up of "petit plats" and hors d'oeuvres, including escargots and fois gras, at much more moderate prices. The lunch menu, served weekdays only, features salad niçoise, quiche Lorraine, croque monsieur, and, in season, a cassoulet. A station on the new light rail line is just steps away.

Portsmouth

✐ ♿ 🦞 **Lobscouser Restaurant** (757-397-2728; www.lobscouser.com), 337 High Street, Portsmouth 23704. Open: Mon.–Sat. Credit cards: Yes. Serving: L (Mon.–Fri.), D. Price: Moderate. Cuisine: Seafood. Handicapped access: Yes. Special features: Early-bird specials, children's menu, lunch specials, wine specials, full bar. Casual family-owned spot in Olde Towne serves fresh seafood, simply prepared in a variety of ways, plus chicken, prime rib, and steak entrées, all at prices that won't break the bank. The appetizer and lunch menus rarely top $5 and feature treats such as a crabcake and Smithfield ham sandwich. The early-bird specials, a lengthy list of seafood and chicken, fried or broiled, served from 5 to 6:30 PM, offers great bargains accompanied by Southern-style vegetables that go way beyond the standard french fries and slaw. Save room for the homemade desserts, perhaps the Drunken Monkey—rum-marinated bananas topped with ice cream, rum coconut custard, and hot fudge.

& 🐾 ⅋ "1" **Still, Worldly Eclectic Tapas** (757-332-7222; www.stilleats .com), 450 Court Street, Portsmouth 23704. Open: Daily. Credit cards: Yes. Serving: L (Mon.–Fri.), D, SB. Price: Inexpensive. Cuisine: Tapas. Handicapped access: Yes. Special features: Beer, wine, and whiskey dinners; vegan options; free Wi-Fi; reservations recommended. Trendy tapas bar in Olde Towne serves a heady brew of menu items distilled from many different cultures. Bourbon-glazed duck shares the table with chicken and waffles and lobster corn dawgs in a speakeasy setting. For dessert you can have cookies and milk, or a Murphy's Irish Stout beer float. Nothing is very expensive (except some of the cocktails, single malts, and small batch bourbons that crowd the bar menu). Still serves until 2 AM on Fri. and Sat., and is the sister restaurant of trendy **Bardo Edibles + Elixirs** (757-622-7362; www.bardoeats .com; 430 W. 21st Street, Norfolk 23517), in Ghent.

& ⅋ **Stove, The Restaurant and Cougar Lounge** (757-397-0900; www.stoverestaurant.com), 2622 Detroit Street, Portsmouth 23707. Open: Daily. Credit cards: Yes. Serving: D, SB (first Sun. of each month). Price: Expensive. Cuisine: Locavore. Handicapped access: Yes. Special features: Seasonal menus, early-bird specials, happy hour, wine pairing dinners, tasting menu, wine club, cooking classes, separate lounge, extensive wine list, small patio, unisex restroom, reserva-

tions recommended. Located in the PoNo (Port Norfolk) neighborhood, west of Olde Towne, this chef-owned and chef-operated spot, very much a personal work of art, earns rave reviews for both its creative cuisine and quirky decor, much of it colorful primitives created by Chef Sydney Meers. The menu, divided into small and large plates, reflects his eclectic tastes, Southern roots, and many career moves, including a Sextuple Truffle selected for the *Death by Chocolate* cookbook, and pimento cheese featured in *Southern Living*. Relishes and dressings, desserts and breads are all made by Meers, who also smokes his own meats and tomatoes, and grows many of the vegetables and herbs in his own garden. Cheeses, meats, mushrooms, and seafood come from Virginia providers, making Stove an outpost of the Slow Food movement.

BAKERIES & COFFEE SHOPS

"1" **A Latte Cafe** (757-625-2326), 321 Granby Street, Norfolk 23510. Coffeehouse on Granby offers outdoor seating, free Wi-Fi. Open weekdays.

Chocollage (757-533-5335), 201 College Place; Norfolk 23510. Little coffeehouse and bakery in the Freemason District is a comfortable spot to relax and enjoy a piece of delicious cake.

"1" **Fair Grounds Coffee** (757-640-2899; www.fairgroundscoffee.com), 806 Baldwin Avenue, #2, Norfolk 23517. Favorite Ghent hangout above the Texture gallery serves fair trade coffee and healthy foods; free Wi-Fi, international newspapers, outdoor patio.

"1" **JoJack's Espresso Bar & Cafe** (757-483-1483; www.jojackscafe.com), 5700 Churchland Boulevard, Churchland Shopping Center, Portsmouth

23703. Free Wi-Fi, plus nice breakfast and lunch menu.

✪ **Rowena's Tea Room** (757-627-8699 or 800-627-8699; www.rowenas.com), 758 W. 22nd Street, Norfolk 23517. A 6-foot-tall white rabbit guards the entrance of this Norfolk institution, where Rowena Fullinwider makes her justly famous almond pound cakes, lemon curd, and carrot jam. In back, a tearoom offers light lunches and afternoon tea. Call for hours and factory tours.

✪ ⌖ **Starboards Coffee Kiosk** (757-478-0056; www.starboards.biz), 101 High Street, Portsmouth 23704. Locally owned stand at High Street Landing serves up iced coffee made with coffee ice cubes, hot coffee drinks, muffins, and breakfast sandwiches, along with maps and tourist info.

BARBECUE ✪ ⌀ ⅋ **Doumar's Cones & Barbecue** (757-627-4163; www.doumars.com), 1919 Monticello Avenue at 20th, Norfolk 23517. Eat inside at the counter or outside in your car at this old-style diner and drive-in that makes waffle cones on a 1907 machine, cooks barbecue on-site, and makes limeades, shakes, and sundaes to order. Open early until very late Mon.–Sat. Cash only.

Rodman's Bones & Buddy's (757-397-3900), 3562 Western Branch Boulevard, Portsmouth 23707. The kind of family barbecue stand you hope will keep cooking pig forever.

⅋ **San Antonio Sam's Texas Grill** (757-623-0233; www.sanantoniosams.com), 1501 Colley Avenue, Norfolk 23517. The locals' choice for ribs and beef brisket, plus other Tex-Mex favorites, in Ghent. **Sam's Texas Sub Shop** (757-333-4098; www.samstexassubshop.com; 4311 Colley Avenue, Norfolk 23508) nearby, serves chili,

oven-baked subs, and beef and pork barbecue.

Wood Chicks BBQ (757-410-9290; www.woodchicksbbq.com), 1620 Cedar Road, Chesapeake 23322. Award-winning wood-smoked meats, and the signature Barbeque Sundae, as featured on the Food Channel and TLC.

BREAKFAST AND CASUAL MEALS ⌀ ⅋ **Broken Egg Bistro** (757-410-8515; www.thebrokeneggbistro.com), 501 Kempsville Road, Chesapeake 23320. Family favorite near Greenbrier Mall serves breakfast and blue plates all day. Second location at Harbor View (757-967-0103; 5860 Harbour View Boulevard, Suffolk 23435).

⌀ ⅋ ⅋ **Brutti's Cafe** (757-393-1923; www.bruttis.com), 467 Court Street, Portsmouth 23704. White-tablecloth spot in Olde Towne Portsmouth offers creative breakfast dishes and fresh pastries, including the popular BagelNutz, plus nights of jazz and a popular Sun. brunch buffet.

⅋ **The Deck Restaurant** (757-398-1221; www.deckrestaurant.com), 10 Crawford Parkway, Portsmouth 23704. Join the locals for Sun. brunch or afternoon cocktails with a scenic water view.

✪ ⌀ ⅋ **D'Egg Diner** (757-626-3447; www.facebook.com/deggdiner), 206 E. Main Street, Norfolk 23510. Restaurateur Phil Decker's downtown diner is a must for homestyle food at breakfast and lunch. Second location in Ghent (757-423-3447; 1170 Lexan Avenue, Norfolk 23508).

⅋ **Donut Dinette** (757-625-0061), 1917 Colley Avenue, Norfolk 23517. For a late-night breakfast after a night of clubbing, Ghent residents swear by the homemade doughnuts at this 1950s-style relic that serves breakfast 6

AM–2 PM daily but opens at midnight Fri. and Sat. nights.

♈ **Frank's Trucking Center** (757-488-8337; www.frankstruckstop.com), 4717 W. Military Highway, Chesapeake 23321. Conveniently located just off the interstates, this family-owned truck stop has been serving breakfast 24/7 for more than 50 years. Try the fried salt herring with corn bread, a local favorite.

Yorgo's Bageldashery (www.yorgos bageldashery.com), two Norfolk locations: **Historic Ghent** (757-623-6609; 2123 Colonial Avenue at 22nd) and downtown at **Selden Arcade** (757-623-3649; 215 E. Plume Street). Freshly cooked New York–style kosher water bagels in many flavors topped with cream cheese, lox, or made into a breakfast sandwich. Lots of vegan choices.

COOKING CLASSES AND COOK-YOUR-OWN Culinary Institute of Virginia (757-858-2433 or 866-619-CHEF; www.chefva.com), 2428 Almeda Avenue, Norfolk 23513. Cooking classes with professional chefs.

The Grate Steak (757-461-5501; www.thegratesteak.com), 235 N. Military Highway, Norfolk 23502. One of the few survivors of the '80s cook-your-own fad lets you pick your own steak, then cook it over charcoal, while enjoying trips to the 40-item salad bar.

Kitchen Koop (757-399-4475; www.kitchenkoop.com), 638 High Street, Portsmouth 23704. Learn Southern cooking secrets at classes on canning and other household skills. Shop also stocks many unusual kitchen utensils and exclusive Olde Towne Blend coffee.

FARMS, FARMER'S MARKETS & VEGETABLE STANDS Bennett's Creek Farm Market and Deli (757-484-9722; www.peanutsandpork.com), 3881 Bridge Road, Suffolk 23435. Locally grown produce, specialty meats from Edwards, plus grab-and-go meals. Look for the cow on the roof.

Chesapeake Farmers' Market (757-382-6348; www.cityofchesapeake.net), Chesapeake City Park, 900 Greenbrier Parkway, Chesapeake 23320. Seasonal, Wed., Sat., and Sun.

✪ ↬ **Five Points Community Farm Market** (757-853-0300; www.5pts farmmarket.org), 2500 Church Street at 26th, Norfolk 23504. Fresh local produce, organic eggs, and free-range meats, plus fresh crabs and seafood. The **Get Fresh Cafe** (757-966-6577) on-site offers smoked fish, ribs, and chicken, as well as dinners to go, healthy cooking classes, and more. Open year-round, Wed.–Sun.

Full Quiver Farm (757-539-5324; www.fullquiverfarm.com), 2801 Manning Road, Suffolk 23434. Organic produce, pasture-raised meats, brown eggs.

Lilley Farms and Nursery (757-484-3448; www.lilleyfarms.com), 2800 Tyre Neck Road, Chesapeake 23321. Pick strawberries from raised beds.

Olde Towne Portsmouth Farmers Market (757-537-9482 or 757-397-2616; www.oldetowneportsmouth .com), Middle Street, between High and Queen, Portsmouth 23704. First Sat. of every month.

Town Point Saturday Markets (757-441-2345; www.festeventsva.org), Town Point Park, Norfolk. Vendors offer local produce, handmade items, and more, Apr.–Oct., plus holiday markets in Nov. and Dec.

FAST FOOD Dog-N-Burger Grille (757-623-1667; www.dognburger.com), 2001 Manteo Street, Norfolk 23517. Hole-in-the-wall sandwich shop, run by the No Frill Grill folks, is a great place for a quick bite in Ghent. Menu runs well beyond dogs to gyros and grilled tuna wraps.

⚓ **Doug's Hot Dogs** (757-587-0370; www.dougshotdogsov.com), 9643 Granby Street, Norfolk 23503. Little stand across from Ocean View beach serves famous chili dogs and local clam chowder.

Moseberth's Chicken (757-393-1721; www.moseberths.com), 1505 Airline Boulevard/US 58, Portsmouth 23707. Try the livers or gizzards, or order up a family pack to go, at this Portsmouth landmark, serving old-fashioned fried chicken (also available roasted or barbecued) since 1940.

Tony Jr's Hot Dogs (757-857-6351), 2611 Lafayette Boulevard, Norfolk 23509. Don't dare ask for ketchup at this little trailer, serving award-winning chili dogs for more than 40 years.

NATURAL FOODS AND VEGETARIAN MENUS As home of PETA's international headquarters, Norfolk has many vegan and vegetarian-friendly restaurants. PETA (www.goveg.com) ranks it the number four dining destination for vegetarians among America's small cities. You'll find the greatest concentration of options in the Ghent neighborhood.

Amalfi Ristorante (757-625-1262; www.amalfiristorante.net), 2010 Colley Avenue, Norfolk 23517. Complete vegan menu, including vegan "meatballs" and cheesecake.

Ⲩ **Bardo Edibles + Elixirs** (757-622-7362; www.bardoeats.com), 430 W. 21st Street, Norfolk 23517. Trendy Ghent tapas bar offers inventive vegetarian and vegan dishes, including a dozen styles of edamame.

Charlie's Cafe (757-625-0824), 1800 Granby Street, Norfolk 23517. Popular

little diner in Ghent serves only breakfast and lunch, with several vegetarian options.

Health Food Center (757-625-6656; www.healthfoodcenters.com), 1701 Colley Avenue, Norfolk 23517. Vegetarian and vegan market in Ghent also stocks organic turkey products, herbs, and supplements. Location at **Wards Corner** (757-489-4242; 7639 Granby Street, Norfolk 23505) has a juice bar.

Kotobuki Japanese Restaurant (757-628-1025), 721 W. 21st Street, Norfolk 23517. Excellent sushi, plus a big vegan menu.

Machismo Burrito Bar (757-624-2424; www.machismoburritobar.com), 409 W. York Street, Norfolk 23510. Burritos and tacos with Boca crumbles, vegan sour cream, and vegan cheese. Additional location in Virginia Beach (757-422-6010; 525 N. Birdneck Road).

Rajput Indian Cuisine (757-625-4634; www.rajputonline.com), 742 W. 21st Street, Norfolk 23517. Full vegetarian and vegan menu, plus vegan buffets and take-out.

Ten Top (757-622-5422; www.thetentop.com), 748 Shirley Avenue, Norfolk 23517. Many vegetarian selections at this Ghent spot, serving lunch, dinner, and Sun. brunch.

PIZZA Amore Casual Italian (757-337-8382; www.amorecasualitalian.com), 606 High Street, Portsmouth 23704. Italian specialties and pizza in Olde Towne.

Ⲩ **Cogan's Pizza** (757-627-6428; www.coganspizza.com), 1901 Colonial Avenue, Norfolk 23517. Cool spot with lots of collectibles and nearly three dozen beers on tap serves Ghent's favorite pizza. Second location, in Suffolk (757-686-9500; 5860 Harbour View Boulevard).

Ψ **Granby Street Pizza** (757-622-5084; www.granbystreetpizza.com), 235 Granby Street, Norfolk 23510. Convenient location in downtown serves New York–style pizza by the pie or the slice, plus burgers, gyros, and beer and wine. Late-night weekend hours. Free delivery, or eat on the outdoor patio.

✔ **Spaghetti Eddie's** (757-484-7301; www.spaghettieddiespizzacafe.com), 3325 Taylor Road, Chesapeake 23321. Family favorite is a consistent winner of local awards.

SANDWICHES & TAKE-OUT
French Bakery & Delicatessen (757-625-4936), 4108 Granby Street, Norfolk 23504. Locals rave about the huge pastrami sandwiches here, complain about the prices and the service. Roll the dice.

21st Street Deli (757-626-3232; www.21ststreetdeli.com), 222 W. 21st Street, Norfolk 23517. Award-winning deli subs and sandwiches in Ghent.

SEAFOOD ✔ Ψ **Captain Groovy's Grill and Raw Bar** (757-965-4667; www.captgroovysgrillandrawbar.com), 8101 Shore Drive, Norfolk 23518. Fun spot in Ocean View specializes in fresh (never frozen or farm raised) fish, daily happy hour, microbrews, Sun. brunch.

Tabb's at Riverview (757-626-0871; www.tabbsatriverview.com), 4019 Granby Street, Norfolk 23504. Local favorite for seafood serves award-winning fried oysters.

SPECIALTY MARKETS Azar's Market & Cafe (757-664-7955; www.azarfoods.com), 2000 Colley Avenue, Norfolk 23517. Healthy Mediterranean food in Ghent.

Gene Walter's Market Place (757-625-2705; www.farmfreshsupermarkets.com), 730 W. 21st Street, Norfolk

23517. Upscale grocery in Ghent offers online ordering and delivery; big selection of microbrews, wines, cheese, sushi, and seafood.

✪ **The Market at Harbor Heights** (757-213-7396; www.harborheights.net), 260 Boush Street, Norfolk 23510. Unique urban market on the Norfolk waterfront offers a variety of gourmet foods, including ready-to-eat items, extensive cheese and wine sections, steamed seafood bar, and free parking on its deck.

SPORTS BARS Ψ Baxter's A Sports Lounge (757-622-9837; www.baxterssportslounge.com), 500 Granby Street, Norfolk 23510. Upscale sports lounge in downtown Norfolk with 70 TVs, outdoor patio, happy hour specials. Dress code. Dancing on weekends.

Ψ "†" ✎ **Roger Brown's Sports Bar** (757-399-5377; www.rogerbrowns.com), 316 High Street, Portsmouth 23704. Enormous sports bar owned by a former NFL star boasts booths with speakers, stadium seating with HD TVs, even TVs in the restrooms, plus pool and arcade room, patio, free Wi-Fi, and a reasonably priced menu, including the local classic chicken and waffles.

Ψ **Shula's 347** (757-282-6347; www.shulas347norfolk.com), 235 E. Main Street, Norfolk 23510. Located inside the Waterside Marriott, this upscale sports bar has legendary steaks, plenty of flat-panel TVs, and a casual vibe.

WINE SHOPS, WINE BARS, AND BREWPUBS Ψ ✎ Bier Garden (757-393-6022; www.biergarden.com), 434 High Street, Portsmouth 23704. Tucked away in Olde Towne, this fun spot serves Bavarian dishes and a deep list of German and English drafts.

Let's Talk Wine (757-204-4720; www.letstalkwine.net), 236 Carmichael Way, Chesapeake 23322. Wine, cheese, beer, and chocolates from around the world. Weekly wine tastings.

Y ↝ Passion Restaurant and Wine Bar (757-410-3975; www.passionthe restaurant.com), 1036 Volvo Parkway, Shoppes at Greenbrier, Chesapeake 23320. Upscale locavore restaurant offers many wines by the glass; hosts frequent wine tastings and happy hour.

Y ↝ Press626 Cafe and Wine Bar (757-282-6234; www.press626.com), 626 W. Olney Road at Colley Avenue, Norfolk 23507. Wine bar in a big old house in Ghent offers pressed sandwiches, small plates, a build-your-own salad, Sun. brunch, and 50 wines under $50.

Y Tap House Grill At Ghent (757-627-9172; www.myspace.com/the taphouse), 931 W. 21st Street, Norfolk 23517. With more than 40 beers on tap, many vegan entrées, and frequent live music, this is a vegetarian's top choice for nightlife, but it's fun for meat eaters, too.

✳ Selective Shopping

Each of the cities in this region has some special shopping opportunities. Norfolk and Chesapeake are noted for their malls, especially the unique **MacArthur Center** in downtown Norfolk. The neighborhood of **Ghent** (www.destinationghent.com) contains many eclectic shops along the W. 21st Street corridor.

A short ferry ride across the Elizabeth River, a stroll along High Street in **Old Towne Portsmouth** (www.oldetowne portsmouth.com) passes numerous antiques shops, galleries, and museums.

Chesapeake

⊤ **Chesapeake Square** (757-488-9636; www.simon.com), 4200 Portsmouth Boulevard, Chesapeake 23321. Anchored by six major department stores, this mall, located off I-664 exit 11B, contains the freestanding **Cinemark Movies 1** (757-465-0266; www.cinemark.com) and a minigolf course.

Greenbrier Mall (757-424-7100; www.greenbriermall.com), 1401 Greenbrier Parkway, Chesapeake 23320. Located off I-64, this large two-level mall is home to Dillard's, JCPenney, Macy's, and Sears, plus 120 other shops and the popular **Cinema Café** (757-523-SHOW; www.cinema-cafe.com), a discount movie house. Visit the customer service desk for exclusive coupons, complimentary wheelchairs, and rental strollers.

Towne Place at Greenbrier (803-227-1294; www.towneplaceatgreen brier.com), 725 Eden Way N., Chesapeake 23320. Cluster of upscale shops and restaurants hosts a summer concert series on Fri. evenings, art shows, and other events. Restaurants include the three-story **Paradocks East Coast Grille** (757-321-2202; www.paradocks grille.com), with great nightly specials and dining on the deck.

Norfolk

The Gallery at Military Circle (757-461-1940; www.galleryatmilitarycircle .com), 880 N. Military Highway, Norfolk 23502. Shopping complex with a covered atrium and more than 140 shops and restaurants, including a large food court and the **Cinemark 18** (757-461-8200; www.cinemark.com).

⁌1⁍ **JANAF Shopping Yard** (757-461-4954; www.janafshopping.com), 5900 E. Virginia Beach Boulevard at Military Highway, Norfolk 23502. Nearly 1 million square feet of shopping, including national brands such as Old Navy, TJ Maxx, Sports Authority, and Marshalls, plus ample parking and lots of dining options, including **Panera Bread** (757-466-1881; www.panera bread.com), with free Wi-Fi.

✪ ✐ ♿ ♞ **MacArthur Center** (757-627-6000; www.shopmacarthur.com), 300 Monticello Avenue, Norfolk 23510. Located in the heart of downtown Norfolk close to the waterfront, this three-level, 1-million-square-foot shopping destination includes prominent national brands such as Nordstrom, Dillard's, Abercrombie & Fitch, Banana Republic, Pottery Barn, and Williams-Sonoma, plus 140 other upscale shops, and the 18-screen **Regal Cinemas** (757-623-7500; www.regmovies.com), surrounding a 70-foot-tall atrium. Next to the food court on the third level, the unique **Looney Tunes Play Port** features Bugs Bunny and his friends hand-sculpted from kid-friendly foam, and a mural painted by Warner Bros. artists. Complimentary strollers and motorized wheelchairs available. Two decks provide parking for very reasonable fees ($1 for the first three hours); RV parking available at the South Deck off City Hall Avenue and Cumberland Street.

✪ **The Palace Shops and Palace Station** (757-622-9999; www.palace shops.com), 301 W. 21st Street, Norfolk 23517. This distinctive shopping complex in historic Ghent, which takes its inspiration from Madame Pompadour's Petit Trianon at the Palace of Versailles, houses a harmonious collection of boutiques, antiques, gift and craft shops, and restaurants, including a day spa, a bike shop, and **Pasha Mezze** (757-627-1318; www.pasha mezze.com), serving healthy Mediterranean cuisine, including many vege-

tarian and vegan dishes, all close to convenient courtyard parking. Noted Palm Beach architect John B. Gosman designed the Palace's 55-foot tower and Temple of the Winds columns.

✪ **Waterside Festival Marketplace** (757-627-3300; www.watersidemarket place.com), 333 Waterside Marketplace, Norfolk 23510. Located next to the ferry landing, the cruise dock, and Town Point Park, this two-story complex is a favorite for visitors arriving by land or sea. Galleries and specialty shops, such as **All About Virginia** (757-623-4551), rub shoulders with nightclubs and restaurants, including Hooters, Outback Steakhouse, and **Joe's Crab Shack** (757-625-0655; www.joescrabshack.com), with patio dining overlooking the harbor. And if you're looking for something fast, Waterside has an international food court decorated with mermaids.

ANTIQUES

Norfolk and Chesapeake
Creek Emporium (757-485-1006), 919 Canal Drive, Chesapeake 23323. More than 50 dealers feature antiques, flow blue, furniture, and pottery.

Futures Antiques (757-624-2050; www.futuresantiques.com), 3824 Granby Street, Norfolk 23504. Fun store deals in 20th-century art, collectibles, and cultural artifacts, from high style to kitsch.

Randy's Auction Gallery (757-626-1919; www.randysauctiongallery.com), 1300 Monticello Avenue, Norfolk 23510. Estate auctions, business liquidations, and more.

Portsmouth
Antique Adventures Ltd (757-398-8763; antiqueadventuresltd.com), 507 High Street, Portsmouth 23704. Shop at the Governor Dinwiddie Hotel spe-

cializes in signed Tiffany & Co. pieces, including silver, bronze, glass, and clocks.

High Street Antiques (757-397-9007), 623 High Street, Portsmouth 23704. Specializing in Depression glass, Fiesta, and Hall.

Nearthebay Antiques (757-393-3301; www.nearthebayantiques.com), 310 High Street, Portsmouth 23704. Antiques and collectibles displayed in an 1879 jewelry store lined with mahogany cabinets.

The Queen Bees (757-397-3939), 425 High Street, Portsmouth 23704. Sweet shop in Olde Towne carries furniture, jewelry, and kitchen utensils dating as far back as the Civil War, plus a special section of children's toys.

Way Back Yonder Antiques (757-398-2700; www.waybackyonder antiques.com), 620 High Street, Devon Square, Portsmouth 23704. Shop in Olde Towne displays a wide variety of 18th- and 19th-century antiques in a huge showroom.

BOOKS & MUSIC **Bibliophile Book Shop** (757-622-2665; www .bibliophilebookshop.com), 251 W. Bute Street, Norfolk 23510. Shop in the Freemason District stocks used and out-of-print books, including some rare first editions.

The Book Exchange at Wards Corner (757-583-2665; www.book exchangenorfolk.com), 116 E. Little Creek Road, Norfolk 23505. Largest selection of used books in eastern Virginia, plus DVDs, VHS tapes, and CDs.

Book Owl Books (757-638-7323; www.bookowlbooks.com), 5772 Churchland Boulevard, Churchland Shopping Center, Portsmouth 23707. Independent bookstore with new and used books, CDs, and DVDs hosts author signings and monthly poetry readings.

Local Heroes (757-383-6810; www .localheroescomics.com), 1905 Colonial Avenue, Norfolk 23517. Store in Ghent stocks independent and small-press comics, plus graphic novels.

✪ **Prince Books** (757-622-9223; www.prince-books.com), 109 E. Main Street, Norfolk 23510. Located just steps from the waterfront in downtown Norfolk, this cool store has something for all ages, including many regional titles, and hosts frequent book signings. The **Lizard Cafe** (757-622-5973) on-site offers sandwiches, salads, and soups made with local produce, plus coffee and other refreshments.

Skinnie's Records (757-622-2241; www.skinniesrecords.com), 2119 Colonial Avenue, Norfolk 23517. Indie record store carries hard-to-find new and collectible vinyl and CDs, specializing in punk, metal, shredder, Oi, and stoner music.

CLOTHING **Commonwealth Boutique** (757-622-3372; www.cmon wealth.com), 717 W. 21st Street, Norfolk 23517. Cutting-edge shop in Ghent features creative fashion and frequent in-store events combining art, music, fashion.

✪ **Eklectik Funk Boutique** (757-295-3294; www.eklectikfunk.com), 331 High Street, Portsmouth 23704. Jewelry, dresses, and children's apparel, handcrafted by local designers.

CONSIGNMENT **2nd Act Consignments** (757-622-1533; www.2ndact consignments.com), 110-A W. 21st Street, Norfolk 23517. Stylish women's clothing and accessories in like-new condition.

✐ **The White Rabbit and The Wild Hare** (757-627-4169 or 757-622-7465),

334 W. 21st Street, Norfolk 23517. Companion consignment stores in Ghent's Palace Shops feature children's and adult's clothing, plus handcrafted toys and gifts, jewelry, and garden statues.

CRAFTS ✐ ↑ **Color Me Mine** (757-625-1666; www.norfolk.colormemine .com), 1300 Colley Avenue, Norfolk 23517. Paint-your-own ceramics studio in Ghent offers more than four hundred designs.

✐ ↑ **Gläzenfyre** (757-436-9990; www.glazenfyre.com), 501 Kempsville Road, Greenbrier Shoppes, Chesapeake 23320. Paint your own pottery, plus classes in clay, mosaics, and jewelry for all ages. Summer art camps and Kids' Night Out. Second location in Virginia Beach (757-456-2787; Independence Boulevard, Pembroke Plaza Shopping Center).

✐ ↑ **Potts N Paints** (757-436-7373; www.mypottsnpaints.com), 920 S. Battlefield Boulevard, Chesapeake 23322; plus two locations in Virginia Beach. Paint your own pottery, plus classes in clay molding and wheel throwing, summer camps, and clay parties.

FLEA MARKETS & THRIFT SHOPS ✺ **First Saturday Olde Towne Antiques to Flea Market** (757-405-3500; www.oldetowneports mouth.com), Middle Street Garage, corner of Middle and London streets, Portsmouth. Held year-round rain or shine on the first Sat. of each month, this fun event attracts more than a hundred dealers and vendors. Free admission and parking.

↑ **The Flea Market at SoNo** (757-248-1465; www.fleamarketatsono.com), 2425 Bainbridge Boulevard, Chesapeake 23324. Large building full of independent shops and bargains.

Friends of the Library Monthly Book Sale (757-393-8501; www .portsmouthpubliclibrary.org), 601 Court Street, Portsmouth 23704. Buy books by the inch. Held on the second Sat. of every month.

✺ **Hope House Thrift Shop** (757-625-7493; www.hope-house.org), 1800 Monticello Avenue, Norfolk 23517. All the proceeds from this unique shop across from Doumar's go to help people with disabilities.

GIFTS **Emerson's** (757-624-1520; www.emersonscigars.com), 116 Granby Street, Norfolk 23510. Shop near the waterfront carries cigars and tobacco products from around the world in a relaxing atmosphere. Smoking lounge with TV, stereo, and beverage area.

✺ ↝ **Green Alternatives** (757-622-1444; www.greenalternativesstore .com), 2500 Church Street, Norfolk 23504. Earth-friendly general store carries only items that are all natural, sustainable, recycled, biodegradable, or reusable. Frequent free workshops.

✐ **Mystic Mermaid** (757-618-6345; www.mysticmermaid.net), 308 W. 21st Street, Palace Shops, Norfolk 23517. Unique shop in Ghent is full of artful displays and mermaids.

✐ **The Silver Rattle** (757-622-4399; www.thesilverrattle.com), 3822 Granby Street, Norfolk 23504. Toys, gifts, clothing, and furnishings for babies and children, including unique VintageLily items, crafted locally by skilled seamstresses.

Treasures Feathers & Fins (757-588-4443; www.treasuresfeathers fins.com), 9563 Shore Drive, Norfolk 23518. Fun store in Ocean View is chock-full of nautical gifts and home decor, including beach art, mermaid prints, and parrot head merchandise.

HOME DECOR Calvin & Lloyd
(757-626-1742; www.calvinandlloyd
.com), 338 W. 21st Street, Palace
Shops, Norfolk 23517. Unique home
accessories, crafts, furniture, and original art.

DecorEklect (757-622-0771; www
.decoreklect.com), 501 Botetourt
Street, Norfolk 23510. Top brands
offered at factory direct pricing. Additional location in Virginia Beach (757-
430-7628; 1941 General Booth
Boulevard).

Garden Gazebo (757-623-1717;
www.gardengazebo.com), 729 W. 21st
Street, Norfolk 23507. Fun store in
Ghent carries indoor and outdoor
decor. Second location in Pembroke
Mall, Virginia Beach (757-490-8922).

JEWELRY Long Jewelers (757-436-
1920; www.longjewelers.com), 701 N.
Battlefield Boulevard, Woodford
Shoppes, Chesapeake 23320. Largest
selection of designer lines in the
region. Additional stores located in Virginia Beach.

Spertner Jewelers (757-583-1559;
www.spertner.com), 9605 Granby Street,
Norfolk 23503. Mermaids and other city
mascot jewelry in silver and gold.

✳ Special Events

For Norfolk and Ocean View events,
visit www.festeventsva.org. For events
in Portsmouth, visit www.portsva
events.com. **FirstEvents in Olde
Towne Portsmouth** (757-397-7173;
www.portsvaevents.com) are held the
first Friday through Sunday of each
month, including First Friday open
houses at area businesses, galleries,
and museums; the Saturday morning
farmer's market at the Courthouse
Galleries Parking Lot; and the Olde
Towne Antiques to Flea Market in the
Middle Street Garage, Sat. 10–2. On

First Sunday, many Olde Towne
restaurants offer special meal deals.
January: **Martin Luther King March
and Observance** (757-664-4253;
www.norfolk.gov/mlk), Scope Plaza and
Chrysler Hall, Norfolk.

Norfolk Winter Restaurant Week
(www.norfolkrestaurantweek.com).

**"Redeem the Dream" Step Show
Competition** (757-420-3599; www
.betathetazeta.org), Waterside Marriott, Norfolk.

Virginia Festival of Jewish Film
(757-321-2338; www.jewishva.org),
Roper Performing Arts Center, Norfolk.

February: **Chesapeake Bay Wine
Classic Grand Tasting** (757-200-
9463; www.cbwc.org), Norfolk.

Fat Tuesday Mardi Gras Party
(757-441-2345; www.festeventsva.org),
Waterside, Norfolk. Free.

**Ghent Winter Bar Tour Charity
Pub Crawl** (www.ghentbartour.com),
Norfolk.

**Portsmouth Founder's Day Cele-
bration** (www.portsvaevents.com).
Living-history tours of Olde Towne
Portsmouth.

March: ✪ **St. Patrick's Day Parade
and After Party** (757-587-3548;
www.norfolkparade.com), Norfolk.

Suffolk Restaurant Week (757-514-
4130; www.suffolk-fun.com/restaurant
week).

Taste of Hampton Roads (757-627-
6599; www.tasteofhamptonroads.org),
Norfolk.

April: **Hall of Fame Weekend** (757-
393-8031; www.virginiasportshallof
fame.com), Virginia Sports Hall of
Fame & Museum, Portsmouth.

✿ **Norfolk NATO Festival** (757-605-
3073; www.azaleafestival.org), Town
Point Park and other venues. Former
International Azalea Festival cele-

brates the NATO alliance with a Parade of Nations through downtown Norfolk and a free all-day festival at Town Point.

Portsmouth Power in the Park (757-460-2201; www.powerinthepark .com), Portsmouth City Park. Power-boat races.

Portsmouth Restaurant Week (www .eatinportsmouthva.com).

Virginia International Tattoo Parade of Bands (www.vafest.com), High Street, Portsmouth.

May: ✪ **Chesapeake Jubilee** (757-482-4848; www.chesapeakejubilee.org), Chesapeake City Park.

Elizabeth River Run 10k Race (757-393-89831; www.tidewater striders.com).

Gosport Arts Festival (www.gosport artsfestival.com), Olde Towne Ports-mouth. Juried art show benefits EDMARC Hospice for Children.

✪ **Great Dismal Swamp Birding Festival** (757-986-3705; www.fws.gov), 3100 Desert Road, Suffolk.

✪ **Greek Festival** (757-440-0500; www.norfolkgreekfestival.com), Annunciation Greek Orthodox Cathe-dral, 7220 Granby Street, Norfolk. The Tidewater's oldest and largest ethnic festival.

Memorial Day Parade (www.ports vaevents.com), Portsmouth. The nation's oldest annually held parade travels down High Street.

Olde Towne Pub Crawl (www.olde townepubcrawl.org), Portsmouth.

Spring Town Point Virginia Wine Festival (757-441-2345; www.fest eventsva.org), Town Point Park, Nor-folk.

✪ **Stockley Gardens Spring Arts Festival** (757-625-6161; www.hope -house.org), Ghent, Norfolk.

Suffolk Raceway Reunion Car Show (757-514-4130 or 866-SEE-SUFK; www.suffolk-fun.com), Suffolk Executive Airport.

Virginia Regional Festival of Flight (757-923-2487; www.virginiaflyin.org), Suffolk Executive Airport. Oldest and largest "fly-in" in the Mid-Atlantic.

June: ✪ **American Indian Festival** (757-382-8466; www.nansemond.org), Chesapeake City Park.

Bayou Boogaloo & Cajun Food Festival (757-441-2345; www.fest eventsva.org), Town Point Park, Nor-folk.

Big Bands on the Bay (757-441-2345; www.festeventsva.org), Ocean View Beach Park, Norfolk. Sun. evenings Memorial Day–Labor Day. Free.

Cock Island Race (www.portsmouth va.gov), Portsmouth waterfront. Called the Best Sailing Event on the East Coast. Public parties at North Land-ing.

✪ ✪ **Harborfest** (757-441-2345; www.festeventsva.org), downtown Nor-folk waterfront. Parade of Sail with vis-iting tall ships from around the world, plus ship tours, nautical activities, live music, fireworks, and more.

Juneteenth Festival (757-648-8549; www.juneteenthva.com), Dr. Clarence Cuffee Community Center, 2019 Windy Road, Chesapeake.

River Rhythms Seawall Festival (757-393-5111; www.portsmouthva .gov), Olde Towne Portsmouth. Coin-cides with Norfolk's Harborfest.

Willoughby Secret Garden Tour (757-587-8711; www.willoughbyon theweb.com), Ocean View, Norfolk.

July: **Cheroenhaka (Nottoway) Indian Pow Wow** (757-562-7760; www.cheroenhaka-nottoway.org), Southampton County Fair Grounds, Courtland.

❧ **Fourth of July Great American Picnic and Fireworks** (757-441-2345; www.festeventsva.org), Town Point Park, Norfolk. Free.

Ghent Summer Bar Tour Charity Pub Crawl (www.ghentbartour.com), Norfolk.

Norfolk Jazz Festival (757-441-2345; www.festeventsva.org), Town Point Park, Norfolk.

Norfolk Summer Restaurant Week (www.norfolkrestaurantweek.com).

Ocean View Crab and Seafood Feast (www.ovontheweb.com), Ocean View Beach Park, Norfolk.

Sacred Music Summer Conference (757-455-3376; www.vwc.edu), Virginia Wesleyan College, Norfolk. Evening programs open to the public.

Shore Thing Concert and Independence Day Celebration (757-441-2345; www.festeventsva.org), Ocean View Beach Park, Norfolk.

✪ **TGOV—Thank Goodness It's Ocean View Beach Party and Music Series** (757-441-2345; www.festeventsva.org), Ocean View Beach Park, Norfolk. Fri. evenings July–Aug. Free.

THE VIRGINIA ARTS FESTIVAL

A seven-week-long extravaganza of the arts held from mid-April to the end of May each year, the **Virginia Arts Festival** (757-282-2800 or 800-982-2787; www.vafest.org; 220 Boush Street, Norfolk 23510) hosts events throughout the Hampton Roads region with performances in Norfolk, Virginia Beach, Newport News, Hampton, Suffolk, Portsmouth, and a special series in Williamsburg.

Offering something for every taste, the festival includes classical, folk, and world music and dance performances featuring top international groups, plus outdoor events on the Virginia Beach Boardwalk and Town Point Park in Norfolk, a free Caribbean music festival, a Virginia beer festival, theater performances and art exhibits, a chamber music series at regional churches, morning coffee concerts, and performances especially for children, including the free **International Children's Festival** in Hampton.

Many of the events take place in Norfolk, including a jazz series at the historic Attucks Theatre and the festival's signature event—the **Virginia International Tattoo.** Considered the don't-miss concert of the festival, the tattoo is the largest show of its kind in the United States, featuring marching bands from around the world, plus bagpipes and drums, drill teams, gymnasts, Scottish dancers, and choirs, forming a massed band more than eight hundred strong. The night before the tattoo, the bands parade through Olde Towne Portsmouth.

Tickets to Virginia Arts Festival events are available in advance through Ticketmaster (www.ticketmaster.com) or at the festival box office in Norfolk's MacArthur Center. Dinner and a Show packages available. Check the festival Web site for a listing of free events.

August: **Little Creek Offshore Tournament** (757-362-3600; www.little creekmarina.com), Little Creek Marina, Norfolk.

Mid-Atlantic Car Show (www .mustangcluboftidewater.com), Chesapeake City Park, Chesapeake.

✪ **Nansemond Tribal Pow Wow** (252-771-2476; www.nansemond.org), Lone Star Lake Lodge, Suffolk.

Norfolk Latino Music Festival (757-441-2345; www.festeventsva.org), Town Point Park, Norfolk. Free.

Portsmouth Seawall Art Show (757-393-8983; www.seawallartshow.org), High Street Landing, Olde Towne Portsmouth.

September: **Acoustic Music Festival** (757-441-2345; www.festeventsva.org), Town Point Park, Norfolk. Free.

Books in the Park (757-441-2345; www.festeventsva.org), TowneBank Fountain Park, Norfolk. Free.

Mid Atlantic Black Film Festival (757-622-4763; www.mabff.org), Crispus Attucks Cultural Center, Norfolk.

Mid-Autumn Moon Festival (757-441-2345; www.festeventsva.org), TowneBank Fountain Park, Norfolk. Asian festival. Free.

Taste of Suffolk: A Downtown Street Festival (757-514-4130; www .suffolk-fun.com), N. Main Street, Suffolk.

✎ **UMOJA African American Culture and Heritage Festival** (757-393-8481; www.umojafestportsmouth .com), nTelos Pavilion & Festival Park, Portsmouth. Traditional African drum call, African foods and crafts, heritage tours, and live concerts. Free.

October: **Art D'vine Wine Tasting and Art Auction** (757-923-0003; www.suffolkcenter.org), Suffolk Center for Cultural Arts, Suffolk.

Chesapeake Bay Art Association Outdoor Art Show (757-588-4805; www.chesapeakebayartsassociation.com, Ocean View Beach Park, Norfolk.

✪ **Great Chesapeake Bay Schooner Race** (757-480-4402; www.schooner race.org), North Ferry Landing,

TALL SHIPS FROM AROUND THE WORLD SAIL TO NORFOLK'S ANNUAL HARBORFEST.

Portsmouth. Annual sailboat race from Baltimore to Portsmouth ends with a festival on the docks.

Olde Towne Fall Charity Pub Crawl (www.oldetownefallcrawl.com), Portsmouth.

Riverview and Colonial Place Front Porch Art Walk (www.cprv.org), Norfolk.

Stockley Gardens Fall Arts Festival (757-625-6161; www.hope-house.org), Ghent, Norfolk.

✪ ✍ **Suffolk Peanut Festival** (757-539-6751; www.suffolkfest.org), Suffolk Executive Airport, Suffolk. Four-day free festival with parade, concerts, arts and crafts, motorcycle rally, fireworks, and more.

TGIF Brewfest (757-441-2345; www.festeventsva.org), TowneBank Fountain Park, Norfolk. Free.

✪ **Town Point Virginia Wine Festival** (757-441-2345; www.festeventsva.org), Town Point Park, Norfolk.

100 MILES OF LIGHTS

Each year, the cities and towns from Richmond right down to Virginia Beach put on their party clothes and light up for the holidays. A special Web site (www.100milesoflights.com) makes it easy to find holiday events for the entire region from November 1 through early January, and special tour packages are available.

Highlights of the 100 Miles of Lights include lighted boat parades in Richmond, Hampton, Yorktown, and Portsmouth; holiday markets; museum open houses; candlelight home and plantation tours; ice skating, Kwanzaa celebrations; seasonal plays; Santa parades; and Scottish bagpipe strolls. The skylines of Norfolk, Portsmouth, and Richmond are outlined with millions of sparkling lights throughout the holidays. Drive-through light displays can be found at Richmond's **Lewis Ginter Botanical Garden** (www.lewisginter.org), in **Newport News Park** (www.nnparks.com), at **Norfolk's Botanical Garden** (www.norfolkbotanicalgarden.org), and on the **Virginia Beach Boardwalk** (www.beachstreetusa.com), where cars travel through a tunnel of lights past more than 250 displays ruled by King Neptune himself.

Colonial Williamsburg (800-447-8679, www.history.org/christmas) kicks off its holiday season with a free **Grand Illumination** celebration with old-fashioned fireworks, fife and drum music, and bonfires in the street. Every year, Williamsburg's residents compete to create the most unusual decorations made entirely from natural greens, fruits, and other materials, from shells to feathers. The results of their efforts are displayed on doors and windows throughout the Historic District, and visitors can participate in special classes to make their own Williamsburg holiday decor. Other special holiday events range from candlelight tours of historic homes to wine dinners hosted by a Thomas Jefferson look-alike.

Call 888-493-7386, ext. 100, or visit www.100milesoflights.com for more information.

✐ **Virginia Children's Festival** (757-441-2345; www.festeventsva.org), Town Point Park, Norfolk.

December: **Battle of Great Bridge Reenactment** (757-482-4480; www.gbbattlefield.org), Chesapeake.

New Year's Eve Lighted Boat Parade (757-650-3052; www.portsvaevents.com), Portsmouth waterfront.

Norfolk Santa Charity Pub Crawl (www.norfolksantacrawl.com).

✐ **Olde Towne Holiday Music Festival and Santa Parade** (www.portsvaevents.com), Portsmouth. Carolers, music performances, and children's activities.

✪ **Olde Towne Scottish Walk** (www.tidewaterscots.org), downtown Portsmouth. Free.

Suffolk Nansemond Historical Society Annual Candlelight Tour (757-539-2781; www.suffolkhistory.org).

✐ **Winter Wonderland: The Coleman Collection** (757-393-8543; www.courthousegalleries.com), Courthouse Galleries, Portsmouth. Annual display of animated figures.

THE OLD DOMINION'S SEASIDE
PLAYGROUND—VIRGINIA BEACH

P eople have visited the shores of Cape Henry, today the site of Virginia Beach, since well before Christopher Newport, John Smith, and their cohorts first climbed the sand dunes in 1607. Members of the Chesepioc tribe lived in the Great Neck region in the years before European contact. The name of the greatest natural harbor in North America, Chesapeake Bay, preserves their memory.

Today, Virginia Beach is the largest city in Virginia, with a year-round population of nearly a half million people. *Guinness World Records* recognizes this as the longest pleasure beach in the world, and many visitors come to "VB" (as locals call it) to enjoy the quintessential beach vacation—sun, sand, and sea—to fish or sail, Jet Ski or surf, eat seafood, build sand castles, or simply lie in the sun.

In recent years, however, the face of the traditional resort has changed with upscale properties both along the oceanfront and inland at the newly developed Town Center catering to both business and upscale luxury travel.

The region also attracts a growing tide of ecotourists, who come to enjoy the many and varied opportunities to kayak the quiet local waters, observing the rich variety of birds and wildlife that frequent the area.

Now a year-round destination with sophisticated nightlife, world-class dining, and an array of attractions appealing to every age and interest, Virginia Beach continues to satisfy all comers, hosting the free Beach Street USA music festival every night of the summer, grooming its 300-foot-wide beach daily, and investing millions in improvements to its 3-mile Boardwalk, public parking, concert venues, bike paths, and many other amenities.

For an outstanding overview of the Virginia Beach area, visit the observation tower on the fourth floor of the **Virginia Beach Convention Center** (757-385-2000; www.vbfun.com; 1000 19th Street, Virginia Beach 23451). Here amid the piped-in songs of dolphins you can scan the beachfront to the east or look south to Rudee Inlet, west to the skyscrapers of Town Center, and north to Chesapeake Bay.

HISTORY

English colonization of the Virginia Beach area, known as Princess Anne County for more than 250 years, began soon after the settlement of Jamestown. Adam

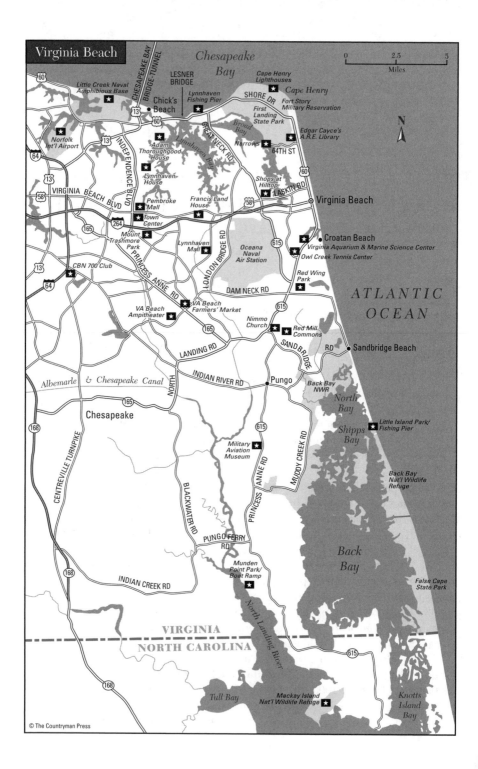

Thoroughgood, a former indentured servant and native of King's Lynn in Norfolk-shire, England, received a land grant in the area in 1635, and others soon followed, settling along the Pungo Ridge, the highest and most fertile land in the region. Some of these families still farm their original grants.

During the 18th century, activity centered on the Lynnhaven River and its many bays and inlets. Plantations, trading stations, chapels, and busy wharfs lined the shores, and shipments of tobacco made the region prosperous.

The Lynnhaven originally could be accessed from the bay only by way of Little Creek, a reportedly torturous trip. At one point, however, the river was separated from the waters of the Chesapeake only by a narrow sandbar. One early settler dug a ditch wide enough for a canoe through the sandbar to shorten the route. No sooner was the ditch finished than a storm swept huge tides through the opening, widening it into Lynnhaven Inlet, today spanned by the Lesner Bridge. In the process, the Lynnhaven River became a bay itself, stretching across 64 square miles. The infusion of seawater gave rise to the region's most popular product in colonial times, the Lynnhaven oyster, noted for its salty tang.

During the years following the Civil War, a belief in the healthful benefits of salt water brought many to the oceanfront, and several hotels were built to wel-come them. These early visitors arrived at the new resort by train beginning in 1883, but in 1922, **Virginia Beach Boulevard** (US 58), the first paved road to link Norfolk with the VB oceanfront, opened the era of the automobile. Many of the city's earliest neighborhoods, as well as the popular Hilltop shopping area, grew up along its route. In the 1960s, a toll road paralleling the Boulevard opened, speeding traffic to the oceanfront. Today, this is the free expressway, I-264, the major east–west artery of the area.

The military occupies an important role in VB history, both past and present. **Fort Story,** an artillery post since 1917, remains a U.S. Army training and test site, as well as housing Cape Henry's two lighthouses and the **First Landing Cross.** The U.S. Navy has a training center at Camp Pendleton/Dam Neck on the coast south of the resort area and an amphibious base at Little Creek, to the west along the Chesapeake shore. At **Naval Air Station Oceana,** the world's largest master jet base, more than a quarter million flights take off and land each year. Hornets and Super Hornets from the base are frequently seen—and heard—above Virginia Beach. Locals refer to the often ear-splitting roar as "the sound of freedom."

OCEANFRONT RESORT AREA

I-264's eastbound lanes end just a few blocks from the ocean, becoming 21st Street. Here you'll find the main **Virginia Beach Welcome Center,** the glass-enclosed convention center, and the Contemporary Art Center of Virginia.

Running from Fort Story to Rudee Inlet, a distance of about 6 miles, the main resort area is relatively narrow, often less than four blocks wide. **Atlantic Avenue** (US 60) is the main drag running along the oceanfront for the entire 89 blocks, and most hotels are located here.

VB's famous Boardwalk, now paved and 28 feet wide, plus a separate bike path, runs about 3 miles from Rudee Inlet to 40th Street and is considered one of the finest seaside promenades in the world.

Atlantic and Pacific avenues merge at 41st Street, just in front of the **Cavalier Hotel** (757-425-8555; www.cavalierhotel.com), the last and most lavish survivor of the resort's "gilded age." The so-called Queen of the Beach opened in 1927 to national acclaim and soon racked up a roster of guest celebrities, including F. Scott Fitzgerald, Judy Garland, Will Rogers, Bette Davis, and Betty Grable, as well as seven U.S. presidents, and was the largest employer of big bands in the world. Today the Cavalier continues to welcome guests—and bands—as it is restored to its original glory.

CHESAPEAKE BEACHES AND SHORE DRIVE

Past Fort Story, Shore Drive passes through **First Landing State Park,** formerly called Seaside State Park, before reaching the Great Neck area. West Great Neck Boulevard, the only major street to cross from Hilltop to Shore Drive, is the first major intersection.

Just beyond, the **Lesner Bridge** over Lynnhaven Inlet provides a distinctive landmark. Marinas offer charter and head boat fishing, parasailing, and sunset cruises. Several popular restaurants, including **Bubba's Crab House** (757-481-3513; www.bubbasseafoodrestaurant.com), the **Dockside Inn** (757-481-4545; www.fishingvabeach.com), and **Chick's Oyster Bar** (757-481-5757; www.chicks oysterbar.com), are located on the eastern side of the bridge off Vista Circle.

A few miles farther west, Shore Drive crosses US 13, the access road of the **Chesapeake Bay Bridge-Tunnel (CBBT),** leading to Cape Charles on the Eastern Shore and the Delmarva Peninsula beyond. Shore Drive itself continues along the bayshore to the Ocean View and Willoughby Spit neighborhoods of Norfolk.

THE WIDE BOARDWALK WELCOMES ALL WHETHER ON FOOT OR WHEELS.

HILLTOP AND TOWN CENTER

The city's first gas station was built on high ground at the northern end of the Pungo Ridge. Today, the numerous shopping centers and restaurants located in the **Hilltop Plaza** area on Laskin Road (31st Street), just a few blocks from the resort area, are a favorite destination for both locals and visitors.

Past Hilltop, Laskin Road merges with Virginia Beach Boulevard and heads on toward Norfolk. **Town Center** (www.vabeachtowncenter.com), a massive mixed-use project, provides Virginia Beach with a new downtown halfway between the oceanfront and Norfolk, at the intersection of Virginia Beach and Independence boulevards. The development contains Virginia's tallest skyscraper, the **Westin Virginia**

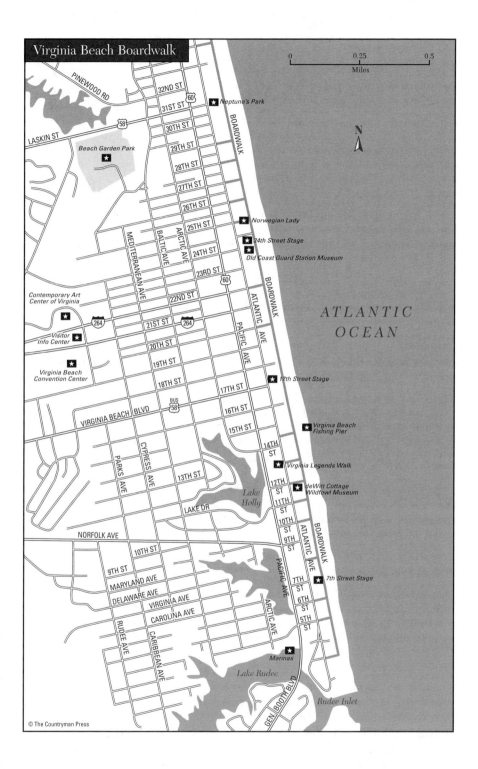

Virginia Beach Boardwalk

PINEWOOD RD
32ND ST
US 60
31ST ST
58
30TH ST
LASKIN ST
29TH ST
Beach Garden Park
28TH ST
27TH ST
26TH ST
25TH ST
24TH ST
23RD ST
60
22ND ST
Contemporary Art
Center of Virginia
264
21ST ST
264
Visitor
20TH ST
Info Center
19TH ST
Virginia Beach
18TH ST
Convention Center
17TH ST
BUS
58
VIRGINIA BEACH BLVD
16TH ST
15TH ST
14TH ST
CYPRESS AVE
13TH ST
PARKS AVE
LAKE DR
Lake
Holly
NORFOLK AVE
10TH ST
9TH ST
MARYLAND AVE
DELAWARE AVE
VIRGINIA AVE
CAROLINA AVE
RUDEE AVE
CARIBBEAN AVE
Lake Rudee

MEDITERRANEAN AVE
BALTIC AVE
ARCTIC AVE

BOARDWALK
ATLANTIC AVE
PACIFIC AVE

Neptune's Park

Norwegian Lady
24th Street Stage
Old Coast Guard Station Museum

ATLANTIC
OCEAN

17th Street Stage

Virginia Beach
Fishing Pier

Virginia Legends Walk

deWitt Cottage
Wildfowl Museum

12TH ST
11TH ST
10TH ST
9TH ST
8TH ST
7TH ST
6TH ST
5TH ST

BOARDWALK
ATLANTIC AVE
PACIFIC AVE
ARCTIC AVE

7th Street Stage

Marinas

GEN. BOOTH BLVD

Rudee Inlet

N

0   0.25   0.5
Miles

© The Countryman Press

Beach Town Center (757-557-0550; www.starwoodhotels.com or www.residences attowncenter.com), topping out at over 500 feet and visible for miles.

Free concerts are frequently staged in Town Center's open plaza, and the **Sandler Center for the Performing Arts** (757-385-2787; www.sandlercenter.org) provides a busy schedule of performances by national and international groups, with plenty of free parking close by.

RUDEE INLET

The protected waters of Rudee Inlet mark the southern limit of the Boardwalk. A saltwater estuary, the inlet is home to much of the resort's charter fishing fleet and some of VB's most popular restaurants, including **Big Sam's Inlet Café and Raw Bar** (757-428-4858; www.bigsamsrawbar.com), **Rockafellers** (757-422-5654; www .rockafellers.com), and **Rudees on the Inlet Restaurant and Raw Bar** (757-425-1777; www.rudees.com). All offer daily specials, great seafood, and superb views of the sunset. You can parasail, Jet Ski, or kayak from the docks out front.

Continue south on Pacific over the high-rise bridge that spans Rudee Inlet, and you'll be on General Booth Boulevard, the main artery on the south side of town.

PUNGO

Historic **Nimmo Methodist Church** (pronounced *nih-mo*), at the intersection of General Booth Boulevard and Princess Anne Road, marks the entrance to the southern reaches of Virginia Beach, including the districts of Pungo and Sandbridge. The church, built in 1791, was one of the pulpits visited by the famous Bishop Francis Asbury during his long ministry.

Princess Anne Road leads to the little crossroads of **Pungo** (www.pungoliving .com), its "downtown" marked by a single traffic light. The center of the region's agricultural industry since the earliest days, the village today is home to numerous truck farms, vegetable stands, and horse stables, as well as the annual **Pungo Strawberry Festival** (www.pungostrawberryfestival.info). Continuing south, Princess Anne reaches **Knott's Island, North Carolina** (www.knottsislandonline .com), boasting several wineries.

SANDBRIDGE

Occupying a narrow neck of land between the ocean and Back Bay, Sandbridge is often called Virginia's Outer Banks. Reached via the relatively narrow, winding Sandbridge Road, the beach community contains many vacation cottages, plus several restaurants, RV parks, a grocery, and two public beach accesses. Outfitters provide kayak tours into the ocean for dolphin encounters and into Back Bay for bird-watching.

Little Island Park, a city facility with a fishing pier at the southern end of Sandbridge, is a favorite destination for surfers, families, and fishing enthusiasts. South of the city park, the paved road ends at **Back Bay National Wildlife Refuge,** winter home to thousands of tundra swans. Beyond, **False Cape State Park** stretches to the North Carolina border. Access to this remote park is limited to foot, bicycle, and boat traffic or via the public tram from Back Bay park headquarters.

Located at the geographic center of the city of Virginia Beach, the Princess Anne Commons area was once the county seat of Princess Anne County, established in 1691. City, state, and federal offices, including the historic 1823 **Princess Anne Courthouse,** continue to operate at the corner of Princess Anne and North Landing roads.

In recent years, Princess Anne Commons expanded to include many other services, sports facilities, and attractions, as well as the Sentara hospital complex and Tidewater Community College. Here, within a few blocks, you'll find the **Virginia Beach Amphitheater,** the Virginia Beach Sportsplex, the Virginia Beach Farmer's Market, and the new Landstown Commons Shopping Center.

A note on addresses: Along the Boardwalk from First to 40th streets, you can determine the block where Atlantic and Pacific avenue hotels, restaurants, and shops are located by looking at their street addresses. The first one or two numbers are the number of the cross street: 1410 Atlantic would be near the intersection of Atlantic and 14th Street; 610 Pacific would be near the intersection of Sixth Street.

In our listings, all addresses are in the Virginia Beach zip code 23451, in the resort area, unless otherwise noted.

GUIDANCE Accomack County (757-787-5700 or 757-824-5444; www.co .accomack.va.us), 23296 Courthouse Avenue, Accomac 23301. On the Eastern Shore.

Cape Charles (757-331-3259; www.capecharles.org), 2 Plum Street, Cape Charles 23310.

Cape Charles/Northampton County Chamber of Commerce (757-331-2304; www.ccncchamber.com), P.O. Box 87, Cape Charles 23310.

Chesapeake Bay Center and First Landing History Museum (757-412-2300; www.dcr.virginia.gov), 2500 Shore Drive, Virginia Beach 23451. Located in First Landing State Park, it is is open daily, all year. In addition to tourism information, the Bay Center provides a quick introduction to the area's natural and cultural history.

Eastern Shore of Virginia Chamber of Commerce (757-787-2460; www.esva chamber.org), P.O. Box 460, Melfa 23410.

Eastern Shore of Virginia Tourism (757-787-8268; www.esvatourism.org), P.O. Box 72, Tasley 23441.

Greater Hampton Roads Black Chamber of Commerce (757-628-5300; www.ghrbcc.org).

Hampton Roads Chamber of Commerce (757-622-2312; www.hamptonroads chamber.com), 420 Bank Street, Norfolk 23510. Includes Chesapeake, Norfolk, Portsmouth, Suffolk, and Virginia Beach.

Hampton Roads Hispanic Chamber of Commerce (www.hamptonroads hispanic.org).

Hampton Roads—America's First Region (www.americasfirstregion.com).

Information kiosks, on the Boardwalk at 17th Street and on Atlantic Avenue at 24th Street, Virginia Beach. Operate from May to September.

Northampton County (757-678-0440; www.co.northampton.va.us), P.O. Box 66, Eastville 23347. On the Eastern Shore.

Virginia Beach (757-385-3111; www.vbgov.com), 2401 Courthouse Drive, Virginia Beach 23456.

Virginia Beach Visitor Information Center (757-437-4919 or 1-800-822-3224; www.vbfun.com), 2100 Parks Avenue, Virginia Beach 23451. Open daily 9–5 and until 7 PM from mid-June to Labor Day. You'll find it at the end of I-264.

GETTING AROUND ✤ **Seven Cities Rickshaws** (757-417-5595; www.seven citiesrickshaws.com), corner of Market and Bank streets, Town Center. On an evening out in Town Center, hail a pedicab to get you from your restaurant to the movie theater or Sandler Center, for just the price of a gratuity. Call for pickup.

✤ **The Wave** (757-222-6100; www.gohrt.com). During the summer season, hybrid electric shuttles on three routes make travel around the Virginia Beach area easy and inexpensive, and eliminate parking hassles, as well. Route 30 travels the oceanfront, from Rudee Inlet to 40th Street, every 15 minutes, 8 AM–2 AM, May 1–Sept. 30. Transfer at 40th Street to HRT Bus 33 for the A.R.E. campus and First Landing State Park. Route 31 travels south to the campgrounds and attractions along General Booth Boulevard, including the Virginia Aquarium and Ocean Breeze Waterpark. Route 32 is the Shopper's Shuttle, traveling out Laskin Road to the shops at Hilltop and Lynnhaven Mall. Per-ride fares on the Wave are $1 for adults and children over 38 inches tall, $0.50 for seniors and the disabled. All-day passes are a real deal, offering unlimited rides aboard any HRT vehicle for $2 adults, $1 seniors. Children under 38 inches tall always ride free.

MEDICAL EMERGENCY First Choice Medical Care (757-671-7777; www .beachmedicalcare.com), 4876 Baxter Road, Virginia Beach 23462.

Sentara Bayside Hospital (757-363-6100; www.sentara.com), 800 Independence Boulevard, Virginia Beach 23455.

Sentara Princess Anne Outpatient Center (757-507-0000; www.sentara.com), 1925 Glenn Mitchell Drive, Virginia Beach 23456.

Sentara Virginia Beach General Hospital (757-395-8000; www.sentara.com), 1060 First Colonial Road, Virginia Beach 23454.

Shore Memorial Hospital (757-414-8000; www.shorehealthservices.org), 9507 Hospital Avenue, Nassawadox 23413. Full-service hospital on the Eastern Shore.

✱ To See

With more than four hundred years of recorded history and the state's largest year-round population base, Virginia Beach offers travelers a rich cultural mix that includes historic houses; excellent museums; vibrant art galleries and events; outstanding performances by local, national, and international groups; and nightlife that just won't quit.

ARCHITECTURE With its long history, Virginia Beach can boast architecturally significant buildings from every era back to the late 1600s. The earliest houses dating to the colonial era are generally built of brick, with thick walls to withstand possible Indian attacks. The **Adam Thoroughgood House,** circa 1719, and

Lynnhaven House, circa 1725, are fine examples of this Virginia-style house type, with massive end chimneys, bricks laid in Flemish or English bond, and many post-medieval features. Both are open to the public.

Several significant examples of Georgian- and Federal-style homes, once the plantations of the region's gentry, lie scattered around the municipality, usually on the shores of the Lynnhaven River. Several are open to the public, including **Upper Wolfsnare,** a three-story Georgian, circa 1759; and **Ferry Plantation House,** a three-story Federal house, circa 1830. **Church Point Manor** (757-460-2210; www .churchpointmanor.com; 4001 Church Point Road, Virginia Beach 23455), a rare survivor of an 1860s Victorian farmhouse, has been adapted into an inn and restaurant.

After the Civil War, a resort community colonized the oceanfront. A few early buildings survive, including the **Old Coast Guard Station** (1903); the **deWitt Cottage** (1895), now the home of the Atlantic Waterfowl Heritage Museum; the **Barclay Cottage,** an 1895 golf clubhouse with wraparound porches, today a bed & breakfast inn; and the circa 1925 Craftsman cottage on 35th Street occupied by Edgar Cayce when he first arrived in Virginia Beach.

Another rather unusual survivor is the 1905 **Greystone Manor,** on the shores of Crystal Lake, an eastern branch of the Lynnhaven. The imposing residence, built of blue Vermont granite in the Scottish Baronial style, housed a gambling casino and notorious nightclub from 1936 to 1939. Today privately owned, its crenelated tower is best viewed from the water.

The **Edgar Cayce Hospital,** circa 1928, located at Atlantic Avenue and 57th Street, resembled the typical beach hotel of the day. Contrast its construction with the magnificent **Cavalier Hotel** (757-425-8555; www.cavalierhotel.com) at 42nd Street, and you'll see why the six-story brick Cavalier, which opened in 1927, earned the name Queen of the Beach. The interior, under careful renovation, features handsomely proportioned public rooms, including a parlor with balconies overlooking the indoor pool, and extensive sunporches. A small museum in the lobby preserves artifacts and newspaper stories from the hotel's early days.

Several architecturally interesting churches also remain in the region, including the 1736 **Old Donation Episcopal Church** (757-497-0563; www.olddonation .org; 4449 N. Witchduck Road); the 1791 **Nimmo Methodist** (757-427-1765; www.nimmochurch.org; 2200 Princess Anne Road); and the **Eastern Shore Chapel** (757-428-6763; www.easternshorechapel.org; 2020 Laskin Road), a modern Episcopal church containing the pews, stained-glass windows, and baptismal font from a 1754 chapel.

The **Virginia Beach Historical Preservation Partnership** (757-385-5100; 3131 Virginia Beach Boulevard, Virginia Beach 23452) publishes a book, *The 50 Most Historically Significant Houses and Structures in Virginia Beach,* with pictures and descriptions of these and many more privately owned buildings, available in the gift shops of the city's historic house museums. The Web site of the **Princess Anne County/Virginia Beach Historical Society** (757-491-3490; www.virginia beachhistory.org; 2040 Potters Road, Virginia Beach 23454) details many of historic buildings.

ART GALLERIES From May through Oct., the **First Friday ArtWalk** (757-498-0215) lines the sidewalks of Town Center with the works of more than 30 area artists, plus live entertainment, from 5 to 8 PM.

The Artists Gallery (757-425-6671; www.theartistsgallery.org), 608 Norfolk Avenue. Some of the finest artists in Virginia Beach exhibit here and work in studios on-site. Opening receptions bring out the art crowd.

Art Space at Pembroke Mall (757-434-3876 or 757-497-6255; www.pembroke mall.com), 4554 Virginia Beach Boulevard, Virginia Beach 23462. A half dozen galleries, plus a dance troupe and theater company, clustered in the North Wing of Pembroke Mall near the Regal Cinema, host openings and a variety of classes.

Beach Gallery (757-428-3726; www.beachgallery.com), 313 Laskin Road. Originals and fine-art prints of duck stamps, sporting dogs, waterfowl, nautical, landscape, and surfing themes.

The Glass Act (757-420-3560; www.glassact-vb.com), 5350 Kempsriver Drive, Virginia Beach 23464. Stained-glass artworks, classes, and supplies.

Jones Art Gallery (757-557-6868; www.jonesart.com), 4549 Virginia Beach Boulevard, Virginia Beach 23462. Town Center gallery displays the work of local landscape artist Herb Jones and his son Louis Jones, famous for his work in the book *Conversations with God*.

Mellow Mermaid Studio (757-287-5151; www.mellowmermaidstudio.com), 2645 Dean Drive, Barrett Street Antique Center, Virginia Beach 23454. Local artist Lori Goldwag crafts a wide variety of fun artworks, seaside souvenirs, and nautical holiday ornaments.

Ocean Art Gallery (757-425-1666; www.oceanart.com), 1628 Laskin Road, Hilltop North Shopping Center. Prints and posters of local scenes by photographer William Harris include many aerial views.

Pembroke 4 Art Gallery (757-499-9900; www.pembroke4artgallery.com), 219 Independence Boulevard, Pembroke Office Center, Virginia Beach 23462. Town Center gallery hangs works by local artists and hosts opening receptions.

Richard Stravitz Sculpture and Art Gallery (757-305-9411; www.sculpture -bronze.com), 1217 Laskin Road. View the bronze-statue-making process in action as well as the work of many fine artists.

21st Street Art Gallery (757-491-2943; www.21startgallery.com), 615 N. Birdneck Road. Cool gallery displays original oils and watercolors, pottery, and jewelry.

Virginia Beach Central Library (757-385-0150; www.vbgov.com/library), 4100 Virginia Beach Boulevard, Virginia Beach 23452. Changing exhibits of local artwork, live concerts, and storytelling. Free Wi-Fi access.

DANCE Dirt Cheap Blues (www.dirtcheapblues.com). Blues dance lessons, workshops, and exchange weekends. Blues bands are featured on Thurs. in July and Aug. on the 17th Street Stage.

Magic Moments Dance Studio (757-498-5110; www.magicmomentsdance.com), 2224 Virginia Beach Boulevard. Studio at the corner of Great Neck Road and Virginia Beach Boulevard offers nightly group classes and several social dances every week. Drop-ins welcome.

Seven Cities Salsa (757-513-4341; www.sevencitiessalsa.com). Comprehensive listing of salsa and latin dance nightclubs and lessons, many of them free, in the Hampton Roads area.

THE DOLPHINS OF VIRGINIA BEACH

All over the city, fiberglass dolphins, each unique, each beautifully decorated by local artists, swim for a worthy cause. Look for them in front of restaurants and hotels, museums, schools, and businesses. A whole pod can be found in front of the Virginia Aquarium and Marine Science Center. They are part of *A Dolphin's Promise,* committed to raising $1 million to help find a cure for cancer. To find out more or to contribute, call 757-573-5272 or visit www.adolphinspromise.com.

THE MANY DOLPHINS SEEN AROUND THE REGION REPRESENT A CHARITY RAISING FUNDS TO CURE CANCER.

Swing Dance Virginia (www.swingvirginia.com). Sponsors dance events all across the Hampton Roads area, including a free swing dance every second Sat. at the **Upper Deck** (757-428-0048; 206 16th Street) in Virginia Beach.

Two Step Tidewater (www.twosteptidewater.com). Ballroom dances open to the public on Sun. at **DanceSportVA** (757-473-3267; www.dancesportva.homestead.com; 5721A Arrowhead Drive, Virginia Beach 23462).

Virginia Beach Ballet (757-714-2997; www.vbconservatoryofdance.com), 4716 Princess Anne Road, Virginia Beach 23462. Performances of classical and modern dance combine the talents of local dancers with touring professionals, including the annual *Great Russian Nutcracker* (www.nutcracker.com) with the Moscow Ballet.

Virginia Beach Lindy Exchange (www.vblx.com). Annual weekend held every June gets Hampton Roads jivin' with dances on the Boardwalk and on the deck of the USS *Wisconsin,* Battle of the DJs, and late-night blues sessions.

Virginia Beach Shag Club (www.vbshagclub.com), P.O. Box 3098, Virginia Beach 23454. Weekly dances at area clubs, including a Wednesday Mix and Mingle at the **Upper Deck** (757-428-0048; 16th Street and Atlantic Boulevard).

SOUTHSIDE

HISTORIC HOUSES AND MUSEUMS ✪ **Adam Thoroughgood House** (757-460-7588; www.virginiabeachhistory.org/thoroughgoodhouse.html), 1636 Parish Road, Virginia Beach 23455. Open: Tues.–Sun. Admission: Adults $4, seniors (60-plus) $3, students (six-plus) $2. Combination tickets to the city-owned Thoroughgood, Francis Land, and Lynnhaven houses: Adults $9, seniors $7, students $5. Surrounded by two-hundred-year-old magnolia trees, the oldest surviving house in Virginia Beach (ca. 1719) is one of the oldest brick homes in America and in remarkably original condition—never renovated or gutted, and furnished with authentic examples of household goods found in the homes of a wealthy planters of the day. Costumed interpreters lead visitors through the paneled common room and open upstairs loft, pointing out unusual features.

✪ ✎ ⊤ **Atlantic Wildfowl Heritage Museum/de Witt Cottage** (757-437-8432; www.awhm.org), 1113 Atlantic Avenue. Open: Daily; closed Mon. during fall and winter. Admission: Free. Housed in the historic de Witt house, the oldest (and only) cottage still located on the Boardwalk, this free museum exhibits carvings of waterfowl and shorebirds from early traditional forms to today's fine-art specimens. Local carvers demonstrate their craft, and the gift shop offers many decoys for sale. Classes available. In the upstairs gallery, old photos and postcards trace the history of the Virginia Beach resort. The area's original one-room library, exhibiting books from the 1930s, is located on the museum grounds, as well as a boathouse and a seaside garden of salt-tolerant plants and lovely sculptures.

A COSTUMED GUIDE EXPLAINS THE LIFESTYLE OF THE EARLY SETTLERS AT THE ADAM THOROUGHGOOD HOUSE, ONE OF THE OLDEST BRICK HOUSES IN THE COUNTRY.

✎ **Ferry Plantation House** (757-473-5626; www.ferryplantation.org), 4136 Cheswick Lane, Virginia Beach 23455. Open: Tues., Thurs., Sat. Admission: Adults $5, seniors and students $2. Federal-style house built in 1830 stands on the site of the area's first ferry, circa 1642. A History Camp for grades 1–6 is offered during the summer months.

Francis Land House Historic Site & History Park (757-431-4000; www.virginiabeachhistory.org/land.html), 3131 Virginia Beach Boulevard, Virginia Beach 23452. Open: Tues.–Sun. Admission: Adults $4, seniors (60-plus) $3, students (six and older) $2. Combination tickets available. This two-hundred-year-old brick plantation home is open for guided tours. The grounds feature herb, formal, and vegetable gardens with plantings typical of the 18th century. A trail with interpretive signs leads through a wooded wetland.

⊤ **Lynnhaven House and Colonial Education Center** (757-431-4000 or 757-385-5100; www.virginiabeach

THE WITCH OF PUNGO

Grace Sherwood, a local midwife living in Princess Anne County in the late 1600s, fell out of favor with her neighbors, who accused her of witchcraft, causing their crops to fail, wearing men's clothes, talking to animals, and assorted other "crimes." Although the magistrates of the day found no reason to try the case, Grace was sentenced to trial by ducking. Tied thumbs to toes, she was tossed into the West Branch of the Lynnhaven River, near what is now known as Witchduck Point, on July 10, 1706. Against all expectation, she floated—a sure sign of guilt to those who believed "pure" water would not accept the body of a witch. Grace spent the next seven years in prison.

GRACE SHERWOOD, THE SO-CALLED WITCH OF PUNGO, MAY HAVE LIVED IN A FARMSTEAD SIMILAR TO THE 1725 LYNNHAVEN HOUSE, LOCATED NOT FAR FROM THE PLACE WHERE GRACE WAS "DUCKED."

Three hundred years to the day after Sherwood's so-called trial, the governor of Virginia granted an official exoneration, restoring her good name. A statue of Grace now stands on the lawn at **Sentara Bayside Hospital** (800 Independence Boulevard, Virginia Beach 23455), near the corner of Independence and N. Witchduck Road.

More information on Grace Sherwood can be found in the children's book *The Witch of Pungo*, written by Louisa Kyle (www.virginiabeach history.org/kyle.html), or at the **Ferry Plantation House** (www.ferry plantation.org), near the site of the infamous ducking.

history.org/lynnhouse.html), 4401 Wishart Road, Virginia Beach 23455. Open: Tues.–Sun. Admission: Adults $4, seniors (60-plus) $3, students (six and older) $2. Combination tickets available. This 1725 brick house with massive chimneys features many Jacobean details and Revolutionary-era graveyard. The adjacent Colonial Education Center offers an orientation video and museum exhibits exploring the influence of water transportation on the history of the region in colonial days.

✪ ♂ ⸸ **Old Coast Guard Station** (757-422-1587; www.oldcoastguard station.com), 24th Street and Atlantic Avenue. Open: Daily; closed winter holidays, and Mon. Oct. 1–Memorial Day. Admission: Adults $4, seniors and military $3, children 6–18 $2. Housed in the 1903 Life-Saving Station right on the Boardwalk, this museum tells the story of the heroic rescues accomplished by the life savers who patrolled this coast from the 1880s. Exhibits include life-saving equipment, histories of shipwrecks, the Battle of the Atlantic in World War II, and the development of the Virginia Beach resort. The on-site library of books and papers on nautical and maritime history, the Life-Saving Service and U.S. Coast Guard, and shipwrecks along the Virginia coast is available to researchers by appointment.

Upper Wolfsnare (757-491-3490; www.virginiabeachhistory.org), 2040 Potters Road, Virginia Beach 23454. Open: Wed. noon–4, July–Aug. Admission: Adults $5, seniors $4, students $3. This white brick Georgian dates to 1759, when Thomas Walke III built it as a setting for his gentry lifestyle. Today it is the home of the Virginia Beach Historical Society.

HISTORIC SITES AND MEMORIALS *Fort Story security information:* To visit any site on the Fort Story Army Base, everyone 16 and older must show a photo ID to enter the gates, where security personnel may search your car. You should also be prepared to show your car registration and proof of insurance.

✪ ♂ **Cape Henry Lighthouses** (757-422-9421; www.apva.org/capehenry), 583 Atlantic Avenue, Fort Story, Virginia Beach 23459. Two lighthouses stand today in Fort Story, near where the English first stepped ashore in 1607. The oldest, the 1792 **Cape Henry Light,** an octagonal stone tower 72 feet high, was the first federally funded lighthouse completed in the new United States of America. Today maintained by Preservation Virginia, the tower is open for climbing from spring to fall. The 191 steps lead to a spectacular view of Cape Henry and the mouth of Chesapeake Bay, once called the Gibraltar of the New World. A second taller lighthouse, built in 1881 and still in use, stands nearby, but it cannot be climbed. Open all year except for Thanksgiving Day, and the Christmas and New Year's holidays. Admission to Fort Story is free; however, climbing the lighthouse costs $4 for adults and seniors, $3 for children 3–12.

First Landing Cross and Battle off the Capes Monument (757-422-9421; www.nps.gov/came), 583 Atlantic Avenue, Fort Story, Virginia Beach 23459. These memorials at Fort Story commemorate two important moments in our nation's early history. A large granite cross marks the point where Christopher Newport and his colonists first set foot on Virginia soil in 1607, before proceeding on to Jamestown. The Order of Cape Henry holds a reenactment of the landing every year near the Apr. 26th anniversary. A statue of Admiral Comte deGrasse commemorates the victory of the French fleet over the British navy on Sept. 5, 1781, a battle that led to the surrender of General Cornwallis at Yorktown and the end of the Revolutionary War.

✪ ✍ Historic Villages at Cape Henry (757-417-7012; www.first landingfoundation.com), Bayside House/Building 711, Atlantic Avenue, Fort Story, Virginia Beach 23459. The Historic Villages re-create both the Native American and the English lifestyles of the early colonial period along a path leading through maritime forest, where reenactors from local tribes explain the lifeways of their ancestors. A spectacular outdoor stage hosts early-evening performances, including *1607: First Landing*, Memorial Day–Labor Day. Admission prices vary.

King Neptune Statue (757-213-3000; www.31ocean.com), Neptune's Park, at 31st Street and the Boardwalk. The 34-foot-tall bronze statue of King Neptune, created by Virginia sculptor Paul DiPasquale, presides over the annual **Neptune Festival** (757-498-0215 or 866-NEP-FEST; www.neptunefestival.com), a monthlong celebration culminating with Boardwalk Weekend at the end of Sept.

KING NEPTUNE RULES THE VIRGINIA BEACH BOARDWALK.

THE NORWEGIAN LADY FACES HER COUNTERPART IN MOSS, NORWAY, BOTH HONORING ALL THOSE LOST AT SEA.

Naval Aviation Monument Park (757-425-7191 or 800-822-3224; www.hrana.org); 25th Street and Atlantic Avenue. Larger-than-life bronze sculptures depict the history of naval aviation, much of which played out in Hampton Roads.

Norwegian Lady Statue (www.virginiabeachhistory.org/lady.html), 25th Street and Atlantic Avenue. After the Norwegian bark *Dictator* foundered off the coast in 1891, the residents of Virginia Beach erected the figurehead of the ship on the Boardwalk as a memorial to the dead. A bronze replica replaced the hurricane-battered statue in 1962. An identical statue stands in Moss, Norway, home port of the *Dictator*, and a Virginia Beach sister city.

POW/MIA Flame of Hope Memorial Park (757-433-3131; www.cnic.navy

THE TIDEWATER VETERANS MEMORIAL LIES NEXT TO THE VIRGINIA BEACH CONVENTION CENTER, WHERE AN OBSERVATION DECK OVERLOOKS THE CITY.

.mil/oceana), Naval Air Station Oceana, Oceana Boulevard. This free public park with an eternal flame dedicated to captured and missing servicemen and women is located near the airbase runways, making it a good place to watch takeoffs and landings.

Tidewater Veterans Memorial (757-385-4303 or 800-822-3224; www.vbgov .com/veterans), 1000 19th Street. A moving tribute to area veterans located opposite the Virginia Beach Convention Center is the scene of a Memorial Day commemoration each year.

Virginia Legends Walk (757-463-4500; www.va-legends.com), 1300 Atlantic Avenue. Landscaped park at 13th Street between Atlantic and Pacific celebrates famous Virginians from Pocahontas to Katie Couric, including eight U.S. presidents, musical stars such as Ella Fitzgerald and Patsy Cline, and tennis star Arthur Ashe. The site is free and makes a pleasant stroll through history adjacent to the oceanfront.

MUSEUMS & ATTRACTIONS ✪ ᛏ Association for Research & Enlightenment (A.R.E) (757-428-3588; www.edgarcayce.org), 215 67th Street. Open: Daily. Admission: Free. The A.R.E. complex at 57th and Atlantic Avenue is the heart of an international organization devoted to research into holistic health, spiritual growth, and ancient mysteries. The institute, founded in 1931, welcomes all comers, offering daily a free video introduction to the life and work of Edgar Cayce, and a tour of the **Visitor Center and A.R.E. Library,** concluding in the serene rooftop **Meditation Room.** Free meditation and prayer sessions and lectures take place daily, and free extrasensory perception demonstrations every weekend. Other classes and workshops, including yoga, tai chi, and astrology, are available for a small fee. The A.R.E. Library, containing transcripts of Cayce's fourteen thousand readings as well as an amazing collection of metaphysical texts, is open to researchers and the general public, and has free Wi-Fi. A bookstore on the ground

EDGAR CAYCE: VIRGINIA BEACH'S SLEEPING PROPHET

In 1925, Edgar Cayce, America's best-known psychic of the time, selected Virginia Beach as the headquarters for his new holistic health institute and research center, basing his choice on a psychic reading that described the area as "a safety land" during coming world upheavals. Today, the **Association for Research and Enlightenment,** located on Atlantic Avenue at 57th Street, attracts many thousands of visitors each year.

Although best known for his past-life readings and revelations concerning Atlantis, Cayce can also be considered the Father of Holistic Health. Many of the natural treatments and remedies he suggested in his trances are today recognized as sound nutritional advice.

Thanks to the presence of Cayce's center and its associated schools of massage therapy and psychic development, Virginia Beach is especially rich in opportunities for spiritual growth and holistic living. The **Heritage Holistic Store** (757-428-0100; www.heritagestore.com; 314 Laskin Road) serves as a center for VB's New Age community, offering classes and bulletin boards of information, as well as books and health foods.

Contact the **Edgar Cayce Association for Research & Enlightenment (A.R.E)** at 757-428-3588 or by visiting www.edgarcayce.org.

floor carries many health-care products, as well as books of and about Cayce's readings.

On the hill above the visitors center, the **A.R.E. Health and Rejuvenation Center's Massage and Day Spa** offers therapeutic treatments based on Cayce's readings to enhance the health of body, mind, and spirit. Appointments are available daily.

Between the two buildings, a meditation garden with a waterfall and benches is open for contemplation or picnics. On the plaza at the top of the stairs you can walk a 42-foot **labyrinth** based on the one in France's Chartres Cathedral, or take off your shoes for a stroll on the short **Reflexology Walk,** guaranteed to activate the pressure points in your feet.

✪ ✐ ↑ **Chesapeake Bay Center and First Landing History Museum** (757-412-2300; www.dcr.virginia.gov), 2500 Shore Drive. Open: Daily. Admission: Free; parking $4 weekdays, $5 weekends per car. Unique facility in First Landing State Park, just across the dunes from the beach, serves as an introduction to the region, with interactive exhibits on the ecology of the Chesapeake Bay. The history room displays statues of famous figures as well as a time line of early contacts between the English and native tribes in 1607 based on journals of the day.

Christian Broadcasting Network (CBN) (757-226-2745; www.cbn.com), 977 Centerville Turnpike, Virginia Beach 23463. Open: Mon.–Fri. Admission: Free. The 685-acre CBN campus includes the TV studio headquarters, **Regent University** (www.regent.edu), and the **Founders Inn and Spa** (757-424-5511 or 800-926-4466; www.foundersinn.com; 5641 Indian River Road, Virginia Beach 23464).

Free tours of the TV studio and Regent University, offered weekdays, take you behind the scenes of this international ministry. To be part of the live studio audience of the nationally televised *700 Club* program, arrive at 8:30 AM.

✪ ♿ ⚲ ↝ **Contemporary Art Center of Virginia** (757-425-0000; www.cacv .org), 2200 Parks Avenue. Open: Tues.–Sun. Admission: Adults $7; seniors, students, and military $5; children 4–14 $3. The only museum in Virginia dedicated solely to contemporary art mounts a continually changing and always interesting series of exhibits in its spacious galleries. Although a noncollecting institution, the center does have one outstanding piece of art on permanent display—a stunning chandelier by glass master Dale Chihuly. Sponsors the **Boardwalk Art Show and Festival** in June and the **Neptune Art and Craft Show** in Sept.

✪ ♿ ⚲ **Military Aviation Museum** (757-721-7767; www.militaryaviationmuseum .org or www.fighterfactory.com), 1341 Princess Anne Road, Virginia Beach 23457. Open: Daily. Admission: Adults $10, seniors (65-plus) and military $9, students $5, WW II veterans and preschoolers free. For fans of warbirds and other vintage aircraft, this museum in Pungo is a must-stop. Housing one of the world's largest private collections of World War II and Korean-era aircraft, including bombers, fighters, trainers, and seaplanes, plus replicas of early Wright flyers and World War I craft, this is a museum with a difference—nearly every one of the planes is airworthy, restored inside and out to its original condition. A staff of dedicated volunteers show visitors around the hangers and fill in the history of each plane and its pilots. The star of the collection is a Curtiss P-40 Kittyhawk painted in the colors of Tex Hill, ace pilot with the Flying Tigers. Flying demonstrations and seminars are held at the museum's private airfield. Call ahead for the flight schedule.

✪ ✒ ♿ ↝ **Virginia Aquarium and Marine Science Center** (757-385-FISH; www.vmsm.com), 717 General Booth Boulevard. Open: Daily. Admission: Adults $17, seniors (62-plus) $16, children 3–11 $12. Combination tickets with IMAX available. Two buildings connected by a nature trail, more than 800,000 gallons of aquariums, more than 300 interactive exhibits, an aviary, and one of the nation's few 3-D IMAX theaters—plus harbor seals, loggerhead turtles, river otters, and great horned owls—are among the many attractions at Virginia's premiere marine science center. In the new Restless Planet exhibit hall, you can create volcanoes and simulate the formation of the bay by asteroid impact 35 million years ago. Following the nature trail, you encounter an archaeological dig, a Native American village, and a 30-foot observation tower offering a bird's-eye view, before reaching the Marsh Pavilion to walk through a salt marsh where plants and animals are 10 times their normal size. Special programs include opportunities to swim with and train harbor seals,

THIS 1941 CURTISS KITTYHAWK IN THE COLLECTION OF THE MILITARY AVIATION MUSEUM RECREATES THE COLORS OF FLYING TIGERS ACE PILOT "TEX" HILL.

whale-watching and dolphin-sighting cruises, behind-the-scenes tours, and a pontoon boat cruise through the salt marsh.

❧ **Virginia Beach City Public Schools Planetarium** (757-648-4940; www.planetarium.vbschools.com), 3080 S. Lynnhaven Road, Plaza Middle School, Virginia Beach 23452. Open: Tues. evening. Admission: Free. Free public star programs at this school facility change monthly. Reservations are suggested.

WILDLIFE ENTHUSIASTS OF ALL AGES CAN GET UP CLOSE AND PERSONAL WITH LOCAL SEA CREATURES AT THE VIRGINIA AQUARIUM AND MARINE SCIENCE CENTER.

MUSIC AND LECTURE SERIES

Friday Night Hoedowns (757-385-4395; www.vbgov.com/farmersmarket), 3640 Dam Neck Road at Princess Anne Road. Free country music concerts under the stars at the Virginia Beach Farmers Market, 7–10 PM, Apr.–Oct.

Natchel' Blues Network (757-456-1675; www.natchelblues.org). Information on concerts, blues festivals, local bands, and venues in Hampton Roads. Sponsor of the annual **Blues at the Beach** festival in Sept.

Sandler Center Summer Concert Series (757-385-2787; www.sandler center.org), Sandler Center Outdoor Plaza, Town Center, Virginia Beach 23462. Free concerts of popular and classical music are offered during the summer season.

Symphonicity (757-671-8704; www.symphonicity.org). Virginia Beach's resident symphony orchestra presents a masterworks series, an annual *Messiah* sing-along, and oceanfront concerts at the 24th Street Stage.

Tidewater Friends of Folk Music (757-626-3655; www.tffm.org), Virginia Beach Central Library, 4100 Virginia Beach Boulevard, Virginia Beach 23452. Folk and old-time music concerts, plus a children's concert series.

Virginia Beach Chorale (757-340-6156; www.virginiabeachchorale.org), Thalia Trinity Presbyterian Church, 420 Thalia Road, Virginia Beach 23452. One of the city's oldest continuing performing-arts groups.

Virginia Beach Forum (757-417-6570; www.vabeachforum.com), Sandler Center (201 Market Street, Town Center, Virginia Beach 23462). Series of lectures explores the stories behind the headlines.

Virginia Symphony Orchestra (757-892-6366; www.virginiasymphony.org), Sandler Center (201 Market Street, Town Center, Virginia Beach 23462). One of the nation's leading regional orchestras presents a series of classics.

NIGHTLIFE From mid-May through the end of September, look no further for evening entertainment than Atlantic Avenue and the Boardwalk, where you'll find **Beach Street USA** (www.beachstreetusa.com) in full swing. Puppeteers, jugglers, and other street performers entertain along the sidewalks of Atlantic Avenue from 17th to 25th streets, while live concerts and theatrical productions take place on outdoor stages at 7th, 13th, 17th, 24th, 25th, and 31st streets along the Boardwalk. Fireworks explode overhead several nights a week. Other Beach Street events are planned on weekends all year long, culminating in the spectacular **Holiday Lights at the Beach,** held nightly from Thanksgiving to New Year's Day, when cars drive down the Boardwalk amid illuminated undersea scenes.

For late-night fun, the party people head for **"The Block,"** bounded by 21st, 22nd, Atlantic, and Pacific, where dance clubs, late-night pizza joints, bars, all-night minigolf, game arcades, souvenir shops, fun houses, and other nighttime attractions line the sidewalks.

Dance Clubs

Ȳ **Central 111** (757-222-1022; www.centraloneeleven.com), 401 N. Great Neck Road, Virginia Beach 23454. High-energy lounge features late-night tapas and salsa music.

Chicho's (757-425-5656; www.chichospizza.com), 2820 Pacific Avenue. High-energy dance music every Sat. night.

✸ **Guadalajara** (www.guadalajaravb.com), five VB locations. Local chain offers some of the area's best Mexican food, plus frequent dance nights, dining under the stars, Fat Tuesday drink machines.

✸ Ȳ **LunaSea Key West Café** (757-437-4400; www.lunaseavb.com), 206 22nd Street. Two-story club has weekend DJs, live music, tiki bar parties, Sun. Bloody Mary bar.

✸ Ȳ **Peabody's Nightclub** (757-422-6212; www.peabodysvirginiabeach.com), 209 21st Street. Party on the largest dance floor in Virginia. Special no-alcohol teen nights all year.

AT VIRGINIA BEACH'S HOLIDAY LIGHTS, CARS DRIVE ALONG THE BOARDWALK THROUGH A TUNNEL OF LIGHT DISPLAYS.

Atlantic Avenue. Hawaiian-themed nightclub and restaurant is a local favorite.

Ϋ **Sky Bar** (757-213-3000; www.skybarvb.com), 3001 Atlantic Avenue. Private club located 21 stories up at the top of the Hilton Virginia Beach Oceanfront, this classy spot hosts full moon parties and DJ dances all summer. Membership required.

Irish Pubs

Ϋ **Conklin's Irish Rover** (757-631-1294; www.conklins-irish-rover.com), the Village Shoppes at Rose Hall, 3157 Virginia Beach Boulevard, Virginia Beach 23452. TVs tuned to European football and international rugby, plus live acoustic music.

Ϋ **Finn McCools Fish House & Tavern** (757-689-0829; www.finnmccoolsvb .com), 3388 Princess Anne Road, Landstown Commons Shopping Center, Virginia Beach 23453. Irish tavern hosts live acoustic music.

✪ Ϋ **Keagans Irish Pub and Restaurant** (757-961-4432; www.keagans.com), 244 Market Street, Town Center, Virginia Beach 23462. Live Irish and acoustic music most nights at this authentic Irish pub.

✪ ✍ Ϋ **Murphy's A Grand Irish Pub** (757-417-7701; www.murphyspub.com), 2914 Pacific Avenue. Live Irish music most nights, and happy hour prices on imports.

Live Entertainment

✪ ✍ "ⵙ" Ϋ ↭ **Abbey Road** (757-425-6330; www.abbeyroadpub.com), 203 22nd Street. A landmark on the oceanfront since 1962, this pub has live music, mostly acoustic, every night; happy hour; free Wi-Fi; and a huge collection of Beatles memorabilia. Full menu served until 1 AM.

✍ **Ammos** (757-313-6083; www.ammosvb.com), 1401 Atlantic Avenue. Authentic Greek cuisine at a café located on the Boardwalk featuring occasional belly dancers.

Ϋ **Baja Restaurant and Bayview Lounge** (757-426-7748; www.myspace.com/ bajarestaurant), 3701 S. Sandpiper Road, Sandbridge, Virginia Beach 23456. Cool spot at the south end of Sandbridge offers great sunsets, seafood, pizza, live music.

Ϋ **Bayside Inn Restaurant and Lounge** (757-460-1593; www.baysideinn.biz), 2104 Pleasure House Road, Virginia Beach 23455. Open mic nights and jazz jams.

Ϋ **Boneshakers Saloon** (757-961-8382; www.boneshakerssaloon.com), 1297 General Booth Boulevard. Biker bar with a difference—live music, blues bands, deck parties, great breakfasts.

✍ Ϋ **DejaBlu Jazz Supper Club** (757-226-7477; www.dejablusupperclub.com), 1910 Atlantic Avenue. Live jazz and N'awlins-inspired menu.

Doc Taylor's Seaside Market Lounge (757-422-0081; www.doctaylors.com), 209 23rd Street at Pacific. Live local and regional bands on Thurs. nights.

Ϋ **15th St. Raw Bar** (757-491-1515), 1400 Atlantic Avenue. Key West–style bar with deck, frequent live music, happy hour, 14 flat-screen TVs, pool, darts, and more.

Ϋ **Five 01 City Grill** (757-425-7195; www.five01citygrill.com), 501 N. Birdneck Road. Live music, happy hour with food specials, wood-oven pizza, spa cuisine.

Funny Bone Comedy Club & Restaurant (757-213-5555; www.vabeachfunny bone.com), 217 Central Park Avenue, Virginia Beach 23462. Enjoy a full menu and cocktails, along with national headliners, in the heart of Town Center.

Y **Green Parrot Grille** (757-460-4640; www.greenparrotgrille.com), 4494 Lookout Road, Virginia Beach 23455. Chicks Beach hangout has daily happy hour with free weekday buffet, live music.

❂ Y **HK on the Bay** (757-605-3024; www.hkonthebay.com), 4600 Lookout Road, Virginia Beach 23455. Chicks Beach outpost of **Hell's Kitchen** (757-624-1906; www.hknorfolk.com; 124 Granby Street, Norfolk 23510) hosts live music on the weekends, including the Sunday Soul Haven Project, a gathering of professional singers, songwriters, and musicians.

Y ❧ **Hot Tuna Bar and Grill** (757-481-2888; www.hottunavb.com), 2817 Shore Drive. Award-winning seafood and live music served up among fanciful Day-Glo sea creatures.

❂ Y **The Hunt Room Grill at Cavalier on the Hill** (757-425-8555; www .cavalierhotel.com), 4201 Atlantic Avenue. Open only from Jan. to Mar., the wood-paneled Hunt Room features jazz every weekend.

Y **Icehouse Restaurant** (757-422-1968; www.icehousevb.com), 604 Norfolk Avenue. Housed in a 1910 building, this landmark South End spot is famous for its ribs, and live acoustic music on Thurs. nights.

❂ Y **The Jewish Mother** (757-422-5430; www.jewishmother.com), 3108 Pacific Avenue. One of the beach's top music venues, home of the East Coast Blues, masquerades during the day as a Jewish deli serving outstanding omelets and giant brownie sundaes.

❂ Y **Lucky Oyster Seafood Grill** (757-430-9600; www.luckyoystervb.com), 2165 General Booth Boulevard, Strawbridge Marketplace. Local favorite hosts live music, popular happy hour, oyster roasts, Sun. brunch.

Y **Regal Beagle Taphouse** (757-428-4695; www.myspace.com/regalbeaglevb), 605 Virginia Beach Boulevard. Local live music on the weekends, huge list of beers, Sun. Bloody Mary bar.

Y **Sharx Margarita Grill** (757-491-4900; www.sharxsportsgrill.com), 211 21st Street. Live music Fri. and Sat. nights.

❂ Y **Timbuktu** (757-491-1800; www.hamptoninnvirginiabeachoceanfront.com), 3107 Atlantic Avenue. Located on the Boardwalk in the Hampton Inn Oceanfront North, this club hosts live music, including jazz, R&B, and calypso, during the summer.

Piano Bars

Y **Aldo's Ristorante** (757-491-1111; www.aldosvb.com),1860 Laskin Road, La Promenade Shopping Center, Virginia Beach 23454.

Y **Bella Monte International Marketplace & Café** (757-425-6290; www.bella montevb.com), 1201 Laskin Road.

❂ Y **Il Giardino Ristorante** (757-422-6464; www.ilgiardino.com), 910 Atlantic Avenue.

Sports Bars

Ɗ Y **A J Gator's Sports Bar and Grill** (www.gatorsportsbar.com), various locations. Take the Gator Challenge, or watch sports on the numerous tubes at this chain with five locations in Virginia Beach, plus Norfolk, Chesapeake, Suffolk, and Carrollton. Live music and karaoke at the General Booth location (757-425-2202; 1485 General Booth Boulevard, Virginia Beach 23454).

✪ ✐ Ÿ **Just George's Sports Bar & Grill** (757-428-3494; www.justgeorges.com), 1956 Laskin Road. Located next to **Capt. George's Seafood Restaurant** (www.captaingeorges.com), one of the beach's most popular buffets, this sports bar has a unique circular layout with more than 50 flat-screen TVs, booths with TVs, and even TVs in the restrooms, all tuned to every major sports event. Order from the extensive bar menu or go next door and fill your plate from the all-you-can-eat seafood buffet for the entire evening—a real deal.

Ÿ **Keagan's Pub and Grill** (757-689-3340; www.keaganspub.com), 2181 Upton Drive, Red Mill Commons, Virginia Beach 23454. Irish pub fare supplemented by 10 flavors of wings, 35 flat-screen TVs, plus a 10-foot big screen, pool, video games, live music after the game.

Ÿ **Parlay's Sports Bar** (757-721-6245; www.myspace.com/parlayszeros), 1615 General Booth Boulevard, Strawbridge Marketplace, Virginia Beach 23454. Watch the game on 32 flat-screen TVs; pool, darts, game room, happy hour, nightly drink specials, food from sister restaurant **Zero's Subs** (www.zeros.com) next door.

✐ ⇴ **Shorebreak Pizza-Sports-Billiards** (757-481-9393; www.shorebreakvb.com), 2941 Shore Drive. Award-winning pizza; 13 billiards tables; 40 flat-screen TVs, plus two 7-foot HD big screens; all satellite sports packages; game room.

PERFORMING ARTS VENUES ⇴ **Sandler Center for the Performing Arts** (757-385-2787 or 888-3-COXTIX; www.sandlercenter.org), 201 Market Street, Town Center, Virginia Beach 23462. Venue in the heart of Town Center stages its own Great Performance Series of concerts and musicals, free outdoor concerts, and a summer film series, in addition to hosting numerous local performing-arts groups and performances of the **Virginia Arts Festival** (757-282-2800; www.vafest.org), a six-week-long celebration of the arts held mid-Apr. to the end of May. More than 3,200 free parking spaces are close by. **Ruth's Chris Steak House** (757-213-0747; www.sizzlingsteak.com; 205 Central Park Avenue) offers Dinner and a show packages.

⇴ **Virginia Beach Amphitheater** (757-368-3000; www.vwvba.com), 3550 Cellar Door Way, Virginia Beach 23456. Outdoor facility in the Princess Commons area hosts performances by major artists. Parking in the well-lit lots is usually included in the ticket price.

THEATER COMPANIES **Angelo's Murder Mystery Dinner Theater** (757-425-0347; www.maverickmurdermystery.com or www.angelosontheboardwalk.com), Angelo's By the Sea, 2809 Atlantic Avenue. Award-winning interactive murder mystery in the Best Western Hotel includes all-you-can-eat buffet with roast beef carving station. Advance reservations required.

Collective Arts Theatre (C.A.T.) (757-905-2895; www.collectiveartstheatre.com), 4554 Virginia Beach Boulevard, Suite 280, Virginia Beach 23462. Community theater company based in the Art Space at Pembroke Mall presents a full schedule of plays, plus workshops and classes.

Little Theatre of Virginia Beach (757-428-9233; www.ltvb.com), 550 Barberton Drive. All-volunteer community theater company six blocks from the oceanfront at 24th Street has been producing classics since 1948.

Mystery Dinner Playhouse (804-649-2583 or 888-471-4802; www.mystery

dinner.com), Double Tree Hotel—Virginia Beach, 1900 Pavilion Drive. Critically acclaimed "killer" scripts unfold while you enjoy a four-course meal. Advance reservations required.

Regent University Theatre (757-226-4245; www.regent.edu/theatre), 1000 Regent University Drive, Virginia Beach 23464. University-level theatrical productions of new and classic works in all genres.

✪ ✿ *1607: First Landing* **Outdoor Drama** (757-417-7012; www.firstlanding foundation.com), Bayside House/Building 711, Fort Story. The beautifully costumed *1607: First Landing,* by local playwright Chip Fortier, recounts the arrival of English settlers on Cape Henry, seen through the eyes of the resident American Indians, on an outdoor stage set against a backdrop of wild dunes and the Atlantic Ocean. Memorial Day to Labor Day. See Fort Story security information under *Historic Sites and Memorials.*

✿ **Theatrix Productions** (757-589-1644; www.kidspaw.com), 821 Sunnyside Drive, Virginia Beach 23464. Nonprofit children's theater offers classes, camps, and full-scale musical productions.

Virginia Musical Theatre Broadway at the Center Series (757-340-5446; www.broadwayatthecenter.com), Sandler Center (201 Market Street, Town Center, Virginia Beach 23462). Well into its second decade of producing musical theater revivals and new works, this locally based group blends nationally recognized stars with local talent.

THE OUTDOOR DRAMA AT THE HISTORIC VILLAGES AT CAPE HENRY TAKES PLACE ON THE DUNES WHERE ENGLISH SETTLERS FIRST MET NATIVE AMERICANS.

✳ To Do

Home of both the most visited (First Landing) and one of the least visited (False Cape) state parks in the Virginia system, Virginia Beach is the state's quintessential oceanfront resort, the place Virginians call "the Beach."

Beyond the Boardwalk, VB is truly a natural paradise. One of the last unspoiled salt marshes in the country lies within its borders, along with more than 120 miles of navigable waterways, more than 200 city parks, and 18,600 acres of protected, pristine habitat.

BEACHES More than 35 miles of waterfront, most of it sandy beach, stretch along the north and east sides of Virginia Beach. The northern beaches lie on the shores of Chesapeake Bay. Here the water is calm and the waves modest, suitable for young children, swimmers, and windsurfers. During

VIRGINIA BEACH AND SANDBRIDGE HOST NUMEROUS SURF SCHOOLS AND COMPETITIONS EACH YEAR.

the summer, dolphin sightings are just about guaranteed in the morning and late afternoon.

The broad oceanfront beaches in the resort area offer the most amenities—and the largest summer crowds. Farther south, stretching nearly to the North Carolina border, Croatan and Sandbridge beaches are favorite destinations for surfers, offering seclusion and a more relaxed beach experience.

Fires, glass containers, and alcoholic beverages are not permitted on any public beach. Pets are forbidden from Memorial Day to Labor Day on the Boardwalk, the sand in front of it, and the grassy strip between the hotels and the Boardwalk.

Detailed information on beach access is available from the **Virginia Beach Visitor Center** (757-437-4888 or 800-446-8038; www.vbfun.com).

Oceanfront Beaches
♿ The Boardwalk and Resort Area Beach. The city's signature sight runs 3 miles from Rudee Inlet to 41st Street, paralleling Atlantic Boulevard. The beach here is 300 feet wide and groomed each day. The Boardwalk, actually two parallel cement paths—one for strolling and rollerblading, another for bikes—is 38 feet wide. Skateboards are not allowed on the Boardwalk. During the summer months, oceanfront stages at 7th, 17th, 24th, 25th, and 31st streets host live music nightly.

Handicapped-accessible beach access points can be found on each block. At 8th, 17th, 24th, and 30th streets, 8-foot-wide wooden walkways reach to the water's edge. All-terrain wheelchairs are available free of charge at 17th and 24th streets.

Lifeguards remain on duty mid-May to late Sept. Public restrooms can be found at 17th, 24th, and 30th streets.

The city provides numerous parking options along this stretch. Metered parking lines the side streets, and municipal lots can be found on Atlantic Avenue at the Rudee Loop and at Fourth Street, and on Pacific Avenue at 19th and 25th streets.

Fees are collected Apr.–Sept. Large municipal garages located between Atlantic and Pacific at Ninth and 30th streets charge fees all year. Daily or overnight RV parking is available at the Fourth Street lot. Call 757-385-2000 for more information.

North End Beach. The stretch of beach between Fort Story and 42nd Street along Atlantic Avenue is mostly frequented by residents and renters in vacation homes nearby. Public access points can be found at the end of nearly every street, but parking can be a problem. Look for a spot on the west side of Atlantic Avenue. No public restrooms or other facilities. Lifeguards are stationed near the Wyndham Hotel at 57th Street, and patrols mounted on all-terrain vehicles roam during the summer months.

Croatan Beach. Quiet beach, favored by locals and surfers, lies south of Rudee Inlet, stretching for a mile to Camp Pendleton. Surfers gather around the jetty at Rudee, where surfing is permitted all day. Public restrooms and changing facilities are available. Lifeguards are on duty during the summer. To find this beach, turn south on Croatan Boulevard off General Booth Boulevard. A large public parking lot ($4–5 after 10 AM) is located at the south end of Vanderbilt Avenue.

✪ ✦ ♿ **Sandbridge Beach.** Located 15 miles to the south of the resort area, this quiet community of vacation cottages, sand dunes, and sea oats has a wide beach, although a clay ledge sometimes exposed by shifting sands can make for slippery footing. Two parks with lifeguards in the summer months offer public access to the dunes at the north and south ends of the strand.

To reach Sandbridge from the resort area, follow Pacific Avenue south to General Booth Boulevard, turn left on Princess Anne Road at the landmark **Nimmo Methodist Church,** then bear left onto Sandbridge Road. Turn right onto Sandpiper Road to reach Little Island City Park. The drive takes about 40 minutes.

STROLLING ON SANDBRIDGE BEACH IS A POPULAR ACTIVITY YEAR–ROUND.

Public restrooms and a municipal parking lot are located near the Sandbridge Market at the junction of Sandfiddler and Sandbridge roads at the north end of the beach. Parking fees (maximum $5 per day) are charged Memorial Day–Labor Day. Another large parking lot and a bathhouse with changing facilities are located at the south end of Sandbridge at **Little Island Park** (757-426-0013 or 800-822-3224; www.vbgov.com/parks; 3820 S. Sandpiper Road, Virginia Beach 23456), a 144-acre city park adjacent to the Back Bay National Wildlife Refuge. The beach here is divided into separate sections for surfing, swimming, and surf fishing. A fishing pier charges a daily fee ($6, Apr.–Oct.). Surfing is permitted north of the pier all day. Lifeguards are on duty Memorial Day–Labor Day.

Amenities include umbrella, beach chair, bike, and body board rentals; a playground; covered picnic area with grills; concessions; basketball, volleyball, and lighted tennis courts; restrooms; and outdoor showers. Balls, nets, and other equipment can be checked out from the park office for free. The fishing pier is handicapped accessible, and a complimentary beach wheelchair is available.

During the summer, the city sponsors free family entertainment at the beach park several days a week. Parking is $5 Memorial Day weekend–Labor Day. A canoe and kayak launch can be found across from the parking lot on Back Bay.

Chesapeake Bay Beaches

Chicks Beach (757-437-4888 or 800-822-3224; www.chicks-beach.com). A favorite with locals who frequent the restaurants and casual clubs found here, as well as the uncrowded, snow white sands, Chicks, an abbreviation of Chesapeake, lies along the bay, well hidden deep in a neighborhood. Public access points are located along two sections of Ocean View Avenue on either side of the Chesapeake Bay Bridge-Tunnel. Lookout Road connects the two sections. To find Chicks from the resort area, head east on Shore Drive (US 60). After crossing the Lesner Bridge, turn right on any road from Indian Hill to Pleasure House Road and head north. Some on-street parking is available, or you can pay ($5 until 4 PM) to park in the lot at **Alexander's On the Bay** (757-464-4999; www.alexandersonthebay.com; 4536 Ocean View Avenue at Fentress Avenue, Virginia Beach 23455), a fine-dining spot with terrific sunset views being rebuilt after sustaining extensive storm damage in 2009. Other establishments at Chicks are **HK On The Bay** (757-605-3024; www.hkonthebay.com; Lookout Road at Fentress Avenue), a casual restaurant with weekend bands, and the **Green Parrot Grille** (757-460-4640; www.greenparrot grille.com; Lookout Road at Seaview Avenue), with daily happy hours and entertainment. All offer outdoor dining. No public restrooms are available.

✪ ✎ ☀ ♿ ✥ **First Landing State Park** (757-412-2300; www.dcr.virginia.gov), 2500 Shore Drive. This wide, clean, generally uncrowded 1.5-mile-long beach combines the quiet waters of the Chesapeake with stunning views of battleships and barges entering the mouth of the bay. This is a great place to swim with dolphins. Parking is $4 weekdays and $5 weekends. Public restrooms and showers are available near the Bay Store, where you can buy food, drinks, and bait, and rent fishing and crabbing gear or bikes. Pets are welcome on a leash. No lifeguards. Boardwalks to the beach are handicapped accessible, and a beach wheelchair is available. Call 757-412-2320 for information.

First Landing has an even quieter, less visited beach. The **Narrows,** considered a secret getaway by many locals, fronts on Broad Bay, the eastern tributary of Lynnhaven Bay. The water here is salty and shallow, the white-sand beach is wide, and the surf nonexistent. To find the Narrows, take 64th Street west from Atlantic Avenue and drive to the end of the road. The beach and its parking lot are on the left, just before the restrooms and boat ramp.

Lynnhaven Boat and Beach Facility (757-460-7590), 356 Piedmont Circle. Park on the western side of the Lesner Bridge over Lynnhaven Inlet, and follow the walkway under the bridge to find **Ocean Park Beach,** a truly undiscovered Chesapeake Bay beach. Bathhouse with changing facilities and showers, fee to park, open 24 hours a day.

BEACH AND BIKE RENTALS Chesapean Outdoors (757-961-0447 or 866-379-5188; www.chesapean.com), 313 Laskin Road. Rentals of beach cruiser and trail bikes, kayaks and surfboards, with delivery available. Bike tours of the North End beaches and Cape Henry.

Moneysworth Beach Home Equipment Rentals (757-468-3999 or 800-662-2122; www.mworth.com), 601 Sandbridge Road, Virginia Beach 23456. Rent beach chairs and umbrellas, linens and towels, baby equipment, rollaways, bikes, and sports equipment by the week. Free delivery and pickup.

Ocean Rentals (757-721-6210 or 800-695-4212; www.oceanrentalsltd.com), 577 Sandbridge Road, Virginia Beach 23456. Sandbridge location rents beach cruiser bikes, kayaks and canoes, surfboards, household goods from gas grills to fans, baby equipment, linens, and beach chairs. Great weekly package deals.

BICYCLING With flat terrain and an extensive system of bike trails, Virginia Beach offers excellent cycling opportunities for all ages. Most of the city's top attractions can be reached by bike. Bicyclists can use any city sidewalk, except those in the resort area and Town Center. You are not allowed to ride on the beach or the pedestrian Boardwalk in the resort area. Helmets must be worn by riders 14 years and younger.

The **Tidewater Bicycle Association** (www.tbarides.org) maintains a busy schedule of rides throughout the region for all ability levels and types of equipment, including tandem and recumbent cyclists. Contact them in advance to join in.

The city of Virginia Beach currently has more than 100 miles of designated bikeways and trails, with more being added each year. Consider joining a guided ride sponsored by one of the local bike shops to become familiar with the local rules of the road. A map of Virginia Beach's bikeways and trails is available from bike shops, the visitors center, or can be downloaded at www.vbgov.com/parks.

The most popular route is the 3-mile paved bike path running alongside the **Boardwalk.** Here you'll find cyclists of all ages, including many families enjoying a spin together in four-wheel surreys, some with fringe on top.

From the north end of the Boardwalk bikeway, you can cut over to the Atlantic Avenue service road, which runs all the way to Fort Story. Bring your picture ID if you plan to bike through the army base. You can also turn west down 64th Street and enter the southern section of First Landing State Park.

The **Cape Henry Trail,** a 6-mile, multiuse path through the maritime forest at First Landing State Park, is a lovely and easy ride for all ages. Access this trail from the 64th Street entrance or the park's Trail Center. Parts of the trail are paved.

Heading south from the resort area, a widened bike path on Pacific Avenue leads over the Rudee Inlet Bridge, connecting with a multiuse paved path running next to General Booth Boulevard past the Virginia Aquarium and Ocean Breeze Waterpark as far as **Red Wing District Park.**

The **Park Connector Bikeway** runs from Princess Anne Park to Mt. Trashmore District Park, about 5 miles away. Another multiuse path runs along Shore Drive to First Landing State Park.

Back Bay National Wildlife Refuge and False Cape State Park, located between Sandbridge Beach and the North Carolina state line, are closed to automobile traffic and popular for longer bike rides. Gravel, sand, and dirt roads lead between the ocean and bay, with many opportunities to see wildlife and historic sites. Be sure to take water, energy food, and a tire repair kit, as neither park offers concessions.

The **Dismal Swamp Canal Trail** in nearby Chesapeake is another great bike ride. Running 8.3 miles along old US 17, now restricted to biking, hiking, and horseback riding, the route parallels the Dismal Swamp Canal, an ecological and historical treasure. The northern trailhead can be found at the intersection of Old Route 17 and Dominion Boulevard.

Mountain bikers looking for off-road adventure can access a complex of single-track dirt trails behind the Corporate Landing School complex on Dam Neck Road.

BIKE RENTALS A cruise along the Boardwalk bike path is a tradition every beachgoer should try. Surrey bikes can hold a whole family—up to 10 people. Convenience and food-mart stores often have the lowest prices for bike and surrey rentals. Most carry groceries, souvenirs, beer, wine, and beach supplies, as well as other beach rentals from chairs and umbrellas to boogie boards, roller blades, and baby strollers. These convenience stores also stay open very late, often until midnight in the summer season. While rental outlets along the Boardwalk typically close down in the off-season, the convenience stores along Atlantic Avenue rent bikes all year.

Atlantic Convenient Mart (757-491-6143), 28th Street and Atlantic Avenue.

Atlantic Food Mart (757-422-3437), 16th Street and Atlantic Avenue.

Boardwalk Convenience and Bike Rental (757-417-7307), 1211 Atlantic Avenue, 13th Street and Boardwalk (inside the Surfside Resort).

Cherie's Bike & Blade Rental (757-437-8888), many locations: 215, 705, 921, 1211, 1909, 2201, 2321, 2417, and 3501 Atlantic Avenue. With numerous locations along the Boardwalk, this family-run company rents bikes, rollerblades, and the popular surrey bikes in several sizes, May–Oct.

NJ Convenience & Gift (757-491-6792), 18th Street and Boardwalk (inside the Howard Johnson Motel).

Quick Food Mart (757-425-1368), 22nd Street and Atlantic Avenue.

Pier Food Mart (757-428-8111), 14th Street and Boardwalk (inside the Sandcastle Resort).

Prise Food Mart (757-437-8381), Ninth Street and Atlantic Avenue.

BIKE SHOPS BikeBeat (www.bikebeatonline.com). Hilltop North location: 1624 Laskin Road (757-491-6151); Kempsville location: 5386 Kemps River Drive (757-424-6151). Road and mountain bike group rides.

Conte's Bicycles and Fitness Equipment (www.contebikes.com).

TOURING IN A KAYAK IS THE BEST WAY TO SEE THE MANSIONS LINING LYNNHAVEN INLET AND ITS BAYS.
Karen Wright

Hilltop location: 1805 Laskin Road (757-491-4085); Red Mill location: 2185 Upton Drive (757-430-1299). Training rides through Great Neck, Shore Drive, and Pungo.

Fat Frog's Bike and Fitness (757-427-9488; www.fatfrogsbikes.com), 1169 Nimmo Parkway, Red Mill Commons, Virginia Beach 23456. Daily training rides on a 21-mile loop through Pungo. Maps online.

BOATS & BOATING To really get to know Virginia Beach, you must see it from the water. Ride along the oceanfront on an excursion boat or a Jet Ski, steer a kayak or a stand-up paddleboard through the mirror-still waters of Lynnhaven Inlet or the reeds of Back Bay, catch a wave down at the jetty, or just hang out with the dolphins.

Boat Ramps and Public Water-Access Points

A map of waterway access points is available from the visitors center or can be downloaded from www.vbgov.com/parks. Another good site to visit is www.kayakvb.com, maintained by an avid local kayaker who lists many of the local put-ins, complete with maps.

Launching into **Lynnhaven Bay,** a great saltwater estuary with numerous inlets, gives access to many miles of usually quiet waters, ideal for kayaking, fishing, and even stand-up paddleboarding. Some of most impressive and historic homes in the area are found on these shores, as well as the latest generations of the famous Lynnhaven oysters.

One of the most convenient launch sites, very close to the resort area, is the First Landing boat ramp at the **Narrows** (757-412-2300), located at the western end of 64th Street. Kayaks and canoes can launch from the wide sandy beach for free. Motorized craft using the boat ramp pay a small fee.

The **Lynnhaven Boat and Beach Facility** (757-460-7590), at the west side of the Lesner Bridge on Crab Creek, also charges a fee to launch motorized craft.

The **Owl Creek Boat Launch** (757-385-1100), next to the Virginia Aquarium on General Booth Boulevard, is primarily used by powerboats headed for Rudee Inlet and the ocean beyond.

The **Hutton Circle** kayak-only launch (757-385-1100), located off Virginia Beach Boulevard, puts you in the water at the far southern end of the Lynnhaven Bay system. Another city-maintained launch at **Carolanne Farm Park** (757-385-1100) gives kayakers access to the Elizabeth River.

Another popular area to kayak is the **North Landing River Natural Area Preserve** (757-925-2318), in southwest Virginia Beach. Good put-in sites include Dozier's Bridge on Princess Anne Road and the dead end of Old Pungo Ferry Road.

Munden Point Park (757-426-5296), a city facility on the North Landing River, has a ramp for motorboats ($5 to launch), as well as kayak and canoe rentals ($6/hour) for use on adjacent Oakum Creek. Waterskiing is a popular activity on this wide part of the Intracoastal Waterway.

Water access points in **False Cape State Park** (757-426-7128), at Barbour Hill, False Cape, and Wash Woods, are primarily intended as spots to dock while you explore this wilderness area. Launch a kayak just north of the park from the parking lot of **Back Bay National Wildlife Refuge** (757-721-2412) or at **Little Island District Park** (757-426-0013), where the trail to the launch, about 30 yards long, is directly across from the parking lot.

Other access points for both motorized and paddled craft are located on the other side of Back Bay at **Back Bay Landing** and **Princess Anne Wildlife Management Area,** both operated by the Virginia Department of Game and Inland Fisheries (804-367-9587; www.dgif.virginia.gov/boating).

Kayakers wanting to explore the northern reaches of the bay, called, reasonably enough, North Bay, have several spots to put in, including **Horn Point,** with handicapped parking and restrooms, and **Lotus Garden Park** on Sandbridge Road, an especially lovely spot when the many lotus plants bloom in summer. From here, you can paddle a loop back to the put-in. One popular destination for kayakers is this area is **Blue Pete's Restaurant** (757-453-6478), a longtime landmark on Muddy Creek.

Motorized boats wanting to access North Bay can put in for free at the boat ramp on Mill Landing Road off Princess Anne Road or pay a small fee to launch at **North Bay Shore Campground** (757-426-7911), off Sandbridge Road.

Many more kayaking and boating opportunities can be found in the southern reaches of Chesapeake along the Northwest River and in the Dismal Swamp. For additional boat ramps, see *Marinas.*

Canoe & Kayak Tours and Rentals

While the crowds rush to the beach and the nightlife of the Boardwalk, ecotourists discover another side of VB. Thousands of little canals, streams, and bays meander through the landscape, quiet back roads paved with water, ready to be explored.

Back Bay Getaways (757-721-4484; www.backbaygetaways.com), 3713 S. Sandpiper Road, Sandbridge. Specializing in excursions into the Back Bay Wildlife Refuge and False Cape State Park by a variety of methods—kayak, bike, airboat, and Jet Ski, with three-day ecocamps that combine them all. Rentals of single and double kayaks, mountain bikes, surfboards; near Little Island Park.

Chesapean Outdoors (757-961-0447 or 866-379-5188; www.chesapean.com), 313 Laskin Road. Kayak and bike tours around the North End beaches and Cape Henry. Dolphin encounters for all abilities are a specialty. Rentals of single and tandem kayaks, surfboards, and bikes with delivery from Owls Creek to the Lesner Bridge, including the resort area. Rent kayaks by the hour from the Chesapean stand at the Wyndham Hotel.

False Cape State Park Kayak Paddle (757-426-7128; www.dcr.virginia.gov), 4001 Sandpiper Road, Sandbridge. Ranger-led tours explore the ecology of Back Bay. Reservations required.

Rudee Inlet Jet Ski (757-428-4614; www.beachparasail.com), 300 Winston Salem Avenue. Rent a single or double kayak by the hour for a paddle around Rudee Inlet.

SouthEast Expeditions (757-331-2680; www.southeastexpeditions.net), 32218 Lankford Highway, Cape Charles 23310. Tours of the Eastern Shore for all abilities, including a popular paddle to a winery.

✪ ✐ ➻ **Surf & Adventure Co.** (757-721-6210 or 800-695-4212; www.surfandadventure.com), 577 Sandbridge Road, Virginia Beach 23456. Located on the road to Sandbridge Beach. The friendly locals here know the surrounding waters well and specialize in ocean kayak trips where dolphins are a given, and sea turtle and even whale sightings are possible. Other tours include sunset dinner paddles to Blue Pete's and explorations of Back Bay.

✪ **Wild River Outfitters** (757-431-8566 or 877-431-8566; www.wildriveroutfitters .com), 3636 Virginia Beach Boulevard, Virginia Beach 23452. Owned and operated by Lillie Gilbert, recognized expert on the local waterways, Wild River offers the greatest variety of paddle tours in the region, from the historic shores of Lynnhaven Bay to overnights in Lake Drummond. Special women's trips available.

Jet Ski & Powerboat Rentals

Back Bay Getaways (757-721-4484; www.backbaygetaways.com), 3713 S. Sand-piper Road, Sandbridge, Virginia Beach 23456. Rentals of Jet Skis, pontoon boats, and jon boats at a convenient location at the south end of Sandbridge Beach.

Dockside Seafood & Fishing Center (757-481-4545; www.fishingvabeach.com), 3311 Shore Drive. Carolina skiffs for rent by the hour at the mouth of Lynnhaven Inlet.

Rudee Inlet Jet Ski (757-428-4614; www.beachparasail.com), 300 Winston Salem Avenue. Rent a single or double Jet Ski, or a powerboat for a fast run up the beach.

Marinas

Lynnhaven Bay: **Bubba's Marina** (757-481-3513; www.bubbasseafoodrestaurant .com), 3323 Shore Drive. Twenty-four-hour boat ramp, transient slips, full-service bait and tackle shop, private fishing charters. **Bubba's Crab House** serves fresh fish and steamed crabs, inside or outside on a covered dock.

✪ **Dockside Seafood and Fishing Center** (757-481-4545; www.fishingvabeach .com), 3311 Shore Drive. Boat slips; rentals; fishing trips with low, family-friendly prices; sunset dolphin watch cruises; groceries and fresh fish market. Out back, the **Dockside Inn Restaurant** offers daily happy hours, outdoor dining, and early-bird specials.

Long Bay Pointe Marina (757-321-4550; www.longbaypointemarina.com), 2109 W. Great Neck Road. Boating resort accommodates craft up to 200 feet; fuel dock, fitness center, salon and spa, bait and tackle shop, and two restaurants on-site, including the highly rated **One Fish-Two Fish** (757-496-4350; www.onefish-two fish.com) and **La Marinella Trattoria Italiana** (757-412-0203; www.lamarinella .biz).

Lynnhaven Municipal Marina (757-460-7590; www.vbgov.com/parks), 3211 Lynnhaven Drive. Public marina on the east side of the Lynnhaven Inlet is home to a charter fishing fleet. Transient slips available by the day or week. **Chick's Oys-ter Bar** (757-481-5757; www.chicksoysterbar.com), a popular local happy hour destination, is just across the parking lot.

The Marina at Marina Shores (757-496-7000; www.marinashores.com), 2100 Marina Shores Drive. Full-service marina near the entrance to Lynnhaven Inlet offers transient slips, swimming pool, TV lounge, bait and tackle shop, fishing charters, and two fun waterfront restaurants: **Kokoamos Island Bar, Grill, and Yacht Club** (757-481-3388; www.kokoamos.com) and the **Surf Rider Grill** (757-481-5646; www.surfridergroup.com).

North Landing River: **Blackwater Trading Post** (757-421-2803), 5605 Blackwater Road, Virginia Beach 23457. Boat ramp and canoe launch, snacks, bait, fishing licenses, restrooms; located on Blackwater Creek, one of the larger tributaries of the North Landing River.

West Neck Marina (757-426-6735), 3985 W. Neck Road, Virginia Beach 23456. Boat and canoe launch, bait and tackle store, snacks.

Rudee Inlet: Anchoring the south end of the resort area, Rudee's is home to most of the offshore fishing fleet, sight-seeing boats, Jet Skis, and parasailing companies in the area, as well as some very popular restaurants. A walkway connects Rudee's with the Boardwalk via Fifth Street.

Fisherman's Wharf Marina (757-428-2111; www.fishermanswharfmarina.com), 524 Winston Salem Avenue. Largest marina in Rudee Inlet has transient slips for boats up to 80 feet, and a charter fishing fleet, including larger boats that can accommodate groups of more than six anglers.

ⓣ **Inlet Station Marina at Rudee Inlet** (757-422-2999; www.rudeesmarina .com), 227 Mediterranean Avenue. Protected berths for craft up to 100 feet are located a five-minute walk from the Boardwalk. Showers, pump-out station, charter fishing on-site, plus two popular restaurants: **Rudee's On The Inlet** (757-425-1777; www.rudees.com), with a popular outdoor cabana bar and free Wi-Fi access, and **Rockafeller's** (757-422-5654; www.rockafellers.com), where sunsets and seafood are the specialties.

Virginia Beach Fishing Center (757-491-8000 or 800-725-0509; www.virginia fishing.com), 200 Winston Salem Avenue. Located at the mouth of Rudee Inlet, with dockage and fuel on both sides of the bridge to accommodate boats that need more than the 28-foot clearance. Large charter fishing fleet; professional fish cleaning; parasailing; Jet Ski, kayak, and boat rentals; and sight-seeing cruises. A convenience store with ATM sells bait and tackle, beer, and souvenirs. **Big Sam's Inlet Café and Raw Bar** (757-428-4858; www.bigsamsrawbar.com) is on-site, with free parking.

FAMILY FUN With more than two hundred parks within the city limits, Virginia Beach has something for every member of the family. City parks typically have playgrounds, walking trails, shuffleboard and volleyball courts, horseshoe pits, picnic tables with grills, and public restrooms, and many have a fishing lake, as well as lighted basketball, softball, and tennis courts. Balls, bats, horseshoes, and other equipment can usually be checked out for free at the park offices with ID. Most parks also have picnic shelters for groups. Call 757-385-2550 to reserve.

In addition, the city operates six community recreation centers, each with indoor pool and gymnasium, plus a full roster of activities. Visitors can use these facilities by buying a one-day pass, $5 for children 3–17, $7 for adults and seniors, with discounts for 10-visit Fun Packs. Contact **Virginia Beach Parks and Recreation** (757-385-0401; www.vbgov.com/parks; 2289 Lynnhaven Parkway, Virginia Beach 23456) for locations, hours, and information.

Amusement Parks, Games & Zoos

🐾 🌴 **Animal Jungle** (757-463-4065; www.animaljungle.com), 4318 Holland Road, Virginia Beach 23452. Visitors are welcome at this huge pet store housing seven rooms filled with birds and critters, two hundred tanks full of fish, and a reptile department ruled by Alexander the Great, a full-sized monitor lizard. Classes are offered in animal care.

🐾 **Back Bay Mining Company** (757-689-3353; www.backbaymining.com), 3640 Dam Neck Road, Virginia Beach 23453. Gem panning fun at the Virginia Beach Farmers Market.

🎯 **Flipper McCoys** (www.vbeach.com/flippers.htm), 2212 Atlantic Avenue. Pac Man and Asteroids fans will find video game oldies here, along with many newer games, pool tables, and a great selection of pinball classics. Open all year.

🐾 **Hunt Club Farm's Petting Farm** (757-427-9520; www.huntclubfarm.com), 2388 London Bridge Road, Virginia Beach 23456. Open daily from Easter through New Year's Eve. Admission $3. Pony rides on the weekends, $5.

🐾 **Jumpin Monkey** (757-306-1334; www.thejumpinmonkey.com), Lynnhaven Crossing Shopping Center, 829 Lynnhaven Parkway, Virginia Beach 23452. Safe indoor playground for babies through age nine has lots of inflatables, separate boys' and girls' areas, and costumes for dress-up.

🐾 **Jungle Golf** (757-425-7240; www.junglegolf.com), 22nd Street and Pacific Avenue. Minigolf course and its game room with pool, air hockey, and video games are open 24 hours during the summer. Parking on 23rd Street.

❂ 🎯 King Neptune's Indoor 3-D Mini Golf (757-422-1742; www.kingneptunes minigolf.com), 213 25th Street. Ten mind-boggling holes of fluorescent fun themed on the Lost Continent of Atlantis. Open all year.

🎯 **Laser Quest Virginia Beach** (757-463-6300; www.laserquest.com), 2682 Dean Drive, Virginia Beach 23452. Overnights, special missions, birthday parties, solo and team games.

Motor World (757-422-6419; www.vbmotorworld.com), 700 S. Birdneck Road. Located behind Ocean Breeze Waterpark, this entertainment complex has something for everyone, from an adult speed track to kiddie rides, paintball battle range, climbing wall, bumper boats, Shipwreck minigolf, Skycoaster, and 11 different go-cart tracks. Hours vary; each activity is priced individually.

🐾 **Ocean Breeze Waterpark** (757-422-4444; www.oceanbreezewaterpark.com), 849 General Booth Boulevard. Just 2 miles from the Boardwalk (look for the giant gorilla), this maze of 16 water slides, a million-gallon wave pool, expansive water playground for the youngest guests, and plenty of shade will keep you cool on a hot day. Adults $25, kids three to nine and seniors $18. Twilight specials and second-day admissions available. Open daily Memorial Day–Labor Day.

Virginia Beach Amusement Park (757-422-2307; www.virginiabeachamusement park.com), 233 15th Street at Atlantic Boulevard. Rides range from the Skyscraper for the extreme thrill seeker to water flumes and trains suitable for all ages. Pay per ride or purchase an All You Can Ride wristband. Open mid-Mar.–Oct.

🎯 **Virginia Beach Rock Gym** (757-499-8347; www.vbrg.com), 5049 Southern Boulevard, Virginia Beach 23462. Climb until 10 PM on the 32-foot wall, rappel tower, or boulder course. Classes in climbing and rappelling.

Bowling

You can bowl at the **Bayside Community Recreation Center** (757-460-7540;

www.vbgov.com/parks; 4500 First Court Road, Virginia Beach 23455) with a visitor
pass. **Pinboy's at the Beach** (757-428-5897; www.facebook.com/pinboys; 1577
Laskin Road) is convenient to the resort area and has pool tables and a game
arcade as well.

361

THE OLD DOMINION'S SEASIDE PLAYGROUND—VIRGINIA BEACH

Disc Golf Courses

The city park department (www.vbgov.com/parks) operates two disc golf courses.
The 20-hole course at **Bayville Farms Park** (757-460-7569; 4132 First Court
Road, near Shore Drive) was the area's first. The tournament-level 18-hole course
at **Munden Point Park** (757-426-5296; 2001 Pefley Lane, off Princess Anne Road
in Pungo) is the most unusual, with water hazard holes on finger piers reaching
into the North Landing River.

Skate Parks

While skateboards are not permitted on any sidewalk or street in Virginia Beach,
including the Boardwalk, the city does provide two outstanding free facilities within its park system. Helmets are required. Bikes must have peg covers. To receive
free wristbands, required to use the skate parks, apply for a free skate park pass by
using the form found on the city Web site (www.vbgov.com/skatepark). Parents
must sign for their minor children.

The **Mount Trashmore Skate Park** (757-473-5237; 310 Edwin Drive), designed
and built by TrueRide, with an extensive street course, 7-foot-deep bowl with a
Skatelite Pro surface, and a competition-sized vert ramp, welcomes skateboarders,
inline skaters, and BMX bikers.

The **Woodstock Park Skate Plaza** (757-366-4538; 5709 Providence Road) features a quarter pipe, vert wall, rails, hubba ledges, radial ledges, stairs, and
handrails.

For skateboarding in cold or rainy weather, visit **Mike'Sk8 Park** (757-480-3483;
www.mikesk8.com; 4247 E. Little Creek Boulevard, Norfolk 23518), a new indoor
facility just off Shore Drive, with open skating sessions and lessons for beginner to
advanced riders.

Playgrounds

Every park in the Virginia Beach system has at least one playground. Visit www.vb
gov.com/parks for a full listing. One unique spot is **Kids Cove** at Mt. Trashmore
Park (757-473-5237; 310 Edwin Drive), a handicapped-accessible playground
designed using children's ideas and input. **Red Wing Park** (757-437-2038; 1398
General Booth Boulevard) has three playground areas. Another city facility, **Seatack Community Recreation Center** (757-437-4858; 141 S. Birdneck Road), has
a climbing wall.

✔ ♿ **JT's Grommet Island Beach Park & Playground for Every "Body"**
(www.grommetisland.org), 100 Second Street. New oceanfront playground and
park at the southern end of the Boardwalk is 100 percent handicapped accessible.

FISHING Located at the convergence of the Atlantic Ocean and the Chesapeake
Bay, the waters off the coast of Virginia Beach are some of the richest fishing
grounds on the East Coast.

The Gulf Stream, just offshore, brings both subtropical and cold-water game fish
to the area, including tuna, blue marlin, wahoo, dolphin (mahimahi), and sailfish.

The Chesapeake, North America's largest estuary system, provides a refuge for numerous species, including cobia, croaker, and red and black drum, and is the breeding ground for an estimated 80 percent of the striped bass (also called rockfish or stripers) on the East Coast.

Spanning the mouth of the bay, the 17-mile-long **Chesapeake Bay Bridge-Tunnel (CBBT)** provides unique opportunities for fishing. Acting as an artificial reef, it is the favorite haunt of flounder, gray trout, king and Spanish mackerel, tautog, and little tunny. Fishing boats gather around the bridge pilings, or, if boats aren't your thing, you can experience deep-sea fishing from the **Seagull Pier,** 3.5 miles out to sea.

Another very productive area, especially for big stripers in the winter, is the concrete boat breakwater off **Kiptopeke State Park** on the Eastern Shore.

Each season brings different species to these waters. Summer is high season for yellowfin tuna, bluefish, and sailfish offshore, with amberjack, triggerfish, sea bass, and mackerel congregating around wrecks and the Chesapeake Light Tower. In fall, flounder and spot are frequently caught at local piers as they migrate out to sea.

As the weather cools, the stripers begin their run. Virginia Beach is called the Striped Bass Capital of the World for good reason. Huge numbers of these hard-fighting fish migrate through the area from November to February, and the state record, a 73-pound monster, was brought to boat here in 2008.

The country's largest striper tournament—the **Mid-Atlantic Rockfish Shootout** (www.midatlanticrockfishshootout.com)—is held each year in January. The **Striped Bass World Championship** (www.stripedbassworldchampionship.com) runs November through December, and the popular **"Rock Around the Clock" Rockfish Tournament** (757-331-2960; www.cbbt.com), a 24-hour marathon at Sea Gull Pier on the CBBT, takes place in late November.

Fishing Charters & Outfitters

Dozens of charter fishing boats make Virginia Beach their home base, and each marina has a number of charter captains working from its docks. In general, boats from the Lynnhaven marinas specialize in fishing Chesapeake Bay and around the CBBT, while the offshore fishing fleet docks at Rudee Inlet. Wreck fishing and inshore fishing are popular from both locations. Some captains also offer overnight trips for swordfish and other Gulf Stream species.

All captains of charters are licensed and typically have years of experience in finding fish. They can take you to legendary hot spots such as Norfolk Canyon, the Fishhook, the Cigar, and the Hotdog, as well as the many wrecks and reefs where the big fish live. To find out what might be biting during your vacation, visit **Dr. Julie Ball's Extreme Sportfishing** Web site (www.drjball.com), where you'll find years of archived fishing reports for the region. Dr. Ball, considered one of the top saltwater anglers in the world, conducts seminars and private fishing lessons.

Charters usually are for a full day offshore, a half day or full day inshore. If you don't care to fish, many boat captains will also take you out for sight-seeing trips, often at sunset after fishing is done for the day.

Check *Marinas* for links to the charter fishing boats working out of each location. Another excellent resource is the **Virginia Beach Sport Fishing** Web site (www.vbsf.net).

Fishing licenses are not required to fish from these piers unless otherwise stated.

&. **Little Island Fishing Pier** (757-426-0013; www.vbgov.com/parks or www.sand bridgepier.com), 3820 S. Sandpiper Road, Virginia Beach 23456. Located at the southern end of Sandbridge Beach, this 440-foot, fully accessible pier is open seven days a week almost all year. Fees of $7/day are assessed Apr.–Oct., when the pier is open until 11 PM.

Lynnhaven Fishing Pier (757-481-7071; www.lynnhavenpier.com), 2350 Starfish Road. Located off Shore Drive just east of the Lesner Bridge, this newly reconstructed pier offers great fishing and crabbing, along with excellent views of Chesapeake Bay. Open 24 hours a day, May–Oct. Admission charged. The famous **Lynnhaven Fish House** (757-481-0003; www.lynnhavenfishhouse.net) and **Pier Café** (open seasonally) are located on-site.

&. **Sea Gull Fishing Pier** (757-331-2960; www.cbbt.com), 32386 Lankford Highway, Cape Charles 23310. Located on the southernmost island on the CBBT, 3.5 miles from the Virginia Beach coast, this 625-foot, fully accessible pier gives anglers an opportunity for deep-sea fishing as well as stupendous views, without ever boarding a boat. No fee is charged for using the pier; however, you do have to pay the $12 bridge toll to get there. Restaurant, cleaning tables, bait shop, and certified weigh station on-site. Open 24 hours a day.

Virginia Beach Fishing Pier (757-428-2333), 15th Street at the Boardwalk. This 1,000-foot-long pier, located in the heart of the resort area, is currently threatened by development. Open Apr.–Oct. and 24 hours a day Memorial Day–Labor Day. Admission charged. **Ocean Eddie's** (757-425-7742; www.oceaneddiesvb.com), a popular seafood restaurant, is located on the pier, along with gift and shell shops.

Freshwater Fishing Lakes

Several lakes in Virginia Beach yield good freshwater fishing. You will need a Virginia Freshwater License to cast your line legally.

Lake Smith (5381 Shell Road at Northampton Boulevard), separated from Norfolk's Lake Whitehurst by US 13, yields citation-sized largemouth bass. The lake itself is owned by Norfolk, so a Norfolk boat permit is required if you want to launch at the dirt ramp. Get a daily pass ($5) in person or by mail from the City of Norfolk, Department of Utilities (757-664-6701; www.norfolk.gov; 400 Granby Street, Norfolk 23510).

Mount Trashmore Park (757-473-5237) has a deep lake harboring largemouth bass, sunfish, white perch, and some fairly large carp. Shore fishing only.

Head or Party Boats

Dockside Seafood and Fishing Center (757-481-4545; www.fishingvabeach .com), 3311 Shore Drive. Low-priced fishing trips for the whole family offered year-round. Half-day, wreck, and striped bass trips available. Children under three free.

Rudee Inlet Charters (757-422-5700 or 757-425-3400; www.rudeeinletcharters .com), 200 Winston Salem Avenue. The three head boats of the Rudee Inlet fleet, holding more than a hundred passengers each, with snack bars, restrooms, and heated and air-conditioned lounges, schedule full- and half-day trips to near-shore and inshore waters. During the fall and winter, they also make "extreme" trips of

16 and 36 hours, venturing up to 80 miles offshore in pursuit of tuna, swordfish, blue fish, tile fish, sea bass, and grouper.

Kayak Fishing

Virginia Beach is a top location for light tackle and kayak fishing. Lynnhaven and Rudee inlets, both saltwater estuaries noted for their speckled trout and puppy drum, are ideal locations for these activities. Shallow Back Bay, with its mix of brackish water and freshwater, produces white perch, channel catfish, and flounder.

Find out more about kayak fishing in the region at www.eastcoastkayakfishing.com and from the **Tidewater Kayak Anglers Association** (757-348-2232; www.tkaa .org; 1230 Lake Point Drive, Chesapeake 23320).

The **Pirates of Lynnhaven** (www.piratesoflynnhaven.org; P.O. Box 61005, Virginia Beach 23466), another group dedicated to the sport, enjoy showing novices the ropes and organize many charity events.

Kayak Fishing with Kayak Kevin (757-572-8048; www.kayakkevin.com). Kevin Whitley is the first kayak angler to be awarded the status of Expert Angler by the Virginia Saltwater Tournament.

Ocean Eagle Kayak Adventures (757-589-1766; www.oceaneaglekayak.com). Four-hour trips for up to two anglers include all gear, rod and reel, fishing instruction, license, and guide. Nature, dolphin, and romantic tours also available.

Ruthless Fishing, Inc (757-403-0734; www.ruthlessfishing.com). Cory Routh, one of the region's first kayak fishing guides and author of the book *Kayak Fishing*, offers classes, private instruction, and kayak fishing excursions, including trophy striper trips to Kiptopeke State Park.

Tackle Shops

Additional bait and tackle stores can be found at the marinas and piers listed earlier in this chapter.

Bruce's Bait and Tackle (757-426-3474; www.brucesbaitandtackle.com), 1650 General Booth Boulevard, Kmart Plaza, Virginia Beach 23454. Everything you need for freshwater or saltwater fishing, inshore or offshore, pier or surf. Licenses for fresh or salt.

Long Bay Pointe Bait and Tackle (757-481-7517; www.longbaypointebaitand tackle.com), 2109 W. Great Neck Road. Shop in Long Bay Pointe Marina has the largest selection of live bait in the area, rod and reel repairs, and hot tips on where the fish are biting.

Oceans East II (757-464-6544), 5785 Northampton Boulevard, Virginia Beach 23455. Located near Lake Smith. Daily and annual boat permits, plus licenses, bass tackle.

GOLF With many courses designed by the top names in golf, and the possibility of play all year, Virginia Beach is a must-do destination for golfers. The courses listed below are public or semiprivate, including three municipal courses operated by the city.

Several companies offer complete golf vacation packages with accommodations and tee times, including **Virginia Golf Vacations** (877-806-8163; www.virginiagolf vacations.com) and **Golf Virginia Beach** (877-246-5382; www.golfvirginiabeach .net).

Virginia Beach Parks and Recreation's three municipal golf courses each offer a driving range, putting green and practice bunkers, golf shop, private and group lessons with PGA professionals, men's and women's locker rooms, and snack bar facilities. Tee times are available up to a week in advance.

Bay Creek Resort (757-331-8620 or 888-422-9275; www.baycreekresort.com), 3335 Stone Road, Cape Charles 23310. Selected by *Golf Digest* as one of the Best Places to Play in 2008–2009, this new resort on the Eastern Shore boasts two signature courses designed by Arnold Palmer and Jack Nicklaus. Two restaurants on-site: **Aqua** (757-331-8660), on the bayfront, and the **Coach House Tavern** (757-331-8631), overlooking the golf courses.

Bow Creek Municipal Golf Course (757-431-3763; www.vbgov.com/parks), 3425 Clubhouse Road, Virginia Beach 23452. Challenging 18-hole par 70, with narrow Bermuda fairways and bent grass greens, set amid mature oaks behind Lynnhaven Mall.

Cypress Point Country Club (757-490-8822; www.cypresspointgolf.com), 5340 Clubhead Road, Virginia Beach 23455. Par 72 designed by Tom Clark. Dining room, lounge, snack bar, pro shop on-site.

Hell's Point Golf Course (757-721-3400 or 888-821-3401; www.hellspoint.com), 2700 Atwoodtown Road, Virginia Beach 23456. Wicked par 72 designed by Rees Jones off Sandbridge Road is considered the area's best.

Heron Ridge Golf Course (757-426-3800; www.heronridge.com), 2973 Heron Ridge Drive, Virginia Beach 23456. Fourteen holes with water hazards make this Gene Bates/Fred Couples–designed course fun to play.

Honey Bee Golf Club (757-471-2768; www.golfhamptonroads.net), 500 S. Independence Boulevard, Virginia Beach 23456. Eighteen holes designed by Rees Jones, putting and chipping greens, a 300-yard driving range, and a unique 40-foot practice bunker.

Kempsville Greens Municipal Golf Course (757-474-8441; www.vbgov.com/parks), 4840 Princess Anne Road, Virginia Beach 23462. City-owned par 70 redesigned by Ellis Maples features a challenging back nine.

Lynnhaven Golf Park (757-468-2137; www.lynnhavengolf.com), 3173 Holland Road, Virginia Beach 23453. Family facility near Lynnhaven Mall with a golf driving range, minigolf, batting cages, picnic pavilions, and snack bar.

Owl's Creek Family Golf Course (757-428-2800; www.golfhamptonroads.net), 411 S. Birdneck Road. Public par 62 executive course is nicknamed the Little Monster. Heated and lighted driving range, club rentals, snack bar.

Red Wing Lake Municipal Golf Course (757-437-2037; www.vbgov.com/parks), 1144 Prosperity Road. Recently renovated George Cobb course now has bent grass greens and Bermuda grass fairways.

The Signature at West Neck (757-721-2900; www.signatureatwestneck.com), 3100 Arnold Palmer Drive, Virginia Beach 23456. Arnold Palmer designed this par 72 with 13 lakes, and scenic beach bunkers. **The Signature Grille** (757-689-0364) offers gourmet fare, as well as Sun. brunch and a casual pub-grub menu.

Stumpy Lake Golf Course (757-467-6119; www.golfhamptonroads.net), 4797

Indian River Road, Virginia Beach 23456. Unique par 72, designed by Robert Trent Jones Sr., is nearly surrounded by water. Completely renovated in 2007.

Virginia Beach National (757-563-9440; www.vbnational.com), 2500 Tournament Drive, Virginia Beach 23456. Designed by Pete Dye with assistance from hall of famer Curtis Strange, a local guy, this tournament-level public course, site of the Virginia Beach Open, is located in the Princess Anne Commons area. Tee times available online.

*✍ **YMCA of Hampton Roads Junior Golf Course** (757-563-8990; www.thefirst teehr.org), 2400 Tournament Drive, Virginia Beach 23456. Nine holes designed by Pete and Alice Dye specifically for kids 5–17 is located next to the Virginia Beach National course, along with a driving range, putting green, and short-game practice area. Special rates for children, seniors, family groups, and YMCA members.

HEALTH & FITNESS CLUBS Staffed fitness rooms equipped with circuit training, free weights, cardiovascular equipment, and fitness classes for all ages can be found at the city's Bayside, Bow Creek, Great Neck, Kempsville, Princess Anne, and Seatack community recreation centers. Visitors can use the city rec centers by buying a one-day pass ($5 for children 3–17, $7 for adults and seniors), with discounts for 10-visit Fun Packs. Contact **Virginia Beach Parks and Recreation** (757-385-0401; www.vbgov.com/parks; 2289 Lynnhaven Parkway, Virginia Beach 23456) for locations, hours, and information.

Hot House Yoga (757-428-0099; www.hothouseyogavb.com), 1952 Laskin Road, Virginia Beach 23454. Calcutta hot yoga method involves postures performed in a heated studio. Beginners' introduction, Vinyasa, and candlelit classes. Drop-ins welcome.

Inlet Fitness Centers (www.inletfitness.com), two Virginia Beach locations: 2101 W. Great Neck Road (757-412-0600), and **Inlet Fitness South,** 2336 Elson Green Avenue in Red Mill Commons (757-689-2446). Classes, steam rooms, tanning, outdoor yoga, boot camps, and more. Daily and weekly rates. Free one-day pass available online.

Oceanfront Yoga (757-233-8000; www.oceanfrontyoga.com), 3316 Atlantic Avenue. Raja, Vinyasa, prenatal, Pilates, and sun salutation classes offered in a peaceful oceanfront setting on the third floor of the Ocean Beach Club Discovery Center. Outdoor classes on the Boardwalk in season. Special classes for men. Free parking.

HORSEBACK RIDING **East Coast Equestrian Training Center** (757-270-5228; www.eastcoastsporthorses.com), 2508 W. Landing Road, Virginia Beach 23456. Lessons and five-day horse camps for ages six to adult in an indoor ring.

Easy Does It Riding Academy (757-721-4646; www.easydoesitranch.net), 3581 Muddy Creek Road, Virginia Beach 23456. Western riding lessons; summer camps for all ages, including a PeeWee Camp with no age limit; and ponies to ride. Beginners welcome.

Morning Star Horse Farm (757-237-2112; www.morningstarhorsefarm.com), 1501 Princess Anne Road, Virginia Beach 23456. Guided trail rides, English and Western lessons for all ages, birthday parties, and camps.

HUNTING Back Bay National Wildlife Refuge (757-721-2412) and **False Cape State Park** (757-426-7128) conduct a shotgun hunt for deer and feral hog every year in October.

Half-day waterfowl hunts take place in **Princess Anne Wildlife Management Area** (804-843-5966) from November to January. Dogs and decoys are allowed, and a special floating blind license may be required. Special hunts for teal ducks and Canada and snow geese, and a special Youth Waterfowl Day in October.

Several spots in the southern sections of the Eastern Shore also offer hunting opportunities. **Mockhorn Wildlife Management Area** (804-843-5966) permits muzzleloader and archery hunting for white-tailed deer. Wild turkey hunting takes place in the spring, with a special Youth Hunting Day in April. The **Eastern Shore National Wildlife Refuge** (757-331-2760) has archery and shotgun hunts for white-tailed deer in the fall.

Visit www.dgif.virginia.gov/hunting for more hunting options and regulations.

SPAS & SALONS Advanced **Fuller School of Massage Therapy** (757-340-7132; www.advancedfullerschool.com), 195 S. Rosemount Road, Virginia Beach 23452. Fully accredited massage school has 40 massage therapists on staff offering a wide range of massage and spa services, often at prices less than you'll find elsewhere.

✪ A.R.E. Health Center and Spa (757-437-7202; www.edgarcayce.org), 215 67th Street at Atlantic Avenue. Services based upon the readings of Edgar Cayce include cleansing and detoxifying packages.

Balance Therapeutic Massage (757-428-2222; www.balancemassagevb.com), 1952 Laskin Road, Virginia Beach 23454. Certified massage therapists at this Hilltop location offer Swedish and deep tissue, hot stone, and Thai massages.

♂ ↝ Flowering Almond Spa (757-424-5511; www.foundersinn.com), 5641 Indian River Road, Virginia Beach 23464. Luxurious retreat at Founder's Inn offers Asian body rituals for men and women, including caviar facials and Thai massage. Special packages for bridal parties.

Sumatra Salon & Spa (757-456-9900; www.sumatrasalon.com), 232 Central Park Avenue, Virginia Beach 23462. Located in Town Center, Sumatra specializes in makeup and haircuts, plus other pampering treatments.

SPECTATOR SPORTS While Virginia Beach has no NFL or NBA teams to brag about, the city hosts top-notch competitions for a number of other sports, including soccer, field hockey, baseball, and volleyball, as well as world-class training facilities.

The best place to check out the action is the **Princess Anne Commons Athletics Village** (757-385-4461; www.vbgov.com/parks; 4141 Dam Neck Road), near the Virginia Beach Farmers Market.

At the heart of the Commons, the **Virginia Beach Sportsplex** (757-427-2990; 2181 Landstown Road) is home to two semiprofessional football teams playing from July to October: The **Southern Virginia Trojans** (757-410-0702; www.southernvirginiatrojans.com) play in the East Coast Alliance Football League. The **Virginia Crusaders** (757-713-7460; www.masondixonfootballleague.com) topped the competition in the Mason Dixon League in 2008.

Next door to the Sportsplex, the **U.S. Field Hockey National Training Center** (757-427-2106; www.usfieldhockey.com; 2181 Landstown Road) is the official headquarters of the USA women's national field hockey team. The facility hosts several championship games each year, while the national indoor field hockey championship is held every March at the **Virginia Beach Convention Center** (757-385-2000; www.vbfun.com/conventioncenter; 1000 19th Street).

Another Princess Anne Commons facility, the **7 Cities Sports Complex** (757-282-9085; www.7citiessports.com, Princess Anne and Dam Neck roads), a state-of-the-art facility owned by major league professional baseball players, offers classes in player development, specialty clinics, and summer camps in several sports.

The **Hampton Roads Soccer Complex** (757-518-5176 or 757-368-4600; www.soccercomplex.org; 2276 Recreation Drive), also in Princess Anne Commons, hosts tournaments and training all year on its 19 playing fields.

Virginia Beach boasts two United Soccer League teams, both named the **Piranhas** (757-641-4460; www.hrpiranhas.com), in the W-League and the PDL League, playing regular season games from May to July at the Virginia Beach Sportplex. The **Virginia Wesleyan College** athletic teams (757-455-3303; www.vwc.edu/athletics), nicknamed the Marlins, compete in the Old Dominion Athletic Conference.

Every summer during the first week of June, the resort area's wide beaches host the **North America Sand Soccer Championships** (757-368-4600; www.sandsoccer.com), the world's largest sand soccer event, with some 10,000 soccer players of all ages from around the world and up to 100,000 spectators in attendance. A kids' clinic with a soccer superstar, Men's Open Championship, and beach lacrosse, wrestling, rugby, and coed flag football are all part of the weekend festivities.

For more action on the sand, look for the nets of **V2 Beach Volleyball** (757-410-0787; www.volleyballva.com) at 33rd Street and the oceanfront all summer long. In addition to league play, V2 offers volleyball clinics and a weekly volleyball club for youths 12–18.

The **Virginia Beach Polo Club** (757-627-1980; www.virginiabeachpoloclub.com) hosts scrimmages year-round, as well as the annual Chukkers for Charity match in the fall, at **Alpha Omega Farm** (2585 W. Landing Road, Virginia Beach 23456). Observers welcome.

The **Dominion Derby Girls** (757-626-0409; www.dominionderbygirls.net) hosts bouts of women's roller derby at **Haygood Roller Skating Center** (757-460-1138; www.haygoodskatingcenter.net; 1036 Ferry Plantation Road, Virginia Beach 23455) and at **Breakaway Skating Center** (757-488-1660; www.breakawayskatingcenter.com; 2850 A Airline Boulevard, Portsmouth 23701).

Seven Cities Boxing (www.7citiesboxing.org) stages the annual Virginia Golden Gloves Championship every March. The **Tidewater Boxing Association** (www.tidewaterboxing.com) sponsors amateur bouts throughout the year.

The **Virginia Beach Academy of Martial Arts** (757-468-6488; www.virginiabeachacademyofmartialarts.com; 3440 Chandler Creek Road) hosts **King of the Ring** (www.kingofthering.org) events.

TENNIS AND RACQUET SPORTS Virginia Beach Parks and Recreation maintains nearly two hundred public tennis courts around the city, available free of charge on a first come, first served basis. Many are lighted from April 1 to December 1, and some have lights all year. For a list of courts, hours, and locations, visit www.vbgov.com/parks or call 757-385-1100.

Courts for handball or racquetball are located at the city recreation centers at Bayside (757-460-7540), Kempsville (757-474-8492), Great Neck (757-496-6766), and Princess Anne (757-426-0022), and at Red Wing Park (757-437-2038). Reserve a court by phone or in person a day before play. You need a visitor pass to use the rec centers' facilities.

Lynnhaven Park (757-496-6742), 1246 Bayne Drive, next to Lynnhaven Middle School. Free play on 12 lighted hard-surface tennis courts.

Owl Creek Municipal Tennis Center (757-385-2695; www.owlcreektennis center.com), 928 S. Birdneck Road. Twelve lighted hard courts outdoors, and two climate-controlled courts indoors, plus a tennis shop, showers, and lessons by certified pros. Call for rates and reservations.

Virginia Beach Tennis Center (757-481-7545; www.hrtennis.com/vbtcc), 1950 Thomas Bishop Lane, Virginia Beach 23454. Thirty outdoor courts, most with clay surface, plus six indoor courts and a pro shop.

TOURING Virginia Beach Vacation Markets (757-502-7170; www.vbvacation market.com), with three locations on Atlantic Avenue at 16th, 25th, and 31st streets, sell discounted tickets to local and regional attractions.

By boat: See also our listings of kayak tours and ecotours in *Boats & Boating.*

Iggy Biggy Adventure Sailing (757-358-5800; www.iggybiggysailing.com). Two-hour sails aboard a 51-foot yacht include refreshments and a chance to take the helm.

Rudee Tours (757-425-3400; www.rudeetours.com or www.rudee rocket.com), 200 Winston Salem Avenue, Rudee Inlet. Board the 70-foot-long *Rudee Rocket* for a high-speed cruise, or catch a ride aboard one of its sister ships for a relaxing sunset tour complete with cocktails. Dolphin- and whale-watching cruises are offered in partnership with the Virginia Aquarium.

Ƴ *Virginia's Jewel* (757-425-6688; www.virginiasjewel.com), 600 Laskin Road. Cruise the calm waters of Broad Bay and Lynnhaven Inlet aboard a luxury yacht with climate-controlled decks, lounge, dance floor, and fully accessible stairways and restrooms. Dinner and sight-seeing cruises available.

By bus or tram: ✪ **Blue Goose Express** (757-721-2412 or 757-721-7666; www.bbrf.org or www.fws.gov/backbay), 4005 Sandpiper Road, Sandbridge, Virginia Beach 23456. Open-sided trams depart from the Back Bay Wildlife Refuge parking lot to False Cape State Park at 9 AM. Call for schedule. Most trips allow time to explore False Cape, returning to Back Bay by 1 PM. Adults $8, seniors (62-plus), and children 3–12 $6. From Apr. through Oct., you must also pay the $5 per vehicle entrance fee to Back Bay NWR.

Naval Air Station Oceana Tours (757-719-3886 or 757-433-3131; www.cnic .navy.mil/oceana). Weekday bus tours of the world's largest Master Jet Base include opportunities to see the resident Hornets and Super Hornets, as well Tomcats and other aircraft in the **Aviation Historical Park.** Tours are offered June–Labor Day at 9 and 11:30 AM. The 11:30 tour includes a stop for lunch (not included in ticket price) at the Officers' Club. Tickets available at the 24th Street Kiosk on Atlantic Avenue. Picture IDs are required for those 16 years old and up. Adults $11, children and seniors $9.

Terra Gator (800-933-7275; www.dcr.virginia.gov), 4001 Sandpiper Road, Virginia Beach 23456. On winter weekends Nov. 1–Mar. 31, this wide-wheeled vehicle makes the trip to False Cape State Park down the beach. $8 per person. Advance reservations required.

By Segway, automobile, or on foot: **Bayside History Trail** (757-431-4000; www.vbgov.com). Self-guided driving tour leads to early sites in Virginia Beach history, including the location of the "trial" of the Pungo Witch. Download a map from the VBgov.com Web site or pick one up at the **Bayside Area Library** (757-385-2680; 936 Independence Boulevard). All the historic buildings on the tour are open to the public on the third Sat. in May.

Histories and Haunts Ghost Walks (757-498-2127; www.historiesandhaunts .com). Walks conducted by actor, author, and historian Al Chewning, based on his book *Haunted Virginia Beach.*

⤷ **Segway of Hampton Roads** (757-412-9734; www.segwayofhamptonroads.us), 2800 Shore Drive, Virginia Beach Resort Hotel. Explore the nature and history of First Landing State Park or Back Bay Wildlife Refuge aboard the greenest form of transportation.

WATER SPORTS Note that no riding, flying, sailing, or boat launching is allowed along the beach in the Boardwalk area from Memorial Day to Labor Day.

Kiteboarding & Windsurfing

Windsurfing, also called sailboarding, is popular along the Chesapeake shore at Chicks Beach and First Landing State Park when winds are in the north or west. The **Windsurfing Enthusiasts of Tidewater** (www.sailwet.com) provide guidance and fellowship for visiting windsurfers. You can view a launch location map at www.windvisions.com.

The sport of kiteboarding is just getting started in the Virginia Beach area, but enthusiasts say that the Chesapeake Bay off the beaches of the Eastern Shore have some of the best—and least crowded—conditions on the coast, with solid southwest and northwest winds setting up epic downwinders. Launch from the public beach in the town of Cape Charles, an ideal spot for beginners with shallow water and consistent sideshore breeze, or south of the fishing jetty at Kiptopeke State Park. When winds are from the northeast, the oceanside barrier islands offer lots of new territory to explore.

The most popular spot for kiteboarding and windsurfing in the area is Sunset Beach, a private stretch of sand at the **Sunset Beach Resort** (757-331-1776; www.sunsetbeachresortva.com; 32246 Lankford Highway/US 13, Cape Charles 23310), on the Eastern Shore. The resort's **Pelican Pub,** located on the beach, is a gathering spot for boarders arriving by water. To launch there if you are not a guest at the resort, get permission through SouthEast Expeditions (see listing that follows), which has its headquarters next door.

For beginner to intermediate kiters, the best spot to launch in Virginia Beach is First Landing State Park. Intermediate to advanced kiters can launch into the

Atlantic at the 45th and 88th street beach access points. Some kiters also sail in Back Bay from the access at Little Island Park.

North End Cyclery Ltd. (757-428-4235; www.northendbikes.com), 3104 Arctic Avenue. Bike shop close to the resort area carries kiteboarding and stand-up paddleboard equipment. Repairs available.

SouthEast Expeditions Kiteboarding School (757-331-2680 or 877-943-8548; www.gogetlit.com), 32218 Lankford Highway (US 13), Cape Charles 23310. The area's first full-service kiteboarding shop offers lessons, excursions, and expert advice.

Parasailing

Soaring high above the water beneath a parachute is a favorite way to see Virginia Beach. The companies offering these trips are highly experienced and can either keep you entirely dry from takeoff to landing or take you down for an exciting dip in the water. The parasail season runs mid-April through October.

Adventure Parasail and Jet Ski (757-422-8359; www.beachparasail.com), 300 Winston-Salem Avenue, Rudee Inlet. Family-owned and -operated company, in business since 1985, has Coast Guard–certified captains and is licensed to fly up to three people at a time. Soar in parachute harness or ride in a unique parasail chair. Free parking. Online reservations. Early-bird specials.

Air America Parasail (757-428-1240; www.airamericaparasail.com), 227 Mediterranean Avenue, Rudee Inlet. Coast Guard–licensed captain and crew. Take off and land on the boat.

Rudee Inlet Parasail and Watersports (757-422-9600; www.rudeeinletpara sail.com), 200 Winston-Salem Avenue, Virginia Beach Fishing Center. Fly high with Captain Mickey aboard U.S. Coast Guard–inspected boats and the "smiley face" chutes, certified by the Professional Association of Parasail Operators. Online reservations; sunset flights. Handicapped- and children-friendly. Free parking.

Shore Drive Parasail (757-478-8246; www.virginiaparasailing.com), 3311 Shore Drive, Dockside Fishing Center. Leaving from the Lynnhaven Inlet area, this company gives you great views of Chesapeake Bay, the CBBT, and the Cape Henry lighthouses, at some of the best prices around. Tandem and early-bird discounts.

Snorkeling & Scuba

Hampton Roads is home to the East Coast's busiest shipping lanes as well as the U.S. Navy. With so many ships coming and going, collisions are inevitable. Add in storms and German U-boats, and you get a richly varied collection of wrecks on the seafloor, both in the ocean and in the bay.

In addition, various government agencies have worked to create an extensive system of artificial reefs in the area, scuttling decommissioned ships, landing craft, barges, tanks, missile launchers, and dry docks. The reefs and wrecks are home to tautog, flounder, sea bass, and lobster, making spearfishing a favorite activity for the scuba crowd.

Spots where you can snorkel or dive from the shore include the 64th Street beach on Broad Bay, First Landing State Park on the Chesapeake Bay, and the cement ship breakwater at Kiptopeke State Park in Cape Charles.

Contact one of the dive shops listed for additional information. The open-water dive season generally runs from April to October in these waters.

DAY TRIPS ON DELMARVA: CAPE CHARLES AND THE EASTERN SHORE

Just a few miles from Virginia Beach across the 17-mile-long **Chesapeake Bay Bridge-Tunnel** (www.cbbt.com) spanning the mouth of Chesapeake Bay lies a surprisingly rural and low-key countryside of farms and fishing villages, dotted with a smattering of interesting shops, restaurants, and wineries. Several wildlife refuges offer excellent birding and kayaking, while kiteboarders claim this will be the next big East Coast destination for their sport. The flat terrain and quiet country lanes are ideal for biking. And the area is renowned for its sunsets, as the sun puts on a show as it sinks into Chesapeake Bay.

This is the southern tip of Delmarva, a peninsula named for the three states that share its governance—Delaware, Maryland, and Virginia. US 13, running down its length, stretches north to the New Jersey Turnpike.

The **Eastern Shore Welcome Center** (757-787-8268; www.esvatourism.org), located in the rest area next to the toll plaza at the northern end of the Chesapeake Bay Bridge-Tunnel (CBBT), provides information on the Virginia portion of Delmarva.

Just 3 miles north of the CBBT, **Kiptopeke State Park** (757-331-2267; www .dcr.virginia.gov; 3540 Kiptopeke Drive, Cape Charles 23310), with a wide beach and lighted fishing pier on the bay, makes a good destination for a day trip or a longer stay. The park boasts an unusual feature—a breakwater composed of partially sunken World War II ships, which creates excellent fishing, as well as scenic views.

A few miles farther north, the **Town of Cape Charles** (www.capecharles .org), once a busy port, now a charming Victorian village, attracts visitors with its small-town personality. The 0.5-mile-long town beach, stretching along Bay Avenue, is clean, shallow, free for all, and welcomes summer sunsets with classical music. Galleries, shops, restaurants, and coffee shops line the quiet streets, along with gingerbread Victorians and Sears catalog houses. Other attractions include a public fishing pier where no license is required, the art deco **Palace Theater** (757-331-2787; www.artsentercapecharles.org; 305 Mason Avenue), a vintage dinner train, and world-class golf courses designed by Arnold Palmer and Jack Nicklaus. Several bed & breakfasts, as well as the luxurious new **Bay Creek Resort** (757-331-8742; www.baycreekresort.com), provide accommodations. Visit the Web site of the **Cape Charles Business Association** (www.capecharles.biz) for listings of galleries, shops, inns, and activities.

The **Cape Charles Museum and Welcome Center** (757-331-1008; www .smallmuseum.org/capechas.htm; 814 Randolph Avenue/VA 184), housed in a former power plant, follows the history of the area from its first visit by John Smith through its days as a port for the train ferry to Norfolk. Technology fans will enjoy the working demonstration of the power generator, and there's a special section for children.

All addresses below are in the Cape Charles 23310 zip code unless otherwise stated.

Arlington Plantation (757-678-7157; www.smallmuseum.org/arlington.htm), Arlington Chase Road, south of Cape Charles off SR 664W. The site of the original Arlington, first Virginia home of the famous Custis family, built circa 1670, is open for self-guided tours. Paths lead to the Custis Tombs and other points of interest. Free.

Bay Creek Railway (757-331-8770; www.baycreekrailway.com), 202 Mason Avenue. Enjoy train travel along the Eastern Shore in a restored 1913 Interurban Dining and Excursion car.

Bay Creek Resort, Marina, and Golf Club (757-331-8640 or 888-422-9275; www.baycreekresort.com), 3335 Stone Road. Selected as the Best Marina Overall from Maine to North Carolina, this new resort offers deepwater access to Chesapeake Bay, slips with full hookups, Wi-Fi, marine store, plus rental properties, retail shopping, Arnold Palmer and Jack Nicklaus signature golf courses, and two restaurants, **Aqua** (757-331-8660) and the **Coach House Tavern** (757-331-8631). Fishing charters, including **Top Dog Charters** (757-647-3017; www.topdogcharters.com), and sailing cruises, including **Fantasea Sail Cruises** (443-262-1161; www.fantaseasailcruises.com), specializing in couples' excursions, available.

THE DISTINCTIVE WATER TOWER ABOVE THE VILLAGE OF CAPE CHARLES RE-CREATES THE TOP OF THE CAPE CHARLES LIGHT.

°ĭ° **Cape Charles Coffee House** (757-331-1880; www.cape charlescoffeehouse.com), 241 Mason Avenue. Coffee shop in a beautifully restored 1910 bank building serves delicious desserts made in-house. Free Wi-Fi.

Cape Charles Farmers Market (757-331-4884), Mason Street, opposite the Cape Charles Hotel. Open seasonally on Sat. afternoons.

Cape Charles Harbor (757-331-2357; www.capecharles.org/harbor.htm), 2 Plum Street. Town facility offering deepwater slips and docks, boat ramp, and a free fishing pier; serves as the home port of several fishing and sailing charter services, including **Sail Cape Charles** (973-479-3346; www.sailcape charles.com).

✐ **Cherrystone Family Camping Resort** (757-331-3063; www.cherrystoneva .com), 1511 Townfield Drive. Full-service campground on Chesapeake Bay offers RV sites, cabins, and rental trailers; boat and golf cart rentals; swimming pools; splash park; four fishing piers; and more.

Chris' Bait and Tackle (757-331-3000; www.chrisbait.com), 28316 Lankford Highway, Townsend 23443. Fully stocked for fishing, plus archery, black powder, and other hunting needs.

Coastal Dune Natural Area Preserve (757-787-5576 or 757-331-1998; www .dcr.virginia.gov), 301 Patrick Henry Avenue. Wooden boardwalk beginning at the Cape Charles Sustainable Technologies Industrial Park leads to a scenic view of Chesapeake Bay, offering good birding in spring and fall.

Eastern Shore Hang Gliding Center (757-752-8811 or 757-442-7519; www .easternshorehanggliding.com), 9114 Bayford Road, Weirwood 23413. Soar high into the clouds in a tandem hang glider towed aloft by an airplane from **Campbell Field Airport** (www.campbellfieldairport.com). Ages four and above can try it.

✪ **Eastern Shore of Virginia and Fisherman Island National Wildlife Refuges** (757-331-3425 or 757-331-2760; http://easternshore.fws.gov), 5003 Hallett Circle. Located just before the toll gates of the CBBT, the Eastern Shore NWR has a fine visitors center, one of the best in the NWR system, with exhibits, films, maps, a gift shop, crafts, and other activities, plus an observation window overlooking a freshwater pond. From the center, short trails lead through a butterfly garden, to the top of a World War II bunker, and past an old cemetery to an overlook of the salt marsh and a distant view of the Cape Charles Lighthouse. The refuge also has a photography blind, boat ramp, and kayak launch.

Fisherman Island NWR, the southernmost island in the Virginia barrier island chain, is an important stopover point for migratory birds, as well as a nesting spot for other species. Although the CBBT crosses its western end, the island is closed to the public. The only access is via free guided tours from the Eastern Shore NWR Visitor Center on Sat. Oct.–mid-Mar. Reservations are required.

Eyre Hall Gardens (757-331-2304; www.esgardentours.com), 3215 Eyre Hall Lane, Cheriton 23316. Planted circa 1800, this magnificent brick-walled garden containing ancient boxwood hedges and 150-year-old crape myrtles is considered the oldest continuously maintained garden in Virginia. Open year-round. Free.

🍷 ⁰ℸ⁰ **Kelly's Gingernut Pub** (757-331-3222), 133 Mason Avenue. Comfortable pub in a historic building in downtown Cape Charles offers an interesting menu, free Wi-Fi, live music, and a nice selection of beers on tap.

✪ **Kiptopeke State Park** (757-331-2267 or 800-933-7275 [reservations]; www.dcr.virginia.gov), 3540 Kiptopeke Drive. This state park offers swimming (Memorial Day–Labor Day) on a Chesapeake Bay beach overlooking the Concrete Ships breakwater, a lighted fishing pier ($1–3) where no license is required, boat launch ($4–8), 4 miles of biking and hiking trails, a butterfly garden where monarch butterflies gather, and the **Kiptopeke Bird Banding Station and Hawk Observatory** (www.cvwo.org), active mid-Aug.–Nov. Day use admission: $2–3. Available overnight accommodations include full-hookup sites for RVs, shady tent sites, rental trailers, and a yurt. The park also rents five large lodges perfect for family reunions or groups, each with six bedrooms sleeping up to 16 people, three baths, fully equipped kitchen, and two porches, but no TVs, telephones, or dishwashers. One lodge is fully handicapped accessible.

THE BREAKWATER MADE OF CONCRETE SHIPS AT KIPTOPEKE STATE PARK, ONE OF THE BEST PLACES TO FISH IN THE CHESAPEAKE BAY, HARBORS HUGE ROCKFISH.

Rayfield's Pharmacy (757-331-1212; http://severn.esva.net), 2 Fig Street. Enjoy the old-fashioned soda fountain and browse the unusual selection of collectibles at this independent drugstore. CD history and architecture tours available.

Seaside Water Trail (www.deq.state.va.us/coastal/seasidewatertrail). Explore this 70-mile corridor behind the Virginia barrier islands by canoe or kayak.

✪ **SouthEast Expeditions** (757-331-2660 or 877-943-8548; www.southeast expeditions.net or www.gogetlit.com), two locations: next to the Sunset Beach Resort (32218 Lankford Highway/US 13) and on the wharf at Onancock (2 King Street, Onancock 23417). Sea kayaking excursions, kiteboarding lessons, and kayak rentals.

✪ **Sting-Ray's Restaurant at Cape Center Exxon** (757-331-2505; www.cape -center.com), 26507 Lankford Highway. Popular with both visitors and locals, this stop along US 13 about 9 miles north of the CBBT offers fresh seafood and homestyle meals at reasonable prices.

♈ **Sunset Beach Resort** (757-331-1776 or 800-899-4786; www.sunsetbeach resortva.com), 33246 Lankford Highway/US 13. Located at the tip of the peninsula just before the CBBT toll gates, this resort includes a hotel, RV resort, and several dining options, including the **Pelican Pub**, with its own beach, live entertainment, and great sunsets.

Windsor House (757-331-4848; www.lewinwindsorhouse.com), 4290 Capeville Drive at US 13. Restored farmhouse displays antiques, local art and crafts, and Windsor chairs handcrafted by owners Kurt and Sally Lewin.

The Wooden Fish (757-331-3474; www.woodenfishcc.com), 555 Mason Avenue. Artist Ryan Dockiewicz carves decoys, fish, and folk art on-site.

For a list of annual events in Cape Charles and the Eastern Shore, see *Special Events*. For additional information, visit the Web sites of **Eastern Shore of Virginia Tourism** (www.esvatourism.org) and the **Northampton County Chamber of Commerce** (www.northamptoncountychamber.com).

Dive Quarters (757-422-DIVE; www.divequarters.com), 1725 Laskin Road, Hilltop Plaza, Virginia Beach 23454. The largest dive center on the East Coast offers dives to a variety of depths, including "mystery dives" to unidentified wrecks, aboard the *Big Time* and the *Pelican II* (www.pelicandivecharter.com). Spearfishing trips, equipment rentals and repairs, snorkeling lessons, Scuba Tuneups for lapsed divers, and PADI classes conducted year-round in an indoor heated pool. Free Discover Scuba sessions.

Dive Services (757-581-8064; www.diveservicesinc.com), 228 Matt Lane, Virginia Beach 23454. Personalized services include private instruction for IANTD and SDI/TDI certification, advanced gas blending, and equipment testing and repairs.

✦ ⬆ **Lynnhaven Dive Center** (757-481-7949; www.ldcscuba.com), 1413 N. Great Neck Road, Virginia Beach 23454. Certified SSI training facility offers boat trips to many different wrecks and reefs aboard a 60-foot custom dive boat with compressor on board, air-conditioned salon, and galley; plus equipment sales, repairs, and rentals. The center's heated pool hosts swimming classes beginning at age six months, snorkeling, and free introductory scuba lessons.

Surfing and Stand-Up Paddleboarding

While the surf off the shore of Virginia Beach is modest compared to Hawaii, or even Hatteras on the Outer Banks, the area is nevertheless a hotbed of surf culture. Because of the uncertain surf, paddleboarding has enjoyed a huge jump in popularity during the last several years, both on the ocean and on the quiet waters of the city's estuaries and bays.

Virginia Beach is the headquarters of the **Eastern Surfing Association** (757-233-1790; www.surfesa.org; 414 25th Street, Suite 21), the largest amateur-surfing organization in the world, with more than seven thousand members. Every August, North America's oldest surfing competition, the **East Coast Surfing Championship** (www.surfecsc.com), brings many top professional surfers to town for a shot at the $10,000 top prize. The four-day event takes place at Second Street next to the Rudee Inlet jetty and includes live music, volleyball, skimboard and skateboard contests, and the famous ECSC swimsuit pageant.

SUNSET AT LYNNHAVEN INLET

Despite its popularity, surfing is somewhat restricted in Virginia Beach from Memorial Day to Labor Day. In the resort area, surfing is allowed after 10 AM only next to the Rudee Inlet jetty and between Fourth and Fifth streets. On the North End beaches, surfing is not allowed 11–4 Friday–Sunday. On Croatan Beach, surfing is restricted to the area next to the Rudee Inlet jetty at the north end of the beach. On Sandbridge Beach, you can surf anytime on the north side of the Little Island Park pier.

For information on current conditions, contact one of the surf shops that follow, visit the Webcams at www.surfline .com, or call the Surf Report Hotline at 757-428-0404, ext. 2.

Austin Surfboards (757-270-8300; www.austinsurfboards.com), 513 19th Street. Buy Austin Saunders's surfboards direct from the factory.

♂ **Corner 24 Surf Shop** (757-428-3389; www.corner24online.com), 211 24th Street. This landmark on the oceanfront since 1989 specializes in long boards. Juniors and girls location at Great Neck Square Shopping Center (757-496-5770).

Freedom Surf Shop (757-491-0266; www.freedomsurfshop.com), 1361 Laskin Road, Hilltop. Center for local surf culture staffed by friendly area surfers, and hangout of the legendary Pete Smith, carries a large selection of new and used retro, long and short boards; surfer art; local and private-label clothing; and surf DVDs. Movie nights bring out the local surf crowd.

Frierson Design Surfboards (757-491-7130; www.friersondesigns.com), 1165 Jensen Drive. Bill Frierson, former owner of Wave Riding Vehicles and an East Coast surfing legend, continues to shape boards, mostly by custom order.

Hotline Surfboards (757-428-6703; www.hotlinesurfboardz.com), 437 Virginia Beach Boulevard. Additional stores at Lynnhaven Mall (757-313-6300) and Red Mill Commons (757-689-3259). Shops owned by shaper Gurney Collins sponsor weeklong surf camps mid-June–early Aug.

Jason Borte Surf School (757-285-9277; www.thesurfschool.com), Fourth Street and oceanfront. East Coast surfing champion Jason Borte heads a staff offering a wide range of surf camps and lessons.

✪ *♂* ↝ **Surf & Adventure Co.** (757-721-6210 or 800-695-4212; www.surfand adventure.com), 577 Sandbridge Road, Virginia Beach 23546. A leader in the paddleboard movement, local surfer Eric Coulson and his experienced staff offer

PADDLEBOARDING INCREASES IN POPULARITY EVERY YEAR, BOTH IN THE OCEAN SURF AND ON QUIET INLET WATERS.

Karen Wright

stand-up paddleboard and surf lessons on the uncrowded breaks of Sandbridge Beach for ages eight and up, plus surf camps and Chica camps for girls. Soft-top and epoxy surfboards, stand-up paddleboards, kayaks, canoes, and bikes for rent. Current surf report online.

Wave Riding Vehicles (757-422-8823; www.waveridingvehicles.com), 1900 Cypress Avenue. The region's largest surfboard manufacturer showcases its products at this shop at the corner of 19th Street, along with top surfer appearances, competitions, surf camps, equipment rentals, and more.

✍ **Wes Laine Surf Camp** (757-630-6055; www.weslainesurfcamp.com), North Croatan Surfing Area. Former top 10 World Tour surfer Wes Laine oversees week-long morning camps for ages six and up, June–Aug.

WILDERNESS CAMPING Primitive camping is available year-round at four locations in **False Cape State Park** (www.dcr.virginia.gov), both along the bay and along the ocean. Campers must bring all their equipment and supplies in and out by foot, bike, or boat. It is between 6 and 9 miles to reach the campsites from Little Island Park, where parking is available. Pit toilets are the only amenity, with drinking water available only in the Barbour Hill area. Advance reservations are required. Call 800-933-7275.

WILDLIFE SPOTTING Beyond the human crowds of the Boardwalk area, Virginia Beach is home to a host of other species, including rare birds, deer, black bears, mink, river otters, and wild horses. Aquatic species are equally numerous, with bottlenose dolphins arriving by the thousands during the summer. During the winter months, fin and juvenile humpback whales looking for an easy meal visit these waters. For loggerhead sea turtles, the undisturbed beaches of Back Bay NWR and False Cape State Park may hold the key to survival, as they return every summer to lay their eggs.

Bird-Watching

The region around Virginia Beach serves as a vital stop on the Atlantic Flyway for many birds, with some three hundred species spotted here regularly. Tens of thousands of snow geese, Canada geese, tundra swans, and various ducks, as well as the shy Le Conte's sparrow, winter over in the Back Bay National Wildlife Refuge. During the spring migration, warblers of many varieties make music from the trees.

The Virginia Beach section of the **Virginia Birding and Wildlife Trail,** the **Seashore to Cypress Loop,** leads to all the area wildlife refuges, plus some sites you might overlook in gardens, city parks, and area golf courses. View an online version at www.dgif.virginia.gov/vbwt or order a printed version ($8.50) through the Web site or by mail (write to 4010 W. Broad Street, Richmond 23230).

For local guidance on where to find the best birding spots, visit the **Atlantic Wildfowl Heritage Museum** (757-437-8432; www.awhm.org) at 11th Street and Atlantic Avenue on the Boardwalk. The Back Bay Birding Club keeps a notebook here listing sightings and suggested bird walks. The **Virginia Beach Audubon Society** (www.vabeach-audubon.org) hosts monthly guided walks and programs open to the public.

BIRDING ON THE EASTERN SHORE

Because of its location, the extreme southern tip of the Delmarva Peninsula serves as an important concentration point every fall for millions of migratory birds, monarch butterflies, and dragonflies, who rest and feed here while waiting for favorable winds to help them cross the mouth of Chesapeake Bay. More than four hundred species have been documented, including many rarities. Migrating raptors and wood warblers are especially prevalent, with some eighty thousand raptors counted in a single season.

Places to observe the migration include **Kiptopeke State Park** (757-331-2267; www.dcr.virginia.gov or www.cvwo.org; 3540 Kiptopeke Drive, Cape Charles 23310) and **Eastern Shore of Virginia and Fisherman Island National Wildlife Refuges** (757-331-3425; 757-331-2760; http://easternshore.fws.gov; 5003 Hallett Circle, Cape Charles 23310). The four-day **Eastern Shore Birding and Wildlife Festival** (757-581-1801; www.esvafestivals.org) takes place in mid-September at the height of the fall migration.

The region has several festivals devoted to birding, including the four-day **Eastern Shore Birding and Wildlife Festival** (757-581-1801; www.esvafestivals.org) in mid-September and the **Great Dismal Swamp Birding Festival,** held in May during the spring migration at the **Dismal Swamp Canal National Wildlife Refuge** (757-986-3705; www.fws.gov/northeast/greatdismalswamp; 3100 Desert Road, Suffolk 23434).

Marine Mammals

Researchers first noticed juvenile humpback whales feeding off the mouth of the Chesapeake Bay in the winter of 1991. They hypothesize that these young whales skip the trip to the winter breeding grounds, where food is scarce, to hang out in the rich waters off Virginia Beach. The humpbacks are often observed making bubble nets and engaging in other feeding behavior. In recent years, they've been joined by a number of fin whales.

Whale sightings are on the increase as the population of Atlantic humpbacks recovers. The Virginia Aquarium staff estimates that whales were spotted on more than 80 percent of their whale-watch cruises in the past several years. According to the experts, February is the best month for whale-watching in the area. Several hotels in Virginia Beach offer whale-watching packages every winter. Visit www.vbfun.com for details.

Bottlenose dolphins are the marine mammal most frequently sighted off Virginia Beach. Pods of up to a dozen individuals leap from the water following boats or schools of fish, and it's the rare dolphin-watch cruise that doesn't spot at least one pod. The area off Fort Story is one of their favorite spots. Most dolphins leave the area in the winter, migrating south, but one pod has recently been hanging out all year off the beach at First Landing State Park.

One of the best ways to have an up-close encounter with a marine mammal is aboard one of the dolphin- or whale-watching cruises operated by the Virginia Aquarium and Marine Science Center. A knowledgeable naturalist accompanies every trip to answer questions and give you insight into these fascinating creatures. Kayak outfitters also offer dolphin trips that nearly always spot a pod or two, and in a kayak you get even closer to the animals.

Harbor seals, usually juveniles, are the most common seal spotted along Virginia's coast, but gray, hooded, and harp seals have been seen here as well. Usually these are single animals taking a rest on the beach during their journeys in winter and spring.

If you find a stranded whale, dolphin, seal, or sea turtle that seems to be in distress, report it immediately to the Virginia Aquarium's **Stranding Response Center** at 757-437-6159.

Wildlife Tours & Charters

For additional ecotour options, see our listings under *Canoe & Kayak Tours and Rentals.*

✪ **The Blue Goose Express, Back Bay Restoration Foundation Tram Tours** (757-721-2412 or 757-426-3643; www.bbrf.org). Open trams take visitors through the Back Bay National Wildlife Refuge to False Cape State Park, identifying birds and mammals, including feral hogs and wild horses, along the way. Special winter trams held twice a month, Nov.–Mar., are the only way to visit the dike trails through the Back Bay impoundments while the migrating flocks of snow geese, tundra swans, and ducks are in residence. Adults $8, children 3–12 and seniors 62 and over $6.

✿ **Dockside Sunset Dolphin Watch** (757-481-4545; www.fishingvabeach.com), 3311 Shore Drive. Enjoy a sunset cruise on Chesapeake Bay, where you'll see dolphins, birds, Navy ships, and more. Adults $16, children $10, under three free.

Eco Images (757-421-3929; www.ecoimages-us.com). Naturalist Vickie Shufer, author of *A Naturalist's Field Guide to Coastal Communities,* offers forest walks, wild root and edible flower seminars, kayak trips, survival skills workshops, and Wild Women Weekends.

✿ **Ocean Collections Cruise** (757-385-3474; www.virginiaaquarium.com), 200 Winston Salem Avenue, Virginia Beach Fishing Center. Aquarium staff trawl the ocean floor, bringing up sea horses, stingrays, crabs, sand dollars, and more on this 75-minute boat trip from Rudee Inlet. Mar.–Nov. Adults $19, children 4–11 $14.

Rudee Explorer Creek Cruise at the Virginia Aquarium (757-385-FISH; www.virginiaaquarium.com), 717 General Booth Boulevard. Leaving from the aquarium's dock, half-hour pontoon boat trips guided by naturalists explore the salt marsh along Owls Creek. Apr.–Oct. $7.

✿ **Seal Splash at the Virginia Aquarium** (757-385-0300; www.virginiaaquarium .com), 200 Winston Salem Avenue. Visitors participate in a training session during this two-hour summer program, the only one in the nation where you get in the water with harbor seals. $125 per person. Reservations required.

Virginia Aquarium and Marine Science Center Dolphin Watching and Whale Watching Cruises (757-385-3474; www.virginiaaquarium.com), 200 Winston Salem Avenue, Virginia Beach Fishing Center. The *Rudee Flipper* makes 90-minute cruises to see the wild dolphins at play, Apr.–Oct., and two-hour whale-watching excursions, late Dec.–Mar., from Rudee Inlet. Onboard naturalist explains marine mammal behavior and research. Dolphin watch:

Adults (12 and up) $20, children 4–11 $14. Whale watch: Adults (12 and up) $28; children 4–11 $24.

✴ Wilder Places

⊙ **Back Bay National Wildlife Refuge** (757-721-2412; www.fws.gov/backbay), 4005 Sandpiper Road, Sandbridge, Virginia Beach 23456. More than 9,000 acres of protected land between the Atlantic Ocean and Back Bay provide a refuge for migratory birds, loggerhead sea turtles, piping plovers, red foxes, river otters, peregrine falcons, and bald eagles. Two boardwalks lead over the dunes to the beach, while a trail leads to the bay front. Dike roads across the marsh provide hiking and biking opportunities but are often closed during the migratory bird season, Nov. 1–Mar. 31. Motorized vehicles are not allowed beyond the Visitor Contact Station. Four miles of undeveloped beach are closed to swimming, sunbathing, and surfing, but surf fishing with a Virginia Saltwater License is permitted.

Nearly three hundred species of birds have been spotted, including the rarely seen Le Conte's sparrow, which winters here. During the migratory season, some ten thousand snow geese, as well as thousands of ducks, Canada geese, and tundra swans gather in Back Bay, while pelagic birds raft off the beach. Wildlife viewing stations throughout the refuge provide excellent opportunities for wildlife photography.

One good way to see the refuge, especially during the winter, is aboard the guided tram tour called the Blue Goose Express. (See details under *To Do—Touring.*) Open daily during daylight hours. Pets on a leash are allowed Oct.–Mar. Admission fees ($5 per vehicle or $2 per person on foot or bike) are charged Apr.–Oct.

Beach Garden Park (757-385-1100; www.vbgov.com/parks), Holly Road, off Laskin Road at Baltic Avenue, in the resort area. Walkways around a pond and wetlands attract songbirds and shorebirds, as well as many butterflies.

⊙ **Chesapeake Bay Bridge-Tunnel (CBBT)** (757-331-2960; www.cbbt.com), 32386 Lankford Highway (US 13), Cape Charles 23310. Built more than 40 years ago, the CBBT, crossing nearly 18 miles of open ocean, remains an engineering marvel and a unique opportunity to see pelagic species without boarding a boat. The islands upon which the bridge rests form the best winter birding sites in Virginia. Also frequently sighted are Navy ships, submarines, and commercial ships entering Chesapeake Bay.

The first island at the south end of the CBBT, closest to the Virginia Beach shore, is open to the public. There you'll find an information center, gift shop, free fishing pier, and the new **Chesapeake Grill** (757-464-4641; www.cbbt.com), a full-service restaurant with outdoor patio seating serving breakfast, lunch, and dinner. Don't miss the soft-shell crabs.

A scenic overlook, restrooms, and viewing machines are located at the north end of the CBBT on the west side of the road. To access the other islands the CBBT crosses, you must apply in advance and pay a fee. See the Web site for details. The CBBT toll for passenger vehicles is $12 each way; a return trip within 24 hours costs $5.

False Cape State Park (757-426-7128; www.dcr.virginia.gov), 4001 Sandpiper Road, Virginia Beach 23456. Camping reservations: 800-933-PARK. Located south of Back Bay NWR and closed to vehicular traffic, False Cape State Park is one of the least-visited parks in the Virginia state parks system. Thanks to its isolation, this relatively undisturbed coast is home to 54 rare and endangered species, as well as feral hogs, wild horses, river otters, and deer. Stretching 6 miles to the North Carolina border, and just 1 mile wide, the park can be reached only by foot, bicycle, or public tram; or in winter by the **Terra Gator** (see *To Do—Touring*); or by motorboat or kayak from Back Bay. The tram brings you to the park office near the **Barbour Hill Interpretive Trail** and gives you about two hours to explore before the return trip. The park has about 15 miles of hiking and biking trails, many of them in deep sand. Trails lead to the ruined church and cemetery of the community of **Wash Woods,** built of driftwood by the survivors of shipwrecks.

Three docks on the bay side are available for motor or paddle craft. Trails from them lead across to the oceanfront beach. Pit toilets are the only facilities available within the park, beyond the Barbour Hill area. Primitive tent camping is permitted year-round, with advance reservations (800-933-7275).

False Cape State Park is open year-round. Rangers conduct many programs, including guided kayak trips, birding hikes, and winter stargazing. There is no fee to enter the park, but you must pay the entrance fee for Back Bay NWR if you come by land.

✪ ✎ ♿ ✈ **First Landing State Park** (757-412-2300; www.dcr.virginia.gov), 2500 Shore Drive. Just a short drive from the resort area's high-rise hotels, Virginia's most-visited state park includes a beach, dunes, upland forest, tidal marsh, cypress swamp, and endangered maritime forest, lying on both sides of Shore Drive. The park has three entrances: the beach and the Trail Center entrances, opposite each other on Shore Drive; and a southern entrance off Atlantic Boulevard at 64th Street.

The park's 19 miles of trails, including the multiuse **Cape Henry Trail,** begin near the Trail Center, where there are exhibits and restrooms. Stands of bald cypress and live oaks covered in Spanish moss, here at the northern limit of its range, make this a pleasant place to hike. Reproductions of Native American dwellings are scattered among the trees. Warblers, songbirds, and several species of woodpecker nest here.

The 64th Street area, on the shores of Broad Bay, with restrooms and and a boat launch, is popular for fishing and Jet Skiing, while the adjacent beach, called the **Narrows,** is a local favorite for picnicking and launching kayaks.

On the beach side of Shore Drive, the park has changing rooms and outdoor showers for beachgoers, in addition to boardwalks over the dunes, a history and ecology museum, and a concession stand where you can rent bikes and fishing gear during the summer. Bottlenose dolphin frequent these waters, including one pod that makes its home here year-round. Rangers offer numerous interpretive programs, including nature hikes, beach walks, and crabbing instruction. The area's biggest paddle-sports event of the year, **PaddleFest,** takes place here in mid-Sept.

First Landing is open all year. Parking: $4 per car weekdays, $5 per car weekends.

Great Neck Park (757-496-6735; www.vbgov.com/parks), 2513 Shorehaven Drive, Virginia Beach 23454. City park on the shore of Lynnhaven Bay has walking trails through pinewoods where you may see pine warblers, an observation deck overlooking a marsh frequented by ospreys and wintering bald eagles, and a restored oyster bank in the bay.

⚓ ♿ ⤴ **Mount Trashmore Park** (757-473-5237; www.vbgov.com/parks), 310 Edwin Drive, Virginia Beach 23462. Located just off I-264 (exit 17), Mount Trashmore, 60 feet high and more than 800 feet long, was the first landfill park in the world, created by compacting layers of solid waste and clean soil. The expansive park, a favorite spot for kite flying, picnicking, and fishing, offers walking trails, two lakes, a skate park, a unique playground, a summer film series, and the **Water Wise Demonstration Garden,** where xeriscaping techniques use a minimum of water.

Munden Point Park (757-426-5296; www.vbgov.com/parks), 2001 Pefley Lane, Virginia Beach 23457. City park lies on the shores of the North Landing River, home of the largest blue heron rookery in Virginia. Trails, gardens, a boat ramp, and canoe and kayak rentals are some of the facilities here, along with a disc golf course.

Princess Anne Wildlife Management Area (757-426-6320; www.dgif.virginia .gov), Princess Anne Road. The Trojan Marsh (off Back Bay Landing Road) has a short trail and a boat launch that accesses the marshes of Back Bay. The Whitehurst Tract (off Munden Road) contains marsh, pond, and woodland edge habitat.

Red Wing Park (757-437-2038; www.vbgov.com/parks), 1398 General Booth Boulevard. Park close to the resort area includes a rose garden, Japanese garden, and fragrance garden, developed by the Council of Garden Clubs of Virginia Beach.

Stumpy Lake Natural Area (757-563-1118), 4797 Indian River Road, Virginia Beach 23456. Causeway at entrance to golf course crosses a cypress swamp that attracts anhingas, migrating shorebirds, waders, nesting bald eagles, and numerous dragonflies. Several miles of trails wander through a mature forest.

Tidewater Arboretum and Display Gardens (757-363-3900; www.hrc.vt.edu or www.vaes.vt.edu), 1444 Diamond Springs Road, Virginia Beach 23455. Located on the Hampton Roads campus of Virginia Tech University, more than 100 acres and several greenhouses are used as trial gardens, including a Bayscape Garden of native plants, a Rain Garden, and a wide range of annuals, perennials, shrubs, and trees being evaluated for their suitability for the local climate. Free.

West Neck Creek Natural Area (757-426-5296; www.vbgov.com/parks), Princess Anne and North Landing roads. Four miles of multiuse trails, including a short paved section, wind through woodlands.

✳ Lodging

Visitors looking for a beach vacation naturally look for accommodations along Virginia Beach's famous Boardwalk, stretching from Rudee Inlet to 40th Street. Dozens of hostelries of every vintage line this strand, with entrances on Atlantic Avenue and beachside access onto the Boardwalk itself. Many restaurants and shops are within walking distance, and from May 1 to October 1, the WAVE trolleys will take you from one end to the other ($1; $2 for an all-day pass).

When making reservations, be aware of cancellation policies and the difference between "oceanfront" and "oceanview" rooms. While oceanview rooms may require some acrobatics to actually see the water, oceanfront rooms should give you an unobstructed view.

Active and retired military can take

advantage of special accommodations available in Virginia Beach, including the **Cape Henry Inn and Beach Club** (757-422-8818; www.capehenry inn.com; 1116 Kwajalein Road, Virginia Beach 23459), a year-round resort on the grounds of Fort Story. Oceana Naval Air Station offers an RV resort, as well as other amenities for military families.

Many hotels and restaurants have pursued accreditation as a Virginia Green property (www.virginia.org/green), designed to minimize tourism's impact on the environment.

All properties listed have air-conditioning and cable or satellite TV, and are open all year, unless otherwise noted.

Price Categories

Rates listed are based on double occupancy and do not include taxes. The range of rates indicates the differences between off-season and high season. Minimum stays may be required, especially on holiday weekends.

Inexpensive	up to $80
Moderate	$80 to $150
Expensive	$150 to $200
Very expensive	$200 and up

HOTELS & RESORTS

Boardwalk & Resort Area

&. ⁇ **Alamar Resort Inn** (757-428-7582 or 800-346-5681; www.alamar resortinn.net), 311 16th Street. Price: Inexpensive to expensive. Credit cards: Yes. Special features: Swimming pool, Wi-Fi access, two rooftop sundecks, daily maid service, game room, private parking. Secluded AAA three-diamond resort two blocks from the oceanfront offers 22 rooms and suites grouped around a landscaped courtyard with heated pool. Rooms are equipped with queen beds, TVs, refrigerators, microwaves, coffeemakers, telephones, hair dryers, and irons. Suites, perfect for families, also have a full kitchen with dishwasher, dining area, and sofa bed. Children stay free. Golf and whale-watching packages, handicapped-accessible rooms, and smoke-free rooms are available.

Angie's Guest Cottages, Hostel and Ocean Cove Motel (757-491-1830; www.angiescottage.com or www.ocean covemotel.com), 302 24th Street. Price: Inexpensive to moderate. Credit Cards: Yes, with extra fee. Special features: Community kitchen, barbecue grill, sundeck, Ping-Pong, exchange library, complimentary beach mats and boogie boards; secure bicycle parking and on-street parking passes available. Located just one block from the ocean, this complex of buildings offers a wide variety of accommodations. The original Angie's Cottage houses charming guest rooms equipped with microwaves, refrigerators, and private baths. Nearby, Cottage Row rooms, with private entrances, porches with hammocks, and minikitchens, are favorites with couples. The Ocean Cove Motel offers weekly family cottage rentals and traditional motel rooms.

Angie's is also a certified **Hostel International–USA** facility with five dorm rooms containing 34 bunk beds, open Apr. 1–Oct. 1. Bunks rent for from $15 to $23 depending on the season to both HI members and other single travelers. Bunk rooms are not air-conditioned but have lots of fans. HI members can also rent a discounted private, air-conditioned room, depending on availability at check-in. Private hostel rooms are available all year. There is no curfew and no age limit for hostel guests. Two-night minimum stays are required. All lodgings are nonsmoking and pet-free. For more information, contact **Hostelling International–USA** (301-495-1240; www.hiusa.org).

"T" ⏀ Barclay Cottage Bed and Breakfast (757-422-1956 or 866-466-1895; www.barclaycottage.com), 400 16th Street. Price: Moderate to very expensive. Credit cards: Yes. Special features: Free Wi-Fi, smoke-free, Virginia Green property. Located on a dead-end street in a historic neighborhood just a few blocks from the oceanfront, this 1895 Victorian beach cottage was the site of several of Edgar Cayce's readings and is the longest continuously operating lodging in Virginia Beach. Today its five guest rooms, decorated with antiques and handmade quilts, are ideal for romantic weekends or laid-back vacations. Breakfasts feature home-baked breads and muffins, fresh fruit, and hot dishes. Special dietary needs can be accommodated. The wraparound two-story porch lined with rocking chairs is perfect for relaxing or enjoying a book from the inn's library. Children under 18 and pets are not allowed.

"T" ⏀ Beach Spa Bed and Breakfast (757-422-2621 or 888-422-2630; www.beachspabnb.com), 2420 Arctic Avenue. Price: Moderate to very expensive. Credit cards: Yes. Special features: Wired access and free Wi-Fi, romance and ecotour packages, Virginia Green property. Innkeeper Greg Nelson transformed this 1937 cottage just three blocks from the ocean into a luxurious and ecofriendly spa resort. Each of the eight antiques-filled guest rooms offers a unique mix of amenities, from jetted tubs, rainfall massage showers, and steamer showers to private balconies and HD TVs. Schedule a massage in the inn's third-floor library tower, or just enjoy the view. The outdoor waterfall spa pool, open all year, provides an ideal spot for enjoying a glass of wine. Homemade breakfasts that change daily, and refreshments served every afternoon,

plus friendly guidance to local hot spots, make this a great alternative to chain hotels.

⏀ ⏀ ⏀ ⏀ "T" ⏀ Hilton Virginia Beach Oceanfront (757-213-3001 or 800-445-8667; www.hiltonvb.com), 3001 Atlantic Avenue. Price: Expensive to very expensive. Credit cards: Yes. Special features: Rooftop infinity pool, indoor pool, 24-hour fitness center, complimentary yoga classes, valet or self parking, Virginia Green property. The four-star, 21-story Hilton is the centerpiece of the **31 Ocean Corridor** (www.31ocean.com), at the northern end of the Boardwalk. The 290 guest rooms and suites have balconies with views of city or ocean, flat-screen TVs, high-speed Internet access, pillow-top mattresses, coffeemakers, and luxurious baths. The Empyrean Club, occupying the top three floors of the hotel, offers rooms with enhanced amenities and a private lounge with complimentary continental breakfast, afternoon snacks, and evening hors d'oeuvres. Two award-winning restaurants, **Catch 31** and **Salacia,** are on-site, as well as the **Sky Bar,** the beach's only rooftop lounge, where hotel guests receive complimentary membership. Room service is available until 2 AM from the hotel restaurants or **Soya** (757-417-7692; www.soyasushi .com), a sushi bar located in the **Shoppes at 31 Ocean,** connected with the hotel via an overstreet walkway. From Memorial Day to the end of Sept., free entertainment is offered in adjacent **Neptune's Park.**

⏀ ⏀ ⏀ ⏀ "T" ⏀ Wyndham Virginia Beach Oceanfront (757-428-7025 or 800-365-3032; www.wyndham.com), 5700 Atlantic Avenue. Price: Expensive to very expensive. Credit Cards: Yes. Special features: Indoor/outdoor pool and Jacuzzi; oceanfront fitness center; children's summer activities; room service; free Wi-Fi; complimentary parking; free shuttles to Boardwalk and airport; bicycle, surfboard, and kayak rentals; Virginia Green property. Located north of the Boardwalk in a quiet, uncrowded portion of the oceanfront, this 17-floor hotel offers 243 rooms and suites, including Jacuzzi kings and pet-friendly patio rooms, each with microwave and refrigerator. The Kid's Cove Activity Center and a life-guarded beach make this a good summer destination for families. Children under 18 stay free. The four-star **Surf Club Ocean Grille** (757-425-5699; www.surfclubvabeach.com) serves breakfast, lunch, and dinner, with ocean views from dining room and patio, an exhibition kitchen, full lounge, and a huge wine selection.

Chesapeake Beaches

✪ ✿ 🐾 ⛱ ♈ ⁏⁏ ↝ **Virginia Beach Resort Hotel and Conference Center** (757-481-9000 or 800-468-2722; www.virginiabeachresort.com), 2800 Shore Drive. Price: Moderate to very expensive. Credit cards: Yes. Special features: Free Wi-Fi in lobby, business center, gift shop and coffee bar, concierge, free parking, full bar with happy hour, outdoor dining, summer children's activities, beach, complimentary tennis and bikes. Located on the quiet shores of Chesapeake Bay, this hotel offers a welcome change from the crowds and traffic of summertime along the Boardwalk. With little or no surf, the beach here is a great place for youngsters just getting used to the water. Summer packages are available at reduced rates, with children's activities scheduled daily.

Each of the 295 units is a spacious suite with separate living room and bedroom; kitchen with granite countertops, microwave, refrigerator, and coffeemaker; two TVs; and a private balcony. The rooms are truly huge,

quite a change from the cramped quarters at many suite hotels on the Boardwalk.

The large indoor/outdoor pool, sundeck, and indoor hot tub are adjacent to a fully equipped health club with sauna. The **Spa and Laser Center** (www.spaandlasercenter.com), across the street, offers special packages.

TradeWinds (www.tradewindsrestaurant.com), the on-site restaurant, serves lunch and dinner daily, featuring Virginia wine specials. Terrific views over the Chesapeake Bay make this a popular spot with locals, especially for Sun. brunch, when a piano player entertains.

Sandbridge & Pungo

♂ ⁏⁏ **Country Villa Bed and Breakfast Inn and Spa** (757-721-3844; www.countryvillainn.com), 2252 Indian River Road, Virginia Beach 23456. Price: Very expensive. Credit cards: Yes. Special features: Adults only, no pets, smoke-free, free Wi-Fi, outdoor swimming pool and hot tub open 24 hours a day. Located on 4 rural acres in the heart of Pungo, the Country Villa provides a romantic spot for getaways far from the Boardwalk crowds. The two luxurious guest rooms each have marble baths with whirlpool tubs; gas fireplaces; down bedding; high-thread-count linens; TV, CD, and DVD players; and complete privacy. Complimentary evening wine and cheese trays and a gourmet three-course breakfast, served on a staggered schedule to ensure the privacy of guests, are included. The innkeepers also provide fresh flowers, candles, candy, home-baked cookies, cotton robes, and rose and herbal bath salts. The inn is located just a few miles from Sandbridge Beach, and guests can borrow beach chairs, coolers, and other gear. Spa services and vineyard picnics are available.

♂ ♿ "♈" **The Sanctuary at False Cape** (757-457-0050 or 866-933-4801; www.sanctuaryresortva.com), 3700 Sandpiper Road, Virginia Beach 23456. Price: Inexpensive to very expensive. Credit cards: Yes. Special features: Free Wi-Fi in library and pool area, Virginia Green property. Located just north of Little Island City Park and Fishing Pier, the Sanctuary is a large, pastel-painted condominium complex renting mostly by the week during the summer season, although three-night rates are available for some units. Condos have up to three bedrooms and sleep up to eight. Each unit is individually owned and offers different amenities, ranging from golf club memberships to Internet access, flat-screen TVs, and video games. Linens and towels are included. Guests in all units can use the several pools and hot tubs scattered around the grounds. All condos also have balconies with stunning views of the ocean or Back Bay.

Town Center

✪ ☃ ♿ ♂ ♈ "♈" ⟿ **The Westin Virginia Beach Town Center** (757-557-0550; www.westinvirginiabeach.com), 4535 Commerce Street, Virginia Beach 23462. Price: Moderate to expensive. Credit cards: Yes. Special features: Complimentary covered self-parking; indoor pool and Jacuzzi; on-site sundries shop; WestinWORKOUT gym; concierge, babysitter, and bellman services; 24-hour business center; room service; lobby lounge; dogs allowed with additional fee; smoke-free. Occupying the first 15 floors of Virginia's tallest building, this stylish Westin is next door to the Sandler Center for the Arts and in the heart of the Town Center urban village, with numerous dining, retail, and entertainment options nearby. The 236 spacious rooms and suites feature high-speed and wireless Internet access (additional fee), flat-screen LCD televisions, free video games, coffeemaker, and the plush Westin Heavenly Bed, Heavenly Bath, and, if needed, Heavenly Crib.

The **Lucky Star** (757-275-7834), long a favorite dining spot on Pleasure House Road, recently reopened in the Westin with its award-winning chef, Scott Bernheisel, at the helm. Famous for his contemporary regional cuisine, Bernheisel brings many of his signature dishes, including Cajun fried oysters and house-made goat cheese ravioli, and an emphasis on fresh, local foods, to the Westin menu. The Lucky Star serves breakfast, lunch, dinner, and a bar menu daily.

BEACH COTTAGE & CONDO RENTALS Affordable Properties
(757-428-0432 or 800-639-0432; www.affordablepropertiesvb.com), 613 21st Street. Unique, fully furnished weekly rentals in the resort area, North Beach, and other beaches.

Atkinson Realty Inc. (757-425-2500 or 800-766-0409; www.atkinsonrealty.com), 5307 Atlantic Avenue. Established company handles weekly rentals for condos in the resort area, and oceanfront houses from North End to Croatan.

Chicks Beach Rentals (757-403-0260; www.chicksbeachrentals.com). Oceanfront properties in the quiet Chicks Beach neighborhood and waterfront properties on the Lynnhaven River.

☃ **Sandbridge Realty** (757-426-6262 or 800-933-4800; www.sandbridge.com), 581 Sandbridge Road, Virginia Beach 23456. Rents more than three hundred properties on Sandbridge Beach, from oceanfront condos to luxurious homes on the ocean or bay, including dog-friendly properties.

Siebert Realty (757-426-6200 or 877-422-2200; www.siebert-realty.com), 601 Sandbridge Road, Virginia Beach

PET-FRIENDLY VIRGINIA BEACH

The city maintains two dog parks, at **Red Wing Park** (757-437-2038; 1398 General Booth Boulevard) and **Woodstock Community Park** (757-366-4538; 5709 Providence Road), where dogs can run free in a 1-acre fenced area. On-site registration ($10/year) and proof of current rabies vaccination required. Children must be at least eight years old to enter the dog park. Call 757-385-4461 for more information.

For boarding, grooming, walking services, dog taxi, or doggy day care, contact **Thee Dog House** (757-289-2700; www.theedoghouse.com; 5503 Virginia Beach Boulevard, Virginia Beach 23462). Boarding and day care for cats and dogs are available at **Shipp's Corner Pet Spa and Resort** (757-301-6941; www.vbpetspa.com; 1515 Drakesmile Road, Virginia Beach 23453), where you can keep an eye on your pet via Webcam.

Pets are not allowed on the Boardwalk, the beach in front of it, or even the grassy area between the Boardwalk and your hotel, from Memorial Day to Labor Day. In other areas, pets on leashes are permitted on the public beaches after 6 PM and before 10 AM. The rest of the year, anything goes. Pet-friendly accommodations along the oceanfront include:

🏨 ⇘ **Residence Inn Oceanfront** (757-425-1141 or 800-331-3131; www.marriott.com), 3217 Atlantic Avenue. Smoke-free, extended stay available.

🏨 **Sea Shell Motel** (757-248-3801 or 866-847-5424; www.seashellmotel.net), 2301 Atlantic Avenue.

🏨 ⇘ **Sheraton Oceanfront Hotel** (757-425-9000 or 800-325-3535; www.sheratonvirginiabeach.com), 3501 Atlantic Avenue. Dogs only.

🏨 ⇘ **Wyndham Virginia Beach Oceanfront** (757-428-7025 or 800-365-3032; www.wyndham.com), 5700 Atlantic Avenue. Pet-friendly patio rooms.

23456. More than four hundred beach home and condo rentals on Sandbridge Beach. Some three-night bookings outside the summer season.

🏨 **Wynnhaven Properties, Inc.** (757-321-1491 or 757-685-0264; www.wynnhavenproperties.com), 2316 Red Tide Road. Luxury condos and homes on the oceanfront and bay side. Some pet-friendly properties.

RV RESORTS AND CAMPING CABINS Virginia Beach is a favorite destination for camping families. Two of the largest campgrounds, KOA and Holiday Trav-L Park, are located along General Booth Boulevard to the south of the Boardwalk, near Ocean Breeze Waterpark, the Virginia Aquarium, and the Owl Creek Tennis Facility. During the summer, WAVE trolleys make frequent trips along this route. These campgrounds, as well as First Landing State Park, are also connected with the Boardwalk by paved bicycle paths.

✪ ♿ ✈ First Landing State Park (757-412-2300 or 800-933-7275 [reservations]; www.dcr.virginia.gov), 2500 Shore Drive. RV and tent campsites located amid the maritime forest next to Chesapeake Bay include electric and water sites for RVs up to 50 feet, and dry sites for tents, RVs, and pop-ups. Amenities include a history and nature museum, boardwalks to the beach, coin laundry, dump stations, and convenience store with bicycle and fishing gear rentals in season. Twenty two-bedroom cabins with baths, kitchens, fireplace, screened porch, deck with grill, heating, and air-conditioning—but no TV, telephone, or dishwasher—are located across Shore Drive in private, forested sites. Cabins sleep four, six max, and rent by the week during the summer. Open all year. Handicapped-accessible campsites and cabins available.

✦ ⛺ ♿ "¶" Holiday Trav-L Park Virginia Beach (757-425-0249 or 866-849-8860; www.campingvb.com), 1075 General Booth Boulevard. The largest campground in the area, this Good Sam park 1.5 miles from the Board-walk offers full hookups with 50 and 30 amp outlets, including new "supersite" pull-throughs for rigs up to 60 feet, rustic tent sites, and 34 cabins. The 100-acre wooded park includes five swimming pools, game room, minigolf course, dog park, and propane sales, plus nightly music, bingo, and a café during the summer season. Wi-Fi access and cable TV available for a fee. The campground has its own parking area for campers about a block from the ocean at Ninth Street.

♿ North Bay Shore Family Campground (757-426-7911; www.northbay shorecampground.net), 3257 Colech-

ester Road, Virginia Beach 23456. Quiet RV and tent campground about 3 miles from Sandbridge Beach and 10 miles from the Boardwalk sits along canals connecting to North Bay, with fishing and crabbing from most sites. Air-conditioned cabins with showers, pool, store, laundry, game room, boat launch, rental canoes and jon boats, and handicapped-accessible sites available. Open seasonally.

North Landing Beach Riverfront Campground and Resort (757-426-6241 or 888-283-2725; www.north landingbeach.com), 161 S. Princess Anne Road, Virginia Beach 23457. Arrive by road or water at this RV resort with a private beach; boat ramp; deli; pool; 16 cabins, including 10 with bath and kitchen; waterfront tent camping for boaters; and rental kayaks, canoes, paddleboats, and fishing boats.

Sandbridge Outdoor Resort and Beach Cottages (757-721-2020 or 800-333-7515; www.outdoor-resorts .com or www.sandbridgebeachcottages -outdoorresorts.com), 3665 Sandpiper Road, Sandbridge, Virginia Beach 23456. Luxury RV facility in the Outdoor Resorts of America family on the bay side of Sandbridge Beach. Weekly rental units available.

Sandy Point Resort Campground (252-429-3094; www.knottsislandonline .com), 176 Sandy Point Drive, Knotts Island, NC 27950. Located off NC 615 (Princess Anne Road), just over the North Carolina border, this quiet campground has a variety of RV and tent sites, as well as log cabin, mobile home, and camper rentals, at reasonable rates. Bait and tackle store, boat ramp, pier, and sandy beach on-site.

✦ ⛺ ♿ "¶" Virginia Beach KOA (757-428-1444 or 800-562-4150; www .koavirginiabeach.com), 1240 General Booth Boulevard. This 52-acre campground has 400 sites, including 50 amp sites and rustic tent sites, as well as Kamping Kabins and RV rentals. On-site activities include a seasonal pool, jumping pillow, outdoor cinema, playground, minigolf, K9 dog playground, camp store, laundry, game room, planned activities, banana bike rentals, and trolley to the Boardwalk. Wi-Fi and LP gas available.

TIME-SHARE AND APARTMENT RENTALS Several of the hotels along the Boardwalk have been converted or rebuilt as time-share properties, available for exchange through RCI or Interval International. Availability is good, except during the summer season, when everything in Virginia Beach maxes out in terms of price and demand. Many time-share resorts also offer rentals independently.

Several of the time-shares listed below belong to **Gold Key Resorts** (800-254-3009; www.goldkeyresorts.com). In addition to the amenities on-site, guests can use the facilities at all the other Gold Key properties. Low-cost intro packages available.

Check-in times typically are not until 4 PM or even later, and summertime travelers arriving earlier may find themselves sitting in the lobby as their vacation time ticks away. Avoid this by packing a beach bag and making a stop at First Colony State Park, where you'll find changing rooms and showers.

⁰ᵀ¹ ⇝ **Barclay Towers** (757-491-2700 or 800-344-4473; www.barclaytowers timeshare.com), 809 Atlantic Avenue. Two-room suites, although somewhat cozy for four adults, all have oceanfront balconies. Large indoor heated pool, hot tub, and sauna.

⌀ **The Beach Quarters Resort** (757-422-3186 or 800-345-3186; www.beach quartersvirginiabeach.com), 501 Atlantic Avenue. Gold Key resort at

the south end of the Boardwalk has indoor and outdoor pools, tennis court, and health club. Most units are ocean-front with balconies.

The Boardwalk Resort and Villas (757-213-3099 or 800-317-9432; www.theboardwalkresort.com), 1601 Atlantic Avenue. One of the newer time-shares on the oceanfront, this Gold Key resort has an indoor pool and hot tub, on-site restaurant, and great location in the heart of Beach Street.

The Colony (757-425-8689; www.thecolonyvabeach.com), 1301 Atlantic Avenue. All units are two-bedroom with oceanfront balconies. Outdoor pool and sauna.

Ⲩ **The Four Sails** (757-491-8100; www.foursails.com), 3301 Atlantic Avenue. Oceanfront high-rise with indoor pool, sidewalk café and lounge, health club. Most units have balconies and whirlpool baths. Penthouses available.

Ocean Beach Club (757-213-0601 or 800-245-1003; www.theoceanbeach club.com), 3401 Atlantic Avenue. The newest Gold Key resort offers indoor and outdoor pools; a variety of units, including three-bedroom penthouses; oceanfront location at the north end of the Boardwalk.

✪ ⁰ᵀ¹ **Turtle Cay Resort** (757-437-5565 or 888-989-7788; www.turtlecay resort.com), 600 Atlantic Avenue. Directly across the street from sister Gold Key resort the Beach Quarters, this low-rise resort features spacious suites and balconies overlooking a pool area with several different Jacuzzis and pools.

⌀ ❀ **VSA Resorts** (800-955-9700; www.vsaresorts.com). VSA manages three resorts available for time-share exchange or hotel rentals: the **Atrium** (757-491-1400; 315 21st at Arctic

Avenue), **Ocean Key Resort** (757-425-2200; 424 Atlantic Avenue, across from the beach), and the oceanfront **Ocean Sands Resort and Spa** (757-428-5141; 2207 Atlantic Avenue). All are older properties, without balconies, but with indoor pools, Jacuzzis, and a nice selection of family activities, including free van trips to regional attractions, and are in the process of being renovated. Ask for an updated room.

✳ Where to Eat

Dining out in Virginia Beach presents a visitor with so many choices that a lifetime of vacations wouldn't be enough to sample them all. Fresh seafood provides the foundation for much of the local cuisine—from simply steamed to elegant new preparations. Dozens of raw bars all over town sell fresh oysters and clams, raw or steamed, and shrimp boiled in their shells. Bites of tuna, fresh off the boat, are as ubiquitous as chicken wings on appetizer menus.

One local delicacy to look for is the Lynnhaven oyster. Once renowned for the salty, fat crustaceans found in its waters, Lynnhaven Bay fell on hard times, and oyster harvesting was suspended due to polluted waters decades ago. Recently, however, local efforts have cleaned up the water, and large stretches of the estuary are now open for shellfish harvesting. Now Lynnhaven oysters, once the favorite of royalty and presidents, can once again be found in local restaurants and seafood markets. Look for them on the menus of fine-dining restaurants such as the Lynnhaven Fish House, Terrapin, and Steinhilber's Thalia Acres Inn.

Another shellfish that has made a comeback in recent years is the hard-shell clam. Virginia leads the nation in their production, with some 200 million clams harvested annually, most farmed

LYNNHAVEN OYSTERS, COLLECTED WITHIN THE VIRGINIA BEACH CITY LIMITS, ARE MAKING A COMEBACK AT AREA RESTAURANTS.

on sandy bottoms off the Eastern Shore by independent lease holders.

If you're on a budget, or have a smaller appetite, you can save money at the numerous happy hours all over town, including many top restaurants, although Virginia law currently does not allow drink specials to be advertised. Generally stretching 3–6 or 4–7 PM, happy hours frequently include specials on appetizers as well as discounts on drinks.

Foodies who want to sample all the area has to offer should visit during **Virginia Beach Restaurant Week** (www.vbrestaurantweek.com), held annually in January.

Price Categories

Inexpensive	under $10
Moderate	$10 to $20
Expensive	$20 to $25
Very expensive	$25 and up

The listings in this section also include information on what meals are served, using the following abbreviations:

B	Breakfast
L	Lunch
D	Dinner
SB	Sunday brunch

DINING OUT

Boardwalk & Resort Area

🐟 ♿ 🍷 **Catch 31 Fish House Restaurant and Bar** (757-213-3472; www.31ocean.com), 3001 Atlantic Avenue, Hilton Virginia Beach Oceanfront. Open: Daily. Credit cards: Yes. Serving: B, L, D. Price: Expensive. Cuisine: Seafood. Handicapped access: Yes. Special features: Wine bar, cocktail menu, late-night menu, children's menu, smoke-free, happy hour, patio dining with fire pits and heaters, valet

parking. Dine outside around the fire pits next to Neptune Park, or inside where the theme is cool, blue, and sophisticated. Both areas offer terrific views of the ocean, and the freshest fish and shellfish flown in from around the world. Try one of the signature seafood towers with Maine lobster, crab, shrimp, oysters, mussels, and yellowfin poke for a sample of all the raw bar has to offer, or select from the menu of creative chowders, heart-healthy salads, wood-grilled fish, hand-cut steaks, pastas, and pizzas. Don't miss the nationally recognized designer restrooms.

✪ 🐟 ♿ 🍷 ➥ **Croc's 19th Street Eco Bistro** (757-428-5444; www.crocs ecobistro.com), 620 19th Street. Open: Daily. Credit cards: Yes. Serving: L, D, SB. Price: Moderate. Cuisine: Locavore. Handicapped access: Yes. Special features: Full bar, green cocktail socials, organic wine list, children's menu, smoke-free, local live music, wine club and dinners, patio dining, online reservations. Award-winning ecobistro was the first restaurant in the state to be certified Virginia Green. The food and drinks here are "S.O.L." (sustainable, organic, and local) in addition to being delicious and beautifully presented. The menu features locally grown vegetables and sustainable fish from regional waters. The Five Pepper Tuna won raves from *Gourmet Magazine*.

♿ **Isle of Capri** (757-428-2411; www .isleofcaprivb.com), 3900 Atlantic Avenue, in the Holiday Inn SunSpree Resort. Open: Nightly. Credit cards: Yes. Serving: D. Price: Moderate. Cuisine: Italian. Handicapped access: Yes. Special features: Reservations suggested, shirts with collar required for men, tableside service. A fixture for decades on Laskin Avenue, the Isle of Capri relocated to the sixth floor of the Holiday Inn SunSpree, where the Arcese family continues its traditions of old family recipes and tableside service. Often overlooked by the crowds on the Boardwalk below, this restaurant is a great choice for couples or those looking for a quiet meal in a sophisticated setting with a fabulous ocean view. Caesar salads prepared tableside are not to be missed. An extensive wine list includes a big selection of "Super Tuscans" by the bottle or glass, perfect with this authentic Italian cuisine.

✎ 🍷 ♿ 🍸 **Mahi Mah's Seafood Restaurant and Sushi Saloon** (757-437-8030; www.mahimahs.com), 615 Atlantic Avenue, in the Ramada Hotel.

Open: Daily. Credit cards: Yes. Serving: B, L, D. Price: Expensive. Cuisine: Seafood, sushi. Handicapped access: Yes. Special features: Children's menu, late-night menu, happy hour, sushi specials, patio dining, live bands. Selected as the best restaurant in any Ramada Inn in the world, Mahi Mah's is a favorite with locals, who gather at the bar to watch sports on the many TVs or to party during the daily happy hour. Fresh fish, served in a variety of tasty preparations, from cedar-planked with honey glaze to pan seared with crab orzo, are the menu mainstays. Surf and turf specials, a full sushi

WINING AND DINING IN VIRGINIA BEACH

These VB restaurants consistently receive the *Wine Spectator* Award of Excellence, the Stellar Cellar award from *Hampton Roads Magazine,* and "Best of" awards in the local press.

Aldo's Ristorante (757-491-1111; www.aldosvb.com), 1860 Laskin Road, La Promenade Shopping Center, Virginia Beach 23454.

Catch 31 (757-213-3472 or 800-HILTONS; www.hiltonvb.com), 3001 Atlantic Avenue, Hilton Virginia Beach Oceanfront.

↝ **Coastal Grill** (757-496-3348; www.coastalgrill.com), 1327 N. Great Neck Road, Virginia Beach 23454.

Cobalt Grille (757-333-3334; www.cobaltgrille.com), 762 Hilltop North Shopping Center.

↝ **Croc's 19th Street Eco Bistro** (757-428-5444; www.crocsecobistro.com), 620 19th Street.

Eat—An American Bistro (757-965-2472; www.eatbistro.net), 4005 Atlantic Avenue.

Fire & Vine (757-428-8463; www.fireandvine.com), 1556 Laskin Road.

The Hunt Room Grill at the Cavalier Hotel (757-425-8555; www.cavalierhotel.com), 4201 Atlantic Avenue. Open winters only.

Il Giardino Ristorante (757-422-6464; www.ilgiardino.com), 910 Atlantic Avenue.

menu, and local James River oysters please the crowds, and the views of the Boardwalk and the ocean can't be beat. Patrons seated on the patio enjoy live music at the adjacent 7th Street Stage every evening during the summer. Great deals on oysters, clams, and wings during happy hour.

& Y "!" **Raven Restaurant** (757-425-1200; www.theraven.com), 1200 Atlantic Avenue. Open: Daily. Credit cards: Yes. Serving: L, D. Price: Moderate. Cuisine: American. Handicapped access: Yes. Special features: Late-night dining, free Wi-Fi, free parking. When the resort razzle dazzle—and the high-season prices—get to be too much, do as the locals do and head for the Raven, perched in the same spot, just across the street from the beach, since 1968. You'll find a dark and friendly bar; burgers, steaks, and seafood that won't break the bank; refreshing frozen libations, and plenty of Raven's own brew to drink here or to take out. A gift store next door sells Raven beer and wine, logo clothing (great for those Edgar Allan Poe fans at home), and a custom line of hot sauces.

& ⊸ **Terrapin** (757-321-6688; www .terrapinvirginiabeach.com), 3102

Mahi Mah's Seafood Restaurant & Sushi Saloon (757-437-8030; www.mahimahs .com), 615 Atlantic Avenue, Ramada on the Beach. Named the best restaurant in any Ramada in the world.

The Melting Pot (757-425-3463; www.meltingpot.com), 1564 Laskin Road, Hilltop.

One Fish–Two Fish (757-496-4350; www.onefish-twofish.com), Long Bay Pointe Marina, 2109 W. Great Neck Road.

⊸ **Rockafeller's Restaurant at Rudee's Inlet** (757-422-5654; www.rockafellers .com), 308 Mediterranean Avenue.

Salacia (757-213-3473 or 800-HILTONS; www.hiltonvb.com), 3001 Atlantic Avenue, Hilton Virginia Beach Oceanfront. Virginia's only AAA four-diamond steakhouse.

Sonoma Wine Bar & Bistro (757-490-9463; www.sonomatowncenter.com), 189 Central Park Avenue, Town Center, Virginia Beach 23461.

Surf Club Ocean Grille at the Wyndham Oceanfront (757-425-5699; www.surf clubvabeach.com), 5700 Atlantic Avenue.

Swan Terrace (757-366-5777; www.foundersinn.com), 5641 Indian River Road, Virginia Beach 23464. Local favorite for holiday brunch.

⊸ **Tautogs Restaurant** (757-422-0081; www.tautogs.com), 205 23rd Street. Housed in a charming old beach cottage. No sign; look for the fish.

⊸ **Zoes Steak and Seafood Restaurant** (757-437-3636; www.zoesvb.com), 713 19th Street.

Holly Road, Pinewood Square. Open: Tues.–Sun. Credit cards: Yes. Serving: D. Price: Very expensive. Cuisine: American. Handicapped access: Yes. Special features: Tasting menu, patio dining, wine tastings, free parking, reservations suggested. Once you're seated at this stylish little restaurant, situated just a block off Laskin Road (31st Street) and four blocks from the Boardwalk, you may forget you're at the beach. The menu, created by talented chef-owner Rodney Einhorn, a veteran of NYC's Le Cirque, is urban, sophisticated, and fun, leaning heavily on seasonal foods from local farmers, so it changes frequently. One ubiquitous dish: the unforgettably creamy truffle macaroni and cheese. Sit at the softly lit zebrawood bar and watch the action in the open kitchen while enjoying a specially priced tasting menu, or take a seat in the contemporary dining room or on the Terrapin Terrace.

✪ ✇ & Ⴤ **Waterman's Surfside Grill** (757-428-3644; www.watermans.com), 415 Atlantic Avenue. Open: Daily. Credit cards: Yes. Serving: L, D, SB. Price: Moderate. Cuisine: Seafood. Handicapped access: Yes, elevator available. Special features: Children's menu, happy hour, early-bird specials, live music, patio dining, free parking, gift shop. Owned and operated by the same family since 1981, Waterman's started life as a simple burger shack catering to local surfers and fishermen. Today, it is one of the few independent restaurants on the Boardwalk, occupying a spacious beach-cottage-style building where wide windows give unobstructed views of the ocean. Try the Waterman's Burger, a half pound of Angus beef topped with a backfin crabcake, or select seafood or steaks from the wide-ranging menu. The bar here makes the best Orange Crush, a favorite local cocktail, on the beach, and the signature Waterman, a rich

blend of rums and lime, is worthy of a pirate captain. Both are on sale during the Sun.–Fri. happy hours, along with fish tacos, oysters, and steamed shrimp.

Hilltop and Town Center

& Ⴤ **Fire & Vine Woodfire Cuisine** (757-428-VINE; www.fireandvine .com), 1556 Laskin Road, Hilltop. Open: Daily. Credit cards: Yes. Serving: L, D. Price: Moderate. Cuisine: American. Handicapped access: Yes. Special features: Pizza happy hour, bar menu, wine bar, online reservations, free parking. Chef Marc Taylor prepares more than 90 percent of the menu at this elegant Hilltop eatery over a live wood fire or in a wood-fired oven. His recipe for the mix of woods he uses is a well-kept secret, but he infuses everything from steaks and shellfish to crabcakes and pizza with smoky goodness. Cleverly named wine flights showcase the cellar's depth. Dinner entrées include hormone-free cuts of beef, wood-fired kabobs, stuffed quail, organic salmon, and other dishes with "farm to table" pedigrees. The uniquely designed wine cellar contains some 5,000 bottles, with more than 40 wines offered by the glass. Most entrées come with access to the 50-item Chef's Table, packed with fire-grilled vegetables and house-cured meats. The Chef's Table is also available as a light meal at lunch, paired perhaps with seafood gumbo and a fresh baked cookie.

✪ & Ⴤ **Sonoma Wine Bar and Bistro** (757-490-9463; www.sonoma towncenter.com), 189 Central Park Avenue, Town Center, Virginia Beach 23461. Open: Daily. Credit cards: Yes. Serving: L, D. Price: Expensive. Cuisine: American. Handicapped access: Yes. Special features: Smoke-free, online reservations, valet parking, wine bar, cocktail lounge, patio dining, weekly wine tastings, monthly wine dinners. Large and small plates of creative cuisine complement the extensive wine list at this elegant bistro near the Sandler Center. Seventy wines by the glass are available in 2- or 5-ounce pours from a climate-controlled Winekeeper at the convivial bar or comfortable sofa seating. Lighter appetites will enjoy the warm Camembert topped with sautéed wild mushrooms, or design-your-own charcuterie and cheese board. Menus change seasonally to take advantage of the freshest ingredients available—no walk-in fridge or fryer in this kitchen.

Steinhilber's Thalia Acres Inn (757-340-1156; www.steinys.com), 653 Thalia Road. Open: Daily. Credit cards: Yes. Serving: D. Price: Very expensive. Cuisine: Seafood and steaks. Handicapped access: Yes. Special features: Riverfront patio dining, full bar. The locals' choice for special occasion dining for more than 70 years, "Steiny's" sits deep in a neighborhood off Virginia Beach Boulevard on the banks of the Lynnhaven River. The cuisine here is the opposite of trendy, full of classic dishes that have stood the test of time. Legendary fantail fried shrimp in a "secret" orange sauce; fresh fish stuffed with oysters, shrimp, or crab; and lobster bisque laced with bourbon all have avid fans. Prime Black Angus steaks, Maine lobsters, and oysters that likely come from the Lynnhaven are menu mainstays, along with bison steak and duck comfit. Built in 1939, the rustic, openbeam dining room features attentive service from formally dressed servers, but the atmosphere is friendly and laid-back.

Lynnhaven & the Chesapeake Beaches

⚓ ♈ **Alexander's On The Bay** (757-464-4999; www.alexandersonthebay .com), 4536 Ocean View Avenue, at Fentress Avenue, Virginia Beach 23455. Open: Daily. Credit cards: Yes.

Serving: D. Price: Expensive. Cuisine: Seafood. Handicapped access: Yes. Special features: Outdoor waterfront dining, cocktail lounge, valet parking, martini menu, Summer Sunset Celebration. Located directly on the sand, this restaurant, rebuilt after being destroyed by a northeaster in 2009, is a favorite with locals who come to enjoy the sunset and fabulous view of the Chesapeake Bay Bridge-Tunnel, or to celebrate romantic occasions. The kitchen prepares many classic dishes with new flourishes: veal Oscar in chicken or tuna versions; barbecued shrimp stuffed with andouille sausage. Alexander's is well off the beaten track in the Chicks Beach neighborhood.

⚓ ♿ **Charlie's Seafood** (757-481-9863; www.charliesseafood.com), 3139 Shore Dr. Open: Tues.–Sun. Credit cards: Yes. Serving: L, D. Price: Moderate. Cuisine: Seafood. Handicapped access: Yes. Special features: Free parking, children's menu, senior discount, all-you-can-eat specials, takeout available, mail order she-crab soup, logo T-shirts, lunch specials Tues.–Sat. Still owned and operated by the same family who started this Shore Drive landmark in 1946, Charlie's is an insider pick for the best and most reasonably priced seafood on the beach. A cup of she-crab soup, so popular that Charlie's ships it around the world, runs just $3.50. Oysters are served raw, steamed, barbecued, or roasted. Fried or broiled fresh fish and shellfish dinners, famous seafood casseroles and crabcakes, as well as steak and chicken plates come with homestyle vegetables and golfball-sized hush puppies. Wash it down with some fresh squeezed limeade.

⚓ ♿ ➳ **Lynnhaven Fish House and Pier Café** (757-481-0003; www.lynn havenfishhouse.net), 2350 Starfish Road. Open: Daily. Credit cards: Yes. Serving: L, D, weekend brunch. Price:

Expensive. Cuisine: Seafood. Handicapped access: Yes. Special features: Children's menu, free parking. The area's most award-winning restaurant, voted Best Seafood in the Tidewater for more than a dozen consecutive years, enjoys a unique location on the Lynnhaven Fishing Pier and the unmatched views to go with it. The restaurant serves a highly praised she-crab soup, supremely creamy and much improved by liberal pours from the carafe of sherry that comes with it. Check the blackboard for a list the day's fresh fish and shellfish options, along with their points of origin. Arrive before 3 PM to sample the restaurant's specialties from the more moderately priced lunch menu. The immense Mediterranean salad; Cape Henry Lighthouse Quiche, filled with lobster, crab, shrimp, and scallops; and the "whale grade" soft-shell crabs are highly recommended. The Pier Café, a more casual spot next door, is only open seasonally but offers even better views of the bay.

Pungo and Sandbridge

✪ ✒ ♿ ♈ **Blue Pete's Restaurant** (757-453-6478), 1400 N. Muddy Creek Road, Virginia Beach 23456. Open: Daily; limited winter schedule. Credit cards: Yes. Serving: D, weekend brunch. Price: Expensive. Cuisine: Seafood. Handicapped access: Yes. Special features: Free parking, boat dock, cocktail lounge, outdoor deck, occasional live music, Wi-Fi, children's menu, reservations recommended. Located on a quiet creek leading to Back Bay, this former fisherman's shack is off the beaten track but well worth the drive. Or come by boat. This is a favorite destination for kayakers. Today under new ownership, the menu features fresh fish in a variety of creative preparations, pasta dishes, and chops and steaks, and the service is welcoming. In winter, the chef adds local wild game to his repertoire. The cozy cocktail lounge with fireplace is perfect for the cooler months, while the outdoor deck and gazebo twined with tiny lights beckon you outside in nice weather, perhaps for a romantic stroll along the stream as the sun sets.

✒ ♿ ♈ **Margie & Ray's Seafood Restaurant, Crabhouse, and Raw Bar** (757-426-2397), 1240 Sandbridge Road, Virginia Beach 23456. Open: Daily. Credit cards: Yes. Serving: L, D. Price: Moderate. Cuisine: Seafood. Handicapped access: Yes. Special features: Free parking, children's menu, lunch and all-you-can-eat specials, full bar, fresh seafood to go by the pound. Join the locals at the Mako Bar, or take a seat at a table for a casual meal of fresh seafood, steaks, or North Carolina–style barbecue at this outpost on the way to Sandbridge Beach. Famous for its she-crab soup, steamed or fried family seafood platters, and surf and turf combos, this is a genuine local hangout, considered a find by visitors who brave the somewhat run-down outside appearance.

♿ ♈ °¶° **Sandbridge Island Restaurant and Raw Bar; Island Pizza** (757-721-2899 or 757-721-2977 [pizza shop]; www.sandbridgeislandrestaurant.com), 205 Sandbridge Road, Virginia Beach 23456. Open: Daily; winter hours vary. Credit cards: Yes. Serving: B, L, D. Price: Moderate. Cuisine: Seafood. Handicapped access: Yes. Special features: Outdoor deck, free parking, free Wi-Fi, full bar with eight TVs, pizza delivery, late-night dining, occasional live music and dancing. Casual spot across the street from the public beach access serves seafood, steaks, and a wide range of appetizers and sandwiches, as well as award-winning BBQ ribs and pizza.

BAKERIES AND COFFEE SHOPS

⁽ᵀ⁾ Baker's Crust Bread Market (757-422-6703; www.bakerscrust.com), 704 Hilltop North Shopping Center. European-style rustic breads, plus a full bar and nice menu. Free Wi-Fi.

⁽ᵀ⁾ ⟜ Bad Ass Coffee (757-233-4007; www.badasscoffee.com), 619 18th Street. Landmark coffee shop close to the convention center serves healthy breakfast and lunch, and organic Kona coffee, with a side of free Wi-Fi. Opens 6 AM.

⁽ᵀ⁾ Daily Grind (www.dailygrind unwind.com), two locations: 168 Central Park Avenue, Town Center (757-228-3907) and Central Library, 4100 Virginia Beach Boulevard (757-965-3121). Free Wi-Fi.

✪ Sugar Plum Bakery (757-422-3913, www.sugarplumbakery.org), 1353 Laskin Road. Bakery dedicated to providing employment for the developmentally disabled offers delicious breakfast pastries and special-occasion cakes. On-site café serves lunch Mon.–Sat.

BARBECUE Beach Bully BBQ

Restaurant (757-422-4222; www.beachbully.com), 601 19th Street. Famous for its beef brisket grilled in mahogany sauce, award-winning ribs, and grilled tuna. Outdoor deck.

Frankie's Place For Ribs (757-428-7631; www.frankiesribs.com), 3333 Virginia Beach Boulevard, Virginia Beach 23452. Best of the Beach winner serves both pork and beef ribs. Delivery available.

Malbon Bros. BBQ & Catering (757-427-9607; www.malbonbrothers bbq.com), 1896 General Booth Boulevard, Virginia Beach 23454. Stop by the Malbon Citgo to fill up your tank and order up some of the best barbecue pork and beef in the area.

Smoked From Above BBQ (757-499-4959; www.smokedfromabovebbq .com), Landstown Commons Shopping Center, 3376 Princess Anne Road, Virginia Beach 23456. Award-winning 'cue with secret sauce, by the sandwich, plate, or pound.

✪ The Smokehouse and Cooler (757-481-9737; www.smokehouseand cooler.com), Lynnhaven Shoppes, 2957 Shore Drive. Featured on the Food Network, CIA grad Rob Murphy's inspired menu mixes smoked meats with sauces from around the world.

BREAKFAST & CASUAL MEALS

⌘ Beach Pub (757-422-8817; www .angelfire.com/va2/beachpub), 1001 Laskin Road. Join the locals for the bargain breakfasts—perhaps a huge crab omelet with side of clam fritters.

Belvedere Coffee Shop (757-425-0613), Oceanfront and 36th Street. The Belvedere Hotel's coffee shop is a favorite gathering spot on the waterfront for local movers and shakers. Open seasonally.

✪ ❢ Big Sam's Inlet Café (757-428-4858; www.bigsamsrawbar.com), 300 Winston Salem Avenue. Tiki bar on the water at Rudee Inlet is best known among tourists for its raw bar and budget lunches, but locals love it for its early-morning happy hour "breakfast cocktails," just $1.99, 7–11 AM.

Citrus Restaurant (757-227-3333), 2265 Great Neck Road, just off Shore Drive. Breakfast 7–3: award-winning omelets, crab or lobster Benedict, signature fruit pancakes, Citrus salad plate. Come early to avoid a wait.

✪ Doc Taylor's Restaurant (757-425-1960; www.doctaylors.com), 207 23rd Street. Serving just breakfast and lunch, this fun and friendly local favorite housed in an old beach cottage serves cleverly named combos, such as the Heart Attack and the Nurse Ratchett Omelet, and discount breakfast cocktails on the sunny enclosed porch or at the convenient counter.

Eddy's Cafe (757-427-6055), 2181 Upton Drive. Café in Red Mill Commons is famous for its Belgian waffles, omelets, and "Eye Opener" fried egg sandwich with grilled tomatoes.

Forbidden City (757-747-2388; www .forbiddencityvb.com), 3333 Virginia Beach Boulevard, Virginia Beach 23452. Long list of dim sum and other Chinese dishes available all day.

❝❡❞ ❦ **Holiday Food Mart Deli** (757-491-2550), 909 General Booth Boulevard. Family-owned convenience store serves bargain-priced breakfasts made from scratch. A favorite with campers from the RV parks nearby, and a great choice for a busy day. Free Wi-Fi.

✪ ❦ **The Jewish Mother** (757-422-5430; www.jewishmother.com), 3108 Pacific Avenue. Jewish deli serves enormous three-egg omelets, bagels and lox, cheese blintzes, and deli specials all day and late into the night.

Mary's Restaurant (757-428-1355; www.marys-restaurant.com), 616 Virginia Beach Boulevard. Local favorite located six blocks from the ocean has plenty of free parking.

Pocahontas Pancake & Waffle Shop (757-428-6352; www.pocahontas pancakes.com), 3420 Atlantic Avenue. Unique Native American decor combines with huge plates of breakfast specialties, including multigrain pancakes laced with pecans. Free parking in the deck on 35th Street.

✪ **Princess Anne County Grill** (757-468-5700; www.pacountygrill.com), 3640 Dam Neck Road at Princess Anne Road, Virginia Beach 23453. Restaurant at the Virginia Beach Farmers Market features country cooking using local produce; fresh veggie plates, blue plate specials, homemade pies. Open daily all year.

CANDY ❦ **Forbes Candies Factory Outlet** (757-468-6602 or 800-626-5898; www.forbescandies.com), 1300 Taylor Farm Road, Virginia Beach 23453. Retail locations at 24th, 28th, and 31st streets along Atlantic Avenue. Recipes for saltwater taffy, peanut brittle, fudge, and specialty candies, such as seafoam and fruit jellies, date back 60 years at this Virginia Beach original.

A ROYAL TEA PARTY

Step back in time with The Art Of Tea: Then and Now, a class sponsored by the **Virginia Tea Society** (www.virginiateasociety.com), then join them for teas throughout the region and the annual Tea Across America. Some places you can enjoy afternoon tea include: **Rowena's** (757-627-8699; www .rowenas.com) and the **Painted Lady** (757-622-5239; www.thenewpainted lady.com) in Norfolk; **Victorian Station** (www.members.cox.net/victorian station), in Hampton; the historic **Jefferson Hotel** (www.jeffersonhotel.com), in Richmond; and the regal **Williamsburg Inn** (www.colonialwilliamsburg resorts.com). In Virginia Beach, have breakfast or afternoon tea at the **English Rose Tea Room** (757-456-2777; www.theenglishrose.org; 404 S. Parliament Drive, Virginia Beach 23462) or discover the mysteries of flowering tea at **Le Thé et Crepes** (757-363-2211; www.tea-and-crepes.vpweb.com; 1801 Pleasure House Road, Virginia Beach 23455), a café combining Asian and European cuisine.

Search out the factory outlet for the best bargains.

Jody's Gourmet Popcorn (757-425-5639 or 866-797-5639; www.jodys popcorn.com), 205 Laskin Road and 2016 Atlantic Avenue. More than a dozen varieties of popcorn, including the signature caramel, plus lots of fudge and chocolate-dipped goodies.

✪ ↝ **The Royal Chocolate** (757-557-6925; www.theroyalchocolate.com), 164 Central Park Avenue, Town Center, Virginia Beach 23462. Fine chocolates from around the world, chocolate fondue available daily, and monthly chocolate-tasting seminars.

DELIS & SPECIALTY FOODS

Aragona Village Specialty Groceries (www.freewebs.com/aragona village), Bayside district, west of Independence Avenue and north of Virginia Beach Boulevard. Those with an appetite for adventure, or a need for ethnic food items, should seek out Aragona Village, an early suburb and today an international community with a tradition of neighborliness. Ethnic grocers located within a few blocks of each other in Aragona include: **Helen's British Shop** (757-769-7670; www.helensbritishshop.com; 676 N. Witchduck Road, Virginia Beach 23462), carrying meats, cheeses, and teas from the British Isles; **Four Seasons Oriental Grocery** (757-499-2173; 311 Kellam Road); **Hana Oriental Market** (757-497-7424; 4885 N. Witchduck Road), offering Korean items; **J Mart Japanese Grocery** (757-201-3520; www.jmartjmart.com; 308 Aragona Boulevard); **Leila's Mediterranean Groceries & Deli** (757-644-6912; www.leilasmed.com; 4505 Virginia Beach Boulevard); **Little Israel Kosher Grocery and Deli** (757-962-3368; www.little-israel.com; 624 Independence Boulevard); and

Swagat Spices & Indian (757-499-7317; 308 Aragona Boulevard), offering Indian foods and Ayurvedic herbal supplements.

✪ ⛾ **Bella Monte International Marketplace & Restaurant** (757-425-6290; www.bellamontevb.com), 1201 Laskin Road. Gourmet restaurant and piano bar also offers catering, a full-service deli, and a great selection of affordable wines.

Country Butcher Shop and Deli (757-468-1583; www.countrybutcher shopanddeli.com), 3640 Dam Neck Road, in the Virginia Beach Farmers Market. Fresh meats cut to order, including buffalo, venison, and duck; frog's legs; deli meats and cheeses; and lunch specials.

La Bella Italia (www.labellaitalia .com), two Virginia Beach locations: 1065 Laskin Road (757-422-8536) and 2133 Upton Drive, Red Mill Commons (757-301-3603). Delis and bakeries operated by an Italian family carry everything you need to prepare an authentic Italian meal, or choose from among the many dishes available for take-out. Lunch and dinner also served on-site.

PJ Baggan (757-491-8900), 960 Laskin Road. Specialty wine, beer, and cigar store offers a walk-in humidor, smoking lounge, and Gelato Gherardini products.

FARMS, FARMER'S MARKETS & FARM STANDS

Thanks to a visionary "green" policy that preserved the family farms surrounding the city back when development began to move in, Virginia Beach today is one of the best vacation destinations in the United States to "eat local." A drive down Princess Anne Road into the heart of Pungo takes you past numerous farms offering roadside stands and pick-your-own. Notable among these are the Vaughan Farm, in the same family since the 1600s, and the Henley Farm, where three generations continue to work the land. Find directions and more details at the Web site of the **Virginia Department of Agriculture and Consumer Services,** www.virginiagrown.com.

This is prime strawberry country, and every year starting usually in late April, you can pick your own strawberries. The **Pungo Strawberry Festival** (757-721-6001; www.pungostrawberry festival.info; 1776 Princess Anne Road, Virginia Beach 23456), held each year on Memorial Day weekend, brings more than a hundred thousand people to enjoy the juicy fruits.

Area farms also offer opportunities to pick your own blueberries, blackberries, sweet corn, and many other vegetables. Find a listing at www.pickyour own.org. Always call ahead to determine if picking is currently available as seasons and hours vary each year.

⌀ **Brookdale Farm and Market** (757-721-0558; www.brookdale-farm .com), two locations: 2060 Vaughan Road, Virginia Beach 23457; 2133 Mount Pleasant Road, Chesapeake 23322. Pick your own strawberries and sweet corn; hayrides and pumpkins in the fall.

Cullipher Farm Market (757-721-7456; www.cullipherfarm.com), 1444 Princess Anne Road, Virginia Beach 23457. Easy-to-find stand in Pungo carries heirloom tomatoes, shelled peas, summer squash, and more, grown using organic practices. Pick your own strawberries.

Henley Farm Market (757-426-6869; www.henleyfarms.com), 1801 Princess Anne Road at Indian River Road. At this farm market in downtown Pungo, you can buy fresh produce grown by three generations of a local farm fami-

ly. Visit the nearby **Henley Farm** (757-426-7501; 3484 Charity Neck Road) for pick-your-own strawberries, blackberries, white corn, and other vegetables, plus cut your own Christmas trees.

Horsley's Blackwater Farm (757-421-3625), 3169 Land of Promise Road, Virginia Beach 23457. Gather your own pecans here in the fall.

↝ **Old Beach Farmers Market** (www.oldbeachfarmersmarket.com), corner of 19th Street and Cypress Avenue, in the parking lot of Croc's ecobistro. Farmer's market in the resort area features products from local farms, wineries, and watermen. Sat. mornings, Memorial Day–Labor Day.

⌀ 占 **Pungo Blueberries, Etc.** (757-721-7434), 3477 Muddy Creek Road, Virginia Beach 23456. Pick your own thornless blackberries and blueberries July–Aug. Handicapped assistance available. Also sells elephant garlic, local honey, and homemade jams and jellies.

Vaughan Farms' Produce (757-615-4888; www.vaughanfarmsproduce .com), 1258 Princess Anne Road, Virginia Beach 23457. Farmed by the same family since the late 1600s, this family-friendly stop offers legendary sweet white corn, pick-your-own strawberries, plus many other vegetables and fruits, local honey, and fresh eggs, all produced using organic practices.

✪ *⌀* 占 **Virginia Beach Farmers Market** (757-385-4395; www.vbgov .com/farmersmarket), 3640 Dam Neck Road at Princess Anne Road, Virginia Beach 23453. Housing numerous produce stands and specialty markets, the city-owned farmer's market showcases the products of the region. Stores open year-round include a butcher shop, dairy store, organic grocery, wild-bird store, and bakery. The **Princess Anne**

County Grill (757-468-5700; www .pacountygrill.com), an on-site restaurant, serves down-home country cooking every day all year. Free Fri. night hoedown, Sat. night Classic Car Cruise-Ins, craft shows, flea markets, and more, Apr.–Oct.

FAST FOOD Aloha Hawaiian BBQ (757-499-9699; www.alohahawaiian bbqva.com), 5260 Princess Anne Road, Virginia Beach 23462. Hawaiian-style plate lunches and noodle dishes, including several based on tofu.

Donkey Dawgs (757-425-3885), 1933 Virginia Beach Boulevard, Virginia Beach 23454. Local favorite serves hot dogs, hamburgers, and North Carolina–style barbecue.

Pollards Chicken & Catering (www .pollardschicken.com), several Virginia Beach locations: 405 S. Witchduck Road (757-519-9000), 3545 Buckner Boulevard (757-416-0003), and 100 London Bridge Shopping Center (757-340-2565). Fried or rotisserie chicken, veggie plates, seafood, barbecue, and famous puffs from one of the largest and oldest catering companies in Hampton Roads. Additional locations in Chesapeake and Norfolk.

HAPPY HOUR FAVORITES See also the *Restaurants* and *To See— Nightlife* sections for additional happy hours.

Baja Cantina (757-437-2920), 206 23rd Street. Locally famous for its 2-4-1 fish tacos.

✪ 🦞 ♈ **Chick's Oyster Bar** (757-481-5757; www.chicksoysterbar.com), 2143 Vista Circle. Spot on Lynnhaven Inlet is popular with locals for its great happy hour menu, nightly specials, winter oyster roasts, and live music in the tiki bar.

♈ **Chix Seaside Cafe and Laverne's Seafood Restaurant** (757-428-6836

or 757-428-2449; www.chix-lavernes .com), 701 Atlantic Avenue. Popular oyster happy hour and early-bird specials overlooking the Boardwalk.

✪ ♈ **Dockside Inn** (757-481-4545; www.fishingvabeach.com), 3311 Shore Drive. Locals crowd the bar here Sun.–Fri for happy hour prices on drinks and oysters. Shag dancing on Sun.

♈ ↝ **Fresh Tapas & Tonics** (757-430-8700; www.freshtapasntonics.com), 2129 General Booth Boulevard, Strawbridge Marketplace. Daily happy hours feature $3 martinis; drink or food specials most nights.

🍴 ♈ **Harpoon Larry's Oyster Bar** (757-422-6000; www.harpoonlarry skillerseafood.com), 216 24th Street at Pacific. Daily happy hours and specials on seafood in a convenient location with free parking.

♈ **Havana** (757-430-8205; www.havana vb.com), 1169 Nimmo Parkway, Red Mill Commons. Sophisticated spot serves a Cuban-inspired menu and sponsors a weeknight mojito happy hour.

♈ **Rockfish Boardwalk Bar and Sea Grill** (757-213-7625; www.theboard walkresort.com), 1601 Atlantic Avenue. Classy bar at the Boardwalk Resort serves happy hour beverages amid an impressive collection of Beatles memorabilia.

♈ **Sushi & West** (757-427-9680; www .sushiandwest.com), 2181 Upton Drive, Red Mill Commons. Known for its sake night and sushi specials. Second location in Renaissance Shopping Center (757-631-1004; 401 N. Great Neck Road).

ICE CREAM AND FROZEN YOGURT 🍦 **Dairy Queen** (757-422-9342; www.dairyqueen.com), 1609 Atlantic Avenue at 17th Street. Said to be the busiest Dairy Queen in the nationwide chain, this neon-bedecked location is the meeting place of the Boardwalk, as much for its outside seating and public restrooms as for the soft-serve masterpieces on its menu.

Kohr Bros. Frozen Custard (757-491-3301; www.kohrbros.com), 1500, 1800, and 2204 Atlantic Avenue. Original frozen custard invented in 1919 is a fixture on the beach, with three locations on Atlantic Avenue.

✍ **The Skinny Dip Frozen Yogurt Bar** (www.ilovetheskinnydip.com), several Virginia Beach locations: Hilltop Plaza (757-648-8800), Landstown Commons (757-689-3433), and Providence Square Shopping Center (757-282-6556). Serve-yourself frozen yogurt in a variety of flavors.

NATURAL FOODS AND VEGETARIAN RESTAURANTS

Azar's Natural Foods (757-486-7778; www.azarfoods.com), 108 Prescott Avenue, Virginia Beach 23452. Mediterranean specialties earned the title of Best Restaurant for Healthy Eating in Hampton Roads.

Fresh Fare Café (757-491-5383), 700 19th Street. Cool sandwich shop close to the convention center has lots of vegetarian options and a smoothie bar.

✪ ✎ **The Heritage Health Foods Grocery, Café and Organic Juice Bar** (757-428-0100; www.theheritage cafe.com), 314 Laskin Road. This fascinating shop offers a full-service natural grocery with many organic and bulk items, and a café serving vegetarian and vegan selections.

Navan Foods (757-965-5422; www .navanfoods.com), 4312 Holland Road, Virginia Beach 23452. Specializes in items for people with food allergies and other special dietary needs.

Organic Food Depot (757-467-8999; www.organicfooddepot.com), 4301 Commuter Drive at Holland Road,

Virginia Beach 23462. Free memberships. Additional location in Norfolk (757-623-8999).

✎ **Virginia Garden Organic Grocery** (757-427-0378; www.vagarden .com), 3640 Dam Neck Road, Virginia Beach 23453. Full-service grocery operated by Virginia's first organic farmer at the Virginia Beach Farmers Market.

PIZZA ♔ **Albie's Pizza & Bar** (757-422-0400; www.albiespizza.com), 200 21st Street. New York–style and stuffed pizzas, and award-winning chicken wings, on "the Block" at oceanfront, stays open until 3 AM many mornings. Delivery available.

♔ **Chicho's Pizza** (www.chichospizza .com), three Virginia Beach locations: 2112 Atlantic Avenue (757-422-6011), 2820 Pacific Avenue (757-425-5656), and 2129 General Booth Boulevard, Strawbridge Marketplace. Chain started by a couple of former lifeguards offers a simple pizza-and-beer menu. Delivery available.

♔ ✎ **Dough Boy's California Pizza** (www.doughboyspizza.com), two locations on the oceanfront: 1700 Atlantic Avenue (757-422-6111) and 2410 Atlantic Avenue (757-425-7108). Restaurants with lots of aloha serve New York, California, and pan pizzas; burgers; gyros; and tropical drinks. Delivery available.

♔ **Pi-zzeria** (757-213-0600; www.pi -zzeria.com), 3316 Atlantic Avenue. Hip spot with outdoor dining, full bar, happy hour, and late hours serves hand-tossed pizzas cooked in a rotating brick oven, paninis and pastas, and daily sangria specials.

♔ ✍ **Planet Pizza** (757-491-1954; www.myspace.com/planetpizza), 812 Atlantic Avenue. Pizzas and pastas served amid out-of-this-world decor. Is that Mr. Spock at the next table? Full bar, patio dining, children's menu, carryout available. Second location at 981 Laskin Road (757-961-3150) has a game room and free parking. Delivery available (757-961-1655).

✔ **Pungo Pizza & Ice Cream** (757-721-4900; www.facebook.com/pungo pizza), 1824 Princess Anne Road, Virginia Beach 23456. Lighthouse-themed building near downtown Pungo offers dine-in on the large screened deck or carryout, game room, low-carb items, carryout.

Ynot Pizza (www.ynotpizza.com), two Virginia Beach locations: Great Neck Square Shopping Center (757-496-9111) and 5257 Providence Road (757-474-6000). Award-winning specialty pies and slices, including white, stuffed, and breakfast pizzas. Order online for delivery or pickup.

SEAFOOD MARKETS Nearly all the seafood you'll find at these local markets is caught on day boats working Atlantic and Chesapeake waters. More than 80 varieties of fish and shellfish are commercially marketed.

Back Bay Crabs (757-237-7518; www.backbaycrabs.com). Jumbo blue crabs straight from the boat. Order 48 hours in advance.

Belanga Fish Co. (757-426-2908), 897 Sandbridge Road, Virginia Beach 23456. Selection here depends on what Mr. Belanga caught that day. Check out his handcarved decoys.

Bonnie & Sons Seafood (757-721-5999), corner of Sandbridge and Princess Anne roads. Steamed crabs are a specialty. Delivery available to Sandbridge.

❂ **Dockside Seafood Market and Marina** (757-481-4545; www.fishingva beach.com), 3311 Shore Drive. Fresh seafood brought in by the marina's captains, plus a wide range of wines and groceries.

Pungo Fish House (757-426-6808), 1973 Indian River Road, Virginia Beach 23456. Wide range of finfish and shellfish, available steamed.

Shellfish Company (757-481-7512; www.bubbasseafoodrestaurant.com), 3323 Shore Drive. Local oysters and clams, live or steamed blue crabs, fresh local fish, plus chowders, salads, crabcakes, Key lime pies, and barbecued tuna, ready to go, at this convenient spot next to Bubba's.

Uncle Chuck's Seafood (757-406-3702), Vendor's Lane, 3640 Dam Neck Road, Virginia Beach 23453. Local oysters, clams, and shrimp, plus unusual soups, bisques, and chowders, such as butternut crab and lobster asparagus, at the Virginia Beach Farmers Market.

Welton's Fresh Seafood Market (757-428-6740), 3621 Pacific Avenue. Seafood at this resort area spot is fresh and local, often caught by the proprietors. Look for Eastern Shore oysters, rockfish, and scallops in season.

TAKE-OUT & DELIVERY Gringo's **Taqueria** (757-961-2987; www.gringosvb.com), 612 Norfolk Avenue. Old-style Mexican recipes with a gourmet twist made from all fresh ingredients. Delivery available.

✔ **Kelly's Tavern** (www.kellystavern .com), several locations: **Hilltop** (757-491-8737; 1936 Laskin Road), **Kempsville** (757-479-3940), **Pembroke Mall** (757-490-7999), and **Strawbridge Marketplace** (757-430-8999). Extensive "curbside to go" menu includes Kelly's famous Humongous Half Pounder, winner of local Best Burger awards for decades.

Mayflower Cafe (757-417-0117), 209 34th Street. Almost hidden behind the Mayflower Seaside Apartments a block from the Boardwalk, this café is a good choice for reasonably priced gyros and other Mediterranean specials at lunch. Avoid the crowds and order to go.

⤙ **Taste Unlimited** (www.tasteunlimited.com). Virginia Beach locations: **Oceanfront** (757-422-3399; 36th and Pacific Avenue), **Bayville** (757-464-1566; 4097 Shore Drive), and **Hilltop** (757-425-1858; 638 Hilltop West Shopping Center). Lunch All Day menu of sandwiches and salads, box lunches, wines, cheeses, coffees, and gourmet items. Free wine tastings on the weekends. Free delivery.

WINE SHOPS, WINE BARS & BREWPUBS ♻ ♈ Eurasia Café and Wine Bar

(757-422-0184; www.eurasiavb.com), 960 Laskin Road. Award-winning café inside PJ Baggan offers a locavore menu, wines by the glass or bottle, and Sun. brunch.

♈ **Gordon Biersch Brewery Restaurant** (757-490-2739; www.gordonbiersch.com), 4561 Virginia Beach Boulevard, Town Center, Virginia Beach 23462. Fresh beer brewed on the premises.

Grape & Gourmet (757-486-9463; www.grapeandgourmet.com), 4000 Virginia Beach Boulevard, Loehmann's Plaza, Virginia Beach 23452. More than 500 wines and 250 microbrews from around the world, plus a wide variety of gourmet foods; weekly beer and wine tastings.

♈ ⍣ **Lubo Wine Bar & Café** (757-216-2900; www.lubowines.com), 1658 Pleasure House Road, Virginia Beach 23455. Neighborhood café and gourmet market with wine flights, beer tastings, cheese boards, award-winning nachos, Sun. brunch, wine tastings, and wine classes. Free Wi-Fi.

Sandbridge Seaside Market (757-426-6594), 209 Sandbridge Road, Virginia Beach 23456. The only grocery on Sandbridge Beach carries a wide range of wine and microbrews, including Pipeline Porter (favored by the surfing crowd), plus fresh shrimp and steaks for the barbee, sandwiches, and everything you need for a day at the beach.

WINERIES & VINEYARDS Blackwater Vineyards

(757-421-9161; www.blackwatervineyards.com), 4280 Blackwater Road, Virginia Beach 23457. Pick 10 different varieties of grapes every fall at the state's largest muscadine vineyard.

Martin Vineyards (252-429-3542 or 252-429-3564; www.martinvineyards.com), 213 Martin Farm Lane, Knotts Island, NC 27950. Tastings available of dry reds and whites, plus fruit wines. Pick your own apples, peaches, scuppernong grapes, and pumpkins in season.

Moonrise Bay Vineyard (252-429-WINE or 866-888-WINE; www.moonrisebaywine.com), 134 Moonrise Bay Vineyard Road, Knotts Island, NC 27950. Scenic views over the water complement dry reds and whites, as well as fruit wines made of berries and cherries. Tastings and tours available.

✴ Shopping

If shopping is your favorite vacation activity, you'll find plenty to do in Virginia Beach. The main drag for shops is Laskin Road, which begins as 31st Street at the oceanfront, then merges a bit farther on with Virginia Beach Boulevard. Driving west on this thoroughfare, you'll pass the trendy boutiques of **31 Ocean;** little shops on Laskin that have been around for years; the **Hilltop Shopping District,** one of the earliest shopping centers in town and still one of the best; the upscale **La Promenade;** and **Chambord Commons,** near where Laskin changes to Virginia Beach Boulevard. Just a few miles farther out, **Town Center** and **Pembroke Mall** sit side by side at the corner of Virginia Beach Boulevard and Independence. Since I-

264 runs parallel with Laskin and Virginia Beach Boulevard all the way to the Norfolk city limits, you can easily access these shopping districts by expressway, if you wish.

Another major group of shopping options lies on the south side of Virginia Beach, where General Booth Boulevard runs past **Strawbridge Marketplace** and **Red Mill Commons.**

SHOPPING CENTERS & MALLS

Chambord Commons Shopping Center, corner of Great Neck Road and Virginia Beach Boulevard, Virginia Beach 32454. Shops include upscale bridal and lingerie boutiques, salons, and galleries.

Countryside Shops (757-427-9009), 3600 Dam Neck Road at Princess Anne Road, Virginia Beach 32453. Located next door to the Virginia Beach Farmers Market, this minimall where all the shops connect inside houses a number of craft and specialty shops, as well as **Bubba's Deli and BBQ** (757-368-6336), serving hand-pulled pork, thick sandwiches, and daily specials.

Hilltop Shopping District. Located at one of the highest points in the city and just a couple of minutes from the oceanfront, this shopping complex centers on the intersection of Laskin (31st Street) and First Colonial roads. On the northeast corner, **The Shops at Hilltop** (www.hilltopshops.com) are home to more than a hundred shops and services, plus a Fresh Market grocery, the Hilltop YMCA, and more than 20 places to eat, among them some of the top restaurants in the city. While most of the jewelry, clothing, and gift stores are locally owned and operated, you'll also find national chains here, including **Blue Ridge Mountain Sports** (757-422-2201) and

TOWN CENTER, HALFWAY BETWEEN THE OCEANFRONT AND NORFOLK, PROVIDES VIRGINIA BEACH WITH NEW SHOPPING, DINING, AND ENTERTAINMENT OPTIONS.

the **SAS Comfort Shoes Outlet Store** (757-425-9915). A branch of the **Virginia ABC Stores** (757-491-5137; www.abc.virginia.gov) is located here as well. On the northwest corner, **The Marketplace at Hilltop** (www .marketplaceathilltop.net; 1744 Laskin Road) hosts many more national chains, among them Borders Books and Music, Michael's Crafts, Total Wine and More, and **Panera Bread** (757-417-7009;www.panerabread.com), with complimentary Wi-Fi. Across Laskin Road on the northwest corner of the intersection, **Hilltop Plaza** is the site of the Virginia Beach **Trader Joe's** (757-422-4840; www.traderjoes .com), the California grocery that's sweeping the nation.

Landstown Commons Shopping Center (757-453-6726; www.thegood mancompany.com), 3312 Princess

Anne Road at Dam Neck Road, Virginia Beach 23456. Located across from the Virginia Beach Farmers Market, this is the newest of the city's big-box shopping centers. Anchor stores include PetSmart, Best Buy, and Kohl's.

La Promenade Distinctive Shoppes (757-422-8839; www.lapromenade shoppes.com), 1860 Laskin Road, Virginia Beach 23454. With wide sidewalks, a central fountain, Victorian-style park benches, piped-in classical music, old-world gas lamps, an open-air flower kiosk, and alfresco dining, La Promenade is a pleasant place to visit day or night. Located 3 miles from the oceanfront, this upscale collection of shops includes Williams-Sonoma, Talbots, Jos. A. Bank Clothiers, and **Simply Selma's** (757-428-2885; www.simplyselmas.com). In addition, two award-winning restaurants are located here: **Aldo's Ristorante** (757-491-1111; www.aldosvb.com) and **Mizuno** (757-422-1200; www.mizuno-

VENDORS AT THE VIRGINIA BEACH FARMERS MARKET SELL MANY TYPES OF LOCAL PRODUCTS YEAR–ROUND.

sushi.com), the area's most authentic Japanese restaurant.

⚓ **Lynnhaven Mall** (757-340-9410; www.lynnhavenmall.com), 701 Lynnhaven Parkway, Virginia Beach 23452. With more than 180 stores and services anchored by three major department stores—Dillard's, Macy's, and JCPenney—this two-story mall is one of the largest on the East Coast. **AMC Lynnhaven 18 Theater** (757-896-2330 or 888-AMC-4FUN) shows first-run films in 18 theaters with digital surround sound. A second-story **Food Court** includes a Johnny Rockets with tabletop jukeboxes, sushi bar, Cajun grill, and noodle shop. Lynnhaven's signature two-story **Island Carousel** (757-631-1925), located at the main entrance, is a favorite with both children and adults. Rides are $2. There's also a nautically themed play area on the second floor overlooking the carousel. Pick up a Premier Passport filled with discounts at the **Customer Welcome Center** (757-340-9410), on the lower level in front of Barnes & Noble.

ⁱ **Pembroke Mall at Town Center** (757-497-6255; www.pembroke mall.com), 4582 Virginia Beach Boulevard, Virginia Beach 23462. Located at the intersection of Independence and Virginia Beach boulevards, this mall predates the Town Center complex, which has grown to embrace it. Recently renovated, Pembroke is home to Sears, Kohl's, Stein Mart, and **Regal Pembroke Cinema 8** (757-671-7469 or 757-671-7664; www.regmovies.com), in addition to more than a hundred specialty stores, a food court with free Wi-Fi, and several restaurants and galleries.

Red Mill Commons and Red Mill Walk (www.redmillcommons.net), 1169 Nimmo Parkway at Upton Drive, Virginia Beach 23454. Located about 5 miles from the resort area and the closest major shopping to Sandbridge Beach, Red Mill is an enormous complex of supersize box stores intermixed with more than 80 specialty stores and restaurants. Anchor stores include a Walmart Super Center, Home Depot, Target, T.J.Maxx, Bath & Body Works, Office Max, and a branch of the **Virginia ABC Stores** (757-427-9650; www.abc.virginia.gov).

Shoppes @ 31 Ocean (877-316-2326; www.31ocean.com), 31st Street and Atlantic Avenue. This hip group of upscale boutiques and gift shops connects with the Hilton Oceanfront Hotel via an overstreet walkway and has its own free parking garage off Pacific Avenue.

Strawbridge Marketplace, General Booth Boulevard and London Bridge Road, Virginia Beach 23454. The **Regal Strawbridge Marketplace Stadium 12** (757-563-9270; www.regmovies.com; 2133 General Booth Boulevard) shares this strip mall with several nice eateries, including the **Atlas Grill and Bar** (757-496-3839; www.atlasgrillandbar.com; 2135 General Booth Boulevard) next door, serving blue plate specials daily.

✪ **Town Center** (www.vabeachtown center.com), Virginia Beach and Independence boulevards, Virginia Beach 23462. This 17-block mixed-use development contains many high-end shopping and dining options clustered around the Sandler Center for the Performing Arts. Among the high-end stores you'll find **The Royal Chocolate** (757-557-6925; www.theroyal chocolate.com; 164 Central Park Avenue), serving chocolate fondue all day. Dining options include many top national chains, including the Cheesecake Factory, PF Chang's China Bistro, California Pizza Kitchen, Red Star Tavern, Ruth's Chris Steak House, Gordon

Biersch Brewery, and **McCormick & Schmick's** (757-687-8686; www.mccormickandschmicks.com; 211 Market Street), with its outstanding happy hour appetizer specials. Several entertainment venues are located in Town Center: **Keagan's Irish Pub and Restaurant** (757-961-4432; www.keagans.com; 244 Market Street), with live acoustic music most nights; the **Funny Bone Comedy Club and Restaurant** (757-213-5555; www.vabeachfunnybone.com; 217 Central Park Avenue); and the **Columbus 12 Regal Cinemas** (757-490-8181; www.regmovies.com; 104 Constitution Drive). Town Center has more than 3,200 free parking spaces, and on some nights, you can get around by rickshaw.

ANTIQUES ⬆ **Barrett Street Antique Center** (757-463-1911; www.barrettstreet.com), 2645 Dean Drive, Virginia Beach 23452. Browse for antique furniture, especially European pine, mahogany, and teak, among the 130 dealers here. Auctions are held about once a month; bidders and browsers enjoy free coffee and doughnuts, and a luncheon buffet.

Cypress Point Antique Mall (757-490-0381), Cypress Point Shopping Center, 928 Diamond Springs Road, Virginia Beach 23455. More than 20 dealers display a wide range of collectibles, glassware, books, and other unique items.

Olde Main Street (757-498-6133; www.oldemainstreet.net), 619 N. Birdneck Road. Vintage clothing and jewelry are the draws at this Best of the Beach winner.

BOOKS & MUSIC **Barnes & Noble Booksellers** (www.barnesandnoble .com). Town Center: 4485 Virginia Beach Boulevard, Virginia Beach

23462 (757-671-2331); Lynnhaven Mall: 701 Lynnhaven Parkway, Virginia Beach 23452 (757-640-2655). Huge selection of new fiction and nonfiction.

Birdland Records, Tapes and Discs (757-495-0961; www.birdlandmusic .com), 957 Providence Square Center, Virginia Beach 23464. Owner Barry Friedman possesses a legendary knowledge of music and stocks the largest selection of 12-inch vinyl in the state, including many rare finds.

The Book Rack (757-496-2470; www.bookrack.org), 2148 Great Neck Square, Virginia Beach 23454. New and used books for sale or trade.

Borders Books, Music, Movies, and Café (757-425-8031; www.borders .com), 1744 Laskin Road, Hilltop, Virginia Beach 23454. Wide selection of new fiction and nonfiction, plus CDs and DVDs.

✔ **Cool Stuff** (757-495-2665; www .myspace.com/coolstuffva), 4239 Holland Road, Timberlake Shopping Center, Virginia Beach 23452. Fun spot for gamers has a great selection of used music, DVDs, MP3 players, game consoles, and game cartridges, for sale or trade.

Edgar Cayce's A.R.E. Bookstore (757-428-3588 or 800-333-4499; www .edgarcayce.org), 215 67th Street. Wide selection of books, DVDs, and CDs on ancient mysteries, dreams, reincarnation, holistic health, astrology, feng shui, meditation, and psychic development.

Heritage Books & Gifts (757-428-0100; www.theheritagebookstore.com), 308 Laskin Road. Browse for uplifting music, videos, and books, all aimed at enhancing body/mind health, at this oasis of calm near the oceanfront.

Smith Bookstore (757-474-9448), 961 Providence Square Shopping Center, Virginia Beach 23464. Independent

store with a wide selection of new and used books, including romances, westerns, and *New York Times* best sellers, many at discount prices.

CLOTHING ✪ **Beecroft & Bull** (757-422-1961; www.beecroftand bull.com), 3198 Pacific Avenue. Venerable men's store continues its 50-year tradition of providing custom and top designer lines of men's clothing. Ranked among the top stores in the United States by *Esquire* magazine. Additional location in Richmond.

♂ **Caribbean Wraps International** (757-495-8003 or 800-495-9105; www .allyouneedtowear.com), 485 S. Independence Boulevard, Town Center, Virginia Beach 23452. Semisheer and hand painted Bali sarongs perfect for vacation, the beach, or weddings. On-site tropical wedding chapel.

Dan Ryan's For Men (757-425-0660; www.danryans.net), 1612 Laskin Road, Hilltop North Shopping Center. Everything for the well-dressed male, from beachwear to business suits, at this longtime local favorite.

Meg's Swimwear (757-428-7945), 307 Laskin Road. Conveniently located two blocks from the oceanfront, this is a local favorite for designer swimwear, or, for those hard to fit sizes, suits custom made by Meg herself.

CONSIGNMENT & RESALE
Echoes of Time Costume Shop (757-428-2332; www.echoes-of-time .com), 600 N. Witchduck Road, Virginia Beach 23462. Fun shop stocks thousands of outfits from the 1800s to the 1970s, for rent or sale.

✔ **Kid To Kid** (757-271-3589; http://virginiabeach.kidtokid.com), 539 Hilltop Plaza, Virginia Beach 23454. Resale store stocks gently used clothing, including many top brands; toys; baby equipment; shoes; and trikes.

Worth the Wait Consignment Boutique (757-498-9051; www.worththe waitusa.com), 3157 Virginia Beach Boulevard, Virginia Beach 23452. A local favorite for new-to-you upscale clothing, plus great prices on jewelry, handbags, and Vera Bradley accessories.

GIFTS ✪ **The Leaping Lizard Gift Shop and Café** (757-363-0161; www.theleapinglizard.com), 4408 Shore Drive, Virginia Beach 23455. Works by local artists in silver, ceramics, and wrought iron crowd this little cottage on Shore Drive. A charming tearoom next door seats 20 for breakfast and lunch, and the red barn out back stocks produce from local farms.

🐾 **Mrs. Bones Bowtique** (757-412-0500 or 877-767-1308; www.mrs bones.com), 1616 Hilltop West Executive Center Shops. The headquarters of Mrs. Bones, the world's top designer of doggie fashion, welcomes well-mannered leashed and carried pets. Second location in Williamsburg's Market Square.

Ragged Robin Gifts (757-428-1831; www.raggedrobingiftshop.com), 325 Laskin Road. Shop with extensive crystal and china selections, and a bridal registry, just steps from the oceanfront.

HOME DECOR Cool & Eclectic (757-428-8000; www.coolandeclectic .com), two locations: 701 Lynnhaven Parkway in Lynnhaven Mall, Virginia Beach 23452, and 4554 Virginia Beach Boulevard in Pembroke Mall, Virginia Beach 23462. Stores packed with far-out decor and fashion. Shipping available.

Heritage Amish Furniture (757-463-3430; www.heritageamish.com), 2738 Virginia Beach Boulevard, Virginia Beach 23452. Browse the timeless furniture styles created by Amish woodworkers, then choose woods and stains. Your furniture is delivered to your door.

House of Capodimonte (757-420-2788; www.1capodimonte.com), 5660 Indian River Road, Virginia Beach 23464. If Italian Baroque is your bag, check out this showroom packed with imported furniture and accessories personally selected in Italy by the owners.

JEWELRY Baker's Fine Jewelry and Gifts (757-422-5522; www .bakersjewelry.com), 972 Laskin Road. Operated by the same family since 1918, Baker's carries the finest lines of jewelry and precious gifts.

Goldworks Jewelry (757-428-7651; www.goldworker.com), 513 N. Birdneck Road. Goldsmith Theresa Parsons creates unique, one-of-a-kind rings and other jewelry in gold, platinum, and precious stones.

Pizazz Jewelry, two Virginia Beach locations: **JodyG at Pizzaz** in Hilltop North Shopping Center (757-422-1201), and Loehmann's Plaza Shopping Center (757-421-0700; 4000 Virginia Beach Boulevard, Virginia Beach 23452). VB's favorite store for costume jewelry carries a large selection of sterling silver pieces under $39.

✳ Special Events

Beachstreet USA plans weekend festivals all year on the Virginia Beach Boardwalk, as well as nightly entertainment during the summer season on a number of stages. Nearly all the events are free. For a complete current listing, visit www.beachstreetusa.com.

January: **Burns Nicht Supper** (www .tidewaterscots.org), Princess Anne Country Club, 3800 Pacific Avenue, Virginia Beach.

THE EASTERN SHORE WINE TRAIL

Wine lovers traveling over the Chesapeake Bay Bridge-Tunnel and up the Delmarva Peninsula, an area with soil and climate conditions that have been compared to the Medoc region of Bordeaux, can visit three wineries.

Bloxom Vineyard (757-665-5670; www.bloxomwinery.com), 26130 Mason Road, Bloxom 23308. Enjoy estate-style wines, cheese, and fresh baked bread on a covered patio.

Chatham Vineyards (757-678-5588; www.chathamvineyards.net), 9232 Chatham Road, Machipongo 23405. Historic farm makes fine Vinifera wines.

Holly Grove Vineyards (757-442-2844; www.hollygrovevineyards.com), 6404 Holly Bluff Drive, Franktown 23354. Award-winning Chardonnays and Merlots.

For additional information, contact the **Eastern Shore of Virginia Tourism** (757-787-8268; www.esvatourism.org; P.O. Box 72, Tasley 23441).

Mid-Atlantic Rockfish Shootout (757-319-5146; www.midatlanticrock fishshootout.com).

Mid-Atlantic Sports and Boat Show (757-222-3999; www.vaboatshow.com), Virginia Beach Convention Center. Largest indoor boat show in Virginia.

Virginia Beach Restaurant Week (757-422-4420; www.vbrestaurant week.com).

Winter Wildlife Festival (757-385-4461; www.vbgov.com), Kempsville Recreation Center, Virginia Beach. Excursions and seminars feature local wildlife, including whales and harbor seals.

February: **Mid-Atlantic Home & Flower Show** (757-420-2434; www .vafgs.org), Virginia Beach Convention Center.

Wine By Design (757-425-0000; www.cacv.org), Contemporary Art Center of Virginia, Virginia Beach.

March: **Back Bay Forum** (757-721-7666; www.bbrf.org), Virginia Beach. Seminars on environmental issues.

Norwegian Lady Ceremony (757-428-5110; www.vbgov.com), 25th Street and Atlantic Avenue, Virginia Beach. Honoring those who died in the wreck of the *Dictator* and Virginia Beach's sister city, Moss, Norway.

○ **Warbirds over the Beach** (757-721-7767; www.militaryaviation museum.org), Virginia Beach Airport, 1341 Princess Anne Road, Virginia Beach 23457.

April: **Blessing of the Fleet and 5K Run-Walk** (757-331-4884; www.cape charles.org), Cape Charles waterfront.

✑ **Celebration of Life for All People Pow Wow** (757-427-2990; www .vbgov.com), Red Wing Park, 1398 General Booth Boulevard, Virginia Beach.

Eastern Shore Garden Tour (757-678-7889; www.esgardentours.com).

Oceanfront Spring Charity Pub Crawl (www.ghentbartour.com), Virginia Beach.

Reel Dreams Film Festival (888-777-7729; www.reeldreamsfilmfest .com), Regent University, Virginia Beach.

May: ✈ **Atlantic Coast Kite Festival** (757-425-3111; www.beachstreetusa .com), Virginia Beach.

Beach Music Weekend (757-425-3111; www.beachstreetusa.com), Boardwalk, Virginia Beach.

Black Drum World Championship Fishing Tournament (757-787-2460; www.esvachamber.org), Bay Creek Resort and Club, Cape Charles.

PANorama Caribbean Music Fest (757-425-3111; www.beachstreetusa .com), Boardwalk, Virginia Beach.

✪ ✈ **Pungo Strawberry Festival** (757-721-6001; www.pungostrawberry festival.info), 1776 Princess Anne Road, Virginia Beach.

Steel Pier Classic Surfing Contest and Surf Art Expo (757-222-2355; www.vbsurfartexpo.com), First Street jetty and the Boardwalk, oceanfront, Virginia Beach.

Virginia Beach Memorial Day Ceremony (757-467-6435; www.vbgov .com), Tidewater Veterans Memorial, 19th Street, across from the convention center, Virginia Beach. A fly-over featuring military and World War II aircraft is often included.

June: **Boardwalk Art Show and Festival** (757-425-0000; www.cacv.org), 17th–32nd streets, oceanfront, Virginia Beach.

Flyway Feast Fund Raiser (757-426-3643; www.bbrf.org), Flyway Hunt Club, Virginia Beach. Benefits the Back Bay Restoration Foundation.

Latin Fest (757-425-3111; www.beach streetusa.com), Boardwalk, Virginia Beach.

July: ✈ **Stars & Stripes Explosion** (757-425-3111; www.beachstreetusa .com), Virginia Beach.

Virginia Beach Tuna Tournament (757-640-8500; www.vbtuna.com).

August: ✪ **East Coast Surfing Championships** (757-557-6140; www .surfecsc.com), oceanfront, Virginia Beach. North America's oldest running surfing competition.

Virginia Beach Billfish Tournament (757-652-8409; www.vbbt.com). Largest offshore event in the region.

September: **American Music Festival** (757-425-3111; www.beachstreetusa .com), Virginia Beach. Labor Day weekend.

✪ **Blues At The Beach Festival** (757-425-3111; www.beachstreetusa .com or www.natchelblues.org), Virginia Beach. Free.

✪ **Eastern Shore Birding & Wildlife Festival** (757-581-1801; www.esva festivals.org).

✪ ✈ **Neptune Festival** (757-498-0215; www.neptunefestival.com), Virginia Beach. Monthlong celebration includes concerts, midnight bicycle ride, sand sculpting competition, arts and crafts show, seafood fair, wine festival, parade, and fireworks.

✪ ✈ **Oceana Airshow** (757-462-8382 or 866-615-9204; www.oceanaairshow .com), Naval Air Station Oceana, Virginia Beach. Free admission and parking.

Plein-Air Painting Festival (757-331-3669; www.stagedoorgallery.com), Cape Charles.

Tomato Festival (757-331-4884), Cape Charles.

October: **Harvest Festival** (757-787-2460; www.esvachamber.org), Sunset

Beach Resort, Cape Charles.

Oktoberfest (www.thenoblemen.org), Oceana Master Jet Base Main Gate, Virginia Beach.

Southern Virginia Celtic Festival (757-572-2835; www.irlusa.org), Murphy's Irish Pub, 2914 Pacific Avenue, Virginia Beach.

Virginia Fashion Week (757-407-0477; www.vafashionweek.net), Virginia Beach and other venues.

November: **de Witt Cottage Auction** (757-437-8432; www.awhm.org), Virginia Beach. Annual auction of hand-carved decoys and other bird-related art.

○ **Eastern Shore Artisan's Guild Open Studio and Vineyard Tour** (www.easternshoreartist.com), P.O. Box 531, Onancock 23417. Held annually on Thanksgiving weekend.

Cape Charles Museum Annual Oyster Roast (757-331-1008; www.capecharles.org), VA 184, Cape Charles.

✍ **Cheroenhaka (Nottoway) Indian Inter-Tribal Corn Harvest Fall Festival Pow Wow** (757-417-7012; www.cheroenhaka-nottoway.org), the Historic Villages at Cape Henry, Virginia Beach.

Veteran's Day Parade (757-491-7866 or 800-822-3224; www.vbfun.com), Virginia Beach.

December: ✍ **Holiday Lights at the Beach** (757-425-3111; www.beach

---

STRIPED BASS WORLD CHAMPIONSHIP

Striped bass, otherwise known as stripers or rockfish, are the most sought after sportfish for both commercial and recreational anglers in Chesapeake Bay, thanks to their delicious taste and fighting spirit. After spawning upstream and feeding off schools of menhaden and anchovies in the bay, the stripers head for open water in the fall and winter, passing close to the piers, bridges, and charter boats of Virginia Beach, acknowledged as the Rockfish Capital of the World. Many of these fish top out at 30 to 50 pounds, or even larger. In 2008, the state record striper of 73 pounds was brought to boat just off the coast.

The **Striped Bass World Championship** (757-638-7400; www.stripedbass worldchampionship.com) is a two-month event from Nov. 1 to Dec. 31, offering $10,000 in cash and prizes, along with a special Thanksgiving Striper Weekend tournament. Other special events scheduled during the championship include:

Kiptopeke Rockfish Riot (757-331-3000; www.rockfishriot.com), Kiptopeke State Park, Eastern Shore.

Lynnhaven Marine Trophy/Bayliner Rockfish Tournament (757-460-1900; www.lynnhavenmarine.com).

Rock Around The Clock—24 Hour Sea Gull Pier Rockfish Tournament (757-638-7400; www.cbbt.com), Chesapeake Bay Bridge-Tunnel.

streetusa.com), Boardwalk, Virginia Beach. Cars cruise the Boardwalk past dozens of light displays.

✍ **Holiday Parade at the Beach** (757-425-3111; www.beachstreetusa .com), Atlantic Avenue, Virginia Beach.

Sandbridge Craft Fair and House Tour (757-721-2815; www.sandbridge christmastour.com), Sandbridge Chapel Community Center, Virginia Beach.

APPENDIX A:
AREA RESOURCES

NEWSPAPERS AND OTHER PUBLICATIONS

For an abbreviated list of major area publications, see "What's Where in Virginia Beach, Richmond & Tidewater Virginia."

HAMPTON ROADS COMMUNITIES *Beach: The Magazine of Virginia Beach* (757-385-4679; www.vbgov.com), 2401 Courthouse Dr., Building 1, Virginia Beach 23456.

Chesapeake Angler Magazine (804-453-7511; www.chesapeake-angler.com), P.O. Box 233, Burgess 22432.

CNU Captain's Log (757-594-7196; www.thecaptainslog.org), 1 University Place, Newport News 23606. Official paper of Christopher Newport University. Published weekly on Wed.

Colonial Williamsburg: The Journal (888-CWF-1776; www.history.org), P.O. Box 1776, Williamsburg 23187. Excellent history magazine is mailed to donors who support the Colonial Williamsburg Fund.

DoG Street Journal (757-221-7851; www.dogstreetjournal.com), Campus Center, P.O. Box 8793, Williamsburg 23187. Monthly publication by the students of William and Mary.

Flagship (757-222-2865; www.flagshipnews.com), 143 Granby St., Norfolk 23510. Free weekly for the military services and their families.

Gloucester-Mathews Gazette-Journal (804-693-3101; www.gazettejournal.net), P.O. Box 2060, Gloucester 23061. Covers the Middle Peninsula. Published weekly on Thurs.

Hampton Roads Live Magazine (757-271-8462; www.hrlonline.com). Local news in print, on TV, and online.

Hampton Roads Voice (757-244-5654; www.voicenewspaper.com), 205 E. Clay St., Richmond 23219. Free weekly is the largest African American community newspaper in Virginia. Published on Thurs.

Independent-Messenger (434-634-4153; www.vancnews.com/emporia), 111 Baker St., Emporia 23847. Covers Emporia, Greensville, and surrounding area. Published twice a week, on Wed. and Sun.

Inside Business: The Hampton Roads Business Journal (757-222-5353; www **417**
.insidebiz.com), 150 W. Brambleton Ave., Norfolk 23510.

Jet Observer (757-433-3360; www.oceanajetobserver.com), 1750 Tomcat Blvd.,
CODE 12, NAS Oceana 23460. Weekly covers Naval Air Station Oceana in Virginia Beach.

Norfolk New Journal & Guide (757-543-6531; www.njournalg.com), 974 Norfolk
Square, Norfolk 23502. Weekly covers African American society and culture.

ODU Mace and Crown (757-683-3452; www.maceandcrown.com), 2101 Webb
University Center, Norfolk 23529. Weekly of Old Dominion University.

Peninsula Warrior (757-222-3990; www.forteustiswheel.com), 143 Granby St.,
Norfolk 23510. Free weekly covers the military community of the greater Fort
Eustis/Fort Story region.

Port Folio Weekly (757-222-3900; www.portfolioweekly.com), 150 W. Brambleton
Ave., Norfolk 23510. Arts and entertainment in Hampton Roads. Print edition discontinued, but event calendar and features still online.

Smithfield Times (757-357-3288; www.smithfieldtimes.com), 228 Main St.,
Smithfield 23430. Published weekly on Wed.

Southside Sentinel (804-758-2328; www.ssentinel.com), 276 Virginia St., Urbanna
23175. Weekly covers the Middle Peninsula and Northern Neck.

Splash Magazine (757-248-3009; www.splashmag.com), P.O. Box 3606, Virginia
Beach 23454. Free monthly covering the nightlife scene in Hampton Roads.

Suffolk News Herald (757-539-3437; www.suffolknewsherald.com). Published six
days a week.

Sunny Day Guides (www.sunnydayguide.com). Virginia Beach and Williamsburg
(*The Colonial Guide*) editions, available by mail or online, contain maps and
coupons.

Tidewater News (757-562-3187; www.tidewaternews.com), 1000 Armory Dr.,
Franklin 23851. Covers Franklin, Southampton County, and Isle of Wight County.

Tidewater Parent Magazine (757-222-3905; www.mytidewatermoms.com), 143
Granby St., Norfolk 23510.

Toano-Norge Times (757-250-3195; www.toano-norgetimes.com), P.O. Box 6,
Norge 23127. Published every other week on Fri.

The Virginia Gazette and *Williamsburg Magazine* (757-220-1736; www
.vagazette.com or www.williamsburgmag.com), 216 Ironbound Rd., Williamsburg
23188.

Visitors Guide Network (757-422-8979 or 800-422-0742; www.vgnet.com), 1264
Perimeter Pkwy., Virginia Beach 23454. Editions available by mail or online cover
Chesapeake, the Eastern Shore, Hampton, Newport News, Norfolk, Portsmouth,
and Virginia Beach.

Vow Bride (757-222-3900; www.vowbride.com), 150 W. Brambleton Ave., Norfolk
23510.

W&M Flat Hat (757-221-3283; www.flathatnews.com), Campus Center, P.O. Box
8795, Williamsburg 23187. William and Mary student newspaper published twice a
week.

York Town Crier/Poquoson Post (757-898-7225; www.yorktowncrier.com), 4824 George Washington Memorial Hwy., Yorktown 23692. Weekly.

RICHMOND REGION Advertising Concepts (804-639-9994; www.flavor calendar.com), 6301 Harbourside Dr., Suite 100, Midlothian 23112. Publishes several free lifestyle publications: *Chesterfield Living Magazine* (www.chesterfield livingonline.com); *Heritage Rivers Magazine* (www.heritageriversonline.com), covering Petersburg, Hopewell, and Colonial Heights; *Hanover Lifestyle Magazine* (www.hanoverlifestyleonline.com); *River City Magazine* (www.rivercity richmond.com); *Shopper's Express* (www.shoppersexpressonline.com); and *West End's Best* (www.westendsbest.com).

Appomattox Times Virginian (434-352-8215; www.wpcva.com/appomattox), 589 Court St., Appomattox 24522. Weekly published on Wed.

Brick Reloaded (804-649-6252; www.brickweekly.com), 300 E. Franklin St., Richmond 23219. Free weekly covering music, arts, and entertainment.

Central Virginian News (800-969-0368; www.thecentralvirginian.com), 89 Rescue Lane, Louisa 23093. Weekly covers Louisa and Fluvanna counties and the Lake Anna area.

Fredericksburg Free Lance-Star (540-374-5000; www.freelancestar.com), 616 Amelia St., Fredericksburg 22401. Daily.

Goochland Courier (800-969-0368; www.goochlandcourier.com), 89 Rescue Lane, Louisa 23093. Weekly published on Wed.

Goochland Gazette (804-746-1235 or 877-888-0449; www.goochlandgazette .com), P.O. Box 1118, Mechanicsville 23111.

Greater Richmond Grid (www.richmondgrid.com). Free quarterly with an online presence covers regional arts news.

Hanover Herald Progress (804-798-9031; www.herald-progress.com), 11159 Air Park Rd., Suite 1, Ashland 23005. Weekly published on Thurs.

Henrico Citizen (804-262-1700; www.henricocitizen.com), 4807 Hermitage Rd., Suite 204, Richmond 23227.

Hopewell News (804-458-8511; www.hopewellnews.com), P.O. Box 481, Hopewell 23860. Daily covers Hopewell, Prince George, Colonial Heights, Petersburg, and Fort Lee.

Mechanicsville Local (804-746-1235; www.mechlocal.com), 6400 Mechanicsville Tpke., Mechanicsville 23111. Weekly tabloid.

Midlothian Exchange (804-379-6451; www.midlothianexchange.com), P.O. Box 420, Midlothian 23113.

Petersburg Progress-Index (804-732-3456; www.progress-index.com), 15 Franklin St., Petersburg 23803. Daily, first published July 4, 1865, was the first paper in Virginia with an African American editor.

Powhatan Today (804-598-4305 or 877-888-0499; www.powhatantoday.com), P.O. Box 10, 3229 Anderson Hwy., Powhatan 23139.

Richmond Chic (804-357-3330; www.richmondchic.com).

Richmond Community Weekly (804-464-2200; www.tcweekly.com), 301 Southlake Blvd., Suite 102, Richmond 23236. Weekly news and free classifieds in 12 separate geographical editions.

Richmond Free Press (804-644-0496; www.richmondfreepress.com), 422 E. Franklin St., Richmond 23219. Weekly.

Richmond Voice (804-644-9060; www.voicenewspaper.com), 205 E. Clay St., Richmond 23219. Richmond edition of the largest African American community newspaper in Virginia.

Tidewater Review (804-843-2282; www.tidewaterreview.com), 425 12th St., West Point 23181. Weekly covers West Point, King William, King & Queen, and New Kent.

University of Richmond Collegian (804-289-8483; www.thecollegianur.com), 40 Westhampton Way, University of Richmond, Richmond 23173. Student weekly.

Virginia Business (804-225-9263; www.virginiabusiness.com), 1207 E. Main St., Richmond 23219.

In addition, Richmond possesses an extremely active blogosphere. Some of the best Web sites to visit include: www.richmondgoodlife.com, www.weeklyrant.com, www.rvanews.com, and www.tarichmond.com.

RADIO AND TELEVISION

RADIO STATIONS For an abbreviated list of major area radio stations, see "What's Where in Virginia Beach, Richmond & Tidewater Virginia."

WFOS 88.7 FM (757-547-1036; www.cpschools.com/departments/radio/index .php), Chesapeake. Local news, plus blues, beach, oldies, and R&B.

WDCE 90.1 FM (804-289-8790; www.wdcefm.org), University of Richmond. Jazz, new music.

WHRO 90.3 FM (757-889-9400; www.whro.org), Norfolk public radio. Classical, big band, swing, old radio.

WCWM 90.9 FM (757-221-3288; www.wm.edu/so/wcwm), Williamsburg. College of William and Mary, student run, alternative music radio.

WNSB 91.1 FM (757-823-9672; www.nsu.edu/wnsb), Norfolk State University. Urban contemporary radio, jazz.

WVST 91.3 FM (804-524-6725; www.vsu.edu), Virginia State University, Petersburg. Jazz, blues.

WCDX 92.1 FM Power921 (804-672-9299; www.ipowerrichmond.com), Richmond. Mainstream, urban.

WNOB 93.7 FM (757-640-8500; www.bob-fm.com), Chesapeake. Hits from the '70s, '80s, and '90s.

WRVQ 94.5 FM (Q94) (804-474-0173; www.wrvq94.com), Richmond. Today's hits.

WVKL 95.7 FM (757-497-2000; www.957rnb.com), Norfolk. Urban contemporary.

WRIR 97.3 FM (804-649-9737; www.wrir.org), Richmond. Indie radio, jazz. Live local DJs.

WNOR 98.7 FM (757-366-9900; www.fm99.com), Norfolk. Rock.

WWLB Liberty 98.9 FM (804-345-0989; www.989liberty.com), Midlothian. Adult hits (top 40 and classics from the '70s and '80s).

WXGM 99.1 FM (804-693-2105; www.xtra99.com), Gloucester. Today's hits and yesterday's favorites.

WKJM 99.3 FM (804-672-9299; www.kissrichmond.com), Richmond. Urban adult contemporary.

WLGQ 99.5 FM (252-538-9790), Emporia. R&B, oldies.

WVHT 100.5 FM (www.hot1005.com), Virginia Beach. Adult contemporary.

WZEZ 100.5 FM (804-796-2WIN; www.ezfmradio.com), Richmond. Easy listening, smooth jazz.

WDYL 101.1 FM (Y101 Richmond's New Rock) (804-330-5700; www.y101 rocks.com), Chester. Alternative rock.

WWDE 101.3 FM (757-497-2000; www.2wd.com), Norfolk. Adult contemporary.

WOWI 102.9 FM (103 Jamz) (757-466-0103; www.103jamz.com), Norfolk. Hip-hop.

WNRN 103.1 FM (434-979-0919; www.wnrn.org), Midlothian. Public radio via translator. Modern rock, acoustic.

WNVZ 104.5 FM (Z104) (757-497-2000; www.z104.com), Norfolk. Top 40.

WPZZ Praise 104.7 FM (804-672-9299; www.praiserichmond.com), Richmond. Gospel music.

WKUS 105.3 FM (KISS 105) (757-466-1053; www.1053kiss.com), Norfolk. Urban contemporary.

WUSH 106.1 FM (US106) (757-248-7106; www.us106.com), Poquoson. Country music.

WBTJ The Beat 106.5 FM (804-474-0000; www.wbtj.com), Richmond. Hip-hop.

WAFX The Fox 106.9 FM (757-366-9900; www.1069thefox.com), Suffolk. Classic hits.

WBBT Big Oldies 107.3 FM (804-345-1073; www.1073bbt.com), Richmond. Oldies of the '60s and '70s.

WJCD 107.7 FM (757-466-0009; www.smoothjazz1077.com), Norfolk. Smooth jazz.

WBACH 107.9 FM (757-565-1079; www.wbach.net), Williamsburg. Classical station.

WNIS 790 AM (757-640-8500; www.wnis.com), Norfolk. News radio.

WRNL 910 AM (804-474-0000; www.sportsradio910.com), Richmond. Sports radio.

WXGI 950 AM (Richmond's ESPN) (804-233-7666; www.espn950am.com), Richmond. Sports radio.

WRVA 1140 AM (804-474-0000; www.wrva.com), Richmond. News radio.

WTPS 1240 AM (804-672-9299; www.urbanpetersburg.com), Petersburg. News talk radio and solid gold R&B.

WGH 1310 AM (757-671-1000; www.espnradio941.com), Newport News. ESPN sports radio.

WHAN 1430 AM (804-798-1010; www.whan1430.com), Ashland. Business news, local sports, jazz.

WCLM 1450 AM (804-231-7685; www.wclmradioonline.com), Richmond. Local talk shows and local music, plus a variety of music from country, classic soul, and oldies to gospel, R&B, and Latin jazz.

WHKT 1650 AM (757-488-1010; www.radiodisney.com), Portsmouth. Radio Disney.

TELEVISION STATIONS

Hampton Roads

WAVY-TV 10 (www.wavy.com), Portsmouth. Local news.

WGNT-TV CW27 (757-393-2501; www.cw27.com), 1318 Spratley St., Portsmouth 23704.

WHRE-TV 21 (www.tbn.org), Virginia Beach. Affiliate of TBN carries religious broadcasting.

WHRO-TV (757-889-9400; www.whro.org), 5200 Hampton Blvd., Norfolk 23508. PBS station.

WPXV-TV 49 (757-499-1261; www.ionmedia.tv), 230 Clearfield Ave., Virginia Beach 23462. ION Television affiliate.

WSKY-TV 4 (757-382-0004; www.sky4tv.com), 920 Corporate Lane, Chesapeake 23320.

WTKR-TV NewsChannel 3 (757-446-1000; www.wtkr.com), 720 Boush St., Norfolk 23510. CBS affiliate.

WTVZ-MYTVZ (757-622-3333; www.mytvz.com), 900 Granby St., Norfolk 23510.

WVBT-FOX43TV (757-393-4343; www.fox43tv.com), 243 Wythe St., Portsmouth 23704.

WVEC-TV 13NEWS (757-625-1313; www.wvec.com), Hampton.

Richmond Area

WCVE-TV PBS (804-320-1301 or 800-476-2357; www.ideastations.org), 23 Sesame St., Richmond 23235.

WRIC-TV (804-330-8888; www.wric.com), 301 Arboretum Place, Richmond 23236. ABC affiliate.

WRLH-TV Fox (804-358-3535; www.foxrichmond.com), 1925 Westmoreland St., Richmond 23230.

WTVR-TV CBS 6 (804-254-3600; www.wtvr.com), 3301 W. Broad St., Richmond 23230.

WUPV CW Richmond (804 230-1212; www.cwrichmond.tv), 5710 Midlothian Tpke., Richmond 23225.

WWBT Television/NBC12 (804-230-1212; www.nbc12.com), 5710 Midlothian Tpke., Richmond 23218.

APPENDIX B:
RECOMMENDED READING

BIOGRAPHIES, DIARIES, ORAL HISTORY

Cashin, Joan E. *First Lady of the Confederacy: Varina Davis's Civil War.* Cambridge, MA: Belknap Press, 2006.

Chadwick, Bruce. *I Am Murdered: George Wythe, Thomas Jefferson, and the Killing That Shocked a New Nation.* Hoboken, NJ: John Wiley & Sons, 2009.

Crawford, Alan Pell. *Unwise Passions: A True Story of a Remarkable Woman—and the First Great Scandal of Eighteenth Century America.* New York: Simon & Schuster, 2005. Members of the Randolph family face charges of murder.

Fox, James. *Five Sisters: The Langhornes of Virginia.* New York: Simon & Schuster, 2001. Daughters of this Richmond family included Mrs. Waldorf Astor, the first female British MP, and the original Gibson Girl.

Freeman, Douglas Southall. *R. E. Lee: A Biography.* 4 vols. New York: Scribner, 1934. Biography of the Confederate leader written by the editor of the *Richmond News Leader* won the Pulitzer Prize.

Mapp, Alf. *Thomas Jefferson: America's Paradoxical Patriot.* Lanham, MD: Rowman & Littlefield Publishers, 2007.

McGaughy, J. Kent. *Richard Henry Lee of Virginia: A Portrait of an American Revolutionary.* Lanham, MD: Rowman & Littlefield Publishers, 2003.

Nichols, A. Bryant, Jr. *Captain Christopher Newport: Admiral of Virginia.* Washington, D.C.: Sea Venture, 2007.

Walsh, John Evangelist. *Midnight Dreary: The Mysterious Death of Edgar Allan Poe.* Piscataway, NJ: Rutgers University Press, 1998.

CHILDREN'S BOOKS

Amateau, Gigi. *Chancey of the Maury River.* Cambridge, MA: Candlewick Press, 2008. Story of a Virginia horse's life, told through his own eyes. Ages 8–12.

Corbett, Sue, and Henry Cole. *The Twelve Days of Christmas in Virginia.* New York: Sterling Publishing, 2009. Ages five and up.

Denenberg, Barry. *When Will This Cruel War Be Over? The Civil War Diary of Emma Simpson, Gordonsville, Virginia, 1864.* New York: Scholastic, 1996. Ages 9–12.

Devore, Jennifer Susannah. *Savannah of Williamsburg: Being the Account of a Young London Squirrel, Virginia 1705.* Williamsburg, VA: Tall Cotton, 2005.

Fullinwider, Rowena. *The Adventures of Rowena & Carrot Jam The Rabbit: A Children's Story Cookbook.* Great Britain: Stanley Press, 1990.

Hamilton, Virginia. *Anthony Burns: The Defeat and Triumph of a Fugitive Slave.* New York: Laurel Leaf Books, 1993. Ages 9–12.

Harness, Cheryl. *Ghosts of the Civil War.* New York: Simon & Schuster Children's Publishing, 2004. Ages 7–10.

Hunter, John P. *Red Thunder.* Williamsburg, VA: Colonial Williamsburg Foundation, 2007. Juvenile novel takes place during the Revolution. Ages 9–12.

Klima, Charlene. *Cherry Point.* Bloomington, IN: iUniverse, 2002. Novel for young readers set on Gwynn's Island in Chesapeake Bay. Ages four to eight.

Mackenzie, Ross. *My Sailor Dad.* Jacksonville, FL: High-Pitched Hum Publishing (www.patriot-kids.com), 2008. Ages four to eight.

McKissack, Patricia C. *A Picture of Freedom: The Diary of Clotee, a Slave Girl, Belmont Plantation, Virginia, 1859.* New York: Scholastic, 1997. Ages 9–12.

O'Brien, Patrick. *Duel of the Ironclads: The* Monitor *vs. the* Virginia. New York: Walker Books for Young Readers, 2007. Ages 6–10.

Rosen, Daniel. *New Beginnings: Jamestown and the Virginia Colony 1607–1699.* Washington, D.C.: National Geographic Children's Books, 2005. Ages 10–14.

COOKBOOKS

Barrow, Mary Reid, Connie Johnson, and Robyn Browder. *The Great Taste of Virginia Seafood: A Cookbook and Guide to Virginia Waters.* Atglen, PA: Schiffer Publishing, 2007.

Booth, Letha. *Williamsburg Cookbook: Traditional and Contemporary Recipes.* Williamsburg, VA: Colonial Williamsburg Foundation, 2004 (15th ed.).

Bowditch, Marian Hornsby. *From the Kitchen at Hornsby House in Yorktown, Virginia.* Yorktown, VA: The Watermen's Museum (www.hornsbyhousecookbook .com), 1979.

Colonial Williamsburg Foundation. *Colonial Williamsburg Tavern Cookbook.* New York: Clarkson Potter, 2001.

Dolphin Circle of the International Order of the King's Daughter's and Sons. *Gourmet by the Bay: The Virginia Beach Cookbook.* Virginia Beach, VA: Dolphin Circle, www.dolphincirclevb.com, 1989.

Fullinwider, Rowena, James Crutchfield, and Winette Jeffery. *Celebrate Virginia! The Hospitality, History and Heritage of Virginia.* Nashville, TN: Thomas Nelson, 2003. One of Virginia's most renowned chefs, owner of Rowena's in Norfolk, presents blueprints for entertaining.

Junior League of Norfolk–Virginia Beach. *Toast to Tidewater: Celebrating Virginia's Finest Food & Beverages.* Norfolk, VA: Junior League of Norfolk, 2004.

Nunley, Debbie, and Karen Jane Elliott. *A Taste of Virginia History: A Guide to Historic Eateries and Their Recipes.* Winston-Salem, NC: John F. Blair, 2004.

Randolph, Mary. *The Virginia Housewife: Or Methodical Cook: A Facsimile of an Authentic Early American Cookbook.* Mineola, NY: Dover Publications, 1993. Originally published in 1824, this was the most influential guide for housewives in the 19th century, with recipes for pickled oysters, plum cakes, and other period delicacies.

Williamson, CiCi, and Garry Pound. *The Best of Virginia Farms Cookbook and Tour Book: Recipes, People, Places.* Birmingham, AL: Menasha Ridge Press, 2008.

CULTURAL STUDIES

Breen, T. H., and Stephen Innes. *Myne Owne Ground: Race and Freedom on Virginia's Eastern Shore, 1640–1676.* New York: Oxford University Press, USA, 2004.

Dixon, John W. *Gwynn's Island: A Brief History of the Oldest Permanent English Settlement on the Middle Peninsula of Virginia: The 1600s to Present Day.* Gwynn's Island, VA: Gwynn's Island Museum, 2006.

Dunford, Earle, and George Bryson. *Under the Clock: The Story of Miller & Rhoads.* Charleston, SC: The History Press, 2008. The history of Richmond's most beloved department store.

Ford, Charles H., and Jeffrey L. Littlejohn. *Elusive Equality: Desegregation and Resegregation in Norfolk's Public Schools.* Charlottesville, VA: University of Virginia Press, 2010.

Holton, Woody. *Forced Founders: Indians, Debtors, Slaves and the Making of the American Revolution in Virginia.* Chapel Hill: University of North Carolina Press, 1999.

Lee, Lauranett L. *Making the American Dream Work: A Cultural History of African Americans in Hopewell, Virginia.* Garden City, NY: Morgan James Publishing, 2008.

Ross, R. David. *Memory Lane, Richmond, VA.* 3 vols. Richmond, VA: Palari Publishing, 2007, 2008, 2009.

Smith, Brooks, and Wayne Dementi. *The Songlines of Richmond: A Celebration of Performing Arts, Artists and Stages.* Manakin-Sabot, VA: Dementi Milestone Publishing, 2009.

Winthrop, Robert P. *Cast and Wrought: The Architectural Metalwork of Richmond, Virginia.* Richmond, VA: The Valentine Museum, 1980.

FICTION

Cline, Edward. *Sparrowhawk One: Jack Frake.* San Francisco: MacAdam Cage Publishing, 2001. First volume of a five-part historical fiction series that runs through the Revolutionary War.

Jenkins, Emyl. *The Big Steal.* Chapel Hill, NC: Algonquin Books, 2009. Murder mystery solved by a Virginia antiques appraiser.

Jones, David H. *Two Brothers: One North, One South.* Encino, CA: Staghorn Press, 2008. Based on true characters, this historical novel narrated by Walt Whitman discusses the battles around Richmond, and wartime society within the city, including scenes set in today's Linden Row Inn.

McCaig, Donald. *Jacob's Ladder: A Story of Virginia During the War.* New York: W. W. Norton & Company, 2009. The *Virginia Quarterly* called this "the best Civil War novel ever written."

McMillan, Ann. *Chickahominy Fever.* New York: Viking Press, 2003. Part of the Civil War Mystery series, which also includes *Dead March* (1999), *Angel Trumpet* (2001), and *Civil Blood* (2003), set in the hospitals of Richmond.

FOLKLORE

Behrend, Jackie Eileen. *The Hauntings of Williamsburg, Yorktown and Jamestown.* Winston-Salem, NC: John F. Blair, 1998.

Bergman, Scott, and Sandi Bergman. *Haunted Richmond: The Shadows of Shockoe.* Charleston, SC: The History Press, 2007.

Brown, Beth. *Haunted Battlefields: Virginia's Civil War Ghosts.* Atglen, PA: Schiffer Publishing, 2008.

———. *Haunted Plantations of Virginia.* Atglen, PA: Schiffer Publishing, 2009.

Chewning, Alpheus. *Haunted Virginia Beach.* Charleston, SC: The History Press, 2006.

Gilbert, Lilie, Belinda Nash, and Deni Norred-Williams. *Ghosts, Witches & Weird Tales of Virginia Beach.* Virginia Beach, VA: Eco Images, 2004.

Hunter, John. *Witches and Ghosts, Pirates and Thieves, Murder and Mayhem.* Williamsburg, VA: Colonial Williamsburg Foundation, 2007.

Kinney, Pamela. *Haunted Richmond.* Atglen, PA: Schiffer Publishing, 2007.

———. *Haunted Virginia: Legends, Myths, and True Tales.* Atglen, PA: Schiffer Publishing, 2009.

Kollatz, Harry, Jr. *True Richmond Stories: Historic Tales from Virginia's Capital.* Charleston, SC: The History Press, 2007.

———. *Richmond in Ragtime: Socialists, Suffragists, Sex & Murder.* Charleston, SC: The History Press, 2008.

HISTORY

Axtell, James. *The Rise and Fall of the Powhatan Empire: Indians in Seventeenth-Century Virginia.* Williamsburg, VA: Colonial Williamsburg Foundation, 1995.

Clancy, Paul. *Hampton Roads Chronicles: History from the Birthplace of America.* Charleston, SC: The History Press, 2009.

Deans, Bob. *The River Where America Began: A Journey Along the James.* Lanham, MD: Rowman & Littlefield Publishers, 2007.

Egerton, Douglas R. *Gabriel's Rebellion: The Virginia Slave Conspiracies of 1800 and 1802.* Chapel Hill: University of North Carolina Press, 1993.

Hariot, Thomas. *A Briefe and True Report of the New Found Land of Virginia.* Charlottesville: University of Virginia Press, for the Library at the Mariners' Museum, 2007. Originally published in 1590.

Hibbert, Christopher. *Redcoats and Rebels*. New York: W. W. Norton, 2002. War of Independence from the British and Loyalist viewpoint.

Kelso, William M. *Jamestown: The Buried Truth*. Charlottesville: University of Virginia Press, 2006.

Kupperman, Karen O. *The Jamestown Project*. Cambridge, MA: Belknap Press, 2009.

Lassiter, Matthew D., and Andrew B. Lewis, eds. *The Moderates' Dilemma: Massive Resistance to School Desegregation in Virginia*. Charlottesville: University of Virginia Press, 1998.

Parramore, Thomas C., Peter C. Stewart, and Tommy L. Bogger. *Norfolk: The First Four Centuries*. Charlottesville: University of Virginia Press, 2000.

Potterfield, T. Tyler. *Nonesuch Place: A History of the Richmond Landscape*. Charleston, SC: The History Press, 2009.

Rountree, Helen C. *Pocahontas's People: The Powhatan Indians of Virginia Through Four Centuries*. Norman: University of Oklahoma Press, 1990.

Rountree, Helen C., and E. Randolph Turner III. *Before and After Jamestown: Virginia's Powhatans and Their Predecessors*. Gainesville: University Press of Florida, 2002.

Selby, John E. *Revolution in Virginia*. Rev. ed. Charlottesville: University of Virginia Press, 2007.

Smith, John. *The Complete Works of Captain John Smith, 1580–1631*. Edited by Philip Barbour. Chapel Hill: University of North Carolina Press, 1986.

Southern, Ed. *The Jamestown Adventure: Accounts of the Virginia Colony, 1605–1614*. Winston-Salem, NC: John F. Blair, 2004.

Yarsinske, Amy Waters. *Ghent: John Graham's Dream Norfolk, Virginia's Treasure*. Charleston, SC: The History Press, 2006.

———. *Jamestown Exposition*. 2 vols. Mount Pleasant, SC: Arcadia Publishing, 1999.

———. *Virginia Beach: A History of Virginia's Golden Shore*. Mount Pleasant, SC: Arcadia Publishing, 2002.

Yetter, George Humphrey. *Williamsburg Before and After: The Rebirth of Virginia's Colonial Capital*. 10th ed. Williamsburg, VA: Colonial Williamsburg Foundation, 2004.

CIVIL WAR HISTORY

Coffin, Howard. *The Battered Stars: One State's Civil War Ordeal During Grant's Overland Campaign: From the Home Front in Vermont to the Battlefields of Virginia*. Woodstock, VT: Countryman Press, 2002. Unique chronicle follows Vermont troops from Brandy Station to the Siege of Petersburg, paired with developments on the home front.

Davis, William C., and James I. Robertson Jr. *Virginia at War, 1861, 1862, 1863, 1864*. Lexington-Fayette: University Press of Kentucky, 2005–2009. The Virginia at War series covers the war years from both the military and civilian perspectives.

Gallagher, Gary W. *The Richmond Campaign of 1862: The Peninsula and the Seven*

Days. Chapel Hill: University of North Carolina Press, 2008.

Lankford, Nelson. *Richmond Burning: The Last Days of the Confederate Capital*. New York: Viking Press, 2002. An excellent look at the final hours of the Confederacy and the return of Robert E. Lee from Appomattox.

Robertson, William G. *Back Door to Richmond: The Bermuda Hundred Campaign, April–June 1864*. Baton Rouge: Louisiana State University Press, 1991.

Spruill, Matt. *Echoes of Thunder: A Guide to the Seven Days Battles*. Knoxville: University of Tennessee Press, 2006.

Wills, Brian S. *The War Hits Home: The Civil War in Southeastern Virginia*. Charlottesville: University of Virginia Press, 2001. The 1863 battle for Suffolk, Virginia.

MUSIC CDS AND DVDS

Aiken, Mike. *Getaway*. Northwind Records, 2003. Maritime folk rock.

Colonial Williamsburg Fifes and Drums. *Drummers Call, America's Fife and Drum Tradition*. Colonial Williamsburg Productions, 2008. Other discs by the Fifes and Drums include: *4th of July Concert* (2006), *Marching Out of Time* (1989), and *The World Turned Upside Down* (2003).

Colonial Williamsburg Foundation Musicians. *From Ear to Ear: The Passage of African Music through American Slavery*. Colonial Williamsburg Productions, 2006. Other compilations from Colonial Williamsburg include: *Encore! Music from the 18th-Century Theatre, A Numerous and Brilliant Assembly: A Colonial Williamsburg Musical Sampler, Songs for a Williamsburg Christmas, In Freedom We're Born: Songs from the American Revolution,* and *Instrumental Music from Colonial Williamsburg*.

Horton, Bobby. *Homespun Songs of the C.S.A #1–6*. Birmingham, AL: Homespun Music (www.bobbyhorton.com), 1985–2001. Horton performs on Ken Burns's *Civil War* series soundtrack and many others.

Itinerant Band. *Jefferson and Liberty*. Norfolk, VA: Southern Branch Music (www.southernbranch.com), 2001. Eighteenth-century music.

Monaco, Michael. *Keys of the Palace*. Colonial Williamsburg Productions. Concert on the organ, harpsichord, and pianoforte performed in the Governor's Palace.

Shostak, Dean. *Celtic Crystal*. Colonial Williamsburg Productions, 1997. Shostak, master of the glass armonica, invented by Benjamin Franklin, also performs on *Crystal Carols* (1994), *Revolutions* (1995), and *Glass Angels: Traditional Christmas Music for the Glass Armonica* (1998).

———. *Colonial Fair*. Colonial Williamsburg Productions, 1999. Children enjoy the sounds and songs of a traditional fair.

———. *Davy Crockett's Fiddle*. Colonial Williamsburg Productions, 1997. Shostak performs on the actual fiddle used by the early explorer.

NATURAL HISTORY

Ausband, Stephen C. *Outdoors Year Round: A Guide to Fishing and Hunting in Coastal Virginia and North Carolina*. Charlottesville: University of Virginia Press, 2006.

Badger, Curtis J. *Salt Tide: Currents of Nature and Life on the Virginia Coast.* Woodstock, VT: Countryman Press, 1999. Lyrical essays on Virginia's barrier islands.

Badger, Curtis J., and and Cynthia Belcher. *A Naturalist's Guide to the Virginia Coast.* Charlottesville: University of Virginia Press, 2004.

Cones, Harold N. *The Mariners' Museum Park: The Making of an Urban Oasis.* Newport News, VA: Mariners Museum, 2001.

Hugo, Nancy Ross, Jeff Kirwan, and Robert Llewellyn. *Remarkable Trees of Virginia.* Earlysville, VA: Albemarle Books, 2008.

Kavanagh, James, and Raymond Leung. *Virginia Butterflies & Moths: An Introduction to Familiar Species.* Phoenix, AZ: Waterford Press, 2008.

————. *Virginia Trees & Wildflowers: An Introduction to Familiar Species.* Phoenix, AZ: Waterford Press, 2005.

Klingel, Gilbert. *The Bay.* Baltimore, MD: Johns Hopkins University Press, 1984. An easy to read exploration of the ecosystems of the Chesapeake Bay.

Lippson, Alice J., and Robert L. Lippson. *Life in the Chesapeake Bay.* 3rd ed. Baltimore, MD: Johns Hopkins University Press, 2006.

Simpson, Bland. *Great Dismal: A Carolinian's Swamp Memoir.* Chapel Hill: University of North Carolina Press, 1998.

Smalling, Curtis G., and Gregory Kennedy. *Compact Guide to Virginia Birds.* Auburn, WA: Lone Pine Publishing, 2006.

Warner, William W., and John Barth. *Beautiful Swimmers: Watermen, Crabs and the Chesapeake Bay.* New York: Back Bay Books, 1994.

Yarsinske, Amy. *The Elizabeth River.* Charleston, SC: The History Press, 2007.

PHOTOGRAPHIC STUDIES AND ART BOOKS

Bemiss, Margaret P., and Roger Foley. *Historic Virginia Gardens: Preservation Work of the Garden Club of Virginia, 1975–2007.* Charlottesville: University of Virginia Press, 2009.

Beney, Peter. *The Majesty of Colonial Williamsburg: Majesty Architecture Series.* Gretna, LA: Pelican Publishing, 1997.

Carneal, Drew St. J. *Richmond's Fan District.* Richmond, VA: Historic Richmond Foundation, 1996.

Case, Keshia A. *Richmond Then & Now.* New York: Vintage Books, 1997.

————. *Edgar Allan Poe in Richmond.* Mount Pleasant, SC: Arcadia Publishing, 2009.

Driggs, Sarah Shields. *Richmond's Monument Avenue.* Chapel Hill: University of North Carolina Press, 2000. The stories and myths behind the monuments, plus wonderful pictures.

Hunter, John P. *Link to the Past, Bridge to the Future: Colonial Williamsburg Animals.* Williamsburg, VA: Colonial Williamsburg Foundation, 2005. Charming photos of heritage breeds.

Jennings, Chris, and Hank Gardner. *From the Beach to the Bay: An Illustrated History of Sandbridge in Virginia.* Marceline, MO: Walsworth Publishing, 2000.

Mapp, Alf J., and Ramona H. Mapp. *Portsmouth: A Pictorial History.* Rev. ed. Virginia Beach: Donning, 2006.

Sullivan, George. *In the Wake of Battle: The Civil War Images of Mathew Brady.* New York: Prestel Publishing, 2004. More than four hundred pictures capture death on Virginia's battlefields and Richmond just after its fall.

RECREATION AND TRAVEL

Adkins, Leonard M. *50 Hikes in Southern Virginia: From the Cumberland Gap to the Atlantic Ocean.* Woodstock, VT: Countryman Press, 2007. Hikes in southeast Virginia include walks in False Cape, Pocahontas, and First Landing state parks; the Great Dismal Swamp; Hog Island; and Petersburg National Battlefield.

Blake, Allison. *The Chesapeake Bay Book: Great Destinations.* Woodstock, VT: Countryman Press, 2005. A complete guide to the fishing villages and waterfront towns of Maryland and Virginia, including chapters on Virginia's Northern Neck and the Eastern Shore.

Gilbert, Lillie. *Bayside History Trail: A View from the Water.* Virginia Beach: Eco Images, 2003.

———. *Wild River Guide to Dismal Swamp Water Trails.* Virginia Beach: Eco Images, 2004. Local guide details area paddling trips.

———. *Wild River Guide to the North Landing River and its Tributaries.* Virginia Beach: Eco Images, 2002.

Nolan, Andrea J. *Sea Kayaking Virginia: A Paddler's Guide to Day Trips from Georgetown to Chincoteague.* Woodstock, VT: Countryman Press, 2005. A comprehensive guide to paddling trips throughout the Chesapeake Bay region, with personal commentary, excellent maps, and directions.

Olmert, Michael. *Colonial Williamsburg Guidebook.* Williamsburg, VA: Colonial Williamsburg Foundation, 2004.

Routh, Cory. *Kayak Fishing: The Complete Guide.* 2nd ed. Tucson, AZ: No Nonsense Fly Fishing Guidebooks, 2010.

Swift, Earl. *Journey on the James: Three Weeks Through the Heart of Virginia.* Charlottesville: University of Virginia Press, 2002.

Tennis, Joe. *Beach to Bluegrass: Places to Brake on Virginia's Longest Road.* Johnson City, TN: Overmountain Press, 2007. Motoring guide follows US 58 across Virginia.

Wennersten, John R. *25 Bicycle Tours on Delmarva: Cycling the Chesapeake Bay Country.* Woodstock, VT: Backcountry Guides, 1995. Detailed itineraries explore the back roads of the Eastern Shore.

Wright, Renee. *North Carolina's Outer Banks and Crystal Coast: Great Destinations.* Woodstock, VT: Countryman Press, 2008.

INDEX